Many hands, many hearts, many heads toiled and prayed and planned to bring the Army where it now is. History will record but a small part of the events, and many of the actors will be completely forgotten, but from God's history, on the Great Muster Day, every heartache, every tear, every agonizing prayer, every day and night of toil will be read out and credited to the proper persons. God won the victory, and to Him we give the glory. It was not an uninteresting fight.

The War Cry, PACIFIC COAST EDITION,
JULY 16, 1892 ON THE NINTH ANNIVERSARY OF
THE SALVATION ARMY IN CALIFORNIA

Shout aloud salvation, and we'll have another song;
Sing it with a spirit that will start the world along;
Sing it as our comrades sang it many a thousand strong,
As they were marching to Glory.

March on, march on! We bring the Jubilee.
Fight on, fight on! Salvation makes us free;
We'll shout our Saviour's praises over every land and sea,
As we go marching to Glory!

How the anxious shout it when they hear the joyful sound!
How the weakest conquer when the Saviour they have found!
How our grand battalions with triumphant power abound,
As we go marching to Glory!

So we'll make a thoroughfare for Jesus and His train;
All the world shall hear us as fresh converts still we gain;
Sin shall fly before us for resistance is in vain,
As we go marching to Glory.

WORDS BY GEORGE SCOTT RAILTON, 1880;
TO BE SUNG TO THE TUNE *Marching through Georgia*
BY HENRY CLAY WORK, 1865.

Marching to Glory

The History of
The Salvation Army
in the United States, 1880-1992

SECOND EDITION
REVISED AND EXPANDED

E. H. McKinley

WILLIAM B. EERDMANS PUBLISHING COMPANY
GRAND RAPIDS, MICHIGAN / CAMBRIDGE U.K.

© 1995 Wm. B. Eerdmans Publishing Co.
2140 Oak Industrial Dr. N.E., Grand Rapids, Michigan 49505
P.O. Box 163, Cambridge CB3 9PU U.K.
www.eerdmans.com

Printed in the United States of America

14 13 12 11 10 09   8 7 6 5 4 3 2

Library of Congress Cataloging-in-Publication Data

McKinley, Edward H.
Marching to glory: the history of the Salvation Army in the
United States, 1880-1992 / E. H. McKinley. — 2nd ed., rev. and expanded
        p.   cm.
Includes bibliographical references and index.
ISBN 978-0-8028-6468-0   (pbk: alk. paper)
1. Salvation Army — United States — History. I. Title.
BX9716.M32 1995
287.9'6'0973 — dc20   95-17414
                                             CIP

COVER PHOTO:
Cadet Welcome march, "Soul Winners" session,
Friday, September 10, 1954. Bronx, New York City.

To Martha,
my dear wife and faithful comrade

Contents

Foreword by the National Commander

Marching to Glory represents an intriguing, insightful, and inspiring kaleidoscope of the stirring saga of The Salvation Army in the United States. Initially commissioned and written in commemoration of the Army's centennial in the United States in 1880, this volume updates the earlier work with the inclusion of the years 1980 to 1992. This dynamic period witnessed a major expansion of the Army's evangelical thrust and its service to others.

"History is essentially biography," wrote Emerson. This history of The Salvation Army is, above all, a record of an innumerable company of ordinary men and women, of their courage and compassion, of their daring and dedication, and of their unselfish commitment to the will and work of God in this God-ordained movement.

These pages will lead the reader on a vicarious journey from the Army's inauspicious beginnings to its current status as one of the most respected organizations in America. You will see the uniform of The Salvation Army on the front lines, among the hungry, the homeless, the hurting, and in times and places of disaster, as well as welcomed into the office of the president of the United States.

We are indebted to our Salvationist historian, Professor Edward H. McKinley, for his astute research and meticulous attention to the details that constitute this history, presented in a vigorous and compelling style. This history is definitive as well as descriptive. It eloquently articulates the dual nature and mission of the Army as a major evangelical movement and foremost human services agency. We believe this volume will not only preserve the record of our rich heritage but also serve as a reminder of our mission under God. May it be a witness to its readers of the redeeming love and power of Jesus Christ, which has been the inspiration and motivation for the story recorded in these pages.

Commissioner James Osborne
NATIONAL COMMANDER, 1989-1993

Preface

This volume was originally prepared and offered to the public as part of the national commemoration in 1980 of the one hundredth anniversary of The Salvation Army in the United States. Since 1980 a number of scholarly writers, both within and outside the organization, have turned their attention to the Army. These writers have broadened our understanding of the contexts in which The Salvation Army has developed over time. In addition, the Army's own archival resources, both on the national and on the territorial level, have been greatly expanded. The volume now before the reader is a major revision and update of the original six chapters of the 1980 edition with the addition of a seventh chapter on events since that year.

It is unlikely that any literate American is wholly unaware of The Salvation Army, nor are many completely indifferent to it. At least some vague image of the organization is impressed on nearly every mind. In several national surveys conducted over the past decade, The Salvation Army has been declared the most popular charity in the United States. Its name alone is sufficient to draw encouragement and support from a generous and grateful public.

Yet The Salvation Army is both more and less than most people suppose it to be. The Army is more than blandly beneficial, more than a mere charity. It is a religious crusade, an evangelical Christian denomination; its sole purpose is to secure the redemption of lost sinners through faith in the Atonement of Christ. The Salvation Army recognizes, however, that before some people — those who are hungry, lonely, helpless, frightened, sick or poor, too young or too old for others to care much about — can be told of His grace and love, they must first be given some assurance, in practical form, that God and His children love them and will not leave them in want and despair. The Army is fiercely evangelical, but its approach to evangelism has always been kindhearted and based on common sense.

The Salvation Army is not, however, a legion of angels or martyrs or saints. Salvationists have not given themselves so completely to comforting the poor and saving souls that they have had no thought for their own happiness. The Salvation Army has always been, and continues to be, made up of quite ordinary human beings. They are, admittedly, willing to do the most extraordinary things, but even the most zealous are neighborly, hard-working, common people. The officers are the ministers, the soldiers are the members, but much of their lives is spent outside of Army service in the commonplace activities of life in America. Salvationists like to eat and to take naps on Sunday afternoon. They enjoy being young and being around young people. They are delighted when their children make the team or win a scholarship. They like band music, and they like to sing. They love and are loved; they grow old and would prefer to grow older still. In the end, there are no trumpets for them, no heavenly visions: they die of the ordinary afflictions that carry us all off sooner or later.

Salvationists are set apart from their fellows not by unnatural saintliness, spiritual transports, or narrow, hopeless asceticism but by the recognition that in giving many hours of the week, a bit of courage, and a large amount of very human energy to the service of God and their neighbors in The Salvation Army, they are allowing God to endow their lives with the only meaning those little lives will ever have, to be in their brief day on earth the embodiment of the supreme truth that Christianity is love in action.

The fact that The Salvation Army is well regarded in the United States makes its history an attractive subject. The fact that the Army is a crusade for Christ makes its history important. The fact that its members are such ordinary people makes its history inspiring. The story of The Salvation Army proves that there is something good in the hearts of the American people that no amount of cynicism and national self-doubt has yet spoiled; if it does not prove, it at least strongly suggests that there is a God after all and that anyone at all can serve Him well. The story of The Salvation Army provides objective grounds for optimism; if things do not naturally turn out well, at least they can be made to turn out better.

Acknowledgments

The work of revising and updating this volume has required the active cooperation of a large number of persons both within and outside The Salvation Army. Although the author did not anticipate it when he set out on the work of revision, it has required as much time and energy as the preparation of the original edition. The author is glad to acknowledge that, just as in the case of the original project, he has been given not only the fullest cooperation in the work of revision but a great amount of kindness, encouragement, valuable advice, and hospitality as well. One of the most valuable results of the project from the author's point of view is the great personal pleasure he has found in interviews and correspondence with scores of Salvationist comrades. For all these boons he can offer no adequate payment except to state that he is, and shall always remain, profoundly grateful for them.

Without casting the contributions of hundreds of helpful persons into a shadow, the author feels bound in gratitude to acknowledge in a special way those whose assistance was particularly beneficial. At the conclusion of these words of thanks is a list of all those who made a contribution to the preparation of both the 1980 and 1995 editions of this book.

The author expresses special thanks and personal respects to Comm. James Osborne, national commander of The Salvation Army, 1989-1993, and to Comm. Kenneth Hood, national chief secretary, for their personal interest and encouragement and for their complete cooperation at every stage of this project. Commissioner Osborne kindly reviewed portions of the manuscript and made very helpful suggestions. Particular notice is due to Lt. Col. Myrtle V. Ryder, assistant national chief secretary, who supervised the production details for this book, under the auspices of Commissioner Hood. Col. Leon Ferraez, national communications secretary, and Col. Henry Gariepy, national editor-in-chief, made special efforts on the author's behalf during his visit to headquarters and afterward. Special thanks, too, are due to Maj. Judith B. Small, resource center director at national headquarters, whose knowledge of the entire body of records there and whose prompt and cheerful response to numberless requests for assistance will never be forgotten by the author. In addition Major Small made several suggestions regarding the direction of research that proved to be of special value. The four territorial commanders during the period of the most extensive research, Commissioners Harold Shoults, Robert E. Thomson, Kenneth L. Hodder, and Paul A. Rader, have given steady interest and support and, like the national headquarters leaders, have placed the resources of their headquarters at the author's disposal. Each of these territorial leaders has provided materials, answered questions, and offered words of personal advice and encouragement.

Commissioner Thomson, an experienced editor, reviewed portions of the manuscript with special care and made a number of suggestions of special insight and value, taking considerable time from pressing administrative duties to give the author this valuable assistance.

Top administrative officials at all four territorial headquarters, the staffs of three of the four territorial Schools for Officers' Training, and every divisional commander in the United States during the years 1991 to 1992 took the time to respond to a detailed survey, and a large number of these officers supplied additional materials, much of it of great value to the project. Special thanks are due as well to Maj. Mrs. Florence Moffitt, Maj. Lyell Rader, and Capt. Roy Edelman, who allowed the author to have access to valuable materials in the Central, Eastern, and Southern territorial museums and the libraries at the Schools for Officers' Training in these territories. Lt. Col. William MacLean, literary secretary, and Mr. James C. Kisser Jr., assistant to the literary secretary of the Eastern territorial Literary Department, reviewed portions of the manuscript.

The author is particularly grateful for the invaluable assistance of Maj. Dorothy Breen, retired eastern territorial literary secretary, who graciously agreed to accept the responsibility of serving as supervising editor for this project under the auspices of national headquarters, rendering to her grateful author the same splendid service she gave from 1978 to 1980 during work on the first edition of this book. Mr. T. A. Straayer, who further edited the manuscript for the William B. Eerdmans Publishing

Company and supervised its final production, provided additional very valuable service to the proeject.

A number of retired officers, many of them of high rank, including territorial and national commanders, have corresponded and talked with the author in connection with the preparation of this revision. The author is a soldier in The Salvation Army who looks upon these officers not only as persons who assisted him in research but as his leaders in the great work of the Army. To them he is glad now to extend not only his gratitude but his heartfelt personal respects. The author takes complete responsibility for the text, which is entirely his own.

Dr. Richard E. Holz, southern territorial music secretary, and his brother Dr. Ronald W. Holz, professor of music at Asbury College, expended large efforts in assisting the author, the former in collecting and understanding the details of the Army's contemporary music program, and the latter, who is a valued faculty colleague, in assisting the author toward a better understanding of early Army music. The staff at the Army's national Archives and Research Center in Alexandria, Virginia, widely known for their prompt and cooperative response to researchers, outdid themselves to allow the author to gain the maximum benefit from his research trip to that facility in 1992. He wishes particularly to thank Susan Mitchem, Connie Nelson, and Vicky Bish for all their many kindnesses to him. In addition, Ms. Mitchem has answered many inquiries by letter and telephone, always with the same prompt and courteous professionalism.

The author takes personal pleasure in thanking Lt. Col. and Mrs. Warren H. Fulton not only for their years of precious friendship, for which no words will suffice, but also for their generous hospitality to him during his visit to national headquarters and to the national capital divisional headquarters in 1992, and to the Georgia divisional headquarters in 1990. In addition, Lieutenant Colonel Fulton provided invaluable insight into the functioning of a modern divisional headquarters and kindly reviewed portions of the manuscript. Warm thanks are due as well to Robert A. Watson Jr., who at the time of writing was a cadet in the USA Eastern territorial School for Officers' Training, and to Dr. Robert R. Moore, chair of the Bible and Philosophy Division at Asbury College. Both persons are treasured friends whose extensive and detailed reviews of portions of the manuscript were much appreciated by the author.

The author acknowledges with thanks the support of the administration of Asbury College in granting him a reduction in teaching responsibilities in the spring semester 1992 and the patience of his colleagues in overlooking his lapses in the conduct of regular academic duties during the hectic weeks in which the final manuscript was prepared for submission to the publisher. Wendy Jones rendered much valuable secretarial help throughout.

It is not possible in the brief compass of these acknowledgments to cite all those scholarly works that have illuminated the author's research and sometimes guided it in new, rewarding directions. Full citations of all materials appear in the notes. The author does wish, however, to call special attention to the important insights gained from a careful study of the work of Roger Green, Lt. Col. Philip Needham, David Rightmire, Norman H. Murdoch, and Maj. John Rhemick. All are authors of doctoral dissertations on the Army, and all but Rhemick have written a number of scholarly articles as well, all of which have contributed in major ways to the author's understanding of The Salvation Army. The author has also attempted to draw broadly on other new research on the historical development of movements such as the Army, on the role of women in evangelical activities and the effect of religious activity on the expansion of opportunities for women, and on several aspects of the historical context in which the Army grew and developed rapidly in the United States.

Lt. Col. David R. Allen

Brig. Evelyn Allison

Lt. Col. and Mrs. Harold J. Anderson

Lt. and Mrs. Michael A. Anderson

Capt. Thomas Applin

Lt. Col. Kenneth Baillie

Lt. Col. Cyril Barnes

Col. Giles Barrett

Lt. Col. Donald V. Barry

Lt. Col. W. Todd Bassett

Comm. David Baxendale

Brig. and Mrs. Ernest Baxendale

Lt. Col. William Bearchell

Aux. Capt. William Bearchell

Vicky Bish

Sr. Maj. and Mrs. Carl W. Blied

Maj. Jorge Booth

Maj. Walter Booth

Bandmaster Ivor Bosanko

Lt. Col. and Mrs. Wesley Bouterse

Capt. Mrs. Jacalyn Bowers

Maj. Dorothy Breen

Maj. Kenneth Brewer

Brig. and Mrs. Cecil Briggs

Maj. Howard Burr

Lt. Col. William Burrows

Lt. Col. John Busby

Maj. Tyrone G. Butler

Maj. Mrs. Betty Campbell

Capt. Terry Camsey

Maj. Donald Canning

Comm. Edward Carey

Mrs. Lt. Col. F. William Carlson

Brig. Lawrence Castagna

Ralph E. Chamberlain

Comm. William E. Chamberlain

Maj. Mrs. Marlene J. Chase

Col. George Church

Mr. Philip Collier
Brig. Ruth Cox, RN
Maj. William Crabson
Brig. Fred Crossley
Capt. Dalton Cunningham
James E. Curnow
Brig. Bernard Ditmer
Comm. Stanley E. Ditmer
Brig. Henry Dries
Maj. George Duplain
Capt. and Mrs. Roy Edelman
Brig. Emma Ellagard
Lt. Col. Houston Ellis
Lt. Col. and Mrs. Howard Evans
Mrs. Peter R. Falbee
Maj. and Mrs. James Farrell
Col. Leon Ferraez
Lt. Col. William W. Francis
Lt. Col. and Mrs. Warren H. Fulton Jr.
Capt. Herbert E. Fuqua
Col. Henry Gariepy
Pat Germany
Maj. Marshall Gesner
Dorothy Gilkey
Comm. W. R. H. Goodier
Prof. Roger Green
Col. Frank Guldenschuh
Lt. Col. Bruce Harvey
Brian Masuru Hayashi
Mrs. Brig. Elsie Henderson
Lt. Col. Gary L. Herndon
Col. M. Lee Hickam
Maj. Dale Hill
Staff Bandmaster William Himes
Col. Harold Hinson
Comm. Kenneth L. Hodder
Lt. Kenneth G. Hodder
Mrs. Col. Edmund C. Hoffman
Lt. Col. Peter Hofman (I)

Lt. Col. Peter Hofman (II)
Lt. Col. David Holz
Comm. Ernest W. Holz
Comm. Richard E. Holz
Bandmaster Dr. Richard E. Holz
Bandmaster Dr. Ronald W. Holz
Comm. Kenneth Hood
Brig. Diana Houghton
Lt. Col. Ray Howell
Col. Rowland D. Hughes
Maj. R. William Hunter
Brig. and Mrs. Masahide Imai
Maj. Travis Israel
Lt. Col. Stanley Jaynes
Wendy Jones
Col. Edward Johnson
Judith Johnson
David Johnston
Comm. Paul J. Kaiser
Col. Paul M. Kelly
James C. Kisser Jr.
Maxine Kreutzinger
Lt. Col. and Mrs. Edward Laity Sr.
John Lawson
Prezza Lee
Maj. B. T. Lewis
Maj. Herbert Luhn
Lt. Col. Olof Lundgren
Lt. Col. William D. Luttrell
Bandmaster Kenneth E. Luyk Sr.
Capt. Kenneth E. Luyk Jr.
Corps Sgt. Maj. E. G. Madsen
Col. William Maltby
Dr. Louis Marchiafava
Jane Mardis
Laurence Martin
Comm. Norman S. Marshall
Maj. Paul Marshall
Col. J. B. Matthews

Capt. and Mrs. Ward Matthews

Maj. Earl G. McInnes

Brig. Olive McKeown

Lt. Col. William D. MacLean

Rev. Douglas H. McMahon

Mr. and Mrs. Douglas McMahon Sr.

Tom McMahon

Brig. Christine McMillan

Eric P. Merriam

Maj. John Merritt

Lt. Col. David Mikles

Comm. Andrew S. Miller

Col. Ernest A. Miller

Mrs. Brig. Phylis Miller

Susan Mitchem

Mrs. Maj. Florence Moffitt

Prof. Robert Rood Moore

Lt. Col. Mervyn L. Morelock

William J. Moss

Lt. Col. David W. Moulton

Lt. Col. David Mulbarger

Prof. Norman Murdoch

Col. G. Ernest Murray

Comm. John D. Needham

Lt. Col. Philip Needham

Connie Nelson

Col. C. Emil Nelson

Comm. George Nelting

Maj. Joe Noland

Capt. Nestor R. Nuesch

Lt. Col. Eric Newbould

Capt. Faye Nishimura

Mrs. Col. Lillian Hansen Noble

Maj. Norman Nonnweiler (II)

Comm. and Mrs. James Osborne

Lt. J. Grant Overstake

Maj. James Pappas

Col. John Paton

Lt. Col. Leroy Pederson

Maj. A. S. Peters

Lt. Col. Dennis L. Phillips

Col. Dorothy D. Phillips

Comm. Arthur Pitcher

Comm. Will Pratt

Lt. Col. Lyell Rader

Maj. Lyell Rader

Comm. Paul Rader

Mrs. Col. William Range

Maj. John R. Rhemick

Lt. Col. R. Eugene Rice

Comm. and Mrs. Robert Rightmire

Prof. R. David Rightmire

Col. Bertram Rodda

Brig. Ronald J. Rowland

Maj. Edward C. Russell

Maj. and Mrs. Reginald Russell

Lt. Col. Myrtle V. Ryder

Maj. Lorraine Sacks

Sr. Maj. Charles A. Schuerholz

Comm. Albert Scott

Dean Seiler

Col. and Mrs. Paul D. Seiler (I)

Col. Paul D. Seiler (II)

Sr. Maj. Bertha Shadick

Maj. and Mrs. Gordon Sharp

Capt. Lawrence Shiroma

Comm. Harold F. Shoults

Maj. Judith B. Small

Capt. and Mrs. Jeffrey Smith

Brig. Lloyd Smith

Sr. Maj. Magna Sorenson

Lt. Col. Charles Southwood

Mr. Harry Sparks

Sr. Maj. and Mrs. F. Railton Sprake

Col. and Mrs. C. Stanley Staiger

Lt. Col. Ray Steadman-Allen

James T. Stillwell

Lt. Col. Marcus Stilwell

Rose Stortzman
T. A. Straayer
Bandmaster Alfred V. Swenarton
Col. B. Gordon Swyers
Lt. Col. and Mrs. Chester O. Taylor
Comm. Orval Taylor
Bandmaster Garfield Thomas
Comm. Robert E. Thomson
Col. Robert Tobin
Comm. Bramwell Tripp
Col. Florence Turkington
Maj. Richard Ulyat
Lt. Col. Alfred R. Van Cleef

Staff Bandmaster Ronald Waiksnoris
Comm. John D. Waldron
Corps Sgt. Maj. Berton Warren
Maj. James Watson
Col. Robert A. Watson
Cadet Robert A. Watson Jr.
Mrs. Sr. Maj. George Watt
Brig. James Watt
Maj. Charles Wikle
Brig. Victor Wilson
Lt. Col. Norman Winterbottom
T. E. Wood
Miriam Zeigler

CHAPTER 1

1880-1890

"All the world shall hear us . . ."

They came to launch a great crusade. By all odds, they should have failed on the spot, outright and finally. Led by an amiable eccentric as single-minded as an arrow in flight (who nonetheless proved in the end to be as ill-fitted to this grand endeavor as he was to many smaller ones) were seven women so graceless that their leader referred to them affectionately as "half-a-dozen ignoramuses." This was the pioneer party of The Salvation Army. They struggled with a flag, luggage, and the other passengers down the gangplank of the steamer *Australia* at Castle Garden, New York City, on March 10, 1880, to claim America for God.[1]

George Scott Railton, the leader of the "splendid seven," was a pioneer in more ways than one. His arrival in New York made him the first officially authorized Salvation Army missionary, the first sent by General William Booth to carry the gospel of his militant, rapidly growing East London crusade beyond the confines of its native Britain. Railton, thirty years old and a bachelor, had been responsible for many of the innovations that led to the creation of the new Army. The orphan child of Wesleyan missionaries who had perished gallantly nursing the sick during a fever epidemic in Antigua, Railton had been a zealous Christian since the age of ten. In 1868, at age nineteen, revolted by the tedium and the many small compromises that made up the daily life of business — Railton was a clerk — he determined to lose himself in the larger cause of world evangelism. He acquired a huge banner inscribed "Repentance — Faith — Holiness!" and, thus armed, threw himself, penniless, ignorant, and unafraid, into an abortive one-man campaign to win Morocco for Christ.

Victorian evangelicals found this charming, and Railton was encouraged to become a full-fledged minister. He was drawn to the Reverend William Booth by the twin allurements of a pamphlet entitled "How to Reach the Masses with the Gospel" and the knowledge that Booth, the author, was searching for an assistant to organize his Christian Mission, a flourishing evangelical crusade that Booth had started among the working class and poor of East London in 1865.

The genesis of The Salvation Army in the land of its birth is well known, one of the cherished fixtures of Victorian history. In the late twentieth century, several scholars have drawn attention to the history of the Army in fresh ways. Yet however often told the tale, it must be told again: not even a casual understanding of the work of the Army in America is possible without a knowledge of its beginning in the experience, personality, and theology of William Booth and those closest to him in his work.

He was born in 1829 in Nottingham, the son of a small-scale building contractor. His father's bankruptcy while Booth was still a child forced the boy into a mean and lonely life. His one solace was religion. Converted at the age of fifteen in meetings conducted by a traveling American evangelist, James Caughey, Booth soon joined the Wesleyan Church. He gave all the time he could spare from employment that he despised — he was a pawnbroker's apprentice — to lay preaching and street evangelism. He moved to London, where he soon resolved to escape from the pawnshop trade altogether to give himself entirely to evangelism. In this attempt he was encouraged by the members of the small chapel he attended, one of whom, a sympathetic Christian with the unlikely name of Rabbits, paid him a small weekly salary for his evangelistic activities for a period of three months. Booth met his future wife, Catherine Mumford, at the same chapel.

The crusades of the youthful preacher were crowned with success. Booth himself was far more than a mere zealot: he was a colorful and fervent speaker with a sense of the effectiveness of the carefully chosen phrase. Well informed from his own experience about the despair and poverty of those who listened to him, indoors and outdoors, he could explain the promises of Christ in a manner that was compelling. Striking in appearance, with piercing eyes and a face — even as a young man — like that of an Old Testament prophet, Booth adopted out of sincere conviction a theology that was itself highly attractive: the doctrine of holiness. This theology, which is associated with John Wesley but is not exclusive to him, is based on two premises: (1) that conversion — accepting in faith that each person is born under the power of original sin and can escape from its consequences only by accepting that the grace of Christ on the Cross alone is the sovereign cure — is an absolute and inescapable necessity and (2) that after conversion sinful tendencies remain, but God offers His children a kind of perfection in grace whereby His love, and theirs for Him and for each other, purges the last traces of selfishness, self-will, and pride. The growing army of Booth's converts were generally vague on theological details, but the great majority of them understood the basic doctrines of the movement. The compulsion to win others to Christ and to live lives of holy love were the twin mainstays of Booth's London mission, and later of The Salvation Army (see Appendix III for the complete doctrines of The Salvation Army).

Railton found in The Christian Mission the cause to which he could at last abandon himself in delicious zeal. In the Founder's wife, Catherine, he found the perfect collaborator. Following her marriage to William Booth in 1855, Catherine exercised an influence over her husband that was entirely in keeping with her strength of character and her sterling qualities. Indeed, Catherine Booth was that rarest of historical beings: a legend that survives scrutiny. As devoted as her husband to the salvation of souls — whom she, like Booth, visualized as perishing in sinful droves, ignorant of the saving truths of Christianity — Catherine was far more interested than the practical William in theology and social causes, such as the elevation of women to places of responsibility and usefulness in Christian endeavor. High-minded and noble — she was first attracted to her future husband during his recitation of that timeless temperance classic "The Grog-Seller's Dream" — Catherine was also prudent, patient, kind-hearted and sensitive, mother and tutor to seven remarkable children, and an efficient organizer of people and money. Booth was quite correctly amazed at his excellent wife and remained touchingly devoted to her throughout their thirty-five years of marriage with a childlike love that was one of his truly endearing qualities.

Guided by the Booths, Railton, and increasingly the Booths' eldest son Bramwell, the work of the Mission progressed swiftly. The single-minded leaders never allowed the movement to stray from its soul-saving purpose. They were, however, willing and even eager to experiment with new means to the great end. Sometimes these changes in organization reflected the personal inclinations of the guiding personalities. The Booths, Railton, and most of the other leaders favored an autocratic structure as opposed to the more democratic control of groups like the Methodist New Connexion, the denomination from which William and Catherine had departed years before because of a vote that denied them the privilege of full-time evangelism. William Booth felt strongly drawn to urban crowds — the working-class poor, desperate people struggling to gain and hold a place for themselves among the respectably employed, orphans, the helpless, the pensionless aged, prostitutes, and the clods and cast-offs, broken wheels and ne'er-do-wells of Victorian England. It was to these that Booth carried the gospel of redemption.

Booth and his fellow workers were convinced that God was blessing this work, because when they began, as the truest expression of the gospel of love, to provide the poor with such small-scale, practical charities as cheap, wholesome food and shelter, The Christian Mission attracted an increasing number of converts and volunteer helpers. Unable to coordinate his burgeoning spiritual empire without stern organization, which he in any case found congenial, Booth and his closest confederates were prompted — inspired, judging by the results — to transform their volunteer army into a real one. In 1878 they sallied forth in their new guise: The Salvation Army was born. Within a year, the now-familiar accoutrements of the "Great Salvation War" began to appear; others were added piecemeal in the following months: church halls became corps, and flags, ceremonial, military badges, ranks, brass bands, and the rudiments of uniform were added with encouraging results. Thus could an Army pioneer write of this vital year, "Guided, doubtless, by Providence, and prompted by the Spirit of God, one new departure had succeeded another, until the Mission had become what it was ultimately designated — an Army."[2]

Even before these inspired and profitable transformations in their affairs, Booth's converts had been remarkably loyal to him and to the principles on which his Mission was based. Leaving the mother country behind did not dampen their zeal, and so the occasional Mission convert was found among the waves of immigration that left the British Isles in the nineteenth century. As early as 1872 a determined Christian Missioner named James Jermy all on his own planted a seedling from the mother plant in Cleveland, Ohio, although the work withered and died when Jermy returned to England in 1876. In December of that year, another

Mission associate wrote from New Jersey, pleading with Booth to send emissaries to start the great work in America. In fact, the dramatic effect of Railton's beachhead landing might have been diluted — as it was in his own estimation if not in the more sober eye of history — by the fact that the "Pioneer Party" was met in New York by Salvationists and supporters of the work, which had been established in Philadelphia by a family named Shirley six months earlier.[3]

American Salvationists rightly venerate the name of Eliza Shirley and her parents Amos and Annie, who unofficially commenced Salvation Army operations in the United States in 1879. They faced obstacles that would have daunted cooler heads — and cooler hearts. Convinced, however, that they were the agents of God's sovereign will and that America needed an organization like The Salvation Army, and unable to find anything even remotely similar to their beloved work, which they sorely missed, they decided to launch a branch of their own. Interest in the cause of urban evangelization was growing rapidly among clerics and reformers in the 1880s, but even later, when such activities were far more widespread, they reached only a small fraction of the urban poor. In any case, the Shirleys knew nothing of these developments in 1879. Annie recalled later that they started the Army in America because "we could not live without it."[4]

Eliza Shirley was an early convert, won by the fledgling Army in 1878 at the age of sixteen. Her zeal for souls was sufficient preparation to enter the work on a full-time basis; she was commissioned a lieutenant and sent to join the great crusade as an assistant officer during a period of rapid expansion. In April of that year her father, Amos, also a Salvation Army convert, immigrated to America, leaving his family behind at home in Coventry but holding forth to his wife and daughter the allure of better times in the New World. A skilled silk worker, he secured a position as foreman in the firm of Adams & Company, silk manufacturers in Kensington, a suburb of Philadelphia. He promptly sent for his wife and Eliza, urging them to join him in order to begin The Salvation Army in America. Whatever his motives had been for going to the New World, once there Shirley was inspired by a vision of what the Army could do for the Christless masses in Philadelphia. Eliza and Annie were naturally anxious to go. But when the seventeen-year-old lieutenant asked William Booth — now General Booth — for a transfer to Philadelphia, of all places, he expressed surprise and disappointment. He demurred and tried to dissuade her, flourishing the girl's vows, the great need for workers in England, and, as the trump, Matthew 10:37: that whosoever loveth mother and father

Eliza Shirley, who, as a young single girl in 1879, conducted (with her parents) the first unofficial Salvation Army meeting in the United States
Source: The Salvation Army National Archives

more than Christ is not worthy of Him. Still, he could not stand in the way of the family's reunion. Encouraged by Eliza's zeal, Booth relented: if the girl was determined to go, she might start a work in Philadelphia along Salvation Army lines. "If it is a success," he added, "we may see our way clear to take it over." Then the General hesitated again; his poetic and charming son Herbert was dispatched to try to dissuade the Shirley women, but in vain. At last Lieutenant Shirley and her mother were given a regulation Salvation Army send-off from Coventry. No doubt filled with gratitude by the General's last and greatest concession — that they might actually name their new work in America after the parent body — the women sailed. They were told to report any successes to headquarters. The family joined hands in August and, true to their word, set out at once to redeem the General's grudging confidence in them. They did not fail.

While Amos spent his working hours at the silk factory, Annie and Eliza searched the poor neighborhoods of Philadelphia for a hall they could afford to rent. They finally located an abandoned chair factory between Fifth and Sixth on Oxford Street, large enough and affordable but filthy, floorless, and unfurnished, with picturesque holes in the roof. The ever-cheerful Eliza compared it favorably to the manger of Bethlehem, and the women attempted to close the deal on the spot. The owner, not surprisingly, had never heard of The Salvation Army and expressed misgivings about the reliability of rent payments, to say nothing of his shock at being addressed by two "female preachers." Amos arrived with a month's rent in advance, drawn from his wages, and the hall was secured.

The family worked late into the night for weeks, preparing their fort for the first assault on Satan and his minions. The walls were whitewashed, sawdust was strewn on the dirt floor, and a platform was built of low-grade, unplaned lumber. With the family's small savings entirely expended in these endeavors, the Shirleys in perfect faith petitioned the Lord for the exact sum necessary to purchase lumber to build benches to hold the expected crowds. When a man arrived with the very sum in hand — he informed the rejoicing Shirleys that God had told him while at prayer to carry such a sum to this address — the cheerful militants naturally took this as further proof of the righteousness of their crusade. Nothing could stop them now!

Sunday, October 5, 1879, was set for the opening of the new work. Amos had plastered the neighborhood with posters announcing that "Two Hallelujah Females" — neither "women" nor "lassies" sat well with father Shirley — would "speak and sing in behalf of God and Precious Souls." The heading ran, in large and florid type, "Salvation Army," and the times and location of the meetings were given. "Rich and Poor, Come in Crowds."

The great day dawned, and the heroic trio marched out with hearts full of high promise. On the way to the "Salvation Factory," the Shirleys held a short service on the corner of Fourth and Oxford, singing, "We are bound for the land of the pure and the holy." Reminiscing about the event forty-six years later, Eliza could not recall if anyone stopped to listen to them. Thus do great events, those much sought-after turning points and watersheds in human affairs, pass unnoticed. For this gallant little scene surely was a great event: the first Salvation Army street-corner meeting in American history. No unprejudiced observer can fail to be touched by it: these obscure and unimportant people, favored by nothing in this life, unknown and unsupported even by their distant comrades, possessed of nothing but a love for God and their fellow sinners, held up the Cross of Christ over the manure and cobblestones of a Philadelphia gutter in 1879.

SALVATION ARMY!

TWO HALLELUJA FEMALES

FROM ENGLAND,

will speak and sing on behalf of GOD and PRECIOUS SOULS,
Commencing

SUNDAY, OCTOBER 5TH, 1879,

IN THE

Salvation Factory,

Formerly used as a Furniture Factory,

OXFORD ST., between 5th and 6th Streets.

Service to commence in the morning at 11 o'clock, afternoon
three and evening at seven.

Other Cristian friends will take part in the meetings.

RICH AND POOR, COME IN CROWDS.

EXCELSIOR PRINTING HOUSE, 1646 Germantown Avenue.

Poster advertising the first Philadelphia meeting held by Salvationists
Amos, Annie, and Eliza Shirley, on October 5, 1879
Source: The Salvation Army National Archives

The indoor meeting was, alas, an anticlimax after such a courageous beginning. Not even the plucky Eliza could make a "crowd" out of the twelve persons waiting on the platform for the service to begin — the more so as these were "Christian friends" who had taken an interest in the Shirleys' pioneer work and offered to help them conduct the first official meeting. Undaunted, the Shirleys were convinced, as were later pioneer officers, that multitudes secretly hungered for Christ and had only to be confronted with the gospel to embrace its saving grace. Clearly another street meeting was required. This time the Shirleys took up their stand at Five Points, a cheerless but crowded intersection of five slum streets. The sound of "We are going to wear a crown, to wear a starry crown" emptied the nearby saloons, much to the joy of the missionaries. But when they tried to deliver a message to the gathered crowd, it dispersed in a cloud of oaths and jibes. And when they gamely returned to the same corner at 7:00 P.M., they were greeted by many of the same crowd with a shower of insults, mud, and garbage. The audience gathered inside the hall for the evening service was again small and consisted of sympathetic Christians.

Confused and discouraged, especially by the perilous developments at Five Points, the Shirleys asked the mayor for protection. In what was to become a pattern in early Salvation Army history in the United States, city officials were unsympathetic to the Army's outdoor evangelism. The Shirleys were told that any disturbance caused by their work was entirely due to its eccentric and annoying character. They were ordered in future to hold forth in some place other than the public streets. The pioneers were finally reduced to trudging eight blocks from their hall to hold their open-air meetings in a vacant lot, where no one listened. In the meantime, the interest of the few "Christian friends" dwindled, and even the indoor services were held in an empty hall. Four weeks passed, with the Shirleys' hopes for the future of their mission sinking daily lower. Penniless, friendless, and discouraged, they prayed for some sign from the Heavenly Commander that He favored their dying crusade and would yet bless it.

Arriving at their dark and lonesome lot one evening, the trio were amazed to find flames, smoke, noise, and — most dazzling of all prospects to their hungry hearts — a crowd! Several boys had set fire to a barrel of tar in the Shirleys' lot, and the horse-drawn fire engines had arrived. Fire was a desperate threat in the crowded, wooden, gas-lit American cities of the late nineteenth century; fear, along with the self-important clang and bustle of fire engines, always drew large crowds to fires. The Shirleys were certain the fire was providential and threw themselves on the startled crowd with thankful hearts, singing, "Traveler, whither art thou going, heedless of the clouds that form?" Their curiosity naturally aroused, the crowd stayed to listen to Amos's brief, simple homily on the grace of Christ. At the end of it, a drunken, rumpled man, who proved later to be a notorious local known only as "Reddie," struggled forward to ask, in his bewilderment, if such Good News could be for the likes of him. Tearfully the Shirleys assured him that it was, and embraced the man, bearing him off in triumph to the Salvation Factory, "ten thousand hallelujahs" in their hearts. The crowd, now thoroughly amazed, followed the quartet into the hall. Reddie was allowed to sleep while the Shirleys sang, prayed, and spoke to the crowd, which now occupied all the seats and filled the hall to overflowing. Reddie was revived, and in the presence of the large and enthusiastic crowd — Eliza later remembered the number to have been over eight hundred — he was soundly converted. Sobered by his experience, Reddie promised to come again the next day to explain in his own words what had happened to him — giving his "testimony," an act the Army encourages to this very day. Many in the crowd had been deeply affected by all that happened — that Reddie was suddenly a changed man none could deny — and they promised to return to hear him. The Shirleys took up a collection and raised enough to carry on for a few more weeks. Though exhausted, they were overjoyed: the work was saved. The Salvation Army had been launched in the United States after all.[5]

At least it was launched so far as the Shirleys were concerned. The Salvation Army in Britain as yet knew nothing of these momentous events. Spreading rapidly in that country amid hurricanes of controversy and with every resource stretched to the thinnest possible point, the movement took no thought of the departed Eliza Shirley and her mission to the New World. But the movement did not remain unaware of the work in Philadelphia for long. With the Salvation Factory an assured success, to which crowds — and, far better, converts — repaired in ever larger numbers, Amos and Annie sent Eliza in January 1880 to open a second mission station — or corps, to use the new military terminology coming into use — on Forty-Second and Market Streets. Delighted at their success, the Shirleys collected newspaper clippings about the new mission and sent them triumphantly to General Booth, along with letters requesting him to take command of The Salvation Army in America officially.

Booth was naturally pleased, and he resolved after the first batch of good reports to promote Eliza Shirley to the rank of captain. But the Shirleys' continued importunities presented the General with a dilemma: he knew that the press of demands on the swelling Army in England made it almost impossible to spare any qualified officer to go to America. It would be a time-consuming and expensive trip to a country of which most people in Britain, the General included, knew little. On the other hand, if he did not act to graft this spontaneous American offshoot back onto the mother Army, he would lose control over it altogether. And Eliza had gone out with something like his promise that he would look at whatever she was able to start.

  The influence of George Scott Railton was crucial at this juncture. His motives for pressing himself on Booth as the leader of an American expedition were complex. Railton was a visionary for whom merely practical considerations like time and money meant nothing. He would throw himself on the American shore as he had on the Moroccan, his innocence untarnished by knowledge of the country. Railton was undeniably touched, as were William and Catherine, by the fact that the "war" had "broken out" in America as a consequence of the "unconquerable, unalterable essence of its nature"; it was "like a plant of God's own sowing." To deny it the sustenance that only headquarters could provide would be sinful and irresponsible. The Scriptures demanded a zeal for souls that transcended natural boundaries. In addition, early Salvationists in England had some reason to feel warmly toward the distant republic to which their attention was now so forcibly drawn: the Founder had been converted by an American evangelist, James Caughey, and in the 1870s he was much influenced by the holiness messages of Robert Pearsall Smith and Hannah Whitehall Smith. Charles Grandison Finney's *Revival Lectures* was the single most popular book in the small personal libraries of British officers. Booth had in his turn adopted preaching methods that some of his contemporaries criticized as "American." In addition, Railton was increasingly frustrated in his role as Booth's secretary; as the Army adopted an ever more consistent and inflexible military structure, the duties of the second-in-command to William Booth shifted from Railton, general secretary of The Christian Mission, to Bramwell Booth, newly installed chief of the staff of The Salvation Army.[6]

  Railton had a powerful ally in Catherine. The two had much in common: both were fond of theology (the practical-minded General regarded them both as bookish), both were zealously loyal to the General and his mission, which they had done so much to organize and guide, and both were committed to a broader program for the Army's evangelistic activities than the General was willing to embrace in this hectic period. First among these was the advancement of women into positions of usefulness and leadership in religious work. From the beginning the Army had attracted women in large numbers, and many were pressed into service as officers. Railton now hit upon the idea of offering to make up the American expedition entirely of women, with himself as leader. This would show what women could do, and it would ensure, through the simple fact of the marriages he confidently expected each to arrange for herself on the other shore, that the Army in America would be self-supporting from the

outset. It is also likely that the kindly Catherine, sensing a clash between Railton and Bramwell, favored an independent command for Railton away from London. Railton's arguments, Catherine's endorsement, and the plain fact of the Shirleys' success carried the General. Whether or not Booth was "forced by circumstances," as Railton wrote later, the decision was made: America for God and the Army![7]

The preparations for the send-off of Railton and the "Hallelujah Seven" were characteristically flamboyant. Collecting the lucky seven had been dramatic enough. Railton selected sturdy, stable women, with a ten-year veteran of the war, Capt. Emma Westbrook, to lead them. The first telegram she had ever received — a memorable event in itself — informed her of her appointment "to America" and instructed her to send in her measurements "for a uniform." Westbrook thought she was having a hallucination: she had never heard of wearing a uniform and had no certain notion where America even was, let alone why she should go there.

The first of several farewells held for the departing pioneers was no more reassuring: the speaker prayed for God to "drown 'em" on the way if they were going to fail Him when they got there! As there were several other meetings in the same spirit, the ladies could at least be grateful that the arrangements for their departure were quickly concluded. Notices of the Shirleys' success and the departure of the new American expedition appeared within two weeks of each other, on January 31 and February 14, 1880.[8]

The "Farewell Celebration" at Army headquarters in Whitechapel was historic in more ways than one. Over a period of time the Booths had resolved to clothe their Army in military uniform. The details of the uniform had yet to be settled, and in fact have been changed many times since — Salvationists have appeared in a bewildering array of ranks, stars, crests, frogs, cords, and colors over the years. The principle of uniform-wearing, however, has been maintained since 1880. It had great merit: Salvationists would thus declare to the world their Christian witness and loyalty to the great cause, and soldiers too poor to purchase decent clothing would acquire a measure of self-respect. All were equal in the Great Salvation War. In fact, even without a religious motivation, the trappings of military ceremonial were widely popular among working-class men in the late nineteenth century in Britain. At the Whitechapel farewell, Railton was the first officer to appear in full uniform. He was also the first man to bear the exalted rank of commissioner, specially borrowed for the occasion from the lexicon of the British Empire. An exquisitely formal oath of loyalty to Booth and the Army was also created especially for the big send-off, an oath that Railton, who was nothing if not a good sport, gamely recited on the eve of his departure. To cap the testimonies and speeches, Catherine handed Railton two new Salvation Army flags: one for the Shirleys in Philadelphia, and one for the "Blood & Fire New York No. 1," which as yet existed only in hope. The party sailed on the Anchor Liner *Australia* on February 14, 1880, after a march to the dock, which — as usual — stopped traffic. Railton looked "as happy as an angel" on the deck. His heart soared at the prospect ahead. As the ship prepared to drop her pilot at Dover, Railton scribbled a last note to the General: "The fact is we are so thoroughly satisfied that Filled with God, we'll shake America that all that lies between us and that result is marvelously insignificant."[9]

The pioneer party rejoiced at the sight of the scene of their future triumphs as the *Australia* berthed at Castle Garden on March 10, 1880.

But then, mused Railton in the first American *War Cry* in January 1881, any country would have looked inviting after "four weeks' tossing" on the sea. The trip had been unusually eventful, even for heroes. The seven women promptly collapsed with seasickness, their agonies punctuated by storms and a cracked cylinder in the engine that nearly caused the ship to turn back. Then there were unsettling rumors that the first-class passengers regarded Railton, who was holding services all over the ship, as a lunatic; the steerage passengers — "card-playing Germans" — didn't regard him at all. The high point of the voyage had been the commissioner's attempts to cheer the ladies by singing hymns through their cabin door. The pioneers were glad to see the New World at last.[10]

March 10, 1880. That subsequent events made it a day of significance no one, even over a century later, can deny. Railton and the "seven sisters," however, were determined to make their arrival in the United States significant without waiting for subsequent events. They marched down the gangplank, holding aloft one of their Salvation Army flags, to which a small American flag had been affixed in the union corner. The commissioner and the women were in their new uniforms, he in "dark blue suit, cutaway coat and a high peaked hat," the ladies in short blue dresses, blue coats trimmed in yellow, and "Derby hats." Each hat carried a red band upon which "The Salvation Army" had been worked in gilt letters. Their walk down the gangplank was a bit unsteady, but the pioneers literally leapt from the bottom step into action. The Army flag was planted with dramatic postures, and the country was claimed for God and the Army. They began to sing. The first hymn — which survived subsequent revisions of the songbook of The Salvation Army until 1987 — was characteristically to the point: "With a sorrow for sin, let repentance begin." Not surprisingly, a "curious throng" formed around the little group: the general impression that this was some kind of "travelling concert troop" was dispelled by the singing of another hymn, "You must be a lover of the Lord, or you won't go to Heaven when you die." This "drill" was cut short by the arrival of Amos Shirley, who had come from Philadelphia to meet the official party and who now hurried forward to greet Railton. The historian notes sadly that their remarks were neither recorded nor remembered, although a reporter who was on the scene noted that, oddly enough, Railton treated Shirley "rather coldly." The pioneers were also greeted by the Rev. and Mrs. James Ervine, former members of The Christian Mission who had written to the General in 1876 asking for missionaries. These people, who like the Shirleys were overjoyed at the long-awaited arrival of Army emissaries, had come to take them to their home in Jersey City.[11]

But not before Railton had spied the reporters. With an instinct that continued to serve the Army well, Railton began to converse with several newspaper reporters who happened to be present. Just as the Ervines and the "Christian friends" who helped the Shirleys with their first meetings demonstrated that the Army did not have to make its way entirely alone in starting its work in the United States, so Railton's eagerness to discourse at length to the reporters, who to his happy surprise were all around, shows that the Army recognized from the beginning the value of publicity — especially newspaper publicity, which was free. Reporters in those days had the habit of showing up at Castle Garden to watch the steamers unload their colorful and often newsworthy immigrant cargos, and the novel arrival of The Salvation Army was an unexpected boon to the New York press. Railton was delighted: "The press took us up with characteristic energy." The commissioner pleasantly remarked to one wondering reporter that The Salvation Army, "did not consist of wild and thoughtless fanatics and that its members had no idea of making a mockery of religion. On the contrary, it consisted of pure men and women, who were devoted to Christ and who had agreed to sacrifice their lives to making converts." He invited other reporters to look The Salvation Army up again when the pioneers had located a meeting hall. Captain Westbrook triumphantly reeled off statistics — another shadow cast back from the future — that demonstrated the success of the Army in England. Before leaving the dock area with the welcome party, Railton asked if there were any printing shops nearby that would produce free posters for the new arrivals.[12]

Exhausted from these endeavors, the eight Salvationists gratefully repaired to the Ervine home in Jersey City. Railton, however, could not rest: he was anxious to return to New York City to find a hall to rent. Ervine brought him to a group of prominent Christian businessmen and ministers who gathered weekly at the venerable Fulton Street prayer breakfast. These kindly men were touched by Railton's passion for lost souls and offered him the use of various churches. He refused. Railton was determined to carry the gospel to the unchurched masses: the Army, like The Christian Mission from which it developed, was at this stage wholly given over to evangelism, much of it on street corners and in music halls. The commissioner intended to maintain this tradition in America. So when the newspaper accounts of the landing brought an invitation from the enterprising Harry Hill, owner of a popular concert saloon, to "do a turn" on Sunday — which horrified the Fulton Street clerics — Railton jumped at it. The Christian Mission had made effective use of theaters and music halls in London. The audience was certain to be made up of just the sort of people the Army was after. Harry Hill's Variety, which stood on Houston Street a block east of Broadway, thus gained additional notoriety. It was already among the best-known dives in New York, a place to which cab drivers routinely took tourists looking for a thrill. Now Hill's achieved a kind of historic importance its amiable proprietor could not have anticipated. There, amid the low lights and stale beer, The Salvation Army held its first official meeting in the United States. The circumstances were not auspicious — Hill and most of the audience regarded the Army as a joke — and the meeting closed without visible results. Yet a beginning had been made, and in the right place. The only regrets that Railton ever had about the meeting were that he had refused the manager's offer of money and that he had asked the men in the audience not to smoke during the service: it only made them uncomfortable. It was clear to him that a standing rule against tobacco in Army meetings might repel from the doors the very sort of people the Army was after.[13]

The details of that first meeting, which was held on Sunday, March 14, 1880, have been preserved. The service was well attended by the Variety's usual clientele and — again — by the Army's "Christian friends," who were "drawn thither by a decent mingling of curiosity and sympathy." It was also well reported. The *New York World* called it "A Peculiar People amid Queer Surroundings." The first hymn was "Lover of the Lord," which had saved the day at Castle Garden. After each song — "Will You Go to the Eden Above?" was applauded — Railton would exhort the crowd, then kneel to pray. His female assistants surrounded him in "various and curious positions." When the lieutenants delivered their testimonies, which were obviously memorized, the crowd grew restless. Railton circulated among the crowd and put his arm around several of the men, which embarrassed them. For the Variety regulars, the novelty of the Salvation Army act had passed. After a fruitless invitation to repentance, the crusaders and the sympathizers who had come to hear them left together.[14]

The next morning, at the Fulton Street prayer breakfast, Railton was greeted with condescension. Predictions were confirmed: the Variety "turn" had been a humiliating fiasco. But the bread thus cast upon the waters did not sink. One of the prayer group, Richard Owens, was touched by the Army's zeal and offered the pioneers the free use of his own Hudson River Hall, at Ninth Avenue and Twenty-Ninth Street, for a month. That very night Railton's party secured its first convert. Ash-Barrel Jimmy (or "Jemmy," as he was sometimes called) was a homeless alcoholic who had earned his nickname when he was found by a policeman drunk in a barrel, his hair frozen to the bottom, and was dragged thus encumbered to the police court. The magistrate was in a jocular mood: he ordered James Kemp to attend The Salvation Army act at the Variety. Ash-Barrel lacked the twenty-five cents admission, but he dutifully — and drunkenly — found his way to the Hudson River Hall the next night. After making several efforts to get past the policeman patrolling in front of the hall, Ash-Barrel was finally gathered up in Railton's loving arms and carried over the threshold. Kemp was soundly converted — a turning point in more lives than his own. Ash-Barrel was a well-known local hard case, and word of his "getting saved" brought crowds. Enough money was collected by the Army pioneers to rent a hall of their own, the Grand Union on Seventh Avenue, which became the "Blood & Fire New York No. 1" corps for which Catherine Booth's flag had been destined.[15]

The meeting at Hill's gave the Army publicity among the growing number of clerics and lay Christians who were inspired to carry the gospel to the urban poor. The Salvation Army had, in fact, arrived in New York at a time when public interest in evangelization among the urban poor was increasing. Many Protestant clergy and religiously minded reformers viewed the cause of urban evangelization as the greatest crusade of the age. As America's cities swelled in population after the Civil War, Protestantism in all forms failed to keep pace. The future of the country, the church, and the cause of Christ itself seemed threatened. The traditional emphasis among most Protestant denominations had been on foreign missions; this now appeared to have been misplaced, even dangerous: the concern for the "heathen world," wrote one churchman in 1886, had "led to a fearful neglect of our cities." Urban centers were perceived as rapidly filling with immigrants and the working poor, few of whom knew or cared anything about Protestant religion. Samuel Lane Loomis, whose alarming lectures on this topic at Andover Theological Seminary were published in popular book form in 1887, lamented that Protestantism had "no following among the workingmen. Everyone knows it." Protestants had so far neglected the poor sections of America's large cities as effectively to have abandoned their inhabitants to Roman Catholicism or to no religion at all. The problem was "much discussed" in the 1880s; by the end of that decade one writer was happy to observe that the cause of urban evangelization had "aroused to an unusual degree the interest of the Christian world."

These sentiments were in fact widespread in the 1880s and 1890s, which helps to explain the public support that often nurtured the Army's development in major American cities. Owens's loan of the Hudson River Hall reflected this concern. Other missions opened their doors to The Salvation Army as well.[16]

The chronology of these first few days is difficult to trace. Even in a settled command with regular procedures, Railton took a cavalier view of record-keeping. Now a pioneer with a dozen things to do at once, flying around the city like some wild evangelical bird, he kept no records at all. Nor did his lieutenants, stalwart women with great hearts but little ability: none of them could even read competently, and they had no interest in details. Fortunately, some knowledge of events can be gleaned from reminiscences, contemporary newspapers, and a handful of fragmentary records. On March 15 Railton held one of several meetings in a converted brothel at 44 Baxter Street, in a desperate slum. The floor was spattered with tobacco spittle, and the place was crammed with "the refuse of the Fourth Ward dance cellars," stinking, smoke-filled, and noisy; "a yellow fever pest house could not have been less attractive." But the Army "did not seem to mind" and held a full meeting. Other halls may have been used as well. There is even confusion as to where Ash-Barrel Jimmy was actually rescued. It is certain, however, that large crowds attended Army meetings. It is also certain that Railton traveled beyond New York City, renting halls and theaters to "open fire" on the lost cities of New Jersey. He also sent some of his helpers on these missions; three of the Army women started the Great Salvation War in Newark in the Odeon Theater on March 21. It was their first experience in conducting activities without Railton's personal leadership. Camden and Atlantic City were opened later in that same month.[17]

This was success beyond hope, but it presented Railton with a problem: the halls could not hold the crowds, and police were forced to bar the doors for fear of suffocation or fire. Railton sensibly decided that the moment had arrived to carry the good news to the street corners, an idea to which he was already devoted in principle. Outdoor preaching was the mainstay of the Army's work in Britain, where its effectiveness had been proved beyond question. The corner outside the Hudson River Hall would be perfect: there would be no limitations on space there, and plenty of potential converts were right at hand. Mayor Edward Cooper thought otherwise: city law allowed only ordained clergy to hold religious services on the public streets, and then only by special permit. Railton exploded.

Cast down in an instant from ecstatic heights, never a lamb except in love, the commissioner delivered an ultimatum in the form of a proclamation on the city hall steps. It contained a dire threat: if the authorities would not relent on this position — Railton considered it no more than "etiquette" — he would remove his "headquarters" to another, friendlier city. Unmoved, Cooper refused again. Railton's statement that the "entire Salvation Army in America" would pray Cooper around likewise failed to produce anything but a cartoon in the New York *Graphic,* which portrayed the mayor sitting in a circle of praying lassies with the caption "Past Praying For!" Even though another permanent convert — Louis Pertain, a man who remained faithful for forty-two years — was saved the night before Railton's departure, the matter was decided: if the Army "could not develop in perfect liberty that line of action which more than any other has made and will make this Army a delivery force for the multitudes," the Army would go to Philadelphia. And, after scattering the seeds of salvation on the fruitful soil of New Jersey, to Philadelphia the Army went.[18]

The commissioner arrived in his new headquarters city on March 24, 1880. The Shirleys had not been idle since their first gallant little open-air meeting nearly six months before. A special public meeting was held for the ceremonial presentation by Railton of the Salvation Army flag sent by Catherine Booth to Amos and Eliza Shirley. When he arrived at the hall, Railton was stunned: it seemed to him to be "the biggest meeting of my life." There were over two hundred cheering soldiers on the platform, each with a Salvation Army hat band. Fifteen hundred people crowded into Athletic Hall, hired for the festivities. For the rest of his life Railton retained a vivid memory of the three Shirleys singing to the crowd the notable black American spiritual "My Lord, What a Mourning, When the Stars Begin to Fall!"

Philadelphia was clearly a center of lively interest in the Army; the city remained the official headquarters of the movement in the United States for another year. In May, when Railton reported to the General that there were eight corps in America, six of them were in Philadelphia. The two Shirley corps were mined to provide leadership for four more. One of the Philadelphia corps, in the Frankford section, produced a notable convert. Jennie Dickinson, a woman with only six weeks' experience as a Salvationist, was appointed to assist the officer who opened the corps and accepted a commission as an officer — the first native-born American to be commissioned an officer in The Salvation Army. Convinced that this hospitable city was the ideal place for a national headquarters, Railton opened one — the first ever in America — at 45 South Third Street. A large sign hung across the front announced to the world that this was "The Headquarters for The Salvation Army in America." The actual office was in the basement, dank and dirty, and it was here that Railton lived and worked.[19]

The summer of 1880 was an odyssey in the Homeric style for the Army pioneers. Railton was indefatigable, and he loved the United States. The heat of the summer and the vast size of the country (which combined to stupefy most English officers), the variety of races, languages, temperatures, and scenes all stimulated his energies to new levels. His vision was global — Scandinavians, Germans, blacks, all would be drawn in by the Army net: "If I can get the Americans, Germans, and Africans all fairly started, I hope by stirring such up to hearty rivalry to keep them all at full gallop."[20]

A newspaper, *The Salvation News,* was started on July 3, 1880. By chance, a copy of the entire second number (July 10) and a fragment of the third survive. The first edition was sold out in a few hours, but Railton admitted he could not offer "any regular terms" for the *News:* it was "merely a pioneer of our American *War Cry,*" soon to appear. The *News* is nonetheless a historical gem. It contains a hymn by Amos Shirley; news of the valiant fight being waged by "brave Captain Westbrook," who had been left to command New York No. 1 on Seventh Avenue, where she preached the gospel and collared roughnecks; advertisements of Army books written by Catherine Booth; and little snatches regarding several Fourth of July picnics, marches, and the testimonies of various converts.[21]

Railton embarked on long train trips to find likely places on which to "open fire." He traveled light and left almost no record; we do not know how many cities he might have visited. Meanwhile, the hectic pace and the heat were proving too much for the pioneer women; three of them collapsed and returned to England. Other English officers were sent to replace them, and American officers like Lieutenant Dickinson arose to join the ranks. The first "officer's councils" were held by Railton in Philadelphia and New York in May to encourage the staff and plan strategy. Although the staff in New York was entirely prostrated by the heat, Railton judged the councils a huge success. Penniless, often facing active physical hostility, jeered at, and mimicked, the Army advanced through that exciting summer. By the fall there were twelve corps in the United States, and fifteen hundred souls had been saved. Franklin, Pennsylvania, was opened as the "7th Pennsylvania," and in October two converts traveled on their own to "open fire" on Baltimore. It was the first anniversary of the Shirleys' street-corner evangelistic service in Philadelphia.[22]

Clearly the commissioner had made a wise move in joining the Shirley forces and consolidating the success in Philadelphia. Railton was not a practical man, however: for reasons that remain obscure, he decided in November to transfer headquarters to St. Louis! He had traveled widely in the summer, covering 4,200 miles, speaking eighty times, "living a real soldier life," scouting the terrain for future attacks. St. Louis was the gateway to the West, and Railton was not alone in believing that this was where the future greatness of the country lay. The city would be the perfect headquarters for a western campaign. The fact that The Salvation Army was unknown in the city, that a savage midwestern winter was rapidly descending, and that he had advanced 959 railroad miles from the rest of his troops did not trouble Railton — in fact, he does not seem to have been absolutely certain where his troops were. Baltimore had opened spontaneously the month before, and the war seemed to be spreading out of control. Railton was delighted. In January 1881, he wrote from St. Louis that he would "welcome the War news from any quarter and shall be thankful to strangers in any State, who are actually carrying on aggressive efforts, quite as much as to any of our own people, who may visit us with information." In St. Louis, as in so many other places where Railton opened fire, he found encouragement and support and gladly acknowledged these "good folk" and "sympathizers."[23]

But he still did most of the work by himself: he remembered St. Louis as "the place where I learnt most to fight alone." He was penniless and would have suffered actual want if a Mr. and Mrs. George Parker had not taken him in for the winter simply because he was a Christian worker. After his first meeting he could not rent a hall for weeks: the crowd had spit tobacco on the floor, and the owner would not have Railton back, despite his offer — he was now clearly repentant of his misjudgment at the Variety meeting — to provide spittoons. There were rumors of broken benches as well. One of the major obstacles that early officers had to overcome was the fact that few people would rent or loan them meeting halls: the crowds they collected for their indoor meetings tended to be drunks and rough customers who amused themselves by smashing the landlord's furniture when they lost interest in the proceedings. Railton spent all of November and December searching for a hall to rent. He succeeded, of course, but not before New Year's Day 1881. On January 1, he opened his crusade at Sturgeon Market Hall with a program advertised like a train excursion: "The Old Reliable Repentance, Faith and Holiness Line." Crowds were small — in Railton's language, "not large" — and there was no money. In February 1881 he wrote privately that he had "every reason & inducement to go back to London," but he could not bring himself to give up the struggle: "For the Lord's sake we must try to make the best of it all."[24]

There was never enough money. Even when he gave up meals and slept on old newspapers at headquarters, there was not enough to pay for posters, rent halls, and launch the American version of *The War Cry.* He had cherished this last project since July, but when an edition finally appeared on January 15, 1881, it was only on an "irregular" basis, like *The Salvation News* it replaced. And if hostility and poverty were not enough, the city authorities refused to allow the Army to preach on the streets of St. Louis. Railton was undaunted through it all: "Difficulties are created by the devil and his helpers solely." Reasoning that the mayor had "no power over the iced Mississippi, especially on the Illinois side," Railton went out on a Sunday to speak "plainly" to the skaters. He reported that it was "quite a novelty to have a congregation come skating around." There have been few individuals more zealous for Christ, more willing to suffer loneliness and humiliation for Him, than George Scott Railton, whose short but seminal sojourn in American history was now at an end. On January 1, 1881, he was ordered to return to London. His abilities as an organizer of advance-guard attacks were needed there: the home front was advancing rapidly, and outposts had been thrown open in France and Australia.[25]

Railton protested the order when it first came. He loved the United States despite the weather, which he now privately admitted to be subject to discouragingly un-English extremes. He had applied to become a naturalized citizen at Independence Hall almost as soon as he arrived in Philadelphia. He was concerned for the future of the American Army, filled with visions of the destined greatness of the country and of the Army if he could only stay to catch the rising tide. His missionary project had only just begun: surely the General would relent. Surely not: the second cable said simply, "Come alone."[26]

The loss of Railton to the pioneer work eventually had serious consequences. An immediate effect was the disappearance of the Army from St. Louis; Railton's work left not a trace. Recent research by Comm. John D. Waldron has uncovered the name of an officer, a Capt. Nancie (or Nancy) Weaver, who apparently carried on the work in St. Louis for a short time after Railton left, before Railton's replacement in overall command brought her East to one of the more promising centers of Army activity. No record has yet been found of what happened in St. Louis after Weaver left, or of Weaver herself, whose appearance on the stage of Army history seems to have been, like those of many others in the hectic pioneer days, brief. She was heard from once again, in Philadelphia in October, before she disappeared from the surviving records. When the Army re-opened in St. Louis in 1887, the officers thought they were making a "first appearance." One scholar states that the "recall of Railton, a man of great ability, threw the organization into complete confusion for five years." It is questionable that William Booth's ability to remain deaf to the pleas of those nearest to him was a kind of strength; that deafness would be at least partially responsible for two major crises in the affairs of The Salvation Army in America.[27]

At first, however, the dramatic speed with which the Army spread throughout the country — seemingly springing up in a half-dozen places at once — obscured the departure of Railton from the public eye. Frederick Booth-Tucker, himself a national commander in later years, correctly assessed Railton's singular year: the "foundations" had been laid. The work was carried on after Railton left with "signal success." The departing commissioner left Capt. Amos Shirley in charge, pending the arrival of a new leader from London. It was to be the only recognition that the pioneer captain ever received. When Maj. Thomas E. Moore arrived to take command in June, he made Shirley his aide-de-camp as a kindness, but Shirley quarreled with Moore for reasons now unknown and resigned after a month. His wife, however, remained an active officer. Several years after Amos drowned in the sea at Asbury Park, New Jersey, on August 12, 1884 — "wafted home on a wave of the Sea," was the cheerful way *The War Cry* reported it — she married an English officer, Maj. John Dale, with whom she enjoyed several more Army adventures on the American field. The courageous Eliza, who left the United States in 1881 for a rest from her pioneering labors, married Capt. Philip Symmonds while in England. They returned to America in 1885. Widowed early, she remained an active and successful officer the rest of her long and happy life and left behind children, grandchildren, and great-grandchildren who are to this day loyal soldiers in the crusade that she once launched on a dirty Philadelphia street corner.[28]

With or without these pioneers, the Great Salvation War went forward on several fronts. When Railton's party arrived in 1880, *Harper's*

Weekly dryly observed that they had a "gigantic and ambitious scheme of travelling all through this country, and establishing branches of their organization in every city and town." It did not remain a "scheme" for long: even critics of the Army and its ways were amazed at its "earnest zeal." Eighteen eighty-one was admittedly a year of consolidation. In 1882, however, a bridgehead was thrown into Ohio, and the Blood-and-Fire flag flew over fallen Steubenville. The crusade spread into Brooklyn, the "City of Churches," where four corps opened in rapid-fire order. Encouraged by this hospitality, Major Moore transferred national headquarters to Brooklyn in July, in the newly rented Lyceum, which soon became a well-known center of Salvationist activity. In 1883 the Army extended its operations to Connecticut and California (where the Army had blossomed forth spontaneously) and then to Kentucky, Indiana, Michigan, Massachusetts, and West Virginia. The rock-bound coast of Maine came under fire in 1884; in December of that year Akron opened as "Ohio No. 10." By January 1885 Columbus became the "15th Ohio."[29]

The year 1885 was especially auspicious. In February Capt. William Evans, his wife, and a lieutenant began operations on a Chicago street corner with a drum and a concertina. Despite "storms of violence," the city eventually took to the Army and became for a few years the greatest center of Salvationist activity in the country; by 1892, the year of the Chicago World's Fair, there were more corps in Chicago than in any other city in the world except London. Washington, D.C., was opened in 1885 as well; and Janesville, Wisconsin, was attacked single-handedly by sixteen-year-old Lt. Edward Parker. Five other states were "pioneered" in 1885. (Early officers were casual grammarians; the Army used several nouns as verbs, and one form of polite address — "farewell" — was — and is — employed as both a verb and a noun: to "farewell" [verb] an officer is to transfer that person; a "farewell" [noun] is the letter informing the officer of the transfer.) Corps were proliferating. The Army abandoned its practice of numbering them by state (as in "Ohio No. 10") and began numbering them by city; the one hundredth corps in the United States, opened in April 1886, for instance, was named "Chicago No. 3 Corps." The Army began to acquire real property as well, very slowly at first and at long intervals (detailed records of some of the earliest transactions appear not to have survived).[30]

By the end of the decade The Salvation Army was triumphantly operating its evangelical crusade — and the beginnings of a social welfare program — in forty-three states. Increases were being reported so rapidly that the national headquarters could no longer maintain effective direct control of the field. In 1884 eight "divisions" were created and put in the charge of divisional officers in order to supervise the burgeoning spiritual empire more effectively. These officers were themselves eventually swamped by a rising tide of converts, and in 1890 it was decided that henceforth the field officer — the person actually operating the individual corps — would have the privilege (hitherto reserved to the divisional officer) of swearing in the new recruits as soldiers.[31]

The Salvation Army arose in the far West in a manner that confirmed the General's confidence in extending the war to America. All the elements of the dramatic were present in the California story: colorful personalities, Herculean energies, obstacles that would have chilled the heart of a dragon, sweeping conversions, and — especially cherished by Army leaders — spontaneity. The Army burst forth on the Golden Shore almost of its own volition, like a wild plant growing up from a forgotten seed carried far away on the wind. Railton would have loved it.

San Francisco is a city that lives in a fog of nostalgia. It seems always to have basked in a golden sunset casting its beneficent rays on a charming mixture of Victorian row houses, reeling seagulls, and cable cars. The truth, alas, is less golden. In the 1880s San Francisco was as nasty a place as thugs, derelicts, and prostitutes could produce on short notice. Before the Gold Rush of 1849, the site had been a Spanish townlet. Gold had created the city, and gold kept it alive. The rich lived on Nob Hill in an opulence that still seems dazzling. Although many prospered in various levels of honest endeavor, others were shipwrecked on the Golden Shore, driven to desperation, begging, prostitution, and even violence to prolong their lives a few days at a time. Old San Francisco, for all its gilding and sterling, was cruel and sordid. Yet zealous Christians believe that where need is great, God's grace is greater. The spirit of compassion was not entirely extinguished; a few persons endeavored to bring the gospel of love to the streets of San Francisco.

In the summer of 1882 a group of Bay Area "holiness men," already convinced that their theology of love demanded action on behalf of the lost and dying on every hand, were galvanized by the blessings of a camp meeting in Oakland and the fortuitous appearance of one copy of the London *War Cry* to transform themselves by unanimous vote from the Pacific Coast Holiness Association to the "Salvation Army." George Newton was chosen as "Commander," and meetings were held — the first on the first Friday in October 1882. The little group held nightly street meetings in San Francisco, on Kearny Street on the Barbary Coast. They published five issues of a *War Cry* of their own, edited by J. B. Knight. The first edition in November predicted ten thousand recruits in thirty days and asked for musicians to form a brass band, which was already regarded as a characteristic feature of the Army's street warfare they had read about. At the outset the group could muster only a drum and a triangle, but, undaunted, they marched out in a long single file, carrying torches and a "transparency" — a sign painted on gauze stretched over a frame, illuminated from within by a kerosene flame — and singing gospel songs. This activity attracted the attention of young John Milsaps, who began attending the indoor meetings held on Eddy Street in the Children's Hall (loaned by a group of Adventists on condition that the "Army" pay the gas bill). Here Milsaps learned that this "Army" was an imitation of one in England conducted by a man named Booth and that the San Francisco branch "sprang at a moment of enthusiasm" from the now defunct Holiness Association. Milsaps felt inspired to join this little group; struggle as he might, he was hooked: on January 15, 1883, he was enrolled as a soldier.[32]

Milsaps was like many early Salvationists. Until he joined the Army — even this rump version — he had found no outlet for the wellspring of energy and devotion hidden within him. Hitherto a drifter and a sport, he found in the Army a long-sought channel for a life of service and purpose. Already a nominal Christian, he found no difficulty in becoming a wholehearted one. Milsaps set to work at once cleaning the hall, testifying in the street-corner circle, and serving as secretary to Commander Newton, for which service he was soon promoted to "sergeant." He showed warm enthusiasm for his new crusade. Outposts were opened in Oakland across the Bay and San Jose to the south. The leaders were former church people. The editor, Knight, was a Baptist, and the "Captain" in San Jose was the son of William Taylor, the Methodist missionary bishop to Africa. Few actual reprobates were saved; San Francisco remained the new Sodom. Enthusiasm began to flag in the face not only of dwindling returns but of poverty, ridicule, and threats.[33]

By July 1883 the original forty members had been reduced to thirteen; Sergeant Milsaps remained among the faithful. Commander Newton felt called to other, more promising, fields. He wrote to General Booth not once but several times over a period of time, offering him the command of all Salvation Army forces on the Pacific Coast. To Newton this seemed only fitting; to Booth, it was the call of Heaven — again. This time he

Maj. John E. T. Milsaps on his seventy-fifth birthday, January 3, 1927
Source: The Salvation Army National Archives

did not hesitate: he accepted Newton's offer as soon as a suitable officer could be selected and sent. The problem was finding someone who was able, aggressive, and replaceable. The General finally settled on a young captain, Alfred Wells, whom he astounded with a promotion to major and orders to open the war in California.[34]

Wells arrived in San Francisco on July 21, 1883, after a meandering trip across the country from New York during which he conferred official flags on outposts in Louisville, Kentucky, and New Albany, Indiana, and was offered a flourishing rescue mission in Chicago if he would take it over for The Salvation Army. The new commander was soon joined in California by reinforcements from England. Volunteering for America was becoming a less terrifying prospect for Booth's officers. Capt. Harry Stillwell arrived in October; a year later, both Wells's and Stillwell's fiancées followed. Thus strengthened, and with the still-shrinking remnant of the holiness group in hand, the Army began a vigorous campaign. The first official corps was opened in Oakland. Although California No. 1 did not always have regular officers in the early months, Oakland Citadel Corps quickly became — and remained for over a century — a vibrant center of Army activity on the West Coast. The corps moved with great jubilation, hallelujahs, and horn-honks into its own newly built wooden "Salvation Castle" on English and Webster in December 1885. Because it was the most handsome Salvation Army facility west of Chicago, California Divisional Headquarters promptly moved in with the Oakland soldiers.[35]

The more feeble San Francisco operation seems to have languished for a while, but not before Sergeant Milsaps won his most notable convert, an Armenian shoemaker named Joseph Garabed (or Garabedian), known to his friends and to The Salvation Army as Joe the Turk. A volatile eccentric, Joe served for two years as "doorkeeper" — a combination of head usher and bouncer — for San Francisco No. 1 corps, until he became an officer himself. Wells promoted Milsaps to captain and sent him to pioneer Stockton, while Stillwell took over the corps in San Jose, where he "had a hard rub but never flinched." In November 1883 a struggling western version of the official *War Cry* appeared for the first time. It became a monthly in March 1884 but was not published on a weekly basis like the eastern edition until November 1889. Milsaps, whose highly colorful accounts of the war had become expected features of the new paper, was made editor in December 1886.[36]

The Army in New York continued, with a fine disregard for geography, to list two "divisions": America and California. National headquarters rejoiced over reports of "California salvation gold dust" and in 1885 noted that the work on the Pacific coast "never looked so well as at present." Unconnected to the rest of the American Army, reporting directly to General Booth in London, The Salvation Army in California struggled on. Progress was slow, against "terrible difficulties." California was so wicked that the air seemed "filled with devils." In July 1884, on the first anniversary of the western branch of The Salvation Army, there were only four corps. In 1886 the Army had one hundred corps in the United States; only eight of these were in the Western states, and four of these were barely flickering.[37]

A welcome development came when the Pacific Coast Division was taken under the mantle of the national headquarters. Major Wells left for England in May 1886, leaving Captain Stillwell — the root of a still flourishing Army family tree — in charge. In August Mrs. Stillwell traveled north to open the work in Portland, Oregon. Maj. J. H. Britton arrived in October from New York to take command, allowing Stillwell to join his wife in Oregon in December, when a new division was organized there. The war gained more ground once the Army was unified. On May 8, 1887, two officers — one of them "Happy Joe the Turk" — opened fire on Los Angeles in a tent in a vacant lot on the corner of Fort and Temple Streets. In June Salt Lake City was assaulted. The first Salvation Army officer to die in the West, Cadet J. M. Burns of Oakland, succumbed to typhoid fever in Salt Lake City in November. By July Seattle had a corps; in August, Boise, Idaho; in July 1888, Helena, Montana; and in September 1889 Reno fell to a Blood-and-Fire squadron. By 1890 there were forty-two corps in the West, and "several hundred soldiers."[38]

Meanwhile, the Army in the eastern states suffered the near disaster of a major secession of officers and soldiers. It recovered only slowly through a sequence of events that seemed almost miraculous to friends of the struggling movement. The principal agent in the crisis, Maj. Thomas E. Moore, was an unlikely villain. Sent to replace Railton in June 1881, Moore was a devoted and enthusiastic officer. Born and raised in London's East End, formerly a divisional officer in charge of a number of corps in London, Moore was flattered by his selection to "command American forces." He was determined to carry the Salvation War to the farthest corners of this benighted land. He was an indefatigable traveler, opening new corps, encouraging the embattled hosts, and sending cheerful messages to places such as California that were too distant to visit at once. A man whose motto seems to have been summed up in one of his several original songs, "Victory or Death," Moore was popular and respected by his officers. He was colorful, obviously sincere, and a successful evangelist, under whose ministry many were converted. Railton, always the gadfly, tried to be fair even in the face of Moore's later official disgrace at international headquarters, stating that Moore had "certainly pushed the war forward with all diligence."[39]

Unfortunately, Major Moore had two defects — one minor, the other catastrophic — in his equipment for the post of national commander. The minor defect was that he had only limited ability, and no interest, in the practical side of administration. He was an evangelist first and last, caring little for fund-raising and bookkeeping, which he seems mostly to have ignored. The more important defect was that Moore never understood the mind of General Booth, who regarded The Salvation Army as a living entity encircling the globe and his own authority over it as sacred and inviolable. These potential rubs became real at a logical point: the question of who owned the material wealth of the Army.

Under American law in the 1880s, someone — a "person" — had to hold legal title to everything of value. The courts had speeded the process of industrial consolidation by defining corporations as "persons" entitled to "own" property. The difficulty, as far as General Booth and British law were concerned, was that all property given or deeded to The Salvation Army was owned by General Booth. As fate would have it, American state laws differed widely on the matter of the ownership of property by foreign citizens; it was difficult and complicated for one foreign citizen to own property throughout the United States. Thus Major Moore, who became a naturalized citizen for this very purpose, held legal title to all properties given to or purchased by The Salvation Army in the United States and all funds collected by it. He did this solely as the agent of General Booth, as far as the Army was concerned; but in the eyes of the law, the Army's wealth and property, which showed early signs of becoming considerable, belonged outright to Maj. Thomas E. Moore — as did the liabilities that might accrue against those properties. Only corporations offer limited liability to their investors and agents; there was no limited liability for individuals such as Moore.

It is clear now, and ought to have been clear to everybody at the time, that the Army should have been incorporated in the United States, most logically under the state laws of New York, site of national headquarters. It was clear to Moore, who began as early as 1882 to try to convince the General of the point. But it remained unclear to Booth for years to come. In July 1883, the major filed a preliminary petition for incorporation under the statutes of New York. This was partly to protect headquarters against the novel project of the corps in New Brunswick, New Jersey, to incorporate itself under the generous corporation laws of that hospitable state. The corps leaders wished to avoid charges, which had become public, that money being raised by the "5th New Jersey" to build a new hall was going to Moore personally or to Booth in London. These charges and the resultant incorporation of the corps alarmed Moore, and with good reason: as an incorporated body, the 5th New Jersey could demand the funds already collected and deposited in the regulation way in the headquarters corps account. Should the demand of the "rebel" leaders be refused, as it surely would be, Moore was liable to arrest for civil suit anytime he happened into New Jersey — which, considering the furious pace of the Great Salvation War along the Jersey Shore, was inevitable. The major, Captain Westbrook, and another veteran officer sailed for England to urge the case for incorporation on the General in person. Unfortunately, they were unable to convince Booth of need for the legal action. The principle of divided ownership of Army property was utterly repugnant to him, and the three returned in defeat. Then the inevitable happened: Major Moore was arrested in December 1883, while holding a preaching service in the corps at Rahway, New Jersey.

Moore was driven to drastic action by the events of 1884. The loyalty to international headquarters of many in the ranks was becoming clouded. American Salvationists were disappointed when neither General Booth nor Bramwell came to the gala fourth anniversary festivities in Brooklyn. Eliza Shirley Symmonds recalled that the failure of the Booths to expose themselves to an American Army that knew nothing of them personally, and of whom they seemed to have known almost as little, was a major cause for the widespread support given to Moore in the October crisis. This conclusion seems to be warranted by contemporary facts. Two staff captains sent by the General in July to give him a firsthand report on the situation in Brooklyn managed to throw fuel on the embers. They discovered to their chagrin that The Salvation Army in America did not yet command sufficient popular support to enable it to apply for special legislation with any hope of success, and under existing laws of incorporation in New York, any act obtained would place full control of all assets in the hands of the local trustees. The auditors therefore suggested that Moore retain legal title to all Army property but that these properties be mortgaged to William Booth for more than their market value (thus giving Booth first and full claim — in effect, ownership — to any property that was the object of a suit). This subterfuge was unlikely to deceive anyone for long, however, and once discovered would bring humiliating publicity on the heads of the American Army leaders. At the same time, the visiting officers gratuitously reported that Moore was not adept at business matters generally, and, even putting aside the incorporation heresy, his accounts were "in confusion." Several of the eight new divisional officers created that very summer added their complaints about this side of Moore's leadership to the official report that the two emissaries carried back to London.[40]

In July 1884 the American *War Cry* carried a "notarized statement" from the General, reaffirming that the legal foundation of the Army — the Deed Poll of 1878 — vested "control and direction" of the organization solely in the person of William Booth, that all properties of the Army were to be "conveyed to, and held by, the General," that Moore was his appointed commissioner to direct all Salvation Army activities in the United States, "including the State of New Jersey," and that Moore would be "acting unfaithfully to his high trust" if he handed over one cent to "certain persons in the city of New Brunswick." Moore was neatly caught: "faithfulness" to the General meant jail in New Jersey. But Moore was not left dangling between extremes for long. Convinced by the report of his auditors that Moore was a well-meaning bungler, and certain after the Rahway arrest (to which another, in Newburgh, New York, had been added) that the major was going to incorporate the Army despite his orders, Booth decided to transfer Moore to South Africa.[41]

Moore still did not wish to cause an open rupture with the General. He was convinced that incorporation was essential for the salvation of the Army and that given time — and a *fait accompli* — the General would come to accept this fact. A rupture, however, was hard to avoid. Sensing rebellion, Booth ordered the commander of the newly created Canadian territory, Maj. Thomas B. Coombs, to hasten to Brooklyn to relieve Moore of his command. Refused admittance at headquarters, Coombs telegraphed to the American field officers that Moore was deposed and that he, Coombs, was in charge. Moore wired soon after with orders to disregard communications from Coombs. Interest among officers was aroused by these events. When Moore called a conference at headquarters in October to explain his position, as many as were able to disentangle themselves from their work attended the meeting — from which Moore had taken the precaution of excluding Coombs and the discontented divisional officers who had joined their complaints to those of the staff captains in July. Moore declared himself willing to accept any assignment, even South Africa (which he regarded as an undeserved demotion), once the General accepted the necessity of incorporation. Even if the officers present voted to approve incorporation and Moore proceeded with it, he assured his listeners that General Booth would still be in absolute spiritual

A War Cry *office located on State Street, New York City.*
Richard Holz is in the top row, third from left; "Ashbarrel Jimmy,"
fourth from left; and Thomas Moore, fifth from left
Photo: Joseph Guthorn, New York City
Source: The Salvation Army National Archives

command of the American Army. The vote was 121 in favor and 4 against incorporation. The Salvation Army was incorporated on October 24, 1884. In a rare burst of business acumen, Moore also registered all Salvation Army insignia, including the crest, and copyrighted *The War Cry*.[42]

The resulting confusion, which lasted for five years, caused serious difficulties for Salvationists and sympathizers alike. The General, outraged at Moore's treason, dispatched Maj. Frank Smith to take command of the Army in the United States. Smith was a man of ability, like Moore an experienced divisional officer in London, loyal to the General, and an effective public speaker. He was keenly interested in social problems and, rare for a Salvation Army officer, was willing to advocate a definite political program. His appointment was nevertheless a mistake: Smith was fiercely zealous and lacked tact and patience. Setting up a rival "loyal" headquarters near Battery Park and issuing a "loyal" *War Cry*, Smith, who was given the high rank of commissioner, dismissed as rebels the large majority of officers who still innocently believed Moore to be in charge or who chose to follow him on principle. Richard E. Holz, a German-American convert who was to become one of America's most distinguished officers and head of a long line of such, was one of many who sought Smith out for advice and information only to be rebuffed as a dupe and a traitor. Ignoring Moore's very real contribution to the war effort, Smith stated that his rival had incorporated the Army only to cover his "mismanagement and insubordination." Five of the eight divisional officers and seventeen corps, several of them desperately poor in soldiers and funds, declared their loyalty to Booth and the international Army in response to Smith's demand for "full surrender." The rest remained with Moore or faded away as the sympathy of the public — at first surprised, then amused, and finally bored at the prospect of two Salvation Armies struggling over the same ground — dwindled and cooled.[43]

Major Smith was not, however, merely a martinet or a fool. He regarded it as his duty to represent the General's viewpoint exactly, and he did so consistently. Booth believed The Salvation Army was a living whole, one movement, above local laws and international boundaries. He believed that he had been called by God to organize this crusade, which God was surely blessing; Booth could not in conscience lay aside this sacred trust by sharing authority or allowing subordinate parts of the "world-wide Army," as he liked to call it, to secure autonomy on any point, however minor. The General was absolutely sincere. Everything William Booth did, he did for the Great Salvation War. He gave his every moment to it, he sacrificed his children to it, and — old, blind, dying — he gave his last and most noble public statement to it. In a series of open letters in the American *War Cry,* Booth pleaded with wavering soldiers to rally to him — everything must be for "the ONE Salvation Army," every book and chair (and heart and mind) must be "nailed to the one Salvation Army flag." Smith himself, who has been slighted in official Army histories, made a considerable contribution toward regaining some of the immense ground lost in the secession. A man of social compassion — he later pioneered the Army's social welfare program in England — Smith planned various campaigns to win the poor and neglected and began several abortive schemes to reach urban blacks. He clearly misjudged the character of the would-be prodigals whom he rebuffed without a hearing, yet he wore himself out in a ceaseless campaign to advance the cause of the loyal Army. In this endeavor, despite all, he largely succeeded.[44]

For his part, Moore assumed the rank of general over the forces that remained loyal to him, which he named the "Salvation Army of America." "Moore's Army" started with several advantages. Many of his officers were noble souls, zealous for Christ. The organization experienced its share of heartbreak and victory, as the editions of his *War Cry* and the scattered surviving reports and private papers of his officers attest, but slowly, inexorably, it withered and died. There were several reasons for this failure. Despite initial hard work and sacrifice, most of Moore's officers did not attract sufficient funds or converts to survive. The loyalists were convinced that God had raised up The Salvation Army for His own purposes, which were not yet fulfilled. Though both groups propagated similar doctrines, used the same techniques, sang the same songs, and were almost identical in appearance, Booth's Army, marching under a new crest cleverly crowned with a gallant eagle (which was officially supposed to refer to the biblical promise that the redeemed "shall mount up with wings as eagles" [Isa. 40:31] but which Americans found gratifyingly patriotic anyway), grew and prospered, while Moore's Army languished.[45]

The excitement caused by the secession seems to have been localized and, in many places, brief. Even in 1884, at the height of the controversy, the young convert Adam Gifford in McKeesport, Pennsylvania, had not heard of either Moore or Coombs. The Army in the West, an area of vast potential, was unaffected by the secession. The Pacific Coast Division was simply informed by wire that Comm. Frank Smith was their new commander. Chicago was opened in February 1885 by Capt. William Evans, who had come with Smith from England along with a number of other "reinforcements." Evans was an able and attractive officer, and the Army in Chicago grew rapidly amid scenes of great excitement. Every convert was a loyalist.[46]

A major factor in the Booth triumph was Booth himself. Effective in print — his *War Cry* letters were widely read — the General was overpowering in person. His first trip outside the British Isles came in the fall of 1886, when he arrived in America, via Canada, to survey this distant front and to encourage the loyalists. The Army was not only encouraged: it was delirious. The General's visit became a triumphal course amid explosions of tambourine rattling, the East Liverpool brass band, and "Hurrah[s] for Jesus." The pandemonium in Chicago in the newly captured Rink was broken only by Commissioner Smith repeatedly blowing on a police whistle. Everywhere the General spoke lovingly of Christ, the sinner's Friend, and of his own vision of the redemption of the world through the self-sacrifice and loyalty of The Salvation Army. From Danbury, Connecticut, in November (where he was in town at the same time as his fading rival, General Moore), to that Elysium of piety, Ocean Grove, New Jersey, in January 1887, William Booth was cheered, adored, quoted — and believed. The decline of Moore's troops became precipitate.[47]

Moore's own lack of administrative skill played a part in his army's decline. His self-elevation to stellar rank had not made him a financial wizard. Money dried up, the rent on his headquarters was not paid, and in December 1888 the board of trustees — Moore shortsightedly made his army more democratic than Booth's — asked him to resign. When he indignantly refused, they deposed him in January 1889. The command was offered to another, who refused, then to Colonel Holz, who accepted reluctantly, only as a means to his long-cherished goal of reconciliation with the worldwide Army; for this reason, Holz did not accept the rank of general with his new command but remained a colonel. He promptly opened informal negotiations with the genial Evans, fresh from his Chicago triumph and now installed as chief of the staff to the new national commander, Ballington Booth. Commissioner Smith, worn to the thread by his labors, had returned to England in 1887 to be replaced by the General's second son. Ballington was conciliatory toward the Moore rebels from the beginning. He made reconciliation not only possible but attractive. He invited Holz to share public platforms with him and acted as though Holz were already restored. On October 5, 1889, Holz wrote to the officers of the "American Salvation Army," declaring that the Holy Spirit had led him to "enter the ranks of the parent Salvation Army" with "as many as I could influence" to do the same, praying to God to "hasten the day when there will be but one Salvation Army throughout the United States." All was speedily arranged. On October 16, 1889, in Saratoga, New York, Holz and twenty-nine other officers, including that doughty pioneer Capt. Emma Westbrook, were restored to The Salvation Army in a tearful and "powerful" public meeting. Holz (taken back as a major) was promptly appointed divisional officer for the New York State Division. Other officers followed Holz's lead and returned to the Booth ranks. The Army had weathered its first real crisis.[48]

CHAPTER 2

1880-1900

"Come, join our Army, to battle we go."

William Pearson (1879), Salvation Army *Song Book,*
1890 ed., song no. 528

The Great Salvation War advanced steadily in the last two decades of the nineteenth century. Progress was often dramatic. Within the first year after the Army opened in Chicago in February 1885, 547 separate conversions were reported in *The War Cry* — and this figure represents only thirty-six weekly reports; at the same rate for fifty-two weeks, there would have been eight hundred converts. When Comm. Frank Smith visited Chicago in January 1886, he claimed that a thousand souls had been saved in the Army's meetings since it opened fire on that city. Four months later the Army opened its third corps in Chicago — its one hundredth in the United States. There were many critics of The Salvation Army in the early years, but no one could deny that it was succeeding in attracting large numbers of people to its services, and that many of these were being "rescued from sin."[1]

The reasons for this were complex; any attempt to explain the rapid growth of The Salvation Army in these years must proceed carefully. It is never possible for believers to separate entirely the direct work of God from the many effects for which there is a natural explanation. Much serious, detailed, and persuasive scholarly attention has been devoted to this period in the history of urban reform. In addition, in the 1980s several Salvationist writers produced important studies of the relationship between Salvation Army beliefs and practices on the one hand and the extent of its growth on the other. In the last two decades of the nineteenth century, however, Army officers operated on the old adage that men (and women) should act as though everything depended on them and pray as though it all depended on God. Salvationists certainly knew human nature and used that knowledge in shrewd and effective ways; yet they were convinced that every advance was led only by God, that every convert was a "Trophy of Grace." The songs of the era declared these beliefs to the world: "Jesus Is Our Captain," "God Leads the Dear Army Along." Salvationists were "Soldiers of Jesus" in the "Army of the Lord."[2]

The General and his leading officers were certain that God was the prime mover in their success: it was His reward to the Army for preaching the true gospel to all who would listen. The Army had, in fact, very definite doctrinal views, a fact that many contemporary observers discounted. Studies by Leicester Longden, Philip D. Needham, and Roger Green have shown that William Booth had a thorough knowledge of orthodox Wesleyan doctrine. All three studies argue effectively that Booth's concept of the Army and its mission sprang directly from his theological beliefs.[3]

Salvationists were convinced that their doctrines were based solely on the Bible. Ballington Booth, national commander in the United States from 1887 to 1896, wrote that the Army preached "a plain and simple revival of the teachings of Christ and His Apostles," while his wife, Maud, spoke of "no new doctrines" but those of Paul, Luther, and Wesley. The Army believed that the people of the world lived under the curse of sin. Every person who was not made to recognize that fact and claim the forgiveness and salvation that God offered through Christ was cast at the end of life into eternal torment. "We must awake to the fact," wrote William Evans in 1892, "that tens of thousands are dropping into a never-ending hell each day we live." Salvationists were driven by a sense of responsibility almost too awesome to bear; the energy and fervor with which they preached touched the hearts of pathetic and lonely people who were all too aware of the price mankind paid for sin and who, informed at last of a cure, flocked forward, outdoors and in, to be "washed in the Blood of the Lamb."[4]

Once rescued, the new convert was immediately pressed into the war for souls, as a testifier and supporter if not as a soldier. "We are a salvation people," William Booth wrote in 1879; "this is our specialty — getting saved and keeping saved and then getting somebody else saved." Activity filled the life of the new convert. Ballington Booth proclaimed in 1888 that "people who are casual onlookers feel surprised that salvation can keep so many people busy, but it can." The lives of converts were given new meaning — the highest possible meaning: they were not only saved but given the privilege of saving others. Here was the world's great cause, and these new "blood-washed warriors," lonely and obscure no longer, were given a part to play in it. Professor Green makes an additional suggestion: the fact that Booth was a "post-millennialist" further explains the zeal with which the Army committed itself to its work. If Christ would come again in glory only after the millennium — the reign of the saints on earth — then the sooner the world was won for Christ, the sooner He could come again to claim His own. The Salvation Army, by winning souls in places where the Army's leaders believed that other evangelistic efforts had not penetrated, was hastening the Second Coming! Booth went so far in 1890 as to refer to the millennium as "the ultimate triumph of Salvation Army principles."[5]

And there was more: after salvation, converts were urged to dedicate their hearts to Christ without reservation, so that His love would pour in and purge all selfishness and pride. The "sanctified" soldiers could then spread the love of God abroad in an ever more brightly burning desire to save souls, to share love, and to provide some kind of physical or emotional comfort to the miserable and desperate people they daily encountered. Needham points out that, for the Salvationist, the work of grace was never purely individual: there was always a communal dimension — those who were saved felt compelled to commence at once the work of saving others. This was the Army's understanding of the Wesleyan doctrine of "holiness," which had served as its foundations from the beginning. It was not without pitfalls — several pioneer officers withdrew, for instance, after seeking in vain for the gift of "sinless perfection," a quest based on the odd idea that the love of God in the heart removes one's capacity to commit sin — but officers quickly learned to steer their converts toward a practical holiness, couched in terms of zeal and compassion, which was eagerly accepted. Many friends of the Army, no less than Booth and his officers, attributed the success of The Salvation Army to its direct and earnest preaching of this gospel of salvation and love. An organization that had been created and controlled from the beginning by a "conception of life as an opportunity to save souls for heaven" and by "a basic sympathy for all men that suffer" could not fail.[6]

Comm. Samuel Logan Brengle in the 1930s
Source: The Salvation Army National Archives

For many years the Army's leading, and still most famous, exponent of practical holiness was Samuel Logan Brengle, a graduate of Boston Theological Seminary who became an officer in 1887. Severely injured in Boston by a drunken man who tried to kill him with a paving stone, Brengle spent a long convalescence writing articles on holiness for *The War Cry*. These articles, which were later collected together in a book entitled *Helps to Holiness* (part of the "Red Hot Library" of devotional classics personally selected by General Booth), established Brengle's reputation as the Army's leading exponent of the doctrine. Brengle was a kindly man, easily approached, eloquent, remembered for decades after his death in 1937 as a flesh-and-blood saint who faced real problems. His personal correspondence and references to him in private journals kept by other officers reveal remarkable spiritual consistency over his long career. He explained holiness in terms of Scripture and his own experiences; his preaching and his writings — which ran to many volumes — had a straightforward, conversational style and were anecdotal and full of stories and analogies to which the average Salvationist could relate. Generations of them found blessed relief in Brengle's homey explanations:

> There are people who fail to get the blessing, because they are seeking something altogether distinct from Holiness. They want a vision of Heaven, of balls of fire, of some angel; or they want an experience that will save them from all trials and temptations, and from all possible mistakes and infirmities; or they want a power that will make sinners fall like dead men when they speak. They overlook the verse which declares that "the end of the commandment is love out of a pure heart, and of a good conscience, and of faith unfeigned"; which teaches us that Holiness is nothing more than a pure heart, filled with perfect love, a clear conscience toward God and man, which comes from a faithful discharge of duty and simple faith without hypocrisy.[7]

A large part of the motive and the success of the pioneer Army can thus be explained in terms of doctrine; yet contemporaries spoke condescendingly of the Army's "singularly meagre 'theology.'" The explanation for this paradox lies in the fact that officers themselves spoke slightingly of "mere" theories and boasted with Catherine Booth that they were "not very intellectual" or "learned." The General and his officers had no time for idle disputations: life was a struggle, and the Christian religion was a perpetual and bitter warfare. Railton dismissed "theory" in the first American *War Cry:* "The world has ten thousand times too much of that already. Let us force war."[8]

The Great Salvation War was no mere metaphor to the Army. "What is this battle? Is it born of fancy — a mere allegory? No! No!" Booth adapted his creed to the "exigencies of the soul-saving task," and, according to Philip Needham, it was this rather than any lack of mental powers in

Army leaders that explained the directness and simplicity of official theology. Anything that stood in the way of a universal call to repentance was
eliminated. The Army abandoned the practice of sacraments in 1883 once
Booth, strongly influenced by Catherine and Railton, came to believe that
participation in sacraments is not essential to salvation. A recent study by
David Rightmire has demonstrated that this decision was based on serious
and well-informed theological considerations. In addition, it was easy
enough to be convinced that these practices were confusing to the ignorant
and that communion wine constituted a dangerous temptation to the
salvaged drunkard. The Army insisted repeatedly that the only real religion
is that which is believed heartily and lived out daily: "Christ in the heart,"
declared *The War Cry* in 1881, "is worth more than a world full of
theories." Ballington Booth proposed substituting "heartology" for the
dread word "theology." An image of itself cherished by the Army in these
years was that of a refuge in a rising tide of sin, in which thousands were
drowning on every side. The Army was variously an island, a lighthouse,
or a lifeboat: in every case Salvationists, dry and secure, were shown
bending to the work of saving the lost, tossing out ropes and nets. It used
hymns like "Throw Out the Lifeline" and "Rescue the Perishing" so often
in street services that these became associated in the public mind with the
Army's outdoor crusade and were thought of as "Salvation Army songs."[9]

It is small wonder, then, that people already disposed to be critical
of the Army would regard its theological resources as thin. Pioneer officers
sometimes added credibility to the charges. Most early officers were recent
converts who knew little of theological matters. Men and women were
pressed into duty as officers with no preparation, commissioned on the
spot by enthusiastic divisional officers, and sent off to command a station.
Although Mrs. Ballington Booth took pains to refute allegations that
Salvationists were "not Bible-students" by stating that "nowhere in the
world are there such Bible-readers" as the Army has made of its converts,
the truth often fell short of her claim. In 1890 an official Salvation Army
handbook boasted that the fact that Salvationists were "unquestionably
very deficient in *earthly* knowledge" made them like the original apostles.
Many officers displayed little knowledge of the Scriptures, memorizing or
quoting Bible texts only as a means to convince sinners that all was lost
without Christ. The same handbook declared that the organization was
not opposed to Bible classes as such (although the ordinary "theoretical,
speculative and controversial" type was forbidden) but preferred to teach
the Bible by preaching and modeling. Pioneer officers sometimes noticed

that their rough congregations would sit happily through testimonies and cheerful songs but grew restive when a speaker began to read from the Bible.[10]

No matter how important or attractive the Army's doctrines were, however, they were not self-propagating. Theology alone cannot account for the rapid spread of the Army over the face of the land. The exuberance of the soldiers, the very joy they found in fighting, won attention for them. "Other sects have professed cheerfulness," observed one magazine, "but none have so openly embraced the spirit of jollity." The hallelujah battalions advanced to sprightly tunes that told the world there was "joy in The Salvation Army: 'Tis Blood and Fire give the Army joy, And victory all the way." The Army was a "living protest against all mere formal religion, all mere ceremonies, creeds, or professions which have no life in them." A meeting in Brooklyn in 1889 was described by a witness as "a right glad, jolly, happy hallelujah time." If The Salvation Army had anything, it had life, a contagious, bumptious vitality that filled the streets of America with "loud joyful songs of praise."[11]

The pioneer Salvationists had discovered with Railton that "there is no cause so hopeless as one without enthusiasm." Officers were not so much enthusiastic as they were impassioned: only a high level of excitement could have produced the prodigies of work that were required to push the constant expansion of the war front. The first thing the *Louisville Courier Journal* noted about the Salvationists who started work in that city in April 1883 was that they were "indefatigable and wonderfully zealous." Similar tributes appeared in scores of contemporary newspapers. Captain Stillwell and his "Hallelujah wife" announced from Oakland: "My wife and I are fully saved, and mean to leave this city better than we found it; if hard work and holy living can do anything much will be done." In New Brunswick, the 5th New Jersey braced itself for "incessant war," holding services "every night without a break." Officers sometimes conducted fifteen meetings each week, indoors and outdoors. Preaching a dozen times a week was not uncommon, although the record of young Capt. Harry Ironside was more nearly typical for the officer of the early 1890s: in his first year as an officer in California, he preached four hundred sermons. The quality of some of these homilies must have been dubious. The officer's daily schedule, which called for hours on the street selling *The War Cry*, collecting money, paying encouraging visits to the soldiery, and doing a host of other undramatic things, left little time for sermon preparation. One retired officer remembered his corps officer in Waterbury,

Connecticut, in 1893, who was so tired he could not preach at all but only sit on the platform and weep for souls. The General warned his troops in 1885 that the work was not all glamour: "Be a Salvation Plod" he ordered. Still, the soldiers who had to listen to almost as many sermons as the officer delivered had to be considered; officers were transferred every few weeks or months so that their stock of sermons would always seem fresh to their listeners. Ironside, for instance, commanded three successive corps in his first year, and Brengle served at Danbury, Connecticut, for just three weeks in 1888. In July 1895 the Army established a fixed rotation of officers, announcing that they would be reassigned four times per year on definite dates. In March 1898 the minimum appointment in a corps was lengthened to four months, which was confirmed in November of the next year as "three general farewells in each year."[12]

It is hardly surprising that a number of pioneer Salvationists worked themselves into a state of collapse. So many persons of all ranks fainted in Army meetings because of "exhaustion or starvation" that in 1892 Maud Booth wrote an article in *The War Cry* explaining to her officers how to tell "sham faints" from the real item ("the patient always changes color . . ."). The Army was inspired to open special "homes of rest" for its sagging warriors, one on a hillside in Sausalito, California, in 1890, the other in North Long Branch, New Jersey, in 1891. Although the occasional officer — a woman from a refined background, say — might succumb to the fashionable nervous condition known as "neurasthenia," the vast majority of officers were simply exhausted. Whatever the cause of their collapse, however, many pioneers viewed the idea of taking a vacation while sinners perished as too selfish for contemplation. Officers refused to leave their posts to avail themselves of the new rest homes until they were in an advanced state of exhaustion. Headquarters was forced in June 1891 to order every officer to take at least twelve days of vacation ("furlough") during each year in order to prevent "serious break-downs of health." The demands on an officer's time and energy remained unrelenting, however: Headquarters regretfully registered many resignations due to "failing health" during the twenty years after 1880.[13]

The Army's greatest task in these years, and the one into which officers channeled most of their strength, was opening new corps. In the summer of 1880 there were eight corps in the United States, six of them in Philadelphia: in the summer of 1890 there were 410 corps in thirty-five states. One might suggest, as several scholars have, that by spreading into suburbs and small towns the Army moved away from its original promise

and the Italian work consisted of a single family of three Italian converts named Natino working valiantly, and in the long run unsuccessfully, against great odds at 201 Hester Street in Mulbery Bend. In 1897, the second-in-command for Sweden, Col. George Sowton, replaced Holz, and the Army's foreign-language work came to center on Scandinavians. Ten years later, in 1906, there were seventy-seven foreign-language corps in the United States; of these, fifty-five were Swedish, eleven German, four Finnish, four Norwegian, and one each Danish, Spanish, and Italian.[37]

On the Pacific coast, Salvationists likewise looked on the vast numbers of Chinese immigrants as fields ripe for harvest. Attempts were made from the beginning to "save the Chinaman." The Army's hopes were boundless: not only would California have a "Chinese Division of The Salvation Army" but the Army would train Chinese officers to "attack China's four hundred millions" in their homeland. The first Chinese convert, Wong Ock, thought to have been saved in 1884 in San Francisco, caught this vision. After several months of fruitless street preaching, Wong, the "hallelujah Chinaman," decided to go to London to prepare himself to lead an invasion force to China. He departed in full Chinese costume, sailing for London on April 18, 1885. Alas, he returned not to China but to San Francisco, where it was reported in 1887 that he was still valiantly preaching to indifferent crowds in Chinatown.

Fong Foo Sec was converted in Sacramento in 1889 and became an officer. He agitated for permission to open fire on his fellow Chinese in San Francisco. In 1896, he was promoted to Ensign, the first Chinese in the world to be raised to staff rank in The Salvation Army (and, sad to say, at that time one of the few ever to have heard of the Army). Fong apparently had staff or clerical duties, because when a Chinese corps was finally opened later the same year, the pioneer officer was Capt. May Jackson. With its gaslights, two "little dragon flags," and John 3:16 in Chinese characters on the wall, the Chinese corps was a triumph from the start; by the end of the year thirty-six Chinese had been saved, and a second Chinese corps was opened in San Jose. Prominent Army visitors to San Francisco always wanted to visit its exotic Oriental outpost. Booth-Tucker, who loved going about in disguise, once showed up at the corps in full Chinese regalia! A Chinese *War Cry* was started in 1896, designed to explain basic Christian truths to the Chinese. Fong, long revered by Chinese Salvationists, finally returned to China and became the English-language editor of the *Shanghai Commercial Press,* but not before the Chinese corps was permanently established in San Francisco. In 1900

to concentrate on the urban masses, but it cannot be denied that these figures represent human effort on a Herculean scale. The Army's national leadership took an encouraging view of expansion, officially assuring divisional officers in 1896 that they were "perfectly at liberty" to open as many new corps as they liked, so long as the monthly hall rent did not exceed thirty dollars — in which case special permission was required for the opening. The process by which the Army opened fire on a place, refreshingly straightforward in theory, was often hair-raising and always exhausting in practice. Headquarters provided nothing in the way of funding to those who were sent to open new corps beyond what they would require to tide them over for a few days, and often they were expected to raise even that small sum on the spot. No effort was made in the early days to determine the extent — or the existence — of local support for the Army's ministry: pioneer officers assumed the Army was needed everywhere.[14]

The attacking party wasted no time. From the moment the pioneers arrived in town, they set about attracting as much public attention as possible. There could be no sneak attacks on the devil and all his works; as his triumph had been public, so must his ruin be. Besides, had Christ not warned His soldiers that whosoever denied Him before men, the same would be denied before His Father? Officers sometimes announced that they had come to town to offer salvation to the worst elements; the Salvationist who began Army work in Adrian, Michigan, in 1883 told the local newspaper that he didn't even want respectable people to show up at the meetings: the Army wanted only "the unbelievers, the roughs, the toughs, the sots of the city." No sooner had lodgings been secured — a cheap rooming house or a pew in a friendly church — than the Blood-and-Fire flag was unfurled, literally. Although corps were occasionally opened by warriors acting alone — John Waldron opened the Buffalo No. 4 Corps in 1896 by himself, marching in the street with a bass drum — the Army attacked *en masse* wherever possible. The officers actually sent to open a place were often reinforced for the first few days by a group of officers and soldiers from nearby corps or divisional headquarters. The party would march, playing musical instruments if they had them, singing if they had no horns, banging a drum and tambourines, to some conspicuous spot such as a busy intersection or the town square. The arrival of The Salvation Army would be announced, along with warnings directed to listening sinners to repent, after which a barrage of songs and prayers would be laid down. The group would then disperse to find a hall to rent, which would then often serve as both meeting place and sleeping quarters. If the place was heated by a stove, as most were, simple meals — usually coffee, fried potatoes, and bread — could be prepared; otherwise the militants ate where they could, often in cheap boardinghouses, sometimes on stale bakery goods or unsold leftover portions from restaurants given to them or sold for a pittance. One pioneer was forced to live for weeks on eggs, wild strawberries, and limburger cheese; another had nothing more to eat than week-old crackers thrown into an empty kerosene box at the back of the hall.[15]

Even securing the hall was not always easy. It was often difficult for pioneer officers to rent furnished halls: the risk to gaslight fixtures, chairs, and other breakables was so well known to prospective landlords that officers sometimes went in disguise to rent halls. A staff officer in San Francisco wrote in 1892 that "skirmishers, on the alert for 'To Let' signs, were dispatched in all directions, but, like the dove of biblical days, found no resting place for themselves or for us." Unfurnished meeting rooms were more generally available and cheaper, but taking such a place entailed the added burden of collecting money, mostly from indifferent passersby, to buy lumber to build benches and a platform. The halls were usually on the second floor of business establishments, very often at the back, with windows looking out on a backyard or alley. The Army's frontage on the street was only the door at the front of the stairs, although audacious officers sometimes paid extra for the privilege of painting the name of their organization in bold letters across the front of the building. Suitable halls designed for meetings were not always available, furnished or not. In such cases, large indoor rooms were often pressed into service. Soldiers were asked to watch for "buildings likely to suit" as "barracks." Philadelphia No. 1 opened in an abandoned chair factory, Newark in a theater, Peoria over a livery stable, Danbury and several other notable early corps in skating rinks. Once the fortress had been secured and regular meetings announced, most of the attack party returned to their regular duties, leaving the appointed officers — sometimes a man or woman alone, a matched pair, or, less often, a married couple — on their own to carry on the salvation war.[16]

The energies expended in proliferating corps are not the only explanation for the rapid spread of the Army. The organization's military structure itself was novel and appealing. The Salvation Army evolved slowly in England, bearing the stamp of William Booth's powerful and autocratic personality; of his militant redemptive theology, which viewed all of life as a struggle, a "holy war"; and of the fact that he received "more practical help from the regulations of the British Army than . . . from all the methods of the churches" in organizing his Mission followers into an effective fighting force. Philip Needham has demonstrated that in addition to providing obvious practical benefits, the military analogy was rich in theological meaning to Booth and his followers, a constant reminder that the Kingdom of God was not yet at hand, that there were many battles yet to fight. In America, however, the transforming process by which The Christian Mission had become The Salvation Army mattered little to new converts. In America, the Army arrived full-blown, freshly sprung from the forehead of Zeus, or, to quote Ballington Booth, "phoenix-like," it had "formed itself from the ashes of depraved and outcast society" — and in America, it worked. Within two years of the official landing, a professor at Lutheran Seminary in Gettysburg wrote that part of the appeal of the new movement was that it allowed people to play at being an army. He denounced this as "sensationalism," but to little avail: everyone seemed to find something about the pioneer Salvation Army appealing.[17]

Everybody loves a parade, especially from the inside. The appeal of special uniforms, of identifying in dramatic and visible ways with a popular crusade, while not universal, has always been widespread, transcending class lines. For those who have little else in life, the appeal is irresistible. To take up the poor and forgotten, dress them in handsome blue uniforms (often the first suit of clothes they had owned that gave them pride), promote them to a colorful variety of different ranks, each with its own distinctive trim, in a crusade in which victory is divinely assured — all this is not only compassionate but reveals a remarkable knowledge of human nature. Maud Ballington Booth, writing in 1889, proudly admitted that the Army drew on what was common to human nature.

> A very interesting suggestion was made by a friend at Washington, D.C., with reference to our military nomenclature and customs which will bear repeating. His theory is that it satisfies the military instinct that almost every race possesses, that inborn enjoyment of marching movements, music, uniform, processions, and all the "Pomp, pride and circumstance of war," without injury or bloodshed; in point of fact, bringing peace instead of war. Perhaps the motive of the Army could not be better expressed: To take man's natural instincts and pleasures which have been perverted, and to gratify them in a manner which will bless and not curse the race, and will glorify, not dishonor God, has been from the first the aim and method of the work.[18]

The Army adapted to militancy with characteristic thoroughness. Salvationists of all ranks were expected to be in uniform every time they were on duty, which for the soldiers meant fifteen times per week, and for the officers meant always, by official order in 1889. At first the traditional high-collar blue tunic for men and women was not regulation uniform: the faithful appeared in an exotic collection of makeshift and multicolored apparel that was consistent only in being eye-catching. The first Salvationist that young Adam Gifford saw on the streets of Pittsburgh wore a "fireman's leather helmet, with a hatband on which were the words, 'Prepare to meet thy God!'" At first the Army did not operate a special department to supply uniforms. In 1886 a new officer such as Lt. Edward Parker simply purchased some trim in something close to the correct color at a dry goods store and sewed it on his civilian jacket; other pioneers had uniforms made locally.

Even when the trade department for uniforms was established at Army headquarters, the matter of ranks and trims was never permanently settled. The basic Army colors were adopted early: blue for purity, red for the Blood of Christ, yellow for the fire of the Holy Spirit. Uniforms were generally blue and hat trim generally red, recalling that day in 1880 when Railton appeared in the first official uniform on the eve of his departure for America. But against that somber background, a rainbow of colors have played over the years, to accompany a bewildering array of ranks and titles that in their brief day were the cynosure of many Army eyes. The black straw bonnet for women appeared in 1880, the invention of Catherine Booth. It was widely worn from the earliest years. Cheap, durable, protective, and solidly unworldly, the bonnet with its red band and huge bow and ribbons became a symbol of the Great Salvation War. Men continued much longer to display a certain individuality in headgear. Pith helmets, toppers, cowboy hats, derbies, sailor hats, and discarded military band helmets proudly appeared, each with its Army hatband, until 1891, when a stern rebuke from headquarters brought the troops under regulation caps, one style for officers, another for soldiers.[19]

Of such things as Army ranks, of course, the public knew and cared little. Salvationists were urged to wear their uniforms not in order to display rank but in order to be "outwardly known when passing among worldlings." *The War Cry* declared in 1885 that a uniform was of great value in "standing out for Jesus." Soldiers who did not at first enjoy this sort of attention were urged by the Army to accept their new notoriety as "an act of direct obedience to God Himself." The great majority of pioneer Salvationists, however, were proud of their uniforms, proud to be associated with the great crusade for which the uniform stood. Partly because of this pride and partly because of economic necessity (officers and soldiers alike had to purchase their own uniforms, and an officer's uniform cost almost three weeks' salary in the late 1890s), many soldiers wore their uniforms even when not on Salvation Army duty — anywhere formal clothing would be expected: school commencements, neighborhood weddings and funerals, when visiting relatives, for family photographs. One old comrade in the 1890s slept in his uniform so that if death came in the night he would be found "in the uniform he loved so well."[20]

Every aspect of the soldier's life and work was displayed in battle array. Salvationists were to prepare for "a warfare of real battles — a real, desperate, hand-to-hand battle for God against the powers of darkness." To Salvationists the "Salvation Fight" was "no mere figure of speech." The one book, beside the Bible, that every soldier was expected to read was the *Soldier's Manual,* which was full of the "true spirit." "There has been plenty of preaching, talking, and praying, but none of these ever won a battle, unless backed home by a real, practical activity in the holy war." The birth of a child to a Salvationist couple was hailed as the arrival of "reinforcements"; the death of a comrade was a "promotion to Glory." Daily devotional readings were "rations." Prayer was "knee drill." To interject an "amen" into a service was to "fire a volley." The soldier's weekly contribution in money was a "cartridge," which was not paid but "fired." Short, snappy testimonies in the meetings were "small shot." The Army's weekly newspaper was *The War Cry.* A series of planned revival meetings was a "siege." The officer's home was called "quarters," and vacations became "furloughs." A staff officer's travel itinerary was a "War Path." A new convert was a "captive," and officers were judged by their superiors not on the basis of Sunday school attendance or funds raised but on the "number of prisoners captured." The devil was no abstraction: he was the enemy commander, as real as sin and death. A jubilant report from Oakland in 1884 declared, "We are learning how to load and fire hot shot and are bringing down some of Satan's best soldiers." Jubilance was indeed the tonic chord. However serious the business at hand, the Great Salvation War was never joyless. Victory was assured, with palms and crowns laid up on high for those who did not falter. So with "charges upon enemy ground," volleys, hot shot, and small shot, the happy Army advanced, "marching on with the flag unfurled" and a brass band playing.[21]

Especially with a brass band — or with such bits and pieces of a band as the pioneers could gather together. Never did an organization become more closely identified by the public with one part of its activity than did The Salvation Army with its street-corner bands. And with good reason: no other part of the Body of Christ in history has demonstrated with more dramatic certainty the effectiveness of music in winning converts and holding them.

The Army had learned the value of bands in England in 1878, when four sympathetic musicians in one family named Fry joined a beleaguered street-corner service in Salisbury. Even in the absence of the British laborer's fondness for bands, the lesson learned in Salisbury transferred easily to America, where band instruments served the Army's purposes ideally. With zeal, even the least adept convert could produce a sound and, with practice, a melody. This was especially true of percussion instruments, the use of which conveniently spared the convert, eager to join the fray, the necessity of practice. With instruments it was possible to carry the sound of a street service over the rattles and clops of horse-drawn traffic. Bands were military, adding a brave and stirring note to the street marches that preceded every evening service and charging the singing indoors to new heights of enthusiasm. Playing an instrument gave the soldier a feeling of belonging, of fulfilling a role in the great salvation crusade. The alto horn or valve trombone was a badge of merit, visible proof to the world that that convert was no longer an unimportant drudge but a bandsman in The Salvation Army, a person of consequence. In addition, playing in the band was fun — a fact the Army gladly emphasized. In 1893 officers were instructed to tell their young people that a crusade planned for that year would be "better than football. Saving is exciting work."[22]

As a movement struggling for whatever support came to hand, the Army was glad to have any instruments at all in the early days. When Major Moore staged a third anniversary parade to the New York City Hall in 1883, the Army band consisted of two kettle drums, a bass drum, and a fife, none of which — alas — played together during any part of the march. Saco, Maine, fell in 1884 to a hallelujah onslaught led by four drums, five triangles, and twelve tambourines. The high musical standards of a later day were notably absent in the 1880s. There is even uncertainty as to when the first actual Salvation Army band — the kind with instruments other than drums — was formed in America. Col. Brindley Boon states in an authorized history of Salvation Army bands that the first official Army band in the United States was the National Staff Band, made up of headquarters officers and employees, which played for the first time on June 18, 1887, at the Brooklyn Lyceum. The new Staff Band received considerable attention at the time, and in later years, when this band had become the Army's premier musical aggregation in the United States, some Salvationists mistakenly believed it to have been the first in time as well as in prestige. The honor of being the first Salvation Army band in the United States, however, arguably belongs to the corps in Grand Rapids, Michigan. A photograph exists which is believed to show the band of Grand Rapids No. 1 Corps in 1884; the picture is of a group of instrumentalists of both genders in a variety of early Salvationist uniforms. Almost alone in Salvation Army history, the Grand Rapids band had its own drum major, Mr. Casey deBlond, the man who delivered the officers' trunk when the Army came to town and who became the Army's first convert there.[23]

Ronald W. Holz has recently contributed new information on the early history of Army bands in this country. East Liverpool, Ohio, had a sizable corps band by December 1884; in 1934 an article in *The War Cry*

Grand Rapids, Michigan, Band, 1884 — the first commissioned band in the United States Source: Central Territorial Museum

suggested that this had been the Army's first American band. By 1885 Oakland Citadel had a fourteen-piece band, Danbury had a "new brass band," and *The War Cry* had begun to advertise band instruments for sale to its readers. The East Liverpool Band had progressed sufficiently in just over a year that by 1886 it sported a full complement of players; it played at the dedication of the new Chicago Temple that year and filled the air "with angels' whispers." Most corps had to struggle along with considerably less: even New York No. 1 had no regular band until 1888. Typical accounts told of meetings and marches accompanied by a trombone, bass drum, and snare drum or a cornet, drum, and pair of cymbals. Banjos, guitars, a "picalo," concertinas, "clarionets," violins, autoharps, and cowbells were all pressed into service. An 1895 service in southern California was led by Comrade Comstock and his "famous fife," which he had played at the capture of Vicksburg. When the Army was sufficiently established in a location to be able to afford the luxury of a choice in the matter of instruments, the official choice was for brass instruments exclusively. It was easier for the complete novice to coax sound out of a horn, and metal instruments were far less likely than woodwinds to be damaged by the rigors of frequent outdoor use in all kinds of weather and sometimes in the midst of blows and missiles. The Army offered a set of the traditional instruments for an all-brass band for sale as early as 1888 — the year that Chicago acquired its first Army band — but it was well into the twentieth century before woodwinds and strings ceased to appear in Army bands. Massachusetts even had a "Divisional Orchestra" in 1891.[24]

Proficiency in these pioneer aggregations counted for less than zeal and holy living. "If a man is not right in his soul, or is not loyal to the Army, or is not a true Blood-and-Fire Soldier, he must not be a Bandsman, whatever his musical abilities may be." Officers were strictly warned to watch "against professionalism" in their bands. There seems to have been little danger. When Capt. Edward Parker was appointed bandmaster of the new Illinois Divisional Band in 1889, he could not read a note of music. And in San Francisco in 1891, the No. 3 Corps' band sallied forth after one week of practice to astonish the world with its rendition of "Rescue the Perishing." Small wonder that a Chicago band was said to have produced a "delirious uproar" in 1891, or that two years later an Army band in Portland, Oregon, was described as "a sort of little German band affair." When Brooklyn No. 1 Corps launched its first band in March 1896, the seven members practiced for several weeks before they noticed that they were all playing the wrong parts. In 1910 in Valley City, North

Dakota, young Lt. Phil Gerringer played "I'm a Soldier Bound for Glory" at a street meeting after only six days of self-instruction on the cornet. The musical reputation thus gathered to The Salvation Army lingered for years and became part of the stock-in-trade of American humorists. One author made a typical observation in 1893 that there was "always a humorous side to the Salvation Army and its methods." The pioneer Army cared little about such criticisms. Let the world laugh: people were attracted by the music, and souls were won. Sympathetic observers agreed: "Honest success of such gigantic dimensions is sublime," declared one writer in *Scribner's Magazine* in 1896, "won though it may be to an accompaniment of ill-blown trombones and kettle-drums off the key." Then, too, there was always the possibility, from the Army's point of view, that the dubious quality of its instrumental music might cause quality players to join the movement out of pity. Edward Trumble, a cornet player in the Elyria, Ohio, Grand Army Band in the 1880s, ridiculed the Salvationists' incompetent little band when the Army came to the town. Soon ashamed that he made fun of the Army when he, a talented player, was willing to do nothing to help the cause of Christ, Trumble was converted and joined The Salvation Army. Later, as "Trumpeter" Trumble, he was a featured soloist in Army meetings and in 1893 became bandmaster of the National Staff Band in New York City.[25]

Part of the appeal of Army music lay in its popular nature. Booth loved the traditional hymns of the church, and these were never abandoned, but they were soon joined by songs set either to sprightly tunes of original Army composition or to popular secular melodies that the Army shamelessly expropriated. The General brushed aside objections with Charles Wesley's question: "Why should the devil have all the good tunes?" The idea was simple: join some lines of religious verse (preferably "snappy" or "red-hot," although the words of many traditional hymns were also used) to a tune already well known to the audience, so they could sing along without feeling awkward or self-conscious. For this purpose, "any serviceable tune" would suffice. If this combination touched the hearts of the people, who could gainsay its use? If it did not, the Army would try another — there were plenty of tunes from which to pick. The Army published a list of usable tunes in 1893 under the heading "Contraband of War." That list and others like it contained an amazing range of airs and melodies from which the pioneer Salvationists might make selections for their musical adventures — everything from "Captain Jinks of the Horse Marines," the Cornell University alma mater, and "O Dem Golden

Delegations to the 1892 Congress line up on 58th Street in New York City
Source: The Salvation Army National Archives
(reproduced from the collections of the Library of Congress)

Slippers" to "The Vacant Chair." Railton was particularly fond of American Civil War songs, but barroom ballads, love songs, and vaudeville and minstrel tunes were no less eagerly adopted. Small wonder that critics and friends alike expressed the conviction that The Salvation Army was likely to be mistaken for a circus parade — as indeed it was when Railton and the heroic seven landed at Battery Park in 1880. Identification can be double-edged, of course: when a circus parade rode into Danbury in 1885, local drunks mistaking it for an Army procession treated it to a "shower of rotten apples."[26]

Striking as the effect of bands must have been, music was not the only arrow in the Army's quiver. The devil had more reason than one to tremble: there was very little in the way of the dramatic or comical that pioneer Salvationists would not do to attract a crowd to hear the gospel. Respectable people might quail before this avalanche of "clap-trap" and "rowdyism," but the Army was not greatly concerned; what did it matter if the Army complied with established customs so long as it attracted sinners. Let the newspapers ridicule them: all the better — it was free publicity. Everything was explained by the "first necessity of the movement, which is TO ATTRACT ATTENTION!" It is difficult to imagine how the Army could have failed with such devices as burning the devil in effigy in front of national headquarters (after dissecting its various body parts, including a huge red tongue marked "gossip"); or parading down San Francisco's Market Street covered in sheets and pillowcases, singing "A Robe of White, a Crown of Gold"; or marching forty bridesmaids down a Chicago street dressed in star-spangled sashes and red liberty caps (complete with Army hatbands), preceded by a torchlight parade! Then there were the umbrellas with red-hot gospel mottos inscribed on every section; announcements painted on the sides of wagons, upon which lassies were perched precariously, beating drums or ringing handbells; and huge palm fans, sandwich signs, transparencies, giant boxes, bottles, and barrels with messages on the outside and hardy Salvationists on the inside, dancing along the street. The variations were endless, the effect the same.

John Rhemick has suggested in several recent studies that there was an additional reason for the Army's attractiveness in the first twenty years of its existence: it appealed to the unsatisfied longing among many of the subliterate working poor for color, image-stimulation, and emotional faith. In this respect, the processions, flags, and colorful rituals of the Salvationists had an appeal similar to those of the Roman Catholic Church. Both organizations proved especially attractive to the urban poor, the last "remnants of an image-oriented culture" that once dominated Western civilization. A contemporary writer noticed the same similarity, comparing the Army's pageantry to medieval Catholic "miracle plays and rude symbolism." The Army's appeal was real enough, whatever its cause. To quote one who observed the San Francisco sheet-and-pillowcase parade, people were "desperately interested." Not surprisingly.[27]

The religious meetings to which these allurements pointed were hardly less energetic. The same principles held for all meetings, outdoors or indoors: "Everything short, sharp, striking, vigorous." The order of service varied considerably, but lively and enthusiastic singing with much hand-clapping and volley-firing, a gospel message, and testimonies were part of every service. The testimonies were regarded as the most important part of the meeting. Testimonies from the soldiers and converts advertised the power of grace in a manner more effective than any sermon. Converts were encouraged by the experiences of their new friends, and sinners were given hope. The testimonies of converted reprobates, especially those who were well known locally, caused crowds to gather at street-corner meetings and fill Army halls. One sympathetic and perceptive writer commented in *The Andover Review* in 1884 on the appeal of testimonies, which she regarded as accounting "in a good measure for the Army's success. . . . But the great charm of these meetings and that, indeed, which secure for them the perpetual freshness and attractiveness, keeping their halls filled, night after night, is contained in the personal testimonies of the converts as to the joy and strength which they have received in the 'great salvation' from sin and its bondage."[28]

Some of the stories of these early trophies of grace would have melted hearts of stone. Maude A. Harris, the "Saved Bare-Back Rider," had been raised as an orphan in a circus with only an elephant for a friend. After a flashy, sordid life as a bareback rider, professional baseball player, rower, and jockey, she was converted at age nineteen at the Army in Albany and became an officer. Another convert had been drunk so long that on the night he was saved he no longer owned a shirt, and there was not enough food in his room "for two mice." Wife-beaters, cheats, bullies, prostitutes, boys who had stolen the family food money, unfaithful husbands, burglars, and teamsters who had been cruel to their horses all stood for their brief and glorious moments in the limelight of grace. Then there were the more colorful characters, those trophies who became regular features at Army meetings: one corps alone, in Haverhill, Massachusetts, had three: "Happy Jenny," "Smiling Alice," and "Hallelujah Pickles." Comm. Frank Smith listed still more, including the "one-armed converted opium eater," "Swearing Billy," and the "Saved Drunkard of Shenandoah." *The War Cry* offered the most complete catalogue of all, including Capt. John O'Brine, the "Saved Seal" (showman), "Orange Box George," the "Dutch Volcano," "Hell Fire Jack," the "Welsh Hallelujah Midget," the "Hallelujah Baggageman," and a host of assorted and long-forgotten "devil-drivers" who now reign with Christ in glory.[29]

Beyond the standard use of songs, message, and testimonies, the content of Army meetings varied. The Army, which produced a regulation governing practically every other aspect of its work, placed no limits on its religious meetings. On the contrary, officers were encouraged to experiment. Imaginations thus stimulated produced remarkable results. Adjutant Wallace Winchell subpoenaed the devil to a mock trial in Chicago in 1894, while Staff Captain Thomas launched a revival at Los Angeles No. 1 in 1896 by preaching on eternity while standing before an open, empty coffin. Both of these techniques became Army favorites. One successful innovation stimulated many others: officers wore prison garb in the pulpit, rode horses onto the platform, or released flocks of canaries in the meetings. The use of the "stereopticon" — a kind of lantern-show with slides of Bible verses and dramatic scenes — was so popular that headquarters had to issue an order in 1897 that only "approved" slides could be used. Staff Capt. John Milsaps introduced the "phonograph service" to the Pacific coast in 1897, a novelty item that soon had national appeal. Special books of instruction were prepared for drills with flags, tambourines, and Chinese lanterns.[30]

Despite these entertaining diversions, The Salvation Army laid down the gospel with what Catherine Booth called "unerring accuracy." The meetings were conducted for one of two purposes only: the conversion of sinners or their growth in grace. However bizarre the attraction or enjoyable the service — and the Army *was* fun — no one came away without knowing that Jesus was the sinner's hope. Not only regular services but special ceremonies, such as the dedication of infants, weddings, and funerals, ended with a period of invitation — the "altar call," during which people who wished religious counseling were asked to come forward to kneel at the "mercy seat," a special rail or bench set aside for that purpose. Dramatic transformations were often the result. Occasionally a penitent would leave a symbol of a former sin at the altar: jewelry, tobacco, bottles — even weapons. Brengle collected a dagger, a revolver, and a tomahawk during the course of his career as an Army revivalist. The great majority of converts left nothing more wonderful at the altar than their broken lives and blasted dreams, now gilded with hope.[31]

Salvationists were convinced that their message was universal. They did not hesitate at the command of their Heavenly Captain to take the gospel to all the world. They were encouraged to discover that in America sizable portions of all the world were conveniently at hand, and more were arriving every day. Uprooted from all that was cherished and familiar, jammed into unhealthful tenements, ignorant of the language, and confused by the manners of their new homeland, many immigrants sought an enhanced religious commitment to preserve some sense of ethnic identity. Into these teeming waters the Army threw its nets. Contemporary church reformers pointed out the necessity of preaching the gospel to immigrants in their native languages. The Salvation Army was actively committed to attracting members of foreign-language populations from its earliest days in this country. The "Foreign Department" produced some of the Army's great saints, and — particularly in the Scandinavian division of the work — traditions that have remained alive and beloved by Salvationists well into the late twentieth century.[32]

The mission to Scandinavian immigrants began in a characteristically spontaneous way. In the winter of 1887 four Swedish laundresses, soldiers at Brooklyn No. 1, began holding services in their native language after the regular services were over. When these Swedish services became popular among churchless and lonely Scandinavian domestics and sailors, the women rented a storefront on Atlantic Avenue. As these still-unofficial meetings grew daily larger, two Swedish-American officers, Annie and Mary Hartelius, arrived — or, rather, rearrived — on the scene. The two sisters had been converted at a street service in Brooklyn in 1882 and had quickly volunteered to return to their native Sweden as missionary officers in 1883. Having departed as the first Salvation Army missionaries to be sent abroad from the United States, the Hartelius sisters now returned to throw themselves into the burgeoning Swedish mission in Brooklyn, which had hopelessly outgrown the resources of the valiant but exhausted laundresses. Ballington Booth appointed the sisters to command the new corps, Brooklyn No. 3, which opened on December 23, 1887. The work progressed with amazing rapidity; clearly *The War Cry* was right in boasting that the Swedes were "a nationality peculiarly affected by our methods and doctrines."[33]

The "Saved Swedes" of Brooklyn No. 3 soon had company. Other cities with large Swedish populations promptly opened missions among them. The first west of New York was in Minneapolis, in April 1888; then came St. Paul and Chicago, where Scandinavian work prospered for generations. *The War Cry* began printing a column and songs in Swedish as a prelude to a full-fledged Swedish edition, the *Stridsropet,* which was launched in February 1891. The next year the already flourishing Swedish work was stimulated to a new level of energy by the arrival of Comm. Hanna Ouchterlony, the heroic officer who had pioneered in Sweden a few months before the Hartelius sisters had arrived to help her. The Commissioner held two hundred meetings, to which Swedish people came in large numbers. Her services in Chicago were particularly successful: by 1894, there were six Swedish corps in that city, crowned by the famous Chicago No. 13. On the tenth anniversary of the opening of Brooklyn No. 3 (which had become a kind of shrine to Swedish Salvationists, revered among them as *Osterns stjarne,* "the Star of the East"), the Scandinavian branch of the work comprised 49 corps, 103 officers, 12 brass bands, and

Capts. Annie and Mary Hartelius, Swedish immigrant sisters who commanded the first Scandinavian corps in the United States (Brooklyn No. 3)
Source: *Genom 45 Ar,* by Karl Walden, commemorating forty-five years of Scandinavian work in The Salvation Army in the United States

a special training garrison in Chicago to prepare officers. The Scandinavian ministry was extended to the Pacific Coast on February 26, 1899, when a mission was opened in San Francisco to reach Swedish sailors.[34]

The success of the Scandinavian work is partly attributable to factors unique to the Swedes. The Salvation Army had made many converts in Sweden, and thousands of these joined the tide of immigration to the United States. Many were delighted to find their beloved *Fralsingsarmen* when they arrived, the one familiar thing in the strange New World. In addition, a large number of the Swedish immigrants were single women, many of whom found employment as domestic servants. Trapped in a dull and lonesome occupation, they delighted to hasten at night to the gay and hearty company of the Army corps. The other large group touched by the Army's Scandinavian ministry consisted of Swedish and Norwegian sailors, who came ashore in such port cities as Brooklyn, San Francisco, and Seattle for periods ranging from overnight to several weeks. These men were grateful for company in their native language and looked forward to seeing the Army women, enjoying the singing, and eating the enormous quantities of food that were characteristically provided by the Scandinavian corps in their heyday.[35]

Work among other ethnic groups was launched with equal fervor but failed to gain similar ground. Railton had a peculiarly strong affinity for Germany and Germans and entertained great hopes for the results of Army work among them. He went after them at once, wiring the General on the latter's twenty-fifth wedding anniversary in June 1880: "American

Old Brooklyn No. 3 Corps, opened on Atlantic Avenue on
December 23, 1897, was the first corps in the United States
to hold services in the Swedish language.
Source: Newspaper clipping in a scrapbook owned by the
New York Central Citadel Corps

Army salutes you. First German battery opened New York on Sunday. Gloriously grand celebration." This was premature, like all Railton's pronouncements on the Germans. Two days later he wrote to Booth that he hoped to "get the Americans, Germans, and Africans all fairly started." But success eluded the pioneers. Moore's *War Cry* offered a column for the *Deutschen Kameraden* written by Staff Capt. Richard Holz, but it wasn't until 1887 that the Booth Army opened a German corps. Railton, by then territorial commander in Germany, sent stirring accounts of conversion there to readers of the American *War Cry*, urging his comrades to start German corps among the millions of Germans in America. An occasional German *War Cry* was offered (first in October 1892), but permanent corps failed to materialize on the scale of the Scandinavian success, and few German corps survived long into the new century. At the Columbian Congress in 1893, the perpetually optimistic Railton as guest of honor spoke in German, mostly about his work in the Fatherland, and once again announced that the Army planned to start German corps in America. Patience was rewarded suddenly but, in the end, only briefly. A German corps was opened in Buffalo in 1893, and then a second in New York. Within five years there were twenty-one German corps in America, located in cities with large German populations such as Buffalo, Hoboken, Cleveland, Cincinnati, Milwaukee, and San Francisco.[36]

The German Salvationists, however, proved to be different from the Swedish in several basic ways. For one thing, despite Railton's abiding affection for all things German, the Army did not prosper in the Fatherland as it had in Sweden; few of the Germans who emigrated to America were Salvationists. In addition, German-Americans did not cling to their native language with the tenacity of the Swedes. The few German converts secured by the Army preferred to attend English-speaking corps in order to learn the new language. Half the soldiers in Cincinnati's two flourishing American corps spoke or understood German in 1894, for instance, while the two small German corps languished. Finally, it was difficult to convince Germans to become officers in sufficient numbers to sustain the German corps work. The attrition rate among the few Germans who did become officers was high. One German-American who did become a successful and prominent officer was Richard E. Holz. A fair number of German Salvationists followed him into and out of the ill-fated Moore Army. In 1896, Holz was placed in charge of the "Scandinavian, German and Italian Department" set up by the new commander, Booth-Tucker, to coordinate all foreign-language work. The German work declined rapidly, however,

San Francisco Chinatown Corps, 1896   Source: Western Territorial Museum

Capt. Millie Banks, stationed at the Army's Home of Rest near Pacific Grove, established a storefront mission in a Chinese fishing village between Pacific Grove and Monterey. Milsaps, who was invited by Banks to speak there, called it "the Chinese 'Christian S.A. Parlour,'" used by "Salvation Army Chinese for private meetings and mutual encouragement." Attendance was sparse but apparently eager enough: Milsaps recorded eight conversions out of nine Chinese at his meeting. There is no evidence that this informal station survived the transfer of Captain Banks.[38]

The story of the Army's repeated efforts to draw blacks into the ranks during these years is an important one. To the many obstacles that stood in the way of Army work generally was added the insurmountable fact of racial antipathy, against which even God's grace was not proof. James Jermy, the Christian Missioner who began an abortive work in Cleveland in 1872, often preached to small black or racially mixed congregations. Railton hoped from the beginning to get the "Africans . . . fairly started" but found the few blacks he encountered indifferent to his appeals. No details of his efforts in this regard are known. Maj. Frank Smith was as zealous as Railton had been in believing that the Army should be the "first Christian community in America" that would "faithfully and wholly break down the wall of partition" separating the races, but, unlike Railton, Smith formulated and attempted to carry out definite plans to reach African Americans.[39]

Major Smith was an officer with a heightened sense of social responsibility; his commitment to evangelizing the "Freedmen," as he called them, was prompt and genuine. It is to the credit of his troops that he secured the cooperation of so many of them for a campaign that was certain to be long, difficult, and unpopular among the poor and working-class whites who formed the real bulk of Army supporters. He announced the opening of the Army's "first colored station" in Baltimore in November, 1884, but nothing came of it. The corps band in Grand Rapids, Michigan, which was apparently organized in 1884, had at least one black male instrumentalist and perhaps several black women who wore uniforms and played the tambourine at Army meetings in that city. The following summer, Smith launched the "Great Colored Campaign and Combined Attack upon the South." A black officer had arrived providentially to take command of the expedition. Capt. W. S. Braithwaite, a Methodist pastor from British Guiana, had been saved at a Salvation Army service in Asbury Park, New Jersey. Special meetings were held in New York, New England, and Michigan to secure funds, volunteers, and prayers for the work. All who believed that "the colored race settled in our midst" was "possessed of immortal souls" were asked to donate. Considerable momentum must have been generated, because when Braithwaite was dismissed in November after the Army had investigated mysterious "circumstances and charges," the "Great Colored Campaign" did not falter. When the Fredericksburg, Virginia, corps was opened in November 1885 (it was identified as the first corps in Virginia, but in fact it was the second: Alexandria had been open for three months), two of the four pioneer officers were black: Captain Johnson, described in *The War Cry* as a "bright mulatto" born in Maine, and Lieutenant Minor, "a handsome colored woman" who had been born a slave in Virginia. The majority of the people in the congregations at their first meetings, indoor and out, were black. This was encouraging. Ambitious plans were laid to open black corps in Washington, Frederick, Richmond, and Norfolk. The Army tried to enlist more volunteers with what it called "colored skins and white hearts" in the crusade. All went well at first. A visiting officer found a mixed crowd of five hundred at Fredericksburg in January 1886. When General Booth visited the "colored corps" in 1887, he found forty "Blood-and-Fire Soldiers," mostly in uniform, on the platform and a packed hall. The Frederick No. 2 Maryland corps was listed by the Army as "colored" as well, but apparently the officer in charge was white. There were two officers named Jones, listed as "colored," on the staff of the Brooklyn Rescue Home in March 1888, then one, "Mrs. Jones, colored," described as a "special" (an official evangelist, stationed at headquarters, available to do "special" meetings in corps) in April.[40]

Black converts were welcomed throughout the Army, and were often featured in the meetings as testifiers and entertainers. The black soldiers were popular as "specials" and were enthusiastically received by congregations. "Special George," a black soldier who played cornet, harmonica, and guitar, was popular in eastern cities, while groups called "colored jubilee singers" sang and testified at Chicago No. 1 in 1889 and in all three Los Angeles corps in 1896. Other black soldiers did valiant service for the cross in their local corps, often enduring the misunderstanding and indifference of both races. Isaac Smith, converted in 1885, became the Color Sergeant at New York No. 3 and did not miss a single open-air meeting for the next fifteen years. When Brengle was in Danbury, a black soldier named George Washington was one of only two members of the local corps willing to accompany him to street services — the other was a disabled child. Capt. and Mrs. Alex Beck, listed as "colored," were in charge of the corps at San Luis Obispo, California, in 1896. The couple was transferred to Pacific Coast Divisional headquarters early the next year as "staff" and withdrew from the Army in 1898, apparently after a disagreement with the divisional commander. Major Milsaps confided to his diary his sorrow at their departure but did not list the reason for the rupture. It is true that the African American "specials" were often made to appear comical, and *The War Cry* sometimes printed poems in "darkie dialect," but the magazine also printed many straightforward testimonies from the "colored comrades." Research by Ronald Holz has confirmed that black spirituals were popular with early Salvationists and were used reverently for serious purposes. The Army's attack on race prejudice was genuine, if somewhat hampered by stereotypical thinking and inertia in its own ranks.[41]

Certainly Ballington Booth's motive in taking five blacks as part of the American delegation to the Army's international congress in England in 1894 was at least partly to demonstrate official endorsement of evangelism among blacks. The men themselves were certainly sincere; they held a spontaneous revival meeting on the ship. The next year the Army took a courageous official stand, both on the spot and later, against the rising tide of lynching that blighted the 1890s. In 1895, the two white officers in command of Frederick, Maryland, now a forlorn relic of the "colored campaign" of earlier days, threw themselves into a valiant but fruitless attempt to rescue a black man from a lynch mob, following and pleading with the mob all the way from the jail to the tree. In the end, hoping to shame the crowd into a change of heart, the officers asked to pray with the doomed man. All in vain: the mob respectfully uncovered their heads for the prayer and then proceeded to hang the man. "Salvation Army, be quick!" stormed *The War Cry:* the "Lynching craze" must stop. The victims of black crime were to be pitied, certainly, but that was no excuse for lynching — and in any case, readers were reminded, African Americans were "also victims of terrible cruelties and assaults." Lynching was "horrible . . . atrocious."[42]

The solution to these problems was clear: all individuals of all races must be saved. The Army was called to step up its campaign to redeem the South. "The Children for God! There must be no Distinction of Color or Class!" declared a *War Cry* cover in July 1894, which portrayed a crowd of black, Asian, and rich and poor white children reaching up to the General. The Army was as good as its word — or tried to be: in 1894, and again in 1896, expeditions were announced to extend "Salvation Army work among the colored population of the Southern States." These proved abortive. Meanwhile, the original black stations languished. Funds could not be raised, African American officers were not available, and white officers delegated to lead the new campaigns were soon called to other assignments that headquarters considered more urgent. The Army's commitment to spreading its work among blacks remained official policy, but the actual results were largely in the realm of hope. Perhaps that was enough to win the gratitude of African Americans for whom even hope was encouraging: Booker T. Washington wrote in 1896, "I have always had the greatest respect for the work of the Salvation Army, especially because I have noted that it draws no color line in religion."[43]

The Salvation Army clearly took a broad view of its function in America. Salvationists were convinced that they were called to preach a universal gospel, that all must be saved, and that any means that would work to that great end ought to be tried. They likewise believed with their General that theirs was the particular destiny to carry the word of redemption to the masses of churchless, Christless urban poor. It was inevitable that an organization of practical zealots propagating a gospel of universal love to large numbers of mostly indifferent, often needy, sometimes hostile people would be drawn to recognize one supreme fact: there is no true religion that is not acted out in compassion for the real problems of real people. There is no piety without love, and love that is merely abstract is not love at all, but mere sentiment. The gospel message must be accompanied by expressions of love so unmistakable that no potential convert could miss them; then only will the good news of God's grace seem real. The Army's evangelical heart was warmed, while its practical head was stimulated. It was only half enough to declare that God is love: The Salvation Army had to show that He is.

Pioneer officers were little concerned with theories of social justice; they knew only that their Heavenly Commander had ordered His soldiers to take in strangers, visit the sick and imprisoned, and offer drink to the thirsty and food to the hungry. They also knew that there were souls dying all around and that the first step in saving some of them was to lift them up so they could hear that such a thing as salvation existed. Social welfare was both biblical and practical: Salvationists needed no more elaborate arguments than these. The Army did not offer a developed theory for its social welfare program for many years. Each part evolved piecemeal, over the years, in response to immediate practical needs that were uncovered in the course of the evangelical crusade.[44]

A variety of small-scale relief operations — more like little kindnesses — must have been started in many corps almost from the day they opened. It is almost certain that "much genuine and wholly fruitful . . . work" was done for unwed mothers and rescued prostitutes in the corps officers' private quarters long before formal "rescue work" was launched. The first recorded and official social program in the Army came in 1885, when the chaplain of the Hartford jail asked the local corps to hold a meeting for the prisoners. He correctly reasoned that his charges would be encouraged by the testimonies of several former inmates now saved and serving in the Army. In Sacramento soldiers began holding services in the jail in August 1886; by March of the following year, two officers were "conducting meetings regularly in the Stockton jail." Other beneficial programs developed spontaneously. In April 1887 the officer at Danbury invited seventy-five poor children off the street for a hot meal served up by the beaming ladies of the corps.[45]

A major program — and the one that came to be the Army's most beloved and successful — was inaugurated in October 1886, in Brooklyn.

The War Cry carried a front-page announcement: "Rescue Home for Fallen and Homeless Girls. The Salvation Army to the Rescue." Operated on a shoestring (donations of food, old clothes, cast-off furniture, and a used sewing machine were gratefully recorded over several months) and without experienced supervisors, "Morris Cottage" was nonetheless a Godsend. Unmarried pregnant women faced desperate alternatives in the Victorian era: they could choose between certain and ruinous scandal or almost certainly suicidal abortion, or they could choose to flee, alone and penniless. Likewise, a young woman, pregnant or not, who wished to escape from a life of prostitution had to have a place to live until she could acquire more honorable work, a place in which she would be safe from the very real danger of being physically maltreated — or worse — by her disgruntled former employers. The gilding on the good old days wasn't very deep. A rescue home was therefore an indispensable adjunct to street-corner evangelism in the slums. Such homes spread inevitably with the expansion of the Army's religious ministry. "Beulah" opened in Oakland in February 1887. The house was small and soon overcrowded. The usual gifts of small change, old shoes, and a jar of preserves were acknowledged. The young women threw themselves into the spirit of their new haven by making three Army flags for the officer pioneers to Oregon. Refuges opened in Grand Rapids in 1888 (helped along by the gift of a box of live chickens) and in Los Angeles in 1890. The rescue home ministry was placed on a more certain footing in 1892, when an experienced English officer, Captain Denison, opened new homes in Cleveland and in New York, on 123rd Street, where a "training garrison" was established to instruct women for rescue work.[46]

The great charm in these enterprises lay in the fact that they were absolutely practical and provided a service made infinitely more welcome by the absence of practical alternatives. The same was true of much of the Army's welfare ministry in this period. The Army was not the only agency providing relief (a major textbook written in 1888 states with regard to city missionary work in the United States that "the full record of these labors would fill many pages with the most significant statistics and evidences of astonishing results"), but the need was so great and the combined resources so slim that pioneer Salvationists could with good reason imagine themselves alone in the field. In 1889, the Army opened a "crèche" on Cherry Street in New York to provide care for infants whose mothers were forced to work, were in jail for short terms, or who had simply neglected them. Soap boxes served as cribs. This original day-care center operated, like the rescue homes, on pennies and donated baby clothes, farina, and rice.[47]

A remarkable and equally practical ministry began the same year when Capt. Emma J. Bown first sent her "Slum Sisters" in pairs into the streets of New York in 1890. These girls simply did whatever came to hand; their sole ministry was to be helpful and speak of Christ when asked their motive. They bathed and fed helpless stroke victims, washed and cuddled the extra baby or two in a crowded flat, cooked meals, made beds, patched clothing, scrubbed floors, bundled returning drunks into bed, washed and dressed the dead for undertakers (who simply delivered a coffin, took payment, and departed). The slum sisters wore no Army uniform but passed unobtrusively among their beneficiaries dressed in faded nondescript clothes. The slum officers encountered the worst poverty imaginable. "No food, no fire, no comfort — filth, vermin, cold and despair were all we found that day," wrote one in 1895. By that year the slum-sister program had spread to Brooklyn, Boston, Buffalo, Philadelphia, Chicago, and St. Louis. Even the Army's worst critics fell silent before this ministry, which the many more sympathetic observers regarded as close to angelic.[48]

The Army's social work in America was still in a fledgling stage, confined to women and children, when it received an enormous boost and a new dimension by the arrival in 1890 of William Booth's long-awaited statement on Army relief policy. The General's book, *In Darkest England and the Way Out* (which was actually mostly written by W. T. Stead, a London journalist friendly to the Army), caught the attention of the American public as much for the novelty that still attached to his movement as for the simple force of his arguments. Booth's purpose, as usual, was the salvation of souls; his premise was the "Cab-Horse Charter: . . . When he is down he is helped up, and while he lives he has food, shelter and work." His solution was the "Social Scheme," which consisted of three connected parts: (1) the City Colony, where men and women from the "submerged tenth" of the industrial society could be housed, trained, and helped upward to honorable and useful lives; (2) the Farm Colony, where those who wished to do so could be strengthened and trained for agricultural work; and (3) the Over-Seas Colony, envisioned as large, self-supporting Christian farming communities in South Africa, Canada, or Australia. Booth's "Social Scheme," audacious and in the long run impracticable, generated widespread public interest in The Salvation Army. The City Colony and, later, the Farm Colony were implemented in the United States by officers who never ceased to regard the arrival of *In Darkest England and the Way Out* as the major turning point in the development of an Army social program. This was especially true for the City Colony plan, which was aimed directly at relieving the destitution of the large urban population of homeless, penniless men, mostly chronic drinkers or alcoholics. Their plight in large American cities was a problem of desperate proportions.[49]

In Darkest England and the Way Out has not ceased to attract serious attention more than a century after its publication. It is the only major publication of The Salvation Army that has been widely read, or even known, outside the Army, and it has held a special interest from the beginning for historians of religious social reform. The book and the scheme for social redemption that it outlines were widely discussed by contemporaries. An article in *The Congregationalist* in January 1891 was typical. Noting that much had been written praising and condemning the scheme, the author asks readers to consider that no one had yet appeared with a better plan to help the urban poor or was better qualified to do so than William Booth. Other authors criticized the "Darkest England" scheme on the grounds that Booth seemed to overlook the fact that many other agencies besides The Salvation Army were at work among the poor, and the Army's dramatic willingness to shoulder the entire burden of rescuing the urban poor ignored not only these other missions but the complexity of the problem of modern urban poverty itself. W. J. Ashley, writing in *Political Science Quarterly*, expressed such a viewpoint: "To suppose that any one force or group of forces is going to completely change [society's] character within a brief space in time, is utterly to misapprehend the nature of social problems."[50]

The controversy has not disappeared. In 1963 K. S. Inglis, in a study of religious charity in Victorian England, charged that Booth turned to the "Darkest England" scheme only when it became clear to him that his efforts to evangelize the urban poor by more traditional methods had failed. Inglis claimed that earlier in his career Booth had denigrated his own first feeble social work activities as mere "pauperism." An important element in this argument is the observation that The Salvation Army had much greater success among the working poor — what Railton called the "laboring masses" — than among the truly destitute, in terms of both evangelization and recruitment. Contemporary writers made the same point, which The Salvation Army did not deny. Army leaders were glad to point out that "all kinds of people are Salvationists," that members came from every social class, and that most officers had respectable backgrounds. Maud Booth chastised those who claimed her women officers had "questionable" pasts. Such attacks "cut deeply," she wrote in 1890, "the pure, devoted young girls who have left father, mother, home and all, to seek Christ's lost ones." Two years later Ballington declared of the Army that "this military crusade of aggressive rescuers was raised from, by and for the people." Scholarship has revived the claim that the Army appealed mostly to working-class populations and gained relatively few converts from among the destitute, alienated, and criminal classes. Inglis, Victor Bailey, and Norman Murdoch have all argued along these lines, Inglis and Murdoch in order to support their contention that the Army's elaborate social relief scheme, which these writers claim was launched on a large scale only with the publication in 1890 of *In Darkest England and the Way Out,* was no more than a "confession of failure" that the Army's urban evangelism had failed. They maintain that the "Darkest England Scheme" was simply an attempt to restore the Army's flagging fortunes.[51]

Roger Green, on the other hand, contends that it is not the case that Booth switched to social reform only when it had become clear that his evangelism among the urban poor had failed. Green argues persuasively that The Salvation Army can be understood only in theological terms and that a large-scale enterprise like the "Darkest England Scheme" was con-

Christmas dinner at Cripple Creek, Colorado, 1898
Source: Western Territorial Museum

sistent with Booth's understanding of his mission from the start. Booth and his followers were committed to evangelism and personal holiness from the days of The Christian Mission. With the establishment of The Salvation Army in 1878, however, and especially in the years 1889 and 1890, says Green, Booth expanded his beliefs to include social salvation as well, either as a means of bringing in the physical kingdom of God on earth or as a prelude to personal evangelism among the desperately poor. Philip Needham likewise argues that the Army's evangelistic and socially redemptive functions both flow from the same "Salvationist theology of mission," a commitment to the universal gospel that also helps to explain the "uncanny ability" of the early Army to traverse social, cultural, and national barriers.[52]

The first relief work among homeless or drunken men was as practical as the rescue homes and the crèche. The Salvation Army's original "Cheap Food and Shelter Depot" opened on December 23, 1891, on the first floor of the building shared with the No. 2 Corps at the corner of Downing and Bedford Streets in New York. The depot provided thirty-six box beds and wholesome meals at very low prices, which were strictly collected: the Army believed that people who paid even a few pennies received the benefit and retained their pride. An immediate difficulty was that many people had no pennies at all. How should the Army respond to people who were not in the market for an inexpensive service but were in need of direct support? All urban relief agencies faced the same difficulty; indeed, an important and widespread debate about the policy to be adopted in such cases was carried on by the leaders of social relief and charitable agencies during these very years. Amos Warner, in a major treatise on American charities written in 1894, stated the obvious: there were only four ways to deal with the homeless poor: send them away, arrest them, give them the aid they request indiscriminately, or refuse to give them the aid "without applying the work test." The Charity Organization Society, which had been established in many American cities to coordinate urban social relief activities, denounced indiscriminate charity as "promiscuous alms-giving" that obscured the distinction between the "worthy" and "unworthy" poor. The Salvation Army officially rejected this distinction, however. Capt. Joseph McFee reminded critics that "God has not rewarded us according to our inequities." The straightforward Army solution to the problem of the penniless applicants for relief was to provide them with work — not because the Army supported the idea that only those who would work were worthy of help but simply because it was the

only practical means of continuing the new branch of the mission. When
the second "Lighthouse" — as such depots were soon renamed — was
opened in San Francisco December 1892, McFee ordered the clients to
collect discarded corks from saloons to make into life preservers. The next
year saw the enterprising McFee, pressed for funds, borrow a waterfront
crab pot and tripod and ask passersby to "Keep the Pot Boiling!" — an
enduring legacy. A far more common means of financing the lighthouses
and providing work at the same time — a means used by many other
agencies as well — was the woodyard. Men who received food and lodging
were asked to saw, split, and bundle wood for delivery at low prices —
five cents a basket, twenty-five cents a barrel — to local families for use
in the kitchen stove.[53]

It was an easy, natural step from the woodyards to the "Salvage
Brigades." The idea of collecting old clothes and discards, hiring the poor
to repair them, and then selling the improved results to other needy persons
was not original with the Army, but the Army was the first agency to
employ it on a large scale and bring it to widespread public attention. The
salvage brigades began in New Jersey in 1896. Refuse was collected in
handcarts. In Chicago the salvage project grew directly out of the cheap
hostels: individuals who received lodging were asked to respond by sorting
out junk and rags given by local merchants. Occasionally items were
uncovered that could still be useful to impoverished families. These were
rescued and sold for a pittance, so that the recipient, like the worker,
retained self-respect: the buyer was a customer, not a beggar. A full-fledged
salvage program was in operation in Chicago by mid-1897. The work
blossomed. The glossy black or dark-green wagons trimmed in red with
"The Salvation Army Industrial Department" in gilt letters on the side
became as much a fixture of American city life as the Army's parades and
street bands. Many an officer's son got his first taste of the thrill of warfare
on a daily round of collections, driving a freshly washed wagon, proudly
yet gingerly trying to keep the rear wheels out of streetcar tracks, which
could jam the wheel and cause a spill.[54]

Soon the Army couldn't do enough. No sooner had a start been made
on meeting one desperate need than another was uncovered, and officers
were sent or volunteered to deal with it. There was the "Prison Gate
Brigade" to offer salvation to prisoners and lodging and help in securing
employment for those who were released. The multiplying Rescue Homes
for Fallen Women claimed that 70 to 85 percent of "these daughters of
sorrow" were restored to lives of virtue." Many programs launched on a

Chicago Industrial Home Wagon, 1908
Source: Peter Hofman

small scale during these years expanded mightily in the early years of the next century: Thanksgiving and Christmas dinners for the poor; the "cheap ice" ministry for the sweltering slums and coal for the winter; steamboat excursions for tenement families; employment bureaus; secure, cheap, and respectable hotels for single working women; "fresh-air camps" and special projects to reach the "inebriate classes." These programs were relatively easy to begin; after all, Army officers lived on a pittance, and most materials used or given away in social projects were donated. The only limit on new projects was ingenuity, a quality that people who marched in pillowcases and preached from coffins did not lack. Headquarters was finally forced to act in 1897: "In view of the rapid development of the Social Work . . . no new shelter, Prison Gate or other Social scheme" was to be "promised or commenced" without the national commander's consent.[55]

The country was in a receptive mood. The revelations of reformers and journalists made it increasingly difficult for middle-class city dwellers to ignore the poverty and vice all around them. Painters and photographers, poets and novelists began to portray the alienation and degradation of city life. Many of those who were indifferent or hostile to the Army's religious message and its means of propagating it now expressed sympathy with its program of social amelioration. Many of these people were disappointed later when the Army did not adopt distinctly political or economic solutions to the problems it attempted to solve. Among religious thinkers there was a similar reaction to the Army. The years in which The Salvation Army was coming to public attention were years in which many religious and educational leaders, horrified by the all-too-obvious bad effects of urbanization, were beginning to perceive certain traditional Christian beliefs, such as a reliance on individual salvation, as too facile. "Higher criticism" of biblical texts and Darwinism added to their anxiety. They developed an alternative to strict orthodoxy, the "Social Gospel," which was based on the conviction that Christ had come to bring what the influential Walter Rauschenbusch called "social restoration and moral salvage." The leaders of the Social Gospel movement were at first sympathetic to The Salvation Army, seeing it as a stirring rebuke to conventional religious indifference. They were touched by the earnestness and kindliness of Salvationists working in the slums. Many more orthodox Protestant and Roman Catholic writers also praised the Army for these things. Later some leaders among the Social Gospel were chilled by the Army's biblical literalism and its insistence that salvation was the ultimate cure-all; they became convinced that, for the problems of urban society, the Army could offer no solution worthy of the name. The writings of the Social Gospel movement nonetheless helped the Army: as the journalists and reformers had made social awareness popular, now the Social Gospel made it intellectually fashionable. Both helped in the 1890s to prepare a broader reception for the Army's requests for public support for its own practical programs.[56]

Less helpful to The Salvation Army was the prolonged argument between its leaders and the Charity Organization Society (COS), which began soon after the Army landed in the United States and continued well into the twentieth century. The first Charity Organization Society was organized in London in 1868 and in the United States in Buffalo in 1877. Within two years there were branches in six other American cities. The COS began in New York City in 1882, just as The Salvation Army was becoming well established in that city. The purpose of the COS was to provide for cooperation among urban relief agencies and coordination of their efforts. The Society called for an end to indiscriminate charity and endorsed efforts to collect information on poor people so that the causes of their poverty could be addressed and practical assistance could be directed to those "worthy" of receiving it. Among the sorts of help the COS promoted were literacy training and education in home hygiene, employment agencies, day care for the children of working parents, and social clubs for wholesome recreational activities (e.g., debating, and choral music) in local churches. The agency hoped that applicants determined to be "unworthy" could be forced to perform work for their assistance, find outside work, or be dismissed without obtaining assistance. The COS particularly warned against almsgiving. A writer in the first issue of *Charities,* the new journal of the National Conference of Charities and Corrections (an organization established in 1874) laid down the official manifesto in 1897: giving handouts "without exacting money, work or information is . . . the plan of unorganized charity with its obvious abuses and social dangers. The absence of charity is an evil. The practice of impulsive, thoughtless, inconsiderate charity is likewise an evil." The Salvation Army accepted some of the principles of the COS but refused from the start to accept the distinction between "worthy" and "unworthy" poor, preferring to apply such categories, if at all, only after the needy had been given immediate relief. The line between the Army and the COS was not always a clear one. By the late 1890s, COS organizations in many cities had begun to give alms — which is to say that they had, as one official put it in 1899, "degenerated" into "mere dole-relief societies." For their part, many Army officers believed that repeated indiscriminate charity was harmful to the recipient, and they endorsed the work test not only for practical but also for moral purposes. Generally, however, the Army and the COS did not cooperate and were often at odds publicly, especially over the Army's fund-raising techniques and its refusal to join federated charity boards officially. A detailed scholarly study of The Salvation Army in 1909 concluded that the Army's refusal to cooperate with the COS was widespread, based partly on the Army's confidence in its own fund-raising appeal and partly on the COS's prejudice against the dominant religious element in the Army's relief operations.[57]

Army officers were fully aware that theirs was not the only solution to the problems of industrialization. Serving on the street, their ministry mostly among the working class and poor, Salvationists were witness to the swell of labor unrest that marked the last twenty years of the nineteenth century. The Salvation Army never strayed from its insistence that personal salvation was the only ultimate remedy for all human misery; it had little interest in merely economic and political solutions and took a neutral position on such issues. Its energetic goodwill was offered freely to all in need, and people of almost all persuasions came to trust its evenhandedness. When a group of respectable Chicagoans wanted to distribute food to the families left destitute in the autumn of 1893 due to a sharp reduction in employment caused by the closing of the Chicago World's Fair and the national financial panic of that year, the *Chicago Mail* selected the Army to conduct the business, commending its "thoroughly equipped corps of charity workers." In the Pullman Strike of the next year, The Salvation Army threw its small resources into action to relieve the suffering of the strikers, who faced starvation. Gov. John P. Altgeld accepted Staff Captain Winchell's offer to collect and distribute food. Amid the bloodshed and riot of that terrible summer, the Army reaffirmed its lofty independent view that both employer and employee needed the "salvation of Jesus Christ," while wagons borrowed by the Army carried food through the police lines.[58]

The Army's official position on the labor movement was neutral. Leading officers were more ambiguous: labor leaders found reasons both to praise and to condemn the movement. The Salvation Army displayed at least some affinity to radical labor causes in the 1880s, both in London and in the United States, especially during the administration of Comm. Frank Smith (1884-1887). In an age when the working classes were alienated from many Protestant denominations, the Army's appeal to the working poor was an important factor in the growth of the organization. When a strike occurred in the mines of western Pennsylvania in 1888, the divisional officer referred to the strikers as "our class of people." The Salvation Army was cheered by labor unions when both groups marched in Fourth of July parades. The Army's social welfare activities developed rapidly during the widespread unemployment that followed the Panic of 1893; the strain on all charity and relief organizations was very great during this period. In 1897, the Army issued a special "Labor Day" number of *The War Cry,* in which there appeared very warm endorsements from the United Mine Workers, who praised the movement for the "interest taken in the working people," and from Eugene V. Debs, leader of the Pullman strikers, who called the Army "Christianity in action." The Army's relief activities, however, were directed at individuals, not at social classes; the Army continued to avoid, and often ridiculed, political solutions to social problems. The single exception was the Army's commitment to legalized prohibition. Some officers were critical of labor agitation. Officers declared that businesspeople ought to support the Army because it improved the workforce by transforming workers into honest, sober, and cooperative citizens. On his first visit to San Francisco in 1895, General Booth told two Salvationist employees of the Army printing plant — who approached him to request that the plant be operated according to union rules — that they had to resign from either the Army or the typographical union. The next issue of the *Pacific Union Printer* called the Army a "rat institution" and blacklisted *The War Cry.* "Abusive pamphlets" condemning the Army were distributed for several years by local socialists throughout the western states.[59]

Socialists had reason for concern: there was little in the official posture of the Army to comfort those who advocated radical reform of the American economic system, although, as in the case of attitudes toward labor, some officers were ambiguous in their attitudes toward the wealthy. Major Smith issued a daring statement in 1886 condemning the "overshadowing inequities, the gross selfishness, the hard un-Christian spirit" of the rich — daring, but far from typical: Smith later resigned from the Army to devote his considerable energies entirely to socialist politics in England. The Pacific Coast *War Cry* frequently carried cartoons in the nineties that personified sin and portrayed the devil as an imp in top hat and tails and in other ways ridiculed fashionable dress and customs. Generally, however, officers took the economic order as they found it. And how they found it was in the hands of the rich, to whom they increasingly had to turn for the large sums of money required to operate the Army's ever-expanding social program.[60]

Field officers were expected to finance their own corps by whatever means came to hand. The financial secretary at national headquarters reminded Salvationists and friends of the movement in 1895 that "one of the fundamental principles of The Salvation Army is that of self-support." At the same time, officers were aware that on the whole Salvationists contributed little in the way of money to the Army's support; it was reported in the same year that the weekly contribution of American and British Salvationists was "remarkably low" even given the fact that the majority of Salvationists were poor and working-class persons. The average in both countries was an English penny (about two cents) per week, far less than the biblical tenth. This meant that officers and soldiers had to raise funds by whatever means came to hand. Selling *The War Cry* produced over half the Army's income in the 1880s; collections were taken at every meeting indoors and outdoors, and Salvationists were often reduced simply to begging on street corners and in saloons. Major Milsaps complained to his diary in 1901 that "with each recurring year" he abominated "more and more these money collecting schemes of the Salvation Army," which had resulted in "universal dissatisfaction" in the ranks. Such means could not begin to produce sufficient funds to finance the Army's burgeoning relief projects, which at first showed no profit; the Army admitted that "certain departments of Social work form exceptions to the rule" of self-support.[61]

The answer was the Auxiliary League, which after several false starts — it was launched in 1883 for a slightly different purpose but languished during the Moore secession crisis — was revived in 1887 as a means of enlisting the support of the fashionable for the Army's "social wing" without expecting their endorsement of the Army's religious doctrines and evangelical techniques. Some officers regarded it as a serious misjudgment, if not something worse, that the Army was willing to distinguish between its social and spiritual selves and to appeal for funds solely for the former. It is a concern that lingers to the present. For the time being, however, most officers put aside objections in the face of the triumphs of Maud Ballington Booth, who assumed control of the Auxiliary League in 1887. A woman of passionate sincerity, charming, quick-witted, and graceful, Mrs. Ballington Booth presided over the drawing-room meetings of the League in an elegant uniform "of fine material and neatly made" and a bonnet "trimmed with broad silk ribbon," sometimes alone, sometimes with a slum officer, a singer, or an instrumentalist. Women were so affected by her accounts of the Army's "great work of reclaiming drunkards, rescuing the fallen, and saving the lost" that they wept, opened their purses, and even donated their rings and jewelry on the spot. The Auxiliary League became fashionable and spread to the Pacific Coast. There were two types of Auxiliaries — the "subscribing" group, members of which agreed to donate five dollars per month (a considerable sum in those days), and the "collecting" group, members of which agreed to collect at least $2.50 per month. Together they counted six thousand members by 1896.[62]

Auxiliaries were expected to support the Army not only with money, but in word and print as well. Among the thousands who agreed to these things and who carried the "small leather ticket bearing the official recognition of headquarters" were some of the richest and most influential people in the United States. From 1892 through 1897 the Army published a special magazine, *The Conqueror*, designed "for the promotion of the interests and work of The Salvation Army." Well written and illustrated with photographs and artists' renderings, the magazine was intended to carry the Army's message to middle-class readers willing to support the movement financially. Members of the Chautauqua Library and Scientific Circle learned in 1893 that The Salvation Army had "become a potent factor in changing the conditions of the lower strata of society. . . . To dismiss it as unworthy of study or notice" was "to confess ignorance of social matters." President Cleveland received Smith and a delegation at the White House on the sixth anniversary of Railton's landing, and President Harrison sent a vaguely worded endorsement to be read at the Army's huge Columbian Congress in New York in December 1892. The support of William McKinley, both as candidate and as president, went beyond the merely formal, however: a kindly religious man, McKinley gave the Army genuine sympathy. Buoyed by the support of the rich and the powerful, the Army arrived socially.[63]

Yet this story of public acceptance has an ironic, darker side. The years that saw The Salvation Army wafted into the drawing rooms of America on wings of praise also saw it advance into dives and gutters against a gale of abuse. This was the time of the Army's trial by fire. The catalogue of hostile acts committed against the Army from 1880 to 1896 is depressingly long, and some of it makes grim reading. At least five Salvationists were martyred (in Colorado Springs, San Francisco, Spokane, St. Louis, and Pittsburgh); a mob tried to lynch young Capt. Adam Gifford in Rockville, Connecticut; officers in Los Angeles and Leadville, Colorado, were shot at repeatedly; several soldiers in Brooklyn had their arms broken in 1885; and at least three officers were struck full in the head with bricks thrown at short range: Richard Holz and Capt. Mary Powell in Brooklyn in 1885 and Samuel Logan Brengle in Boston in 1888. A young female officer in Portland, Maine, permanently lost her hearing after being knocked unconscious by a large chunk of ice. Many crusaders were badly cut and bruised by direct assaults; several were burned deliberately with cigars and firecrackers. A mob rushed into a meeting at the Chicago No. 3 corps, upset the wood stove, and rushed back outside and locked the door in an attempt to burn the crowded hall. Attempts were made to burn the corps in Sacramento and a shelter in Los Angeles, and in 1886 a crowd wearing hoods succeeded in burning down the Army hall in Bristol, Connecticut. In Napa, California, the officers were warned to leave town before somebody blew them and their work into atoms with "Dina might."[64]

The large majority of assaults were not aimed at killing or crippling Salvationists or burning down their halls, but the effect of attacks on the victims was unpleasant enough. Young Capt. Harry Stillwell came to the end of his first meeting at the San Francisco No. 2 Corps covered with tobacco spit. William Brewer, the divisional officer in Boston, was accosted while strolling with his infant son in his arms by a man who slapped the baby in the face! Attacks on parades and street-corner meetings were widespread and frequent. The weapons varied: stones, bits of broken brick, old bottles, mud, pears, apples, tomatoes, eggs of various ages, garbage, small dead animals, horse manure, and water collected from handy barrels and horse troughs or dispensed from the occasional accommodating fire engine. Indoor meetings were hardly more secure: windows, lamps, chairs, and pictures were smashed, and flags and banners were torn down — the latter usually not without stiff resistance: the corps flag was sacred. And there were odd variations on the disruptive theme. In San Francisco, enemies dumped pepper over the floor; in Buffalo they smuggled pigeons into the hall and released them during the meeting; in Napa, dead cats and rotten eggs were pitched into the meeting hall through open windows; in Newark, skittle balls were rolled over the floor of the Music Academy above the Army hall, creating a racket. Even where meetings were not attacked, a hostile environment hampered the Army's work, and its reputation for attracting vandalism often made it impossible to rent rooms or buildings in which to conduct its services. Meetings outdoors or indoors that were not physically attacked were jeered and mimicked, which was often harder to bear. Railton never forgot "the clever and biting sarcasm of the United States, in which all classes and professions can more or less unite."[65]

The intensity of this vituperation, and the fact that it so often issued in actual physical violence, requires explanation. For one thing, the success of the Auxiliary League should not obscure the fact that not all respectable and fashionable opinion supported the Army. The pioneer Army with its hallelujah hoopla offended many church leaders. Many of these later accepted the Army's bizarre antics as well suited to reach the urban poor (an editorial in *The Homiletic Monthly* declared in 1883 that the power of The Salvation Army was "not in its extravagances, but in spite of these. Its power is in its devotion to the poor"), but the initial negative reactions lingered for years and provided encouragement to those whose dislike of the Army was less principled. Some church leaders advocated the adoption of some of the Army's methods by their own denominations. Other ministers declared from the pulpit and the press that the Army made a "mockery" out of sacred things and degraded the heritage of Christianity. Many others, ministers and laypersons alike, disagreed with the Army's fundamentalist doctrines quite apart from its methods of presenting them. There were, after all, many people on the streets who held different views on religion. Roman Catholic writers were generally favorable to the Army, praising it for its zeal in carrying religion to the urban poor and for its social welfare activities among them, but even some of these writers condemned what the Church regarded as the Army's wrongheaded doctrine and, as one writer put it in 1882, the Salvationists' repeated introduction into the sacred sphere of religion of "those scenes that may be described as half-painful and half-profane." There must have been large numbers of people who regarded religion as a personal matter, or a matter of no importance, who were repelled by the overtures of street preachers. Many idle, irresponsible men and boys lounged around the scenes of the Army's activities, men with no regular employment, bored and hopeless, drifting along on the edges of criminality, often drunk. Such people viewed an attack on a Salvation Army parade as a welcome diversion, a kind of cruel sport they could excuse as harmless fun if nobody actually died.[66]

At about the same point on the social scale were those who found the Army threatening: persons whose livelihood depended on the drinking, gambling, and sexual appetites of others. Saloon keepers were particularly liable to feel the adverse effects of the Army's street-corner revival. It is a mistake to suppose that most taverns in the 1890s were elaborate and well-endowed places with long mahogany bars, gas chandeliers, and cornet, piano, and violin trios. In fact, most were shoestring operations with little in the way of furniture and no music; a survey of 163 saloons in Chicago's 17th Ward conducted in 1900 revealed that only eight had music of any kind. Although the great majority of saloons offered a "free lunch" and had some value to the neighborhood as the only social club available to the immigrant and working poor, most of these establishments were dark, smoky rooms for hard drinking on a small margin; the loss of a half-dozen faithful brought financial ruin to them. The same was true for those who lived on the earnings of prostitution. The conversion of a prostitute or two, with subsequent flight to a Rescue Home, meant disaster to most procurers or madams. The Salvation Army's doctrines would have meant little to such people had the Army been content to dispense them in fashionable churches. But the Army gave out the call for repentance — with flags, posters, and a brass band — on the street corner, the very doorstep of those engaged in the behaviors it opposed.[67]

In many cases, its enemies could attack The Salvation Army with impunity. Many American cities had inadequate numbers of police, and sometimes none at all in the worst districts after dark. Even when the police were present, they often offered the Army little protection or joined in the attack by arresting the Salvationists for disturbing the peace or blocking the sidewalk — or, when all else failed, for violating a hastily enacted ordinance against marching, playing band instruments, or beating drums without a license. In larger cities, mayors and police commissioners simply denied the Army the privilege of holding services outdoors. Official persecution was not a universal problem, however, and for the most part it did not last long. Many police officers were sympathetic from the first; in general the police provided adequate security to the Army when asked, and public opinion and the courts did not abide blatantly discriminatory legislation forever. The generally favorable attitude taken toward the Army by the Roman Catholic Church may have encouraged some police officers on their own initiative to take a more benign attitude toward individual Salvationists even during periods of official persecution. But the fact remained that saloons played a major role in municipal politics, and their owners expected favors from city police and fire personnel as part of the arrangement. Ballington Booth complained in 1888 that local laws were made and enforced by "liquor dealers, politicians, and other influential authorities." Saloons were the most common locations for big-city political meetings. Of the 1,003 political rallies and meetings held in New York City as part of the November 1884 election, 633 were held in saloons and 86 were held next door to saloons. Where law enforcement officials were indifferent or hostile to the Army or where they favored the cause of the saloon keepers in whose establishments important political operatives conducted much of their business, Salvationists faced a severe trial. The Army was convinced that police persecution was caused almost entirely by pressure from liquor dealers with political connections. For a while, arrests were common. Many Army meetings were broken up by police, and many Salvation Army officers and soldiers were arrested — some of them often.[68]

It was as the "Hallelujah Jail Bird" that Joe the Turk earned his niche in Salvation Army history. A pugnacious, fearless man with no administrative ability and little actual knowledge of religious matters, Joe was called as much to flamboyance as to religion. Dressed in his "full Turkish costume," he became a kind of happy wanderer, traveling around the country challenging anti-Army statutes, being arrested, and demanding jury trials. The Turk (actually an Armenian) had discovered early that juries of respectable persons, many of them churchgoers, were more sympathetic to Salvationists than to saloon keepers and lowlife plaintiffs. He was usually acquitted, whereupon the statute used to arrest him ceased to have practical effect. Even when convicted and sent to jail for a few

Joseph Garabed, better known as "Joe the Turk," an enthusiastic traveling officer who "went to jail for Jesus" many times
Source: The Salvation Army National Archives

days or weeks in lieu of the fine (which he always refused to pay, however small the sum), Joe triumphed. He held revival services in his cell, sang, prayed aloud, and decorated the walls, sheets, and other prisoners' clothing with his special "Jesus Saves" rubber stamp. Once, in the Portland, Oregon, jail in 1890, Joe amplified his motto-stamping ministry; having brought his cellmate to Christ, he discovered to his great joy that the convert was a sign painter. The two worked through the night, emblazoning the walls of the cell, which shone forth in the morning with "Jesus is the Drunkard's Friend" and "Where Will You Spend Eternity?" Not all arresting officers and jailers were gentle, however, and Joe was stoned by mobs several times. The work of this odd, contentious man required courage and brought great benefit to The Salvation Army. The publicity that resulted from his escapades made it difficult to take the offending statutes seriously.[69]

The wave of persecution crested in the late 1880s and then began to ebb. By 1892 Ballington Booth was encouraged by the changed attitude of the press and the public and felt it necessary to warn of the opposite "dangers attending the universal well-speaking of all men." Congratulations and statements of support poured in to the Army "from Pulpit and Press, from President and Policemen." By the end of the decade an Army publication declared that "a noticeable and decidedly felicitous feature of the War in the United States" was the "increase in friendliness displayed by almost every newspaper and periodical towards the Army." Persecution had accomplished little even in immediate terms, and nothing permanent. The opposite had been the effect in many places: the Army grew stronger. Touched by the courage of the beleaguered Salvationists, angry and embarrassed by discoveries of special statutes and police persecution, public opinion became more favorable to the Army. For this reason, and because they regarded opposition as good for the soul and proof that The Salvation Army must be on the right track for the devil and his stooges to be so worried, leading officers welcomed persecution. Commissioner Smith added a practical note in 1885 by reminding the troops in Newark that it was better to have a crowd pelt them than not to have a crowd at all.[70]

Encouraged by approval and strengthened by adversity, the Army broadened its war front. In the West, a mounted branch was formed in June 1892 and thrown into the war. Dressed in top-boots, red shirts, "mouse-colored corduroy inexpressibles," and sombreros with hatbands in Army colors, the "Salvation Army Cavalry" hit the trail in California. The "Mounted Foes of Satan" consisted of Maj. Philip Kyle and ten young bandsmen (including Lt. Fong Foo Sec as cook and bass drummer). The plan of campaign required the men to ride to the vicinity of a town, make camp for the night, mount up in the morning, instruments more or less at the ready, and "storm the town." In between camping and storming, the cavalrymen painted uplifting mottos on large rocks and enjoyed miraculous cliff-hanger escapes from various dangers — crashes, storms, wild animals, and so on — which enthralled the readers of their weekly dispatches to *The War Cry.*

The results of this endeavor were very encouraging — although total success eluded the valiants because none of them could actually ride a horse. The next two summers an old concord coach and six horses were enlisted, and the group set out again as the "Charioteers." The efforts of these "twelve godly musicians" led by Ensign Sam Wood were crowned with glory: eighty-seven souls were saved the first summer out. One of

"The California Charioteers" evangelistic group pose with their Salvation Army
"war chariot" in California, July 1893. Their leader was Ensign Samuel A. Wood,
standing third from right.   Source: Miss T. E. Wood, Ocean Grove, New Jersey

these was a young Jewish storekeeper, Julius Abrams, who was brought to Christ at a Charioteer open-air meeting in a Mojave Desert mining town. Abrams spent thirty years as an officer and Army evangelist. Thus graced by the blessing of God, the old stagecoach was kept in San Francisco as a souvenir and driven in parades. Army visitors from "back East" were thrilled to see the "War Chariot" waiting for them at the ferry slip. Nor did cavalrymen and charioteers exhaust the possibilities: a regular series of circuit riders called the "Outriders" was established. These heroic officers traveled alone or in pairs, carrying the salvation war into the back country of California.[71]

Well might the famed artist of the Old West Charles M. Russell lament that Dame Progress and Father Time were consigning his beloved gamblers and bushwhackers to oblivion — and not without help! One of Russell's 1898 pen drawings showed Progress and Time lording it over a dispirited crowd of doomed heroes — but in the background, under a "Salvation" flag, the lead woman is clearly carrying a *War Cry*. The Old West was dying indeed, and the Army was doing all that valor could ask to minimize the number of souls that died with it.[72]

The prospects were bright before these soldiers of Christ in the waning years of the nineteenth century. The plantation owners who ruled the Hawaiian republic invited the Army to send an advance guard in 1894 to evangelize the pineapple workers who had not been touched by the churches already on the scene. Convinced that their "enlivening methods" would create "a wonderful stir" in the islands, a pioneer party of five officers led by the indefatigable Staff Captain Milsaps landed in Honolulu in September. The party was kindly received by their hosts, introduced to the editors of the three newspapers in town, and provided with a large hall equipped with electric lights and seven hundred seats. Sanford B. Dole, president of the Republic of Hawaii, invited the pioneers to the palace and set upon their brows the seal of official approval, which did not dim when the republic was annexed to the United States in 1898.[73]

Those were the years in which the Army offered its first tentative spiritual overtures to men in the ranks of the American military. National headquarters was concerned that Salvationists who joined the U.S. armed forces would drift away from true religion without the vivifying fellowship of their "Blood-washed comrades." In the case of the Salvationist crew of a U.S. revenue cutter stationed at New Bern, North Carolina, in 1888, there seemed to be little to fear: the crew conducted Army meetings wherever the ship cruised or docked. With Salvationists who found themselves alone, or with only another comrade or two in a regiment or ship, the case was far different. Shortly after their arrival, the Honolulu pioneers went aboard the *USS Charleston* to seek out Salvationists (and to sell *War Crys* — sixty-three of them). In 1896 an official Naval and Military League was established at New York headquarters, under Brig. Alice Lewis. Its primary purpose was to locate Salvationist men serving in the national military, establish contact with them by letters and visits, and hold special services for them on their base or ship or at the nearest corps. Such services were of course broadly evangelical, and other servicemen were converted. In 1896 two converted sailors on the *USS Adams* asked to be enrolled as Salvationists on the deck — and were, in the presence of the entire crew.[74]

The Spanish-American War, which began in April 1898, caused a rapid expansion of American military forces. Many Salvationists were among the volunteers. The one-woman Naval and Military League was suddenly hard pressed to perform its duties, and many officers were enlisted for the duration. The Salvation Army was, in fact, enthusiastic about the spiritual possibilities of the war. In the summer of 1898 *The War Cry* produced a "War Special," and the picture on the cover was captioned "The Battleship 'Salvation' Opens Fire on Fort Sin." After bureaucratic objections were resolved by the kindly intervention of the wife of President McKinley, Brigadier Lewis and an assistant were sent to minister to the troops assembling at Tampa and Key West for the invasion of Cuba. The women were received gallantly, their meetings greatly enlivened by the superb playing of the band of the 9th U.S. Cavalry, a black regiment that was said to have the finest band in the U.S. Army. Thus encouraged, the Salvationists petitioned to follow the troops to Cuba but were denied permission to do so. They continued to pour energies into ministering to the armed forces where they could, sending detachments to the new camps at Peekskill and Hempstead. In California, three officers held services in a tent for the fifty Salvationists among the troops waiting to depart from San Francisco for the Philippines. In Sacramento, the Army joined the Red Cross in handing out a loaf of bread and a mug of coffee to each of the five thousand men in training there.[75]

Troops on the Pacific Coast were being collected and dispatched in such large numbers that the government facilities were swamped. The Salvation Army was likewise overwhelmed in its attempts to establish some sort of helpful contact with members of this enormous and transient mass. Many men, like those on the flagship *Olympia* who wired that they were holding Army meetings on their own aboard ship, were already out of reach, reduced to such spiritual resources as they could provide for themselves. Clearly an officer would have to accompany the troops to the Far East if the "spiritual welfare of all Salvationists serving as soldiers in the Army" was to be attended to properly. Staff Captain Milsaps was again selected. Maj. Gen. Wesley Merritt, commanding the Philippine expedition, agreed to allow Milsaps free transportation on the troopship *Newport* but let him know that he would be on his own for everything else, including food on board and facilities for his work in the Philippines. Although Milsaps was not a military officer or in any legal sense a chaplain, he was regarded as such by himself and The Salvation Army.[76]

Nor was Milsaps a missionary to the Philippines, which he reached in July 1898. His work during the twenty months he stayed in Manila was entirely among American servicemen, almost all of them Salvationists, although he did send to San Francisco for some copies of the new Chinese *War Cry,* as he apparently hoped to begin work among the Chinese in Manila. Whatever he was doing, he received little official encouragement. After a full day of walking and asking permission to begin his work, Milsaps and a friendly Salvationist sergeant from Oregon held an impromptu open-air meeting on the old walls of Cavite, singing and testifying to a hundred men as the setting sun gilded the wreck of the Spanish flagship *Reina Christina* in Manila harbor. Milsaps soon opened a "Soldiers' and Sailors' Reading Room" in the city, a place where soldiers could meet, read Salvation Army literature (the only kind Milsaps could provide on his limited funds), and avail themselves of free stationery and ink. Milsaps provided Salvation Army services regularly for the eight Salvationists who visited him faithfully. While the Army operated a resting station in New York for convalescent veterans of the completed Cuban expedition, Milsaps remained with his little band of soldiers in Manila, uncertain as to what the Army's long-range plans for the Philippines might be. As it turned out, the Army had no plans for the Philippines, but that did not detract from the official conviction that Milsaps's Philippine expedition had been a complete success, further proof to headquarters that The Salvation Army was an agency through which God was changing the world.

Milsaps's return to San Francisco in March 1900 was the occasion for a tremendous rally, one more tribute to the nineteenth century, which had ended so full of promise for The Salvation Army. Had it not grown wonderfully? And, even more wonderful, had it not survived, through the good Providence of God, its greatest defection, a secession even more lamentable than Moore's, and passed on to greater things?[77]

CHAPTER 3

1896-1914

"How the weakest conquer . . ."

By the mid-1890s The Salvation Army was a familiar sight on the streets of America. The open-air ministry remained at the heart of the Great Salvation War. The Army's formidable arsenal of weapons could not be wielded with maximum effectiveness inside its own halls, where the devil hardly dared to venture. The Army's commitment to the "method of Christ and the Apostles" did not depend on brass bands for fulfillment — Ensign J. C. Ludgate offered detailed instructions on carrying on a street meeting single-handedly — but a band was employed wherever one could be mustered. These were the years that saw the beginning of the long and still-revered era of the street parade: there were few commuters hurrying home on the streetcar, few tenement dwellers strolling the sidewalks to escape the fetid darkness of a windowless room who did not hear the joyful thump and blare of The Salvation Army out for the evening march. This remained, according to an official statement, the Army's first means of attack — "holding meetings out of doors, and marching singing through the streets, in harmony with law and order." When law and order ceased to offer their vain resistance and the Army had added its charitable programs of relief and uplift, the movement became not only familiar but popular. More, The Salvation Army was on the way to becoming respectable. In 1892 a young graduate of Baker University in Baldwin City, Kansas, James Marion Price, extolled the work of the Army in an oration

entitled "Honor to Whom Honor Is Due" at the June commencement
exercises. Charles Augustus Briggs, an influential professor at Union Theological Seminary, was enthusiastic about the Army and gratified to note
in 1894 that "no religious organization in history" had "enjoyed such a
marvelous growth as the Salvation Army in so short a time."[1]

The Army continued to offer the world an encouraging set of statistics. Critics who had predicted that it was no more than a transient fad
were silenced, while soldiers and supporters swelled with pride at repeated
proofs of the blessing of God: every new tally revealed an increase, and
growth was often phenomenal. In 1892 Marshal Ballington Booth, the
national commander, enrolled the fifteen hundredth officer in the United
States; three years later there were two thousand officers serving in six
hundred corps and twenty-four slum and rescue stations. Granted, the
precise meaning of these figures was cloudy to all but the most sanguine
view. There was, for instance, no easy way to determine how many people
were reached by the Army's ministry, nor in what way they were helped;
it is certain that only a small percentage of those rescued by the Army ever
joined its ranks or offered financial support to the war. Few corps could
be supported by the contributions of their own members alone; almost all
depended on constant solicitation of the public in some form. Nevertheless
there were increases, clearly and unmistakably, in the number of officers
and stations, and these facts alone were enough to stimulate the marshal
to fresh outbursts of enthusiasm: in 1895 he ordered a one-third increase
in every statistic.[2]

The Army still owned little real property. Most corps went forth to
war from rented barracks. A major exception to this gypsy maneuverability
— and a symbol of the Army's new prestige — was the national headquarters building at 120 West Fourteenth Street in New York City. This
"imposing if not . . . beautiful structure" was Ballington's pride and joy.
He and his wife had expended every energy to raise the huge sums necessary
to secure the lot — $160,000 — and to raise the eight-story structure —
another $200,000. The Army had not yet developed any systematic means
of raising large sums of money. Except for bequests, which were not yet
large, the movement had no internal means for acquiring properties of its
own. The support of the six thousand Auxiliaries was consumed by the
rapidly spreading social work, and the many new corps programs were
hard-pressed to find the pennies and nickels necessary to survive. For three
years the marshal diverted part or all of the funds raised by the annual
"Self-Denial Campaign" toward the new building. The "Self-Denial

The national headquarters of The Salvation Army on 14th Street in New York City (built while Ballington Booth was national commander) was officially opened in June 1895.
Source: The Salvation Army National Archives

Fund," which was started by William Booth in 1886, was based on a special voluntary levy raised by the soldiers in addition to their weekly "cartridges" and was supposed to be sent to International Headquarters in London to finance special evangelistic projects, such as supporting the Army's overseas missionaries. In any case, the new building was finished and opened in June 1895. Complete with crenelated towers and a mock-Gothic battlement frieze draped with flags, its eight stories glowered over Fourteenth Street like a fortress, its presence periodically reconfirmed for startled pedestrians by the firing of a signal cannon on the roof.[3]

The life of an officer on the field remained hard, full of labor under trying and often humiliating circumstances. The soldiers in the corps were too few and too poor to support the work financially, or they were unwilling to do so, so in order to keep the doors open, officers were reduced

to what one of their ranks called "the everlasting beg" in one form or
another. The officers had no claim on the Army for their penurious
allowances: they could draw their salaries out of the meager collection only
after all other outstanding debts were paid. Many officers lived without
complaint in grinding poverty. When Emma Westbrook and two cadets
opened a corps in Haverstraw, New York, the three carried all they owned
in a single peach basket. And when young Adam Gifford's infant son died,
Gifford had to dress and bury the child himself, in a donated grave. In
addition to the poverty they endured, officers were circumscribed by a
web of regulations that controlled every part of their lives, including whom
they could marry (only another officer) and when (with permission,
granted only after the couple had endured a long period of separation and
reflection). These valiants, many of whom were barely literate, threw
themselves with high hearts into the struggle after a brief exposure to the
rigors of a "training garrison," which consisted almost entirely of scrubbing
floors, memorizing selected passages from the Bible, and selling *The War
Cry*. From dawn — the cadets in New York were awakened by a slide
trombone at 6:30 A.M. — until the gaslights were turned down late at
night, the emphasis was on "practical training in field service." By 1893
there were ten of these garrisons scattered around the country, each under
the control of the local divisional headquarters. There was no standard
curriculum or fixed term of attendance. Living conditions were often grim.
Meals in the Jersey City Training Garrison in 1894 consisted of breakfast
(oatmeal, day-old bread, and "milk" — a concoction of one can of evaporated milk in a gallon of water), lunch (stew or fish), and supper (bread,
butter, and tea). Nothing in these training garrisons, nothing in the zeal
of youth or the new hope of the redeemed prepared these warriors for the
months and years of heartbreak and lonely toil that awaited them as
officers. Many fell by the wayside. Many did not, and it is to those
long-forgotten captains and ensigns and adjutants who gave up their
obscure lives, which is all they had to give, in the service of Christ and
His Kingdom that history shall give credit for all The Salvation Army was
enabled to accomplish for its Lord. Modern-day Salvationists look on these
pioneers gratefully as they stare out in formal piety from faded photographs. From their lips ascended the clouds of prayers and from their eyes
flowed the ocean of tears that provided the Army with a measure of
strength for the Great Salvation War.[4]

By 1896 the Army had reached the point at which its growth no
longer depended exclusively on national headquarters. The Army was no

longer a tender seedling requiring constant careful attention from New York or London; its roots had gone deep into American soil, and its branches grew daily stronger. Leadership was important in 1896, but it was no longer nearly so indispensable as it had been in 1884, when the defection of Major Moore had almost destroyed the Army. These changed conditions were the background against which the next — and happily, the last — major crisis in the leadership of The Salvation Army in the United States took place: the resignation of Marshal and Mrs. Ballington Booth as national commanders in January 1896.

The news came as a complete surprise to the Salvationists in the American field. The commander and his wife, Maud Charlesworth Booth (she often added "Ballington" to her last name), seemed to be highly successful leaders. Certainly they were well liked. Both were officers of exceptional ability whose administration was marked by advances that the rank and file were eager to attribute to their leadership: the reconciliation of Colonel Holz and most of the remnant of the Moore rebels; the construction of the new national headquarters on Fourteenth Street; and the origin, by Maud, of a range of activities designed to convert convicts and to help them into honest and useful lives on their release from prison. One of the Ballington Booths' most important contributions to the future of the Army was the rejuvenation of the Auxiliaries, who formed the first stage of the massive public support upon which the Army's social programs would come to depend; among the numerous wealthy and influential Americans who became attached to the cause of the Army during these years were George S. and Carrie Judd Montgomery, California philanthropists who became active soldiers in the 1890s. Beulah Camp near Oakland was their gift to the Army, along with the loan of several other rural properties for social service activities. The Booths were powerful public speakers who could electrify large crowds, holding a jammed auditorium almost motionless for an hour, or alternatively convulsing it with laughter, tears, and applause. They were the first of the Army's national leaders to be well received outside the ranks. Indeed, Maud became so well known to the general public that at least one manufacturer sought, and obtained, her endorsement in advertising his product, the "Vapo-Cresolene Lamp." It was as a speaker to ladies of fashion that Maud became fashionable herself, while Ballington edified Chautauqua audiences and charmed the dowager saints of Ocean Grove, New Jersey, on a regular basis.[5]

As effective in print as on the platform, the Booths were prolific writers. In addition to the much-treasured *Soldier's Manual* and several

Comm. and Mrs. Ballington (Maud) Booth. Ballington was national commander from 1887 to 1896, when he resigned and formed the Volunteers of America.
Source: The Salvation Army National Archives

jointly authored books, manifestos, articles, and songs (including "We Shall Win America" and "The Cross Is Not Greater Than His Grace," which is still used in Army meetings), each wrote weekly columns for *The War Cry.* Hers was winningly entitled "Sunbeams from Mother's Office" and contained helpful and practical hints for her "precious and faithful" women officers; his column was likewise practical: a sermon outline offered to help the hard-pressed officer over at least one of the week's obstacles. Nor did these writers confine themselves to print: both were indefatigable correspondents. Maud wrote regularly, personally, to every woman officer in the country, signing each letter "Your Affectionate Mother in the Holy

War," and reams of friendly and encouraging letters went to officers over Ballington's florid signature.[6]

Ballington and Maud were clearly an engaging pair. Devoted to the Army's evangelical mission (Ballington once described himself as one "who daily yearns for the Salvation of the worst of our great cities"), both were dramatic and whimsical, which further endeared them to Salvationists, who took it as evidence that their courageous leaders were not concerned for their own reputations. Ballington spent weeks during the winter of 1890-1891 flitting about New York in disguise, collecting impressions for a series of lurid articles he produced for the *Herald,* by which he privately hoped to stimulate contributions to the Army's new social relief program. He also did eccentric things with the long-suffering National Staff Band, which trailed after him on his speaking tours. The band must have dreaded the Marshal's semiannual expeditions to Ocean Grove: he ordered them out of the train to play on the platform at every stop down the North Jersey Shore route. Although a spellbinder as a speaker, Ballington was less comfortable on the platform than when engaged in more active forms of warfare, such as parades (day and night — with torches), mass rallies, and "All-Night for Jesus" meetings. Maud was equally colorful, dividing her copious energies between melting the hearts of the rich with her tales of the life of a slum sister and riding five hundred miles in the cab of a locomotive, gathering material for a special Army ministry she proposed to launch among railroad engineers and firemen (an occupation she felt had been too long neglected). Yet all was not well with the Marshal and Mrs. Booth.[7]

The difficulties that overtook them in 1896 sprang from several sources. Minor problems included Ballington's reservations about the official rejection by the Army of sacramental observances and his inclination to dwell on the benefits that ordination would bring to Army officers. A few officers were also uneasy about sacraments: Col. J. J. Keppel, who resigned in 1898, called the Army's position "shifty and unexplainable." Some of Ballington's prestigious clerical friends were still detectably condescending toward the Army on these points.[8]

There were other, more profound problems. If the ancient Greeks were right, tragedies are not accidental but inevitable: there are situations in life that, given the conditions, cannot but turn out badly, regardless of the character and motives of the principals. The Salvation Army crisis of 1896 is a tragedy in the classical sense. A family quarrel, patriotism, and the high-minded stubbornness that is characteristic of power struggles within religious institutions were joined in an unhappy mixture. The results were predictably disastrous.

General Booth promoted his remarkable children to positions of authority within the Army and decorated them with special princely ranks — Ballington, for instance, was the "marshal" — but his motive for doing so was not merely dynastic. The General was a visionary, convinced that God had given him a large part to play in the redemption of the world. With the zealot's sense of urgency, he had little time when selecting officers for high command to gratify the ambitions of the headquarters staff or to concern himself with their merely human feelings. He turned naturally to his children: they were an exceptional brood, energetic and clever. They knew his mind. They had been raised in the hothouse spiritual environment of Catherine's household and had absorbed the Army from infancy. They were loyal to him as General and father, in that order, and he counted on them without further thought. Booth relied especially on his oldest son Bramwell, whom he elevated to the rank of chief of the staff, a position in the Army second only to his own. The thought that his other children, no less zealous and more full of ideas than Bramwell, might resent their brother's eminence over them, which was military and increasingly absolute, does not seem to have occurred to the General.[9]

The seeds of discord thus sown among these high-strung siblings were nurtured every year, as Bramwell's ascendancy over the others became complete. The General spent more and more time traveling over the world, surveying his vast spiritual domain, and inspiring the troops with his presence; during his long absences from London, he left the detailed administration of the Army in Bramwell's loyal and capable hands. This was especially true after 1890, the year that Catherine Booth died of cancer, for which the medicine of the day could offer neither cure nor relief, while William watched in helpless desperation. He was overwhelmed with grief at her death. He never fully recovered from the loss of the one who was the daystar of his life, but he dealt with it to some extent by plunging into an ever more hectic and unrelenting round of tours and meetings, while the Chief's domination of the organizational structure of The Salvation Army became perfect.

These developments pressed on no one with more galling constancy than Ballington Booth. As the triumphant years in America lengthened, the Marshal became suspicious, then convinced, that his elder brother was not prepared to give him the proper credit — or, as it turned out, *any* credit — for the wonderful progress of the Army in the United States.

Little of an encouraging nature came from the General; the London headquarters as a whole seemed to display an alarming lack of knowledge of the United States and the triumphs of the Army here. By 1894, Ballington had come to regard the increasing isolation of New York from London as the one cloud on his otherwise golden horizon. He arranged a gala visit to the United States for his father in hopes that it would serve a double purpose: the General would see how splendidly the war was going in America, and the two men could reestablish a properly warm relationship beyond the interference of Bramwell, whom Ballington regarded in an uncharitable light.[10]

These hopes proved vain: General Booth's Jubilee Tour, which took place from September 1894 to February 1895, was a disaster for Ballington and his wife. In public, all went well: the General was lionized, and his trip across the country was triumphal, accompanied by the usual thunders of tambourines, volleys, and hallelujahs. Booth was a captivating speaker, but he never played up to a crowd: he was always the General addressing his troops, no matter who the audience was. For his final series of meetings in Carnegie Hall, he had a sign of his own design hung from the pulpit warning people not to leave while he was speaking. The crowd loved him the more for it, half-convinced that his military gruffness was part of the act. Privately, in small groups of officers, things were far different. The General was morose and difficult to please, a tiresome and demanding guest and a fussy eater who suffered from chronic indigestion. More important to some was the fact that despite the importance of American religious influences on his spiritual development, the General seemed to have developed an aversion to the "Americanization" of the Army in the United States in general and to Ballington in particular that the latter was unable to charm away. The General was not reconciled to that legacy of the Moore secession, the eagle-topped version of the Army crest, used only in the United States. He also disliked the use of the American flag beside the Army colors in street parades — a tactic Ballington himself had introduced shortly after his arrival in 1887, in order to offset the charges being hurled by the still-active Moore army that the loyalists were the tools of British tyranny. The General viewed The Salvation Army as a worldwide, organic unity, above mere national boundaries; he wrote to his daughter Emma that he was "disgusted" by "all the 'Yankee Doodleism'" he found in the American branch of the Army.[11]

It is suggestive of how wide the chasm between London and New York had grown that the General was unaware, or unconcerned about, the feeling among some American officers — and many persons outside the Army as well — that the Army leadership in the United States had been dominated by "foreign" officers from the beginning and remained so in the mid-1890s. The extent of this resentment cannot be known, but the Army leadership in New York took it seriously enough to attempt to defuse it with official pronouncements. In 1889 Maud Booth declared that the Army "is and desires to be distinctively American" and that "two-thirds of its officers are American born." Three years later, the editor of *The War Cry* felt called upon to answer the "foolish question" of whether or not American-born officers were "ever promoted to the ranks of staff officers" by listing ten prominent examples (including Brengle, Brewer, Fielding, Milsaps, and Parker). Although the article did not touch on the unhelpful fact that only three of the Army's eighteen administrative divisions were led by native officers in 1892, the author was able to say that of the non-American leading officers, most were Canadian or naturalized and loyal in spirit. Another article, in the *Conqueror* in 1893, a column that was a regular feature intended to answer "correspondents' questions," stated that of the one thousand officers in the United States, "only about 200 have come from other countries, and of these there are probably not fifty who have not taken out citizen's papers." The hostility, such as there was, was apparently centered on British officers; Salvationist leaders born in Scandinavia or Germany attracted little criticism on that basis alone. There is no evidence that the majority of Salvationists objected to British leaders in the early days or that press comment tended to be unfavorable to the Army solely because of the nationality of some of its officers. At most, newspapers occasionally commented on the fact that while many Army leaders were English, almost all the converts were native born. On the other hand, the chorus of a song that the Salvationists themselves used in the 1890s proclaimed, "The Salvation Army is a wonderful thing. It's English, you know — it's foreign, you know."[12]

Ballington, Maud, and the General had several private conferences while the latter was in the United States, but the exchanges did not bear out the younger man's high hopes for them. Nothing was settled. The General was convinced that Ballington had lost the vision of the worldwide Army and had become too entrenched in the affection of the American people. He regarded it as somehow sinister that his son had become an American citizen, even though the General must have known that Ballington could not hold title to Army property otherwise. The Ballington Booths, for their part, were proud of their American citizenship and made frequent public references to it. The General professed to believe that the success of his son and daughter-in-law in securing the support of the Auxiliaries was a base denial of all the Army stood for — a kind of playing-up to the rich — although the world leader himself regularly addressed audiences of business leaders in America in order to attract their financial support. And when he learned how thoroughly Ballington resented his brother, the chief of the staff, the General was horrified, denouncing it as practically treason to the flag. He spoke of dividing the American territory into three parts, each joined to a part of Canada, or of mortgaging all Army property in America to finance missions elsewhere. This was not a proposal likely to soothe the inflamed sensibilities of the Ballington Booths, fresh from the plaudits of the crowds, which they believed had been as much for them as for the General. Still, all might not have been lost: Ballington was no fool, and he was blessed in ordinary circumstances with a sensitive and compassionate heart. He might have reflected that his father was very tired, a chronically uncomfortable, grief-stricken old man whose blazing passion for the lost souls of the world — a passion that had consumed his entire energy for fifty years — excused a large amount of snappish behavior on the sidelines. The General had always been irascible in private, and he counted on his loyal, loving children to forgive him, as no one knew better than Ballington. Better counsel, however, did not prevail on either side, nor was the Spirit allowed to heal the wounded hearts. The General departed in February 1895 unreconciled to the Ballington Booths.[13]

The order relieving them of the American command reached Ballington and Maud on January 6, 1896. It could not have come as a complete surprise: they had six months, unrelieved by a single word from the General, in which to contemplate the expected blow. Nor were they alone in receiving "farewell" orders: twenty territorial commanders, including all the Booth children (except Bramwell) were being transferred in a general shuffle. Nevertheless, the commanders prepared to resist, first writing to Bramwell (over whose name, unfortunately, the transfer orders had gone out) asking for a reconsideration, then writing again stating that they planned to "quietly retire" rather than accept a transfer out of the United States. Whether this was a bluff and whether Bramwell used all the patience and tact that common sense suggested to reconcile the Ballington Booths are issues that continue to invite speculation. Three important peace emissaries were sent to New York on behalf of the General: two of them were his children Commandant Herbert Booth and Field

Comm. Eva Booth, and the third was Col. Alexander Nicol. Apparently the presence of his brother and sister chilled all thought of reconciliation in Ballington: he had asked especially when he resigned that no member of the family be sent to speak to him. Meetings were held between these three and the Ballington Booths. What passed between the principals cannot be reconstructed with any certainty.[14]

Many leading American officers were saddened and alarmed by these developments, fearing that the public would turn against the Army if it could be made to appear that Ballington's transfer reflected an anti-American attitude on the part of London headquarters. By unhappy coincidence, a controversy then raging between Britain and the United States over a border dispute between British Guiana and Venezuela, whose side America championed even at the risk of war, lent credence to these fears. *The Nation* noticed that the rupture between the Booths had "precipitated the element of nationality into the question of salvation," and *The Homiletic Review,* which had published a number of articles favorable to the Army in the past, now criticized the Army's "absolute despotism" as "contrary to the genius and spirit of the American people and of American institutions." Loyal Auxiliaries sponsored public rallies in an effort to retain the charming Booths. The press gave considerable coverage to these events, which included several suitably dramatic moments: Eva trying to persuade a crowd of confused staff officers to remain loyal to her father and silencing an unruly crowd at the Cooper Union by waving an American flag.[15]

Following these colorful incidents, the debate declined in quality. After the first three weeks of the crisis, both sides abandoned all serious efforts to convince the other, and each turned its energies toward drawing public opinion to its side. This period of mutual vituperation, which lasted several months, accomplished nothing except to confuse and sadden the ranks of humble Salvationists who were eager to look upon their commander, the Chief, and the General as models of piety and zeal. The affair dragged to its inevitable conclusion. Despite the pleas of such officers as Gifford, Brengle, and even the Turk, Ballington resigned in the end, regretfully and with many backward glances, and in March 1896 he formed a new organization called the Volunteers of America. It was much like the Army in military style but featured a more democratic form of government. It also provided for sacramental observances and the ordination of its officers. The Volunteers offered a range of social relief programs something like the Army's but with a special emphasis on the kind of prison ministry that Maud had so lovingly nurtured while she was still in the Army.[16]

Thus ended a tragic episode that cost The Salvation Army in America its two most popular officers and proved nothing. No real principle was resolved. Attempts to make the General appear as a tyrant, willing to sacrifice even his own son in order to maintain his authority, fell down in the face of Ballington's own well-known autocracy, which many subordinate officers had felt. The issue of British control added to the acrimony of the discussion, but it clouded the real issues at hand. Ballington and his wife had often maintained before 1896 that The Salvation Army in The United States was an American operation and that London allowed the American commander great latitude in making decisions. That the General should eventually wish to transfer his son to another post raised no basic question of principle: the General said repeatedly that the whole system of military control, which he believed to be a major factor in the Army's success, would be compromised if it appeared that he did not impose it evenly on all his important subordinates. Maj. T. C. Marshall, the editor of *The Conqueror*, who was still loyal to William Booth, declared that the General's decision to transfer Ballington was "one of the grandest examples of sacrifice for principle" in the history of the world. Ballington's tenure in America was already exceptionally long by 1896; it was inevitable that he would be transferred. The truth is that Ballington had no wish to go, no wish to leave a place where he and his wife had been happy and successful, especially in response to what they unfairly regarded as the whim of the ungrateful old General, who in any case was being manipulated by Bramwell. Ballington had no important disagreement with the Army; he had nothing to say against its military system until he was transferred. His love for The Salvation Army was, and remained, genuine; there is evidence in the recollection of elderly retired officers that Ballington occasionally regretted his decision to resign. It is certain that during the crisis of 1896 he consistently urged officers to stand by the General and the flag. The only officer with major administrative responsibilities who followed Ballington out of the ranks at once was Brig. Edward Fielding, the chief divisional officer in Chicago, who resigned in April along with some of the staff. "Trumpeter" Trumble resigned from the National Staff Band to follow Ballington, along with so many other musicians that the loyal remnant could not cover the parts, putting the Staff Band temporarily out of business. Of the few who trickled out in later years, the most noteworthy was Col. J. J. Keppel, chief divisional officer in Minneapolis, who joined the Volunteers in 1898. Despite the official hostility with which he was regarded by the Army after his resignation, Ballington tried to maintain courteous, if formal, relations with his old comrades. Col. Richard Holz, for one, never ceased to recall Ballington with gratitude and fondness.[17]

When Ballington first arrived in 1887 to replace the ailing Frank Smith, *The War Cry* declared that "the old chariot, after but a moment's pause for change of drivers, has resumed its rapid journey and is hurriedly rattling along." Now, in 1896, the old chariot suffered more than a "momentary pause": for a few weeks, work was almost halted. Most officers and soldiers were confused; many didn't know whom to follow, especially in Chicago. Army leaders averted disaster by following the inspired course of ignoring the schism and pursuing with redoubled zeal their old objective of winning the salvation war. Eva Booth, left in command during the few days before the new commanders could be sent, confined herself to purely religious themes when she addressed Army meetings open to the public, making only an occasional oblique allusion to "this time of sorrows." In places where corps officers resigned, officers from large, loyal corps or from staff positions were rushed to the scene to carry on the work until more permanent replacements could be secured. These officers, too, spoke only of Christ and His redemption, refusing to gratify local reporters with more than general statements about Army discipline and loyalty. William Brewer, the corps officer in Morristown, New Jersey, and Samuel L. Brengle, an officer on the newly reformed divisional staff in Chicago, were typical of many loyal officers during the first tense weeks after Ballington's new movement had been launched. Captain Brewer forcibly reminded local supporters of the Army and his own soldiers that discussion of the Ballington affair only detracted from the Army's true and only purpose, which was saving souls. Brewer's stand was effective: Morristown was the only corps in the division that did not lose a single soldier in the crisis. For his part, Brengle used his energies almost entirely in speaking and writing on spiritual themes and counseling with wavering officers. His theme, like Brewer's, was constant throughout the crisis: concentrate on the work God has given the Army — the salvation of the lost. Without ever referring specifically to Ballington, Brengle raised in a hundred ways the question of how it could matter to the rank and file who the national commander was or why he had refused his orders when souls were dying all around for want of someone to speak to them. His messages and *War Cry* articles on the theme of single-minded dedication to evangelism were influential in holding many waverers in the ranks. These materials later joined the little shelf of Brengle's red-bound books in a volume entitled *The Soul-Winner's Secret.*

The soul-winner, then, must once and for all abandon himself to the Lord and to the Lord's work, and having put his hand to the plough must not look back, if he would succeed in his mighty business; and if he continues faithful in this way, "he shall conquer though he die."

He must love his Lord and love his work, and stick to it through all difficulties, perplexities, and discouragements, and not be given to change, for there is no discharge in this war.[18]

The new national commanders were on the scene by April 1: Frederick St. George de Lautour Booth-Tucker and his wife Emma — the "Consul" — second daughter of the General. The imperious old Founder was unwilling to see his daughters merely absorbed in marriage: he insisted on the hyphenated name for the three who married and gave these women rank and authority independent of, and only grudgingly subordinate to, that of their husbands. For his part, Frederick Booth-Tucker gave the lie to the notion that the Army recruited its officers exclusively from dives and gutters; he was the son of an important British colonial official in India. An officer of education, ability, and experience, having spent nine dramatic years as the Army pioneer in India, he came to the American command from London, where in 1893 he had been made the first editor for *The Officer,* a new international magazine for Army officers one of the stated objectives of which had been "to place within the reach of every officer the best and newest plans for saving the world." Since 1894 he had served as the Foreign Secretary, supervising the details of administering the Army's now imperial domain. The new commander was clearly zealous, and he tried to be flamboyant. Given to thinking in intense spurts, he had a particular penchant, almost a mania, for catchy phrases. Essentially a practical man, he had an odd, other-worldly air about him (he was something of a health faddist), and, lacking Ballington's warmth, he never achieved the popularity of his predecessor with the public or rank-and-file Salvationists. Yet he was kindhearted, showed a special interest in the young cadets, and came to be much admired by the officers on his staff. Booth-Tucker was greatly assisted in regaining the support of American officers by the new chief secretary, Col. Edward Higgins, an industrious and generous-spirited officer. The Consul, Emma, was a warm, approachable woman who had taken her role as "mother" of the London training garrison as a kind of divine commission and continued to regard her new role as national commander in the same maternal way. Far plainer than Maud in appearance and

Frederick St. George de Lautour Booth-Tucker, national commander from 1896 to 1904 Source: The Salvation Army National Archives

manner, the Consul included among her resources a quiet earnestness and an adaptable intellect.[19]

The Booth-Tuckers arrived at a critical time in Army history. The defection of Ballington and Maud did not itself endanger the ultimate success of the Army's work, which depended on the hard work and sacrifice of the officers and soldiers; yet the mistaken ideas that gained circulation at the departure of the Booths and resentment against "British autocracy" caused some resignations among the soldiers and field officers so essential to the success of the Army's work, and financial contributions from the general public dwindled during the confusion. First impressions of the new commanders were thus important. Some waverers stood by them when it was learned that their infant son, whom they had been forced to leave in the care of a servant in London to recover from a fever, had died while they were crossing the Atlantic. The Booth-Tuckers regarded the matter as personal and unintentionally gained sympathy by their refusal to refer to the loss in public. Then, to the relief of American staff officers, both the Booth-Tuckers proved to be competent public speakers. Their first large meeting in Carnegie Hall was a success. The new commanders professed themselves eager to become American citizens to thunders of applause. They made various other welcome announcements: that they wished to hold out the hand of reconciliation to Ballington and his followers and that the General himself would shortly visit the United States for the same purpose. Personal correspondence indicates that the General continued to hope for a reconciliation through the summer of 1896. There were further encouraging signs from the new commanders: Booth-Tucker's practical-mindedness appealed to hardheaded politicians and businesspeople much as Ballington's charm had appealed to socialites. The Army's cause gained prestige when Emma and Booth-Tucker secured the support first of Cleveland millionaire Myron T. Herrick and then of Sen. Mark Hanna of Ohio, through whom they gained access to the newly elected President McKinley, a genial, thoroughgoing Christian who sincerely endorsed the Army.[20]

The Booth-Tuckers were never entirely successful in reconciling the dissidents, nor even of winning the affection of all the loyalists. The Consul's maternal instincts, so appealing to the girls at the London training garrison, impressed some Americans as tiresome condescension. The Booth-Tuckers' eccentricities eventually lost the engaging quality that novelty had bestowed upon them. Resentments against British paternalism, even of the General's nepotism, were voiced in the field and are

preserved in letters and diaries of officers who were among the hardest
working and most willing to sacrifice themselves to the rigors of the war.
But on the whole, the Army rallied, with some grumbling, around the
new commanders. They embarked at once on national tours, with important results, especially in Chicago — a hotbed of secessionist sentiment —
and San Francisco. There were few resignations after 1898. The Army
continued to ignore the Volunteers. *The Conqueror* magazine was discontinued in 1898 and replaced by a less expensive small magazine called
Harbor Lights, which was aimed at a broader audience; this, too, expired
in 1900. The Great Salvation War was pushed into new areas. Social
programs were launched, and some old difficulties were at last eliminated.[21]

There was no more talk about mortgaging the Army's property in
America to finance international projects or of dividing the American
command jointly with segments of Canada. Moreover, the Army's world
headquarters finally agreed to make the ultimate concession to strengthen
the position of the new commanders and allow the Army to incorporate
itself in the United States. The Chief of the Staff must have shuddered
when he reflected on the ease with which his brother, now officially listed
as "deserted," might have bankrupted The Salvation Army when he left
it in 1896. As an American citizen and the sole trustee of a foreign
corporation, Ballington was the outright legal owner of every atom of
Army property in the United States, and he could have decamped with
everything as Moore had done in 1884. Booth-Tucker was instructed to
proceed rapidly in the matter. He found the situation "very propitious":
The Salvation Army was famous and could request a special act of incorporation of the New York legislature with some prospect of success. (A
corporate charter granted by one state is valid in all states, and the location
of national headquarters in Manhattan made it necessary to secure incorporation in the state of New York.) Booth-Tucker privately regarded the
legislators with whom he had to deal as a collection of low politicians;
still, he had not been sent to America to remake the political system, and
he admitted privately that "even the worst of the boodlers respect The
Salvation Army."

The Army secured the services of a prestigious and influential law
firm headed by Benjamin F. Tracy, a distinguished former secretary of the
Navy. The governor, Theodore Roosevelt, was known to smile upon the
Army's militant and aggressive variety of evangelism. On April 28, 1899,
The Salvation Army was incorporated in the state of New York under

Chapter 468 of the laws of that year. The Salvation Army (the capitalized article became part of the official title) was defined as a "religious and charitable corporation" governed by a Board of Trustees competent to hold and control all the temporalities and property, real and personal, belonging to that corporation, the purposes of which were stated with crusading frankness: "For the spiritual, moral and physical reformation of the working classes; for the reclamation of the vicious, criminal, dissolute and degraded; for visitation among the poor and low and the sick; for the preaching of the Gospel and the dissemination of Christian truth by means of open-air and indoor meetings."[22]

The Army remained a "protest against the conventional methods of the churches," and the salvation war continued to rage unabated. It was not curtailed any more than briefly by the desertion of Ballington, nor was it stimulated by incorporation, about which most soldiers knew little more than what the brief, glowing accounts in *The War Cry* elaborated and in any event cared nothing. The hallelujah jesters still cavorted in the streets, making captives for Jesus. Brigadier Brengle was released from staff duties and allowed to spend the rest of his career as an official Army evangelist and writer of articles on the doctrine of holiness. Major Ludgate produced a new version of his classic instruction for conducting open-air meetings single-handedly. It was really quite simple: one climbed on a chair, beat a drum, and sang songs from *The War Cry,* prepared to exhort the crowd that would certainly form. The long transition from horsecar to trolley, from gaslight to electricity, offered no new obstacles to parades and street meetings. The Army eagerly adapted every new fad to the great work. After the stereopticon and the phonograph came the bicycle, which became so popular for mobilizing the forces that the formal uniform began to fall into "declension": the commanders had to issue a stern warning to the peddlers that bicycle hats could be worn *only* "when actually bicycling." *The War Cry* still edified its readers with such testimonies as "The Confessions of a Crib-Cracker . . . How I Burgled Alderman Beasley's Plate." Indoor meetings were as fervent as ever: "From the start," read one gloating report, "stiffness departed and formality was laid on the high shelf." The Army was given extensive, respectful treatment in the late 1890s in the important textbooks and journals of social reform. In 1898 it was featured in a major Broadway play, "The Belle of New York," which moved to London the following summer for a long, successful run. Crusades, revivals, and "sieges" followed one upon another, from the commander's "Century Advance" plan of 1899 to the "Red Crusade," which the Consul launched in 1903, dressed in a flaming red costume and preaching before an open coffin — a technique that she was certain "would be calculated to awaken the careless and make them think of eternity." The General made a third visit to the United States in 1898. The tour was a coast-to-coast success in every respect save one: the old man met Ballington in Montclair, New Jersey, to effect a reconciliation. His account of the sad, futile encounter was brief: "We met and prayed and parted" — forever.[23]

The Booth-Tuckers were essentially practical people with an eye for easy solutions. The Consul was a skillful publicist, decisive and clever, her one ambition being to advance the Army. She wrote, directed, and delivered in over fifty cities an elaborate illustrated lecture called "Love and Sorrow," described as a "skillful combination of the stereopticon, the living tableau, music and song," which lasted for almost three hours. She had no interest in the feminist cause of her day, and, according to a household servant, she read nothing, not even a newspaper, but she kept a complete list of the children of all the officers on the American field, with the name, age, and clothing sizes of each, so she could send every child a Christmas present. At the time of her untimely death in 1903, the list had eight hundred names. For his part, Booth-Tucker was able, despite his authentic eccentricity, to convey an impression of commonsense ingenuity that people of influence found reassuring. The commander established rewarding contacts with business and political leaders. At the same time, the work of scores of slum sisters and rescue officers was bearing fruit at last: the social wing of the Army was producing a return in souls harvested, in operating revenue, and in public prestige. Booth-Tucker effectively sprinkled the social programs with helpful suggestions and directives. In the end, the flow of official minutes on all subjects from headquarters was only briefly interrupted by the schism of 1896.[24]

On top of many innovations, Booth-Tucker made substantial improvements in the officer-training program. In 1896 the number of divisional "training garrisons" was reduced and the field-training component strengthened in those that survived — which was not for long: in 1899 the remaining divisional "training garrisons" were closed, and two "central training homes" were established in New York and Chicago. (Actually there were two schools, one for each gender, in both places — and two divisional garrisons, in San Francisco and Portland, Oregon, were allowed to linger a little longer as junior branches of the central schools.) The new central training homes were placed under the control of national headquarters and given a standard program. The curriculum remained "sternly practical." It was divided into two parts: a "secular" portion, which offered training in reading and writing, arithmetic, and single-entry bookkeeping, and a "spiritual" portion, which consisted of Bible lessons and instruction in the doctrines and disciplines of The Salvation Army. In addition, the cadets received the "rudiments of musical notation" and were favored by occasional lectures by the commanders and other national staff officers.[25]

Booth-Tucker presided over a major expansion of Salvation Army social service activities, including salvage operations. Cheap, safe, and convenient hotels were opened for the needy working woman — "only women of thoroughly respectable character are received." Some of the rescue homes were gradually transformed into regulation maternity hospitals, while those that retained the old status were given a comfortable, homey look and made less institutional for the residents. The "Penny Ice Philanthropy" reached its peak in 1901, when five tons of the "precious crystal" were given away daily in New York City and Chicago through the summer; benefaction on that scale proved too costly, even with the assistance of the Knickerbocker Ice Company, however, and ice donations on these levels were never repeated in Chicago. The Army's "Cheap Coal for the Multitudes," given away or sold for a pittance in bushel baskets, was a boon for the poor, but as with the ice ministry the enormous amounts of material that were needed put a strain on the Army's resources. During the peak year of the coal ministry, the winter of 1903, the Army gave out a thousand tons of coal in each of three frozen cities: New York, Chicago, and Boston. The prison ministry grew and prospered. An outpost opened in San Quentin prison in 1894 by Oakland Salvationists at the request of a few prisoners who had read *The War Cry* became a full-fledged Salvation Army corps with thirty soldiers by 1897. At various times Booth-Tucker, Emma, and Brengle all visited the corps; Booth-Tucker was so touched by a bouquet of flowers given to him by the convicts that he dried the flowers and kept them. The Consul was strongly drawn to prison work as well and became famous for her interest in it. She was riding one day in a streetcar when the car was boarded by a policeman handcuffed to a prisoner. In a flash Emma was at the captive's side, only to learn to her delight that he had recognized her and had hoped that she would speak to him. In 1897 Adjutant McFee and Brigadier Keppel opened a small but innovative hostel for discharged prisoners in San Ramon, California.[26]

The Army enjoyed other major advances as the nineteenth century gave way to the twentieth. After twenty years, the Army had acquired a second generation. Just as veterans' sleeve stripes (one for each five years in the fight) became necessary with the passing years, so too did organized activities for young people. At first children were simply ignored, partly on the strength of the still-current Victorian theory that children were tiny adults (and thus free to enjoy the privilege of sitting through adult programs) and partly because the ferocious evangelism of the pioneers left little time and energy to devise extra activities to interest children. The pioneers sometimes turned in reports from the "Little Forts," testimonies of the "real saved little Soldiers," but the emphasis in these reports was on how similar to adults the children were in their courage and zeal. Even this amount of interest apparently fluctuated: in 1887 *The War Cry* lamented that interest in the children of the corps had waned. Occasionally, particularly eager young people would ask for religious services that they could understand and enjoy, but they were kindly but firmly rebuffed. Yet young people were drawn to the Army by its life and color. When these young converts were joined by the increasing numbers of soldiers' children who began to attend the corps, the lack of programs for young people became too obvious to overlook.[27]

In 1891 headquarters ordered that each corps conduct two meetings for young people per week, on Sunday afternoons and Wednesday evenings. These were called "company meetings" and were instructional in nature, to prepare the children in doctrine, singing, and the Army's methods of warfare. After a period of preparation, the young people signed an affirmation of the Army's eleven doctrines and joined the ranks as "junior soldiers." In 1894 the "Band of Love" was added to provide for children drawn to the Army from non-Salvationist families. The Band was designed to be a magnet for erring youth: it offered useful instruction in things that appealed to the children of the nineties, such as "overhead scarf waving drills" (a kind of practiced routine in which a group synchronized its movements in time to music) and the proper technique for rolling double hoops down the street, while it exacted from the little trainees a pledge of good living, which included a promise to be kind to animals. Some of the children became quite zealous, tottering down the street laden with buckets of water for overheated draught horses and endangering life and limb to climb trees in order to rescue stranded kittens, orphaned baby birds, and the occasional escaped canary.

These programs were a good beginning, but in many places youth work languished for lack of the interested and qualified adult leadership upon which headquarters vainly insisted. In 1898 headquarters announced that "the irregularity of the past must be improved upon" and ordered each division to appoint a "Junior Soldier Staff Secretary" to oversee the work of the "junior corps" in that division. In addition, there was to be a special noncommissioned officer in each corps, called the "Young People's Sergeant-Major" (YPSM), to take charge of the youthful recruits. The pattern of two youth meetings per week became the minimum standard. Those among the young soldiers who felt inspired to offer themselves as officers in the Army were expected to enroll for further instruction as "Corps Cadets." The local sergeants placed in charge of these programs often lacked experience — when Mrs. Helen Hoffman asked for help in preparing herself to serve as a YPSM in the late 1890s, she was told that "God will help: Pray to Him!" — but zeal and consistency seem in the end to have overcome other difficulties. By the turn of the century, Army youth work was well established: *The War Cry* reported 396 regularly organized junior corps in June 1899.[28]

The Army extended its operations to include children other than those who came to its meetings. The need for child care in that era was very great. An Army writer observed as the old century ended that it was no longer possible to think that "old age in poverty and neglect was the awfullest reproach that existence offers"; on the contrary, the "most tragic pathos" was "at the portal, not at the exit." The young children of the working poor had to be left to their own devices, toddling among the horses' legs and playing alone on sidewalks that were far more crowded and noisy than streets in the same neighborhoods today, and at least as dirty. The Army opened what its leaders believed was "the first day nursery in the down-town slums of New York" in 1894. It was filled to capacity at once and remained so. The first home for orphans — "these little atoms of human wreckage" — was opened on Washington's Birthday, 1897, in Fordham, a suburb of New York City, but was soon moved to Rutherford, New Jersey. The opening date suggested the name, the Cherry Tree Home for Waifs and Strays, an inspiration conveyed to the Consul by the young wife of President Cleveland. The home was small — thirty small, single bedrooms — but at that it was a burden on badly strained Army finances because it produced no income. From all accounts it was a cheery place, despite the haphazard manner in which it, like the rescue homes, was financed — mostly by donations in kind. In the case of Cherry Tree, the staff depended on local women to invite the children to home-cooked suppers and on the profits from the desultory sale of the Army's own brand of tea. Cherry Tree was eventually eclipsed by the Army's other orphanage, at Lytton Springs, California. The western home became a regular community, with its own classroom (decorated with encouraging mottos like "Try Again!"), dairy, chicken farm, and brass band. Nor are the annals of the children's work without their true heroism. In October 1900 there was a fire in the Salvation Army Children's Shelter in Cincinnati. The two officer-matrons, Staff Capt. Selma Erickson and Capt. Bertha Anderson, gave up their lives in a vain attempt to rescue their five little charges. All seven were buried together in a common grave, over which the city government maintained an Army flag for decades.[29]

Not everything in the Army showed change or improvement during those years. There were still a few arrests, from which not even the commander was exempt. In fact, Booth-Tucker was arrested twice, a distinction no other national commander has earned since, even once. In 1896 he was arrested for skulking about New York at night disguised in his "slum toggery"; although this was practically the traditional Army way to learn more about slum conditions — and in fact, was a common practice among journalists, reformers, and even tourists — it was technically against the law. In 1897 he was hauled into court for disturbing the peace — and convicted: a hallelujah "All-Night for Jesus" at national headquarters had been heard "all over the Ninth Ward," banishing sleep and the devil together. There were other problems. A chronic shortage of officers was the major obstacle to effective expansion in the late 1890s. The Corps Cadet Brigade, which numbered five hundred by 1900, was designed to prepare youth to fill this need in the future. Attrition among officers varied, and at times was high. Some of those who remained were not consumed with zeal: some officers groused about filling in statistical forms for headquarters, and others relished the rumors about impending transfers and promotions that filled the air every few months.[30]

Finance remained a serious problem. In 1899 the Army's main sources of income were still collections taken at every meeting, the "donations of friends," and profits from the sale of *The War Cry,* books, and uniforms. Collections were often dismal, even at large meetings: a collection among three hundred Salvationists at San Francisco No. 1 in November 1897 yielded an even five dollars. Officers being transferred from one station to another were sometimes forced to take up a collection at their "Farewell Meeting" in order to raise funds for the journey. Various innovations were introduced to supplement these meager resources. Ballington and Maud Booth's auxiliaries had been one such attempt, and the auxiliaries were maintained by subsequent national commanders, although the membership fee was reduced to five dollars per year in order to maintain the number of members at a high level. (Many auxiliaries had supported Ballington during the secession.) Booth-Tucker tried "Mercy Boxes," which sympathizers could take into their homes, to collect a weekly donation of a penny. The "Merchant's League Box" was designed to stand invitingly on a store counter. The rich were approached directly with requests for outright gifts, loans, or bequests. Local corps often took up these ideas for their own use: the enterprising Adjutant Maltby in Meadville, Pennsylvania, launched his own "Helpers' League" in 1900.[31]

The national staff was determined to secure a balance of income against expenses while maintaining the expansion of the salvation war at its current gratifying rate. There were two ways the budget could be balanced: by raising income in every category or by requiring that social programs such as the corps work become self-supporting. Eventually both of these strategies were implemented, but one immediate result of the campaign to balance Army accounts was the farm colony scheme, which had various other things to commend it as well. The purpose of the farm colony was to provide a refuge in the country for the worthy poor of the cities, a place to which entire families could repair together, the father learning an honest, useful, and healthful trade as a farm worker while the mother and the children fed chickens, chopped kindling, and basked in the pleasures of country life. The farm colony was, it will be remembered, a central part of General Booth's "Darkest England" scheme, which advocated the training of individuals and families for life in an "overseas colony." The farm colonies, in a modified form, became Booth-Tucker's pet project.[32]

As we have noted, The Salvation Army officially broke ranks with many other late nineteenth-century charity reformers by refusing to make a distinction between the "worthy" and the "unworthy" poor. By general definition, the worthy poor consisted of decent folk who were willing but unable to find honest employment and the truly helpless, including the aged, invalids, and children; the "unworthy poor" were the vicious and lazy, the prodigals, idlers, and tramps who sought to maintain themselves by crime, begging, or as unproductive recipients of charity. The Army never refused help to anyone or promoted the assertion that anyone who wanted work could find it. On the other hand, the Army did offer work to all who came for relief; if there was no other work, the Army would create jobs in its own shops and woodyards in order to spare those too poor to pay even the few cents that the Army asked for its ministrations the humiliation of "pauperization." When the editor of *The War Cry* went

in disguise to the Army's new "Lighthouse" in New York, he pretended
not to have the seven-cent price for food and lodging. He was lectured on
the "evils of indiscriminate charity" and told that he could have a meal
and stay overnight only if he agreed to saw wood in the morning. In effect,
the farm colonies were designed to provide more systematic relief for
"worthy" poor men and their families.[33]

The General and many leading officers — the Booth-Tuckers
emphatically among them — believed that city life was inherently unnatural and corrupting. This was a popular notion in the late nineteenth
century. One of the most popular charities in New York City in the last
half of the nineteenth century had been the Children's Aid Society, which
transferred thousands of impoverished children to "Western homes." "No
treatment which man could devise," proclaimed *Harper's Magazine* in
1873, "could possibly be so beneficial to the laboring children of this city
as that offered by Western farms." Many writers and reformers, influenced
mainly by Henry George's famous book *Progress and Poverty*, struggled to
understand the relationship between "progress" (in the form of urban
concentration) and increasing poverty. Part of the appeal of Populism and
William Jennings Bryan twenty years later stemmed from distrust of city
life. That this essentially romantic notion should have lingered so long in
the minds of officers otherwise so practical will not seem so strange when
one reflects on the fact that Salvationists found little to quarrel with in
the political and economic systems of the countries in which they served.
They believed individual salvation was the sovereign cure for all social
evils. These officers did not confront the fact that urban life on a massive
scale was here to stay: they did not presume that *any* merely human system
was here to stay. If it were easier for a man to be saved outside the crowded
city with its evil influences, then he should by all means be removed from
the city; presumably, capturing him for Jesus would hasten the day when
cities and evil influences would cease altogether. The goal was escape and
salvation, not reform. For the purpose of redemption, the country offered
many advantages: families could be rescued together, and the problems of
mass unemployment and urban congestion could be solved at a stroke. In
addition, the colonies would begin to provide a solution to many of the
Army's financial problems practically overnight: the farms would be self-
supporting from the first and would eventually begin to generate surplus
income.[34]

Booth-Tucker was fond of pithy sayings of his own invention; his
favorite motto summarized the colony scheme: "The Landless Man to the

Manless Land." Both he and the Consul became increasingly enamored of the idea, until by 1903 they were devoting most of their time to the farm colony enterprise. The commanders became rustic, knowledgeable about crop yields and irrigation, possessed of reams of production statistics that they unloaded on dazed Army audiences. Booth-Tucker liked to think of himself as "The Man behind the Plow," as a cover on *The War Cry* portrayed him — in full uniform — in 1900. This enthusiasm for redemption through agriculture was so great that the Army toyed briefly with the idea of opening tiny farms on vacant city lots to provide work and food for those among the worthy poor who did not seek a complete escape from city life. This idea was originally put forth by Mayor Hazen S. "Potato Patch" Pingree of Detroit, who turned the patches over to the Army in 1897 when destiny called him to the governor's office. This project, and others to "Pingreeize" Chicago and the Bronx, were on a modest scale compared to the farm colonies proper, which were launched with considerable fanfare at a huge meeting in Carnegie Hall in December 1897.[35]

There were three colonies: Fort Herrick, in Ohio, on land twenty miles from Cleveland that was donated by Myron T. Herrick, the banker-politician for whom it was named; Fort Amity, in eastern Colorado; and Fort Romie, near Monterey Bay in California. Administered by the "National Colonization Department" under Col. Thomas Holland, who also served as manager at Amity, the three farms together housed about five hundred people on three thousand acres at the height of occupancy. Headquarters was convinced that the farms would be a "practical, com-monsense-business-like venture," and early developments encouraged the wildest optimism. The Army received "thousands of applications" at the special farm colony recruitment offices opened in several large cities. No one was turned away because of "religion, caste, or sex or nationality." There were one thousand applicants in New York City alone, almost five thousand from Chicago. Many prominent persons, including the governors of New York, Colorado, and Michigan and the mayors of Boston, Denver, and San Francisco, publicly endorsed the scheme. The Sixth Annual National Irrigation Congress in Lincoln, Nebraska, called it a "grand, noble and patriotic work." At the height of the crusade in 1904, Sen. Mark Hanna of Ohio agreed to Booth-Tucker's request to prepare a bill to launch farm colonies on a federal scale; after Hanna's untimely death, the bill (S.5126) was introduced into the Senate by Sen. George Hoar of Massachusetts. Unfortunately, public enthusiasm failed to take into account the practical problems that beset the colonies from the outset and eventually caused the Army to abandon them.[36]

Amity was located on 1,830 acres in the well-watered Arkansas River valley in eastern Colorado, on the main line of the Santa Fe railroad. Most of the sixty original colonists were from Chicago, unemployed and so poor that the Army had to pay their fare to the site and give them something to eat on the train, but they were brave and willing enough. The Army provided ten acres and supplies, the cost of which the colonists were to repay. A range of crops were planted and harvested, and the population swelled to 450. A town with several stores, a post office, Salvation Army corps, and depot grew up. In 1902 the Cherry Tree home was transferred from New Jersey to a new stone structure at Amity, the finest building in the county. The rigors of the first years passed. Amity became comfortable, almost restful. Major Stillwell, the California pioneer, was sent there with other officers to recover his strength after he had collapsed from overwork. Yet there were snakes in Eden: the orphanage could not operate without medical and school facilities nearby, and there were few employment or adoption prospects for children so isolated. In 1905 the orphans returned to New Jersey, and the Amity building became a tuberculosis sanitarium, which failed almost at once. There were grave financial difficulties: the Army confidently advanced large sums on the hope of a return, and it had to borrow these sums at the then-ruinous rate of 6 percent. Worst of all, the river backed up, and alkali seepage poisoned the soil. The colony went into an irreversible decline and was sold at a loss in 1909.[37]

Booth-Tucker opened Fort Herrick with a brass band and a mass rally in September 1898, but it was a failure from the start. The 288 acres near Cleveland sold to the Army by Herrick at a bargain rate were surrounded by land that was far too valuable for the Army to purchase: expansion of the colony was therefore impossible, and the original farm was too small to support the eight or nine impoverished families who moved there. The Army attempted to raise livestock that required little space — pigeons, bees, chickens, and rabbits. Unhappily, these activities required experienced workers, which the colony lacked; a good part of the breeder stock simply flew away. When Colonel Holz visited the colony in March 1899, he discovered a "good deal of grumbling and dissatisfaction" among the few colonists, occasioned no doubt by the fact that all the houses had been shoddily built on low ground and were standing in three inches of water. He suggested starting all over with new houses, new families, and a new manager. Instead the Army converted the colony into an "Inebriates' Home" under the redoubtable Major McFee; the clients would come from nearby Cleveland. This likewise proved too costly to operate, and Fort Herrick became a "fresh air camp" for slum children in 1909.[38]

The beginnings in California were no less auspicious, and no less certainly doomed, at least as a means of redeeming the poor. Enthusiasm for the project was especially high in the West, and many prominent San Franciscans supported the Army colony. Fort Romie contained 520 acres near Soledad, about 150 miles south of San Francisco. Purchased with the help of the San Francisco Chamber of Commerce in 1898, Romie was actually the first piece of property acquired by the Army for a colony. It was to form "the first link forged in the chain of colonies" that were "to girdle our continent and constitute our Salvation Army Workingman's Paradise." The eighteen indigent families selected from among the Bay Area "worthy poor" departed from Oakland in two wagons decorated with banners: "Ho for the Salvation Army Colony!" Difficulties awaited. The land was rich and loamy, but it required irrigation even in the best of times — which the next three years, alas, were not: a drought brought "utter failure" to the colony. The Army was undaunted. In 1901 a steam pump was installed to carry water from the Salinas River to the colony, which was redivided into 20-acre tracts and offered to local families at one hundred dollars per acre on a twenty-year mortgage, with encouraging terms for stock and supplies. Many families, "practically destitute" but with some farming experience, hurried forth to seize the opportunity. The little farms prospered, but the officers' delight was short-lived: the colonists made so much money on their farms that they all paid off their mortgages by 1905, and the colony ceased to exist. The Army made $12,000 net profit and many grateful friends in Romie, but the site had failed as an experiment in uplifting the urban poor through farming.[39]

The Army's farm colonies failed not out of any lack of zeal for the project, nor because the distinction between "worthy" and "idle" poor was subject to criticism, nor even because the belief in the salutary effects of country living was romantic nonsense; the colonies failed because successful farming required skill and experience that the unemployed urban poor, worthy or not, did not possess. The colonies did nothing to relieve the causes of urban poverty, nor did they assist its worst victims. Critics of the colony scheme argued that none of the Army's colonists had ever really been desperate, their families had not been in danger of breaking apart, and none of them had been the objects of charity when the project began.

In fact, the Army soon began to require settlers on the California project to be able to support themselves until the anticipated crops had been harvested. Major Milsaps complained to his diary about the irony that "the poor cannot go on our farms without money." These criticisms were valid; in fact, five of the twenty-eight colonists at Romie, and a dozen of those at Amity, were former Salvation Army officers who had resigned because of poor health and who had been sent to the farms as a rest cure. Mismanagement by well-intentioned, inexperienced officers also contributed to the ruin of the Fort Romie project. The problems of city poverty had to be solved in the city or not at all. Even if a sufficient number of poor families had entered the system with enough agricultural skill to make a farm colony work, the Army lacked the financial resources to acquire large enough tracts of land to provide for more than a handful of the city poor as yeomen farmers, and the local agricultural markets would in any case have been unable to support them.[40]

Frederick Booth-Tucker's personal interest in farm colonies had mostly evaporated before their failure was finally revealed. The Consul was returning from an inspection trip to Amity when she was the only fatality in a train wreck on October 28, 1903, at Dean Lake, Missouri. The commander was inconsolable, barely able to struggle through the several mass memorial meetings and the three enormous public funerals — one in Chicago, where Booth-Tucker had been waiting for her when he received the news of her death, and two in New York — that Army tradition demanded. The funerals in New York were held in Carnegie Hall and the Army's own national headquarters; the latter was a memorable affair, the hall tightly packed, the close air heavy with solemn band tunes, a beautiful wreath on hand touchingly sent by the "Bowery Boys," the open coffin at the foot of the podium, from which Booth-Tucker, most memorable of all, sang his own truly noble testimony:

> Thou knowest all things, my heart Thou canst read;
> Master, Thou knowest I love Thee indeed.
> Ask what Thou wilt my devotion to test,
> I will surrender the dearest and best.

In keeping with the Army's single-minded devotion to salvation warfare, which could not be tempered by any merely personal sadness, no matter how exalted the victim, the Chicago funeral and the one in the Army hall in New York ended in public invitations to accept salvation or, for those already saved, a fresh spiritual blessing; the two services netted sixty-two new converts and "hundreds for consecration." Salvationist families treasured the little funeral programs, trimmed in mournful purple, for years. And in London the General, his grief-stricken heart plunged lower still by the loss of his beloved daughter, experienced a new — and lasting — wave of affection for the country that was to be her home forever: "Indeed, as the Comrade of the Commander, she won a place for herself and The Army in the confidence and appreciation of all that was noblest and best in that great nation."[41]

Exhausted by grief and by the round of meetings and tours into which he plunged in vain to escape from grief, harried by six young children, distraught and dispirited, Frederick Booth-Tucker continued as national commander only a few months longer. In August 1904 *The War Cry* announced his farewell, and in November he departed, leaving behind an impressive record: between 1896 and 1904, officers and employees had increased from some 2,000 to almost 3,800, the number of social service institutions had increased from 25 with accommodations for 600 persons to 267 with room for 10,000, and annual expenditures for social relief had risen from $20,000 to $900,000. The total value of Salvation Army property had increased substantially, from $473,000 to $1,520,000. Even allowing for debate over the exact significance of these figures, they represented an increase in Salvation Army social welfare activities on an important scale. Booth-Tucker was a difficult act to follow, but circumstances allowed the General to appoint the ideal choice: his fourth daughter, Eva. He could not have known that he was bestowing upon The Salvation Army in the United States its most colorful, exciting, controversial, and certainly its most durable commander. Christened Eveline and called Eva by her father, she was inspired by a dramatic impulse to select a more euphonious name. It was as Evangeline Cory Booth that she reigned — no other word will do — over the American Army for the next thirty years.[42]

That the General had succumbed to an inclination to nepotism could no longer be denied. Some American officers privately registered their dismay at what seemed to be an almost dynastic succession at national headquarters. Miss Booth was English, thirty-nine years of age, and unmarried, known in this country only from her brief and not altogether successful role in the Ballington schism. Yet Eva had enjoyed considerable experience before coming to America to command: harassed and battered in the Army's pioneer combat days in Britain, she had superintended the training garrison in London; then, as the "Field Commissioner," she had overseen all Army work in London for four years; and from 1896 to 1904 she had been national commander in Canada. Her Canadian command had been punctuated by three dramatic trips to the Klondike, where the Canadian branch of the Army had sent an advance guard to rescue some of the thousands of people who were drawn by the gold rush and were otherwise certain to fall into the clutches of the bad element that had flocked to the mining camps to take advantage of them.

Evangeline Booth proved to be a complicated woman. Raised as a kind of junior princess in her father's hectic household court, she was allowed — even encouraged — to abandon herself to her strong, inherited dramatic impulses. The young woman was placed in positions of authority over thousands in which she was responsible to no one save God and her father (who usually left her to the Former). Thus it is natural that at age thirty-nine Evangeline was imperious and willful. She was also somewhat vain, impetuous, given to emotional flourishes, and addicted to dramatic poses. When she came from Canada to Buffalo in October 1903, to join the train bearing Booth-Tucker's party and Emma's body from Chicago to New York, she announced herself exhausted by a long confinement for nerves — unrelated to her sister's sudden death — and had to be given Booth-Tucker's private room on the train. During her entire career, Eva arranged to be surrounded by a staff of officers who were little more than aides and servants. Chief of these was her private secretary, Maj. Richard Griffiths, a discreet bachelor who came with her from Canada and spent his life in her personal service. She was at the same time a compassionate soul, thoughtful, full of little kindnesses, genuinely sympathetic with the poor and lonely in their sufferings, and a dedicated, fearless evangelical. A clever administrator, well informed, decisive, with a good eye for details, she gave her subordinates considerable latitude. Above all else, Evangeline was an exceptionally effective public speaker and could hold large audiences spellbound for hours. As her years in the United States lengthened, her English accent became more diluted; at the height of her powers, her voice sounded rather like those of the upper-crust dowagers portrayed in comic movies in the 1930s, smooth and sweet, yet consciously dignified by studied pronunciation and rolled *r*'s. Nor did her abilities as a publicist end on the platform: she was particularly adept at charming the rich and securing large contributions to the Army. Into the bargain she played the harp well and wrote creditable music. Take her for what she was in fact and in fancy, Eva Booth was a phenomenon of historic proportions.[43]

The commission the General issued to Eveline Cory Booth on November 9, 1904, gave her the rank of commissioner and the title of Commander. Her authority, subject only to his interposition, was absolute — "subject nevertheless at all times to my direction countermand qualification and veto absolute command and control over all Officers and Soldiers in the Salvation Army in the said United States of America." Her first official meeting as commander took place at Carnegie Hall on December 6. The faithful and curious alike jammed the hall and were suitably transfixed by the latest Booth, bracketed by flags, flowers, and a brass band and buoyed up by volleys and hallelujahs. Settled into her office, she immediately set a tone by writing a personal note to every officer of staff rank in the United States. Eva did well to lay a firm foundation for her administration, although her first few months were necessarily tentative, partly because her appointment coincided with a major change in the administrative structure of the Army. Rumors had circulated among staff officers for almost a year that Army administration in the United States was going to be divided into Eastern and Western parts in some way, with Chicago as the second headquarters center. Several explanations were offered for the impending division, which was opposed by some staff officers. The work of overseeing the Army's activities had become too demanding and complicated for a single person to perform efficiently. Eva's predecessors had been married men who shared major responsibilities with their wives, but even a married couple could no longer supervise the entire Salvation Army in the United States from a single center, even if both had been willing and able to spend almost all of their active careers riding in trains. In November 1904 the rumors were confirmed: the United States was divided administratively. A "deputy commissioner" was appointed whose primary responsibility was to serve as territorial commander of the West, with headquarters in Chicago. The new commissioner, George Kilbey, was directly responsible to the Commander, but there was considerable uncertainty among Salvationists as to his authority to make the sorts of important decisions in his new territory that had traditionally had been made by national headquarters.[44]

The public, of course, did not share the Army's concern with these matters. In many ways, in fact, the Army that Eva inherited had ceased to be controversial at all. The press had been mostly friendly since the late 1890s, and Army leaders moved comfortably in the highest circles almost as a matter of course. During a visit to the United States in 1898, General Booth felt no hesitation in writing a personal letter to President McKinley

in order to encourage his efforts to find a peaceful solution to the Cuban
crisis that eventually led to the Spanish-American War. When the General
paid his fourth visit to the United States in 1902-1903 to inspect the
still-promising farm colonies, he opened the U.S. Senate in prayer, lunched
with President Roosevelt, and spent a memorable afternoon at the Arling-
ton Hotel with Senators Hanna and Hoar, the vice president, and the
speaker of the house. Who could doubt, an officer asked the delegates to
the Army's first Western Territorial Congress in 1906, that God had
"blessed and prospered" the Army in its "effort to help the weak. No! It
is no longer an experiment." The Army figured in public entertainments
with increasing frequency: its entertaining evangelistic activities and strategies were sufficiently known to the public that the organization could be
portrayed without additional explanation in the plot as to its purpose. A
popular magazine carried a story in 1903 of a fictional young Salvation
Army musician who saves his town from a flood by beating his bass drum,
and in 1908 Edward Sheldon's play "Salvation Nell" became a major hit
on Broadway, an important step toward greater social realism in drama.
One year later the Army was featured in a commercial motion picture,
"The Salvation Army Girl," made by Biograph Studies and directed by
D. W. Griffith — the first of many portrayals of the Army in commercial
motion pictures. Salvationists made their own contributions to the entertaining effects; in April 1902 the Army published the first full-scale march
written exclusively for its own bands. The public's acceptance is largely
attributable to the open-minded approach toward conversions shown by
the Army's genial street-corner evangelism and by its social program, which
expanded steadily, its way smoothed by a generous public and accommodating civic officials. The Army even worked out an uneasy peace with
grafters and ward heelers: one of Chicago's slum posts was on South Clark
Street, right across the street from Alderman McKenna's "Hinky-Dink
Saloon."[45]

The "workingman's hotels" prospered and spread. When Brig. Edward J. Parker was appointed National Metropole and Relief Secretary in
October 1903, much had been accomplished, but without national over-
sight or long-range planning. A survey of cheap lodging houses in Chicago
in 1900 praised the Army's "Harbor Light" hotel as "the best of these
houses" in the city. Some of this sort of encouraging information was
known at headquarters, but little in the way of details. Parker knew only
that "the Army was forging ahead" with this work, providing decent
lodging at low rates for underpaid urban workers and the temporarily

unemployed. Parker provided effective leadership. Within five years there were over seventy such hotels for men and four for women, with a total capacity of 8,700 beds. The capstone in this arch was the new Boston People's Palace, a five-story grey brick building opened in 1906. The Palace had almost three hundred single rooms, a swimming pool, labor bureau, library, and, on the ground floor, a soon-to-be famous Army corps. Social work spread into the Scandinavian branch of the Army when the Scandinavian Sailors' Home was opened in Brooklyn in 1902; by 1905 it was flourishing, flanked by the Brooklyn No. 6 corps in a converted theater. Labor bureaus were set up in several headquarters as part of the now obligatory "relief departments" that formed a regular activity at every divisional and territorial office. The "rescue homes for fallen women," now supplemented by maternity services, conducted their expanding programs in an atmosphere that, at the Army's insistence, was kept small, comfortable, and "homey." Even the sharpest critics of the Army social program called the rescue homes the most effective of their kind in the country. These good reports encouraged public support for an innovation: in 1914 the Army opened a small general hospital in Covington, Kentucky, a suburb of Cincinnati, in order to offer the local population a service and to train nurses for the thirty-one Army rescue homes. The credit for the success of the rescue work went to the indefatigable matrons; the day-to-day operation of a rescue home was backbreaking and heartbreaking at the same time. Many touching stories were tucked away in the admissions files of these rescue homes. In Chicago in 1910 a young woman who had somehow been duped by a department store employment agency into becoming a prostitute fled from her madam as the two strolled past an Army street service, throwing herself into the ring of Salvationists and begging for their protection. She was taken up lovingly and borne away but died later receiving medical treatment.[46]

Perhaps the most engaging aspect of the Army's expanded relief work in the years before the First World War was its ministry to children. The days were now long past when a young person had to beg to be allowed to become a convert. Officers now threw themselves into the work of reaching and uplifting poor and helpless children. A great day in the lives of many children, and a scene forever fixed in the memories of the few surviving octogenarians who experienced it, was the annual Salvation Army excursion. Across Long Island Sound, Chesapeake Bay, and Lake Michigan, up the Hudson, down the Monongahela, steamed the white sidewheelers, an Army flag at the jackstaff, a band on the hurricane deck, hundreds of cheering "little slummers" leaning over the triple railings, hair tossing, faces damp in the mist of the bow waves. To spend one day in every year in the sun and salt spray, with a box lunch and lemonade thrown in, was no small thing for children who spent months in the noisome dark of back alley flats and dingy schoolrooms. And there were variations on this happy theme: in 1908 Colonel Holz sent out eleven thousand mail appeal letters to finance a grand all-day trip for fifteen hundred poor Cleveland children, who filled seven chartered streetcars for a trip to Euclid Beach, where an amusement park, lunch, movies, ice cream, and a game with the encouraging name of "bun-eating" awaited them. In Chicago, the equally innovative Col. George French, "a boy among the boys," acquired the loan of fourteen automobiles — which in those days were still regarded by most average people as expensive, exciting novelties — filled thirteen of them with 225 poor slum children and one with the new Chicago Staff Band, and proceeded, with much backfiring, flag waving, cheering, and unevenly played march music, to a nearby camp for the day. Not to be outdone, the corps officer in Meriden, Connecticut, tried the same thing a month later, with thirty cars and two hundred children. Such excursions became common in the first decades of the twentieth century.[47]

Army efforts to redeem the lives of the children of the poor were not confined to day trips, of course. It was clearly necessary to expose the young ones to the sacred truths of Christianity in a more relaxed and unhurried setting. Despite the inexorable decline of the farm colonies that followed the departure in 1904 of Booth-Tucker, who had been their only important champion on the American field, the Army remained of the opinion that country life had much to recommend it. With the colony zealot gone, it was possible to concentrate on more practical forms of sylvan relief. It was only natural that officers would begin to perceive the benefits of children's camps. It is not certain which was the first official Salvation Army summer camp; the best evidence gives the honor to the "Fresh Air Camp" pitched in twenty tents in Kansas City's Fairmont Park in the summer of 1897, the brainchild of the divisional officer, the ubiquitous Harry Stillwell. The Chicago auxiliaries donated the beautiful lakeside acreage at Camp Lake, Wisconsin, in 1904; the property remains in Army hands today, the organization's oldest continuing camp in the United States. As we have already noted, the Army's last remaining farm colony, Fort Herrick, after a brief interlude as an inebriates' refuge, became a fresh air camp for Cleveland slum children in 1909. Nor was fresh air the only stimulant offered to young hearts: weekly programs for the young people of the corps were developed through these years as well, culminating in the first "Young People's Council" in Chicago in 1913, which offered three days of rallies and lectures for corps young people and their leaders.[48]

The Army's multiplied activities in the field of good works won it widespread attention, most of it favorable. Many church leaders, reformers, and professionals in the field of charity praised the Army during these years; a typical comment came from a professor of sociology at Syracuse University, who referred to the Army in 1908 in an important textbook as "redemptive in purpose as well as social in aim," with a "world-wide organization and successful work" worthy of study and praise. The movement was not without critics during this period, however, and some of them were determined and outspoken. The criticism fell largely on three aspects of the Army's activities: its failure to cooperate with other agencies, especially the Charity Organization Society; its unreliable — or worse, misleading — statistical reporting; and its habit of spending some of the funds that had been collected for its social operations on its evangelistic activities. Many leaders of the Charity Organization Society movement had never been reconciled to the Army's reluctance to cooperate with it in screening applicants, weeding out the "unworthy," and joining the COS in its advocacy of political and social reforms and its condemnation of almsgiving. Writers condemned the Army's famous Christmas dinners for the poor on the grounds that since the guests were not investigated, the dinners were no better than handouts. One denounced the Army's "shivering bell ringer" and "suggestive pot" for raising money for the Army's holiday dinners in Madison Square Garden; if the diners there "could only be sorted and sifted, those honestly worthy would be a pitiful minority." Others condemned the Army's statistics, which offered the public a baffling array of duplicated counts of welfare recipients, and which, when referring to evangelism, seemed to show large numbers of conversions while, as these critics pointed out, the movement remained small and struggling except in a few large corps. The criticism that The Salvation Army collected money under false pretenses was the most commonly heard and the most damaging. C. C. Carstens, secretary of the Massachusetts Society for Prevention of Cruelty to Children, published a harshly critical report on Army finances in 1907, charging that the Army obtained "large funds" on the strength of its social programs and then used part of these funds "in the furtherance of its religious plans with which . . . many of its largest donors have little or no sympathy." In *The Salvation Army and the Public,* a book cited by several critics of the Army, John Manson supports this charge, although the book refers only to Army activities in London. Edwin G. Lamb, a researcher who was generally favorable to The Salvation Army, lamented this aspect of Army finances in a report published in 1909. That same year, the city officials who regulated charitable activities in Boston placed severe restrictions on Salvation Army fund-raising at the start of the holiday season; only the intervention of a friendly newspaper, the *Journal,* saved the day by offering to accept donations for the Army. Although friends of the Army often refuted criticism of its accounting procedures, some officers were privately alarmed at the confusion in Army fund-raising techniques.[49]

In the front lines — the corps themselves — the Great Salvation War made uneven progress. The initial excitement of a pioneer crusade had waned. By the time Evangeline Booth assumed command, The Salvation Army had been in the United States for a quarter of a century. Officers boasted that the Army was no longer an experiment; more to the point with regard to corps work, it was no longer a novelty. After the initial ferment had dissipated, converts were no longer added by hundreds or dozens in a few weeks, but by ones and twos at long intervals. For the large, well-established corps, this tranquil period before the First World War was healthy; it provided a needed interval for the soldiers and their families to become rooted and grounded in their faith. A few corps, like the one in Flint, Michigan, grew at a handsome rate due to immigration of Salvationist laborers from Europe into the local job market. In 1909 Flint acquired an entire brass band through the agency of Bandmaster Beacraft, who was also — conveniently — the manager of the Buick Motor Company. The growth that most large corps experienced was due to the prodigious efforts of officers and soldiers; the weekly schedule of such corps as Chicago No. 1, Boston Palace, Flint, or Oakland would seem staggering by today's standard. In May 1906, for instance, a week's activities for the band of Chicago No. 1 included five open-air meetings, five indoor services, three musical programs for bandless neighboring corps, and two rehearsals. An extra obligation for that month only was a weekly three-hour concert on State Street to raise money for the victims of the San Francisco earthquake. Nor did bad weather stay soldiers from their duty: in January 1904, Chicago No. 8 held thirty-nine outdoor services. Any corps capable of meeting the regulation schedule, which called for an indoor meeting every night of the week and three on Sunday (all but two of them preceded by an open-air meeting and a march), was expected to do so. This was no easy task, as a glance at the official corps cash account book then in use reveals: not counting special seasonal appeals, there were 132 separate columns to complete each week, covering attendance, finance, visitation, and social relief activities. Yet the officer who merely "kept things together" without bringing the corps at least "slightly up" received mediocre marks from his superiors.[50]

With many corps — the majority — the case was far different from what it was for the large ones. The early growth registered at these small stations in pioneer days did not last. In 1906 the average number of Salvationists per corps was thirty-five, and this number counted officers, employees, and all other persons over the age of thirteen on the rolls; it says nothing about average attendance, which was almost certainly considerably smaller. The comparable figure for all Protestant congregations in the same year was 104. Many of those whom the Army rescued were part of a transient population, moving from job to job, place to place, in an endless quest for a better life. A survey of seven officers taken in 1906 revealed that, together, they had seen seven hundred souls saved, of whom 136 became soldiers — roughly one in five. Brigadier Walter Jenkins, who reported this phenomenon, speculated that the major cause of it was the transient nature of the converts. In 1908 Col. Richard Holz surveyed his vast provincial command, which ran from Cleveland to Key West, and concluded that the Army's failure to build up its soldiery was due to the "migratory character of the working people" who were the main object of its outreach efforts. The result was often small, understaffed corps, which in itself worked against growth: Brigadier Jenkins cited as another cause for the reluctance of converts to join the ranks "the smallness of our corps and consequent disinclination to stand with it."[51]

The small corps was doubly crippled. The Army did not accept inactive membership. Officers depended on their soldiers, who were expected to take on the rigors of warfare without hesitation and to abandon job, home, and family if these stood in the way of total consecration to God and the Army. The Army was built on such soldiers and field officers. Advances depended principally on them, only indirectly on the staff, and not at all on the convert who shrank, however understandably, from the sacrifices that warfare required. Soldiers were given special passes, depending on their support of open-air meetings and "knee drills." These passes were highly prized: without one, a soldier could not attend the weekly soldiers' meeting at which corps problems were discussed and war strategy planned. Officers were warned that the Army could not long survive if it did not make more of its converts into soldiers. Getting people saved was no longer enough: the Army had to reach "the people who are more fixed in their abode and habits." The need for soldiers did not cease with the need for warriors. Soldiers were called not only to wage the war but to finance it with their cartridges, their peddling of *The War Cry,* and their faithful support of the open-air services at which money was collected. A corps with just a few soldiers was not only too weak in personnel to advance the war but was also in constant, desperate financial difficulty. Officers commanding such places — and there were hundreds of them — faced poverty that was often severe and occasionally so extreme as to endanger their health.[52]

The solution was to attract into the ranks what General Booth called "the better sort of mankind." In addition, the families of the Army's existing membership had to be secured if the organization was to have a future. The Salvation Army had to build a second generation. The many innovations in youth work that characterize these years indicate a recognition of this fact. At the same time, officers began to undertake rudimentary family counseling, and corps offered small-scale relief designed to hold corps families together, such as small loans or short-term jobs with the Army itself so that fathers would not have to go on the road to find work. Sometimes these fledgling family services required courage: when Lt. Col. William Bearchell was a small child in 1910, he saw a man shoot his wife then himself after Bearchell's father, the corps officer in Huntington, West Virginia, had failed to reconcile the couple. Yet the benefits of securing entire families were too obvious to be abandoned because of a few setbacks. In 1908 Maj. John Bouterse built a large and active corps in Asheville, North Carolina, by making soldiers out of the families attracted to the Army by a series of winter revival meetings. The Salvation Army launched the Home League on a national basis during the years 1913 to 1915. The League, a new program to reach wives and mothers, was started in London in 1907 by Mrs. Bramwell Booth; the first branch in the United States was probably the one in Pen Argyl, Pennsylvania. The League offered Christian fellowship and useful household instruction and was a success from the beginning. In 1915 Chicago's first Home League was officially commissioned at the Chicago No. 5 corps by the wife of the Territorial Commander of the West, Mrs. Comm. Thomas Estill.[53]

Despite the discouragement of small corps, from which even the saintly Brengle was not immune — "I felt I could have had larger crowds in a church, but I should not have had needier souls" — the Army's crusading zeal did not disappear during these years of slowed advance in the field. The Army continued, for instance, to offer plans to win the African American population of the South. General Booth had visited Mobile, Alabama, in February 1903 during his farm-colony tour; while there, he spoke at the city's largest black church. His old heart had melted at the sight of the "weeping penitents," which reminded him of his experiences as a revivalist in Cornwall almost a half-century before. The Army declared its continuing interest in southern blacks but urged patience. Plans for an "advance" were "not quite ready." The Army had very few black officers in the North, and none in the South. There were two black officers working in the New York rescue home in the early 1900s: "Sisters in Race, Sisters in Grace," they had both been saved at open-air meetings (in St. Louis and Manchester, New Hampshire), and both had served briefly as slum sisters in Philadelphia. In the South, however, there had been very little success in recruiting black soldiers and no progress in establishing black officers. In 1908 the provincial officer stated frankly in a private report that "Our work is exclusively among the white population, we do not touch the colored element. This of course limits our scope for Soldier-making etc." The difficulty was "the strong antagonistic feeling between the two races," which made it "practically impossible to do anything among the colored people there." Rescue homes were segregated, and in Greenville and Birmingham there were facilities only for white women. Given the legal and social structure of southern life in the early years of the twentieth century, the Army had only one alternative to segregating its facilities, which was to close them altogether and withdraw from the region. Official hope for an evangelical advance among African Americans remained high despite the many obstacles. In 1912 a black corps was opened in Washington, D.C., and the next year Colonel Holz, now in command of the Atlantic Coast Province (which included much of the South), announced that once again the time was "deemed ripe for The Salvation Army to start a regularly organized work among the hundreds of thousands of colored people" of the southern states.[54]

Nor did the Army's ill-fated African American crusade exhaust its interest in the South. The state of Kentucky exerted a powerful allure, despite several false starts (when officers "invaded" Kentucky in 1894, opening in Newport and Louisville, they imagined themselves to be pioneers: in fact Louisville had been "pioneered" twice before, in 1883 and 1887). Once permanently installed in the Blue Grass State, however, the Army did all in its power to make good its claim that "Kentucky shall be won for God!" The Army was invited to hold meetings in 1895 and 1896 at the camp meeting grounds at High Bridge, south of Lexington. Specials and musicians were gathered from several states, with gratifying results: local congregations, who had never seen the Army before, regarded it as a "revelation." In the fall of 1903 a more daring invasion was launched. Colonel Holz and eight others, mounted on horseback and clad in special khaki uniforms, braved gunfire to bring the gospel to the feuding hills of eastern Kentucky. The mountain people, solidly religious, were friendly and hospitable, and open-airs were held along the roads and in courthouse squares in perfect safety. Once the Salvationists held forth on Beaver Creek to a group of men operating a moonshine still, who listened politely. The Army found it difficult to get more than a toehold in Kentucky, however: the people were "Hardshell Baptist of long and approved standing," and a state in which the main sources of income were bourbon whiskey, horse racing, and tobacco was not fertile ground for The Salvation Army.[55]

Other areas were more congenial. The Scandinavian work continued to prosper, although the steady growth in Scandinavian membership did not match that of the Army as whole: from 1906 to 1916, membership in the Army's foreign-language corps (70 out of 74 of which were Scandinavian) grew by 25 percent, while overall the Army grew by 57 percent. The number of Scandinavian immigrants to the United States from 1900 to 1917 was nearly three-quarters of a million persons, greater by almost a hundred thousand than the number who arrived in the years between 1887 (when the Scandinavian work began) and 1900. Secure in its large eastern nests — by the end of World War I, New York No. 2 corps was the largest Scandinavian corps outside of Sweden — the Scandinavian work advanced across the country, nurtured by the enthusiasm of its cheerful minions and guided by such leaders as the sweet-spirited Col. Ben Nelson, who commanded Scandinavian operations in the western territory from 1908 to 1920. The Scandinavians had their heroes, too. On February 11, 1907, the steamer *Larchmont,* en route from Providence to New York City, was struck by a coal schooner in stormy weather in Long Island Sound. Aboard were ten Scandinavian Salvationists on their way to a rally in New York. When it became clear that the ship would sink before all the lifeboats could be lowered and that no one would survive more than a few minutes in the freezing water, the Army soldiers calmly knelt in a ring on the listing deck, urging their terrified fellow passengers to prepare to meet God and singing "Jesus, Lover of My Soul, Let Me to Thy Bosom Fly" as the waves closed over their heads. All ten were drowned, but not in vain. The testimony of their faith caused a revival to sweep the Scandinavian ranks, and the funeral at New York No. 2 — only three of the Salvationists' bodies were recovered — turned into a hallelujah free-for-all at which many souls were saved.[56]

Another disaster — the San Francisco earthquake and fire in April 1906 — brought the Army into the news as well and gave it its first opportunity to provide large-scale and systematic emergency relief, which assumed a large role in later years. The Army's earliest connection to public emergencies may have been the dauntless George Elliott, a Chicago convert who in 1889 hastened to fires carrying drinking water to the thirsty firefighters and directing the attention of the crowd to the flames as a sample of what awaited the unconverted soul. More temporal measures were taken as well. In 1900 national headquarters offered first aid instruction to officers and soldiers so that they might be ready to offer physical as well as spiritual rescue as they went their rounds in busy streets and back alleys. That same year a hurricane drove a flood over the town of Galveston, and the Army literally threw out the lifeline. "Mother" Thomas, a Houston Salvationist, traveled to the scene to care for the "storm refugees" who had fled to the outskirts of the city. Booth-Tucker quickly sent after her a relief expedition of twelve officers under Brigadier Stillwell and Major Galley, the first aid instructor. They set up tents for the homeless in Texas City and helped to clean, feed, and shelter some of the thousands of refugees.[57]

These helpful activities served as a kind of prelude to the Army's participation in the massive relief operations in California. On April 18, 1906, the San Andreas fault shifted, causing severe earthquakes along part of the California coast. The Army itself was badly hit by the quake. The Beulah rescue home in Oakland was wrecked, the Lytton orphanage was severely damaged, and the Santa Rosa corps hall collapsed. Fortunately, Ensign and Mrs. Jensen were able to extricate themselves from the rubble at Santa Rosa. Mrs. Anna Butler, the Salvationist matron of the orphanage, was not so lucky; in San Francisco on business at the time, she was killed. The worst damage in San Francisco — and, temporarily, the Army's various religious and industrial activities in it — was produced not by the earthquake but by the fires that raged in the aftermath. The "City of the Argonauts" was still partly illuminated by kerosene and gas in 1906: spilled lamps and broken chimney pipes caused numerous fires, which spread unchecked through the splintered wreckage. The fire department could do nothing: all the city water mains had ruptured in the quake. Within three days the better part of a city that housed 400,000 people burned to the ground.[58]

With nothing material left on the scene — the industrial home, lighthouse, and the corps were gone, and all that remained of California provincial headquarters was the safe and one melted cornet — The Salvation Army limped into the breach. It had no organized plan for disaster relief: most of what was done was spontaneous and practical. While Commissioner Kilbey announced from Chicago a territory-wide campaign to raise funds and collect food and bedding, Oakland Salvationists opened the Citadel (which had lost its plaster ceiling in the quake) and the Beulah Park camp meeting grounds to some of the refugees who streamed by the tens of thousands across the Bay seeking safety. Chinese refugees were given their own little corner of the camp and proved so receptive to the Army's ministry that several were converted — enough to open a Chinese corps in Oakland in 1907. Eventually, most of the San Francisco Army arrived in Oakland, and the Citadel became temporary headquarters for relief operations. The San Francisco soldiery had already performed one heroic service during the worst of the fires by rescuing hundreds of injured people who had been placed for safekeeping in the Mechanics' Pavilion, a large hall supposedly well away from the flames. By the time it became clear that this building, like most of the rest of the city, would eventually be consumed, the injured there had been forgotten except by their panic-stricken relations. The Army came to the rescue with its small fleet of industrial home wagons. Once this heroic operation was completed and the injured were safely aboard the Oakland ferry, the military government of the city took the Army's horses for its own supply wagons. Temporarily disconcerted by this development, most Salvationists repaired to Oakland to formulate new plans. They did not have long to wait: the military governor detailed all willing Salvationists to help in refugee camps and emergency hospitals. In addition, the military assumed part of the duties of maintaining the Beulah camp, freeing more Salvationists for service in San Francisco. The soldiers streamed back across the Bay and into action.[59]

Meanwhile the Commander herself, not content with staging a mass fund-raising rally in Union Square in New York, nor with channeling to Oakland the hundreds of letters and telegrams of prayer and support that daily poured in at national headquarters, decided to hasten to the scene in person as a surprise to her hard-pressed western troops. The delight in her visit was reciprocal. Her pleasure at all that had been done was unfeigned. Almost thirty thousand persons had been fed, over nine thousand given beds, a new one-story wooden provincial headquarters had already been erected on the old site, and the Army was singing and testifying in the refugee camps every night. For their part, San Francisco's soldiers beamed with pride as Evangeline, at the top of her form, charmed the city and captivated a mass meeting on May 30 in Golden Gate Park. Thus rejuvenated, the Army continued its relief efforts through the summer. A group of volunteers sponsored by William Randolph Hearst, the eccentric millionaire publisher, arrived in June from Los Angeles; the party's organizers had turned down many volunteers but accepted all nine Salvationists who had offered themselves. By the fall of the year the city was functioning again, rubble had been cleared away, and the Army's emergency relief operations were closed down. By the summer of 1907, The Salvation Army, like the rest of the city, was conducting business at the old stands: the industrial home wagons were plying neighborhood streets, and the band of San Francisco No. 1 was marching nightly through the newly restored Barbary Coast, almost as if nothing had happened.[60]

The Army's work in the California disaster received considerable attention in the press and helped to reinforce the image of the movement as an agency for good. The Great Salvation War, the direct assault on Satan and all his works, was thus indirectly aided in the last years before the First World War. There were more direct and straightforward advances as well. The old General paid two visits to the United States in 1907: in March a "flying visit" while en route to Canada and then Japan, and an official American tour in the fall. Obviously failing in health, almost certainly making his last trip to the United States, the General was lionized, greeted everywhere by enraptured crowds. He and Eva were received in state by President and Mrs. Roosevelt at the White House. The president was genial, chuckling his approval of the Army's street ministry: "I thoroughly believe in a brass band." These sunny remarks, and others of a similar nature, failed somehow to dispel the gloom into which November's falling leaves had plunged the General. So many friends had passed from the American scene — his old friend Mark Hanna, President McKinley, then Mrs. McKinley, all of whom had given sincere and highly valuable support to The Salvation Army at the height of their careers. (To honor the martyred president, the Army paid for a costly stained-glass portrait window in 1907 when it built a new corps building in Canton, Ohio, McKinley's hometown.) Eva found that she could not charm her father out of this mood in the White House, and she became concerned. But on the platform, as the apostle of the poor and lost, Booth still flamed forth,

Gen. William Booth with his daughter Evangeline
when she was national commander in 1907
Photo: Falk Studios, New York City
Source: Mr. Tom McMahon, Ocean Grove, New Jersey

the old giant a giant still. At his last address in New York, he commended
Eva to the United States as one whose "only ambition is to see you a holy,
happy and useful people, one of the strongest, bravest and most effective
wings of this great organization," and then he departed for England amid
a tornado of volleys and cheers.[61]

The effect of the General was always electric. The Army redoubled its attack on sin in the streets and stepped up the percentage of hot-shot being fired at the "drink traffic." Since the 1880s the Army had supported the principle of the legal prohibition of all alcoholic beverages but deliberately avoided a public commitment to any political party — including the Prohibition Party itself, which canvassed in vain for Salvationist support. The Army's traditional view was that Christ alone was its Candidate, who alone could solve the problems of the world; any more mundane advocacy would only alienate one or another part of the public. The Army preferred to attack Demon Rum by direct assault.[62]

The great attack opened on Thanksgiving Day 1909 with a parade in New York City. The general idea seems to have sprung spontaneously from several minds, but the details of what was guilelessly called the "Boozers' Convention" were devised by the provincial officer Col. William McIntyre, a wellspring of novelties, aided in this case by Maj. G. W. Baillie. The double-deck buses that were to grace Fifth Avenue for many years had just come into service; the Army borrowed some of them and filled them with idlers, many with chronic drinking problems, collected off the city streets. A parade was formed of these buses, a ten-foot papier-mache whiskey bottle, and five brass bands, and the whole was led by a municipal water wagon to which were willingly chained one-time "bona fide bums," now sober converts. The parade ended at headquarters, where participants and observers were offered a free dinner and an evangelical meeting was addressed by notable saved drunkards from all the New York corps. The Boozers' Convention became an annual event and spread to other cities. In 1910 this straightforward technique netted a particularly noteworthy captive. Henry Milans was a former editor of the *New York Daily Mercury* whose career had been ruined by his alcoholism. Discharged from Bellevue in 1908 as a "hopeless incurable," Milans fell literally into the gutter, where the Army found him. He was powerfully converted, miraculously purged of his taste for drink, and went forth as a glorious "Trophy of Grace" whose testimony in meetings and in print became an important part of the Army's growing temperance crusade. Milans's contributions were joined in the arsenal by a variety of pamphlets portraying the effects of drink on body, mind, and soul, by parade floats depicting "The Drunkard's Home" (suitably forlorn), and by thousands of broadside song sheets offering homespun truths that touched many hearts: "The pail that holds the milk, sir, he used to fill with beer."[63]

To the public in these years, The Salvation Army must have seemed like its old self, the zeal and dedication — even the hallelujah buffoonery — much the same. Certainly the Commander did all that lay within her nearly inexhaustible dramatic powers to inspire the troops. She developed a series of illustrated lectures — more like tableaux with gestures and music — which she delivered from memory to large crowds. Of these, "The Commander in Rags," loosely based on her pioneer experiences in London slums, and later "The World's Greatest Romance" were public favorites. Her zeal for the old Army never waned; she even kept alive the Victorian Army's fondness for photographers. Her enwreathed picture graced the Christmas *War Cry,* and the fine portrait of Eva kneeling beside her father, taken at the Falk Studio in New York on his last visit in 1907, became an Army classic.[64]

The passing years nevertheless brought changes to the Army, each of which had its subtle effect on the movement. One source of uneasiness for some Salvationists, at the same time it was an occasion for official pride, was the acquisition of permanent property. The purchase of land and the construction or purchase of corps buildings and social institutions represented a major change in Army policy. The pioneer Army owned little real estate. Army halls were rented, and seldom for long. Officers felt that the ownership of property would tie the troops down, and imperil the crusade's vital mobility. In 1885 the national commander wrote that "much of the Army's future achievements for good" would be "found in its ability to form flying columns, and to deliver sharp and rapid strokes upon the slumbering consciences of one city after another." Pioneer officers cherished the flexibility given them by a policy of renting their meeting halls by the month. In 1890, for instance, the Army owned only twenty-seven pieces of property in the entire United States, with a total value of $38,150; only 7 percent of the Army's corps locations were owned by The Salvation Army. In the next few years the Army took steps toward a new policy regarding real estate. In 1892 an official decree required local officers to secure permission from national headquarters for any real estate purchases, and in 1894 the first "Property Board" was set up at national headquarters, but if these changes represented a new policy, it was implemented slowly at first. With the single major exception of the national headquarters building on New York's Fourteenth Street, the Army acquired little in the way of property until the end of the administration of Ballington Booth.[65]

Frederick Booth-Tucker and the Consul gave an important stimulus to the acquisition of real estate, with dramatic results. By 1906 The

Salvation Army owned 159 pieces of property, valued at more than $3,000,000 (83 times the valuation in 1890!). Many of the new properties were social institutions, but the number of corps properties increased rapidly as well: by 1906, 23 percent of corps were in Army-owned buildings. There were several causes. For one thing, from the beginning the General had required that all bequests to The Salvation Army be used in some permanent manner, as a memorial rather than as operating funds; by the mid-1890s this policy had resulted in a large accumulation of money. Many Army leaders even during Ballington's administration had advocated spending these funds on buildings; Booth-Tucker took up these suggestions with enthusiasm. The national financial secretary, writing in 1895, stated that the advantages that would come to the Army by owning property "must be apparent to all thinking people"; for one thing, "real estate has a tendency to contribute to the permanency of the work." Many soldiers in big city corps registered dismay at the gypsy-like wandering around town that was a part of their service in the Army. These persons — who were often in the majority — felt that such an organization was "insecure and impermanent"; they craved the comfortable assurance of a fixed congregational home. The large numbers attending Army meetings in the early days had necessitated the renting of large halls; as the numbers fell off, the soldier remnant made their demands for regular meetings halls felt. Officers could point out that monthly mortgage payments on a building were usually less than rent on a comparable property. Finally, several aggressive officers came into positions of authority during the years when sentiment was building to replace rented halls with corps buildings. These men became convinced that the procurement of property was an essential step, upon which the future progress of the Army as a stable and respected force for good in American life depended. This became official Army policy, and in 1907 *The War Cry* declared that the fact that the Army was gaining properties was a sign of "the lofty pedestal of public confidence upon which we stand today." Col. William McIntyre and Col. Richard Holz, among the most influential of the provincial officers and both leaders among those who wanted the Army to acquire property, were fast movers. When McIntyre began in Buffalo in 1898, the Army in his province owned only the national headquarters, worth $400,000, and a small frame shop used as a hall in Addison, New York; by 1920 property in the province was valued at $3,000,000. In the Ohio, Pittsburgh, and Southern Province Holz purchased thirty-two properties during his years of command, from 1899 to 1908. When he arrived, the Army had owned nothing; the book value of its holdings at his departure was $536,000. Everywhere the Army was moving into splendid new barracks of brick and masonry, like the new citadels in Oakland (1902) and Flint (1911). Although the total number of Army properties increased by only eight from 1906 to 1916, a disproportionate number of acquisitions were made for corps, so that by 1916, 40 percent of the corps in the United States were in Army properties.[66]

The old-time "flying columns" were not only becoming tied down in fixed locations but were also becoming entangled in increasing confusion over money and the purposes for which it was collected. The Salvation Army never ceased to be an evangelistic crusade, with the redemption of the unchurched urban masses its sole function. Yet the means to this glorious end had expanded and prospered in their own right. At first spontaneous, haphazard, and immediate, the social programs had been organized on a massive scale, requiring a constant influx of money and donations in kind. These activities were not confined to (and in some cases not even concentrated at) the Army's official social relief institutions. It is clear from contemporary professional writings, from the Army's own voluminous literature on this subject, and from the personal observations of many officers at the time that by the first decade of the twentieth century Salvation Army corps had become clearly established in the public mind as centers of many kinds of social relief activities. In its obituary for General Booth in 1912, the influential *Christian Advocate* observed that "of late years there has appeared to be a larger emphasis on social ministries than upon distinctly evangelistic effort. But no decline in spiritual activities has been permitted." Field officers were expected to perform both functions under the most trying circumstances. Lt. Phil Gerringer, stationed alone in Brainerd, Minnesota, spent the evening of December 23, 1910, preparing twenty-five Christmas baskets for needy families, then stayed up all night to keep the stove alight so the food would not freeze before he could deliver it the next day. Officers and friends of the Army were fearful that the demands of administering these good works would absorb energies badly needed for the evangelistic crusade. Colonel Holz spoke officially: "Unless care is taken, there is danger that our Field Officers will become fully absorbed in the Charity and Relief work, to the exclusion of the Spiritual side of things."[67]

Despite these reservations, of which the public — and indeed, many Salvationists — knew nothing, and despite the occasional appearance in the press of criticism of some aspect of Army administration, the Army

The Salvation Army Industrial Home for Men, New York City, ca. 1916
Source: The Salvation Army National Archives

had become so well-established in the years before World War I that no one could seriously deny its place in American life both as a successful working-class denomination growing at a rate well in excess of that of the population at large and as a major agency for good works. The Army's industrial homes developed rapidly during these years: from 1911 to 1913 the total number of homes increased from 107 to 124, and accommodations increased from 2,421 to 3,139. The Army's men's social services branch possessed the two largest buildings in the Army's American holdings after the national headquarters — New York No. 1 Industrial Home on W. 48th Street (opened in 1906) and the Booth Memorial Hotel on Chatham Square (opened in 1913).

The industrial home officers were not behind in their taste for dramatic innovations: in 1913, Adjutant Ray Starbard purchased the first motor vehicle ever owned by The Salvation Army — a 1913 Koehler chain-drive truck for the use of the Worcester, Massachusetts, Industrial Home. When the *Titanic* sank in April 1912, it was only natural for the public to expect The Salvation Army to play a role in the national response. There was a series of memorial services held in corps across the country, and several Army bands, making heavy use of the "Dead March" from Handel's *Saul,* put on concerts in aid of the official Titanic Disaster Relief Fund. Interest in these events may have been stimulated by knowledge that two English Salvationist immigrants had been among the rescued — and that Evangeline had booked passage on the *Titanic* for the return trip to England![68]

The death of the General on August 20, 1912, might have been a serious blow. Predictions were heard when The Salvation Army began in the United States that its success, dependent as it was mostly upon the personal leadership of its famous Founder, would not outlast his lifetime. Some pioneer officers expressed the same concern, but these predictions were far from the mark by 1912, after the Army had been at work in the United States for over thirty years. The pioneer American sociologist Edward Allsworth Ross was more prescient; writing in 1897, he compared the Army to the Franciscans, confident that the Catholic example gave grounds for optimism regarding the Army: "With age the vitality of an order comes to reside" not in the "ascendant personality of its founder," he wrote, but "in its models or ideals." The death of William Booth was, of course, an important historic event. It received widespread sympathetic coverage by the popular American press and professional and religious journals. The death was a blow to the American Army not so much because it was unexpected as because it left an absolute void. No one had ever known another General. The Army, in one form or the other, had existed for forty-seven years under the sole leadership of William Booth, who had long since been recognized as one of the great men of his times. American Salvationists, who had seen Booth only during his official state visits to the United States, if at all, and were of necessity less captivated than their English comrades by the General's constant physical presence, were nonetheless saddened by the loss of the great human fixture that had for so many years symbolized the movement.

Memorial services were held from coast to coast. Eighty-three, blind, and dying, William Booth had spent most of his last months preaching the gospel with all his old power. His heart seemed to flame up once more before its fire went out forever: his last public address, which is still cherished by Salvationists, was heard in May by seven thousand people, Evangeline among them, at the Royal Albert Hall in London. It was the triumph of the spirit that built The Salvation Army:

> When women weep, as they do now, I'll fight; while little children go hungry, as they do now, I'll fight; while men go to prison, in and out, in and out, as they do now, I'll fight; while there is a poor lost girl upon the streets, while there remains one dark soul without the light of God, I'll fight — I'll fight to the very end!

In Los Angeles Vachel Lindsay, a struggling poet who had sheltered with the Army in his travels, wrote what became his most famous poem as a tribute to the old General; "General William Booth Enters into Heaven" was soon published in *Poetry* magazine and gained wide notice. *The War Cry*, bordered in mournful black, carried more conventional tributes. Photographs were circulated showing the General lying in state, his hands folded over Evangeline's last cable to him: "Kiss him for me."[69]

The next General was Bramwell, chosen by the Founder in 1890 for that honor according to the legal procedures designed by himself in 1878, which made the selection of a successor the privilege of the reigning General — a procedure, incidentally, that a new edition of the Army's official catechism for cadets was careful to praise. The new General was generally unknown to Americans; even his name was obscure except to staff officers. He was a man of exceptional administrative ability whose careful and painstaking organizational work had enabled his crusading, eloquent, and peripatetic father to gather in the masses on a worldwide basis. Bramwell was loyal to his father — whom he never ceased to refer to as "the General" even after he had become General himself — and to what he conceived his father's wishes to have been on certain matters of Army policy. Bramwell was intelligent, a man of conviction and high principle, and he had a fine prose style; his printed messages and devotional writings were widely read and much beloved. Nevertheless, many Americans were uncertain about the character and ability of the new international leader and his attitude toward the Army in general and their branch of it in particular, an uncertainty that was transformed into anxiety by their first sight of him in his new august capacity. The new General's first official visit to the United States in 1913 was a disappointment. Bramwell lacked presence on the platform. It is only fair to grant that the Founder was a hard act for Bramwell to follow; the contrast between the old man's impassioned eloquence and his son's lackluster delivery was striking. Bramwell was partially deaf and wore a wobbly pair of pince-nez, which made him appear fussy and uncertain. His views on Army administration were even more unsettling than his presence. However pure his motives may have been, Bramwell Booth was a thoroughgoing bureaucrat — Ballington had called him a "systems man." The new General had a narrow and inflexible conception of the Army's hierarchical structure, fatally combined with the mystical notion that he had inherited from the now glorified Founder a sacred trust to preserve the powers of the General indivisible and inviolate.[70]

Seven hundred American Salvationists went to London in June 1914 for a great International Congress. Led by the Commander on horseback, the American delegation (in cowboy hats) included the two staff bands and the Flint Citadel Band and a small group of elderly African American Salvationists assembled by Colonel Gifford, the Boston provincial commander. The joy that was shared by the fifty-eight national delegations was genuine, and no group enjoyed the Congress more than the Americans, who cheerfully regarded it as an honor that their place in the parade was as the last national unit (just ahead of the employees of the Salvation Army Assurance Society and staff clerks): clearly the General wanted a grand finale — and what could be more grand than Eva on a horse, three brass bands, seven hundred Americans waving cowboy hats, and the black soldiers, who appeared for the occasion in special star-spangled costumes? What indeed could be more grand? Patriotism itself was grand, a harmless display of camaraderie in the engaging context of a world evangelical crusade. Patriotism appeared less harmless, however, in Sarajevo, where on June 28, 1914, a Serbian nationalist shot the visiting heir to the Austrian throne and his wife. The fifty-eight delegations to the Salvation Army International Congress paid no official attention to this event and departed from the Crystal Palace still in a euphoric mood, unaware that the beginning of a great world war was at hand.[71]

CHAPTER 4

1914-1929

"Fresh converts still we gain."

No hint of coming war in Europe appeared in the pages of *The War Cry* during the summer of 1914; all talk was of the big Salvation Army congress in London. When the Great War began in Europe in August 1914, the United States remained neutral, and the American branch of The Salvation Army was at first little affected by the hostilities. The regular spiritual and social activities went forward and were supplemented by new programs. The open-air ministry continued to characterize the Army. "Born in the street," the Army continued to thrive "in the place of its nativity, and its power to prevent evil and encourage purity by this means" was, according to a modest official statement, "beyond computation." In 1915 an ice dealer in San Bernardino, California, asked the local Salvation Army band to play in front of a notorious house of prostitution, with happy results: seven years later he saw the former operator of the house leading an Army band on a street corner in Arizona! Corps activities, augmented now by the new Home League, filled every night of the week. Salvationist immigrants continued to augment the native ranks; in 1915 young Erik Leidzen left Stockholm for the United States, heading straight for the New York No. 2 (Swedish) Corps on 49th Street. Youth work in the corps was expanded by the addition of two British transplants — the Life-Saving Scouts for boys in 1915 and the Life-Saving Guards for girls in 1916 — only one of which, the Girl Guards, managed to flourish in the United States.[1]

New York: Bowery open air, 1915. The slogan on the drum is "Every Beat for Jesus."
Source: The Salvation Army National Archives

The penny ice and cheap coal benefactions spread rapidly and far. By 1915 these good works were no longer confined to the larger cities: individual corps officers in cities both large and small plied the poor sections in hired wagons dispensing this seasonal boon. At the same time, major innovations were introduced in the Army's expanding activities among homeless alcoholic men: motor vehicles to operate salvage routes began to make an appearance (seventeen were in use in the eastern half of the country by 1917), and programs aimed directly at counseling and evangelizing heavy drinkers were started, most notably by Maj. Wallace W. Winchell in the Jersey City Industrial Home in 1911, followed in 1912 by a national program of fellowship and encouragement for clients willing to pledge themselves to abstinence. Participatory burial and medical insurance and a nationwide client registration system were introduced during the years 1912-1915. The next year saw the first use of a new name for the Army's industrial homes, which eventually became uniform and lasted for over sixty years: in 1916 Evangeline Booth opened the new Philadelphia "Industrial and Social Service Center." The Army's prison ministry, so tenderly nurtured by Maud Booth, grew steadily under her successors, especially Commander Evangeline, who took a great personal interest in its development. A converted former convict, Ensign Thomas Anderson, formed the Brighter Day League in 1904 to offer spiritual service to prisoners and to help them prepare for that "brighter day" when they would be free. In 1916 Anderson began the "Lifer's Club" to convert and comfort those with no such hope — men serving life sentences. The club's first president, Jesse Harding Pomeroy, spent his life in the Massachusetts State Penitentiary for a murder he committed at the age of fifteen. Prison visitation became part of the duties of every nearby corps; the annual Prison Sunday saw scores of visits to prisons. In February 1917 Evangeline took the entire National Staff Band with her to play before she preached at Sing Sing.[2]

The years of American neutrality in the World War, which ended in April 1917, seemed propitious for the Army. It is true, as the Army itself admitted, that the public accorded it only "passive acceptance" so far as its evangelical crusade was concerned and that much of its spiritual work lapsed "into comparative obscurity, from which there seemed to be no escape. Few knew the Army for what it was, and few cared." Yet the social programs drew public praise and financial support in increasing amounts, so that the Commander was inspired to act on an idea with which she, and her father before her, had toyed for years: the "University of Humanity" to train officers on a national scale. The old General put the idea forward regularly, starting in the Consul's day, but he insisted — oddly enough — that the proposed new college be in London, which ruined the prospects, so carefully cultivated by the Booth-Tuckers, of sufficient American funding, without which no such project would be possible. Mrs. Leland Stanford, the California philanthropist, withdrew her offer to finance the "university" on this ground. Commander Eva made no such mistake; once the Founder had passed from the scene, the idea of the University of Humanity reappeared in a more congenial and familiar form: a national training college for American officers, to be combined with an old people's home and two social institutions, in downtown New York. The Army planned to launch a national fund-raising campaign in 1914 but postponed it at the request of the YMCA, which had long planned a national campaign of its own for a somewhat similar project. When the Army began its campaign to raise $500,000 for the "University of Humanity" in 1916, the YMCA offered its full support, as did a wide segment of the public, including former president Theodore Roosevelt, still as warm as ever toward the Army.[3]

If imitation is the sincerest form of flattery, then The Salvation Army had reason to congratulate itself during these years. The problem of imitation "armies" had troubled the Army since the Moore era. In August 1892 an organization called the "Industrial Christian Alliance . . . meeting somewhat on S.A. lines" solicited funds in the Ocean Grove Auditorium: the vacationing Colonel Holz, in the audience by chance, glumly gave a nickel. The press called public attention to several "bogus 'armies' " in San Francisco in 1898. The phenomenon continued to plague officers into the 1920s, especially in Chicago. In 1922 the problem of "Fake Armies" was placed on the agenda of the second annual meeting of national leaders, called the commissioners' conference. Yet these imitation armies continued to appear in cycles; during the years between 1913 and 1917 in particular, the number of these "spurious concerns" grew to alarming proportions. In December 1913, Brig. A. E. Kimball, provincial commander for Michigan and Indiana, wrote in despair to the national chief secretary, pleading for "some way out of the present difficulty we have in connection with so many Armies." There was the Afro-American Army in Philadelphia (an especially disreputable swindle), the Good Samaritan Army in Detroit, and the Christian Army in Nashville and Louisville. In Baltimore there were the American Rescue Workers and the Volunteers of America (both of which were legitimate organizations, descendant from the Army schisms of 1884 and 1896), the Samaritan Army, the American Gospel Band, and the "Salvation Army Church (not connected with The Salvation Army)," all operating in the year 1915. Davenport, Iowa, had a Calvary Army, while Chicago produced the Redeemer's Army, the Christian Army, and the Samaritan, Saved, and Volunteer Rescue Armies. These agencies, which used uniforms, flags, and brass bands wherever they could muster them, caused great confusion to the public, which naturally mistook them for The Salvation Army. Most of these tiny "armies" were either frauds or the work of sincere but deluded individuals who did not have the resources to provide the charitable services for which they collected money. The Army's legal secretary, Brig. Madison J. H. Ferris, secured assistance from the courts in banishing the most flagrant examples from the streets.[4]

Meanwhile the war raged on in Europe, a disaster of appalling magnitude. There were few who imagined — or hoped — that the United Stated would become a belligerent, but the country was nevertheless drawn increasingly into the conflict. The United States was the leading supplier of war materials to the Allies, and to that extent American prosperity had become tied to an Allied victory. At the same time, many Americans were moved by the accounts of atrocities and casualties that increasingly filled the newspapers. These developments caused great excitement among the millions of Americans whose ethnic loyalties were still strong. Although The Salvation Army in the United States was not heavily involved in war relief work before the country entered the war in 1917, American Salvationists were never indifferent to the suffering, physical and mental, caused by the war. Salvationists were urged to pray for peace, to "affect the battlefields of Europe by way of the Throne of Heaven." The American branch of the Army remained absolutely neutral: soldiers were warned not to pray for any "particular side, but . . . in the interest of our great humanity." American Salvationists were saddened to learn that the Army work of their European comrades was "quite prostrate" as a result of the war, which affected the working people — the mainstay of the Army — more than other classes.[5]

In November 1914 the Commander announced the "Old Linen Campaign" to aid victims of the war. Corps personnel were asked to collect and clean old linen, fold it into bandages and surgical pads, and send these items to divisional headquarters. National headquarters would mark each package in English, French, and German and ship them to Europe for distribution by neutral parties. Funds and old clothing for Belgian refugees were collected as well, starting in 1915. In October of that year, the Army's international headquarters requested that an American officer — a citizen of a neutral state — be dispatched to conduct the Army's relief work in Belgium. That country was occupied by the Germans, who were willing that the relief work be continued but refused to accept an officer from an enemy country like Britain. The Commander sent Major Winchell, the energetic industrial home officer and colorful Chicago pioneer who twenty years earlier had subpoenaed the devil and operated the Army's food relief program during the Pullman strike.[6]

Major Winchell arrived to find some Army centers already at work, and he opened a wide range of additional practical charities, which were financed by subscriptions at home and funds from London. Clothing and money grants were given to destitute families, soup kitchens were opened for schoolchildren, and milk was given to babies. The Major, always a fan of Booth-Tucker's agricultural panaceas, secured lots upon which unemployed Belgians could grow potatoes. Winchell took no sides in the war, which he diplomatically attributed to original sin. He found the Germans efficient and cooperative and discounted Allied propaganda about German atrocities. Some of Winchell's religious activities were unfamiliar to the

Belgians: while holding an open-air meeting in Brussels he was attacked by a wounded Belgian who mistook him for a German. The excitement of his war work caused Winchell to lapse into periods of hallelujah whimsy, during which he planned to borrow military trucks to take the poor children of Brussels into the war-ravaged countryside as a novelty or to bombard the Allied lines with bouquets of flowers flung over from the German side as the first stage in a massive peace plan of his own devising. Despite these lapses, Winchell accomplished much in the way of practical good work and departed before his privileged status as a citizen of a neutral power had evaporated.[7]

The United States declared war against the German Empire on April 6, 1917. There were several reasons for this action, for which diplomatic and military developments during March had only partially prepared the public, but the basic principle upon which the administration of President Wilson decided for war was the defense of American maritime rights, which had been endangered by Germany's unrestricted submarine warfare. The Salvation Army was caught off guard at first. American Salvationists had been officially instructed for years to value the Army's international status, which had sustained it through two domestic schisms. As late as March 1917, *The War Cry* had admonished American Salvationists to put aside the question of "whatever there may be of merit or demerit in the contending camps arraigned upon Europe's bloody fields" and concentrate on The Salvation Army's "great war against sin, this fight for God." Initially it was difficult for Americans to write off their comrades in Germany, for whom Railton had worked so lovingly after he had left his pioneering labors in America, as bloodthirsty militarists determined to conquer the world. The Commander's statement of April 21 was equivocal: the Army was "international" and could glory only in the struggle against "sin and strife." Still, The Salvation Army was ready to stand by the president, and the Commander placed at his disposal the services of her "disciplined army" of thirty thousand Salvationists for Red Cross work — her enthusiasm causing her to offer the entire membership of the Army in the United States. "The Salvation Army, as a unit," she pledged, would "move to meet the utmost demand upon us." *The War Cry* lost its elevated tone within a few weeks of the American declaration of war, although the magazine was never fierce in its nationalism, and the anti-German tone was, considering the times, muted. In May 1917 the magazine reprinted a British cartoon showing the German Kaiser — the wreath he had sent to the Founder's funeral in 1912 now forgotten — with the legend "the spirit of militarism bursts its tomb," but such items were rare. Later that same month Colonel Brengle reminded readers to beware of hatred, wrath, and careless speech; the war would not bring a better world — only the "progress and triumph of the spirit of Jesus in the hearts of men" could do that.[8]

Beyond making dramatic pronouncements, it was not at first clear what the American branch of the Army proposed to do in the war. The chief secretary, Col. William Peart, wrote in the April 21, 1917, *War Cry* that the Commander was still "considering the steps The Salvation Army in the United States, in harmony with our principles, is likely to take." That week the Commander placed Col. E. J. Parker in overall command of Salvation Army war relief activities, as part of a new top-level "Emergency Board" to supervise war work at headquarters, chaired by herself. The Army decided almost at once to open "a number of huts or restrooms" at military training camps in the United States. Salvationist nurses, men with motor-vehicle experience, and bandsmen ("for the cheering, blessing and saving of the soldier boys") were invited to volunteer for service in these canteens or to join the "Salvation Army unit of the Red Cross" to serve in France. Lt. Col. William S. Barker, in charge of Army properties at headquarters, was given the additional responsibility of organizing the "Soldiers of the Soil," a national campaign to enlist civilian volunteers to farm vacant land and city lots to help increase the nation's food supplies at a time when many regular farmhands were going into military service.[9]

The government was hesitant at first to accept the Army's services. Congress authorized and the high command issued a general order that the American Red Cross should provide all "relief work" for the U.S. Army — that is, services for the sick and injured — while the YMCA was given by the same means an official monopoly on "welfare work," which included social, recreational, educational, and religious activities for the able-bodied troops. These grants of authority were not intended to be absolute, however: when other, smaller agencies offered their services, they were not automatically rebuffed, so long as they were willing to coordinate their efforts with those of the two officially chartered agencies. Civilian war work was divided into two areas: training camps at home and services to the American Expeditionary Force (AEF) in France. The Salvation Army was eventually included in both, but only after a period of negotiation and uncertainty. Most government officials knew little of The Salvation Army, looking upon it as vaguely beneficial, with little capacity for efficient war service. The same feeling was common among military officers in

France. No one, in The Salvation Army or out if it, anticipated the impact that its war service in France was to have — not only on American soldiers but on the reputation and prospects of the movement itself. Considering the languid official response to the Army's first offers of service, it is ironic that in 1951 Prof. Herbert Wisbey, preparing a doctoral dissertation on the history of the Army, concluded that World War I "probably" marked "the climax of Salvation Army history in the United States."[10]

On the home front the Army was designated as one of several "auxiliary welfare agencies" authorized to operate canteens and "huts" at military training camps assigned to it by the YMCA. Activities at these stations varied, from enlisted men's clubs, in which lounges and reading rooms had to be maintained and entertainment and baked treats had to be provided, to full-scale soldier's hostels in which dining rooms and clean overnight lodging had to be supplied. There were evangelical services on Sunday in all the Army facilities, and in all of them the officers maintained the cheerful domestic atmosphere for which the rescue homes had long been famous (at least to their beneficiaries). Ninety-one such clubs operated at one time or another by the time the last of them was closed in 1919, after the Armistice. These clubs varied greatly in size. The largest was the Army "Hut" at Fort Dix, New Jersey, a major, multi-story structure that opened on November 21, 1918. Many others were small, part-time affairs. In fact, the Army lacked officer personnel for large-scale war work in the camps, and its contribution to the total home front war service in the First World War was not great. The Salvation Army cooperated fully with other agencies, avoiding all forms of sectarian competitiveness. It loaned its kettles and tripods to the Red Cross for fund-raising and distributed among the needy thousands of pieces of civilian clothing left at YMCA canteens by arriving military trainees. Although the Army was officially recognized as one of seven agencies — the "Seven Sisters" — that made up the Commission on Training Camp Activities, its share of the national budget was only 2.05 percent, the same as that of the Jewish Welfare Board and the American Library Association. There is nothing in this record to explain the impact of Salvation Army war service on the later history of the movement in the United States.[11]

The turning point came in France. The Army's war work there in 1917 and 1918 showed the movement at its old-time best — joyful, fearless, practical, and immediate. The spirit of the Great Salvation War was again brought before a sizable number of people who had forgotten, if they had ever known, the capacity for self-sacrifice of the Army pioneers.

The Commander appointed Lt. Col. William S. Barker to be the "pioneer to blaze the way for the work in France." The Commander's plan was typically simple: find the troops and "mother" them as resources permitted; details were left to the officers on the spot. Barker proved a remarkable choice. His headquarters position, while involving important responsibilities for the selection and purchase of properties, had been routine; the "Soldiers of the Soil" campaign was an additional duty. But service in France was an opportunity to play a part on the stage of great world events. Barker warmed to his exciting new assignment and set off for France in June 1917 in high spirits with Ensign Bertram Rodda as his assistant with the assignment of reconnoitering U.S. Army camps to learn where and how Salvation Army volunteers could be used most effectively.[12]

Barker presented his credentials, which consisted mostly of a general letter of introduction secured by Evangeline from President Wilson's private secretary to any official who would receive him in France. The American ambassador to France and the several other military and civilian officials whom he met were cordial but offered little encouragement: the government had granted a monopoly on welfare work to the YMCA, and while this grant was admittedly not absolute, nobody in authority could see anything special for The Salvation Army to do in France. Gen. John J. Pershing, the commander in chief of the AEF, was more helpful. He, too, understood that the YMCA was to be responsible for all of the kind of work the Army might do. But, unlike other officials in France, Pershing had a warm personal recollection of The Salvation Army. In 1915 his home at the Presidio in San Francisco had burned, killing his wife and family. The Army's provincial officer, Col. Henry Lee, had shown great personal interest and sympathy, as had many Salvationists, while the respectable Bay Area churches had somehow ignored the incident, failing to offer even perfunctory condolences to one who was not part of the local community. Pershing never forgot the Army's kindness, which touched him deeply. He decided after meeting Barker in August to allow The Salvation Army to open its own huts and offer whatever ministry it had in mind in the military district of the First Division.[13]

Evangeline borrowed $25,000 — and later another $100,000 — to finance the Army's war work, for which no other source of funds was at first available: certainly no corps or headquarters budget contained large extra sums for that — or any — purpose. In June 1917 the Army launched the "War Service League" and invited 500,000 people to join up. Each member would pledge fifty cents a month to Army war relief work and promise to pay encouraging visits to nearby military camps and produce knitwear and bandages for the troops. A subscription to a news sheet, the *War Service Herald,* was included in the membership fee. Barker returned to the United States and participated in an official send-off at national headquarters on August 10, along with a small contingent of eleven officers (seven men and four women) who were to sail two days later for France. Each was equipped with a special commission signed by Eva for "Service with the American Expeditionary Forces in France" and with an enthusiasm for service that was as yet undiluted by knowledge of the dangers of the front. Pershing ordered the Salvationists into regulation khaki-colored private's uniforms, with the red Salvation Army shield on caps and epaulettes. Barker spent the borrowed $25,000 on a large tent and a touring car. A quick tour of the district had already convinced the colonel that women were needed to carry on proper "mothering." He believed that the troops were already bored with the informal, "slangy" Christianity of the YMCA workers, all of whom were men, and yearned for respectable and sympathetic female companionship. Barker quickly wired home for more women officers.[14]

The Commander, at first surprised by this request, quickly perceived the wisdom behind it. The Army's officer ranks were promptly sifted for corps assistants, all single female officers in their twenties, and this number was augmented by soldier volunteers. Colonel McIntyre wrote to one appointee, Ensign Helen Purviance, that war work needed "a woman of your type, who is full of good horse sense and yet possessing those womanly qualities that are so helpful and attractive." He added, needlessly, that he did not consider the appointment to be a "soft snap." These indefatigable, warm-hearted, and adaptable women showed courage even in going to France. Few had ever been on the ocean before, and the terrible novelty of a first voyage was made more frightening by the knowledge that the dark, cold sea was infested with German submarines. Officers bound for France sent off mournful farewell telegrams to their families and boarded the troopships filled with dread. Their arrival in Bordeaux was thus doubly providential. There were never very many Salvation Army soldiers abroad during the war; Professor Wisbey concluded that the popularity of the Army's work in France was "greatly out of proportion to its quantity." There was a total of perhaps 250 Salvationists in war service in France, compared to over 10,000 YMCA workers. Yet the women transformed the Army's ministry, which at first was little different from that of the YMCA, into the uniquely welcome and long-remembered service that won The Salvation Army a special place in American life after the war.[15]

The Army carefully placed its huts in places where the YMCA had no work so as to avoid duplication in France as it had in camps at home. The first Army hut was at Demange. When women arrived, Army work became more popular with American troops. Of course there were several other reasons for this improvement in the Army's status, although the women were the major part of the explanation. Even before women Salvationists began to arrive in significant numbers, the Army huts had started to gain a loyal following on their own. The government provided the troops with nothing in the way of toilet articles, sweets, or writing materials. This service was regarded as part of the "welfare" for which civilian agencies were responsible. The Salvation Army charged either nothing for the kit items it offered to the men or prices far lower than those at YMCA counters. In addition, the Salvation Army freely offered credit not only to individuals who were short of funds but to entire companies whose pay was delayed. The terms for this credit were not rigorous: pay when you have it, no notes to sign, no interest added; if your unit is moved up before you get the money, give what you owe to any Salvationist anywhere. These policies gave the Army a reputation for open-handedness that spread from unit to unit. It hardly mattered to the American forces that the YMCA was chartered by the government and was expected to keep careful accounts of its finances, while The Salvation Army dispensed the bounty of its own loans, appeals, and street-corner collections; what mattered was that the Army gave items away or charged very little, while the YMCA seemed to be making a profit from its canteen sales.[16]

Nor was this all that mattered to the troops. The Salvation Army's interpretation of Christianity had wide appeal. The women officers and soldiers only enhanced this ministry; they did not create it. The Army was the Army, even in France. It remained staunchly evangelical. Attendance at Salvation Army religious services was in no way required of the men who availed themselves of the services of its huts, but those who chose to attend were presented with the gospel unvarnished: in Christ alone is life and hope. The music at these services was the same as one might hear at an Army corps on a Sunday evening back home: the taste of the doughboys ran to lively numbers such as those the Army had made famous on street corners across America — such favorites as "Brighten the Corner Where You Are," "When the Roll Is Called Up Yonder," and "The Battle Hymn of the Republic," accompanied by a piano and often a cornet. Fred Stillwell, son of the California pioneer, drove an Army canteen truck and played cornet in France. Occasionally a regimental band would play hymn tunes for a Salvation Army meeting. The troops appreciated the Army's straightforward approach to the Christian religion and the fact that Salvationists — men and women alike — did not drink, smoke, or use profanity and would not sell liquor or tobacco (although the Army did distribute gift packages of cigarettes to wounded men who asked for them). Many American soldiers were confused by the religious posture of the YMCA workers (viewing it as compromised by an irreverent tone) and the commercial practices of the YMCA huts. The leaders of the YMCA were aware of the widespread failure of the religious part of their service but were unable to recruit a sufficient number of committed Christians to offset it; faced with the need to find thousands of workers in a few months, the YMCA often settled for persons of merely "Christian character" who lacked formal church affiliation before coming to France.[17]

For all the genuine good it was doing, however, the Army would have remained merely one of several welfare agencies serving the troops in France had it not been for the "lassies" who "mothered" the troops by the thousands. The women received no formal instructions in what was expected of them in France; they simply served as the slum sisters had served before them, doing every useful, kindly thing that came to hand. They darned socks, sewed on buttons, wrote letters, kept money for the men, and sent it home for them via hometown corps officers. Regimental officers asked Salvation Army women rather than regular chaplains to break bad news to the younger men. One of the hardest jobs Helen Purviance had to do in France was to tell a seventeen-year-old soldier that his mother had died back home. The women sang at all the Army religious services — one doughboy's haunting memory of the war was of a young Army woman singing "a hymn" in a bombed-out church at the front on Good Friday, 1918. The Army women tidied up the hasty wartime graves and decorated them with wild flowers. And they baked. Above all, they baked.[18]

The role of the doughnut in the history of Salvation Army work in the First World War has survived in popular memory through to the end of the twentieth century. What Commander Evangeline liked to describe as "the winsome, attractive coquetries of the round, brown doughnut" practically eclipsed the rest of the Army's welfare service, and that of other agencies as well. Colonel Barker and four newly arrived lassies set out in the touring car in September 1917 looking for some boys to mother. Their plans were necessarily vague; no officer, including the colonel, had any training for war relief, and no instructions other than to make themselves "available and helpful." At Montiers they came upon the camp of the 1st Ammunition Train, 1st Division. The women piled out, set up a Victrola, and held a little service and sing-along. When they made as if to leave, the men, young and homesick, were reluctant to let them depart. Two of the officers, Ensign Helen Purviance and Ensign Margaret Sheldon, Purviance's assistant, suggested that the women would bake something "American" for the boys if they would let them go. This jolly offer was taken up with enthusiasm, but there were difficulties in the face of the original project, which was to make pies: no stoves, no proper pans, only a bit of flour, grease, baking powder, and sugar. The resourceful Sheldon, a former slum sister who was ready for anything, suggested that they make doughnuts. The noble work was performed by Adjutant Helen Purviance, who cut the dough into circles with the top of the baking-powder can and popped out the holes "with a camphor ice tube." Purviance offered the first hot item to an Alabama private, one Braxton Zuber, with the observation that if it did not kill him she would keep making doughnuts. Success! With a stroke, the Army's reputation was made. The doughnut proved ideally suited both to the insatiable craving of the troops for hot, fresh homemade treats and to field conditions in France, where the chronic shortage of field stoves, pans, and supplies made it difficult to produce

Capts. Geneva Ladd and Signa Saunders serve doughnuts to American soldiers during World War I. Source: The Salvation Army National Archives

more elaborate baked goods such as pies and cakes. Doughnuts could be produced in large numbers in lard melted in any sort of pot or bucket, placed over a fire built in a hole dug in the ground, while hot chocolate and coffee to go along could be made in galvanized trash cans heated over the same heat source.[19]

The doughnut ministry also included delivery. Here practicality combined with courage. When the AEF was ordered up to the front lines from its base camps, The Salvation Army volunteered to follow them. The Army placed its new huts and field kitchens as close to the fighting as the military authorities allowed. Salvationists often baked and sewed in the secondary trenches that connected the front to staging areas, and they often came under fire, literally dodging and ducking — and occasionally diving — to avoid shot and shell as they carried hot food to the men in combat. Several times Salvation Army canteen trucks were caught by German artillery and abandoned in the road — although daring sorties by hungry doughboys often rescued the contents before all was lost. Several Salvationists were gassed, and most suffered extreme fatigue, parasites, and nervous prostration, but only one died in service — Major Barnes, of pneumonia in 1918. Not only did most women refuse to allow the difficult conditions at the front to deter them, a few failed altogether to grasp the seriousness of the situation. Several of the doughnut girls dashed out of their dugout one day to see a German airplane, and in a moment of laughing high spirits shot at it with a borrowed rifle, thus exposing the whole position to unpleasant artillery fire. Most Salvationists, however, were aware that they were working in perpetual mortal danger and managed to smile only despite constant terror. Commandant Joseph Hughes, almost paralyzed with fear, unable to think, filled a car with goodies and drove it, eyes closed, hands clenched on the wheel, straight up to the front lines and into a surprised and delighted artillery company that cheered him as they continued firing away at the enemy.[20]

If all of this were not enough to endear The Salvation Army to the men in the ranks, the Army's policy toward military officers secured its popularity. The Army still regarded itself as the church of the working class and the poor; few financially successful or educated people had been drawn to it, except as supporters of its social welfare activities. In France the Army aligned itself officially with the enlisted men, much to their satisfaction. Officers were welcome, but they were not given precedence — an unusual policy in the conscript army of 1917. "Officers and soldiers take their places in the line," wrote a Salvationist in France, "as our work is particularly for the enlisted men." Evangeline regarded it as one of three "cardinal principles which were deemed necessary to success in this work" that Salvation Army personnel should share hardships with the enlisted men, eat with them in their messes, and associate with them rather than with the officers; the other two principles were "consistency" in religion and taking the Army's work into the actual fighting zone. She recounted with pride stories of Army officers who, in order to "stay with the boys," turned down invitations from regimental commanders to lunch at chateaux. Most American troops were new to military life and looked on the military caste system as a degrading and unpleasant novelty. These men especially relished the democratic policy of The Salvation Army.[21]

The Salvation Army had secured an official place for itself in American military life. On September 12, 1917, the U.S. army's Judge Advocate General declared officially that The Salvation Army was a denomination of the Christian Church, with its own "distinct legal existence," creed, form of worship, "ecclesiastical government," doctrines, discipline, ministers, and members — the first such legal recognition in the Army's history in America. The declaration made Salvation Army officers exempt from the draft; far more importantly, it meant that they could be enlisted as chaplains with formal military commissions. Five officers served as chaplains during World War I. The first was Ensign Harry Kline of the Omaha Industrial Home, who was appointed chaplain to a Nebraska National Guard regiment with the military rank of first lieutenant. Kline was the first Salvation Army officer to become an official military chaplain; interestingly, he had been one of several young Salvationists among the American troops in the Philippines during the Spanish-American War and had often supported Major Milsaps's efforts in Manila in 1898. The other Army chaplains were John Allan, Ernest R. Holz (son of the famous colonel and father of two later commissioners, one of them a national commander), Norman Marshall (who would later become a national commander and the father of another), and J. A. Ryan. There was also one "unofficial chaplain," Maj. John E. Atkins. Sent to France as a hut worker, Atkins set up shop in the camp of the 26th Infantry, commanded by Maj. Theodore Roosevelt, son of the former president. When the unit was ordered into the trenches, the courageous Atkins closed his kitchen and followed them, offering spiritual counsel, caring for the wounded, bringing treats, and running errands behind the lines for men who could not leave their posts. He was enormously popular.[22]

In fact, the whole Salvation Army was enormously popular. Company officers, who had to censor all homeward-bound mail from enlisted personnel, noticed that praise of The Salvation Army appeared more and more frequently. Soldiers wrote to their families and friends back home extolling the Army for its frontline service. "It is always in the places where the boys need help and the closest hut to the lines you'll find is the Salvation Army." By 1918 the current of tributes had become a flood, which a surprised military general brought to the attention of the *New York Times* in October. Salvationists in the United States were at first modestly surprised at the spreading news about the success of their comrades' work in France: had the Army not always "reduced the theory of Christianity to action"? Had it not always waged its own salvation war in the front lines of sin? Modest surprise turned to delight as the home front public's approbation took on a practical form: the grudging trickle of pennies and nickels upon which the Army had eked out its beneficial existence now became a golden stream. The Army's begging and borrowing days were over. Fund-raising drives were oversubscribed by large amounts. In the spring of 1918 The Salvation Army asked the country for the then-unheard of sum of one million dollars for its war work — and $2,370,000 was donated! A later campaign, conducted jointly with other war relief agencies, was interrupted by the armistice in November. The Commander was elated, declaring that the Army now had excellent references for its mammoth fund-raising projects: "The average man in the trenches — the military authorities at headquarters" — even the president and the secretary of war![23]

The Army's prospects on the home front were clearly improving. It is true that the Commander had been forced to brave certain difficulties in connection with the Army's war work. She was convinced at one point that German spies, thinly disguised as "women," had tried to penetrate national headquarters late one night as she sat at her desk, planning the Army's war relief strategy. A fire later at the training college, next door to national headquarters, was attributed to saboteurs: national headquarters was certainly their next target. Thus alerted, Evangeline had cleverly avoided giving a direct answer to a hotel porter's question about Salvationist work in France: another spy! Still, these dangers proved fleeting, and the excitement bubbled away, to be replaced by the greater and more lasting thrill of triumph that seemed to presage a new day — a new era — for The Salvation Army in America. The newspapers were full of war news, mail homeward from the front glittered with praise for the Army, and support for the movement from the American public, based now on sentiments both grateful and patriotic, grew daily warmer and more widespread. Old friends such as John Wanamaker, who as a director of the War Welfare Council had a "particularity for the Salvation Army which he did not conceal," were joined by many new ones. The war occupied an increasing portion of the Commander's attention. The public seemed to expect so much, and there was so much to do.[24]

In addition to its operations in France, The Salvation Army administered a burgeoning military welfare program throughout the country. The Army gave away thousands of "camp kits" filled with the toilet articles that the government did not provide. The *War Service Herald* was distributed in the camps. The "War Service League" enlisted corps Salvationists and outside volunteers to contribute funds toward Salvation Army war work and to serve as home-front auxiliaries, visiting wounded veterans in hospitals, bringing good or bad news to families, and knitting warm clothing. Eventually 31,000 people joined the War Service League, all busily knitting socks, helmet liners, and scarves. Such a large quantity of knitted material was produced that the Army had to donate twelve Ford ambulances to the military in France to facilitate delivery of the warm things to the men at the front. And if providing these practical blessings was not enough to keep the Army busy, its leaders conducted a national publicity campaign calling for the prohibition of alcoholic beverages in the United States for the duration of the war. Beer was denounced for being hardly less German than the Kaiser's mustache, and it was argued that the elimination of distilled liquor would conserve precious grain and sugar. Prohibition would preserve the morals not only of the troops but of the country as a whole during these stressful times, and the curse of drunkenness would cease at a stroke. A cause the Army had advocated for years now became patriotic and popular — like the Army itself.[25]

Difficulties seemed to evaporate one after another. It is true of course that each of the Army's war projects cost money; each new project placed an additional drain on funding for the Army's regular evangelical and social welfare programs, all of which continued as before. In May 1917, still early in the war, for instance, the Eastern Territory staged a massive congress in Philadelphia, the "cradle" of Salvationism in the United States. The commander placed a plaque on the site of the Shirleys' triumphs thirty-seven years before, and Col. R. E. Holz led the crowd in singing "We're Bound for the Land of the Pure and the Holy." Colonel Brengle assured Salvationists that successful revivals could and should be held in wartime, and a national spiritual campaign was conducted in 1918. These activities, too, had to be financed. The work of the men's industrial homes was curtailed as a result of sharp declines in clients, public funding, and donations of salvage materials (it was suddenly patriotic to collect old newspapers for the war effort, reducing the Army's share of that important market). A number of industrial homes were closed, not all of them small or marginal: in April 1918, the Army closed and offered for lease the largest industrial home in the United States, New York No. 1.[26]

Indeed, the extra burden of the war work staggered the Army initially, and the Commander cast about desperately for ways to increase revenue. She first borrowed large sums and asked the hard-pressed corps and divisional headquarters for increased support; next she turned to the War Service League; finally, the daring million-dollar campaign of 1918 was launched, which meant a large extra workload for many officers. Then the golden tide began to flow. Evangeline had been confident from the beginning, when some of her staff had argued against the first loan, that the American public would support The Salvation Army's war work once it was underway and they came to see that the Salvationists in France counted life less than duty and would make any sacrifice for the AEF. She was right. Sums that would have dazzled officers in 1915 now came to be regarded as too modest, almost a refutation of faith in God's bounty. By the time of the Armistice, November 11, 1918, The Salvation Army seemed to have passed forever beyond the necessity of begging in the streets and taverns to finance its war on sin. Confident in the grateful affection of tens of thousands of returning doughboys, who had promised the lassies in France that they would "always have a good word" for the Army, Evangeline opened the Army's first peacetime national appeal in May 1919. She asked for enough money to run every part of the Army's program except the corps; the money would finance the "maintenance, supervision and the extension of the work," pay off all mortgages, buy new buildings, and cover all general and headquarters expenses. Called the "Home Service Fund," the national campaign asked the public for the astronomical sum of thirteen million dollars. The Fund was launched at a mass rally held in Madison Square Garden, at which Vice President Thomas D. Marshall, New York's Gov. Al Smith, and a host of other dignitaries spoke in glowing terms of the Army and a popular new song was sung — "Salvation Lassie o' Mine." The campaign was a huge success.[27]

The Armistice did not bring an end to Salvation Army service to the American troops: Salvationists continued to minister in all the old ways to the thousands gathering in staging camps waiting to be shipped home, and young Army women waited with coffee and doughnuts to greet returning troopships. The men who disembarked from these ships had very little time at dockside before they were put on trains for demobilization camps; as a result, many could not telegraph their families with the welcome news that they were safe at home. The Salvation Army women provided this service thousands of times, taking the names and addresses of the men as they waited in line for the trains, then sending the telegrams in batches. The Army also operated huts and "rest rooms" in the demobilization camps themselves. Nevertheless, November 1918 was the high-water mark, and The Salvation Army wound down its war work as rapidly as the federal government discharged its victorious troops. Even so, the public's new affection for the Army did not dissipate. A new day had arrived, for the Army no less than for the country. *The War Cry* announced new projects of the "utmost value to the county."[28]

The postwar decade began with Salvation Army officers in a confident mood. The signs were certainly encouraging. The "Salvation Lass" had become "a kind of doughboy's goddess" whose name, "sure of gaining the loudest applause," was enshrined already in popular song ("Salvation Lassie o' Mine" was, in fact, only one of perhaps a dozen ephemeral musical tributes to the Army that appeared in the postwar years), poetry, and on the bow of at least one freighter — the *SS Salvation Lass*. The Army was officially invited to send five delegates to the lavish patriotic ceremonies held in Washington to honor the Unknown Soldier on Armistice Day in 1921; the Salvationists were instructed by their headquarters to wear their official war-service "overseas uniform." A war-time photograph of Stella Young, wearing a smile of truly heroic proportions and holding a large pan of fresh doughnuts, was widely used for publicity purposes after the war and became famous. The Army's "nightmare of finance" was over: "The Salvation Army will probably never again appeal in vain for popular support." Other old battles had been won, too. Wartime prohibition became permanent in January 1919, when Congress ratified the Eighteenth Amendment to the Constitution. The saloon — that nest of devils and old-time provoker of police attacks — suddenly disappeared from the scene. Progress was evident everywhere. The Army adopted a new slogan in 1919 and a new ethnic ministry. Elmore Leffingwell, the publicity director of the Home Service Fund campaign (and the author of the words of a briefly popular song called, appropriately, "Don't Forget The Salvation Army") is credited with coining the phrase "A man may be down, but he's never out" as a new slogan for the Army's social programs. (The line may have come originally from Bruce Barton, the famous publicist.) Like such cherished pioneer mottos as "the Great Salvation War," the new slogan embodied the spirit of the Army perfectly. And in California, the Army "opened fire" on the Japanese community with all its old-time blare and fervor.[29]

The Salvation Army had periodically thrown out the lifeline to California's growing Japanese population since 1896, when the "Articles of War" were hopefully translated into that language. In 1898 the Army opened a mission to reach the Japanese in the Hawaiian Islands. A Lieutenant Loxton, who spoke Japanese, was sent from San Francisco to Honolulu to start the work in August of that year. The mission promptly folded but was reopened permanently in 1920. Real success in establishing a Japanese branch of the Army came in 1919, when Masasuke Kobayashi turned his admirably disciplined zeal to the task. Kobayashi was a Presbyterian minister and general secretary of the Japanese interdenominational Board of Missions in California when he came under the powerful influence of Col. Gunpei Yamamuro. The founder of the Salvation Army in Japan, Yamamuro had earned a well-deserved reputation as one of Japan's Christian statesmen and was twice decorated by the Emperor. Kobayashi admired the work of the colonel from afar for years and in 1917 arranged a series of revival meetings for him among California's Japanese. In two weeks — all the time the colonel, en route to London, could allow — 842 Japanese were converted. Kobayashi was astounded and became convinced that The Salvation Army could win the Japanese in America for Christ. He and his wife resolved to begin the work and abandoned all that home and career could offer to sail for the Army training college in Yokohama. The pioneers returned to California on July 24, 1919, accompanied by two officers from Japan, and were joined by three Japanese-American converts from the Chicago training school. These seven visited every Japanese home in San Francisco. Five hundred Japanese attended the official opening of the Army's Japanese Corps in the United States, in San Francisco on August 16, 1919. Los Angeles followed in September, Fresno in October, and Stockton by Christmas.[30]

Ensign Kobayashi was a dedicated evangelical whose preaching brought gratifying results. An indefatigable worker, he was gifted with the ability to win and hold the loyalty of subordinates, a quality without which no officer could succeed in command of Japanese workers. Within 17 months, 12 officers, 18 noncommissioned officers (called "local officers" in the Army), and 208 soldiers had enlisted in the Japanese Salvation Army, and a special rest home had been established in San Francisco for ailing Japanese, who fell prey to charlatans in disproportionate numbers because of their fears of Western medicine. Kobayashi faced several obstacles. Although regarded at first as something of a home-mission field — Gen. Bramwell Booth donated an initial $5,000 from headquarters' funds — the Japanese corps were required to be self-supporting as soon as possible, on the same basis as other corps. Officers were frugal, however, and fund-raising among the hospitable Japanese was seldom the major obstacle to progress. There were two more significant difficulties, however. One was associated with the tendency of the Japanese to view themselves not merely as individuals but as members of families that stretched generations into the past. They were especially sensitive to the wishes of their parents. To sever all ties with one's family was difficult enough for Occidentals; for Japanese it represented a sense of loss that was almost unendurable. Yet any Japanese who contemplated conversion to Christianity — a religion regarded by many older Japanese as illogical, weak-minded, and above all foreign — had to face just such a loss. Beyond this, joining The Salvation Army entailed wearing an outlandish uniform and parading in the streets behind a brass band, which for the Japanese amounted not merely to an abandonment but to a humiliation of one's family and a sacrifice of personal dignity as well. It was a supreme sacrifice. Every Japanese Salvationist was thus not only a trophy of grace but a monument to courage.[31]

The other difficulty faced by Japanese Salvationists came with an increase in anti-Japanese sentiment on the West Coast in the 1920s. Although this unhappy sentiment was not so widespread in this period as it would become in the years surrounding the Second World War, it accounted for the first public hostility toward the national background of Salvationists that had surfaced since the excitement over Ballington's resignation twenty-five years earlier. The Japanese Salvationists' response is therefore of considerable interest to the historian of the movement. Brian Hayashi, working with documents Kobayashi wrote in Japanese in Tokyo in 1933, has shown that the leader of Japanese Salvationism in America developed an official policy to help his troops cope with public rejection based on their nationality. Kobayashi called this *Choteiko Shugi,* "the Principle of Super Resistance," patterned on the passive resistance of the Savior. "Super Resistance" had three components: "personality," "moral character," and "capability." These three together constituted the best in Japanese character, and Kobayashi contended "openly" that the Japanese

Salvationist's best defense against racial misunderstanding was to exhibit these qualities in the face of every difficulty.[32]

The Japanese ministry prospered on the Golden Shore despite these difficulties. Corps were opened in Sacramento in 1920, the same year that Capt. and Mrs. Soichi Ozaki were sent from San Francisco to commence operations (again) in the Hawaiian Islands. The Visalia corps was pioneered in 1921, and on November 6 of that year a full-fledged Japanese divisional headquarters was dedicated in San Francisco by none other than the elderly Commissioner Booth-Tucker, assisted by the new territorial commander and various civic and Japanese dignitaries. A Japanese post was opened in Seattle in 1922, and in Oakland in 1923. Like every Army event in Oakland, the movement's premier city in the West, the opening of the new Japanese corps there was enthusiastic and supported by "the famous Oakland No. 1 Band, who rendered most delightful service." By 1924, when San Jose was launched, the Japanese ministry boasted, in addition to the nine Japanese corps and the Home of Rest, a medical clinic, children's home, and day-care center in San Francisco, a summer camp near Seattle, and a Japanese-language version of *The War Cry* with a weekly circulation of five thousand. The success of the Japanese division seemed assured. Many West Coast officers came to share Kobayashi's prediction — once regarded as commendably overly enthusiastic — that the Army *would* save America's Japanese.[33]

The Salvation Army's commitment to its "strong Scandinavian work in America" continued into the peacetime era as well. The Army claimed to have eighty Scandinavian corps in the United States in 1919, almost all of them Swedish. In 1920 Scandinavian ranks were joined by Fritz Nelson, an officer in the U.S. Merchant Marine who became a Salvation Army officer. In 1919 Nelson had founded the Christian Mariners of the World, an organization "to promote the principles of Christianity among the seafarers." The embryo of the Christian Mariners organization was thus brought into The Salvation Army; Fritz, energetic and persuasive, overcame all obstacles in lobbying Army leaders to officially adopt his idea for a special mission to seamen. In 1927 The Salvation Army Mariners' League was formally inaugurated "as an Official Branch of the International Organization." The league's founder was Ensign Fritz Nelson; its announced motto was "Truth, Justice, Courage, and Temperance," and it was intended to "organize all Christian mariners" for the purpose of fellowship, worship, and wholesome recreation (which seems to have meant mostly singing and eating). The program was aimed at Christian

Scandinavian sailors in American ports. Nelson was able to attract notable endorsements for his program. In 1927 the famed Norwegian explorer Roald Amundsen joined the league as an "honorary member." Two years later, after the Mariners' League had been renamed, it secured an even more newsworthy endorsement: Commander Richard E. Byrd, preparing for his famous flight over the South Pole, was besieged by over 1,500 requests to take various emblems and flags with him, but in the end he took only the flag of The Salvation Army Naval and Military League and his own college fraternity pin.[34]

By 1920 the Great Salvation War had seen many battles won. The Salvation Army was popular, and while some officers had been warning since the 1890s that success brought special dangers of its own, the consequent easing of the long-standing financial strain was welcomed by all. The Army had acquired millions of dollars in property and had created in the Home Service Fund the machinery for collecting millions more on an annual basis. A regular retirement program for officers was established on August 30, 1919, calling for mandatory retirement at certain ages with a pension after a required period of service. The training of Salvation Army officers was strengthened by the purchase of new facilities in the Bronx, Chicago, and San Francisco; there were 450 cadets in training by middecade. The years 1916-1926 saw the Army's greatest growth in relative terms for any comparable period in the twentieth century, and the greatest for a similar period since the pioneer decade of 1880-1890. The trend toward Army ownership of corps facilities continued as well; by the mid-1920s the proportion had reached 63 percent. Roughly equal in property value to the corps facilities were the Army's 239 social service institutions, 3 training colleges and territorial headquarters buildings, and 30 camps.[35]

There had been indications before the war that the growing complexity of Salvation Army operations, spread over the huge territory of the United States (the vastness of which continued to astonish European Salvationist visitors), put a strain on national headquarters that the creation of a deputy commander in Chicago in 1904 had only partially and temporarily relieved. A further division of administrative responsibility was required. The end of the war made it possible to effect the change, which the Commander welcomed — for, in addition to its other benefits, the new structure would enable her to reward several faithful senior officers with commands and higher rank. Gen. Bramwell Booth may also have contemplated transferring the Commander to another position elsewhere in the Army empire; the new administrative structure would make any transition go more smoothly.

In October 1920, three separate territorial commands were created, and the historic dominance of national headquarters came to an end. The leaders of the new commands were still "directly responsible" to the Commander but had considerable independent authority of their own. The position of national chief secretary was ended (although it was revived after World War II; each territory was given a chief secretary of its own. Col. Walter Jenkins replaced Comm. William Peart as second-in-command to Evangeline Booth in 1920 and was called "national secretary." A study of The Salvation Army conducted for the Rockefeller Foundation in 1924 found that only matters of "large importance" were referred to national headquarters, which had "a very small staff of but ten and administers no activities." Except for the few matters directly handled by the Commander's office, the routine administration of The Salvation Army was now in the hands of the three territorial commanders. These officers could either take action on their own or agree with their peers on a common policy. The territorial commanders and selected staff officers began to hold annual meetings at national headquarters in order to discuss common problems and plan national strategies. The first of these Commissioners' Conferences, which continue to the present day, was held on January 3-4, 1921. The new territorial command units were the Eastern territory, under Comm. Thomas Estill, who since 1908 had skillfully commanded the old Department of the West; the Central territory, still headquartered in Chicago, under Commissioner Peart, who had been serving as national chief secretary since 1905; and the new Western territory, under the command of Lt. Comm. Adam Gifford, the heroic pioneer who, as a young captain, had lacked the few dollars to pay for his infant's grave. Gifford came to San Francisco, the new territorial headquarters, from Boston, where he had served since 1908 as provincial commander. All three of the new commissioners were officers of exceptional experience and ability. The apportionment of states within the new territories was mostly based on geographical proximity and had little historic significance: the East comprised the Union east of Indiana, from Canada to the Gulf Coast; the Central ran from Indiana to the Dakotas, including Texas, Oklahoma, Arkansas, and Louisiana; the West included Montana, Idaho, and the nine western states.[36]

The War Cry had grown more sedate by 1920. While it maintained a militant form of reporting about the salvation war, the "jubilee boomlets" and "small-shot" of pioneer days were seen no more in its pages. The

Billings, Montana, band, 1923
Source: Western Territorial Museum

change did not obstruct a great increase in circulation stimulated by the Army's war work, publicity for the Home Service Fund, and the increase in Army membership, however: weekly circulation almost tripled from 70,000 in 1918 to 200,000 in 1920. The bulk of the issues continued to be distributed through individual sales rather than subscriptions. Corps officers were still expected to boost *The War Cry;* circulation contests were part of a "drive that never ends," and this despite the announcement in October 1920 that the price of the magazine had to be increased — doubled, in fact, to a dime — to compensate for higher production costs. The new territorial commands began to produce *War Cry* editions of their own. The Western territory had sponsored a Pacific coast version since 1883, while national headquarters had published the American *War Cry* since January 15, 1881. The Pacific coast edition now became *The War Cry,* Western Territorial Edition — the new "white winged messenger of the West" — on January 1, 1921. The new Eastern and Central territorial editions appeared on the same date.[37]

Although staff officers knew that behind all of these gratifying developments certain difficulties were developing between New York and London headquarters, these were unknown to the rank-and-file Salvationists and had no effect on the Army's work. Commander Evangeline's public references to her brother, Gen. Bramwell Booth, were infrequent and unexceptional. Privately, the Commander regarded her relationship to her brother as anything but encouraging. She and Bramwell had shared an abiding affection for the now-glorified Founder; of the Booth children, these two had been closest to the old General. Beyond that and a thorough-going commitment to the evangelical purposes of the Army, however, they had little in common and were, in fact, suspicious of one another.

Bramwell must have felt that once the war was over he could safely transfer the Commander; the triple-territorial reform may have been part of that overall plan. After all, by 1920 Evangeline had been national commander in the United States — the Army's premier appointment, excepting only the Generalship itself — for sixteen years. The difficulty was, of course, that she did not wish to be transferred. Furthermore, she disliked being ordered about by Bramwell as much as her brother Balling-ton had. Unlike Ballington, though, Evangeline was absolutely loyal to The Salvation Army and apparently never considered setting herself up in a rival organization. She was in a strong position. She did not have to threaten resignation or schism: the war work and the Home Service Fund — and after 1920 the territorial fund drives that replaced it — along with the new Advisory Board system and its new Community Chest support made the American branch of the Army the richest and most powerful in the world, and Evangeline Booth — patriotic, winsome, and fiercely evan-gelical — was its living symbol. Rumors that her transfer was being con-sidered produced cyclones of protest from the American public. One such flurry occurred in 1922, when the national convention of Elks cabled Bramwell that Eva had become the "angelic personification" of all the Army stood for in America.[38]

The General could, however, insist on small concessions: when he reappointed the Commander in 1924 to another three years in America, he took from her the right to approve any promotions beyond the rank of staff captain or to approve medium-level territorial headquarters ap-pointments without submitting them to international headquarters for ratification. This did not leave her without resources in making promo-tions, however. The Army possessed an impressive array of ranks in 1924; three had been added in recent years (commandant in 1916, lieutenant commissioner in 1920, and field major in 1923), and none of the old favorites had been eliminated, so that there were thirteen different slots from commissioner to lieutenant, seven of them from staff captain down. Evangeline nevertheless resented the orders about promotion and staff appointments and treated the new restrictions as mere formalities. These small concessions aside, the General could not, without wrecking the Army in America, transfer her if she insisted in public on staying. At the time, Bramwell Booth could not have been certain that his sister would not refuse outright to obey an order, although from our perspective today it appears that such a refusal would have been extremely unlikely. But she might have succumbed to "nervous prostration" under the strain of what she interpreted as her brother's enmity and jealousy; or the issue might have been raised again of London's attempts to "Anglicize" the American branch of the Army; or the matter of the General's "autocratic" powers, or his "dynastic" susceptibilities — the suspicion (which has never been substantiated) that he planned to name his daughter Comm. Catherine Bramwell Booth to be his successor — might have been broadcast through the American newspapers. And the results of any of these courses of action would have been as disastrous as an outright refusal to obey an order.[39]

Territorial-level staff officers knew of the unfortunate state of affairs between the General and the Commander — her letters to the territorial commanders were remarkably frank; she even devised a code name for Bramwell ("Brown") and herself ("Cory") — and a few lower-level officers guessed. Most officers and soldiers, however, knew nothing of these matters. When the breach between New York and London began to widen and occasionally became public, the rank and file were shocked or refused to believe that anything could seriously divide two such trusted leaders.[40]

In March 1925, the first of several "manifestos" appeared (by an odd coincidence, they arrived simultaneously at many Army headquarters in Britain and America) signed by "W. L. Atwood," supposedly a soldier at the Wichita Falls, Texas, corps but apparently written by another hand. These statements denounced the General as an autocrat and a dynast and demanded on the one hand that he relinquish the privilege of naming his own successor, and on the other that he give vastly increased independent powers to Commander Evangeline Booth and the American branch of The Salvation Army. Once the danger was past that the Commander would be transferred in the foreseeable future, the chief grievance of those who publicly upbraided the General was his undoubted legal right to name the next General, as he had himself been named by the Founder. This was a grievance, however, that affected only the Commander and those in her circle whom loyalty or interest prompted to support her. The rank and file continued to celebrate the General's birthday as an Army holiday, and in 1923 E. Irena Arnold, something of an official Army poet, composed a birthday poem to the General entitled "Oh, America Is Loyal." The work of the Army, which as always was carried on by the faithful field and social officers and their soldiers, progressed at an encouraging rate as the roaring twenties unfolded.[41]

The decade opened auspiciously enough in 1920, when The Salvation Army was asked to contribute a brass band to the annual Rose Bowl Parade in Pasadena. The Army was in a great many parades in the 1920s — particularly those held to commemorate Memorial Day, the Fourth of July, or Armistice Day. The theme of the Army float or entry was almost always the same: a sign on the Army's truck-bed display in a 1923 Nashville parade declared that "Some say it was the doughnut, But the Boys know that it was the Spirit Behind It." In Hattiesburg, Mississippi, the Army's entry in the 1927 Armistice Day parade was an enormous coffee cup on a Model-T Ford flatbed, while in 1925 in Shreveport The Salvation Army distributed doughnuts along the parade route from a float helpfully marked with a sign that read, "Salvation Army. Just a Reminder." The doughnut was rapidly becoming the new symbol of the Army. When Col. Edward Parker asked a professional artist for a proposal for a Salvation Army exhibit for the 1926 Philadelphia Sesquicentennial Exposition, he was presented with a sketch of a huge lassie holding high a doughnut: Parker was horrified to discover that the artist assumed that The Salvation Army had begun in France as a doughnut-making crusade![42]

The Army remained highly popular among veterans' groups. The Commander, who had been decorated with the Distinguished Service Medal in 1919 for the Army's contribution to the war effort, was no doubt gratified by the handwritten inscription on a photograph of General Pershing that she received from him May 1921: "To Commander Evangeline Booth, the members of whose Army gave such generous aid and comfort to their brothers in the A.E.F. Much high esteem and sincere regards." The Army was given a place of honor in the parade and ceremonies that were held to commemorate the Unknown Soldier in Washington on Armistice Day, 1921. Booth was correct in telling a huge ten-year convocation of the American Legion in 1927 that The Salvation Army's "substantially bettered financial condition, and the unqualified blessings of the people we enjoy today under the Stars and Stripes" were largely due to the support of veterans. The boosters, too — those civic and fraternal organizations that drew upon so much of the loyalty and energy of middle-class Americans in the twenties — took up the cause of The Salvation Army with lively enthusiasm. Many of the members of these clubs were grateful veterans; in addition, the Army's practical and efficient community services, combined with the familiar trappings of homespun Protestant religion, appealed to the booster ethic of the time. The Elks, Eagles, Rotarians, and members of the Lions, Kiwanis, and the Civitan Club in towns from Passaic to Santa Monica put their energetic hands to the Army's wheel, raising funds for new buildings, donating Ford touring cars, and providing legions of bellringers for annual Christmas kettle campaigns. Older officers who could still remember the hailstorm of abuse that greeted the Army in the 1880s reflected wonderingly on "the great change" that had come about. Officers hastened for the first time to join civic clubs, and territorial and divisional budgets began to include officers' club dues as a regular item.[43]

The golden glow of public approval in which The Salvation Army basked in these years was too widespread to come from civic clubs alone and too valuable to the Army as a resource for any important portion of the good will to be overlooked for long. In January 1920 the Army established the local "Advisory Board System," which was designed to enlist local professionals and business and civic leaders to provide the Army's field officers with advice on local business decisions and useful contacts for fund-raising purposes. Board members were usually willing contributors themselves as well. The advisory board system was well suited to channel community support for The Salvation Army, and it rapidly developed into one of the most important of all Salvation Army support systems. Within one year there were advisory boards in 1,500 counties in 24 states; Army leaders decided at their first commissioners' conference in January 1921 that the advisory board "in principle was generally conceded to be good as in practice the institution has proved its value." By 1925 Col. Richard Holz was happy to declare that there was "an army of not less than 20,000 business and professional men . . . linked to The Salvation Army" as advisory board members.[44]

Field officers and soldiers were gratified by the new popularity of the Army, based though much of it might have been on doughnuts, especially when they needed to raise money, but they did not allow themselves to be deflected from their zeal for souls. Evangelism remained the Army's chief purpose, and the Great Salvation War raged on. A reviewer in an important social-service journal warned its readers in 1924 that anyone "who would understand the Salvation Army must first realize that its uncompromising aim is the salvation of souls." A new edition of *Orders and Regulations for Officers* declared that the "ingenuity of the all-alive officer, inspired by the Holy Spirit" should always be at work devising new "attractions [to draw] fresh people — at first out of curiosity." Open-air meetings remained the Army's most reliable "attraction": there were over 200,000 such outdoor meetings in 1926. Many corps continued to have six such meetings each week; the standard corps schedule called for an open-air on Saturday night, when large numbers of city dwellers were out window shopping. There were three street meetings on Sunday. The weekend open-air meetings were preceded by a lively street parade, with all the soldiers marching behind the band, jingling tambourines, firing volleys, and singing militant songs unchanged from the days of pioneer warfare — the official anthem of the Army's national revival crusade in 1925 was "Storm the Forts." In 1921 and 1922 Capt. Rheba Crawford conducted open-air meetings from the side steps of the Gaiety Theatre on Forty-Sixth Street in New York City. The captain was a strikingly beautiful woman whose presentations drew large — at times enormous — crowds. Although her dress and theology were unorthodox (so much so that the Army soon felt it necessary to order her on a "rest furlough"), her unique ministry lasted long enough to win the heart of the young reporter Walter Winchell, and through his good offices to win for Captain Crawford a kind of immortality as the "doll" from the "Save-a-Soul Mission" in Damon Runyon's classic short story "The Idyll of Miss Sarah Browne." It was this story that, combined with another Runyon sketch, "Pick the Winner," gave Frank Loesser the inspiration for the popular musical comedy *Guys and Dolls*.[45]

Other established methods besides the open-air ministry survived or were revived in a new guise. In the West the Charioteers appeared again in 1922 and 1923, this time in a motor bus. The six officers, all in special trooper uniforms, displayed the old-time horse-drawn zeal as their gypsy mission traversed California. On a smaller scale, Capt. Fred Brewer of East St. Louis carried the gospel to mining camps in a Model-T Ford truck covered with such inspiring slogans as "Where Will You Spend Eternity?" The campaign saved 120 souls, and the captain earned special commendation in *The War Cry* for "this wide-awake method."[46]

Nor was Brewer alone in inventiveness. In November 1922 Commissioner Gifford, in goggles and scarf, flew from San Francisco to Sacramento in a DeHaviland U.S. Army observation plane, the first Salvation Army officer to use air transport on official business. Other leaders eyed Gifford's daring with misgivings: "Don't risk too much," warned the Commander on the eve of the big flight. But Gifford enjoyed the experi-

Cadet William Maltby leads singing in an open-air meeting held by cadets in 1921.
Source: Col. William Maltby (R)

ence hugely, and vainly urged his nervous colleagues to indulge in air travel. Innovation was in the air. The automobile did not immediately replace the horse in Army work, of course. The ice and coal ministry depended on horses throughout the decade, and the Army's industrial homes used wagons until 1946. A sufficient number of officers acquired cars, however, that the Army had to issue a special memorandum: cars must be modest, black, and inexpensive to operate. Radio, the popular wonder of the decade, was also pressed into service in the salvation war. In 1922 the Chicago Staff Band began playing over station WDAP, broadcasting from atop the Drake Hotel.[47]

The Army was advancing socially as well as technologically. A new generation of Salvationists arose. Saved drunkards and rescued roughnecks had always shared the ranks of the Army with a majority of conventionally respectable working-class persons, but by the mid-1920s even the image of soldiership was changing. Many second-generation Salvationists now attended high school. Ensign Wesley Bouterse assured this new class of soldiers that the Army understood that the temptations that faced them were as real as those that faced the saved miners and millhands of former days. There were even a few Salvationists who ventured beyond high school into the rarified atmosphere of college. At this development, so completely unforeseen by the pioneers, some veteran officers feared the worst and expressed their alarm: how could the guileless faith of the Army withstand the disdain of higher culture, the criticism of sophisticated academics? Desertion of the disillusioned young person would be the inevitable result. If teenaged soldiers in their charge still insisted on higher education, officers urged them to reflect on the benefits of small, rural, Christian colleges in which faith and holiness would be part of the course of instruction. Especially favored in this regard was tiny Asbury College in Wilmore, Kentucky, a hospitable little institution near Lexington. Its doctrinal foundation in Wesleyan holiness made it especially congenial to The Salvation Army. The saintly Brengle, still the National Spiritual Special, spoke several times in the college auditorium.[48]

The fear that educated officers and soldiers would shrink from the ardors of warfare fortunately proved groundless; yet such fears were not unnatural. The life demanded of a Salvationist remained hard, with few tangible rewards. The career of a social officer required years of relentless sacrifice. At the same time, the constantly increasing welfare programs administered by the corps frequently threw the newly respectable soldiers into the company of the socially undesirable sorts from which some at least of the first generation of Salvationists had been drawn. Despite these problems, the Army's social programs grew and became more diversified in the 1920s.

Alongside the services provided by the Army's regular social institutions, a large number of corps offered special social welfare services of one sort or another addressing a wide range of human needs. The help offered was typically immediate and practical: a day-work employment service to connect needy individuals with local odd jobs; the loan or gift of small sums to purchase kerosene, coal, or food; a warm cup of coffee, soup, and a place to sleep; simple, kindly family counseling; sheltering (and helping to trace) runaways; and directing especially desperate persons to Salvation Army institutions better equipped to provide long-term attention. Nor was this beneficence dispensed only at the corps: the League of Mercy, founded in Chicago in 1905, flourished after the war. Its members were corps personnel who brought many forms of kindness — baked goods, reading materials, flowers, kind words — to nursing home residents, prison inmates, and asylum patients. In 1928 these short-term welfare services were extended to areas in which there were no Army corps, through the creation of the Rural Service Units, the first of which was in Bennington, Vermont. Groups of local volunteers would collect and distribute social relief funds in the Army's name, or an employee from divisional headquarters would oversee the operation of one or several service units.[49]

And yet the heart of the Army's social welfare program did not lay in short-term, small-scale activities on the local level, however welcome these might have been to the recipients. The regular social institutions of The Salvation Army offered both social and spiritual redemption and assistance; their programs were not only ameliorative but provided rehabilitation designed to lead the beneficiary to a permanent change. Social officers met together on a regular basis to discuss problems common to their branch of the Army. The necessity of centering every welfare program on Christ was emphasized at these large meetings, at the same time that new techniques — new means to the traditional redemptive end — were freely discussed. The Salvation Army social program prospered in the 1920s; old programs were strengthened, and new institutions were built. After the armistice in 1918, the Army opened a number of new hotels for men, partly to accommodate discharged servicemen. Named after the site of a major American victory in the war, the "Argonne hotels" were designed for respectable laborers who wanted clean, secure, convenient, and economical lodgings; they were not intended as a form of social welfare. By the mid-1920s the Army operated seventy-nine hotels of different types for men, an additional nineteen hotels and boarding houses for working-women, and thirty-three maternity homes. The Army's industrial homes increasingly were listed in official literature as "social service centers" after 1924. It is not possible, in retrospect, to arrive at a clear statistical accounting of the volume of the Army's social program in the 1920s; the Rockefeller study of 1924 found that the Army's published statistical tables of beds, meals, pounds of materials, and hours given away had "little significance." It is nevertheless certain that tens of thousands of individuals were helped, and hundreds of these — including the poet Charles Taggart — were rescued permanently and became fervent Christians.[50]

Although officially restyled in 1920 as "The Salvation Army Home and Hospital," the Army's rescue home continued to provide a popular and effective welfare service during these years. What had originally been a refuge for all kinds of homeless, vulnerable women changed into a ministry exclusively for unwed mothers. These homes offered modern prenatal, delivery, and recovery care, infant care, and a discreet adoption service. The emphasis, beyond the medical care, was on discipline, religion, and the traditional homey atmosphere, complete with the obligatory Victrola in the front parlor. Officers detected a change in the nature of their charges: they were getting younger. At the turn of the century, most of the clients had been "mature"; by 1926, 42 percent were schoolgirls, and the average age of a client was only sixteen. The head of the Women's Social Service Department, which administered this branch of Army welfare, blamed the automobile: the unwanted pregnancies were the result of "automobile flirtations" rather than the poverty and prostitution of the old days. Whatever the cause, Salvation Army Homes and Hospitals claimed to provide the cure. The Army noted with pride that 85 percent of the girls who passed through its maternity homes went on to live "wholesome lives." Objective outsiders agreed: the Women's Social Services were the least criticized of all Salvation Army social activities. The Rockefeller study of 1924 concluded that "these Homes collectively [were] without question the Army's most successful contribution to the social field."[51]

The Army also continued to rescue alcoholic and homeless men. The Industrial Homes offered residents a wholesome living environment and practical work therapy. Although the social secretary, Colonel Parker, acquired a car, the Army wagons were still mostly horse drawn. The cleaned and patched used clothes and repaired furniture were a welcome boon to the needy but proud householders who acquired these things for a pittance at the Army's salvage stores. The Army still drew welcome revenue from the sale of waste paper, which had to be sorted into thirteen grades. The difficulty in the industrial home program was not in sales but in production. Prohibition had practically ended public drunkenness, at least in the first flush of popular enthusiasm that accompanied the enactment of the Volstead Act to enforce the Eighteenth Amendment. The Salvation Army's ministry to problem drinkers seemed almost to evaporate in the years immediately after 1919: before that year, 75 percent of the 19,000 men in the Industrial Home shops had been habitual drunkards; after the Act took effect, the Army could not "corral a handful" for Boozers' Day, and "dead calm" reigned in deserted Industrial Home dormitories and workrooms. The Army had to hire laborers to keep its industrial operation afloat.[52]

Yet many rootless men were still at large, and the Army opened its doors to them. The cheap "workingman's hotels," such as Boston's Peoples'

Palace and the Workingman's Palace in Chicago (one of three hostelries operated by the Army there) provided a badly needed service, especially in the brief, sharp recession that came in 1920 on the heels of peace. These older institutions were augmented by the new "Argonne" chain. There were still migrant workers, homeless transients, beggars, and rootless, desperate men in America, and The Salvation Army cared for a large portion of them — perhaps as many as half of the total number. Alcohol did not disappear completely — Canadian and Scotch whiskey, the cocktail party, and the speakeasy proliferated — but access was largely restricted to a class of people over whom the Army had never exercised much influence. The saloon and its most popular lines of merchandise, beer and cheap watered liquor, were gone, and gone with them was the working-class victim of excessive drinking who had been the main object of the Army's street-corner appeal.

The Army hardly regretted the end of that part of its ministry. Officers from the Commander down were loud in their determination that Prohibition should remain the law of the land. Evangeline endorsed the Eighteenth Amendment "without hesitation." This remained the Army's official position, fully supported by Gen. Bramwell Booth and international headquarters, until repeal came in 1933. The Salvation Army believed so completely in "the beneficent influence of prohibition" on the United States that it abandoned, for the only time in its history in this country, its nonpartisan stance. In the presidential election of 1928, the Army endorsed the candidacy of the Republican nominee, Herbert Hoover. In 1931 Evangeline publicly praised Hoover for his "magnificent conflict with the forces of organized and defiant disorder" who were working for repeal of the Eighteenth Amendment. Officers were urged to combat "reactionary forces" that sought to ignore or annul the prohibition laws. Evangeline herself was a tireless speaker on behalf of legislation for which the Army had prayed for years. Lower-ranking officers spoke to local rallies, and many Army units paid for advertisements on radio and in the press. E. Irena Arnold, the gentle officer-poet well known in the Southern states, produced a short poem with the opening line "We thank God for Prohibition in America today." Out in Honolulu, in an outburst of reciprocal solidarity, the Hawaiian Anti-Saloon League elected as its president Brig. C. W. Bourne, the new divisional commander.[53]

This is not to say, of course, that The Salvation Army was preoccupied with Prohibition. The readers of the Central *War Cry* were assured that even with Prohibition on the books, the Army was still eager to help the down-and-outer: it was "the same old Army," and many of its programs were unaffected by Prohibition. The Army's social welfare ministry had begun in the Hartford jail in 1885; work among prisoners continued to expand and flourish after the world war. The Army's prison ministry was probably second only to the Women's Social Services in the number of souls it rescued and in the approval it gained from professional observers. The Lifers' Club, formed in 1916, was rejuvenated in May 1920, still under its first and most famous president, Jesse Pomeroy. There were several branches, the largest of which, in the New Jersey State Prison in Trenton, had 142 members in 1929.[54]

Entire corps, with sergeants, flags, and brass bands, sprang up spontaneously in several prisons, nurtured after the first burst of enthusiasm by regular visits from nearby corps officers and from representatives of the Salvation Army Prison Department at territorial headquarters. The first of these corps was at San Quentin, established in Maud Booth's day; the next was at the Michigan State Prison in Marquette. In 1920 a Salvation Army open-air meeting was held in the yard of the Indiana State Boys' Reformatory at Jeffersonville, which touched off a religious revival among the youthful inmates. Many came forward to be rescued from sin. The prison chaplain, Lucien V. Rule, and the Army officers were naturally overjoyed; the former "worked like a Trojan" to prepare the six hundred boys who wished to join the Army's Brighter Day League. Sixty-five of these wanted to become full-fledged soldiers in the Army. A corps was promptly started, supervised by Adjutant Ladlow of Louisville No. 1. By 1921, when Commissioner Booth-Tucker came to conduct the ceremonial enrollment of the new soldiers, their number had swelled to ninety. The corps movement spread to other prisons, and soon there was a corps in the Oklahoma State Prison at McAlester. The seventy soldiers of "McAlester No. 2" corps marched through the prison yard with flag, drums, and a guitar band and secured over seven hundred converts. In 1924 these soldiers fitted out a Ford truck with a van body, suitably covered with evangelical appeals, and proudly presented it to their comrades at McAlester No. 1 as the "Salvation Army Gospel Truck." The corps officer used it for many years to conduct meetings in outlying districts. Corps were added at Folsom Prison in California and in state prisons in New Jersey and Kansas, bringing the total of these prison corps to seven. This is touching and remarkable evidence of the Army's appeal to the cast-offs and lost souls of life. Soldiers in these corps valiantly held their services in the prison yard, amid the kind of abuse and skepticism that had greeted the salvation war everywhere in the 1880s.[55]

The Salvation Army did not coddle these warriors: they were told outright that prison was not the "cause of the prisoner's calamity" but the "consequence of his crime." Individual officers did what they could to alleviate especially brutal conditions, but the Army had little to say about basic prison reform: its "real work" was to bring the sinner to Christ and thereby to "change the inner mind of the criminal." Men who joined prison corps or the Brighter Day League were expected to witness to their new faith in Christ, to abandon drink, drugs, and gambling, and to obey prison officials. The latter, naturally pleased at these requirements, beamed approval on Army work within their walls. The approbation of the guards sometimes made things difficult for the prisoner-converts — the other inmates harassed converts, accusing them of feigning religion to ingratiate themselves with the authorities — but many of these convict-soldiers nevertheless remained doggedly faithful to their newfound Lord and continued to live within the law when they left prison, some of them forever.[56]

Many released prisoners passed again into the hands of The Salvation Army. The decade of the 1920s saw "an increasing reciprocity between the Bench and The Salvation Army" as the latter developed parole programs in New York, California, and Massachusetts. Almost half the men released to the Army in these programs had been convicted of violent crimes. Officers made much of this fact, convinced that it reflected the Army's reputation "of being a sort of sociological sieve for getting the best out of the worst." Formal parole programs were supplemented in many places by Army personnel who acted as unofficial probation officers for youth in legal difficulties, especially for first offenders and those who appeared to the Army to have been driven to crime by poverty. Army prison work gained full judicial recognition when officers were appointed as chaplains in the federal prison at Atlanta and at McNeill Island near Tacoma, Washington. The McNeill chaplain, Ensign C. W. Burr, conducted himself like a Salvationist in his new appointment. He counseled the seven hundred men with the Army's lively, practical version of Christianity and conducted the prison band using a full set of *The Salvation Army Band Journal* that had been given by Commander Evangeline, who had a great interest in prison work.[57]

It was the "same old Army" in other ways, too, as the twenties roared along. The Great Salvation War, whether fought in corps, street, social institution, or prison, was buoyed up as always by the Army's own brand of music. The decade saw widespread improvement in that bane of the devil, the Salvation Army band. After 1921 all three territories had headquarters' staff bands — the Western Territorial Staff Band, the Chicago Staff Band, and the Eastern Territorial Staff Band (actually the former famous National Staff Band, which used the new name more and more frequently beginning in 1921). There were new regional ensembles as well, such as the New England Divisional Staff Band in Boston and the Washington Headquarters Band in the nation's capital, both bands led in turn (in 1923 and 1925) by the gifted young Erik Leidzen. And in 1921 the Army opened its first music camp, at Long Branch, New Jersey. The camp leader was Capt. John Allan, safely returned from his chaplain's duties in the war. Many corps mustered large bands of considerable proficiency, able to perform concerts and put on handsome parades in addition to their street-corner and congregational accompaniment duties. Some of these bands had been long established, including those of Oakland No. 1; Flint, Michigan; East Liverpool, Ohio; Brooklyn Citadel; South Manchester, Connecticut; and a dozen large corps in both New York and Chicago. Others, including those of Los Angeles No. 1, Boston Palace, and the Honolulu Girls' Home Band, developed fully only after the war. Gradually the colorful variety of instruments — the keyed bugles, valve trombones, and fifes of pioneer days — disappeared from the scene, as a regulation brass instrumentation was ever more widely adopted. Clarinets and saxophones held on longer — in a few places into the 1930s — but only doubling parts written for brass. (Woodwinds ceased to have an *official* place in Army bands in 1902, when the Army published for the last time a part for the "clarionet.")[58]

The Salvation Army's willingness to steal tunes from the devil continued into the 1920s, although on a reduced scale. It remained difficult to acquire material in sufficient quantity at reasonable prices that met the Army's requirements for its music: it had to be religious, every arrangement and selection had to contain a recognizable strain of Christian hymnody, and the music had to be written entirely in the treble clef, even the bass parts. This was a British custom for all brass bands, Army or not, but the Army adopted it eagerly for the practical benefits — in a pinch (which often occurred), a player could be switched to any instrument without learning new fingerings for the valves. It was also much easier to start a band from scratch if there was only one set of fingerings to explain to everyone. Army bands used only brass instruments, another British device The Salvation Army in America gladly adopted for practical reasons — it was easier for a beginner to squeeze those exciting first feeble notes from a brass horn than from a woodwind, and brass instruments held up much better to the rigors of street warfare. Unfortunately, music arranged in the treble clef for all-brass bands was not easily obtained in the United States.

So the Army published its own band music. At first this consisted merely of familiar hymn tunes arranged to accompany congregational singing. Gradually selections, marches, and "meditations" were added. By 1920 the Army was publishing three series of band journals: the "Festival" series, made up of intricate pieces requiring a full band; the "Ordinary" (later "General") series, which consisted of pieces that were difficult but still playable by a smaller, slightly less proficient band; and a still-easier "Second" (later "Triumph") series. By the end of the decade the Army had collected "a combined body of literature which was remarkably diverse in nature." The familiar set of straightforward hymn tune arrangements, playable by four or five bandsmen of indifferent skill, were published periodically in sheets as part of the "Ordinary" series; these sheets were later collected together, supplemented with other tunes, and published as *Band Tune Books,* the first of which appeared in 1900. The increasing number and ability of Army bands did not allow the music publishing branch, located in London, to rest on past accomplishments. The director of the London branch, Col. Frederick Hawkes, who maintained a special sympathy for the needs of the small band, resolved to produce a new improved version of the *Tune Book.* He sent melody lines in bunches to his many bandmaster friends throughout Britain, asking them to supply band arrangements, while he produced the remainder at his desk at headquarters. The results were published in 1928 as The Salvation Army *Band Tune Book,* a collection of 541 hymn tunes. Bound in a complete set in red-varnished cardboard covers, it was a remarkable collection, with many curiously beautiful little pieces, some somber and sonorous, other sprightly and full of hope. The *Band Tune Book,* which was in regular use until it was replaced by a revised edition in 1987, may well have contained the most widely heard band music in world history. In the almost sixty years that it was in use throughout the Salvation Army world, the arrangements were played tens of thousands of times, indoors and outdoors.[59]

Although quite content to use the lovely *Band Tune Book* for hymn tune playing — which was all that many small bands played — serious Army musicians in the United States wanted a band journal of their own in which to publish meditations and selections of their own composition. The Commander, who was by now so thoroughly American in her sentiments that no one but Bramwell remembered that she had ever been English, easily secured the approval of the territorial commanders for an

American Band Journal in 1928. American bands would, of course, continue playing the material published by London as well. Thus supplied with an endless stream of music from England and America, the Army's bands multiplied. Every corps capable of mustering a band did so. The bands of older, established corps were staffed no longer by fresh converts who had received a few rudimentary lessons on a horn but by second-generation Salvationists who were skilled instrumentalists. But no matter the size of the band or its musical ability, it was expected to play in the street five times per week, while larger bands held numerous additional concerts and special musical weekends throughout the year. The quantity, variety, and charm of Salvation Army music came to the favorable attention not only of the public but of professional musicians and critics as well. By the mid 1920s, the Army's street-corner bands had become common sights in the United States: "One of the most familiar sights in America is a little knot of Salvation Army preachers at a street corner blaring fundamentalist hymns on brassy horns." Their zeal and ability won the affectionate respect of America's finest musicians. "The next time you hear a Salvation Army Band, no matter how humble," declared John Philip Sousa in 1930, "take off your hat."[60]

The Army's place in public esteem seemed assured. Yet this happy state of affairs failed to penetrate entirely to the level of corps finance. The social institutions, camps, and territorial and national projects were able to draw on the benefits of the annual Home Service Fund and its territorial successors. But the corps were excluded from these schemes; as denominational congregational units, they were expected to be self-supporting, in the same way that the local churches of other denominations were self-supporting. Not all of the corps were as successful in sustaining themselves financially as leading officers had hoped or predicted. To make up the shortfall, many corps participated in annual fund-raising campaigns that solicited contributions from the local community to finance all the major charities and good causes in the area. The most common of these was the annual Community Chest, which began on a spotty basis after the war but spread rapidly because of its convenience and practicality and its appeal to bumptious community spirit and the boosterism of the decade. Many local Salvation Army corps participated from the beginning; within a few years some units had become, or imagined themselves to be, dependent upon the Chest. In 1922 the commissioners' conference took official notice of these facts and authorized continued participation: "As the benefits are so generally recognized and the alternative is so precarious it was the uniform judgment of the conference that cooperation — with great caution — is the correct course."[61]

For many corps the Chest was a welcome boon. What the Home Service Fund was to the rest of the Army, the annual community appeal of the "Red Feather" (the symbol of the Community Chest) was to the corps. Before the arrival of the Chest, officers in small corps had been hard-pressed to meet expenses. Young Bertha Shadick, sent to Saratoga Springs, New York, found the corps — and herself — penniless. When an elderly soldier died, the fledgling lieutenant had to find an undertaker who would bury the departed sister for the few dollars her pathetic possessions had brought. Mr. Otis S. Carr agreed; he was a kindly sort of man who was touched by Shadick's courage and resolved to help her by arranging on his own a kind of community appeal on behalf of the Army. Many officers in small corps sustained themselves in the early Twenties as the pioneers had, on stale bakery goods, and walked long distances in all weather to save carfare of a nickel.[62]

The "Red Feather" changed all that. The welfare services offered in the corps qualified them as a public charity, which entitled The Salvation Army to a share of what the Chest raised — funds that in some cases made the difference in a corps's survival. And yet there were questions. From the beginning, Salvationists had never shown much enthusiasm for providing financial support for the corps out of their own pockets. This disinclination, the one recurring blot on the soldiers' otherwise admirable record for loyalty and service, was a constant source of irritation and embarrassment to Army officers. It was partly due to soldiers' own poverty, of course, but it was now exacerbated by the ready availability of outside funding. Nor were the concerns on this point all internal. The Army was subjected to repeated public criticism over the years for the fact that a portion of the funds it raised for social welfare activities was used to finance its corps operations. In any event, the amount given in the individual soldier's cartridge packet was often "ridiculously low." Despite official Army policy, which required that corps be self-supporting, the Rockefeller investigation in 1924 found only one corps in the entire eastern half of the United States that attained the goal — despite the fact that the same study estimated that any corps with one hundred soldiers could be self-supporting on much less than 10 percent of their combined salaries. (Like other evangelical denominations, the Army accepted 10 percent — the biblical tithe — as a reasonable donation from its members.) The fact that almost no soldier returned more than a pittance to the salvation war was attributed by officers to the availability of community appeal funds.[63]

Still, it was difficult for officers to become too depressed over the meagerness of the weekly cartridge collection when the Home Service Fund or the Community Chest made up all deficiencies and more. In fact, the prospects before the Army in the 1920s were bright. Prohibition had eliminated the saloon and most public drunkenness. The Army's standard for membership was among the highest of any evangelical sect, and the ranks continued to increase faster than the population — the Army's membership increased by 38 percent in the decade after 1926 — albeit more slowly than in the past, and with a much larger percentage of new soldiers coming from the second and third generation of converts rather than from an influx of freshly rescued sinners. Although there was occasional controversy and some disappointment about the source of its funding, an overall lack of money was not a problem for The Salvation Army in the 1920s. The Army's social programs, evangelical activities, bands, and summer camps all flourished. The Life-Saving Guards and its charming junior branch, the Sunbeams (added in 1925 as the successor to the Band of Love), attracted many girls with their stirring mottos "To Save and to Serve" and "Do Right!" and their varied programs. In 1928 these included a wide range of religious, camping, and domestic exercises, along with helpful household hints such as how to use the telephone and simple recipes for things like stewed rabbit and "boiled macaroni." The leaders of other denominations, worried over declining attendance, urged their members to adopt Salvation Army tactics, a Catholic writer noting in 1929 that the practical benefits of "street and platform work by qualified laymen" had been "amply demonstrated." Yet the Army's spiritual program was not confined to evangelism; by the 1920s the Army's leaders stated frankly that the Army had two purposes — to "win souls and make Soldiers." Evangelism was not enough; corps officers must build the Army's membership as well. Cadets in training were told that the only proven way of increasing membership was by house-to-house visitation. The results of Salvationist activities during these years were rapid large-scale growth. One writer declared in 1926 that the Army had experienced "a rapidity of March [that was] in many aspects . . . little short of phenomenal." The first half of the decade recorded dramatic statistical increases in net assets, buildings, total seating capacity, and "senior soldiers" (adult members). From 1916 to 1926, for instance, the number of corps in the United States increased from 742 to 1,052, an increase of 42 percent. At the same time, the Army's total membership (including soldiers of all ages and officers) more than doubled, increasing from 35,954 to 74,768. Thus, while the number of corps grew rapidly, the average size of each corps was increasing even more rapidly, from an average of 48 members per corps in 1916 to 71 in 1926! As encouraging as these overall statistics must have been to Army leaders, developments on the local level were sometimes even more spectacular. In the fall of 1924, the "entire population of 159 men and women [of Samptown, New Jersey] knelt at the drumhead and in the words of the Army, claimed salvation." This encouraging development followed the labors of a team of officers from nearby corps who held a revival in Samptown at the request of the owner of the town's steel mill. The next year the *War Cry* announced that "drumhead conversions" were "still the style" and reported success in Miami, Pittsburgh, and Batavia, New York.[64]

Caught up in the spirit of advance that her own flamboyant and popular personality helped to reinforce, the Commander decided in 1926 to open a new territorial headquarters for the South. This move would serve several happy purposes at once: it would capitalize on the regional pride of the old Confederacy by giving the Army there its own headquarters, *War Cry,* and training college; it would eliminate the long distances staff officers stationed in New York now traveled on visits and inspections in the South; it would create a group of leaders who could devote their

Girl Guards, 1920s
Source: The Salvation Army National Archives

entire energies to developing The Salvation Army in the South, a region in which overall progress had been slow; and — best of all — it would be dramatically symbolic of growth and progress.

The new territory was made up of the southern parts of the Eastern and Central territories; it consisted of all of the Southern states: Maryland, Kentucky (except for an enclave south of Cincinnati), Oklahoma, Arkansas, and Texas (except El Paso on the New Mexico border, which was left in the Western territory). Atlanta was selected as territorial headquarters after Maj. Bertram Rodda, the Georgia–South Carolina divisional commander, aided by Atlanta's Rotary Club and various local boosters, had neatly disposed of the claims of Birmingham, Memphis, and Washington. Rodda, whose divisional headquarters were in Atlanta, was then appointed to arrange the legal and business aspects of the transition. A cheerful, expansive officer with unlimited energy, Rodda scurried about like a worker ant, pulling a headquarters together out of local materials. He secured the Elks' Temple on Ellis Street for the new headquarters building and arranged with a local printer to publish an inaugural issue of a Southern version of the *War Cry* even before the new editor arrived.[65]

To serve as territorial commander, Evangeline selected William McIntyre and promoted him to lieutenant commissioner. It was an inspired choice. Evangeline Booth had, in fact, a special gift in finding and utilizing individuals of exceptional talent: many of the territorial and divisional officers who served under her were among the most effective and dedicated leaders in the history of the movement in the United States. McIntyre, a provincial commander, was overjoyed at this challenging promotion in rank and responsibility. Another of the Army's amiable eccentrics, a colorful speaker, plain, almost rough in manner, McIntyre was an innovative and courageous leader, a zealous evangelist, and wholly unorthodox in his methods. He occasionally promoted officers on the spot for a good suggestion — he called good suggestions "hat-stretchers" — and drove about the territory in a stately green Graham-Paige sedan (despite the Army's regulation requiring officers to use inexpensive black cars), because he had secured the luxurious car at a low price; he explained that it would have been a shameful waste of the Lord's money to let this bargain escape. The commissioner loved buildings as much as he had when he and Colonel Holz had been pioneer advocates of the purchase of property for the Army before the war. He was devoted above all to the welfare of the corps officer and was determined that each one would have a decent corps, decent quarters, and a regular salary.

There have been few territorial commanders more loved by his officers than William McIntyre.[66]

The new commissioner faced a large task, and he wasted no time in undertaking it. In addition to the normal administrative burdens of establishing an entire division, there were concerns associated with the fact that both the Central and Eastern territorial leaders had been forced to relinquish vast areas and hundreds of officers from their control and that many officers from the Northeast and the Midwest now faced the prospect of being marooned in an unfamiliar region for the rest of their careers. Smoothing the transition required prodigies of tact and patience, which McIntyre produced. He and Rodda responded to objections from Chicago and New York regarding their proposal that cadets destined for Southern appointments be taken at once to form a new Southern war college; it was agreed as a compromise that these cadets would remain in their current training colleges, joining the new Southern training branch only for their last month of preparation. McIntyre knew that the advance of the Great Salvation War would be delayed in the South as long as the feeling persisted among officers that they had been stranded in a strange land. The Southern Territory, officially inaugurated in 1927, was actually born in 1928, when the first big Congress in Atlanta brought Salvationists from the former Eastern and Central parts of the new territory together for the first time.[67]

McIntyre set incredible goals for the first five years of the new territory and then inspired the rank and file to reach them. His "Salvation Offensive" captured the old-time war spirit: he called for 10,000 new soldiers and 150 new corps buildings. It is a monument to the ceaseless toil, sacrifice, and prayer of hundreds of officers that so much of the "Salvation Offensive" was achieved before McIntyre departed for the Chicago command in 1930: 9,000 new soldiers and 163 new Army halls. The first issue of the Southern territorial *War Cry* appeared on March 26, 1927, full of hope — and predicting that the people of the South would soon be disabused of the notion, which seemed to be held nationwide, that The Salvation Army consisted only of street-corner bands and warm memories of the services rendered on the battlefields of France.[68]

A Southern Staff Band was organized and departed almost at once in June on its first tour in a "comfortable touring bus." Brass banding, however, did not flourish in the new territory, despite the gentle climate and the religious disposition of many of the people, which should have encouraged the Army's open-air and marching ministry. The corps were small — the average Southern corps had but six soldiers in 1929 — and poor. There was no tradition of all-brass music in the Southern branch of the Army and little interest in it outside of the Army. There was little immigration into the South from Britain or Canada, from which many Army bandsmen had come to more northerly corps. There were only a few large corps in the South with bands; the largest was the Atlanta No. 1 (Temple) Corps at the territorial center. The bands of other relatively large corps, such as those in Miami, Tampa, Washington, Richmond, and Charleston, West Virginia, were not experienced enough to play the more difficult and challenging Army pieces. When national headquarters optimistically sent one hundred full sets of *Festival Series* music and five hundred sets of the new *American Band Journal* to the new Southern territorial trade department, McIntyre sent it all back with the comment that the South had no bands, except the Staff Band, that were "able to handle this class of music." Still, progress was made even in banding. Within a year McIntyre reported there were forty-two regular and young people's bands in the territory, although these aggregations were mostly very small and unskilled. In other areas success was remarkable: the Army added an average of one hundred new soldiers per month during its first year in the new territory.[69]

The Salvation Army's interest in extending its ministry to African Americans had never abated and was freshly stimulated by the official opening of the Southern territory, where almost 90 percent of American blacks still lived in 1927. Two black corps, in Washington, D.C., and Charleston, South Carolina, had been opened in 1914 on the eve of the World War. At that time Army leaders were confident they could extend "this work among the negroes in the South indefinitely" if only they could "secure capable, devoted, and faithful colored officers." Fredericksburg, Virginia, was reopened in the summer of 1920, a relic of the Army's Victorian "Colored Campaign" reborn in what was hoped were better times. Salvation Army indoor religious services in the South were segregated on the basis of race, but open-air services attracted large mixed-race crowds. This encouraged Salvationists: when it proved impossible in 1920 to buy or rent a hall in Norfolk to open a new black corps, the officers decided to hold open-air and cottage meetings indefinitely, or until a suitable hall was found. The Army encouraged other little cracks in the "color barrier" as well. Spiritual retreats for the officers of a division — called "officers' councils" — and large public youth rallies were officially integrated in the 1920s, although travel, hotel, and restaurant facilities were not, which embarrassed officers of both races. The actual number of black officers involved in these incidents must have been very small; a number of the Army efforts on behalf of the African American population of the South that were started after the First World War did not survive long enough to welcome the new territory: there was only a single "colored Corps" and one Serviceman's Hotel listed in the Southern Territory in 1927, both in Washington, D.C. In fact, few African Americans were won to Christ through the ministry of The Salvation Army in the South in the 1920s. The shortage of black officers was cited at the time as the major obstacle to progress in the South.[70]

Elsewhere blacks were successfully integrated into Army programs in small numbers. There was a sprinkling of dedicated African American Salvationists throughout the country. New York City had three active black corps in the 1920s, and several others had black sergeants. The band at the Brooklyn No. 1 corps — one of the best in the country — had four African American players in 1922. Yet there were several segregated facilities outside the South as well: New York No. 8 was listed as a "colored corps" in 1920, and in 1921 the Army turned the old Chicago No. 2 corps on South Division Street into a black corps, announcing it as the first corps for that race in Chicago. In 1925 a maternity hospital for African American women was opened in Cleveland; in 1930 it was relocated in another part of the city and named the Mary B. Talbert Home and Hospital. In the North as well as the South, the Army's authentically good intentions, the courage of black Salvationists, and the love that is properly the mark of Christian work produced some touching and remarkable results in improving relations between the races, but the overall result of the Army's intermittent efforts to extend its work among black Americans was slight.[71]

The advance of the salvation war was clearly not uniform in the 1920s, but overall The Salvation Army had made encouraging progress as the decade drew to its end. A second, and in some cases third, generation had taken its place in the ranks of the "dear old Army," while the traditional street and welfare ministries had yielded up many remarkable conversions. Occasional protests from local supporters over the transfer of a popular corps officer were politely ignored and do not seem to have weakened public support. The Commander continued to embody, so far as the public and the Army rank and file were concerned, the zealous evangelical spirit of the Army and the booster patriotism of the Republic. Her "World's Greatest Romance," supplemented by that old classic "The Commander in Rags," and her motorcades, lectures, and mass rallies earned Evangeline Booth, and the Army she so consciously represented, a lasting place in the affection, respect, and bounty of the public. It was inevitable that she would require a new

National and Territorial Headquarters building in New York City, dedicated in 1930. The complex consisted of a large auditorium (left), the headquarters building (right), and a residence (rear).
Source: The Salvation Army National Archives

headquarters building, a "Salvation Skyscraper" in the latest style, to replace the Victorian Gothic fortress that had once been Ballington Booth's pride and joy. The official dedication of the new structure was delayed so it might serve as the capstone to the celebration in 1930 of the Army's Jubilee in the United States — "a fitting testimony to the labors of The Salvation Army in America for the last fifty years." As the building went up over the old address on Fourteenth Street in New York City, joined by a new residence for working women — the John and Mary R. Markle Evangeline Residence, named for the Markles, who had donated a half-million dollars — the prestige and pride of The Salvation Army seemed to rise with it. The new year 1929 dawned full of hope for the Army and the country alike.[72]

CHAPTER 5

1929-1950

"How the anxious shout it . . ."

The buoyant spirit that animated the Army throughout the 1920s ought to have been chilled by the events of 1929, when two crises in succession overtook the movement: the deposition of Gen. Bramwell Booth in January and February and the beginning of the Great Depression in October. The fact that the evangelical and charitable zeal of the average officer and soldier did not falter during these troubling events — or during the prolonged years of depression and war that followed — is one more of many monuments to the sense of loyalty to Christ and the soul-saving mission of the Army that inspired the lives of most Salvationists.

The administrative crisis that overtook the leadership of The Salvation Army in early 1929 had been developing for several years. Printed statements on the issues at stake had been distributed among selected staff officers in the United States as early as March 1925. The discussion concentrated on two points: the powers of Gen. Bramwell Booth, who had succeeded his father, the Founder, in 1912, and the procedure by which his successor, the third general, was to be chosen when the time came. The Founder had fixed the conditions of the generalship in the Deed Poll of 1878, an act of Parliament that served The Salvation Army as its legal charter. This act placed in the hands of the General all executive power over the Army, including the rights of a legal trustee in whose personal hands all properties were held (except in the United States, where since 1899 the Army had been separately incorporated) and the right to name his successor. His authority was absolute and final: there were no councils, conferences, or committees that he had to consult or even inform concerning his actions. The appointment was for life; there was no provision for a general to retire.[1]

There was, however, a means for removing one. In 1904 William Booth had accepted the advice of legal counsel and added a Supplementary Deed to the 1878 Deed Poll. It did nothing to diminish his autocratic powers, but it did provide for the removal of an insane, morally corrupt, or bankrupt general or one whom three-quarters of all active commissioners and territorial commanders, meeting together as a High Council for that purpose, declared to be "unfit for office." This High Council could be summoned by the "joint requisition" of the chief of the staff and any four other commissioners or by *any* seven commissioners. The Council could elect by a two-thirds majority a successor to a general deposed in such a manner; all powers of the one overturned ceased at once, including the right to name a successor. Thus far had the Founder tempered the absolutism of his office, and no farther. The monarchy remained autocratic and almost certainly hereditary. The contingencies under which a High Council could be summoned were regarded by the Founder and later by his chosen successor Bramwell as fantastically remote.[2]

Others, alas, did not take such a relaxed view. To them, the prospect of summoning a High Council and deposing the General seemed increasingly more practical and appealing. The problem in their eyes was, in general, Bramwell, and, in particular, the widespread belief among senior officers that he had named a member of his immediate family to succeed him. At first speculation centered on his wife, Florence Soper Booth, and later on his eldest daughter, Comm. Catherine Bramwell-Booth. No one could deny that the General was a man of extraordinary administrative skill: much of the structure of The Salvation Army, which has survived in almost its original form until the present day, was the work of Bramwell Booth. He was a wholehearted evangelical, an able writer, and a kindly, well-spoken man. Many of his immediate subordinates as well as the rank and file held him in great personal affection. Bramwell had a high — indeed, a mystical — conception of his office, which he viewed, perhaps naturally, as a sacred and inviolable trust placed in his hands by the glorified Founder.

That he had defects, however, was undeniable. While less marked than his virtues, they led him and the Army into the tragic affairs of 1929.

Some of his faults were mere foibles. Those who were around the General knew him to be fussy, rigid in his habits, and old-fashioned in little ways to the point of eccentricity: he signed his name with a quill, for instance, and blotted the ink with sand, and refused to use pencils that were not of exact dimensions. There were more serious disabilities. Bramwell had a remarkable taste for flattery; the official Salvation Army telegraph code book, issued by international headquarters in 1925, provided a convenient list of fulsome phrases, some of them almost Byzantine, with which officers could congratulate their General on his activities — "magnificent," "marvellously successful," "splendid" were among the more commonplace of these stock phrases. Many high-ranking officers who loved Bramwell as a person believed him to be too autocratic in his official conduct, inviting no advice or argument and brooking none, except from members of his own family. These officers feared, rightly or wrongly, that criticism of the General would bring swift transfer to some less prestigious position, far from the center of power. The case of Col. George Carpenter, the international literary secretary, was widely regarded as confirmation of these suspicions. After a period of chilled relations with the General, Carpenter was transferred to the editorship of *The War Cry* in Sydney, Australia, in January 1927. These officers were also alarmed by what they regarded as the General's unfortunate predilection for relying largely on members of his own family for advice on Army matters great and small and favoring them with appointments beyond their abilities. These critics did not suggest that the General's children — especially Catherine, Bernard, and Wycliffe — were not dedicated and talented officers; they simply took exception to the children's deportment, which seemed breezy and presumptuous, their easy assumption of being destined for great things, and their access to the ears of power when other, more senior officers were consulted on nothing.[3]

The feeling that the Army's system of government should be changed was widespread among leading officers. This was not merely a matter of concern about the personality traits of Bramwell and his children; it was a concern about the future of the Army. Many officers were convinced that the autocratic military system developed by William Booth in the days of rapid advance and terrible warfare was no longer practical in the enlightened 1920s and that it certainly could not be allowed to pass intact into the hands of Commissioner Catherine (who was only forty-five in 1928) for what might be a very long reign. In fact, a majority of the commissioners felt this way. Highly principled individuals in every regard, sincere in their devotion to God and the Army, they had no consciously selfish motive for advocating change. There were others who had less noble motives, however. Some had, or imagined they had, personal grievances against the General or one of his children. Frederick Booth-Tucker, the General's brother-in-law, had been retired in 1926 at age seventy-three, very much against his will, according to a policy introduced by Bramwell in 1919 that set age limits, according to rank, for active service. Booth-Tucker, who still had a warrior's heart, had volunteered for the Army in the days when officers expected to serve for life; now he felt cast aside and useless. His resentment against Bramwell and the system was great. Still other officers sought the General's office for themselves or for some candidate other than the supposedly predestined Commissioner Catherine.[4]

National feelings were involved as well. Evangeline Booth and the four American territorial commanders made it clear to the General and to the chief of the staff, Comm. Edward J. Higgins, who knew America and loved it, that they felt the American branch of the Army — which they considered to be the richest and most powerful segment of the movement — should be given considerably more autonomy in administrative matters. There is abundant evidence to demonstrate that Commander Evangeline had negative feelings toward Bramwell as a person and resented on principle his authority over her and the American Army. There is evidence as well that strongly suggests that she craved the office of general for herself, which would of course have been impossible had Bramwell been allowed either to remain in office indefinitely — she was sixty-three herself in 1928 — or to name his own successor, who most likely would not be Evangeline.[5]

The events that led to the first meeting of the High Council of The Salvation Army on January 8, 1929, can be traced with some accuracy. It is far more difficult to trace the motives of the principal actors in those events, and more difficult still to describe or explain the sadness and confusion that lingered around this story in Army circles for more than half a century. Two things are certain. First, although Bramwell Booth's poor health was a factor in the crisis of 1929, the issues of his autocracy and the succession dominated in the calling of the High Council. Agitation on these subjects began long before the General fell seriously ill. Second, from the beginning, the movement to reform the Army in both of these particulars was organized by American officers, including Evangeline Booth, who rapidly came to dominate that movement.[6]

Bulletins, manifestos, and "blasts of a trumpet" appeared regularly from 1925 to 1928 from the pen — more accurately, the mimeograph — of the mysterious Atwood, supposedly a local officer in Wichita Falls, Texas. Commissioner Brengle was horrified at these bulletins, which denounced the General as a tyrant whose pretensions were practically criminal and whose nepotism was laughable. Brengle condemned these charges as "absolutely ridiculous." One of the bulletins called for its readers to "fight" for the "interests" of the Commander and urged that all of the General's authority over the American branch be vested in her. Brengle exchanged letters with Booth-Tucker over the subject matter of the Atwood bulletins in June 1927. The latter's reply, defending Atwood and adding more charges of his own to the indictment, was printed and widely circulated; it convinced Brengle (and the Booths) that Booth-Tucker and Atwood were at least exchanging correspondence, if not more closely associated.[7]

The opposition to the General, however, did not make use of subterfuge for long. In October 1927, the Commander called on the General in London. Fresh from the triumph of an important address in Paris delivered before the Ten-Year Convocation of the American Legion, she delivered a sort of manifesto of her own in the form of typewritten "Notes for Interview with the General, October 11, 1927," which were likewise widely and judiciously circulated in mimeographed form. There were fifteen points in this important document, which can be distilled to the familiar two: the General's exercise of "absolute power" was no longer acceptable to leading officers, and it was time that he transfer his authority to appoint his own successor to the "High Council or some such body within the Army," which would make the choice more democratically. "The conviction is growing everywhere that the time has arrived when some change must take place in the Constitution of the Army," she declared, "particularly with respect to the appointment of its General."[8]

The General responded on November 24 with a seven-page typewritten letter (which Evangeline also distributed among the staff) in which he rejected all of the Commander's arguments and announced that he was now convinced that British law did not allow a trustee (such as himself) to alter the Deed Poll under which his trust was held: the system created by the Founder in 1878 and bequeathed to Bramwell was eternal and inviolate; the Supplementary Deed of 1904 had not altered but rather strengthened the 1878 trust. Bramwell also touched on a fact that must be kept in mind when reading about this unhappy quarrel: he noted that he might have taken the concerns of his critics more seriously if the great work of preaching the gospel had been "really suffering" under the existing system. He was quite right: the extent of the General's authority and the question of the succession to it mattered not at all to the great majority of Salvationists, who made their daily contributions to the salvation war quite unaware of a war of a different, less creditable nature, slowly brewing above them.[9]

The Commander responded to her brother with a twenty-one-page letter, which inevitably followed the others into print and distribution among staff officers. Her remarks were to the point: the General's belief in the inviolability of the 1878 Deed was "utterly repugnant" (she used the term *repugnant* twice in the letter); there were "widespread questionings consequent upon the nepotism existing." There were dark hints in the letter as well: the "present conditions" were "filled with those very things that threaten, ultimately if not speedily, to break out in internecine war." To this ominous remark she added the even more pointed observation that the sacred Deed Poll of 1878 was in any case a piece of British law: it was "alien" and had "little or no standing" in the United States! Finally, on page eighteen, she stated her position openly to the General: if the "claimed provision" in the Trust Deed that allowed the General to name his successor were not removed, "then disturbance or rupture seems inevitable." These remarks were circulated by the Commander herself among the American territorial commanders. It was hardly surprising that the General and his family regarded Evangeline as actively disloyal and ambitious for the generalcy herself. What the General did not realize was that dissatisfaction with him was widespread among high-ranking officers.[10]

In April 1928, the seventy-two-year-old Gen. Bramwell Booth fell ill with what he supposed to be a mild case of influenza. In May he was well enough to lay the foundation stone for the new International Training College at Denmark Hill in south London, but it was his last public appearance. Always nervous by nature, and now burdened by age and the conviction that the American branch was a nest of enemies, the General grew weaker. He availed himself, as his father had before him, of the water cure at Matlock, likewise in vain. In October he was ordered to bed by his doctor. The daily administration of Army business passed into the hands of the General's wife and Edward J. Higgins, the chief of the staff. The General's illness gave the officers who wished to alter his powers their opportunity to call the High Council on the grounds that he was physically unable to continue in office, but it also placed them in a quandary. They did not wish to appear to be taking advantage of a sick man by acting against him in his absence; on the other hand, they did not know the extent of his illness. If he should die before they could act, all would be lost: his chosen successor would rise to power automatically, healthy and alert, and there would be no excuse for calling the High Council. The chance to make the Army government more democratic, and the generalcy elective, would be lost for years, perhaps forever. On November 14, 1928, after several meetings and considerable soul-searching, seven commissioners made a formal request to Commissioner Higgins that he summon the High Council to declare William Bramwell Booth unfit for the office of General of The Salvation Army and to elect a successor to his office.

The events of the next few months were marked by confusion, rancor, and heartfelt anguish. The dispute now became public knowledge. *The War Cry* began to carry noncommittal news briefs about the General's health and the calling of the Council. Salvationists were horrified. So was the General, who had recovered enough to receive the bad news that the Council had been summoned; it was only then that he learned for the first time that dissatisfaction was not confined to the Americans and Booth-Tucker but was widespread among senior officers.[11]

Worse news was to come. A letter signed by all but seven of the commissioners assembled for the Council urged Bramwell to resign with dignity and allow the High Council to choose a new general. Later a small delegation (which included two of the Army's saints, Yamamuro of Japan and Brengle of the United States) visited the General in his sickroom to make the same request. He refused through Commissioner Catherine, who was a member of the Council and allowed to speak for her father at their deliberations. On January 16, 1929, Bramwell Booth was declared to be unfit for his office by the three-quarters majority required by the Supplementary Deed, and he was deposed from his position as General.

Surprised, horrified, and still convinced that he must preserve the Founder's system at all costs, the falling leader sought the intervention of the British law courts. His case was in part a good one: the commissioners, wishing to spare both the General and themselves unnecessary humiliation, had refused to allow his legal counsel to address the High Council on his behalf, and the British court regarded this refusal as a violation of natural justice. On the strength of that charge, an injunction was granted that prevented the commissioners from meeting again to elect a successor until they had been addressed by the General's attorney. The General also requested the court to invalidate the Supplementary Deed Poll of 1904

— which created the High Council — on the grounds that a trustee (even the Founder!) cannot alter the terms of his trust.

The commissioners were shocked and dismayed by the General's action. So far as they were concerned, the legal merits of his case mattered nothing compared to the fact that he had brought a case at all. Almost all of the commissioners were literal-minded Christians who regarded any attempt by one Christian to bring the secular arm of the law to bear on fellow believers as a clear violation of the teachings of St. Paul, who in 1 Corinthians 6:1-8 instructed the followers of Christ to allow themselves to be defrauded rather than "go to law one with another." His lawsuit damned the General in the eyes not only of the Council but of almost all Salvationists who read of it in *The War Cry.* American staff officers, led by the national secretary Col. Walter Jenkins, cabled a protest from the United States denouncing the lawsuit as "disastrous combat," calling the General a "recreant," and pledging full support to the "constitutional" High Council. On the Council itself, the handful still loyal to the General shrank to the four members of his family and one other. The General's lawyer was courteously heard on February 13, after which a second vote confirmed the first: the General was deposed.[12]

Later that day Commissioner Higgins was elected as the third General of The Salvation Army. "Poor Commander!" wrote Brengle to Colonel Jenkins. "She is sadly cut-up & feels humiliated by the smallness of her vote [Higgins was elected with forty-two votes to her seventeen] & she wants to lay it to anti-American feeling, but in that she is wrong." On the contrary, declared Brengle, "They just didn't want the Commander." If Bramwell had underestimated the opposition to him, so too had Evangeline. The American commissioners (except Brengle) and a few international supporters, including Comm. Henry W. Mapp, had made her confident of election without knowing the hearts of the majority. Her flowery speech accepting nomination and her self-glorifying publicity releases had disturbed many commissioners, while Higgins did not campaign at all. The prize eluded her, but she was soon consoled: the precedent of election was established and would inevitably become a principle. Many commissioners favored a mandatory age limit, even for the General. Higgins might not serve for life. There was hope. Evangeline's confidence returned: she was still in charge of the Army's most powerful branch and would soon be back among her dear American comrades. The day after the election she cabled Col. Alexander Damon, chief secretary in Chicago, that she would be "delighted to get back. We must now go ahead for biggest advances" in the Army's history. What mattered far more to Salvationists around the world was that the Army's greatest crisis had passed. The Salvation soldiers, alarmed and confused by the many press and *War Cry* reports about the High Council, lawsuits, and electioneering, now gratefully turned their hearts' energies back to the street corners and penitent forms where The Salvation Army still lived and had its being.[13]

Four months after being deposed, Bramwell Booth died, on June 16, 1929, at the age of seventy-three. His illness had been genuine; when the group of seven officers called on him in January, Bramwell had received them in bed, able to move only his eyes and his "trembling, feeble hand." Brengle, a member of the visiting group, had been convinced by this sight that the General must either retire or be deposed — and that he, Brengle, must vote against him; still, overcome with respect and sympathy, Brengle tearfully kissed the old General's hand as he left the room. Whether Bramwell, given sufficient time and untroubled by the crisis of the High Council, would have recovered sufficiently to conduct the duties of his office cannot be known. His death removed the last major figure who had supervised the birth of The Salvation Army. No one except Catherine, the Army Mother, who died in 1890, or Railton, who joined them in death in 1913, had known William Booth more intimately or understood him better, and no one still living in 1929 had wielded a greater or, for the most part, more constructive influence on the Army Founder. The highly efficient administrative structure of The Salvation Army is still accounted one of its strengths, and that structure was almost entirely the work of Bramwell Booth. It remains his legacy.[14]

Back in the United States, Evangeline was hailed as a heroine by the American staff. "The leader of the Reform Cause," announced the Eastern *War Cry* in March, "was our Commander Evangeline Booth, whose return as the leader of a cause that triumphed is hailed from shore to shore. God bless the Commander." Commissioner Holz introduced her to a huge welcome rally in New York as "the Joan of Arc in this Reform Movement." The press offered overwhelming endorsement of the victory of the "democratic" side in the conflict. "Admiration for the work of the Salvation Army" ran through "all the American comment" on the High Council. Yet many sympathetic observers were troubled and expressed the hope that the conflict would leave no permanent damage. Writers declared their fears that "a mighty Victorian impulse [had,] perhaps, spent itself," that deposing the old General would cost the Army its old-time "crusading air," the "wholly unworldly martiality" of its pioneer days.[15]

The Army's friends need not have feared for its future. The great strength of the movement lay as always in the thousands of soldiers and officers who fought on for Christ after only a brief, confused pause to contemplate in wonder the activities of the High Council, whose deliberations might as well have taken place on another planet for all they affected the life of the corps and rescue work in the United States. The American commissioners were glad to return to what was, for them as well as for their troops, the end and purpose of their calling as Salvationists: the redemption of the world through the Blood of Christ — or at least as much of the world as could be drawn to the Savior by the Army's unique combination of evangelism and practical charity. It is well that the Army did not lose sight of its mission. In late October the values on the New York Stock Exchange collapsed.

The severity of the crisis was not immediately recognized, however, and the worst was still in the future when The Salvation Army celebrated a grand and glorious event in March 1930: the Golden Jubilee of Salvation Army work in the United States, celebrating the fiftieth anniversary of the arrival of George Scott Railton and the "Hallelujah Seven" on March 10, 1880. Commissioner Holz held a mammoth open-air meeting on March 10, 1930, at the very spot in Battery Park on which Railton had stepped from the *Australia* on that memorable day. The last surviving Salvationist among the pioneer party, Field Maj. Emma Westbrook, overwhelmed by the cheering and the multitudes of Salvationists all around, exclaimed in wonder, "What hath God wrought!" A National Congress was held in May, with mass rallies and an enormous parade up Broadway by four thousand soldiers and twenty brass bands. With Evangeline in her open car rode the beaming Major Westbrook, alongside still another who had reason to feel humbled by what the Army proclaimed to be the faithfulness of God: retired Commandant Eliza Shirley Symmonds. Prizes were offered for commemorative songster and band music, and two gems took the honors: "My Keeper" (a choral piece by William Bearchell) and the march "Army of God" (by Emil Soderstrom, a Danish-American Salvationist). The new Salvation skyscraper on Fourteenth Street, housing national and territorial headquarters, was opened officially, and jubilant Salvationists swarmed into the new Memorial Temple to sing and cheer (which doubtlessly produced a pleasantly deafening effect in a hall acoustically designed by the Commander so that a pin dropped on the platform could be heard anywhere in the auditorium.)[16]

The Army would shortly need all the encouragement it could find. The economic slide that started in October 1929 became a general col-

Emma Westbrook, one of the seven lassies who accompanied George Scott Railton to America in 1880, at the Golden Jubilee celebration in New York City
Source: The Salvation Army National Archives

lapse. By March 1933, fifteen million Americans were unemployed, nine million bank accounts had vanished, and the national income had fallen to less than half of its level in 1929. The Great Depression settled over the country, and The Salvation Army passed into a time of desperate and prolonged struggle, as taxing and heartrending in its way as the salvation warfare of pioneer days.

The traditional mainstay upon which The Salvation Army relied for the contributions required to support its social and evangelical programs was the working class — the very people upon whom the Depression bore most heavily. The Army's membership increased during the 1930s, but there was little growth in the number of corps in the same period. There was a 38 percent increase in membership in the ten years ending in 1936, but only a 3.4 percent increase in the number of corps: the result was a sizable, 34 percent increase in the average size of each corps, from an average of seventy-one members to ninety-five members. The Army's membership, however, was not built on complete families; the proportion of men to women among members of The Salvation Army had been declining for years. In 1906 there were slightly more men than women in the Army, but an imbalance in favor of women became noticeable with the passing years. By 1926 there were only seventy-seven males for every hundred females in the Army; ten years later, the figure was only sixty-five men for every hundred women. In addition, nearly a third (29 percent) of the membership figures reported to the government in these studies were children under the age of thirteen. A large number of Salvationists thus had no access to family income, which overwhelmingly remained at the disposal of the male family head, and in any case a sizable majority of those Salvationists who were breadwinners displayed little inclination to support the Army financially. The result was that contributions did not increase at the same rate as the membership. Income was far below what was required to fund the increasing demand for social relief, especially in the early years of the Great Depression.[17]

From 1929 to 1932, Salvation Army emergency relief expenses, counting the drain from social institutions and corps together, increased

Depression-era relief line at the Detroit Men's Social Service Center
Source: Detroit Adult Rehabilitation Center

by 700 percent. It was not surprising that *The War Cry* reported in 1931 that the Army was "strained to the utmost to successfully cope with the tremendous emergency relief load suddenly placed on it in addition to its normal work of social salvage." Indeed, a considerable part of the "normal work of social salvage" ground almost to a halt. The Industrial Homes (renamed Men's Social Service Centers in 1931-1932) had begun to show a small profit in the 1920s, as had the laborers' hotels. Now both of these institutions were swamped with the homeless, penniless, and desperate. Many facilities were converted into soup kitchens and free sleeping shelters, and regular rehabilitation programs were temporarily set aside. Little of what was being given to the Army after 1930 could be fixed or resold anyway, and there was almost no market among the poor for the few cleaned and repaired articles that were processed. The financial circumstances of the industrial homes grew daily more desperate, as funds from every source evaporated and expenses multiplied. Social officers characterized it as a "nightmare." There were days in which there was no food to offer applicants and no money to pay those in the Army's rehabilitation programs even their miserly standard wage: twenty-five cents a week over board. The Army consolidated or eliminated several administrative positions within the Men's Social Services Department during these years as a money-saving expedient, and a number of center managers delayed the long-discussed replacement of horse-drawn vehicles with motorized ones: whatever the benefits brought by motor trucks, the old horse and wagon was cheaper. The Salvation Army vied with a dwindling number of local dairies and the occasional junk dealer for the honor of being the last commercial users of horse-drawn transport in the United States.[18]

The Women's Social Service Department fared somewhat better. The Army's maternity homes were at least not besieged by homeless, jobless women. It was nonetheless impossible to raise enough in traditional ways to finance the Army's maternity program. Women officers were reduced to begging for food for their hospitals. Young Magna Sorenson traveled around a circuit of farms near Boise, Idaho, in a borrowed truck in the 1930s collecting free vegetables for her pregnant charges in the city. In New York City, Emma Ellegard was forced to make a long weekly trip by streetcar to a fish market to get a basketful of donated fish for the patients in her hospital. All officers in the Women's Social Service Department accepted large reductions in their meager salaries, and many served for nothing except their board and lodging. Unlike the hard-pressed men's social programs, however, there was no curtailment of services in the

Army's thirty-six maternity hospitals during the Depression — a fact of which veteran officers are still proud — although the small general hospital in Covington, Kentucky, was forced to close from 1932 to 1937.[19]

Financial problems pressed heavily on the Commander and the commissioners. General Higgins wrote from London in June 1931, gamely assuring the territorial commanders that the Army hoped to avoid "lowering the Flag" anywhere because of the Depression, which was worldwide, but instructing them to curtail all expenses beyond what was "absolutely essential." By 1931 the commissioners may well have wondered what was *left* to curtail. Buildings had been mortgaged, and in some cases — such as that of the seven-story hotel in Norfolk "snapped up" by Commissioner McIntyre in happier times — the Army could not even pay the interest. Officers who had comforted evicted families faced the prospect of joining them on the curb, surrounded by office furniture and one of the ubiquitous framed portraits of the Commander. Staff officers' salaries were reduced several times. Divisional officers lost even the small bonuses that they were used to receiving for maintaining *The War Cry* circulation in their districts: that journal recorded a "gradual decrease in circulation" throughout the Depression years. The territorial commander of the West pared the headquarters budget so close to the bone that the territorial staff band was forced to disband, and officers wrote new memos on the backs of old ones to save paper. In Chicago, Commissioner McIntyre had to take out a loan on his beloved Graham-Paige in order to pay the headquarters staff part of their (reduced) salaries. In 1932 the commissioners' conference officially recognized "the overwhelming demands made upon the organization by the present economic conditions and our high status in the welfare field" and announced the Army's determination to maintain assistance levels and reduce all other Army expenses. All four territorial training colleges were closed for the school year 1931-1932, and officers' salaries were reduced an additional 10 percent. (Disappointed candidates were urged to use the year's delay to prepare themselves by being faithful soldiers in their corps and by studying up on useful subjects.) At their 1933 conference, the commissioners renewed their pledge that the Army would carry on "with its utmost diligence" but acknowledged that fund-raising activities were suffering. Many of the Army's traditional supporters were faced with ruin themselves. "A reason given for the difficulty in securing funds," declared the commissioners, "was the fear in people's minds that they might themselves soon be without money." The commissioners' conference itself, held annually during the years 1921-1933, was suspended for the years 1934-

1936; its next meeting was on November 13, 1937. The Depression blighted even some programs that were still capable of producing revenue. The day after a new Evangeline residence for working women was opened in Detroit — a project begun before the hard times — the facility's entire operating budget disappeared when the city's banks failed.[20]

It was on the corps that the Depression bore with the most severity. Never a part of the national and territorial fund campaigns that followed the First World War, the corps had become dependent in the prosperous twenties on the Community Chest and the soldiers' usually meager cartridge contributions. This pattern continued into the 1930s. An audit of seven corps in Minneapolis in 1936 revealed, for instance, that 49 percent of their support came from the Community Chest and 51 percent from "Corps efforts," which included not only soldiers' personal contributions but *War Cry* sales and all sorts of public solicitations as well. All these sources except soldiers' contributions were dependent in some form on public support, and this was sharply reduced almost everywhere during the Depression. In many cases it dried up altogether, so that even without the extra demands caused by the hard times many corps would have been faced with debt just to maintain their regular activities. As it was, of course, concern with financing their regular activities was the least of the officer's problems: homeless, jobless men, worried families, and tens of thousands of anxious, penniless transients were joined by more thousands of neighborhood unemployed and hungry people at the doorsteps of the corps, drawn in their desperation by the promise held out to them by the name of the organization.[21]

Corps officers distributed to the jobless all manner of things that they had collected from kindhearted local merchants and farmers — coal, firewood, flour, milk, day-old bakery products, vegetables, and leftover food from restaurants. Many corps halls were used at night to house homeless men, who slept under newspapers on the seats or on the hardwood floors. In Roanoke, Virginia, where the Army hall was one block from the yards of the Norfolk and Western Railroad, a hundred men a day swamped the little corps. Young Capt. Ed Laity housed them all in an empty dance hall upstairs over the chapel and begged enough scraps from restaurants and a local vegetable market to provide soup or stew daily for the men. In the worst months of the Depression, the officer and his family had nothing for themselves but this soup and had to sleep with the transients when they could no longer pay the rent on their living quarters. On one of his tours, Commissioner McIntyre found that the two young women officers in International Falls, Minnesota, had lost their house and were forced to live in the Army hall and use a nearby filling-station restroom, drawing their water from its sink. For his part, Comm. Alexander Damon, territorial commander in the South during the Depression, visited a corps in Waycross, Georgia, in January 1933 where the "single boy officer" was so poor he could "hardly live." Even officers in better circumstances lost all or most of their salaries during part of the Depression years, and some officers received no salary through the entire period. Corps, like headquarters, fell into prolonged debt; a national survey in 1936 revealed that although the trend toward increasing the percentage of Army-owned corps had continued from the 1920s, the percentage of those corps that were listed in debt had increased slightly faster: 77 percent of corps were now in Army-owned properties, and almost 70 percent of them were in debt. The very few stations that could find adequate financing were forced to share the general privation: Commissioner Damon would not allow two officers to purchase new Dodge cars for their corps in March 1933 even though they had the necessary money in the proper account: it "would be serious in these days," he recorded in his diary, "to have new autos moving about different cities as S.A. cars." He imposed the same restriction on divisional officers whose staff cars had used up their mileage limit.[22]

The Army's financial difficulties in the Depression did not curtail its religious activities, however. While the volume of relief work often frustrated the efforts of Salvationists to provide spiritual and personal counseling to the recipients, traditional Army evangelistic programs were pushed with renewed vigor during these trying years. The Army sponsored a national revival crusade as part of the celebration of its fiftieth anniversary in the United States, for example. Called the "Golden Jubilee Crusade," the campaign was a great success, and Army leaders decided to declare similar campaigns for several more years, each with an encouraging motto designed to speak to the needs of the troubled times. The "Fight It Through" revival meetings came in 1931, and in 1932 the even more popular "Try Religion: Everything Else Has Failed" campaign. This theme proved so attractive to the public that the Army continued it into 1933 as well. The theme for 1935 was the most optimistic yet: "The World for God!" Readers of the Central *War Cry* in 1934 were urged to keep the wolf of fear from the door with a wall built of bricks of faith. "In spite of traffic and other conditions" which went "to make open-air evangelism more difficult than in days gone by," the Army succeeded in holding 163,991 such meetings in 1937. The automobile that had replaced the

"World for God" session of cadets, Eastern Territory, Bronx, New York, 1935-1936
Source: The Salvation Army National Archives

horse on city streets might even be used for the Lord's purposes: Adjutant Victor Dimond reported an encouraging incident at a street meeting in Boston in 1938, at which a man had driven up in a taxicab, thrown himself on the drum, been converted, jumped back into the cab, and dashed away! "Who can estimate the eternal worth of that open-air service?" The Salvation Army identified itself so willingly with its street-corner ministry in the Depression years that it chose that aspect of its program to symbolize the Army's religious activities in a mural painted by the religious artist Warner Sallman in its exhibit in the Hall of Religions at the Chicago World's Fair of 1933.[23]

It is true that the attitude of a portion of the public toward The Salvation Army had changed. Those who received assistance at the Army's hands during the Depression differed from those who had received help before 1930. Most of those who came forward for relief now had been working- and middle-class people, decent and respectable in their own eyes, whom, innocent and unprepared, economic disaster had overtaken. These people were unaccustomed to charity and to the poverty that preceded it, and they found it humiliating to ask for assistance. Many were discouraged and bitter, and they transferred their natural resentment onto the agency to which they were forced to go for relief. This was especially true when delay or inconvenience was encountered. John Steinbeck's powerful novel of the Depression *The Grapes of Wrath* expressed the confusion and hostility of these newly poor in graphic terms: a hungry family that was treated badly by The Salvation Army in some unspecified way complains, "If a body's ever took charity, it makes a burn that don't come out. . . . We was hungry — they made us crawl for our dinner. They took our dignity. They — I hate em!" On the other hand, The Salvation Army was clearly portrayed in an attractive and sympathetic manner in two major motion pictures of the Depression era: *Laughing Sinners,* with Joan Crawford and Clark Cable, made in 1931, and *She Done Him Wrong* released by Paramount in 1933, starring Mae West and Cary Grant, who played the part of an Army officer — the film made him a star.[24]

Criticism of the Army's charity did not negate the fact that the organization produced prodigious relief work on behalf of the Depression-poor, most of it practical and timely and given out with tact and kindness, even if the old-time personal counseling was set aside in the press of applicants. Commissioner McIntyre reported to the National Conference of Social Work in Detroit in 1933 that a national survey conducted by the Conference in March of that year concluded that The Salvation Army was caring for 20 percent of the homeless and transient population of the United States — more than any other agency. Huge shelters were opened in major cities for homeless men drawn there in a vain search for work. In 1930 The Salvation Army Mariners' League obtained the loan of an old river steamer, the *Broadway,* and berthed it at a Brooklyn pier as a hostel for stranded unemployed merchant seamen. That same year, the Army launched Wrigley Lodge on Union Street in Chicago. Operated by the veteran Brig. Sam Wood (once a California Charioteer), the facility enabled Army workers to feed eight thousand people a day. In New York the "Gold Dust Lodge" (named for a brand of flour) opened its doors in 1932 on the corner of Corlears and Cherry Streets in a factory donated by the Hecker Flour Company. The Lodge was presided over by Maj. and Mrs. Andrew Laurie and another graduate of zany pioneer adventures, Lt. Col. Wallace Winchell. These huge facilities were donated, and partly supported, by sympathetic wealthy individuals in the desperate days before the federal government began massive and varied attempts to relieve the unemployed. The Hutton Food Station at Thirty-sixth and Tenth Avenues was another such facility, operated by the Army to provide breakfast and supper to two hundred needy schoolchildren every day. These programs and scores of smaller ones operated throughout the country in institutions and corps were intended by the Army to serve as an expression of Christianity in practical form. They provided food and shelter at a time when no adequate large-scale government welfare existed.[25]

The Army was aware that those who came to its doors now were not accustomed to charity, and efforts were made to ease their humiliation. The cover of the Eastern *War Cry* proclaimed in October 1931: "Mr. Citizen, Temporarily Embarrassed, The Salvation Army Understands — and is Your Friend. Every Salvationist is pledged to extend to you, during these anxious times, as always, the right hand of aid and fellowship." To spare the feelings of such persons, the Army set up a Confidential Counselor's Bureau in New York to offer advice: in two days there were one thousand applicants.[26]

The Army, in fact, was full of advice during the Depression, most of it cheerful and filled with hope: the Depression would end when people regained their confidence, took control of their lives, and accepted Christ as Savior. Although the Army held out the hand of charity to all who needed it, even to those whose viewpoint its leadership regarded as extreme — when 400 Communists were felled by food poisoning at a convention in Massilon, Ohio, in 1932, the local Army gamely rushed on the scene with cots, overnight shelter, and a temporary soup kitchen — large-scale political and economic solutions no longer interested it. In fact, the Army abandoned the only political platform it had ever embraced — its official advocacy of the Eighteenth Amendment — even though it continued to view Prohibition as a definite success. Officers reported in many forums and journals that the incidence of public drunkenness had sharply declined following the ratification of the Eighteenth Amendment. Col. George H. Davis in Chicago was quoted as saying that the persons applying to the Army in 1932 were "almost entirely drink-free" and that "poverty from drink" was "a negligible factor in the current depression." Lt. Col. Wallace Winchell staged a public campaign in Easton, Pennsylvania, to warn the public against "the ravages of the old saloon." Nevertheless, it was clear that Prohibition had no future. The Republican Party, which supported it, was unlikely to remain in power after the next national election. It was time for the Army to take up again its traditional position that political solutions did not touch the central need of the heart. Evangeline, whose officers had endorsed Hoover in 1928, gladly accepted an invitation to open the Democratic National Convention in prayer in 1932, a fact that she pluckily announced in Chicago while addressing a Prohibition rally.

It was certain that the Democratic platform would demand a repeal of the Eighteenth Amendment; it was almost equally certain that whoever the Democrats nominated would win the election. "The Salvation Army knows nothing of parties or politics," she declared. "Tomorrow I shall enjoy the memorable privilege of opening the Democratic Convention in prayer."[27]

The Salvation Army managed to bring two rival football teams — Army and Navy — together again to play for the benefit of the Army's Depression relief, and in the same spirit the Army's leaders were convinced that religion, hearty good cheer, and a cooperative spirit would soon eliminate the Depression itself. Commissioner McIntyre conducted a "Good Cheer Council" for the officers of the Wisconsin–Upper Michigan Division, whose spirits had been somewhat dampened by the imminent bankruptcy of their division. A writer for the Central *War Cry* declared in 1932 that there was a "glory" in adversity: overcoming it brought a sense of satisfaction, a willingness to help others, and more complete reliance on God. The Eastern version of *The War Cry* encouraged its readers with the proclamation that God was speaking through the Depression to people who had no time or need for Him when the wheels of industry were humming. Adjutant Vincent Cunningham, the talented editor of the Southern edition, offered even more direct instructions on overcoming the unwelcome effects of hard times: "Stop Talking Depression!" Politics and social theories were clearly not the answer. Even a cheerful heart and a willing hand went only so far. The final solution to the Depression was individual salvation in Christ, multiplied many times. "What this country needs," declared Commissioner Brengle in 1932, "is a Revival!"[28]

However it may have appeared to some of its transient beneficiaries, The Salvation Army was not merely — or even primarily — a charity after all. It was an evangelical crusade, and its soul-saving activities continued without interruption through the Depression years. Salvation Army street parades and open-air meetings still attracted crowds. Such large corps as Oakland, Flint, and Brooklyn Citadel divided their musical forces into sections and held several open-air meetings at once, rejoining for a long parade back to the hall. Even medium-sized corps held sway on the streets: in Sioux City, Iowa, in 1933, crowds following the Army band became so large that police had to be called to control traffic. Bands with too few players for effective marching still went forth several times each week to play on street corners. In New York City young Richard Holz (grandson of the famous pioneer) led the tiny band at New York No. 3 out to Times

Square four times a week in 1936 and 1937. The corps, which became known as the "Glory Shop," was commanded by Adjutant Lyell Rader, whose zeal for souls was of the old-time variety. At the top of the Army's musical hierarchy, Maj. William Broughton, leader of the New York Staff Band, eliminated the last of the old-time woodwinds in that famous unit and standardized all instrumentation along British brass-band lines during the years 1932-1935. A writer for *Newsweek* at the end of the decade estimated that there were perhaps a thousand corps bands in the United States, the majority of which had between eight and fourteen members. In the hundreds of corps where there were only two or three players, or none at all, officers and soldiers were expected to sing and pray on the street corners. Carl Blied and his wife bravely sallied forth several times a week for five years in Bridgeton, New Jersey, with only a French horn and a drum.[29]

The Army's indoor activities flourished as well during the Depression. Christians naturally turn to their religion in adversity, and many working-class Salvationists were unemployed. The Army offered its soldiers who had time on their hands a considerable amount of plain fun and good company at no cost. Many who were drawn to the Army for relief became

"The Glory Shop," an open-air wagon, off New York's Times Square in 1937. Adjutant Lyell Rader is behind the two little girls.
Source: The Salvation Army National Archives

interested in the organization itself, and curiosity turned to conviction when they learned of Christ and His claims. If Army membership grew in the 1930s, attendance at Army activities soared. Total attendance in the Eastern Territory, for instance, was higher in 1932 than in any other year after 1927 until 1975. Programs for young people were particularly successful: band instrument classes, Scouts, camps, after-school sports, the Girl Guards, and the Sunbeams all grew rapidly in the 1930s. At the other end of the working years, in areas where retired officers were concentrated, they organized for fellowship and active spiritual warfare during these years. The Salvation Army Retired Officers League was organized in New Jersey in 1928, and The Salvation Army Retired Officers' Association (SAROA) was organized in Miami in 1931. Nor were faithful Salvationist families overlooked in the developing structure of Salvationism: in 1936 General Evangeline Booth inaugurated the Order of the Silver Star to decorate proud Army mothers with a star for each child who served the Army as an officer.[30]

The Scandinavian work celebrated jubilees of its own every five years. At the forty-fifth anniversary in Chicago in 1933 Commander Evangeline Booth was decorated by the Swedish ambassador with the Gold Medal of the Vasa Order — Sweden's highest decoration for a non-Swede. The Scandinavian ministry was strong enough in Chicago to support the opening of a major new corps during the Depression: Chicago No. 20 (Mont Clare) opened in 1935 with Gabriel Skrudland as its corps sergeant major. The Golden Jubilee in 1937 saw the Scandinavian work at the height of its success, providing material relief and spiritual comfort to thousands "who, handicapped by a lack of knowledge of the language, or by a natural reticence and pride, would never have made their physical or spiritual needs known." There were Scandinavian departments in every territory except the South, led during the Depression by individuals of exceptional piety and zeal — Lt. Col. Axel Beckman (East), Col. Tom Gabrielsen (Central), and Brig. Hal Madsen (West). The work was weakest in the West, where Madsen privately urged the Army to consolidate all Scandinavian activities in a single national administration so that weak divisions and territories (like his own) could draw on the strength of the whole. Along with the retired Commissioner Brengle in the American corps, these men traveled widely, holding successful evangelical services. Many Salvation Army corps, in fact, experienced spontaneous revivals in the Holy Spirit during the Depression years and in their joy forgot the rigors of the hard times.[31]

The Commander was at her best during these years. Although nearing seventy, Evangeline had lost none of her flair nor the graciousness in public that made her, year after year, the personal darling of her troops. Her addresses continued to draw packed halls. The "Commander in Rags" — sad to say — had been put aside forever as somewhat inappropriate for a woman well past middle age, but the "World's Greatest Romance," practiced and refined to the level of professional entertainment, remained a popular favorite. Nor was Evangeline dependent on a few set pieces: in 1931 she traveled with the New York Staff Band in a motor tour of New York and Pennsylvania, speaking forty-seven times without repeating herself. The tour was a success for many reasons, not the least of which was a revival of old-time hallelujah clowning. The Staff Band, for instance, paraded into Butler, Pennsylvania, in tiny Austin cars — one car to each bandsman! Evangeline herself had a zany side: she liked to do her personal shopping in what she imagined to be a foolproof disguise, which consisted of dressing in civilian clothes and calling herself "Miss Cory." Once she went incognito to purchase flagstone for a walkway at her cabin at Lake George, New York, only to be spotted by the quarryman at once — by her nose![32]

Several aspects of the Commander's personality could be seen in the development of a series of special weekly Friday evening meetings she arranged for the new Centennial Memorial Temple at national headquarters on West Fourteenth Street. The programs were ably planned by the territorial commander, Comm. John McMillan, assisted by Brig. W. Alex Ebbs, and their quality was superb. The Army's best musicians performed, and there were special compositions for many of the services. The Commander, at her polished and eloquent best, spoke often. A special brass ensemble under the direction of Erik Leidzen, employed by the Army as the divisional bandmaster, was brought together in 1930 to play for these meetings.[33]

Leidzen was a man of rare ability, a zealous Christian whose standards of personal piety and musical performance exerted a profound and long-lasting influence on the lives of many young Army musicians. He did not suffer fools gladly, however; like the Commander, whom he once described as "the Lord's handmaiden," Erik Leidzen could be cranky and was sensitive to the point of fragility. These two Salvationists struck sparks off one another at the end of the last of the Friday meetings at the Temple, in an incident that was once too well-known in Army circles to ignore here.

The last of these special meetings was held on May 26, 1933. An especially prestigious and enjoyable program was offered to the packed hall that included a new march, "Brooklyn Citadel," by Adjutant Bearchell, who led the band at that famous corps; a new composition by Evangeline called "Streams in the Desert"; and a galaxy of songs, duets, and solos. The Commander spoke, but the guest of honor was Edwin Franko Goldman, a band conductor second only to Sousa in accomplishment and fame. Leidzen had written a special march for the guest, "E-F-G," based on Goldman's initials. The great man was surprised by this array of Army music and especially by Leidzen's flattering march. He promptly declared Leidzen to be a "genius" and praised to the skies all that he had heard. A thrill of pride swept the delighted crowd, most of whom were Salvationists and musicians themselves.

Evangeline was caught up in the excitement and felt inspired to end the carefully planned program in a burst of hallelujah enthusiasm with an old-time chorus called "The Salvation Army Doxology." Such alterations are commonplace in the Army meetings, but Leidzen, always stiffly formal about the conduct of public meetings, and with Goldman's praises still tickling his ears, coolly informed the Commander that the band had no music for that piece and would not play it. The song was known to everybody — could they not play along without music? They could not — not after a superb, well-rehearsed, and brilliant evening: it would be a ruinous anticlimax. Perplexed, Evangeline turned to the band and asked them to play the song. Leidzen, now thoroughly irritated, intervened by laying his baton down on his music stand, and the band followed his lead, putting down their instruments. The audience saw none of this, and happily sang the chorus with a single cornet. The following Monday morning Leidzen refused a summons to the Commander's office, and she reluctantly dismissed him from his employment with the Army. He became the arranger for the Goldman Band almost at once and nursed wounded feelings for years, until patience and tact drew his great talents back into Army service. The incident, trivial in itself, caused confusion and resentment at the time among Salvationist musicians, who naturally admired Leidzen for his gifts. It illustrated the dangers to which leaders and Army musicians alike had become prey in the new era of professionalism, when personalities and protocol seemed to replace service and zeal as the forces driving them to action.[34]

The Salvation Army continued to make musical progress, however, despite these little setbacks. In 1934 the Central Music Institute (CMI) opened for the first time at Camp Lake, Wisconsin, north of Chicago. The Eastern Territory launched its own annual camp the next year, at Star

Lake, New Jersey, under Lt. Col. John Allen, who had pioneered the Army's first band camp in 1920. These camps offered sectional rehearsals and several bands, graded according to the players' abilities. CMI and Star Lake each developed its own traditions and proud alumni, and both have proved lasting successes, annual beacons for aspiring young Salvationist musicians. The great distances in the West and poverty of brass music in the South were insuperable obstacles in the path of effective territorial band camps in those regions before World War II. London offered correspondence courses in brass band conducting to adult leaders, but by the end of the decade only one American, Bandmaster Samuel E. Collins of San Francisco Citadel, had completed both the intermediate and advanced courses.[35]

There were other renovations besides music — the *War Cry* editions appeared in a smaller, more modern format in 1939 — and the Army also opened its evangelical work in new fields. In 1937 Capt. Cecil Brown laid the cornerstone of the Maple Springs Citadel in the mountains of North Carolina. It was the first of a string of log cabin and trailer chapels set up to serve the mountain people. Captain Brown, like one of the Outriders of old, traveled alone on horseback over the circuit between the rustic little outposts and declared in word and in many good deeds a simple gospel of love. In that same year The Salvation Army opened fire on the Republic of Mexico, which was promptly annexed, in a spiritual sense, to the Southern Territory. The heroic pioneer was a struggling Mexican evangelist named Alejandro Guzman, who had traveled to Dallas from the Mexican capital to offer his tiny band of coworkers to The Salvation Army, of which he had heard only recently. This "Salvation Patrol" was invited to Atlanta to meet the General, who was in the city to celebrate the tenth anniversary of the opening of the territory. The Mexican valiants were enrolled in the Army and sent off with great enthusiasm to wage spiritual war in their country. The Mexican branch of the Army, although almost entirely financed from American funds, was not considered a foreign mission but a regular division of the Southern Territory. The work remained under the noble Guzman, who struggled on for years with only a handful of soldiers against official opposition and the indifference of the people — proving, like Captain Brown and thousands of street-corner warriors, that the old-time crusading spirit continued to flourish.[36]

Still, the old Army was changing in the 1930s. A quartet of venerable officers' ranks were dropped in 1931: staff captain, field major, commandant, and ensign. In 1935 the traditional system of numbering Army corps was at last abandoned in favor of giving each corps an individual name. A relic of the glorious days when the Army was expanding so rapidly that it was difficult to keep track of all the new corps, the number system was given up with great reluctance by veteran soldiers. The new names had a certain dignity, however, and soon offered competition to the old numbers in younger hearts. New York No. 3 became Times Square Corps, Minneapolis No. 4 became Temple Corps, Washington, D.C., No. 2 became Central Corps, and Los Angeles No. 1 became Los Angeles Congress Hall. Some corps, including Oakland, Brooklyn No. 1, and Flint, had been known as "Citadel" for years before the change became official. Inevitably, there were other changes: pioneers and heroes began to be promoted to Glory and disappeared one by one from scenes they had enlivened and graced. Booth-Tucker died soon after Bramwell in 1929, Maj. John Milsaps and Eliza Shirley Symmonds in 1932, Field Major Emma Westbrook ("the heroine of fifty appointments") in 1933, and Lt. Col. Wallace Winchell in 1934. When Lt. Comm. Edward J. Parker rose to speak at an Army meeting in Chicago the next year, in 1935, he was introduced as "the senior, active American-born officer in point of years." Joe the Turk, the "Sanctified Salvationist Showman," joined the others in Glory in 1937. The Army staged showpiece hallelujah send-offs for each of these departed heroes, and each event caused a flurry of renewed interest in pioneer times. The same interest was stimulated at the end of the decade when it was learned that Emma Westbrook had not been the last living member of Railton's party after all: ex-Captain Emma Morris, now Mrs. Lambert, was found still living in Frankford, Pennsylvania, where she had opened a corps fifty-nine years before. Her extensive interview in *The War Cry* was filled with interesting details.[37]

There was another change as well: the Commander departed the American scene. The "Joan of Arc" of the reformers was elected General at last on September 3, 1934. Her rise to that eminence was long and uneven, but she made it at age sixty-nine on the fifth ballot, with not a single vote to spare. Evangeline had disagreed — blessedly, mostly in private — with her predecessor, Edward Higgins, over certain details in The Salvation Army Act of 1931. Higgins and other Army leaders had prepared the bill for Parliament in order to regularize the election of the General, to set a retirement age (seventy-three), and to create a corporation to assume legal title to Army property (which was still held in the General's personal name). Her objections were that the new bill did not provide sufficient protection for the financial independence of the American branch and that the new structure was not democratic enough. At one point Evangeline's correspondence with Higgins took an alarming turn. Enough of the story leaked out that a few officers became unreasonably frightened, and the territorial commanders had to reassure them. The bill, adjusted slightly to suit the Commander, passed. Higgins was a generous-spirited and honorable officer, and he voluntarily retired at the age he had originally proposed as the limit (seventy), even though the new law did not apply to the incumbent. His graceful departure left the way open for Evangeline.[38]

The Commander's election marked the end of an era. To millions of Americans, she was the symbol and embodiment of The Salvation Army, and the great majority of American Salvationists had never known a different leader. Evangeline had ruled the Army from 120 West Fourteenth Street for thirty years. Her triumphant return to America as General and her farewell parades and congress in New York in November were gala events, marked not only by an avalanche of tributes, from President Roosevelt downward, but by an outpouring of genuine affection that touched the now-elderly General-elect to the heart. She departed these shores in a cloud of ticker tape, fireboat sprays, tugboat whistles, hallelujahs, and tearful farewells.

When the excitement died down, staff officers had time to reflect on the administrative changes the new General had made: her successor, Lt. Comm. Edward J. Parker, would serve not as "Commander" — the title disappeared for a time — but as "national secretary," with reduced powers. The territorial commanders were given additional responsibility at the expense of the now-truncated national headquarters; the commissioners were to answer directly to the General and send copies of all correspondence to the national secretary. The latter was authorized to serve as legal head of the Army corporation and to communicate on behalf of the Army with the federal government in "any great national crisis or in connection with National Efforts on great moral questions and the like." Parker's powers were so diminished that the *Literary Digest* assumed that Evangeline as General had "retained her . . . Commandership of the United States Salvation Army." She certainly retained her command of the worldwide Army: no more was heard from Evangeline about democratic reforms.[39]

For all that, American Salvationists loved her still — the more so, perhaps, when rumors began to circulate that her flair for the dramatic was not having a good effect on the British. Americans knew Evangeline was an American citizen, loud in her praises for this country and for the Army here. She announced early in her period of command in London that she intended to return to her adopted country in retirement. Her one official visit to the United States in 1937 gave American Salvationists a last opportunity to acclaim their old Commander. The highlight of the tour was the ten-year jubilee celebration held in Atlanta in September. American staff officers who knew her well grieved for Evangeline when Lt. Comm. Richard Griffith died suddenly in October 1938. He had been her private secretary and trusted aide for thirty-five years, loyal and discreet. Officers who had been in the Commander's American inner circle cherished their memories of Griffith playing the cello while she played the harp during long evenings before the fire at Arcadia, her home in Hartsdale, New York.[40]

The Army began to improve its operating facilities as the Depression eased. Eva's Atlanta meetings caught the attention of a local businessperson, who offered the Army the entire campus of the Atlanta Theological Seminary on Stewart Avenue for a "remarkably low figure" — too low to resist for the spacious campus, which was ideally suited for a new training college. The Southern Territorial Training College was officially opened there on June 5, 1938, and dedicated by the retired General Higgins, who had settled in the United States.[41]

In San Francisco, the indefatigable Major Kobayashi presided over the opening on February 28, 1937, of a new headquarters building for the Japanese Division. The structure at 1450 Laguna Street represented the culmination of the Major's lifework: he had raised "by far the major portion" of the money for it himself during a heroic five-year campaign in California and Japan. The Emperor of Japan himself donated five thousand yen in 1931 (the equivalent of $1,750 at the time), and a framed decree to that effect hung in the new chapel. The building housed the social service headquarters and a corps and was opened with great ceremony by Comm. Benjamin Orames, the territorial commander, and the consul-general of Japan, who raised the Japanese flag alongside the American and Salvation Army flags. The training college band played American and Japanese patriotic music for the two thousand people who attended the festivities. It was the greatest day in the history of the division.[42]

Evangeline Booth retired as General with little ceremony and returned home to Hartsdale. She had reached the age of seventy-three on Christmas Day, 1938, but remained in office another year in the vain hope that the world situation would become less troubled, allowing the inter-

Groundbreaking ceremony for the Japanese National Headquarters,
San Francisco, 1937 Source: Western Territorial Museum

national commissioners to gather for another High Council. She finally departed London on September 2, the day after the war began in Poland. A writer who had interviewed her during a visit to New York in May predicted that it might be "some time before the amazing momentum that she has acquired in 35 years slows down very much." In any event, the power she held passed from her all at once, into unfamiliar hands. Her successor was George L. Carpenter, whose name had figured in the prelude to the Bramwell crisis ten years before but who was largely unknown in the United States. Several American observers outside the Army's ranks interpreted Carpenter's election, after a lengthy balloting procedure in London, as a further step in the democratization of the Army's autocratic structure. For one thing, Carpenter had agreed that if he were elected General he would consult the other commissioners on important matters — a process that Carpenter did indeed adopt and that was formalized in 1947 as the General's Advisory Council. For another thing, no member of the Booth family was chosen — and none has been chosen since. A report in *Newsweek* appeared under the headline "Salvationists Curb Autocracy with Election of New Leader." Britain's role in the war and the fact that Carpenter had no close associations with the American branch of the Army caused the new General to focus the attention of the beleaguered international headquarters on the Army's other branches. Territorial officers in the United States were given wide latitude. In 1943 the title of national commander was revived and bestowed on the deserving Commissioner Parker shortly before his retirement.[43]

The war began in Europe in September 1939. The attitude of the Army in the United States at first was pacific, that of an international organization with its own agenda. A story in *Newsweek* conveyed the Army's official position that the war would never cause the Army to neglect "its manifold peacetime activities." Army officials kept public attention fixed on the Army's traditional social services, and above all on its evangelistic religious crusade. References by officers and Army writers to world affairs in 1938 and 1939 were to the Army's worldwide network of good works, many of them financed and otherwise supported by the American branch of the movement; glowing reports of the activities of Capt. and Mrs. Clesson W. Richardson, a married couple of American officer-physicians on duty at an Army hospital for women and children in India, were typical. A *War Cry* cover labeled "International Service Station" portrayed The Salvation Army pouring the "Spirit of love" into cans marked "Everyday World." On September 27, 1939, The Salvation Army had a special day at the New York World's Fair, led by Comm. Alexander Damon, the territorial leader, and officially hosted by Mayor Fiorello LaGuardia. The Army's entire display was evangelistic, consisting of open-air services around the Fair grounds and gospel meetings in the Temple of Religion. The twenty-first anniversary celebration of Armistice Day, November 11, 1939, held in the Centennial Memorial Temple on 14th Street, was built around an even more explicitly peaceful and religious theme. The speaker, a local judge, called for peace, and the congregation responded with the song "Peace, Perfect Peace"; the major Staff Band concert piece was a tone poem, "Triumph of Peace."[44]

The Salvation Army's territorial training colleges continued to offer a cross-section of Salvationist life in the United States during the last years of peace. A writer commenting on the Army's school in Morris Heights in the South Bronx in 1937, for instance, touched again upon a lingering popular mistake about the social basis of Salvationism: "Contrary to the widespread misconception, the officers of The Salvation Army are not recruited from prisons, saloons and gutters. About half of them are children of Salvationists, and the rest began attendance at its Sunday Schools at a tender age." An analysis of the "Enthusiasts" of 1937-1938 in New York conducted by Brig. Norman S. Marshall, the training principal, revealed the truth of that contention: out of 75 cadets, 71 had been Army Corps Cadets, 56 had been converted in the Army before the age of ten, 46 had been Army brass musicians, and 41 were the children of Salvationists. Later sessions, the "Dauntless Evangelists" of 1938-1939, and the "Hold-Fast" class of 1940, showed the same patterns. Few cadets had been to college; about half had graduated from high school. Although a few cadets had professional or managerial backgrounds, the large majority of them came from working-class occupations. In the 1940 class, for instance, eight women cadets still listed their previous occupation as "domestic servant," which in Victorian days had been the most common occupation from which women officers were drawn. The Training College Band, led by Cadet Richard E. Holz in 1938, had twenty-five players, all male, but women outnumbered men in every session. Until America entered the war, however, the proportion of women in the Army training sessions was not markedly different from that in the denomination as a whole (over 60 percent). A reporter for *The New Yorker* magazine noted in April 1940, however, that the women cadets were more attractive and "looked some-what more at home."[45]

For many aspects of the Salvation Army program, however, the war in Europe brought rapid and important change. The development of war-related industries geared to supply the needs of the armed forces of the European democracies, and later, in September 1940, the enactment of the Selective Service Act, at first drew thousands and then hundreds of thousands of men out of the labor pool. The Men's Social Centers, so recently swamped with applicants, had difficulty finding enough clients to operate the Center programs in the late 1930s. Within a few years this shortage of clients and employees, combined with restrictions on supplies of materials, forced this department to make decisions that abruptly altered its history. In addition, departmental leaders were forced to develop an official strategy for responding to the requirements of the Fair Labor Standards Act passed in 1938. The new law could be understood to classify the clients in the Army's centers as employees contributing to the profit of the organization rather than as recipients of a program's benefits. In other fields of Army endeavor the European war did not dampen the innovative spirit, but wartime conditions frequently prevented or delayed full implementation of any scheme that required additional resources in funding, personnel, or material. The Army's first serious attempt to broaden systematic rehabilitation of alcoholics, for instance, came in 1939 — not in one of the Army's Men's Social Service Centers but in a new facility, called a Harbor Light Corps, opened in Detroit by the divisional commander, Lt. Col. James Murphy. Full implementation of the Harbor Light program, and the introduction of similar programs on a much larger scale throughout the Army's Men's Social Services Department, had to be postponed because of wartime conditions. This did not prevent the reduced Detroit program from rescuing one of the Army's most notable converts, Tom Crocker.[46]

Services had to be arranged for the rapidly swelling armed forces as well. One national magazine suggested helpfully in 1939 that The Salvation Army might bring back "the coffee and doughnuts that American veterans remember so well." For its part, the Army, which had labored with great success to keep those memories alive for twenty years, was unlikely to forget the First World War on the eve of the Second. Commissioner Parker and Lt. Col. John Allan, who had served as a chaplain in 1917 and 1918, were determined to revive the cooperative spirit of those years in advance of the actual need while praying all the while that the United States would not be drawn into the fighting. A number of American social welfare agencies including Catholic Community Services, the Jewish Welfare Board, the YMCA, the YWCA, and the Travelers' Aid Society responded to the Salvation Army's invitation to join in a spirit of patriotic camaraderie to offer services to the country's armed forces. (The Red Cross, which provided no social or welfare services, declined to join.) On January 31, 1941, leaders of the agencies formed the United Welfare Committee, and on February 4 the group was incorporated as the United Service Organization (USO). In March the commissioners' conference was called together by Commissioner Parker for the sole purpose of discussing Salvation Army activities in government military camps throughout the country; the Army already operated programs in 46 camps, 27 of them in the South and West. Having launched the USO as a cooperative venture, The Salvation Army operated a number of clubs for the USO as well as emergency service centers of its own called "Red Shield Clubs," which offered showers and emergency sleeping accommodations. At first the Army intended to forbid the use of any form of tobacco or dancing in its centers, but it relented to the extent of allowing dances in buildings owned by the government so long as they were sponsored by the YWCA, which, the commissioners were promised, would conduct them "on the highest plane."[47]

Then, too, the growing ranks of soldiers required spiritual guidance. The Army's offer to provide at least part of its quota of military chaplains was accepted at once. In November 1940, Col. John Allan was asked by the secretary of war to join the five-man staff of the chief of chaplains in Washington and was given the Army's official permission to do so. By the end of the war, thirty-two Salvation Army officers had served as military chaplains. All of them were in the U.S. Army and the Army Air Corps: the Navy would not waive its requirement that its chaplain officers have a college degree and three years of seminary, a requirement that no Salvation Army officer could have met in 1941.[48]

On Saturday, December 6, 1941, the Western *War Cry* announced a three-day conference of Salvation Army leaders in New York to arrange broader Army participation in the USO; there were already seventy-five posts and close to a hundred officers dedicated to the work. Still, America was not yet in the war, and Salvationists were instructed to pray for peace. These issues of *The War Cry* went on sale in the lobbies of West Coast corps on Sunday, December 7, although it is unlikely that attendance at services that morning would have reached normal levels: news of the Japanese attack on Pearl Harbor had been on West Coast radios all morning. Salvationists learned later that they had already suffered a casualty: Aviation Ordnanceman 3rd Class John D. Buckley, a Salvationist from Providence and a member of the Future Officers' Fellowship who joined the Navy in November 1940, was killed in action at his machine-gun post.[49]

Another casualty of the war was The Salvation Army's work among Japanese in the continental United States. The Japanese divisional structure itself had been officially terminated almost a year before Pearl Harbor day when the valiant Major Kobayashi died suddenly of heart failure on October 15, 1940. Venerated by his troops and respected by the Japanese community, Kobayashi was irreplaceable as divisional commander: no other Japanese officer would accept the responsibility. In addition, several Army leaders argued that the Japanese Division was too small — it consisted of just eight corps and the two social institutions on Laguna Street — to warrant the expense of a separate divisional structure. The latter argument was not directed specifically against Japanese work; in 1942 the Western territorial commander suggested the amalgamation of Scandinavian work in his territory because there were too few units to justify a separate administration. Kobayashi's funeral was a full-dress Army affair conducted by the territorial commander, Comm. Donald McMillan, and the training college band. Kobayashi had suffered from a bad heart for years, yet despite the knowledge that overwork might kill him, he refused to slacken his pace lest the Army work suffer. The major's funeral was quite correctly a hero's send-off.[50]

The case was, unfortunately, quite different for the remaining Japanese officers. The entry of the United States into the war against Japan in December 1941 immediately made it much more difficult to conduct activities that were publicly identified as Japanese, regardless of the nature of those activities. For the first months after Pearl Harbor, Japanese Salvation Army officers attempted to carry on their normal activities in the face of widespread and open hostility directed not against their religion but their nationality. Even some American Salvationists were caught up in the wartime hysteria: officers now regarded Kobayashi's death, so near in time to Pearl Harbor, as "mysterious." The Emperor's innocent gift to the Japanese building fund, the framed imperial decree in the chapel, the imperial portrait in Kobayashi's office, his "frequent" trips to Japan — all these things now appeared in an ominous light. The fact that the Japanese officers were sometimes shy and reticent around their American comrades was taken as more proof of Oriental perfidy. Dismayed and confused, several Japanese officers resigned or accepted leaves of absence. The Japanese children's home on Laguna Street was placed under American officers from the Women's Social Department. In March 1942 all Japanese on the West Coast, Salvation Army officers included, were transported to relocation camps in the interior, and the Japanese work of The Salvation Army in the continental United States officially ceased to exist.[51]

A few Japanese officers, who had already given up everything for God and the Army, remained loyal through the ordeal of arrest, deportation, and the long years in the camps. Maj. Masahide Imai was in command of the Japanese corps at Fresno (one of only two in the division with a brass band) when the war began. In March 1942 he and his family were transferred to a camp near Little Rock, Arkansas. He resolved to wear his uniform, to minister to any other Salvationists in the camp, and to take his turn to preach "the Salvation Army way" at the united Protestant services held weekly in the camp. Word that an officer was in the camp reached the Salvation Army headquarters in nearby Little Rock, and the divisional secretary and corps officer came at once, greeted the Imais like lost lambs, sang and prayed with them, and offered to take them out of the camp every Sunday so that they might speak in various corps around the division, enjoy Sunday dinner with comrades, and go sight-seeing. The camp commander, a military officer, made it clear from the outset that he admired The Salvation Army and had regretted being forced to imprison any of its officers: the major was free to go whenever he liked, on trust. Imai's faith in the Army was thus rewarded, and he was "so happy, so encouraged." He later attended five conferences in five major cities as a representative of Japanese ministerial groups in the camps to plan for work among Japanese-Americans after the war.[52]

Maj. and Mrs. Tozo Abe, who had been in charge of the Army's Japanese work in Stockton, showed similar courage and zeal during their initial period in the Reception Center at Ponoma, where they conducted nightly open-air services with Army drum and flag (loaned by Salvation Army administration) and their own guitar and trumpet. Later, during the three-year internment at Heart Mountain, Wyoming, the Abes continued to function as Salvation Army officers, wearing regulation uniform, conducting Sunday school classes, visiting the sick and elderly (on a bicycle the major had purchased by mail order), and holding weekly religious services. As in the case of the Imais, fellow Salvationists from nearby Army corps visited the Abes regularly in the camp, took them out for visits to other Salvation Army facilities, and, in the case of the Abes, invited them to be special guests at the annual Divisional Youth Councils. Major and Mrs. Abe later remembered not only that many persons were converted to Christ in the camp but that two Japanese men decided to become ministers as a result of the Abes' example.[53]

The war bore heavily on The Salvation Army in the United States. Providing 32 chaplains and officer personnel for 219 Red Shield clubs and 200 USO clubs placed an enormous strain on the Army's human resources. The administration of this program, under Brig. William Parkins, became an important administrative responsibility. Selective Service and the patriotic impulse combined to draw many young Salvationists who would otherwise have served as officers and lay employees into military service. Up until 1940 the disproportion of women to men among Salvation Army officers had remained around 60 percent, where it had been for many years. A study of the Southern Training College for the war years, however, reveals a marked decrease in the number of male cadets. In 1942 there were four men out of twenty cadets; in 1945 there were three single and four married men out of thirty-one. The situation in the other territories differed only in detail. At the same time, corps officers were asked to take on extra duties for the duration of the war, especially those in corps near military bases, ports of embarkation, and prisoner-of-war camps. The demands of war service, combined with a shortage of officers and recruits, threw a terrible weight on remaining corps and social officers alike. Men's social centers, training colleges, and territorial purchasing and supply departments lost clientele and suffered officer staff reductions steadily throughout the war. Command structures and departments were consolidated in every territory and at every level to conserve officer personnel. In 1942, for instance, the Eastern Training College principal also took on the duties of New York divisional commander, and Comm. Ernest I. Pugmire served as both national commander and Eastern territorial commander after 1944.[54]

The war hit the Men's Social Service Department with special force. The ease with which men could secure profitable employment and the repeated siftings of the male population by local Selective Service boards left few men who were not elderly or of unsteady habits in Army centers. All institutions suffered a loss of clients; most could barely operate even a reduced program. Social officers were forced to reappraise their entire mission. Pioneering work in the adoption of case-work procedures and counseling of alcoholics based on the understanding of alcoholism as a disease was done by Maj. Richard E. Baggs in Philadelphia, Adjutant Peter J. Hofman in Cleveland, and Capt. Cecil Briggs in Kansas City. Their reformist ideas were first made known to a broader circle within the Army by a series of reports based on surveys of several Eastern centers prepared by Adjutant A. E. Agnew, a divisional staff officer with professional social work training. A series of important conferences were held culminating in the Eastern Territory in "Institutes" held in 1944 for all Men's Social Service officers. From a "deliberate and organized reemphasis of the original aims and purposes of our social work with men" there emerged the conviction that the Army must greet the postwar era with a new program for men — one designed to bring together professional counseling, Alcoholics Anonymous, medical advice, and Christian evangelism to focus on men's problems, most of which were caused by alcoholism. In 1944 not a single center had a complete program specifically designed for alcoholics; indeed, the Army's national commander responded in the same year to a nationwide survey of hospital treatment of alcoholism by stating flatly that his organization did "not maintain institutions for alcoholics in this country." In addition, both principle and the practical implications of the new Fair Labor Standards Act caused the Army to abandon not only the idea but the very appearance that its social institutions were a "business" employing men to raise revenue for operations; the purpose of the Men's Social Service Department to make "better men" had to be reaffirmed. Out of the ruins of the "industrial home" concept, which World War II destroyed, there emerged the "Service-to-Man" program, which transformed the Men's Social Service Department in the years after the war.[55]

The Women's Social Service Department, on the other hand, enjoyed something of a boom during the war. The maternity program was already a proven and acknowledged success; wartime romances provided an increased volume of clients. The war did bring its exigencies, of course — two young women in the Oakland home went into labor during the first air-raid practice of the war — but war brought no lasting changes to the department. Individual officers found an opportunity for an occasional innovation, all on their own. When the Army's all-black maternity hospital in Cincinnati was closed by the state of Ohio before the war for violation of recently upgraded safety standards, Brig. Marian Kimball opened the Catherine Booth Hospital in the same city to black physicians — the first nonsegregated medical facility in the city to recognize their professional capabilities officially. The two Army facilities were officially merged in 1940, and the policy of allowing black physicians to practice was courageously continued during the war years, despite the fact that the beginnings of black migration from the South into Ohio in search of war-related employment caused racial antagonism to develop in Cincinnati.[56]

The Salvation Army was placed on "war footing" everywhere on the home front. In the anxious days of January 1942, Western territorial headquarters offered the facilities of all 306 of its institutions and corps to civil defense authorities to serve as bomb shelters. Officers were prepared to assist in the mass evacuation of the West Coast, and the national commander gamely volunteered the Army's entire fleet of 1,125 salvage trucks to military authorities to help in this vast undertaking. In Pittsburgh the divisional commander, Brig. William Harris, ordered a mobile canteen — a panel truck equipped to prepare and serve hot meals, drinks, and sandwiches — to accompany units of the Pennsylvania Home Guard as they defended "strategic points" around the city. Another mobile canteen served the men on the first blackout watch in Tacoma, Washington. A corps officer, Adjutant Henry Dries, convinced pharmaceutical magnate Gen. Robert Wood Johnson to finance the rebuilding of the corps at New Brunswick, New Jersey, into a "model" bomb shelter.[57]

The Salvation Army adopted a positively belligerent tone, even in its spiritual ministry. The Western territory's revival campaign for 1942 was entitled "Enlistment for Christ," and was heralded by such mottos as "Cal V ary for Victory!" The departed Brengle was cited reassuringly as having asserted that killing in battle was not murder. The Army's traditional religious and family activities were not allowed to falter during the emergency. In Racine, Wisconsin, Hester Pottinger began the first of a historic series of Girl Guard Troops in 1942; next year in Augusta, Georgia, Capt. W. R. H. Goodier topped off a full schedule of visiting jails and hospitals, distributing Christmas baskets, and administering family welfare with 142 street-corner meetings, 11 radio broadcasts, and the addition of 69 persons to the body of Army converts. The Army's home-front service lost none of its militancy by being more largely administered by women than during peacetime. Military service, rigorous war industry employment, and the increased demands of Salvation Army service took so many men that many old and long-established corps bands that had previously been bastions of male service, such as Oakland Citadel, were forced for the first time to choose between accepting women musicians and curtailing operations or ceasing them altogether. Encouraged by officers and filled with the same patriotic sentiments that filled their husbands, brothers, and boyfriends in the Army's war work, the women of the Home League threw themselves into the Army's war work. The service they gave or directed others in giving was varied, but it was all typical of the Army: immediate, practical, and free.[58]

In Alaska a "sewing brigade" mended jeepfuls of uniforms as hordes of arriving troops swamped the few civilian tailors. The women of the Freeport, Long Island, corps tended the severely wounded arriving at Mitchell Field, showering them with cakes, cookies, and cigarettes and writing their letters, while another group of volunteers knit scarves and helmet liners for overseas troops. The women volunteers of the Asbury Park, New Jersey, corps supplied goodies and all manner of kindly attentions to the patrols of the Coast Artillery guarding the North Jersey beaches; the grateful young men voted one of the women, Marion Kuster, their favorite pinup. In Atlanta, Georgia, in 1943 the annual "Dixie Divisional Home League Rally War Service Display" consisted of 1,110 patriotically handmade garments. All over the country the members of Home League and non-Salvationist volunteers of the Women's Auxiliaries served throughout the war. The refreshments, letters, knitted garnets (there was even a national "Home League of the Air," with the motto: "Remember Pearl Harbor — Purl Harder!"), utility kits, layettes for service wives, fracture pillows, and afghans produced by these women "reached astronomical proportions." This mountain of good works was the more remarkable when one remembers that Salvation Army women were also called upon to take up many regular corps duties formerly carried out by departed men. Every Home League kept a "Book of Remembrance" that listed the name of every serviceman in the town, so that the ladies could pray weekly for each person individually.[59]

In Hawaii and Alaska the Army's USO and Home League service were especially arduous; conditions sometimes approximated the front-line ministry of the First World War. Among Salvationists, only chaplains were closer to actual combat. Maj. and Mrs. Alva Holbrook, USO officers at Schofield Barracks at Pearl Harbor, came under fire on December 7 and responded by making four thousand doughnuts for hungry defenders. Throughout the war the Army visited hospitals, made bandages, and ran child-care centers for working mothers. Maj. Jeanetta Hodgen comforted frightened children in Honolulu's Damon Tract during air-raid alarms, while the classy little Waioli Tea Room, an auxiliary to the Army's girls home in Honolulu, made thousands of doughnuts before it was taken over in 1943 by a government concessionaire. Although Hawaii was officially

Home League in the Western Territory, working on a service project, ca. 1942
Source: The Salvation Army National Archives

part of the Army's Western territorial administrative unit, the increased demand for officers for war work in the islands necessitated the reassignment of personnel from all over the United States there. Maj. Leah Schmuck, for instance, came from the Central territory, and Capts. Olive McKeown and Luella Larder from the East. The latter two officers operated a Salvation Army mobile canteen on fifteen runs per week around Honolulu, visiting the men in lonely and isolated guard posts near the city. The women also developed a unique ministry among the men working in the U.S. Army mortuary in Honolulu. These men were all sergeants in their thirties who had been undertakers in civilian life. The nature of their work was held against them by other service personnel, and they were usually left alone during periods of free time. Many of them became lonely and depressed, a state from which the Salvationist women's patience and kindness regularly lifted them.[60]

The Salvation Army had arrived in Alaska in 1898 under the auspices of the Canadian branch of the movement. After an initial flurry of heroic evangelism in the Klondike in 1898 and 1899, the work had not gone much further among the small white population of the territory. The case was quite different among the Tlinget Indians, a fishing people who lived in small villages along the southeastern coast. A courageous Tlinget Salvationist, Charles Newton, designated by the special Army rank of "field captain," had carried the gospel and the Army's carefree style of worship everywhere among the friendly and receptive Tlinget before he settled down to command the thriving corps at Kake. By the Second World War there were fifteen corps in Alaska, all of them except one in Anchorage "principally of native identity." These good-hearted soldiers were as patriotic as they were religious, and they were overjoyed when the twin facts of a massive American military presence in Alaska and the difficulties of wartime communication and finance from Toronto led to the transfer of the Alaskan corps from Canada to the Western territory of the United States on June 1, 1944. The first American divisional commander was a genial veteran, Brig. Chester Taylor, who assumed command not only of the cheerful Tlinget but of a varied program of USO and military relief activity in what was still officially considered an active theater of war.[61]

Of course Salvationist chaplains also found themselves in theaters of war that were active not in theory but in fact. Their duties were varied: attending to the religious life and morale of the troops, providing the sort of cultural life available through records, movies, and portable paperback libraries, making regular daily visits to field hospitals and guardhouses, and conducting three to five services on Sunday. Dignified and respectful funerals were an essential part of a chaplain's duties. Salvationists found that their Army background fortified them for the demands of their new duties: comforting the sick and dying, patiently counseling drunken soldiers, holding the attention of crowds of men who were indifferent or hostile to religion often in distracting outdoor conditions, and conducting decent burials with a minimum of funeral furnishings were all part of a Salvation Army officer's experiences in civilian life.[62]

Army experience in the use of music was a boon to at least one officer. Chaplain Richard E. Holz of the 882nd Airborne Engineers found his cornet an invaluable tool. He used music extensively in his ministry, organizing a special choral group on his own in 1944 to accompany a Christmas Eve program on Leyte. When a surprise air raid disrupted the meeting, Holz took the choral group around to sing carols to the freshly wounded men, to their delight. Holz was well regarded by the men around him, but other officer chaplains had to face a kind of mild prejudice when they first arrived at their new commands. Many military officers were unaware that The Salvation Army was a recognized Christian denomination. When Giles Barrett reported for duty as a chaplain at 2nd Army Headquarters, he was asked, "Where's your drum?" This sort of condescension did not last, however, and military officials repeatedly urged The Salvation Army to fill its quota of chaplaincies — although the wartime shortage of officer personnel made this impossible.[63]

The shortage of qualified officer personnel, the difficulties of trans-Atlantic communication during the war, and lingering disagreement among American commissioners and between American and international leaders about the proper structure for the national administration of The Salvation Army combined during the last years of the war to bring about the final resolution of the position of national commander. When Comm. Edward J. Parker, the national secretary, finally retired in December 1943 (after one delay at the General's request), the Army's leaders faced what the General in London, George Carpenter, called a "parting of the ways." Debate over what Chief of the Staff Charles Baugh referred to as "the best means of carrying on the Leadership in the U.S.A." became the "subject of much correspondence and many telegrams." At issue was the need for a national headquarters and the position of national commander.[64]

On the one hand was the viewpoint, favored by the General and his close advisors in London, that when London had committed itself to the territorial commander system at the time the American territories were created, it had also committed itself to giving to those commissioners the authority necessary to operate independently. Added to this argument was the fact that a grave shortage of qualified officers made it difficult to staff both a national headquarters and four territorial headquarters. A "national secretary" with minimal staff would be able to coordinate correspondence and reports between the four territorial commanders and London and call the four commissioners together on those few occasions when some kind of joint decision or statement was required — as had been the case concerning the national coordination of USO programs in the early years of the war, for instance. A different viewpoint was offered by the Army's American legal counsel, the distinguished firm of Cadwallader, Wickersham, and Taft, which contended that the Army's various acts of incorporation required that a single official, a "commander" — the term survived in the New York Act of Incorporation of 1899, upon which other state acts of incorporation had been patterned — serve as ex-officio president; in addition, one figure should have the authority to represent The Salvation Army on national issues and to make decisions on matters affecting the whole movement when there was not enough time to arrange for a commissioners' conference.

Opinion among American commissioners was sharply divided: generally, two of the four territorial commanders favored the looser structure, while Comm. Ernest I. Pugmire, whose position as Eastern territorial commander was regarded as senior to the others, and Lt. Comm. Donald McMillan, territorial commander of the West, favored a proper national headquarters. The General proposed a compromise: each of the four territorial commanders — starting with the senior Pugmire — would have a turn for one year as national commander, whose sole function would be to satisfy the legal requirements of the acts of incorporation and to preside as chair at meetings of the commissioners' conference; a national secretary would also be appointed, whose duties would be the same as those exercised by Parker, including the actual calling of the commissioners' conference in consultation with the territorial commanders and the preparation of the agenda. Having conceded this much, the General insisted on the revival of the venerable title of "commander" as the official form of address for the national leader. It was the very word required, was it not, in the legal instruments cited by the advocates of the stronger position, and it had been venerated by its long association with Evangeline Booth. On December 13, 1943, Carpenter appointed Pugmire commander without removing him from his position as Eastern territorial commander; McMillan was promoted to full commissioner and appointed national secretary.[65]

This arrangement did not prove satisfactory to Pugmire, however. He continued to press the General to establish a national commandership with more authority, including the right to convene the commissioners and arrange their agenda, to speak for the nationwide movement on national issues, and to exercise some actual legal authority in decisions affecting the Army's financial and property interests in the United States. McMillan continued to support him in these contentions, while the other three territorial commanders expressed to London what Baugh diplomatically referred to as "a little natural reluctance" to have their authority diluted in this way. Correspondence and telegrams continued to cross the Atlantic in both directions until after the war — indeed, until the end of Carpenter's term in 1946. In the course of these exchanges, which were often lengthy and very detailed, the position of the national commander was somewhat strengthened and clarified: his name was to be used when national statements, agreed upon by all the commissioners, were issued; he could exercise direction when the commissioners were divided; and he gained some legal initiative in property matters. Pugmire pressed the General to approve the title "National Commander" in order to distinguish the position from the territorial commanders. Carpenter and all the territorial editions of the Army's official *Disposition of Forces* continued steadfastly to use the title "Commander." All parties agreed to put the national commandership in final form during the international meeting of Army leaders held in London in 1946 to elect a successor to Carpenter. The title "Commander" was replaced by "National Commander" in the Eastern and Western *Dispositions* in the summer of 1947, but the venerable form of address survived in the Central territorial edition until 1948, and in the Southern edition until November 1949.[66]

Meanwhile, the Second World War had ended in Europe in May 1945, and in Japan in August. The Christmas 1945 *War Cry* was eloquent: "Home Again to Sing the Songs of Peace." Salvation Army officer participation in the USO continued on a reduced scale for another two years, but for the most part The Salvation Army looked home again, too. American commissioners looked over a scene bright with promise: a rich and powerful country supremely confident in victory, a country in which the reputation of The Salvation Army was assured, in which the Army's evangelical and humanitarian activities during the long years of Depression and war had confirmed its place beyond all challenge. The new General,

Albert Orsborn, who visited this country shortly after his election in 1946, was dazzled by the Army's prospects in the United States. A poet of ability and a zealous Christian, Orsborn selected Comm. John Allan to be his Chief of the Staff, the first American-born officer to rise so high.[67]

There was still much to do. One old ministry was gone: the Japanese Division was not restored after the war, nor were the few Japanese officers who had remained loyal to the Army sent back to California; the valiant Imais and Abes were sent to command Japanese corps in Hawaii. An old familiar rank — adjutant — was dropped in 1948 (although two new ones were added, senior captain and senior major, to confuse the public for another ten years). The Army still maintained a stimulating array of military possibilities for its lay members; an official regulation in 1946 listed no fewer than twenty-eight different ranks to which soldiers could aspire as "Senior Local Officers." The Army's traditional emphases had survived the war, and some achieved a new vitality, such as the Men's Social Service Department, which evolved into the "Service-to-Man" program. When a number of homeless, unattached men began to circulate again in the first year after the war, the Army's centers were ready with a program that included all "that The Salvation Army stood for," applied "in a thoroughly thoughtful, organized and constructive manner, focused on the individual man, according to his individual needs," and aimed at his "permanent rehabilitation" through a "definite Christian experience."[68]

Experts in the field of social work became increasingly aware after the war of the Army's growing reliance on the techniques of their profession. One such writer published a detailed and sympathetic account in 1948 of the work of Maj. Jane E. Wrieden, a highly regarded officer in the Army's Women's Social Service Department. The author confirmed that The Salvation Army was "carrying on social work in the sense in which the term is used in a public welfare department or a family casework agency." The Army had its own "specified goals and attitudes" to be sure, but it made use of "the trained social worker's philosophy and skills" just like any other agency "concerned with the perplexities of human relations." Commitment to professional standards was not entirely new to the Army: Major Wrieden had been encouraged to obtain her degrees in social work by Col. Martha Hamon, her superior in the Army's Brooklyn home in 1933. Now, in 1948, Wrieden could outline the Army's professional casework program, "individually tailored" to each woman and child's need, in all thirty-six Salvation Army Homes and Hospitals nationwide. These maternity hospitals were a far cry from the Victorian Rescue Homes from which they had developed through the years: Wrieden did not employ direct evangelism in her work, relying instead on her own personal Christian faith to work as "part of the daily process, a quiet influence," and although a majority of the babies were still placed for adoption, only approved agencies were employed.[69]

Salvation Army music flourished after the war. The two remaining Staff Bands were mostly made up of officers and lay employees of the Army who had not been subject to conscription into the armed forces; these bands had survived the war with their single-gender status as yet unchallenged. Many large corps bands welcomed home their returning servicemen and resumed their extensive prewar programs — without the women players, who were disappointed to find themselves redundant again. Smaller bands grew and developed as teenaged Salvationists grew old enough to take their places in the ranks, in the sunshine of peace and public approval. The number and proficiency of corps bands reached a kind of peak in the late 1940s. "These organizations [were] the most numerous of their kind in the world," observed a writer in 1949. "Nowhere, other than in the school music program of the United States," could there be found "such a large number of excellent bands as at this level of Salvation Army participation." There were "literally hundreds of these bands." Band camps were popular. Not only the territorial Star Lake and CMI camps but divisional and even corps music camps drew large crowds of youthful Salvationist musicians — five thousand in the summer of 1947 alone. Phonograph recordings of Army brass music on the Regal label appeared, radio broadcasts became routine, and in June 1946 the Los Angeles Citadel Band chartered a DC-3 to fly them to Phoenix to play for a fund-raising drive — the first time a Salvation Army band flew to an engagement.[70]

A large step in the development of Salvation Army music came in 1946. Ex-chaplain, now Capt. Richard Holz was given the responsibility of creating a special music department in New York under the auspices of the Eastern territory (which possessed the necessary funds for the new project). Holz acquired an able assistant in Alfred V. Swenarton, an alto horn soloist with the Staff Band; together these two coaxed Erik Leidzen back into the Army fold, and the department was launched. They must have been a busy trio: Holz was solo cornet with the Staff Band, worked closely with its leader Brigadier Bearchell, and led the Male Chorus; Swenarton had the additional duty of organizing the musical forces at the Asbury Park corps after the war; and Leidzen, whose enthusiasm for the

Corps band of Chelsea, Massachusetts, marching back to the hall
after an open-air meeting in 1946
Source: Lt. Col. David Moulton, Wilmore, Kentucky

musical ministry of the Army had returned with a rush, was active in Army
band weekends and as an annual guest at Star Lake camp. On top of this
activity the department managed to conduct a composers' competition in
the winter of 1946-1947 (it concluded on January 31). It produced thirty-
two pieces that were published as "Band Music for Evangelism," which
became the *American Band Journal* in 1948. The series was later approved
by the Army's international headquarters for worldwide use — the first
American publication so honored. But the competition, publishing schedules, and professionalism did not dilute the Army's main objective in all
its musical activities. When a reporter for *The New Yorker* interviewed
Captain Holz during an outdoor concert in New York City, the latter
declared that, like "the Greek philosophers, we believe the first duty of
music is to ennoble the soul."[71]

During these years the Army confirmed other things than its reliance
on music: the traditional doctrine of holiness was the focus of attention in

Chicago in August 1947, when the first Brengle Memorial Institute was opened. The three-week session was the brainchild of the national commander, Commissioner Pugmire. Its first chairman was the kindly Brig. Albert G. Pepper, the principal of the Central training college, who was himself considered a living exemplar of the doctrine of love. Officers were invited from all four territories on a rotating basis, so that eventually every American officer would be exposed both to an explanation and an experience of the doctrine of scriptural holiness. The first staff included Comm. Norman Marshall, the territorial commander, the feisty old McIntyre, Brig. Edward Laity (whose specialty was a lengthy demonstration of how the Old Testament Tabernacle offered examples of New Testament Christianity), and Maj. Mina Russell. The Institute was a huge — and lasting — success.[72]

The Army had never forgotten entirely its commitment to African Americans before and during the war, nor during the period immediately after the war. Salvation Army USO activities were segregated during the

The Army launching work among African Americans
in Atlanta at a 1948 open-air meeting
Source: Publications Bureau, Territorial Headquarters, Southern Territory

war — as was the U.S. military itself. There were separate Salvation Army USO clubs for black troops throughout the south; in Washington, D.C.; in Harlem; in Junction City, Kansas; in Mt. Clemens, Michigan; and in Ipava, Illinois. The Army's indoor evangelical activities likewise remained segregated in the South in the postwar years. The Army's few traditionally black corps were often crowded, and many lasting conversions were recorded in them. One of the most effective corps ministries in the South was housed in the "Washington No. 2 (Colored) Corps" on Seventh and P streets, commanded for thirty-eight fruitful years by Brig. and Mrs. James Roberts and from 1941 to 1950 by Maj. and Mrs. Lambert Bailey. A small step toward integration was taken in Washington when the National Capital Divisional Band added a black tuba player in 1941. After the war, several white officers made determined efforts to broaden the Army's appeal to African Americans and to provide activities that would not be narrowly racial in participation. The Salvation Army did not have an official national policy imposing, or even suggesting, segregation in its social institutions in the decade of the 1940s, but admission policies differed from region to region and often from institution to institution. Black men were occasionally hired as employees at some men's centers, but there is no evidence that African Americans were admitted as residents or clients at any of them during these years. Adjutant Agnew found in his wartime survey of Eastern territorial men's social centers that all of these units imposed the "usual restrictions" on applicants, one of which was that only white men would be accepted. This was true even in centers located in racially mixed or predominantly black neighborhoods. On the other hand, Major Wrieden proudly pointed to the fact that her Door of Hope maternity hospital in Jersey Center had accepted Protestant, Catholic, Jewish, Chinese, and "several Negro babies."[73]

One promising solution, which utilized another traditional Army ministry that was re-emphasized during these very years, was the open-air meeting. Meetings and activities conducted in public thoroughfares could not be easily segregated along racial lines. Adjutant Vincent Cunningham, editor of the Southern *War Cry*, based in Atlanta, was the driving force behind a campaign to launch open-air meetings, first in the black districts of Atlanta, and then — on the heels of the success that he felt was certain — all over the South. Encouraged by Comm. William C. Arnold and his successor as Southern territorial commander, Lt. Comm. Albert Chesham, both of whom were solidly evangelical in their priorities, Cunningham laid his plans. On April 3, 1948, the entire territorial staff and cadets held an open-air meeting on the corner of Auburn and Bell Streets in the heart of the "colored part" of Atlanta. Four African Americans were converted. Cunningham, overjoyed at these conversions, which he was certain were a sign of divine approval, gave this auspicious beginning full coverage: "The Salvation Army Launches a Program for The Southern Negro." Vaguely congratulatory letters from five Southern governors, the mayor of Atlanta, and Sen. J. Strom Thurmond of South Carolina (who added gratuitously that he regarded segregation as "essential to be maintained in the South") were conspicuously published in *The War Cry.* Thus stimulated, other officers launched smaller efforts of their own. Soon the happy editor was able to publish cheerful accounts of open-air meetings and other outreach programs aimed at African Americans in Gastonia, North Carolina; Alexandria, Louisiana; Birmingham and Tuscaloosa, Alabama; Lawton, Oklahoma; and Little Rock, Arkansas.[74]

The public still admired and supported the Army's social welfare, its outreach to those elements among the poor and helpless who had failed in or been overlooked by other uplifting programs, and its steady dedication to its street-corner ministry. Capt. Tom Crocker at the Chicago Harbor Light Corps and Capts. Luella Larder and Olive McKeown at New York's famous Bowery Corps drew special praise. Yet writers pointed out, with a note of sadness, that the Army had changed since William Booth's day, that it had become "a religious body much like any other Protestant denomination, with an accent on works and service," that it had taken on "respectability in spite of itself, [had] acquired property, a standing in the community, a connection with Community Chests, advisory committees of distinguished citizens." Although *Time* agreed that the Army still stood for "humility and love — and another chance for sinners," the magazine felt compelled to point out in a later article that National Commander Pugmire rode to his New York office in a Buick sedan chauffeured by a Dutch war refugee. The Army's top leadership, long accustomed to associating with the favorites of the fashionable world, were embarrassed when Frank Costello, a reputed crime figure, made a donation at a fashionable hundred-dollar-a-plate dinner given for The Salvation Army in January 1949 — that in fact, Costello was one of the 123 "vice chairmen" of the Army's annual New York City financial campaign. This reminder, however accidental, that the Army had once not been ashamed to work among seedy characters might also have reminded its leaders of their predecessors' practical approach to fund-raising: there is no such thing as tainted money. In any case, the Army kept Costello's $10,000 contribution.[75]

The end of the decade brought an end, at last, to the career of one who had been, in her day, the very symbol of The Salvation Army. After her return to the United States in 1939, Evangeline had lived in Hartsdale, a dowager queen. Invitations to visit her at home were still considered an honor, even if the cause was some trivial piece of business. She regularly arrived late for Sunday morning service at the White Plains corps, knowing the respectful officer would begin the program all over for her. As Evangeline grew older, however, she began to feel abandoned, isolated not only from the reality of power for herself but even from those who held it after her.[76]

Yet American Salvationists still revered Evangeline. The hearts of her old associates enveloped the elderly queen in her growing isolation. Brig. William Maltby, the commander of the New York City Metropolitan Division, had often sung in her religious meetings in the 1920s. Together Maltby, Brig. William Bearchell of the Staff Band, and Captain Holz planned a gala evening to honor her: a whole program for a "Friday Evening at the Temple," featuring the compositions of Evangeline Booth. On Friday, November 19, 1948, they pulled it off, a grand, full-dress affair before a packed house.[77]

Evangeline Cory Booth died on July 17, 1950, at the age of eighty-four. She had done all that a leader could do to make The Salvation Army strong and popular in the United States. She had been proud of Christ, proud of the Army, proud of the uniform, and proud of the thousands of common people that filled the ranks behind her. Whatever difficulties she might have had with those in close association with her, the average Salvationists sensed her pride in them and returned it with love. The Commander left behind a legacy of courage, zeal, kindness, caprice, and a fondness for the dramatic that lurks somewhere in the heart of every Salvationist. She could make an important production out of walking across the sidewalk on Fourteenth Street from her car to the front door of headquarters. She filled the Army with excitement and gave it a sense of important purpose. She loved people for loving her as well as for their souls' sakes. To Americans, her generalcy was anticlimactic: to them she was the woman who had commanded The Salvation Army in the United States for thirty years, the Commander, a presence that returned to them when she came back to America in retirement and that was taken only when she died. With her died the last link with William Booth. She was the last national commander of The Salvation Army in the United States who enjoyed a long tenure in office, and the last such official who was widely known to the American people. She was the Army's last Household Word.[78]

CHAPTER 6

1950-1980

*"Sing it as our comrades sang it,
Many a thousand strong,
As they were marching to Glory."*

The Christmas issue of *Time* in 1949 displayed the national commander of The Salvation Army on the cover, surrounded by a wreath of the little hand-rung bells that had become symbolic of the Army's annual Christmas appeal. When Evangeline Booth died seven months later, the leading magazines and every major newspaper in the country lavished praise on her memory and on the work of the Army. The Salvation Army had become more than respectable, more even than popular: it had become venerable. Certain parts of the Army's mission had especially endeared themselves to the heart of the public over seventy years and had come to represent, in a reassuringly visible way, the wide strain of generous and practical philanthropy that was characteristic of modern American life. The particular scenes in this pageant that were selected as favorites varied with the observer, but included on every list were the doughnut girls in the First World War, the Army's long and valiant struggle to lift up the down-and-out (which had included an enlarged percentage of the population during the Great Depression), the maternity homes, and, best known and perhaps most cherished of all, the little brass bands thumping away once or twice weekly on the nation's street corners. No religious organization had ever become more certainly identified with one part of its ministry than had The Salvation Army with its street-corner bands. Their brassy evangelism had long since become a part of the national life — and the single most effective reminder that despite the public's mistaken notion that The Salvation Army was dedicated solely to good works, the overriding purpose of the movement had always been, and remained, to propagate the gospel.[1]

Officers were not surprised to see the Army's street-corner evangelism portrayed in good-natured (and often very funny) cartoons in the best repositories of that art form, *The Saturday Evening Post* and the *New Yorker.* An even more lyrical expression of the public's bemused but genuine affection for the Army's open-air rescue work was the musical *Guys and Dolls,* which opened to rave reviews on November 24, 1950, at the Forty-Sixth Street Theatre in New York. The still-charming story is built on the encounters of Sgt. Sarah Brown of the Save-A-Soul Mission with a collection of Damon Runyon's choicest Broadway characters. Nor could officers object: had not the Army pioneers conceded a half-century before that it was better to be laughed at than ignored? In 1961 a writer in *Reader's Digest* could still assert that the Army "thrives on mockery." And who could deny that the cartoons, plays, and movie scripts were not mere ridicule but a kind of left-handed tribute, no less real for being indirect. So many high-school drama programs put on productions of *Guys and Dolls* that several Army headquarters laid aside a supply of outdated uniforms to loan out for this purpose. There was even a revival of scholarly interest in *Major Barbara.* When a reporter for *Newsweek* disclosed in 1971 that many Army bell-ringers and Christmas musicians were not actually Salvationists or volunteers but merely paid employees — "mercenaries," in the reporter's words — the revelation had no effect on the Army's popular appeal or on contributions.[2]

The Army took justifiable pride in its unwavering dedication to outdoor evangelism. "Except for the blaring auto horn and the roaring motorcycle," Sr. Capt. Don Pitt observed in 1950 in an official booklet, "the setting in which the officer seeks to win men and women to Christ has changed little" since the Army's early years. "The open-air ministry still goes on." The Army conducted 98,417 open-air meetings during that year. Indeed, there were still prodigies of open-air evangelism in the 1950s: Capt. Morris Richardson arranged more than four hundred open-air meetings every year in Frankfort, Kentucky, mostly with musicians from nearby Asbury College, and recorded 147 "decisions at the drumhead" in five years. The funeral for a Niagara Falls corps sergeant-major who died in the midst of preaching at an open-air meeting in 1954 was far from somber: it was a fitting end for such a "great open-air warrior." And the Army maintained not only its street evangelism but a full schedule of weekday evening meetings and Sunday marches and a complete range of traditional corps and social programs through the 1950s, often with gratifying results.[3]

The Salvation Army's efforts to provide spiritual and social rehabilitation to alcoholic men took place in two kinds of facility. One was a specialized corps program called a Harbor Light Corps, a name extended to all such skid-row and bowery programs in 1950. The other was the Men's Social Service Center. The Army's Harbor Light corps reached out directly to skid row residents with spiritual and material solace. These corps were new and uniquely American: General Orsborn had never seen an Army ministry designed particularly for alcoholics until 1946, when he visited the Army's pioneer Harbor Light facility in Detroit. Capt. Tom Crocker, who commanded the Detroit mission for four years before he was transferred to another on Chicago's skid row in 1948, was especially effective in this type of warfare. In New York Captains McKeown and Larder, the Honolulu "doughnut girls," found themselves after VJ Day in a less dramatic (but no less exciting) form of combat when they were sent to command the Army's Bowery mission in New York. When McKeown explained the nature of their work to a fashionable congregation in 1951, Metropolitan Opera star Jerome Hines was touched and generously offered to "sing for the men." His musical ministry to the down-but-never-out at the Bowery Corps was no transient whim: Hines and his wife Lucia sang at Army services regularly for years, laying their musical talents alongside those of Robert Merrill and thousands of less conspicuous lay volunteers in the service of the Salvation War.[4]

The Men's Social Service Department was revitalized after 1944 by the Service-to-Man program, which was fully implemented in the 1950s by progressive social officers who were in the forefront of reform. Through correspondence and frequent meetings, a growing number of energetic officers, of whom such leaders as Richard E. Baggs, Peter Hofman, Cecil Briggs, William Browning, and George Duplain were typical, kept one another informed of innovations in each center. Hofman and Baggs were early advocates of Alcoholics Anonymous, which stressed self-help, courage, honesty, and group support, to which the Army added its own straightforward religious appeal. AA "anniversaries" — one year without a drink — climbed to 114 in Hofman's Cleveland center in 1956.[5]

The Army needed every human resource — and help from above — in the work of the Men's Social Service Department. Not only were as many as 80 percent of its beneficiaries persons with serious drinking problems, but most of the men also had difficult personalities. A painstaking professional survey of the men in the Men's Social Service Center in Minneapolis in 1958 revealed a personality composite very similar to that of prison inmates: socially maladjusted, subject to depression and self-pity, dependent, dishonest, and often pathological. The Men's Social Service remained a kind of missionary endeavor, and frequent reports of "conversions of old-time trophy caliber" were powerful testimony to loving patience and faith in God's grace together. In rare cases a center convert might aspire to become a full-fledged soldier in The Salvation Army; because these centers (unlike Harbor Light units) were institutions rather than corps, their managers did not have the privilege of enlisting soldiers; Peter Hofman pioneered a cooperative program in the Cleveland center that allowed converts from his program to be instructed and enrolled as regulation soldiers at a nearby corps.[6]

The business side of the social centers was also refurbished in the 1950s. Bins of junk and piles of old clothes were replaced by modern retailing techniques. The Army's retail stores lost the rummage-sale appearance that hard times and war shortages had forced on them and regained the air of respectability they had not enjoyed since the days of Col. Edward Parker, fifty years before. Knowledgeable officers even put aside antiques and art objects for sale to collectors and dealers, who began to frequent the Army's stores for this purpose. Placing these objects in the hands of those who would appreciate their value was a useful service and brought additional income to the Army. Retail sales — and ledger profits — climbed through the decade, surpassing by far the Army's income from waste paper and rags.[7]

This happy development, however, brought problems of its own. The Administrators of the Wages and Hours Division of the U.S. Labor Department, established under the Fair Labor Standards Act of 1938, had maintained from the beginning that the profitable commercial operation of the Army's social service centers made them subject to the prescriptions of the Act. If this contention were upheld in federal court, the Army would be forced to treat its clients as paid employees, entitled to the minimum hourly wage and other benefits. Salvation Army leaders countered, of course, that the clients in these centers were receiving numerous benefits and that any work they performed was part of their therapy. Funds generated by their work were needed to operate the complete program and did not constitute "profit" in the commercial sense. The Department of Labor did not press its claim consistently over the years, but it never abandoned it, and Army leaders remained alert and prepared to defend their position. Army administrators recognized that "surplus" income, or "profit," from center operations damaged the Army's position that its Men's Social operations were purely charitable. Income adequate to fund the Army's rehabilitation schemes was one thing, but anything beyond this became problematic — and the Social Service Department's accounting procedures did not clearly allow for depreciation as a charge against income, so that profits often appeared larger than they actually were. Already in the 1940s the Army began to recognize that it was going to have to make more careful distinctions between "employees" and "beneficiaries." In October 1956 a national conference of Men's Social Service Department officers was called, and a series of regulations was drafted to draw these sorts of distinctions. The Army defined beneficiaries (who were not covered by the labor laws) as individuals with "primary handicaps" — temporary disabilities that the Army center's program was designed to "overcome or alleviate," such as alcoholism, drug addiction, or antisocial attitudes — who voluntarily entered the Army centers as the subjects of religious and social rehabilitation. It defined employees as individuals who worked for the Army solely for financial reward. To maintain this distinction, the Army set an official, nationwide ratio of beneficiaries to employees at two to one. Officers were careful to demonstrate that the Army nationwide invested more in its clients than it received for their services. Individual centers that enjoyed "surpluses" were told to add "new services and facilities for the rehabilitation of the beneficiaries" and to use excess money in worthwhile ways. At the same time, the Army acknowledged the awkward fact that financial practices varied considerably from center to center. The Men's Social Service Departments for the four territories clearly needed to adopt uniform national policies and procedures. Delegates from the four departments met in 1960 for that purpose under the chairmanship of Lt. Col. Peter Hofman. They produced the monumental *Handbook of Standards, Principles and Policies,* which was approved by the five commissioners in October as the first national guide for Men's Social Service Department operations since Colonel Parker's series of *Minutes,* issued in 1910. The *Handbook,* with additional minor revisions, remained the fundamental basis for the Army's social work among men until 1987, when a revised edition appeared.[8]

The venerable Women's Social Service Department remained one of the Army's "most active" social programs in the 1950s, its thirty-seven maternity hospitals operating at nearly full capacity throughout the decade. The 83.5 percent adult occupancy reported for the Buffalo facility managed by Sr. Maj. Jane Wrieden, the Army's best-known expert on maternity care, was a typical figure in 1953. The period was nonetheless a time of change for women's social officers. The traditional maternity home program had provided unwed mothers with hospitality, kindness, and evangelism; in the 1950s officers began to experiment with offering the women educational opportunities through accredited secondary educational programs. Craft classes, group therapy, and professional social counseling were also introduced. The clients were gradually given more freedom to leave the hospital to shop and to visit and receive friends as well. Many officers found an RN degree necessary for an effective and professional ministry. A national conference was convened by the commissioners in 1955 to evaluate the entire department and to recommend changes in the Army's services to unmarried mothers. The result was a national statement issued in September 1955 (and reaffirmed and expanded in February 1960) which declared that there should be "only one standard — good service to the whole person — physical, mental, social and spiritual." The statement noted in passing that "unmarried mothers mirror faithfully the degree of social disapproval existing within the overall cultural setting" — a truism with disturbing implications for the Army's maternity homes that the officers overlooked at the time. The popularity of this program remained high, however. In 1962 applicants to Army maternity hospitals faced on average a two-month wait nationwide. One Army caseworker told a writer for *The Saturday Evening Post* that the nationally syndicated columnist "Dear Abby" was the Army's most influential source of referrals — so much so that Army officials had to remind Abby several times that there were other agencies as well with worthwhile maternity homes.[9]

Although nostalgia has led many today to look on the 1950s as a time of bland tranquility, it was in fact a period of significant change in American life, and The Salvation Army did not escape it, although the movement was never more popular or prosperous. When the Army celebrated its seventy-fifth anniversary in the United States, the Eighty-Third Congress of the United States declared, and Pres. Dwight D. Eisenhower proclaimed, the week of November 28 to December 4, 1954, as the first "National Salvation Army Week." Comm. Norman S. Marshall, Eastern territorial leader, assured Salvationists that the Army was "still 'On the

March.'" Perhaps the last of the active pioneer Salvationists to leave the scene of active warfare was Frank Fowler, who retired in February 1957 from the New York Staff Band after fifty-nine years of service. Trained in an orphanage band, Fowler engaged in his first active duty with a Salvation Army band by participating in a victory parade for Admiral Dewey in 1898. The record of the Army's early activities, never precise, was growing increasingly difficult to reconstruct as the last few pioneers were promoted to Glory, taking the treasure troves of their recollections with them. Letters, diaries, programs, and photographs, the faded relics of lifetimes of spiritual warfare meaningless to distant relatives, were scattered and lost. At the height of the renewed interest in the Army's beginnings generated by the seventy-fifth anniversary celebrations in 1954, Maj. Christine McMillan, a noted Army writer, lamented that precise dates for many early events were now "almost impossible to fix." Old ways were abandoned slowly. Army publications in the Central Territory still used the system of numbering city corps well into the 1950s. But innovation was in the air as well. One prospective officer, Damon Rader, entered a university to study electrical engineering in 1955 to prepare himself to introduce radio to Salvation Army overseas missions; he would be the first "to use electronics to carry the Word of God to the jungle tribes." Salvationists, one-time innovators in the use of lantern sides, stereopticons, and wind-up phonographs, did not confine use of the electronic media to foreign missions. The national commander made himself available for an extensive interview by Dave Garroway on the NBC "Today Show" on March 10, 1960. The Salvation Army in the Western Territory began its own radio program, called "The Army of Stars," which was successfully offered to radio stations across the country, and the staff bands produced records in both 78 and 45 rpm formats and, by the end of the decade, in the new 33 rpm style.[10]

The Salvation Army's work among prisoners — its first social program in the United States — produced variable returns during the first half of the twentieth century. The prison work in the East profited for many years from the leadership of Envoy J. Stanley "Red" Sheppard, who regarded the prison population as "the last virgin ground for Army evangelistic service among the type of men that the Army originally was designed to serve." Agnes Lindsay Nightingale supervised an innovative counseling and probation program for women and girls in San Francisco. Yet some of the Army's most active programs among prisoners had been gradually abandoned. The prison corps had not outlived the original converts, nor did the Army have the officer personnel to provide many full-time prison chaplains. The Salvation Army was represented officially in the American Prison Association, and each territory established a "correctional services" department to coordinate prison visitation, Christmas welfare for prisoners' families (which often took the form of toys selected beforehand by the inmate parent and delivered to the child by the Army), and annual Prison Day band concerts. The Army increasingly interested itself in counseling and probation programs designed to prevent rather than ameliorate detention, especially for delinquent youth. In 1969 the Army divisional correctional services officer in Pittsburgh, in cooperation with state prison officials, started the innovative "Alpha Ins and Outs" program to provide Christian counseling, redemptive outside relationships (the "Alpha Outs"), and parole supervision for volunteer inmates.[11]

Progress was often difficult to evaluate. In some areas advance and retreat occurred together. Youth programs such as the Corps Cadet brigades (a religious training program that was originally more advanced than Sunday school and intended for the young Salvationist who sought to become an officer), Girl Guards and Boy Scouts, the Young People's Legion (a weekly evangelistic program for those aged eleven to eighteen years), and the Young People's (or "Junior") Band still prospered, despite growing competition from television and a captivating array of after-school activities offered in many American high schools. The Army's youth activities were the envy of other denominations, whose young people drifted off in bored distraction. The Army won national recognition for its role in the White House Conferences on Children and Youth in 1950 and 1960. Even so, attendance at Salvation Army Sunday school, which officers at every level regarded as the Army's most important religious activity for young people and a reliable indicator of the future vitality of the corps, did not keep pace with the increase of the national population during the twenty-five years after 1955. The same was the case for adult members: The Salvation Army had nearly the same number of senior soldiers in 1980 as it had in 1954. The number of officers actually declined during the 1950s, and although the decline was later reversed, the number of officers, too, failed to keep up with population increases over the longer period. Attendance figures later began to decline in actual numbers as well.[12]

The Service Extension program spread rapidly in the 1950s; a manual issued in 1958 for nationwide use prescribed in detail a practical program of short-term welfare to be administered by local volunteers in areas where there were no regular Army corps. And although the Army was "not primarily an emergency disaster relief organization," its members were drawn "by tradition and inclination" to scenes of catastrophe, dispensing hot food from the ubiquitous white mobile canteen, offering clothing and shelter to victims, and proffering the consolation of Christ and His love. The obvious lack of bureaucratic delay in these on-the-spot acts of kindness made the Army's emergency services highly welcome to disaster victims and very popular with the public as a whole, although other agencies provided more in the way of systematic, long-term welfare. Yet at the same time that the service extension and emergency relief programs were winning friends for the Army, officers began to encounter difficulties from local Community Chest administrators, who questioned the value to the community of some of the Army's religious programs.[13]

The Advisory Board program flourished in the decades after World War II. Born in the auxiliaries of Ballington Booth's day and more fully developed in the aftermath of World War I, advisory boards became a mainstay of the Army's community service. Local business and professional leaders who sympathize with the Army's total mission serve on these boards, giving their financial support, advice, and encouragement to the officers and soldiers of the Corps. The advisory boards were uniquely American until the 1960s, when the Army in Canada, Britain, and elsewhere began to adopt the idea.

There were also developments in this period that affected the Army internally without the notice of the public. Some of these were highly beneficial to Salvationists. The Salvation Army has always cared for its own. The Army pioneers were relatively young; the organization had been at work in the United States for almost forty years before its leaders established an official retirement policy for officers in 1919. That policy had ensured that retired officers would not be left to languish in obscure poverty, but, as their numbers increased, some more reliable provision had to be made for them. In August 1953 General Orsborn officially opened the Retired Officers' Residence in Asbury Park, New Jersey, within earshot of the corps band's seaside open-air stand and close to Ocean Grove, the Sabbatarian piety of which had drawn many retired Salvationists. In December of that year the Retired Officers' League celebrated its twenty-fifth anniversary in the new residence; three of those who had founded the League in 1928 were in attendance. A later divisional commander, Maj. David Baxendale, took special care to utilize the skills and experience of New Jersey's 250 retired officers as counselors, prayer warriors, and visitors. The Army provided subsidies and special programs for those veterans who settled elsewhere as well, in such silver-haired enclaves as Old Orchard Beach, Maine; St. Petersburg, Florida; and southern California.[14]

There was mere bureaucratic change as well: two Army ranks, senior captain and senior major, were dropped from active use in 1959 (although these, like previously discontinued ranks, were retained by those who held them at the time of retirement). The Army's tendency to keep extensive records was nothing new — a writer in 1893 observed that "Every part of The Army is accurately labelled and pigeon-holed" — but it became more marked with the increasing complexity of Army operations in the fifties. Officers were asked to prepare a steadily increasing number of statistical reports, which Capt. John Waldron of the Western New York division described in 1953 as "statistical measurements of a work that can't be measured, a numerical evaluation of a work beyond human values." Yet for all of its incessant collection of data, outside observers of the Army's administrative structure found it complicated and overlapping. An article in *Business Week* noted in 1965 that while the Army's "increasing size has spoiled the simplicity [of its autocratic command structure] with a maze of staff functions, committees, regional commissions and advisory boards," its leaders were willing to embrace innovations in the interest of efficiency. Col. William E. Chamberlain, the greater New York area commander, installed the Army's first computerized system of accounting the same year.[15]

The Army experienced other kinds of change, too, which no one welcomed. The movement, once so mobile that it was forced to assign numbers to its rapidly proliferating stations in each city in order to keep track of them, had long since settled down in neighborhoods, and in many cases had remained in the same location for decades. These neighborhoods began to change in the 1950s. The average age, income, race, and language of the Army's neighbors changed from what they had been in the communities among which the corps had once flourished. In many places this trend was only beginning, but it was detectable enough to make some officers uneasy. At the same time, the open-air ministry began to decline as television, the decline of public municipal transportation in favor of private automobiles, and a marked shift of retail activity toward the suburbs began to empty the cities' sidewalks of their crowds. The first shopping mall in the United States opened in 1956, but these centers quickly proliferated and began to draw off large numbers of shoppers, who now meandered among shops enclosed within larger structures that the Army's brass-band evangelism could not penetrate. The number of Salvation Army street meetings fell by almost 50 percent in the fifteen years after 1950. Yet officers in many places doggedly stood by their commitment to outdoor evangelism, which the movement still officially regarded as its lifeblood.[16]

One lamented victim of time was the Scandinavian work, which lost its separate administrative identity during these years. The action was necessitated by a steady decline in attendance and support for this branch of the Army's religious ministry, which had once been among the most enthusiastic and successful in the movement. The decline was in turn caused by a drop in Scandinavian immigration and the aging of the resident population; second- and third-generation Scandinavian Americans no longer required or even desired religious activities conducted in the Scandinavian language. The end came first in the West, in 1950, when the fourteen corps of the Scandinavian Division were incorporated into the American divisions in which they were located. The Scandinavian work was larger in the Central and Eastern territories than in the West (although no stronger in evangelical zeal) and lasted through the decade, albeit with flagging confidence. In January 1961 the Scandinavian division of the Eastern Territory ceased operations. The last divisional commander, Lt. Col. Gustav A. Johanson, was given the newly created post of Assistant Field Secretary for Scandinavian Affairs to supervise the remaining ministries, which were now administered under American divisions. In the Central Territory the Scandinavian division was absorbed over a two-year period, from 1963 to 1965. The last divisional commander in the Scandinavian Department, Brig. Stig Franzen, and his second-in-command, Maj. C. Milton Anderson, both staunchly evangelical in their priorities, were placed in charge of the new Northern Illinois division, which combined Scandinavian and English-speaking corps. The separate Swedish-language edition of the *War Cry,* the *Stridsropet,* was discontinued. These administrative changes were accepted by the Scandinavian troops with gloomy resignation; not only did the Scandinavians lose their separate administrative structures but they were also forced to take down Scandinavian national flags from the front of their halls and to display versions of Salvation Army flags, crests, and wall mottos with English wording. Their spirits recovered considerably, however, when it became clear that Army leaders would continue to appoint officers of Scandinavian descent to command these corps and that official efforts would be made to help them keep their festival and special music alive. In 1975 Lt. Col. Olof Lundgren, a (nominally) retired officer, was appointed "Director of Scandinavian Activities" for the Eastern Territory. A list of distinctly Scandinavian corps that Lundgren prepared in 1978 contained ten units in the Central Territory and eight units in the Eastern Territory. The ten units in the Central Territory included six in Illinois (one each in Moline and Rockford and four in Chicago — Mt. Greenwood, Irving Park, Norridge [formerly Mont Clare], and Andersonville) and four in Minnesota (Minneapolis Temple and Central Avenue, St. Paul Temple, and Duluth Temple). The eight units in the Eastern Territory included three in New York (New York Central Citadel on E. 52nd Street, Brooklyn Bay Ridge, and Jamestown), two in Connecticut (Hartford Temple and New Britain), and one each in Massachusetts (Worcester Quinsigamond), Pennsylvania (Erie Temple), and Rhode Island (Providence). The practice of selecting persons with Scandinavian ethnic background for leadership positions in these units continued with few exceptions into the 1990s.[17]

The decline of the Scandinavian work was one of a number of developments that proved unsettling to officers in this period. The Army's very strengths seemed to work against it. The movement had become so popular and so respectable that in 1965, the centennial year of the beginning of William Booth's work in London, the Army in the United States was honored with a commemorative postage stamp. The Army's practical philanthropy had secured widespread support for the organization among a broad range of the American people. A survey taken in a large midwestern city in the same year put the question as to which religious organization "best fulfills the Christian ideal," and The Salvation Army outpolled all other organizations combined. Yet the public who so generously gave its money to the Army was largely indifferent and occasionally even antagonistic to its religious appeals. Officers who felt they had been called by God to a great crusade for souls were frustrated with their role as administrators of a charity, no matter how popular. In addition, the extent and complexity of the Army's philanthropic and financial affairs forced officers to hire an ever-increasing number of professional and clerical employees (the number of the Army's lay employees doubled between 1951 and 1961), and supervising them took more and more time. Other frustrations multiplied as well. The neighborhoods surrounding many corps not only ceased to be filled with persons who were easily accessible to the Army's traditional evangelical methods but became hostile and, in a few places, actually dangerous. The sixties witnessed an increase in violent crimes against city residents generally, and even the most faithful soldiers grew reluctant to venture downtown to corps halls to conduct evening services for the benefit of people in indifferent or hostile neighborhoods.[18]

Like other Christian organizations and denominations, The Salvation Army experienced turmoil in the decade of the 1960s. The old and the new tumbled together as the movement attempted to adapt its venerable and popular ministries to a rapidly changing human context. The attempts met with varying success. On the positive side, the Army officially recommitted itself to its theological foundations and experienced almost none of the internal division over theological matters that marked other denominations in this period. In 1960, as part of its celebration of the 100th anniversary of the birth of Samuel Logan Brengle, The Salvation Army became an official denominational member of the National Holiness Association at the latter's annual convention in Asheville, North Carolina. Messages by William Booth, Brengle, and Railton, officially described as still timely, were reprinted in *The War Cry.* The Army repeatedly declared its commitment to evangelism during this decade. A Laymen's National Evangelism Commission was appointed, made up of leading laypeople from all four territories: Jack Wood from Hollywood Tabernacle Corps, Alfred Swenarton from Asbury Park, Frank O. Staiger from Port Huron, and Milton Servais of Nashville. Its final report called on Salvationists "to use every means to reach this generation for Jesus Christ." In July 1968 the Army held its first annual Laymen's Institute on Evangelism in Glen Eyrie, Colorado. At the same time that officers extolled the value of the Army's traditional approaches to soul-winning — including what one called in 1967 the "lovely, traditional Salvation Army bonnet" — they also authorized a variety of novel programs designed to carry the gospel to hippies and street people. Cadets held street meetings in the Haight-Ashbury district of San Francisco, young Salvationists conducted gospel-rock concerts during the summer on the Asbury Park Boardwalk, and for several seasons the Army operated special coffeehouses, drop-in centers, and shelters around the country. The programs administered by Capt. Judy Moore on Peachtree Street, Atlanta, and Mrs. Brig. Howard (Sally) Chesham's "Old Hat" in Chicago were especially notable examples that attracted considerable attention from national religious and political figures.[19]

Despite these activities, however, the message of The Salvation Army was sometimes clouded by the traditions of the organization itself, even by its very image. Army leaders recognized that the Vietnam war was controversial and that the Army's own young people were divided over national policy regarding the war, but the Army's only official comment on the war confirmed both its historic commitment to support American troops at home and overseas and its refusal to take a stand on issues that its leaders regarded as merely political or social. The Army drew attention to the activities of American Salvationists in Vietnam during the war years. A team of officers operated four refugee camps near Saigon from 1968 to 1971. They cared for almost two thousand people weekly, half of them children, providing rudimentary educational and religious counseling services and distributing resources provided by private donors, the Red Cross, and the U.S. government. Army leaders were especially proud of Capt. Kenneth Hodder, a chaplain serving in the U.S. Navy near Da Nang — the only Salvation Army officer in the history of the movement to be accepted by the U.S. Navy as a chaplain (and one of the few Army officers to have earned a Phi Beta Kappa key!). The majority of the Army's members remained politically conservative during these years, like the majority of members of other evangelical Christian organizations, and thus probably endorsed the government's actions, at least privately. But some young Salvationists were troubled by the war. And some young people within the Army (and many more outside it) viewed the Army's militant image with distaste and rejected its hierarchical administrative structure and what a few critics regarded as its outdated understanding of the nature of human authority. Criticism of the Army in the American press over the dismissal of a popular officer in London on charges of unorthodoxy in 1970 and a lawsuit the same year by an officer in Atlanta based upon claims of gender discrimination did nothing to help. A "Concerned Officers' Fellowship" of indeterminate strength held meetings in the Southern territory and issued "bulletins" on an infrequent basis from 1967 to 1970 questioning the status quo, and during the same years college-age Salvationist youth in both California divisions used official and unofficial Army clubs to discuss agendas that senior officers regarded as radical. There were regional differences in the complaints voiced in these forums, but there was agreement on two points: the need to emphasize the importance of the status and the spiritual role of the corps officer in the Army structure and the need to make the Army more democratic. Correspondence among top leaders shows that several commissioners were sympathetic to these parts of the reformers' agendas.[20]

Despite the increasing difficulty of the social issues with which the Army's officers were forced to deal and the ever-growing diversity and sophistication of the programs sponsored by the organization itself, patterns of officer recruitment changed little during these years. Slightly more than half of officers were the children of officers, and almost all had come up through the corps youth programs. Their experience with Salvation Army life was often confined to traditional religious services. A study of officer training in the West in the early 1960s revealed long-standing patterns: the average training college cadet had been in the corps for six years before coming to the college, and three-quarters of them had been involved in the corps cadet program. The public continued to believe — incorrectly — that most Salvation Army officers had been rescued from lives of Skid Row desperation, but in fact most of the officer-candidates were vastly more familiar with the Army's evening and Sunday meetings than with its day-to-day welfare activities. Many were not exposed to any sort of corps welfare programs until they were appointed to their first command.[21]

Then, too, some officers, particularly in the ranks of lower field officers and administrative support personnel in headquarters, were single women. Women have outnumbered men in The Salvation Army, both as soldiers and as officers, since Victorian times. Although the imbalance in the early days was high, the proportion of women to men in The Salvation Army in more recent years has not been markedly different from that in other religious organizations. From the first days of the movement in the United States, a large majority of Salvationists had been women; from the 1950s through the 1980s, over 60 percent of all Salvationists were women. The difficulty arose from the nature of the demands on an officer's resources and the fact that many single female officers had no practical opportunity to retain their commissions if they married. The Army permits male officers to marry only female officers or women who are willing to become officers at once; thus, even if every male officer married, more than 20 percent of the officer corps would remain single women who would never marry if they wished to remain as officers. In addition, there are officers who are widows. Moreover, the percentage of women officers is highest among younger officers, in their first five years of officership, the very years when discouragement is most frequent, even for a married couple who have the consolation of mutual support and companionship. These problems became more acute after 1945. Because the the number of cadets diminished during the war, the number of new officers was inadequate to make up for losses from retiring officers after the war. Although officers in the United States did not suffer a noticeable decline in absolute numbers, they fell behind the increase of the national popu-

lation at a growing rate, at a time when the needs of the organization were
increasing rapidly. The combined pressures led to resignation, one of the
most frequently cited reasons for which was simply "dissatisfaction."[22]

Even so, there remained a large basis for hope. The Salvation Army
was the Army still, and it valiantly carried on its evangelical crusade in
many places under the banner of the Cross. Although the Army's outdoor
ministry faded steadily during these years — in 1980, for instance, the
Army conducted only a tenth as many outdoor meetings as it conducted
in 1950 (and less than half as many as in 1970) — many bandmasters
held their musicians to the high standards of an earlier day: such individuals as Garfield Thomas of Oakland Citadel, Ron Smart of Hollywood
Tabernacle, Kenneth Luyk of New Kensington, Pennsylvania, and Al
Swenarton of Asbury Park led their corps bands out on street marches and
open-air crusades into the 1970s. Here and there the decline was even
reversed: in 1965 San Francisco Chinatown corps staged its first annual
"parade of witness" assisted by four hundred Bay Area Salvationists. Bands
still marched in the muddy streets of Alaskan villages, and young musicians
still learned the rudiments of street marching at the Army's annual territorial music camps across the United States.

The Army's musical ministry continued to bring life and joy to
Christian worship, and a rich production of band and choral music flowed
steadily into print in the 1950s. This included the several series published
in London, which also produced a supplement to the beloved *Band Tune
Book* in 1954. From New York came *Band Music for Evangelism* scored for
a nine-piece band with four optional parts, a collection of forty-eight pieces
including compositions by Erik Leidzen, Richard Holz, Vernon Post,
Stanley Ditmer, and Emil Soderstrom. The Eastern territorial music bureau
also published a welcome little book of forty-two gospel band tunes called
the *American Supplement to the Band Tune Book* in 1956 and, a year later,
a collection of brass quartet arrangements of Christmas carols by Erik
Leidzen called *Carolers' Favorites*. Ronald W. Holz, in a scholarly study of
Army instrumental music, states that although the serious compositions
of this era were strongly conservative in a technical sense, they were often
of surpassing beauty: the Army's "conservative guidelines" for composers,
imposed by its official editorial boards, did not prevent the introduction
of many innovative techniques and brilliant effects.[23]

The Salvation War advanced on other fronts as well. On the greatest
single social issue of the 1960s, the revolution in race relations, the Army
was unambiguously on the side of change. The Army's honest, if sporadic,

efforts to draw more Southern blacks into the circle of its ministry had not resulted in a direct official assault on racial segregation before 1950; to have done more would have inflamed local authorities and public opinion to drive the Army from the scene. Still, the Army did not simply delay action until after the massive shift in national opinion that slowly followed upon the Supreme Court school desegregation decision of 1954. A scholar pursuing his doctoral research in 1949 and 1950 found that segregation was "not accepted by the Army with an easy conscience." In 1950 a national commission (established along with territorial commissions) to prepare for Army participation in the White House Conference on Children and Youth officially declared itself to be "concerned about continuing legal separation of race," and the Southern territorial commission optimistically reported "an upsurge . . . of good will in a tradition-ridden area of the nation, in point of prejudice and discrimination."[24]

The Army was among the first social welfare agencies in Washington, D.C., to integrate its facilities. After 1946 the Army's summer camp for African Americans in Maryland had an integrated summer staff. In 1952 the camp itself was closed, and the entire program was transferred to the formerly all-white camp in Virginia. The newly integrated and enlarged facility was called Camp Happyland, in honor of the defunct black camp. The first director of the new program, Sam Covington, was African American. Maj. Victor Wilson, a courageous black corps officer in Washington during these years, found that African American youth were willing to participate in the newly integrated divisional programs but that older Salvationists were too laden with unhappy memories of past rebuffs to make risky gestures. During these years the Army dropped the adjective *colored* from official usage. In 1949 the Army responded to the request of Maj. B. Barton McIntyre, in charge of the Cleveland "Colored Corps," that his command be redesignated the "Central Area Corps." In 1951, Washington, D.C.'s Ninth Street "Colored Corps" likewise became the Central Corps.[25]

By 1955 activities conducted on the divisional and territorial level, such as Young People's Councils, Girl Guard, and Home League rallies, were integrated throughout the South, although local units remained segregated. In northern cities the preexisting racial makeup of neighborhoods and the preference of many African American Salvationists for a local center for worship and service combined to keep some corps largely or entirely black; this was the case, for example, at St. Louis Euclid Avenue, Omaha Northside, Cleveland Central Area, Harlem Temple, Brooklyn

Bedford Temple, Pittsburgh Homewood, and Milwaukee West Corps. Where segregation was the result of past policy, however, divisional leaders were allowed and encouraged to eliminate the barriers.[26]

The Salvation Army brought goodwill and a near-military efficiency to successive crises in race relations during the decade of the 1960s and carried most of its soldiers with it onto a new level of understanding of the meaning of Christian fellowship. In May 1964 the territorial commanders issued a joint statement on "racial justice" in which they declared that officership, employment, membership, and participation in The Salvation Army were open to any person regardless of race and that "all social welfare services" would be offered on the same basis. In November the territorial commander of the South had to overrule local advisory board members in Mississippi who had refused to distribute free Thanksgiving turkeys to black families after civil rights activists had collected food for the dinners among supporters in the north. More difficulties followed: the riots in many northern cities placed the Army in a dilemma. The Army was traditionally nonpolitical, wishing only to be of service to all people, and yet, because of the nature of its work, it typically had long-established ties to municipal emergency response agencies and similar groups that unfortunately proved damaging to its reputation with those who objected to the establishment. At scenes of urban rioting and burning, Army officers instinctively moved in and provided canteen refreshment to weary firefighters, police, and members of the National Guard. Those who viewed these authorities as their enemies instinctively resented the Army's activities.[27]

Yet officers attempted to bring help to those whom the fires victimized as well as to emergency officials. In Pittsburgh, during the 1963 riots, Capt. Israel Gaither of the Homewood corps distributed encouragement and groceries to many African American families after local supermarkets had gone up in smoke. Col. Paul Seiler, the territorial men's social service secretary, collected spare trucks from eleven centers for this massive project. In the Cleveland riots of 1966, Col. Giles Barrett, the divisional commander, ordered canteens from three cities to distribute relief to police and riot victims alike. There were many similar accounts. Such evenhandedness, combined with the Army's genial willingness to open its youth programs to neighborhood young people and to distribute its practical welfare with a minimum of red tape, sometimes rescued the movement from condemnation by radical leaders who might otherwise have dismissed the Army as no more than another part of a bigoted and hateful establishment. So it was that several Army centers — including Milwaukee's West Corps — were apparently deliberately spared during the window-breaking and arson that occurred during neighborhood riots.[28]

The Salvation Army was not content merely to escape condemnation; it redoubled its efforts to broaden its evangelical ministry among African Americans, who over time came to constitute an increasingly large percentage of the urban population. Recognizing that "inner city" was often a synonym for black, some officers were convinced that the Army in the city would have to become what one officer called "a largely black organization" in order to survive. Certainly the Army's existing all-black corps showed no signs of abandoning their enthusiastic evangelical outreach. Harlem Temple Corps, under Brig. B. B. McIntyre (succeeded in 1972 by Maj. Abraham Johnson, who served this appointment until 1988), offered helpful programs, hot meals, remedial reading, Spanish-language classes, and gymnasium facilities for the neighborhood and capped it all with an old-time hallelujah street service with a brass band on the corner of Seventh Avenue and 125th Street. The warmhearted evangelical zeal of the soldiers of Brooklyn Bedford Temple, under Sr. Maj. Pearl Hurdle, Maj. Lebert Bernard, Capt. Israel Gaither, and, after 1975, Maj. Lilian Yarde, remained proverbial in Army circles. There are a dozen other lively, hospitable, and flourishing corps under black leadership in Boston's Roxbury, Washington, Philadelphia, Pittsburgh, Chicago, St. Louis, Omaha, Cleveland, Richmond, Little Rock, and Atlanta.[29]

New programs were launched and new ministries devised to meet what several knowledgeable staff officers called the "felt needs" of the ghetto. In 1964 Maj. Mary Nisiewicz, with the pluck and zeal of a Victorian slum sister, began a one-woman rescue crusade on East 125th Street among New York ghetto youth and drug addicts. Two years later, in the aftermath of the riots in Cleveland, the Army returned to the burned-over area with a new ministry — or rather, an old ministry in a new form. Colonel Barrett inspired the city with his vision of a vast new Army center, full of encouraging programs, that would rise phoenix-like from the smoking ruins of the Hough Avenue slums. Contributions were secured from the entire Cleveland community, including a grant from the Leyte Thomas Trust that was the largest gift ever received by the Army in Ohio, and another from the George Gund Foundation. The first contribution from the African American community came in the form of a refund of half the commission on the land acquisition, returned to the Army by the realtor, J. Howard Battle. The Hough Multi-Purpose Center, a kind of religious-recreation-welfare shopping mall, was opened in October 1969 by civil rights activist James Farmer. The first director of the center was Maj. Henry Gariepy, a longtime advocate of a more diverse Army program in the inner city. Gariepy quickly built an effective staff, the star of which was Madeline Manning Jackson, a black Olympic runner and fervent Christian.[30]

A retired Army missionary to India, Col. Dr. William Noble, opened a free medical clinic for African Americans in 1967 in Atlanta's slums; it operated for five years with a volunteer staff and medicines donated by sympathetic pharmaceutical sales representatives. In 1968 a new multipurpose corps was opened in Hartford, Connecticut, named for Henry W. Jennings, a black police officer killed in action. The new center, like several other Army programs, included an extensive schedule of remedial reading classes for slum youths who were functionally illiterate in traditional English. The Army command in Chicago, a major center of Salvation Army activity since the nineteenth century, organized an entire administrative branch for "Inner-City Services." It included several community centers, the Freedom Center complex on West Monroe Street, the Tom Seay Service Center, an old-time rescue shelter called the New Life House, and the Chicago Southside Settlement.[31]

In 1971 the commissioners' conference appointed a task force for each territory to survey Army services to racial minorities. The results revealed a remarkable range of new programs designed to supplement the traditional Salvation Army evangelical ministry: counseling; employment referral; day-care centers for working mothers; assistance in matters of court appearances, parole, and probation; medical clinics; recreational, gymnasium, and camping opportunities; black studies; community planning sessions; vocational training; and even several attempts to organize drum and bugle corps, at the time a favorite activity among many inner-city youth. The official task force report, written by Maj. Robert A. Watson, appeared in 1973. It admitted that the Army faced serious problems in its ghetto ministries: overworked officers; the presence in the ghetto of "militant factions" that deliberately undermined the Army's influence; the transient nature of much of the ghetto's population, which prevented the Army from building a stable following; increasing violence, vandalism, and burglary; and the fact that some inner-city corps were sustained largely by middle-class African Americans who had moved to the suburbs and now had little influence in the immediate neighborhood of the corps, to which they returned only once weekly for Sunday morning services. The report declared twice that the Army faced a "critical need" for more black officers. Still, there were grounds for encouragement: Major Watson was glad to note that there was a "significant evangelical thrust" in many of the new activities, that "traditional programs" continued to play a major role in changing lives, and that "heroic and dedicated service" was being rendered on the inner-city front.[32]

African American officers shared their comrades' concern about the Army's ministry among black Americans as well as their pride in being officers in the movement. Black Salvationists were also increasingly proud of the contribution that they had made over many years and that they were still making to the Salvation War. In 1969 the black officers of the Eastern territory met together for the first time on a formal basis, during a territorial congress in New York. Arranged by Brigadier McIntyre (who had become divisional secretary — second in command — in the Metropolitan New York division) and led by Captain Gaither and Lt. Noel Christian, the meeting heard expressions of loyalty to the Army mixed with anxiety. The African American community "recognized and liked" the Army for the services it provided, but few ghetto youth were joining the ranks as soldiers. It was difficult to encourage young black soldiers to become officers, because black officers were appointed only to the few "black" corps and apparently were not considered for headquarters or training college positions. The congress noted that many black Salvationists were immigrants from the Caribbean, and while it granted that these comrades and many others like them should be actively cultivated for service in the Army, it also urged that "instead of turning to the West Indies when Officer personnel is needed, effort should be made to acquire black American Soldiery and Officers."[33]

A number of the difficulties brought to wider notice by the black officers in 1969, like some of those noted in the Watson report of 1973, proved difficult to overcome in the next two decades. Of these the most critical was the Army's failure to recruit sufficient numbers of African American officers. Problems that were amenable to mutual goodwill and simple administrative decisions were easier to correct: by the 1970s black officers were being considered for promotion and service on the basis of ability alone. B. Barton McIntyre, for instance, retired in 1975 with the rank of lieutenant colonel, his last appointment having been on the terri-torial staff, as territorial evangelist. Capt. Israel Gaither was promoted to a staff position in 1975, and in 1978 he was appointed divisional secretary in the Greater New York division. In March 1979 Captain Gaither led a "Black Heritage Night" at a Friday evening temple meeting in New York

City that included a performance by the New Found Sound — a special band made up of black players from all over the territory — and inspired by a gospel message from Dr. Martin Luther King, Sr. In June the "first all-black brigade of cadets in the history of The Salvation Army" invaded Cleveland; the six cadets conducted evangelical services at the Hough Center and the Miles Park Corps (formerly the Central Area Corps) with heartening results. Israel Gaither's career continued throughout the 1980s to encourage black Salvationists; in 1990, Gaither became the Army's first black divisional commander in the United States (in Western Pennsylvania, with the rank of lieutenant colonel).[34]

The Army made efforts to "throw out the lifeline" to Spanish-speaking immigrants as well, efforts that were no less honest and strenuous for being mostly recent. The Army had operated small Spanish-language missions in Laredo and El Paso, Texas, for many years; El Paso Southside (Spanish) corps began in 1907 with a street-corner meeting in the Spanish language. The Salvation Army did not launch a major Spanish ministry, however, until after the Second World War, when massive Hispanic immigration into the United States began. This significant population movement turned large sections of American cities into Spanish-speaking ghettos, and The Salvation Army had to choose whether it would address its ministry to this new population or abandon still another part of its traditional downtown harvest field.[35]

The Bronx Spanish-American corps opened in 1960, with good results almost at once. Mrs. Gladys Torres was the first to enroll as a soldier there, in January 1961. She was nothing if not enthusiastic about her new religion, and, while home in Puerto Rico for a visit in March, she stirred up enough local interest in the Army that work was soon started on the island. Within a decade there were Spanish-speaking corps in Los Angeles, San Diego, Phoenix, El Paso, Laredo, Chicago, the Bronx, Jersey City, and Paterson. In the Eastern territory the Army organized a Spanish Ministries Committee under Maj. Frank Payton to develop new forms of outreach to the more than one million Spanish-speaking people in the New York–northern New Jersey area. The Inner-City Task Forces of 1971 and 1972 were also charged with surveying Army work among " 'Hispanic' persons," and found that Spanish-language tutoring, casework interviews, counseling, and evangelization were proliferating in Army programs. Inner-city coordinators were appointed for Philadelphia, Cleveland, and Chicago to coordinate and expand both African American and Hispanic ministries. The "critical need" in the Hispanic mission, as in work among African Americans, was for qualified officer personnel.[36]

Another traditional ethnic ministry continued to thrive despite constant changes in leaders. The Chinatown Corps in San Francisco had no fewer than 166 officers from the time it opened in 1896 until 1959 — none of whom could speak Chinese. Until the 1980s it was the Army's only official Chinese corps in the United States. For the first twenty-nine years of its existence, the Chinese ministry was sustained largely by the valiant color sergeant Looey Gooey (the name is almost certainly a poor contemporary transliteration), who provided what continuity he could working with the stream of new officers. In 1959 Capt. Check Hung Yee was given the command, and the corps began to prosper. By the mid-1960s there were almost three hundred Chinese involved in one or another of the many helpful activities offered by the energetic and resourceful Yee: counseling for recent immigrants, family welfare, a small Evangeline residence for working women, a Home League, timbrel brigade, and a complete complement of musical forces all glowing in the gospel fire of the Captain's quiet, earnest evangelism. In 1978 the Chinatown Corps began to produce a fifteen-minute religious television program in two dialects of Chinese and in English, broadcast once a week on Sunday evenings and intended, like the corps's traditional open-air meetings in Chinatown itself, to fulfill the Army's fundamental mission: to carry Christ to those who do not seek Him out.[37]

The high attrition rate among Army officers during their first five years in office and the complexity of social and religious problems faced by even the most veteran officers convinced Army leaders that the program of officer preparation at the territorial training colleges was no longer sufficient. The Army had admitted for years that the traditional nine-month course was a "limited period in which to accomplish much in training future officers," but lack of funds and the incessant demands of the field for fresh officers had delayed expansion of the program. In 1960 the training college curriculum was lengthened to two years, and the institution was renamed The Salvation Army School for Officers' Training. The new curriculum was still largely "practical" — 40 percent of the weekly class hours in required subjects were devoted to "field training" — but courses were added in theology, history, literature, and psychology, and more time was allowed to prepare officers for the bookkeeping and administrative details of their work.[38]

Nor were the benefits of formal higher education proscribed for those young Salvationists who felt called to some form of service that required a baccalaureate degree or who wished thus to prepare themselves more completely before entering the Schools for Officers' Training. The number of soldiers who have attended colleges and universities has increased steadily since 1950. Army collegians have tended to be concentrated in schools near areas in which the Army itself has well-established corps and musical activities, which were major factors in holding young people in the ranks during their college years in the 1960s and 1970s as well. Such areas included eastern Michigan, Chicago, the San Francisco Bay area, southern California, Philadelphia, New York, northern New Jersey, southern New England, the Tampa–St. Petersburg Bay area, and Atlanta.

Other Salvationists have been drawn to small Christian liberal arts colleges. Of this group, the largest number attended Asbury College, near Lexington, Kentucky. More than two hundred commissioned officers and several times that many soldiers and Army employees had graduated from this college between 1924, when the first Salvationist enrolled there, and 1980. The Salvationist students, who are formally organized as part of the worldwide Salvation Army Student Fellowship (SASF), have had a brass band of their own at Asbury since the 1950s and have traditionally taken an active part in the activities of the campus and nearby Salvation Army corps. Prof. Lee Fisher, a longtime Asbury faculty member who was popular in Salvationist circles as a counselor and writer, was a major influence on the development of the Army presence at Asbury. In 1968 a high-ranking Army officer, Col. Andrew S. Miller, was appointed to the college board of trustees; from that time on there have always one or two officers on the board. By 1973 the relationship between the college and the Army had become so congenial that the international chief of the staff, Arnold Brown, commented favorably on the educational influence of Asbury on The Salvation Army worldwide. In 1975 the national commander, Comm. William E. Chamberlain, attached the Asbury SASF directly to national headquarters. A newly retired officer, Lt. Col. David W. Moulton, was appointed to serve as national liaison officer, and two faculty members, E. H. McKinley and James Curnow, were commissioned as corps sergeant major and bandmaster. In 1979 the commissioners authorized the attendance of the Asbury College SASF Band to represent national headquarters officially at the Army's national centenary congress in Kansas City in June 1980.[39]

Asbury was not the only Christian college to benefit from a warm connection with the Army, of course. Other institutions developed official relations with the Army during the decade of the 1970s. In the Central Territory, cadets from the School for Officers' Training were enabled to obtain academic credit by attending selected classes at Olivet Nazarene

College in Illinois. A similar but more advanced arrangement was established in the Western Territory to allow cadets to obtain associate of arts degrees from Azusa Pacific College when they are commissioned as officers. These and similar relationships expanded considerably during the following decade.

The Army's benevolent attitude toward higher education flowed from its century-old determination to adapt its ministry to achieve maximum efficiency. Increasingly this has meant that Salvationists must be seen by others as capable of functioning according to professional standards. Nowhere has this commitment been more apparent than in Salvation Army music. A generation of young American Salvationists composers arose in the late 1960s and gained widespread recognition in the 1970s. Among those who became known outside Army circles were Bruce Broughton, an important composer of scores for motion picture and television productions who produced several pieces for the Army in the 1960s; his brother William, who remained an active Salvationist composer and musician; and James E. Curnow, well known in the field of band composition and conducting. Other Army composers of note within the movement itself in these years were Stanley Ditmer, Vernon Post, William Himes, and Ivor Bosanko. By 1980 there were several Salvationist performers with established professional reputations as well, the most notable of whom was Philip Smith, principal trumpet with the New York Philharmonic. Others worthy of note were Charles Baker, Peggy Paton Thomas, Carole Reinhart, and several arrangers and musicians in the premiere military bands stationed at the national capital, notably Robert Schramm in the U.S. Air Force Band, Patrick Morris in the U.S. Army Band, and Stephen Bulla, principal arranger for the U.S. Marine Band. At the same time, Salvation Army bands maintained a high level of proficiency during these years; although some forms of traditional musical evangelism declined, the quality of Army musicianship did not. The New York and Chicago Staff Bands, territorial music camp instructors' bands, and a few select regional ensembles continued to achieve standards of playing that were admired by Salvationists and outsiders alike. Every Army division maintained a youth band, and several of the larger divisions had an adult divisional band as well. In addition, the Army put into the field every year several bands made up of skilled players from various units for such events as the Tournament of Roses, Cotton Bowl, and big-city Thanksgiving Day parades.[40]

These bands had a threefold purpose: promoting good public relations, performing at ceremonial functions, and supporting the Army's religious ministry. The main burden of the Salvation War continued to be carried, however, by the Army's corps bands, which accompany religious services on the congregational level, both indoors and outdoors, and play for corps weddings, funerals, and the annual Christmas appeal. In addition, many corps bands conducted a regular schedule of visitation to neighboring hospitals and nursing homes. The Army's official definition of a "band" remained unchanged through these years — and in fact, had not changed since the Founder's day: "A group of not fewer than four senior [at least fourteen years old] Salvationists who voluntarily serve together to further the purposes of The Salvation Army by means of instrumental music." Not every Salvation Army band was as small as this, but the Army showed some wisdom in making careful provision in its regulations and in the type of music it published for bands of four or five players: many corps had little more, and a growing number of Army corps had no band at all. Responding with impressive detail in 1967 to pessimists who predicted the Army band was "fading away," Bandmaster Charles Hansen of Montclair, New Jersey, insisted that, on the contrary, the Army's "brass band future is bright." Statistics, alas, did not support this cheerful view: despite enormous effort on the part of officers and soldiers, the number of corps bands in the United States declined. From 1960 to 1980 the number of Army band personnel fell by 35 percent. In 1960 half of American corps had senior bands; twenty years later the figure had fallen to one in three. In the latter year, the nation's 1,056 corps supported only 379 senior bands — which means that fully 64 percent of American corps had no band.[41]

The Army published a wealth of music for the small band in the two decades after 1960, including The Salvation Army *Brass Ensemble Journal* (1960, 1964) and a book of regional tunes published in Atlanta called *Songs of the South* (1975), which was designed to accomplish "a good harmonic balance" using just four musicians. In 1979 the Army's international music department in London ordered a revision of the classic 1928 *Band Tune Book* so that every tune could be played adequately by just four instruments, a process that required much more time than was anticipated and was not completed until 1987. In 1980, 98 percent of corps with bands also had "junior bands," a hopeful sign that efforts were being made to ensure a supply of future players. Despite the preponderance of small bands in Salvation Army corps, there were perhaps seventy-five corps bands of twenty pieces or larger at the end of the seventies. Many of these bands were generations old and exceptionally proficient: citing just one example from each territory in the mid-1970s, one might point to the Cambridge Silver Band in Massachusetts, Atlanta Temple Band, Chicago Mont Clare Band, and a relatively new band at the time, the Santa Ana, California, Citadel Band.[42]

The Army's willingness to adapt its music to the taste of contemporary ears did not depart during these decades. The Army's General reminded the readers of *Christianity Today* in 1965 that The Salvation Army accepted no "beatitude for inefficiency from the Master, Who bade the children of light learn from the world." The twenty years after 1960 witnessed a multiplication of efforts by Salvationists both to write innovative music for the traditional brass band and to form small "gospel-rock" groups of instrumentalists and singers in order to carry the Christian message to a new generation of listeners who were indifferent to the Army's brass-band evangelism. Such officers as Capt. Ernest A. Miller were committed in the sixties to broadening the Army's musical appeal and reminded their fellow officers that, after all, it was still the "function of music to communicate." James Curnow and a group of talented young Salvationists from the Royal Oak, Michigan, Corps formed the "Royalheirs" in 1965, followed by "Second Destiny," which toured the Central territory during the summers of 1969 and 1970, playing in parks and camps. Indeed, the success of the youth and music programs in the Royal Oak Corps in the mid-1960s, culminating in their one-corps production of a major Salvation Army musical entitled "The Take-Over Bid" at an Army territorial congress in 1967, could be offered as a symbol of American corps life at its peak; this is especially true when one considers figures indicating that the mid-1960s represented the historic high point of Salvationist membership in the United States. Other groups sponsored by corps and divisions played in the Army's coffeehouses, which sprang up briefly in the late 1960s as a means of reaching young people on the street, as well as at youth rallies and high schools and on beaches and boardwalks.[43]

In some areas, however, no amount of innovation, no degree of willingness to move with the times could save the Army's ministry. A significant casualty was the Women's Social Service Department. Officers of the department made many efforts to adapt to the rapid changes that overcame them in the 1960s. "Service is not static," declared the official *Handbook* for home and hospital administration in 1962. "Policies and programs must be reviewed and reassessed periodically to insure their effectiveness in meeting the needs of people." The Army's kindhearted service to unwed mothers had always been one of its most effective social programs, but in the sixties it began to die. Discouraged officers watched as social acceptance of teenage and single-parent pregnancy, the ready availability of public medical care, increasingly stringent governmental standards for professional medical care, and — hardest of all for them to bear — abortion emptied their little hospitals. Occupancy in Salvation Army homes and hospitals declined sharply in the 1970s; from 1970 to 1978, for instance, total bed capacity fell by 55 percent to 874, and the number of newborn infants provided for declined by almost 40 percent, to 3,667. Many maternity homes closed, a process that was completed early in the next decade. In October 1978, the Women's Social Service Department of the East was itself closed. Because the pioneer rescue home officers did not keep accurate records of their work, it is not certain how many thousands of children were born in Salvation Army homes since 1887, when the first home was opened, nor how many women left these places of refuge determined to make a fresh start, convinced in their hearts that Christ loved them. The closing of this chapter in Salvation Army history is still regretted by Army leaders.[44]

The end of the Women's Social Service Department was a defeat, and the best public relations efforts could not have made it otherwise. But there were victories as well for the Army's social welfare efforts in the 1970s. Even the Women's Social Service Department had its triumphs: it helped produce ninety-seven conversions to Christ during 1977, for instance, and several of its facilities were adapted to meet contemporary needs and thus survived into a new generation of social welfare activities. In Cincinnati the Catherine Booth Home opened a mother/baby after-care program, a residential day-care center where young single mothers learned to care for their babies, and in Philadelphia the Army converted its hospital to the Booth Maternity Center, which offered a program in midwife training that gained national attention. Other defunct maternity homes were converted to day-care centers and senior citizen facilities. The Army expanded in the general hospital field. Ground was broken in 1955 for the Booth Memorial Hospital in Flushing, New York, which was joined in 1979 by another in the suburban area south of Cincinnati, which, however, was not continued as a Salvation Army facility.

An especially noteworthy advance in the field of correctional services occurred in the 1970s in Florida. In 1974 the Florida state legislature responded to charges that state parole officials were padding their case loads by taking from these officials the legal right to supervise misdemeanant probation cases. This would have left the courts with only two ways of dealing with persons convicted of misdemeanors — jail or fines

— had not a Duval County judge, Major Harding, decided in 1975 to assign a few cases for probation supervision to the local Salvation Army. An Army official in Jacksonville, Jordan Rothbart, developed a small program for this purpose, which proved successful. With Harding's encouragement, the Army expanded its probation-supervision activities to other counties and won in this larger field the same admiration it had gained in Duval. Impressed with the success of the program, judicial and corrections personnel suggested that the Army prepare a state-wide plan. Rothbart contributed to the design of legislation passed in 1976 that allowed the officials of any county to put its misdemeanant program into the hands of "any court approved public or private charity"; the act, in fact, specifically named the Army and was called "The Salvation Army Act." The Army's probation supervision program flourished in this encouraging environment. By 1981 The Salvation Army Misdemeanant Program had become, according to a favorable review in *Corrections Magazine,* "for all intents and purposes, the only misdemeanant probation supervision arm of the Florida criminal justice system." It was the Army's largest corrections program in the United States as well. Surveys conducted by the magazine and by the National Institute of Justice turned up almost universal praise from local officials and corrections professionals for the Army's probation program, which by the end of 1980 was handling 14,000 clients per month in thirty-seven Florida counties.[45]

The Army's ministry among alcoholics developed as well during the 1960s and 1970s, implementing professional, sophisticated multi-staged programs, leading through detoxification to long-term counseling and rehabilitation. The Founder's "Darkest England" scheme, adapted many times since 1890 in order to meet evolving social conditions, remained triumphantly alive in Salvation Army Harbor Light corps. Among the most innovative and successful of these programs were Chicago's Freedom Center; the enormous Cleveland Harbor Light Complex, the veteran director of which, Maj. Edward V. Dimond, pioneered several advanced rehabilitative techniques, including musical therapy; and the three-stage Harbor Light Center in St. Louis, commanded throughout this period by Capt. Jack Bennett, himself a Trophy of Grace, whose efforts produced two genuine and lasting converts out of every hundred "intakes" — a remarkably successful record for rescue work among transient alcoholic men.[46]

The Men's Social Service centers likewise adapted successfully, not only to changing conditions of urban life but to the findings of a proliferation of sociological and medical research on alcoholism and even to such worrisome developments as the neighborhood garage sale, where householders sold items they would otherwise have conttributed to the Army. The official departmental handbook on alcoholic rehabilitation reminded officers that devising programs for clients required "understanding that they may be dealt with intelligently." Careful study revealed, for instance, that most of the homeless, transient problem drinkers who came to The Salvation Army for help were not actually "addictive" drinkers; they drink simply to fill their time, as a compensation for "social deprivation," or for companionship — not from uncontrollable physical need. This revelation naturally raised the hopes of officers that such men might be more amenable to spiritual rehabilitation than they would be if their problem were entirely, or even primarily, physiological.[47]

The Army's alcoholism treatment programs also had to adapt to a change in the demographics of the clientele as an increasing number of alcoholic women appeared, many of them working-class wives and mothers. Army centers also sought to develop programs for married couples. As a result of these trends, and to avoid the stigma that professional social welfare personnel now attach to single-sex programs, The Salvation Army decided in 1977 to change the name of its social institutions from Men's Social Service Centers to Adult Rehabilitation Centers (ARCs), although the territorial departments retained the traditional names. Even so, the great majority of clients were still men, and among these the Army achieved mighty results in these years. In the West, Comm. Richard E. Holz, the territorial commander from 1974 to 1980, encouraged long-term ARC residents to enroll as "adherents" of The Salvation Army, as a formal recognition that they were transients no longer and that the movement that had rescued them was their spiritual "home." (An adherent is defined as a person who attends The Salvation Army regularly, as one would attend any church, but does not become a formal member as a soldier; converts of the Army's Adult Rehabilitation program often do not become soldiers because of the 1975 ruling that soldiers added to the rolls after that date cannot smoke.) In 1978 fully 425 center beneficiaries had become adherents, the more experienced men taking on the new converts as "disciples" in the Christian life.[48]

Programs directed at homeless alcoholics were not alone in experiencing beneficial change in these three decades. Sometimes the innovations appeared paradoxical. On one hand, the commissioners' conference established The Salvation Army Archives and Research Center in New York

City in 1977, to be operated under the auspices of the eastern territorial headquarters. Under its first director, Thomas Wilsted, a professional archivist, the center became the Army's official national depository of historic materials. On the other hand, although the Army has a highly developed interest in its own past, its leaders were not often blinded by sentimentality. Facilities that have outlived their purpose are routinely sold or demolished, a fate that has overtaken many cherished landmarks of the old-time Salvation War. The few soldiers remaining in these facilities sometimes managed to rescue some precious mementoes of past victories. A remarkable stained glass portrait of Pres. William McKinley — a costly tribute to his affection for the Army — was saved when the old corps in Canton, Ohio, was razed, and the Gamble window, a beautiful rendition of the Army crest, with its gallant eagle topping, a gift of philanthropist William A. Gamble to the Cincinnati Citadel in 1905, was rescued for the new Army hall in 1980. A few old halls were rejuvenated for some new form of Salvation Army service: just as some ex-maternity hospitals became day-care centers, so the venerable Oakland Citadel became a Harbor Light mission when the corps moved to a new building in another part of town, and Los Angeles Congress Hall, once the largest corps west of Chicago, became a mission to the Korean population that moved into the neighborhood during these years.[49]

Some change was internal, innovations that served mostly to improve administrative efficiency. The Army's territorial leaders, concerned over the increasing complexity and expense of the bureaucracy that implemented their decisions, commissioned a management analysis in 1968 by Booz, Allen & Hamilton, a New York consulting firm, and implemented many of their recommendations over the next several years. The main result of reforms was that the four territories adopted a uniform, streamlined command structure. The territorial commander, a commissioner, is chief executive. His second-in-command, the chief secretary (a full colonel) supervises the heads of the three main administrative branches: personnel (officers' appointments, records, pensions), program (music, youth, women's organizations, social service activities), and business. The National Planning and Development Committee, chaired by the national chief secretary and made up of territorial and divisional leaders, which makes major policy recommendations to the commissioners' conference, was originally created in 1970 to help the Army adjust to the substantial changes in federated funding that occurred when the new United Way of America replaced the old local Community Chest appeals. The Army rejected the recommendation of a commission of officers in 1970 that it establish a national training college in order to pool training-staff personnel and avoid expensive duplication, but it did make significant efforts in the following years to improve the quality of the four territorial training-school programs.[50]

Training officers and administrative leaders had felt for some years that the Army's system of officer training needed overhauling: not only was the curriculum regarded as inadequate to prepare officers for all that would be expected of them in the 1970s but the very structure of the training colleges themselves was outdated, reflecting the long-gone days when most cadets had been young, single, and accustomed for all of their lives to rigid autocracy. The official impetus toward change came from an international conference of the Army's training college principals that met in London in March 1974, but the American commissioners were already prepared to act on the recommendations with enthusiasm and to add their own changes. In October of that year the territorial commanders endorsed what they called the "Total College Concept" as a "goal to work toward." The new training college program called for major changes in both curriculum and the administrative structure of the schools themselves. The commissioners did not agree on a fixed national curriculum, so they adopted instead a common program with allowances for the situations in which local training colleges might find themselves from time to time in terms of short-term personnel needs or the requirements of future local academic affiliations. The common program was to include three major sections: biblical studies (including Bible, doctrine, and ecclesiastical history), field training (including pastoral ministry, social-work ministry, and public ministry), and administration. The new structure was designed to reflect the major changes in Salvation Army territorial administration; instead of the traditional "side" system, in which cadets were divided by gender and marital status (as in "men's side," "women's side" and "married side," each under the supervision of a "Chief Side Officer"), the school was divided by function, into business, personnel, and curriculum, each under a qualified and experienced officer. The actual titles attached to these new positions varied at first from one territory to the next. In October 1976 the commissioners invited the Western territorial school to conduct a two-year "pilot project" of the new program. When the Western experience proved successful, the commissioners ordered all four territorial training schools to adopt the "Total College Concept" by September 1979. Later the Eastern school requested and received an extension until September 1980 to allow territorial leaders to coordinate changes in the school staff with the movements of other territorial personnel. To ensure the continued vitality of the national curricular "guidelines," the commissioners began to approve all course syllabi for the four territorial Schools for Officers' Training in October 1980.[51]

Another effort at national centralization was more successful: in 1965 the four territorial editions of *The War Cry* were partially merged into a single version; each territory retained control over the last eight pages of the twenty-four-page edition circulated within its own region. In 1970 the vestiges of territorial editorial control were eliminated, and a truly national *War Cry* emerged, published in Chicago under the auspices of national headquarters. Maj. Robert E. Thomson, the first editor, announced in the inaugural issue that "for the first time in 87 years, a single publication becomes the official organ of The Salvation Army in all of the United States." The new version cost twenty cents, up from a dime — the first price increase in over fifty years. The Army launched two other important publishing ventures in the 1970s as well. A new monthly magazine for teens and young adults called *SAY* was started in January 1975, and a journal for Army musicians called *The Musician* (patterned after a British periodical with the same name) appeared in October 1978, under the editorial control of Brig. Ronald Rowland, a noted Chicago instrumentalist.[52]

In 1973 two more Army ranks were eliminated: lieutenant commissioner and brigadier (always a puzzler to the American public, which naturally mistook it for the rank of brigadier general, when in fact the Army's brigadier was subordinate to lieutenant colonel). The elimination of the rank of brigadier differed from the elimination of ranks in the past in that the new policy referred only to new appointments; active officers with the rank of brigadier at the time of the change retained that rank, some of them for many more years. Two traditional Salvation Army youth programs, the Young People's Legion and the Junior Legion, were officially dropped as well in 1973 for being insufficiently innovative, although there was disagreement over this decision, and considerable lingering regret in high places when it became clear that no new programs were forthcoming that precisely replaced the once-popular and effective Sunday-night "Y.P.L." in the life of the corps. A new national system of accounting and record keeping called The Salvation Army National Statistical System (NSS) was introduced in 1977. It was designed to speed the analysis of statistics from the field, but it did not recommend itself to hard-pressed corps officers, who shrank in alarm from the new pile of ledger forms.

Their apprehensions were not groundless: the 1988 issue of the NSS regulations required the "officer in charge" of a Salvation Army unit — such as a corps — to complete one weekly and three monthly ledger series, with a total of 199 different entries. The Mexico Division was detached from the Southern Territory and became a separate territorial command of its own in 1976; this administrative change, arranged in London, was in keeping with plans to form independent Salvation Army commands in sovereign states wherever possible. The change did not reflect any diminished American interest in the success of their Mexican comrades or in the spiritual welfare of Hispanic peoples generally.[53]

The long and convoluted legal history of the American-eagle version of the Army crest played itself out at last in 1976, when it was discovered that the copyright on the crown-topped model (the Army's international symbol, expropriated by Maj. Thomas Moore when he decamped in 1884) had expired irrevocably. The American commissioners, in a spirit of international camaraderie, promptly ordered the reintroduction of the crown crest on a massive scale. The eagle had disappeared from the last piece of stationery, drumhead, and building front in the country by 1980, except for certain examples of the eagle-topped crest that were regarded as especially important as works of art or historical artifacts. Eagle crests survive in stained-glass windows, for instance, in Cincinnati, Boston, Pasadena, and Frankfort, Kentucky.[54]

Of far greater interest to the public was the diversification of Salvation Army social welfare services. Some Salvationists developed new programs in fields long occupied by the Army, while others carried the flag into new areas. The Salvation Army both provided on-the-spot practical relief and coordinated the channeling of personnel and resources on a national scale following the earthquakes in Alaska in 1964, Peru in 1970, and Guatemala in 1976. The last enterprise was unique in that the Army's Southern territory, represented on the scene by Maj. Harold Hinson, not only provided short-term relief but also built 521 permanent blockhouses and a community center in Tecpan. The Army was present in full force at every major domestic disaster as well, from the Gulf Coast hurricanes of 1969 to the floods along the Kentucky, Ohio, and Mississippi rivers in 1978 and 1979. In 1970 the Army joined other emergency service organizations in providing "disaster liaison officers" on a regional basis under the auspices of the Federal Disaster Assistance Administration (FDAA). In 1975 Lt. Col. Ernest A. Miller was made "primary liaison" for the FDAA when he was placed in charge of the Army's new National Public

Affairs and Disaster Services Office in Washington, D.C. Professional analyses of the Army's disaster relief activities during these years pointed out that the Army's greatest strengths lay in its local resources, its flexible, friendly, and practical approach to immediate human needs, and the almost limitless trust reposed in it by the general public. Disaster victims sometimes expressed preference for the Army's approach over that of the American Red Cross, which was hampered in this comparison by the adherence of its officials to strict national accounting procedures, its insistence on keeping more extensive records, and the diminished flexibility associated with its commitment to long-term goals.[55]

Although the internal tensions generated by the Army's official commitment to both a social-welfare program and an evangelistic program were not new in the 1970s, they had become acute and remained so into the 1990s. Salvation Army officers have always been dedicated to evangelism. Although they are aware that the role of a corps officer is more complex than that of the minister of a mainline denomination, they have always seen themselves as pastors, spiritual counselors, and ministers of the gospel of Christ. The entire process by which young Salvationists are recruited for officership emphasizes the spiritual nature of the officer's work. It is only natural that officers would not look lightly on programs bearing the beloved name of their crusade and under their control that were merely good works — charity — not given in the Savior's name and with no clearly spiritually redemptive purpose. Army leaders shared this concern and officially reaffirmed that the "primary purpose" of the Salvation Army officer is "to reach the spiritually and physically impoverished with the gospel of Jesus Christ." Yet leaders also recognized that the Army's reputation for scrupulous accounting and efficiency and the affectionate trust in which many of the disadvantaged continued to hold it attracted increasing sums of public, foundation, and government money for a variety of welfare programs that were often well intentioned, innovative, and helpful — and that these programs brought large numbers of people into Army buildings, a number of whom became interested in its religious work. In June 1971, Brig. W. Kenneth Wheatley was appointed "National Consultant for Agency Relationships and Special Services" in New York. The Commissioners Conference decided in 1972 to move the office to the national capital, and in April 1973 Wheatley was transferred to Washington with the same title. His official duties were described as representing the national commander "to national government officials, departments, and agencies, and to specific national voluntary agencies, as directed." In addition to serving as the Army's official liaison to all government agencies and the United Way of America, Wheatley helped to secure for The Salvation Army an official status as a disaster agency. The Army also negotiated grants for a growing number of new projects in the 1970s.[56]

All of this was a mixed blessing to the Army. The principle of taking money from any source willing to offer it, including the government, was not new to Salvationists. Gen. William Booth was convinced in his day that the British government should pay for his plan to transport the country's urban poor to farm colonies abroad, and in 1904 Frederick Booth-Tucker sought a federal endorsement and financing for the American version of the farm-colony scheme. Yet many modern officers were troubled in the 1970s by an increase in government funding of Army programs. Their concern concentrated on two problems: (1) federal agencies exerted considerable control over the administration of programs they financed, control that threatened the Army's long-cherished independence to carry out its own unique combination of social and religious enterprise in its own way; and (2) the First Amendment to the Constitution had been interpreted by both the executive and judicial branches of government as forbidding federal funding of religious activity. This meant not only that there could be no obviously evangelical purpose to any Army program that received substantial federal money but also that officers would have to calculate what proportion of their resources, including floor space, office supplies, utility bills, and the time of their staff and themselves, was devoted to religious work — and then to deduct that proportion from any budget presentation for many kinds of outside funds. This required officers to divide their programs for budgetary purposes into "religious" and "social" activities, which was distasteful to them and antithetical to the Army's long-standing tradition that its social and spiritual work could not be divided. Worse still, some officers were ordered to remove Christian pictures and mottos from rooms in Army buildings being used for funded social welfare programs. A number of federated funding programs — including the United Way, like its predecessor the Community Chest — made similar demands on The Salvation Army.[57]

Despite such difficulties, the Army's reliance on government and external funding became increasingly widespread during the 1970s. Probation supervision, low-cost housing units, nutritional services, and daycare and drug rehabilitation programs were established under Salvation Army auspices from coast to coast. Some Harbor Light services were almost completely dependent on federal funds. There was also a growing reliance on "purchase-of-service" contracts, by which the public agency paid only for certain parts of the Army program (such as floor space, use of kitchen facilities, utility bills, janitorial services, vehicles, and professional staff time). These contracts were often connected with the employment by the Army of beneficiaries of the federal Comprehensive Education and Training Act (CETA). These persons provided labor in that part of the Army program funded by the government agency but were not responsible to the Army officer nominally in charge of the facility. Some projects were large and promising: in 1978, for instance, USAID bestowed a grant on the Army that enabled it to set up the new Salvation Army World Service Organization to assist in the training of indigenous officer leadership around the world. The first director of the new organization, Lt. Col. Ernest Miller, who had succeeded Wheatley in the national office in 1974, was a firm believer in the Army's evangelical purpose and viewed his new office as a continuation of the purposes of the old Founder himself. The Army's official position on governmental funding was carefully worked out and refined several times in these years as it sought to retain control of the programs administered in its name and preserve the essential unity of its religious and social programs. The commissioners' conference stated the official position in 1972, as part of new guidelines for American corps officers: "There is nothing inconsistent about the Army's receiving governmental funds so long as it would require neither denial of its Christian incentive nor a compromise of its evangelical intention."[58]

At least the influence of the government funding was on the whole limited to the directly sponsored welfare programs that depended upon it: if the funding had been cut off for those programs, almost all of which were new in the 1970s, only they would have suffered; traditional corps programs and many of the Army's own small-scale but long-established welfare enterprises would not have been seriously affected. It was easy in these years to exaggerate the importance of United Way funding on Salvation Army operations. There was no clear nationwide pattern. The percentage of the Army's income coming from United Way allocations differed significantly among the divisions. In the Southern California and Eastern Michigan divisions in the early 1970s, for instance, the overall Army program received perhaps 24 percent of its total revenue from the United Way; in the Louisiana-Alabama-Mississippi division, on the other hand, the percentage was just over 40 percent, which was slightly less than the aggregate percentage for all divisions in the Eastern territory. Similar differences turned up among corps in any given division as well. Large,

well-established corps needed the United Way less than the small, strug-
gling ones. Nor did the Army dominate United Way budgets: in 1976
The Salvation Army nationwide received only 5 percent of the United
Way's total allocations to all agencies.[59]

The remainder of the money for the Army's evangelical and charitable endeavors had to be raised from the public through special project
campaigns, direct mail appeals (a favorite Army method since the turn
of the century), and the vitally important annual Christmas kettle collections, which by 1960 were a national tradition with tinkling handbells
and brass quartets happily playing Leidzen's *Carolers' Favorites*. The
Army's right to continue to use these methods, and the fact that funds
left to the Army in wills are applied to the acquisition or improvement
of permanent facilities in order to provide a lasting memorial to the
generosity of the departed friend, became part of every formal agreement
between The Salvation Army and the United Way. There was also "internal giving" — the "cartridges" of the soldiers and the cash collections
taken up in meetings — although few corps in the United States supported themselves in this way. In fact, American Salvationists remained,
on average, poor financial supporters of their own cause. There were
several explanations for this phenomenon. Most Salvationists were willing
to make up in personal energy and time what they could not contribute
in money: the weekly schedule of Salvation Army activities supported by
the officers and soldiers in corps large and small remained, as it had
always been, prodigious. In addition, most Salvationists remained literally
poor; most were widows, single women, or women who attended the
corps with their children but without their husbands. Nationwide, the
majority of the relatively few complete Salvationist families were, as they
had been for the whole century of the Army's existence in the United
States, from the "respectable working class." Most of the remaining
Salvationists were either elderly or young. One third of the Army's active
membership in 1980 was under the age of fourteen, and a large percentage of the "senior soldiers" over the age of fourteen were still in their
teens. Nevertheless, the anxiety of officers that the Army was becoming
dependent on outside funding might have been eased if soldiers had
given more sacrificially, as the teaching of Christ — and the generous
example of members of other evangelical denominations — suggested.
The Salvation Army wisely required that every corps become self-
supporting as soon as possible, but only a handful of very large corps
had achieved this goal by the Army's centennial year of 1980.[60]

The importance of corps funding lay in the fact that the corps has always been the basic unit of Salvation Army religious activities. It was, and remains, at the corps level — and in its Adult Rehabilitation Centers — that The Salvation Army maintains its front lines in the war for souls. Large-scale jubilees and territorial congresses, with massed bands and a combination of hallelujah excitement and quiet dignity, as though the participants moved every moment to the thrill of leading forward a still-great crusade, continued to punctuate the Army calendar during this decade, but it was in the chapels of corps and institutions that the evangelical work of the Army went forward. Territorial and national leaders were installed in the 1970s in the time-honored flamboyant style that thrilled Salvationists as much as it had when Evangeline Booth presided over similar scenes for the benefit of their parents and grandparents. But Salvationists knew, even as the Army's leaders knew, that it was only when the troops returned to the weekly routine of the corps that the Great Salvation War would be pushed forward again. The corps remained in 1980, as it was in 1880, the "heart of the Army's evangelical mission."[61]

The corps were not free of problems. The most pressing of these was membership, which not only failed to keep pace with the population of the country as a whole but actually began to decline after the mid-1960s. This may not have seemed to be the case when the Army reported a 5 percent increase in membership in 1975, leading religious periodicals to hail it as "the fastest growing U.S. religious body," but these promising numbers were the result of a change in accounting procedures: the Army had begun recording everyone who made use of its community-center youth programs and corps facilities. The figures for actual members — soldiers, recruits, and adherents — were less encouraging as the Army neared the end of its first century of service in the United States. In 1980 the Army had 77,257 senior soldiers (full adult members) and close to 11,000 additional recruits and adherents. The much larger "total membership" figure of nearly 400,000, which was given to such religious publications as the annual *Yearbook of American and Canadian Churches,* represented every name on the corps rolls, plus members of clubs, athletic teams, the Home League, scout troops, and ancillary organizations that made use of corps community centers, most of whom attended the Army's religious services irregularly or not at all and who contributed nothing to the work. (Officers cannot easily remove names of soldiers from the roll; it can be done only for individuals known to be dead or those who request in writing that their names be removed. Moreover, there is a natural reluctance to remove names where there is any question about their actual status, since, among other things, every removal that is not matched by a new enrollment reflects adversely on an officer's record.) The totals for Army membership in 1980 were only 9 percent larger than they were in 1936, although the national population had increased by 70 percent. Returns on the national level for the twenty years after 1960 were even more disquieting: assuming that statistics given to the *Yearbook* were accurate and consistent in their significance over time, The Salvation Army reached its highest level of membership in 1966, after which the figure began to decline, although the losses were concentrated in the Eastern and Central territories. The number of corps had been declining a good deal longer: in 1950 there were 1,380 corps; by 1980 there were only 1,056. The number of bandsmen declined from 6,097 in 1960 to 4,149 twenty years later, and the number continued to decline throughout the 1980s. The number of adult local officers (the most active category of adult member — the sergeants, treasurers, musicians, and Sunday school teachers) declined by 5 percent during the 1970s, from 15,217 to 14,446.[62]

Salvationists at every level were naturally alarmed at these unhappy developments. Nor were their spirits always restored by cheery reports of the Army's many good works. A national soldier's commission that met in 1967 at the request of the commissioners declared its concern: "Without the continuing development of healthy corps spiritual life, all of the splendid, manifold social, community and welfare activities are stripped of their vitality insofar as soul-saving is concerned because of a lack of committed Christian leadership." A number of divisional and local study-groups were established to investigate the causes for the decline of the corps; these efforts were expanded during the 1980s into territorial and national commissions with substantial funding and broad mandates. Those who looked for causes for the long-term decline in The Salvation Army corps found that some of them were general, affecting more than just the Army: the decline of urban areas, which made churchgoers that much more reluctant to drive the long distances from their new suburban homes into the neighborhood of the building, especially after dark; a long, national decline in Sunday school attendance, which afflicted other churches as well as the Army; and the development of alternative forms of social activity, especially in the evenings and on weekends, such as watching television, visiting shopping malls, and, for the more affluent, recreation on boats and at summer homes.[63]

Other factors were unique to the Army. Its image as a social welfare agency sometimes worked at cross purposes with its evangelical ministry, for instance: people are more inclined to seek out more conventional ministers or churches for help with spiritual troubles. Salvationist traditionalists were sad to note that the open-air ministry, once its most famous means of evangelical outreach, and a ministry that clearly established the Army in the public mind as an evangelical mission, declined through the decade of the 1970s, from 23,000 meetings per year in 1970 to 9,190 in 1980. Problems existed inside the hall as well. The pressure on a corps officer to maintain the full range of welfare, public relations, and business activities has always been very great. Maj. Herbert Luhn, a successful and experienced corps officer, spoke for many of his comrades when he told a national Army conference in 1978 that the corps officer "cannot possibly function effectively in all areas of his responsibility." This had been part of the cause of the "declension" of the corps' "Spiritual Mission." Other officers were concerned that some of their colleagues who did have adequate time for their pastoral duties none-theless failed to discharge them. Capt. Philip D. Needham warned his fellow officers in 1972 that many soldiers were "dying spiritual deaths" from a steady diet of shallow and ill-prepared sermons. Others pointed to research on church growth that suggested a close relationship between the length of pastoral tenure and the size of the congregation; they denounced the Army practice of transferring officers frequently from corps to corps and the inevitable promotion to staff positions of many of the most able and dedicated. These points remained germane throughout the decade of the 1980s as well.[64]

Even the smallness of the Army congregation worked against further growth, throwing a heavy burden on the few regular members who continued to attend and causing newcomers to feel conspicuous and awkward. And the Army *was* small, making up only 0.4 percent of all churchgoers in the United States in 1978. A Sunday morning congregation of seventy-five people was considered good for most corps. Even if every man, woman, and child on the rolls in 1980 were to have shown up — despite the fact that many of these names were completely inactive — the average number of soldiers (senior and junior) per corps in the United States would only have been 102, little more than it was fifty years before. The number of corps with as many as two hundred in regular attendance nationwide was very small, perhaps three dozen at the most. It was hardly surprising, then, that Maj. David Baxendale announced in 1971, when these trends were already apparent, that the corps had "come to a crossroads, a time for agonizing reappraisal."[65]

Yet The Salvation Army approached its centennial year with optimism. The Army still had enormous strengths after its first century of service in the United States, strengths that other religious and charitable organizations openly envied. The Army's fundamental Christian principles had not wavered either in doctrine or in practice since the courageous Shirleys unfurled the flag on a Philadelphia street corner in 1879. The Army remained first and foremost a branch of the church of Christ on earth. Twice in the 1970s the Army stated to the Internal Revenue Service, in official and unequivocal terms, that its leaders claimed tax exemption for their organization not because it was a charity but because it was a denomination of the Christian church. During the twenty years after it joined the Christian Holiness Association in 1960, the Army's aggressive and unwavering commitment to its official Wesleyan theology earned for it a role in the nationwide association out of all proportion to the Army's small size as a denomination. Its firmly orthodox Christianity bestowed great strength on the Army's members, who shared a sense of divine purpose, a missionary zeal, and an abiding and warmhearted loyalty to Christ, whom they regarded as their Friend, their Brother, their great Commander, who overlooked and encouraged them in every forward step in His cause. All this seemed quite wonderful to the distracted and divided leadership of mainline denominations in these years, struggling with schisms and identity crises.[66]

The Army remained as firmly committed to noble practice as it was to high principle, and its standards, like its orthodoxy, did much to sustain its high morale. Its accounting and auditing procedures were exemplary. It compromised on nothing. The Salvation Army became formally affiliated with so many major organizations — forty-one by 1977 — that in that year it helped to organize a national council to coordinate them all, the Coalition of National Voluntary Organizations. Yet the Army belonged to no organization in the 1970s that required it to surrender a single moral principle. It officially resigned from the USO, which it had helped to found, when that organization began to serve alcoholic drinks in its clubs in 1976. The Army, already officially troubled over a statement calling for "eucharistic" unity, finally suspended its membership in the World Council of Churches in 1978 after that body authorized a grant of funds to guerrilla organizations in Rhodesia-Zimbabwe, members of which were implicated in the murder of unoffending Salvation Army missionaries in that country.[67]

This decision by the Army's international leaders did not reflect any lack of concern for the problems of the developing parts of the world. By the centennial year, 1980, The Salvation Army had become one of the largest Protestant missionary organizations in the world, carrying on its evangelical and social ministries in eighty-one countries besides the United States. Much of the success of the vast enterprise depended on financial support from the American branch of the movement. The Army in the United States raised large amounts from internal sources to support overseas projects. These "self-denial" funds from the United States, which increased by substantial amounts every decade, have been the largest single source of funds for the Army's foreign missions since before the Second World War. In addition, eighty-five American officers were serving in appointments outside the United States in 1980.

Standards set for soldiers, both in the service required of them and in their daily lives, have remained uncompromising. The life of a Salvationist is a strict one. The Army's *Orders and Regulations for Soldiers,* originally written by the Founder, were finally revised in 1977, making large allowances for changed social conditions but no concessions on fundamental Army principles: soldiers are expected to avoid every sort of immorality, vulgarity, and dishonesty and to treat everyone they encounter in a straightforward and kindly way, like a brother or sister. The "Articles of War" that soldiers must sign were changed only twice during the Army's first century in the United States — the last time, in 1975, only to be made more strict: the Army added the rule that soldiers must not use tobacco. Soldiers were expected to obey their officers in every lawful thing and to support the Salvation War with their time and money, heart and soul. For their part, Army leaders made repeated efforts to demonstrate that they recognize and value the vital role of the lay Salvationist in The Salvation Army. This recognition led on the national level to the annual Soldiers' Seminar on Evangelism at Glen Eyrie, Colorado, and to a number of commissions, committees, and planning councils on the territorial and divisional levels — so many by 1975 that the national chief secretary had to remind the territorial commanders to use the "current names" for them when corresponding with headquarters.[68]

The capacity of its field officers and soldiers for service in the corps has always been one of the Army's most valuable resources. The account of time that the average Salvationist still donated to corps duties at the end of the Army's first hundred years in the United States, even considering the decline in these figures since 1950, remained amazing. While officers often feel that they are sinking beneath the business and social welfare requirements of their assignments, and leaders have tried one expedient after another to relieve or encourage them, the prodigious evangelical and social activity of the corps goes on, maintained by officers and soldiers for whom the Army "Corps Community Center" (the new official name, indicating the broad role of the modern corps, became official in 1973) is a busy place all through the week. This has remained true both indoors and outdoors: in the late 1970s almost one-quarter of American corps still conducted weekly open-air services. Schedules selected at random in the late 1970s from corps in Danville, Kentucky; Kittanning, Pennsylvania; Columbus, Ohio; Warsaw, Indiana; Sheboygan, Wisconsin; Augusta, Georgia; and Redding, California reveal a dozen meetings of one kind or another per week; most soldiers attended at least half of these, and some attended them all — along with the officer or his wife or the assistant officer. These schedules could have been reproduced literally a thousand times; taken collectively they represent quantities of time and energy expended weekly in behalf of the religious work of The Salvation Army in the last years of its first century of activity that must have encouraged even dispirited observers of the Army scene. And what is even more striking is that Salvationists were willing to do more: the capacity for sacrifice and the zeal for souls that marked the early Army crusades was not dead in many hearts; such feelings waited only to be rekindled by a renewed sense of the movement's high evangelical purpose to produce the great revival for which officers and soldiers had so long yearned.[69]

It was only natural that the Army's leaders would have high hopes that great work would be accomplished by the coming generation of Salvationists. In 1978 a number of high-ranking officers of The Salvation Army were interviewed in connection with the preparation of the first edition of this book; included among them were three national commanders, four territorial commanders, and six chief secretaries. Each of these officers declared, without knowing the statements of any of the others, that the dedication, talent, and zeal of the Army's current generation of young people were together the single most encouraging thing about the movement as it neared the end of its first hundred years in the United States.[70]

On the other hand, the centennial year was a time to celebrate the past. The Army had an amazing history, fully capable of supporting grand conclusions, yet rich in colorful anecdotes — whimsical, humorous, exciting, and inspiring. It had taken The Salvation Army almost a hundred years to become even comparatively dull, and even in 1980 there was still much about the movement to attract the attention of reporters, cartoonists, and comedians. The generation of Salvationists that experienced the centennial year in 1980 was made aware of the Army's colorful historical heritage in many ways. Few denominations were prouder of their past or more eager to celebrate its milestones and keep alive its traditions. Although the Army did not begin systematic archival preservation until comparatively late in its history, much that was noble and redemptive was preserved, in one form or another, around the country. Everyone had a scrapbook, a box of letters, and a favorite story, and some Salvationists were serious private collectors. The most successful and important of the Army's amateur archivists was Col. Paul D. Seiler of Ocean Grove, New Jersey, but a large volume of valuable items was preserved by other officers as well, including Brig. Lawrence Castagna in Columbus, Ohio; Maj. Dick Norris, a Southern adult rehabilitation officer; Lt. Col. John Busby of Florida; Comms. Richard E. and Ernest W. Holz, brothers who were grandsons of the Army pioneer; and Mr. Harry Sparks of Los Angeles. The Army's fondness for reminiscing reached a high level in the 1980s, when a large number of divisional and corps centenaries were celebrated throughout the country. But the Army's long memory was not merely nostalgic; it also served to give the soldiers a sense of collective responsibility, as though the departed pioneers had laid a claim upon the lives of those who followed after. Old songs, old sermons, even old advice, revived and widely circulated as part of the official centennial celebrations, did not strike the Salvationists of 1980 as old-fashioned. Members of The Salvation Army were as open to the inspiration of these bequests from long-dead comrades as their grandfathers had been when they heard the originals.[71]

CHAPTER 7

1980-1992

"Come join our Army, to battle we go!"

William J. Pearson, 1879, *Salvation Army Song Book,*
1987 ed., Song No. 681

The National Centennial Congress held in Kansas City in June 1980 to celebrate The Salvation Army's one-hundredth anniversary in the United States was the most lavish series of ceremonies ever staged by the movement. It was the Army's first nationwide celebration since the great congresses of Ballington Booth's day, late in the nineteenth century. In the midst of five days filled with parades, messages from Gen. Arnold Brown, and national and territorial leaders, concerts, the performance of several original musical and dramatic productions, seminars, and reunions, Salvationists did not neglect those expressions of their energetic faith — the testimonies, street meetings, and militant gospel songs — that had characterized their crusade since 1880. One high-ranking officer, unused to such old-fashioned hijinks, was caught without an Army flag to wave at a particularly hair-raising moment during the "Service of Praise and Thanksgiving." Mortified, the same colonel carried a flag in his Bible case for months afterward, for similar emergencies.[1]

The Centennial Congress provided Army personnel with many opportunities to reflect on their past and future. The episodes and personalities from the Army's colorful past that were selected for special attention at the congress in June and throughout the special centennial year were cherished by and long familiar to Salvationists: Railton at Battery Park, Ash Barrel Jimmy, the Slum Sisters, Joe the Turk, Brengle, the Doughnut Girls, Evangeline Booth, pioneer adventures in the Golden West, the Scandinavian work, Vachel Lindsay's famous poem. The Centennial Congress differed from national gatherings of the distant past, however, in that the conventions in the 1890s had been given over almost entirely to celebration and optimistic pronouncements, whereas the centennial in 1980 had an additional, more serious function. Delegates were encouraged to re-enact colorful vignettes and sing martial songs in Kansas City, but they were also called upon to react to a "Battlefield Report," a set of five "Battle Objectives" from the Army's National Planning and Development Commission. The commission, created by the commissioners' conference a decade before, coordinated an extensive nationwide survey conducted for the Army by International Marketing Group, Incorporated, and called for the creation of territorial task forces to develop plans for the implementation of the objectives. Delegates at the congress were invited not only to participate in this process on the spot by submitting suggestions but to spread the word to their home corps that the era of grass-roots participation in major Salvation Army planning had arrived: "In each and every corps, soldiers will participate in the further development of this plan and the affirmation of its purpose."[2]

The territorial task forces met throughout the year. The national coordinator for this effort, Lt. Col. Hartwell B. Fleming, reported in October 1981 on "the countless meetings, accumulation of study materials and research, the intensity of purpose and sincere concern" in each task force as well as the "intense and enthusiastic grassroots involvement" that had been evident. The five "Battle Objectives" of the Centennial Congress, now grown to six, became the Army's official "Second Century Advance" strategy for marching into its second hundred years in America. The new official objectives were first and foremost spiritual in nature. Enthusiasm for the new program was high, partly stimulated by the results of the nationwide surveys, which showed that while the Army was the most popular charity in the United States, relatively few Americans, even among regular donors, realized that it was a religious organization. Even some of those who should have known the Army well, such as its own advisory board members, supported it even though they may not have believed in or even understood its religious purpose.[3]

The first "Battle Objective" called for "affirming spiritual commitment" based on a "Bible-based growth program" for the local corps; the world must also be reminded that "the main purpose of all Salvation Army social services continues to be to lead people to Christ." The second objective was "expanded recruitment" using a variety of means to make the corps more effective in attracting and introducing all kinds of new people to Christ while at the same time nurturing the existing congregations. A major part of this proposal was a call for an "official Salvation Army Mission Statement" to explain to the American public "the broad spiritual foundations and purpose of The Salvation Army." It also endorsed more effective means "to recruit, nurture and train minorities for Army involvement and leadership." The other objectives included expanded programs for training officers, more effective communication, and better funding systems. Clearly, nothing of the Army's militant zeal for souls was being lost in the transition to the computerized format of the 1980s. Even moderate outside observers were impressed: "In a world where many Christians are uncomfortable with militaristic images," noted *The Christian Century* in 1980, "the Salvation Army has held fast to its martial emphasis."[4]

The Salvation Army was, as its own public relations firm announced in the pages of *Christianity Today*, officially "on the verge of far reaching change." Despite the lingering sameness of kettles and uniform styles, Dale Hanson Bourke of International Marketing, Incorporated, was able to predict that her clients would soon "take on a new look" as the Army carried out the plans of the Second Century Advance campaign. The official task teams had generated twenty-five major proposals. The new official Salvation Army Mission Statement, the product of collaboration by lay members, officers, and leaders, was promulgated by the commissioners' conference in 1982 with the intent of re-establishing "the credibility of The Salvation Army as a branch of the Christian Church." The statement, which remained in use throughout the 1980s, described the Army as "an international religious and charitable movement organized and operated on a quasi-military pattern" and "a branch of the Christian church." The "motivation of the organization" was described in unqualified terms as "love of God and a practical concern for the needs of humanity." This motivation was expressed in the Army's religious and social service programs, which were freely offered to all persons "regardless of race, color, creed, sex, or age."[5]

While the Mission Statement was the most important of the proclamations the commissioners issued during the 1980s, it was far from being the only one. In addition to the proclamations issued by the Army's international headquarters in London (the language of which the commissioners "Americanized" before issuing them in the United States), fifteen specifically American "positional statements" were prepared and issued during the decade. Responding to another task force proposal, the Army moved quickly to expand the type and effectiveness of the communications at its disposal. The Office of Media Ministries was opened in Dallas in October 1981. Although this office, which specialized in the production and distribution of videotaped materials for use in corps, was operated as part of the Army's Texas division, it soon developed into a nationwide service. A Salvation Army radio program, started in 1951 and in continuous production in Atlanta since 1975, expanded rapidly after 1980, with the gospel message borne on the airwaves by the gentle voice of Maj. James Hylton, who joined the program in that year. In January 1984, a new position, Director of National Communications, was created at national headquarters in order to develop and coordinate Army communications and publicity activities nationwide. The first director, Col. Leon Ferraez, remained in this position, which continued to change and expand, throughout the decade. The official goal of Salvation Army communications remained the same: "to effectively transmit the message of the balanced ministry of The Salvation Army to the general public" in order to attract more members, volunteers, clients, money, and cooperation from other agencies.[6]

The first half of the new decade was filled with innovation and change. Seeds planted by the Second Century Advance sprouted, and although that campaign itself faded into memory, it was counted a great success by Army leaders for having launched many initiatives. In time it was replaced by a succession of new national and territorial campaigns and by proposals from other, more permanent sources (including the Army's administration). These proposals, too, were built into new policies and programs. One result of lasting importance to come from the Second Century Advance was the official recognition by Army leadership that long-range planning was "essential." The effectiveness of this process was ensured soon after the centennial celebrations were over, when the commissioners decided to make long-range planning one of the central responsibilities of the Army's National Planning and Development Commission (NPDC), which was the most influential and prestigious of the large number of such commissions that made recommendations to the commissioners' conference. In February 1984 the commissioners stated that henceforth long-range planning would be a regular "major agenda item" for the NPDC, and in 1987 the leaders approved the addition of a full-time research consultant to the Commission.[7]

The NPDC was itself strengthened in important ways during the decade. In 1982, while the Second Century Advance Task Force Coordinator (Lt. Col. Fleming) still served on the Commission, two divisional commanders were added from each territory in order to broaden representation from the field. At the same time, the NPDC continued to coordinate recommendations and detailed plans for one of its major projects, the creation of a national advisory board for The Salvation Army. This proposal, which brought enormous benefits to the national organization, began in 1976 when the commissioners accepted the recommendation of Comm. William E. Chamberlain, the national commander from 1974 to 1977, that a new advisory council be formed of some of the nation's leading business leaders. The National Advisory Council (NAC) would bring to national leadership the same counsel, experience, and financial resources that advisory boards had brought to Army units on a smaller scale for sixty years. The acting chair of the NAC organizational meeting, held in New York City on October 18, 1976, was Dr. Jerome Holland; at that meeting the first slate of official officers was elected. The first official chairman was Mr. Robert Sellers of the City Service Oil Company of Tulsa.

A number of prominent business leaders served in the chair in the following years. Mr. Prime Osborn III, who was elected in 1978, presided over developments of particular importance. Osborn, the president of CSX Railroad, encouraged the formation of several active committees to function under the NAC executive committee. Osborn also served as chair during The Salvation Army Centennial celebrations in Kansas City, in which the support of council members played an important role. There were a few awkward moments in the early stages, when the high-powered executives on the council overlooked the Army's commitment to processing recommendations through its own elaborate channels, but these bumps were smoothed over. A highly efficient structure, tuned year by year to function with maximum efficiency in the Salvation Army context, developed over time. Chairs after Mr. Osborn, who served until June 1982, were Mr. John Hanley (Monsanto), Mr. Richard Bertholdt (Price Waterhouse), Mr. B. Franklin Skinner (Southern Bell), Mr. J. Duncan Brown (Iron City Sash and Door), Mr. Harry V. Lamon (an Atlanta attorney), and Mr. Arthur Decio (Skyline Corporation).[8]

The National Advisory Council's influence became, and remained, very great. By the end of the decade, every major decision affecting the Army nationwide was reviewed by these persons, who numbered among the Army's most prestigious supporters in the United States. In October 1982 the analogy with the Army's local boards became complete when the National Advisory Council was renamed the National Advisory Board. The new board was divided into nine committees. Although the names of these committees changed occasionally in later years, the division of labor they represented gave an indication of the scope of the board's interests; the committees were these: executive, nominating, advisory board development, finance and accounting, public and agency relations, investment management, world services, personnel development (related to officer development for the Army), and bequest and endowment cultivation. The National Advisory Board took its role very seriously and played an increasingly important role in the direction of Salvation Army affairs as the decade unfolded. In addition, the board established and sponsored triennial "National Advisory Organization Conferences" that attracted members of local advisory boards and friends of the Army from across the nation. The first was held in St. Louis in 1983, the second in Dallas in 1986, the third in London (amid exciting re-enactments of the Army's East-end beginnings) in October 1989, and the fourth to date in Washington, D.C., in May 1992.[9]

The Army's national publications were improved and expanded during the 1980s. In May 1983 the commissioners appointed a high-level committee chaired by Col. James Osborne, national chief secretary, to study the nature, purpose, and readership of *The War Cry* "and to consider its spiritual focus and use as an evangelistic tool." The commissioners gave much of the responsibility for implementing sweeping changes in the publication to Maj. Henry Gariepy, who became national editor-in-chief in 1981. The eight pages of territorial news (two pages for each territory) that had been regularly appearing were discontinued in an effort to make *The War Cry* into "a *national* publication." (In 1983 the territories were given permission to design and publish their own territorial newsletters. The first to do so was the West, with *The New Frontier;* the others followed shortly with the Eastern *Good News,* the *Central News,* and *The Southern Spirit.*) The venerable *War Cry* emerged from its "year of destiny" in 1984 like the patriarch in a coat of many colors, printed on high-quality paper and filled with spectacular color photography and articles by the country's most prominent evangelical writers. A new magazine for youth called the

Young Salvationist appeared in January of that year, "an all new and exciting teen publication" replacing *SAY* magazine (and reducing the familiar *Young Soldier* to the modest role of an eight-page pullout inserted in the new magazine). Even internal program notes, like those for the Army's Home League, were modernized in 1984, when Mrs. Col. Martha Ferraez became editor of these "Program Aids."[10]

The Salvation Army Adventure Corps was launched in January 1983, not exactly to replace the Boy Scouts of America in the life of Army youth — the Army continued to support the Scouts — but to provide boys with an alternative "where needed." The new Adventure Corps was distinctly Christian, giving out "star awards" for Bible knowledge, the Christian life, and Salvationist-style activities as well as for physical fitness, crafts, and nature lore. The new youth program was well suited to Salvation Army youth; within a few years it had largely eclipsed the Boy Scouts in Army circles, despite efforts by the Boy Scouts' national leadership to reverse the trend. In 1990, for instance, there were 15,974 Salvationist boys in the Adventure Corps, while the Scouts attracted only 2,773.[11]

The Army underwent some important physical relocations in this decade as well, moving its territorial and national headquarters facilities away from downtown locations to suburban sites. This process had started in the previous decade; in 1976 both the Western and Southern territorial headquarters moved to new locations. In 1982 the Army's national headquarters left its hallowed site at 120 West 14th Street in New York City — its most famous address in the United States, which it had occupied since 1896 — to move to a more modern facility in Verona, New Jersey, where it remained for the remainder of the decade. In September 1990 the Eastern territory moved its administrative center from West 14th Street as well, to a new office complex in nearby West Nyack, New York, which the territorial commander, Comm. Robert E. Thomson, described as a new "place of encouragement and enabling for those who fight the salvation war." In the same year the Army's national leadership announced their decision to move national headquarters to Washington, D.C. The Verona location was now seen as only a step in a longer process of movement away from a location shared with a territorial headquarters toward a more central and convenient site. The next year, the general shift from historic urban addresses was completed when the Central territorial headquarters moved from downtown Chicago to new, much larger facilities in Des Plaines.[12]

Some younger officers and Salvationists who were committed to a renewed urban ministry viewed these moves into green spaces as steps in the wrong direction, at least symbolically; but leaders regarded the reasons for these moves as compelling. More space was required for the expansion of administrative support functions; in addition, the new locations provided improved access to highway and air transportation systems, allowed for improved staff housing, and reduced commuting. Furthermore, the value of urban real estate had inflated steadily over the many years that The Salvation Army occupied its downtown addresses, allowing the Army to realize large sums from the sale of the old headquarters properties that could be applied to much more modern, convenient, and comfortable facilities. On top of these general reasons, the Army's national leaders recognized the value to the Army's national administration of proximity to the many government agencies and foundations located in the national capital as well as the symbolic importance of such a location. The national staff was encouraged in this decision by the National Advisory Board, the members of which gave valuable support and guidance. The Army's local Washington Advisory Board was naturally enthusiastic as well; its chairperson, Mr. Richard Carr, personally assisted Col. Kenneth Hood, the national chief secretary, in visiting almost sixty different properties. In the fall of 1991 The Salvation Army's National Headquarters was officially established in a beautiful new facility in Alexandria, Virginia — funded, in the time-honored Army way, by legacies.[13]

Some of the most venerable aspects of salvation warfare were jettisoned in the 1980s. The nostalgia of the centennial celebrations had hardly passed into memory when the commissioners announced in October 1980 that the bonnet and high-collar tunic, which had symbolized the Army for its entire history in the United States, had become "optional" for officers. Territorial commanders could still require the old-style uniform for special events, but only until December 31, 1981. The commissioners were careful to add to their pronouncement that the "stand-up collar uniform" was "always appropriate at any time of year, if the Salvationist prefers. For women, this could also include the bonnet." Although these items of dress survived here and there for a few years longer for ceremonial and public relations uses, the bonnet and stand-up collar virtually disappeared from the American scene. The Army's official brochure on the proper way to wear the uniform was revised in 1985; among other changes, all references to the stand-up tunic and bonnet were eliminated. Territorial headquarters museums collected a few of these dignified relics for display and to assist Salvationists in the production of historic pageants and re-enactments, of which there were a large number in these years. The

National Headquarters, Alexandria, Virginia, 1992
Source: The Salvation Army National Archives

popularity of *Guys and Dolls* among high-school drama departments remained high, but the Army could no longer oblige with a regular supply
of old-fashioned uniforms, for almost none remained by the late 1980s.
Maj. Paul Marshall, director of the Central territorial museum, could only
refer these numerous inquiries to a costume shop in Milwaukee.[14]

More importantly, the Army's traditional open-air ministry declined
rapidly in the 1980s. In 1982 the commissioners decided that the class in
"outdoor evangelism" that was offered as part of the annual Soldiers'
Seminar on Evangelism at Glen Eyrie should be revised: the term *outdoor*

was regarded as "too restrictive, usually being perceived as 'open air.'" The class should "explore all evangelistic opportunities." The Army's leaders did well to explore alternatives to the traditional street-corner meeting, since this form of ministry was rapidly disappearing. The number of open-air meetings held by the Army declined from an annual total of 9,190 in 1980 to 6,710 in 1990. The latter figure represented only a fourth of the total twenty years before. Traditionalists were saddened by the nearly complete extinction of this form of evangelism, although they could not deny that conditions had become increasingly less conducive to street-corner evangelism for thirty years.[15]

Here and there stalwarts revived open-air meetings with a flourish, catching even Army leaders momentarily off guard. Capt. John Purdell caused a stir in the San Fernando Valley in 1988 by holding evangelistic services in a shopping mall, hanging gospel banners over a freeway, and generally reviving the uncompromising spirit of the Great Salvation War of the previous century. Some of the coming generation of officers were willing on their own initiative to engage in old-style street-corner warfare as well, loath to abandon this part of the Army's heritage without testing its effectiveness on a new generation of sin-shackled passersby. In May 1990, a gallant trio of cadets from the Southern School for Officers' Training formed a gospel-rock band (appropriately called "Joyful Noise") and held a curbside service in an area of Atlanta known as Little Five Points, "one of Satan's headquarters." In November of that year thirty cadets in Chicago staged a full-scale old-time march and open-air in front of Wrigley Field, complete with mock funeral. Both of these attacks brought gratifying results: the attention of just the sort of bewildered drunks and homeless people among whom The Salvation Army had been casting its gospel net since William Booth's day.[16]

The decline of the open-air meeting did not mean that the Army disappeared from public view in the 1980s. On the contrary, Salvationists were conspicuous everywhere, often clothed in the style and armed with the mottos and songs of their ferocious predecessors. This was the great age of centennials, re-enactments, and historical revivals, occasioned by the fact that exactly one hundred years had passed since the Army exploded on many of the scenes of its pioneer warfare. So many corps and divisions planned elaborate centennial celebrations that the small staff at the Army's National Archives and Research Bureau was kept busy searching ancient files of *The War Cry* for opening dates and colorful anecdotes suitable for dramatic recreation. Even the American Rescue Workers, that ancient and long-forgotten relic of the Moore split, briefly reappeared in 1982. The Army reminded the group, no doubt with a touch of nostalgia, that by referring to their Army background in their fund-raising materials they were violating a still-valid injunction granted against them seventy years before. One entire territory — the Western — celebrated its hundredth anniversary as well, with a lavish congress on June 2-6, 1983. Local newspapers, television news reports, and Salvation Army periodicals and news releases were filled with reports of these affairs throughout the decade.[17]

The spread of the Army in the 1880s had been dramatic. It "opened fire" on cities in thirty-five states in that decade — each of which commemorated the event a century later in ways that were, if possible, even more dramatic. This was the intention at least, although the public's long-standing approval of the Army lent to the modern re-enactments more an air of congratulation than of the astonishment and hostility that greeted the originals. The revival of the old-fashioned militant style, which was adopted in order to lend the appropriately fierce tone, pleased many officers and soldiers, who still yearned to think of themselves as fighting on the winning side in actual spiritual warfare. Robert E. Thomson, an officer with extensive literary experience, called on his fellow officers in 1983 to maintain the vocabulary of a real army at war, claiming for them and for himself the knowledge of being "called in a peculiar way, to be fighting soldiers of the Captain of the Host."[18]

The constancy of The Salvation Army in the midst of change, and especially its commitment to the principle of militant spiritual warfare, which underlay its willingness — even, at times, eagerness — to embrace the latest innovation as no more than the newest improvement on a means to the Great End, was evident in many individual careers. Many officers still living and active in the 1980s had careers that encompassed the torchlight parade at one end and satellite transmission at the other. The Salvation Army's extensive oral history project, started in the Western territory in 1978 and taken over by the Army's national archives bureau in 1986, was designed to preserve the experiences of these persons. Comm. Edward Carey, an officer of broad administrative ability whose career was capped with the national commandership in the years 1971-1972, had one such epochal career. Commissioned in 1924, Carey knew Eliza Shirley and Emma Westbrook well. His first ten years of active officership were served under Commander Evangeline Booth. He participated in the Army's fiftieth anniversary celebration at Battery Park in 1930. Fifty years later, Carey led an open-air meeting in Laconia, New Hampshire, to celebrate the Army's centennial. A veteran of countless street-corner meetings, Carey pioneered many innovations in Sunday school and youth work and supervised the creation of the Greater New York Command, by which administration of Army activities in that city was separated from territorial headquarters in 1960. As a young officer, Carey fought in a mostly horse-drawn Army; automobiles, radio, and the Community Chest were novelties to most Salvationists in the mid-1920s. Yet as territorial commander in 1969, Carey proposed a reorganization of the Army's international headquarters in ways he lived to see enacted in 1991, and as national commander in 1971 he hosted the first meeting of the Army's international commissioners' conference to be held outside Britain. In his long retirement, Carey served as a faithful soldier in Laconia and chaired the local advisory board. Along with another retired commissioner, John Waldron, with similar research skills and interests in Army history, Carey continued to make important contributions to the study of Army history well into the 1990s.[19]

The Second Century Advance called for "the preparation of a document which explicitly states the basic Biblical presuppositions underlying our social work" for use in "orientation and in-service training" programs. Work on this document went forward during years in which The Salvation Army was generally evidencing a serious interest in its theological foundations, a period that was wholly unprecedented both in terms of the scholarly nature of the inquiries and the widespread interest shown in them by Salvationists. The position paper, entitled "Basic Biblical Propositions," written by Maj. Peter J. Hofman (a social services expert — and son of the Men's Social reformer), was finally approved by the commissioners in February 1988. It affirmed the Army's official commitment to two fundamental scriptural principles: God established the value of human beings by creating a "special place" for them in His Kingdom, and the Scriptures teach that humans have a "redemptive and social ministry." This ministry is based on "the Scriptural position regarding the responsibility of God's people to care for other human beings." The Salvation Army thus has a dual mission, including both religious and social-service elements, which is fulfilled "through proclaiming the Gospel and meeting human needs."[20]

Several influential Salvationists had prominent roles in the theological discussions of the 1980s. Gordon Bingham, a respected figure in Army social services in two territories, prepared an important statement for the commissioners in 1988. In the document, entitled *Structuring Community Service Ministries So That Participants Have an Opportunity to Receive Spiritual Guidance,* Bingham suggested a "continuum concept," viewing all activities in an Army corps as mutually supportive parts of a total spiritual/social program. The most conspicuous writers in this decade were Maj. Philip Needham, a Southern officer with three advanced degrees in theology, and Prof. Roger Green of Gordon College in Wenham, Massachusetts. Both scholars repudiated the assumption, common among critics of The Salvation Army since its pioneer days, that theological ideas more elaborate than simple faith in the redemptive work of Christ were unimportant to Salvationists, who were mostly unlettered, working-class, and practical-minded people. On the contrary, argued Needham and Green, the key to the Army's past success, and an essential factor in its survival as a spiritual force in American life, was the commitment of its members to what Green called the Army's "redemptive theology." This theology called on Salvationists to wage a kind of "war on two fronts" to redeem lost souls and to uplift the neglected poor; the Army's "understanding of redemption" was "both personal and social." Needham, equally committed to the "universal Gospel," was more critical of the contemporary Army for having been led astray temporarily by various forms of bureaucratic self-absorption. He called for a "contemporary Salvationist theology of mission" based on the Army's "heritage as proclaimer of the Gospel to the poor." Needham suggested that a thoroughgoing recommitment to such a heritage might well require a massive overhaul of the Army in America.[21]

The force of these observations was strengthened by several factors. Their proponents were highly respected by their comrades in the Army. Bingham, for instance, relied partly on Needham's work in preparing his own document for the Army. Both were loyal Salvationists. Needham was a successful officer from a venerated Army family (both his grandfather and his father had been officers, the latter having served as national commander from 1982 to 1983). Both men were officially encouraged to publish their studies and were widely invited to explain and discuss them in Army circles. Needham's book *Community in Mission: A Salvationist Ecclesiology* appeared in 1987, and Green's *War on Two Fronts: The Redemptive Theology of William Booth* appeared in 1989, both under Army imprint. In addition, the Army launched several major new social service programs in the 1980s that were intended not only to meet human needs but also to conform to the Army's theological criteria.[22]

The success of these programs was encouraging to the growing number of Salvationists whose minds were turning away from pragmatism and operations toward principles and long-term goals. The critical element in success, as Needham had predicted, was flexibility. A number of writers, drawn to the Army as a subject because of the centennial publicity, praised the Army for this quality in its social services. One noted that the Army had "shown remarkable ability to adapt to changing societal needs." The range and diversity of its services, already considerable, was expanded at an accelerated rate over the next decade: by 1990 client totals in several important categories had increased much more rapidly than the overall population, in some cases more than doubling during the decade. In 1988 the Army established a National Social Service Award at the suggestion of Lt. Col. Beatrice Combs, the Army's national social services consultant, who received support for the proposal from a national board of social service staff officers. The first award went to the Cleveland Harbor Light corps program. Subsequent annual awards were earned by an adult rehabilitation program conducted by the Las Vegas corps, a substance abuse service center in Grand Rapids, and a program in the Georgia Division called SHARE, which administered funds provided by the Georgia Power and Light Company to provide winter energy cost relief.[23]

Army leaders were well advised to encourage zeal and innovation among those who operated the Army's vast system of social welfare, because the strains on the system were great. The 1980s were filled with challenging new demands on the Army's existing programs. An increase in the number of the homeless was perhaps the most noticeable of these new developments. The genesis of the National Social Service Award in 1988 was, in fact, an award designed the year before for the most successful Army program of the decade to provide care for the urban homeless. A large number of programs, both short- and long-term, were developed nationwide. The Salvation Army became a major user of Federal Emergency Food and Shelter funds beginning in 1983. The Army accepted a large number of state and municipal grants as well. By 1987, when the Army's annual National Social Services Conference was devoted to the problems of homelessness, the Army was the largest single private supplier of beds in the country. By the end of the decade the Army was operating twenty-seven full-time emergency shelters in California alone.[24]

On Armistice Day 1987, the Army revived a program that had been advocated by William Booth himself and embodied after World War I in the long-forgotten Argonne hotels. A shelter was opened in Long Island

City, New York, exclusively for homeless veterans and quickly earned special praise. The Army started programs to rescue "throwaway children" in Portland, Oregon, in 1984 and Hollywood in 1988, both at the instigation of the divisional leader, Lt. Col. David P. Riley. The Salvation Army "Grate Patrol," using an Army emergency mobile canteen and local church volunteers, began in Washington, D.C., in 1983 under the direction of Alan H. Ritson, the Army's emergency disaster relief coordinator. The "Grate Patrol" was another revival of the antique idea that elaborate social theories and long-term rehabilitation programs were of less interest to freezing, starving people than the thousands of hot meals and blankets the patrol distributed every year. Another old-fashioned ministry was restored by Mrs. Lt. Col. Fay Howell in New York City, who in "slum-sister" fashion gathered up an elderly homeless man she encountered in the street and saw him safely into an Army residence where he was cared for and soundly converted.[25]

The Salvation Army's official response to the AIDS epidemic showed the movement at its best. At a time when its resources were being stretched to an exceptional degree to satisfy other needs, and when some public religious figures who shared to the last jot and tittle the Army's theological conservatism seemed almost to celebrate the disease as divine retribution, The Salvation Army threw out the lifeline with courage and compassion. To the extent that AIDS was associated with homosexual behavior, the Army had already taken up a relatively charitable position. The Army's official statement on homosexuality, approved in May 1985, condemned only "overt acts," stating that an innate tendency was not the result of conscious choice and by itself could not be considered "blameworthy." The official statement offered lonely and alienated persons "Christian love within Salvation Army fellowship and worship, which is open to all." Official policy statements on AIDS issued by the Army's Eastern territorial headquarters in 1987 and 1988 set forth the basic position. The policies were drafted by a task team chaired by Peter J. Hofman, whose team was broadly representative of the Army's religious, social service, and medical professional staff. The Salvation Army restated its commitment to its traditional standards of behavior, based on biblical principles, including opposition to illicit drug use and endorsement of "chastity before marriage and fidelity within marriage." These were upheld along with the Army's "continuing commitment to help those in need." Long-established guidelines regarding admission to Salvation Army camps, day-care, and adult residential programs were confirmed: "People are admitted who are able to take part and who meet the criteria and the purpose of the program." While no moral judgment was imposed on applicants, Army programs did not knowingly admit people suffering from communicable diseases. Persons who had AIDS or who tested HIV positive were counseled, encouraged, and referred to other agencies with more extensive programs: "pastoral care" was still "the basic in all services of the Army."[26]

Starting in 1989 the Army participated in a nationwide AIDS Education and Prevention campaign for teens. On June 18-19, 1990, the Army conducted the first official Salvation Army AIDS Consultation Seminar, as part of the sixth annual International AIDS Conference in San Francisco. The consultation was coordinated by Capt. Dr. Ian Campbell, the Army's international medical advisor from London. Attention was focused on AIDS programs in adult rehabilitation centers in Los Angeles and Miami, the Fairbanks corps, and Army general hospitals in Flushing, New York, and Calgary, Alberta. Aux. Capt. Michael Olsen, social services consultant in the Army's Southern California division, reminded delegates of the Army's official position, based on its own theology and historic mission: "The life of all persons, whatever their sexual orientation, is sacred and worthy of our non-judgmental love."[27]

The Army's compassionate attitude on social problems did not, however, spare it from criticism. Some activists condemned the Army for failing to propose radical solutions for the ills of society. In 1983 the editor of *The Other Side* wrote disdainfully of The Salvation Army as "very supportive of the political status quo," observing that the Army "makes almost no attempt to deal with the root causes of today's problems." This was an ancient charge, first raised against William Booth (who had announced in *In Darkest England and the Way Out* that he left "to others the formulation of ambitious programmes for the reconstruction of our entire social system") and often repeated throughout the Army's history. Nor did the Army's sympathetic programs protect it entirely from legal entanglements in the 1980s.[28]

In April 1980 New York's Mayor Edward Koch signed Executive Order 50 (EO50), to become effective on January 20, 1982. Among other things, the new order stated that any agency receiving funds from New York City must include in its personnel hiring policy a statement that the agency would not discriminate in hiring on the basis of "sexual orientation or affectional preference." The Army, which received funding from New York City for ten programs worth about five million dollars annually, did not prepare the required statement; in fact, several officers signed service contracts without knowing that the new requirement appeared in them. In November 1983, however, the city's Bureau of Labor Services, conducting a routine review of city contracts, discovered that The Salvation Army was not in compliance with EO50. Now pressed to comply in the matter of a family social service program in the Bronx, local Salvation Army officials, acting on behalf of the territorial administration, publicly refused and withdrew their request for municipal funding for the program. The city then demanded that the Army comply at once or it would withdraw funding from all ten programs. The issue became public, and accounts of the controversy appeared in the New York papers. The *Times* urged both sides to compromise, but The Salvation Army regarded compliance with EO50 as a violation of its own official policy on homosexuality, a position supported by William J. Moss, the Army's longtime legal counsel.[29]

The commissioners were convinced that such an important issue required a national policy statement, so that the Army's response to similar demands would be the same in all territories. In February 1984 the commissioners approved a carefully worded "National Statement by The Salvation Army Regarding Employment," in which they stated that the organization did not discriminate in any way in employment, "with only those exceptions dictated by the religious purpose of The Salvation Army" (and those required by "bona fide occupational qualifications"). The Army's purpose was to "provide humanitarian services consistent with the values and goals of the Christian faith," and the Christian "factor will be considered in the employment of those members of the staff who the organization determines have the responsibility for the transmission of these values." Undeterred, the city included the complete language of EO50 in all city contracts beginning October 25, 1984. The Army was faced with the loss of all municipal funding — until, providentially, a much larger and more powerful provider of humanitarian services joined the Army in publicly protesting EO50 on moral grounds: the Roman Catholic Archdiocese of New York, headed by Cardinal John J. O'Connor. A small Jewish agency, Agudath Israel of America, joined its name to the protest as well. While it would not have been difficult for the city of New York to find alternatives for the Army's ten programs, it would have been much more difficult to do away with the numerous programs of the Roman Catholic Church, which collectively handled an enormous volume of clients. Nor was it easy to ignore the influence of a respected part of the Jewish community. On top of these setbacks, the city lost a critical legal battle in June 1986, when the New York Supreme Court struck down

EO50. A new Executive Order 94 was soon drafted, which gave sufficient latitude to conservative religious organizations that the Army and its influential friends could regard the matter as "settled."[30]

Still, the commissioners were not entirely reassured: the Army administration in San Francisco had signed similar contracts with the city, explaining this action on the grounds that the employees concerned were service and maintenance staff who had little contact with the public, so there was no question of their having "the responsibility for the transmission of these [Christian] values." Clearly times were changing. At their meeting in March 1986, the commissioners expressed official alarm at the fact that there seemed to be a "growing acceptance of untraditional moral values and deviant life-styles" that "challenged the validity of Christian morals in our time." The Army must address this issue as part of its mission in the modern world, "for the sake of its own survival." Grateful to Mr. Moss for his legal guidance in these matters and for his many years of loyal service, the commissioners honored him with a special luncheon and the Order of Distinguished Auxiliary Service in May 1985. Mr. Moss had joined the firm of Cadwallader, Wickersham and Taft in 1949; for years he worked on Salvation Army matters under the tutelage of a senior partner, Robert E. Lee. When Lee died in 1963, Moss became senior partner in charge of the Salvation Army account, and he continued thereafter to serve the Army as its chief counsel, a "good and faithful servant" whose lifelong contribution to the Army was little known to the rank and file.[31]

Public opinion had generally favored the Army in the New York dispute; evangelical leaders, for their part, had been highly vocal in their support. The Salvation Army remained the favorite charity of the American people, who continued to rely heavily on private voluntarism to support essential social relief activities. The public's trust was demonstrated in many ways. On January 16, 1984, "Dear Abby" ran a column praising the Army's missing persons department, and within three weeks the Army had received a record 4,903 inquiries. Broad public support and its own religious convictions were the bases upon which the Army built new crusades as the last darkening years of the twentieth century were drawn out. The Army's large correctional services program in Florida, which was handling over 20,000 cases per month by the end of the decade, and Capt. Walter Booth's "multidimensional correctional ministry" in the Pennsylvania state penitentiary system were part of a nationwide system that visited almost 200,000 prisoners, offering spiritual counsel, specially designed Bible correspondence courses, and help in allowing prisoners to select Christmas gifts for their children in addition to probation and parole planning. In San Francisco, local Salvationists even opened an official branch of the Army Home League in the city-county jail. On other fronts Salvationists increased their commitment to home care for the elderly. In 1989 the National Association of Home Care honored Emily Reno, Home League secretary in the Boise, Idaho, corps, as one of the nation's "Ten Most Caring People." Other programs for the elderly were developed; notable examples were the Tremont Older Persons Program in Cleveland, designed to help frail elderly persons to live independently, and San Francisco's Central Corps and Senior Activity Center.[32]

The Salvation Army's largest program for the elderly came to national attention during this decade as well. The Oklahoma City Senior Center program started modestly enough in 1955, when a few senior members of the corps Home League began to hold weekly meetings on their own. Programs were added gradually, until Army activities for the elderly began to attract not only special United Way and government funding but entire centers previously operated by other agencies and charities. Nina Willingham became executive director of the Senior Center program in 1978, which proved to be a turning point: as the program grew and flourished, Willingham gained national recognition in the field of service to the elderly. In 1980 a Federal Title V grant enabled the Army to hire sixty older workers. By 1990 The Salvation Army Senior Center program had nineteen centers in operation and served 22,000 individual clients annually. The range of benefits offered was diverse, including "well-being clinics" (checkups and health monitoring), daily meals, transportation, advocacy, employment, recreation, and religious activities. The clientele was no less varied: of the nineteen centers in 1990, two were predominantly African American; two were Native American; five were Native American and white in combination; one was Native American, Hispanic, and white together; one was Native American, Korean, and white together; one was entirely Hispanic (with its own "excellent traditional Hispanic band"); and seven were predominantly white. Even these last seven were far from homogeneous: one was made up of Czechoslovakians, and in another center young disabled persons outnumbered senior citizens. When Gen. Eva Burrows visited the United States in December 1990, she included a special visit to two of the Oklahoma City Senior Centers in her official itinerary.[33]

The Army's system of practical social welfare became ever more widespread and intricate in the 1980s, reaching every age group and touching almost every social problem. The Salvation Army Social Services for Children in New York City, a program to expand recruitment for badly needed foster parents, began in March 1988. The Army sent the Indiana divisional commander, Maj. M. Lee Hickam, as an official delegate to the National Consultation on Pornography and Obscenity in Cincinnati in November 1983. Hickam's stirring report confirmed Army leaders in their ancient resolve to fight against an evil that the Army had first attacked in Victorian times. The Salvation Army became increasingly involved in the national campaign against pornography and joined the national Religious Alliance Against Pornography at a White House meeting in 1990 to officially denounce "child pornography and illegal obscenity." Corps officers and local staff members were instructed on how to detect, counsel, and intervene in cases of spouse and child abuse. In March 1986 the commissioners' conference issued a strong statement in opposition to "abortion on demand or as a means of birth control" that carefully outlined a narrow justification for the termination of pregnancy. As always, the Army pledged to "show love and compassion" and offer its "services and fellowship" to persons who rejected its good advice in this matter.[34]

The Salvation Army's residential rehabilitation programs for men, broadened in the 1970s to include women in a few locations, was one of two or three aspects of the Movement launched in pioneer times that had managed to secure public recognition and support and grow more successful and respected with the passing years. Along with its Christmas relief and emergency disaster activities, the adult rehabilitation centers were, so far as the generous public was concerned, the mainstay of the organization. Its trucks and thrift stores were as familiar as Christmas kettles and emergency canteens on the American scene — although familiarity might have suffered a brief setback in 1987 when the commissioners decided to end forever the ancient argument between territories as to which color (red or blue) was best for social trucks by decreeing that henceforth all Salvation Army salvage trucks would be — white! The Salvation Army now operated the largest private residential alcohol rehabilitation agency in the United States. The traditional adult rehabilitation centers (ARCs) were supplemented in the 1980s by a small but growing number of programs operated by local corps. Although smaller than ARCs, these "corps salvage and rehabilitation centers" were held to the same professional standards in program, staffing, and facilities. By 1990 there were thirty-four such units, twenty-two of them in the Southern Territory; their total bed capacity and annual case load were each one-ninth those of the larger and far more numerous ARCs. The combined programs had accommodations for 11,674 people and handled 52,753 cases in 1990.[35]

The 1980s were often a time of trial for the Men's Social Service Department, punctuated by many happy surprises and blessed with noteworthy successes overall. Administrators faced a host of new problems in these years. Urban centers encountered increasing numbers of clients who were addicted to drugs other than, or in addition to, alcohol. In 1989 the Eastern territorial men's social services secretary estimated that 80 percent of the men in inner city ARCs had drug-related dependencies. On average, these men were younger than the Army's traditional middle-aged clientele, often more violent, and lacking in any of the work skills that enabled the older clients to find useful places in the work therapy program. Although relatively few clients had AIDS or were HIV positive, fear of this disease among other residents was enough to cause panic that could empty a center. Increasing government regulation added enormously to operating costs; this in turn reduced funds for capital expansion. Pressure grew on The Salvation Army to submit its local programs to accrediting and licensing procedures. Governmental and agency pressure occasionally hindered the straightforward approach to gospel presentation generally favored by Army officers. Strict local landfill and recycling requirements forced ARCs and corps salvage centers to make much more stringent policies on accepting donations-in-kind. This frequently resulted in the Army truck pulling away from a donor's house with just clothing and small choice items; the useless refrigerators, washing machines, bed springs, and old tires remained, annoyingly, on the curb. Public relations suffered. The Central territorial headquarters began in the late 1980s to encourage local administrators to trade dump trucks for trash compactors.[36]

A disagreeable turn of events came in September 1990, when the Wages and Hours Administrator of the U.S. Department of Labor revived the long-dormant charge against the Army that it was a profitable enterprise required by the Fair Labor Standards Act to pay its "employees" — whom the Army steadfastly referred to as clients — the federal minimum hourly wage. The issue was finally resolved in the Army's favor when the administration ceased to press its claims, but not before many anxious moments and considerable unpleasant publicity for The Salvation Army. Army leaders did not look on any resolution as permanent that did not provide written recognition of the Army's contention regarding clients.[37]

On the bright side, the Army's adult rehabilitation programs enjoyed a genuine revival of religion in the 1980s. The same was true of the large urban Harbor Light Corps, including the famous units in Cleveland and St. Louis, and Booth House II on the Bowery. The selection, training, and assignment of official chaplains in ARCs was given top priority in all four territories. Evangelistic services, spiritual counseling, and a range of nurturing social and educational programs were carefully coordinated. The Pittsburgh ARC even sponsored its own troop of client clowns, who went on regular cheering forays to a nearby veterans' hospital. Most centers had choral ensembles of various kinds; in several centers these groups were regarded as quite accomplished and were invited to sing at large Salvation Army gatherings. The results of these combined efforts were encouraging: between 1980 and 1990 the annual number of converts in ARCs nationwide nearly doubled, to 13,929. At the same time, changed market conditions and more efficient and attractive sales techniques brought increased revenue, enabling the Army to overcome the adverse effect of new tax laws passed in 1987 reducing the amount of allowable deduction for donations-in-kind and continuing competition from flea markets and yard sales. This was encouraging not only to local administrators but to the Army's top administration as well, who cherished the new converts and incidentally relied on revenue from these centers to provide part of the operating funds for all four territorial headquarters.[38]

The prospects of the ARC program brightened with time. A waiting list developed among officers from other branches of Army activity who requested transfer into the Men's Social Service Department. Officers of special ability were attracted to this work, including Aux. Capt. William Bearchell, a former airline pilot with a doctoral degree. Pride in this department was further enhanced in April 1991, when the ancient barrier that prevented ARC administrators, like corps officers, from being promoted above the rank of major was broken for the respected Lt. Col. David Mulbarger, who became administrator of the Ft. Lauderdale ARC. The symbolic significance of this appointment was substantial and was soon matched by several similar appointments in corps. The process that started in 1978 with the change in name of local centers, removing gender-specific names from programs, was renewed and completed on January 1, 1992. The Men's Social Service Department was officially renamed the Adult Rehabilitation Center Command; the department secretary was styled Commander.[39]

An additional charm of the ARC branch of Army operations was that it was self-supporting. To finance the rest of its vast array of social services, The Salvation Army relied on fund-raising techniques of consid-

erable variety. These ranged in sophistication from the simplest possible
approach — a pot placed in some convenient public place into which
persons were invited to throw money — to computerized market surveys,
direct mail appeals, and media campaigns. Even the simplest technique
— the annual Christmas kettle appeal — required constant attention:
Army officers had to submit to prolonged and detailed negotiations to get
their kettles into shopping malls, where most Christmas shopping was
conducted. An important advance came in 1984, when the Edward J.
DeBartolo Corporation agreed to allow Army kettles into its numerous
malls, provided that each kettle was accompanied by "an appropriate
musical group," so that shoppers would have the benefit of Christmas
music. As fund-raising became more extensive, it also became more complicated; Army leaders were particularly concerned that nothing central to
the Army's mission be lost in any arrangements they made with the United
Way or governmental agencies.[40]

In March 1981 the commissioners agreed on an official statement
that "any agency, government or private," that enters into a contract with
The Salvation Army should "clearly understand that The Salvation Army
is an international religious and charitable movement" operated on "a
quasi-military pattern" and is a "branch of the Christian Church." In the
course of the decade the Army developed official "guidelines" for its
financial relationships with other agencies. An agreement with the United
Way entitled "Working Together" was approved in 1983; more general
rules were formulated in a document entitled "Guidelines for Relationships
between The Salvation Army and Other Groups and Organizations,"
which was approved in 1987. Both of these documents were revisions of
previous versions with the same names. They gave the Army considerable
latitude, and they left nothing to chance. They were typical of many similar
arrangements by which The Salvation Army sought successfully to maintain its institutional independence and the integrity of its Christian message while at the same time continuing to exercise its broad-minded
approach to fund-raising. Despite the constant possibility of litigation over
its Christian purpose when the Army signed service contracts with government agencies — New York City's Executive Order 50 was a notable
example — its leaders continued to operate on the official principle, repeated in the new *Corps Community Center Profile* issued in 1983, that
financing from government sources was "consistent with the purposes and
policy of The Salvation Army." It was essential in such cases, of course, to
adhere to the Army's official guidelines. The Army's Founder himself laid

it down as a principle that money was where one found it and that every dollar that came into the Army's hands, whether from private or public sources, so long as no compromise was required, was another dollar the Devil would never use again. Leaving no stone unturned, the Army also placed new emphasis on internal giving, recasting its corps treasurers as "Corps Stewardship Secretaries" and giving them an important role in encouraging their comrades to "fire their cartridges" more regularly and in larger amounts.[41]

Planned giving programs — the cultivation of bequests in advance — were introduced into the Army's financial affairs by several progressive finance officers, of whom Col. G. Ernest Murray in the Western territory was a notable example. The effects of systematic planned-giving campaigns in the Southern territory were particularly dramatic: income from this source increased almost a hundredfold in the decade after 1980. Service contracts, government grants, United Way allocations, and the contributions of its own members were additional sources of income for The Salvation Army. The mainstay of Army financial support, however, continued to come from millions of individual donors with relatively modest incomes who gave small amounts on a regular basis. In many parts of the country annual mail appeal campaigns became the single most important means of reaching these donors in the 1980s. The general public was encouraged to believe that a dollar placed with The Salvation Army would be used efficiently. An important report on American charities that appeared in *Fortune* magazine in November 1987 praised the Army for channeling 86 percent of donated funds into beneficial programs. The authors of the report noted that of the fifteen largest charities in the United States, The Salvation Army was one of only four to spend at least 85 percent of its total revenue on social welfare activities and less than 15 percent on fund-raising and administration.[42]

For The Salvation Army's own members — the junior and senior soldiers, adherents, and recruits — and its new converts, the Army's welfare empire and its enormous prestige and popularity were far less important than its purely religious activities. To the Salvationist, the Army was a denomination, a worshiping community, a kind of church — a fact of which the general public remained, as always, surprisingly unaware. The article on the Army in the 1989 edition of *The Encyclopedia of American Religions* observed that the Army's programs of social services made it "famous and respected by many who are quite unaware of its existence as a holiness church body." Salvationists were accustomed to the divergence between the public's perception of the Army and their own, but they were not reconciled to it. The Second Century Advance that greeted the new decade listed among its top priorities a wholesale recommitment of The Salvation Army to its spiritual mission. Proposals included major publicity campaigns and the redesign of the Army's logo in an effort to advertise the Army's evangelistic purposes. But the heart of the effort involved the revitalization of the local corps.[43]

Second Century campaign materials quoted Lt. Col. Paul A. Rader approvingly at length. Rader, one of several officer sons of the notable evangelist Lyell Rader, was for many years a missionary officer in Korea. In 1984 he returned to serve in the U.S.A., and in 1994 he was elected the first American-born general of The Salvation Army. His diagnosis of the Army in the United States drew heavily on insights he gained in his doctoral research on the causes that led to the rapid growth of the Army in that country. The Salvation Army, according to Rader, was "experiencing a serious identity crisis"; it was time for the movement to reaffirm its total spiritual mission, which meant strengthening both its "service dimension" and its "churchly dimension" (which included all of its activities and programs directed at "enriching and enlarging its own life"). Although there was a "serious question" as to whether the church had ever been "signally successful in holding these two dimensions together in a single structure without sacrificing one to the other," The Salvation Army must accomplish precisely this balance. The corps must not simply survive as an adjunct to the Army's social welfare program: the Army's corps must grow and develop in order to fulfill its special calling. "It would only be as its corps are multiplied and its ranks vastly swelled," reported Rader, that the Army could "hope to reach the masses with the Gospel."[44]

The Second Century Advance task teams proposed a number of specific ways in which this could be achieved. These proposals, and others generated during the next few years from other internal sources, developed into a major theme for the decade: the revitalization of The Salvation Army's spiritual ministry. This was to take place first in the corps and soon thereafter in every facet of the Army's prolific and diverse social services. The call for official new position papers that would illuminate the theological purpose for the Army's service and welfare programs reflected the latter concern, but these papers and several other official attempts to build a sound theological foundation for social welfare used only a small fraction of the energy that Salvationists devoted to the success of the corps. More effective means of evangelism were needed to replace the disappearing street-corner meeting. The Army's annual National Soldiers' Seminar on Evangelism emphasized house-to-house visitation. Seeds were widely scattered that would grow into an official Corps Growth Movement by mid-decade. A number of officers proposed ways in which the Army could evangelize among the vast numbers of persons drawn to its welfare, volunteer, and community service programs. The corps community center could be the new mission field! Others suggested ways to improve the Army's existing religious services. One officer recommended that Salvationists abandon the habit of making windy introductions; another denounced the "archaic practice" of lining out the verses of songs, a custom left over from pioneer times, when many persons in an Army audience could not read.[45]

The various expressions of the Army's revived official awareness that its success as a "balanced ministry" depended on the religious life of its corps centered with remarkable unanimity on the corps officer. These "field officers" (so-called to distinguish them from staff and social-service officers) were The Salvation Army's pastorate. They ministered not only to the soldiers and recruits but to their comrade officers as well: each staff and social officer was expected to "soldier at" (attend and support) a local corps. Lt. Col. Charles Southwood, a veteran staff officer whose experience confirmed in his own mind the vital role of the pastor's heart, addressed Eastern administrative officers at a leadership conference in 1981, reminding delegates that "the caring shepherding of our officers" was "an awesome task" but one that leaders had to fulfill if the Army were to prosper as a spiritual force. The Second Century Advance called for the realignment of administrative responsibilities at divisional headquarters to allow the divisional commander to function as a "shepherd" and pastor to his flock of officers. Ten years later the Eastern territory created a special Pastoral Care Department, under Lt. Col. Damon Rader, to provide spiritual nurture for its officers. All four territories maintained lists of respected officers who served as part-time counselors to their colleagues as needs arose. The annual divisional officers' meetings, called "Officers' Councils," were increasingly devoted to spiritual themes. Many divisional commanders refused to allow the discussion of any purely business or policy matters at these councils. In 1983 the commissioners' conference approved a recommendation from its own Personnel Commission that divisional commanders be freed from one of their traditional responsibilities — the administration of Army activities in the divisional headquarters city — in order to give them the opportunity to engage in more "internal ministry" with their field officers. "Area Coordinators" were to be appointed to run The Salvation Army in the headquarters city.[46]

Salvationists at every level, including top administration, repeatedly called for reducing the frequency of rotation of corps officers in their local appointments. Later, when the Army officially embraced the principles of the Church Growth Movement, five-year minimum corps appointments became an official goal — although top leadership, all too aware of the many difficulties that lurked in the path of this good intention, preferred the term *objective* when referring to the five-year plan. There was much discussion about enhancing the prestige of field appointments. The Personnel Commission reported to the commissioners in February 1983 that "Officers at every level must be aware of, and accepting of, the fact that true success as a corps officer provides the highest fulfillment that can come to any Salvation Army officer." Proposals included the adoption of an official policy that a lifetime in corps work would be recognized by leaders as a successful career choice and that notably successful and respected corps officers could be promoted to the rank of lieutenant colonel, a rank previously reserved for staff appointments only.[47]

Several Army leaders, of whom James Osborne became the most influential, were particularly devoted to this proposal, recognizing its enormous symbolic significance. The policy was adopted at the end of the decade, after Osborne became national commander. Robert Bridges in St. Petersburg, Florida, and Check Yee in tthe San Francisco Chinatown Corps were promoted to the rank of lieutenant colonel in June 1991 and January 1992, respectively — the first two corps officers so honored in the history of The Salvation Army in the United States. Nor were these titles meaningless decoration. Each territory had a fixed quota of promotions to the rank of lieutenant colonel, and each promotion to that rank had to be approved by the General. Although the size of the quotas of lieutenant colonels changed over time, they were never large; every corps officer who was given this rank reduced by one the number of divisional commanders or department heads who could be promoted.[48]

Army leaders recognized at the beginning of the decade that many of their previous manuals, guides, and regulations for corps work were inadequate. Either they were outdated or they did not give proper emphasis to the importance of the work. Editorial work progressed for three years on a new, comprehensive manual for corps operations, under the close supervision of the commissioners' conference. The new *Corps Community Center Profile* was approved by the conference in October 1983 for nationwide distribution. The new manual was intended to "provide a single, comprehensive and convenient reference source" for officers, so that they could "plan and administer Salvation Army services in an intelligent, purposeful and objective manner." The mission of the Salvation Army corps was presented in uncompromising terms: "The Salvation Army seeks to preach the Gospel message of the Lord Jesus Christ to people and to become involved with the problems and needs of individuals on a personal and a community level. Its task is always twofold — spiritual redemption and social service."[49]

As straightforward as this twofold task appeared — and a commitment to "the evangelical purposes of The Salvation Army" appeared throughout the *Profile* — the program that the Army had designed to achieve its double purpose was of daunting complexity and variety. The officer and soldiers were faced with the development and implementation of program objectives, support services, long-range planning, analysis of community needs, and close working relationships with advisory organizations, the United Way, and various other outside funding agencies, in addition to other kinds of fund-raising activities, "Business Administration/Fiscal Management," and preparation of programs for several important annual reviews by visiting headquarters staff officers, among other things. On top of these requirements, the officers and soldiers were expected to adhere to a schedule of official Salvation Army activities that included weekly and Sunday meetings, the corps council and local boards, five "special evangelistic programs" per year (which included holiday activities, visitation campaigns, and series of special evangelistic services), nineteen other local programs, twelve annual divisional events (e.g., Scout Camporees, Home League Rallies, and Youth Councils), and five territorial events (only three of which, blessedly, were actually required). It was clear that The Salvation Army's reliance on the devotion of its officers and soldiers had not abated with the passing years.[50]

When the commissioners proposed that the official *Orders and Regulations for Corps Officers* in the United States should be revised in light of new, expanded demands on those human resources, the author they selected, Maj. Philip Needham, proposed a much more thorough revision — in fact, a new book, in which the officer's role in the Army mission would be explained in terms of the Army's theological commitment. The leaders concurred in this proposal; the result was a major publication, *The Corps Officer: Mission and Method — USA Supplement to the Orders and Regulations for Corps Officers.* The new volume, which appeared in 1992, was less a traditional list of regulations than a treatise on the meaning of Salvation Army officership in twenty-first-century America, something entirely new in Army rule books. It was divided into three parts: the mission of the corps, the corps officer's role as "key missional leader," and the "Corps Officer's Plan of Action." The corps officer — masculine and feminine pronouns were used interchangeably — must be committed, trained, and prepared to lead the corps in fulfilling its mission through outreach, nurture, resources, and strategy.[51]

The program, staff, learning resources, and even the facilities devoted to the training of officers were repeatedly upgraded in every territory in the 1980s. The commissioners' conference set new standards in 1980 for applicants to the Army's four territorial Schools for Officers' Training: they established as an official goal that all candidates should have at least the associate of arts degree "or its educational equivalent" and "two years in a significant work experience." Although the level of pretraining education achieved by cadets rose substantially in all four territories throughout the decade of the 1980s, the commissioners' official goal that every cadet should have at least an A.A. degree has not yet been achieved at this writing. Discussion of a national training institution was revived, briefly and without result. Special relationships between Army training schools and Christian liberal arts colleges were established in three territories in the 1980s. These programs differed in detail, but all involved the granting of recognized academic degrees by the partner college to persons who completed both the Army training program and a number of courses offered by the college. One of these programs, at Azusa Pacific College, which led to the A.A. degree, was dropped in 1984 after the territorial leader, Will Pratt, issued an official reminder that cadets were supposed to have at least this "acceptable standard of education" *before* they entered the officer training program.[52]

A similar agreement with Olivet Nazarene University in Illinois was dropped by the Central territory in 1990 because it required the addition of courses to the Army curriculum that leaders regarded as unnecessary to the work of training cadets. The relationship with Olivet, however, was not only rescued but strengthened by Maj. John R. Rhemick, the territorial education secretary. Rhemick designed an innovative continuing-education program at Olivet that allowed enterprising new officers to take ten one-week seminars leading to a special "bachelor of science in practical ministries" degree. In the Eastern territory the Army had "articulation agreements" with Nyack College that allowed for the transfer of a certain number of credits from the

School for Officers' Training curriculum toward a bachelor degree for officers who successfully completed an additional thirty credit hours in residence at Nyack. Another agreement, with Houghton College in western New York, allowed individuals who completed the Army training program to obtain either an associate of arts degree in applied science (after one year in residence at Houghton) or a bachelor's degree in Bible, sociology, or psychology (after two years in residence at Houghton).[53]

In the Southern Territory the Army established an arrangement with Asbury Theological Seminary by which all enrolled officers completed one hundred hours of credit in specially designed courses of use to them (e.g., in personal spiritual formation, preaching, Bible study, pastoral ministry, church growth) within the first five years of officership; those who wished to complete an additional eighty hours within the first ten years of officership would receive a Certification of Advanced Ministry Skills (CAMS). Of more overall importance, the Southern training school established its own Board of Visitors in 1990, made up of outside friends and philanthropists, who provided the school with the kind of support that a board of trustees gives to a small private college. This arrangement provided considerable benefits to the Southern school, yet nothing similar was attempted in other territories in the early part of the new decade. The West, however, was not behind in other innovations. Official recognition of the academic content of the Army's training program was carried farthest in that territory, where the Western Association of Schools and Colleges granted formal accreditation to the training school at Rancho Palos Verdes in January 1990. Cadets were granted an A.A. degree in ministry on completion of the Army curriculum. This formal endorsement, which was unique in The Salvation Army world, came only after three years of preparation conducted by the training principal, Lt. Col. Peter Chang.[54]

Despite the real and potential success of these programs, many Salvationist youth preferred to obtain an undergraduate degree before entering a Salvation Army training school. The percentage of cadets who had at least attended an undergraduate institution before entering a training school almost doubled during the 1980s. The Salvation Army continued to encourage its collegians to attend one of several Christian liberal arts colleges. The most popular of these among Salvationists continued to be Asbury College, near Lexington, Kentucky. The Army's national commander, John D. Needham, was authorized by the commissioners' conference to supervise the construction of a large, well-equipped Salvation Army Student Center near the Asbury campus in 1983. The project was supervised by Col. G. Ernest Murray, the national chief secretary. Two Generals of The Salvation Army paid official visits to Asbury as well (Jarl Wahlstrom in 1983, to dedicate the building, and Eva Burrows twice, in 1989 and 1992). In 1992 an active officer, Maj. Mrs. Juanita Russell, was appointed director of the Asbury Salvation Army Student Fellowship Center. In 1994 Asbury College enjoyed two additional boosts to its Salvationist image when Comm. Paul A. Rader, a 1956 graduate of the college, was elected general and Professor James Curnow returned to the college as composer-in-residence. The Kentucky college did not have a monopoly on Salvationists, however; in 1986 the Eastern territory recognized an official branch of the SASF at Houghton College, which had a sizable enrollment of Salvationists in the late 1980s. In 1992 the SASF opened an official chapter at Eastern Nazarene University in Massachusetts as well. In that year there was also an official chapter at the University of Mississipi in the Southern territory. There were no chapters of the SASF or official Army student clubs in either the Central or Western territories, but sizable groups of Salvationist students at a number of institutions in both territories laid the groundwork for future developments along more organized lines. Among these institutions were Olivet Nazarene University, Vennard College, the University of Missouri, and several state universities in Michigan, all in the Central territory, and Azusa Pacific University, Seattle Pacific University, and Warner Pacific College in Portland, Oregon, in the West.[55]

With almost no exceptions, graduates of the Army's officer training programs were appointed to "the field" — that is, to corps work. The need for personnel for corps remained critical throughout the decade; approximately two-thirds of all active commissioned Salvation Army officers in the United States were stationed in corps at any given time during this period. There was much to encourage them, even in the face of declining membership. Most Salvationists reported that it was their impression that their particular corps was too small; these members were usually willing, however, not only to discuss but to carry out with a good spirit various means to attract new members. In terms of its enrolled membership, in fact, the Army's average congregational size was not markedly different from the national average for Protestant churches, and it was larger than figures for several denominations to which the Army could be compared in strictly denominational terms (on the basis of doctrine, social attitudes, etc.). There was considerable interest in the small church among American religious leaders and writers during this period, and many of the studies and reports they produced underscored the strengths and possibilities of small churches. Much of this was of great value to The Salvation Army. In addition, friendly observers were glad to point out that although the Army was small, its outreach was far greater than that of many much larger denominations.[56]

There were numerous examples of corps in the United States that had reached impressive levels of attendance, financial support, and congregational activity and outreach in the 1980s. Although the number of such corps was small for a denomination as old as The Salvation Army, the Army drew attention to these successful corps in many ways. They included Atlanta Temple, officially the South's "premier" corps since a separate territorial headquarters was established in that city in 1927 (in 1991 the territorial commander appointed the corps sergeant-major at Atlanta Temple, James Curnow, "territorial sergeant-major," to serve at headquarters as a representative of all the soldiers of the territory); Norfolk, Virginia, which developed the largest Sunday school in The Salvation Army during the aggressive regime of Capt. and Mrs. Dan Delaney; Clearwater, Florida, which attracted a large number of retired and vacationing Salvationists; Fort Lauderdale, where the sparkling "Front Line" programs were launched by Capt. and Mrs. William Crabson; Royal Oak, Michigan; Norridge Citadel (a Chicago suburb); Montclair, New Jersey, where the Army's most famous performing musician, Philip Smith, was the corps bandmaster; Lexington, Kentucky; Santa Ana, California; El Paso Temple, the largest Hispanic corps in the United States; San Francisco Chinatown Corps; and Rockford, Illinois, a still-thriving center of Scandinavian Salvationism. Such corps combined familiar church activities with the Army's traditional neighborhood and service programs (e.g., the Home League, men's clubs, youth activities, and the League of Mercy, a program that organized volunteers to visit local rest homes and hospitals) to achieve effective recruitment. Army leaders who reflected among themselves about the advantages of developing "regional corps" to draw attendance from a large surrounding area usually centered their attention on corps such as these.[57]

However encouraging these star corps were, however, most corps remained much smaller. Relatively few corps were able to increase adult membership in the early part of the decade, and many experienced losses. Overall the denomination did not keep pace with the increase in the population of the United States during the decade. Salvation Army leaders, in whose ears still rang the conquering songs that were revived for numerous centennial extravaganzas, did not look with indifference on the Army's apparent stagnation. Their concerns were mixed with those of many others. In every territory influential younger officers, several with seminary training, introduced leaders to new literature on recruitment and church building. Many corps officers and soldiers, who could see nearby churches apparently similar to their own that were visibly growing, took advantage of every official opportunity to urge innovative approaches on their leaders. By the middle of the decade The Salvation Army in the United States was prepared to look outside its own ranks and experience for guidance: the Army embraced the Church Growth Movement.[58]

Church growth was not a novelty when the American branch of The Salvation Army officially endorsed it. The accepted birthdate of the movement came in 1955 when a missionary, Donald A. McGavran, published a book entitled *The Bridges of God — A Study in the Strategy of Missions.* McGavran founded the Institute of Church Growth in 1959, and in 1965 it became part of the School of World Mission at Fuller Theological Seminary. Publications of growing influence began to flow from the group of experts gathered at Fuller. The Salvation Army first officially interested itself in these developments in Canada in 1976, then in Australia. In 1983 the commissioners' conference in the United States decided that the territories should arrange for each divisional commander to receive training in church growth principles. Soon the four American territorial headquarters made important commitments to the new ideas. Territorial departments to publicize and encourage church growth principles were established; the first was in the South in 1985, then in the West in 1986, under the direction of Capt. Terry Camsey, who soon developed an international reputation for his expertise in the area. The cause of church growth was promoted in the Central territory by the appointment as territorial leader in 1986 of Comm. Robert Rightmire, fresh from scenes of rapid corps growth in Korea. The Central territorial corps growth office was opened in early 1987, and the fourth, in the East, was opened in 1988. Dr. Carl F. George from Fuller Seminary was invited to deliver a series of detailed lectures explaining church growth principles in a Salvation Army context to delegates gathered for territorial congresses and commissioning ceremonies in all four territories in the years 1988-1990. Interest was international: the new General, Eva Burrows, elected in 1986, had introduced church growth concepts to her Australian command before coming to the international office, and she officially committed herself, as General, to the movement. In 1988 Col. John Larsson, a British staff officer, wrote a corps growth manual in which he drew heavily on North American literature and experiences. An international conference on growth strategy was held at Army headquarters in London in August of the next year. Manuals, tapes, and articles and regular features in all four territorial newsletters were widely distributed. The Central territory even had a special growth newsletter, *The Beanstalk.*[59]

The operating premises of the corps growth program in The Salvation Army were clear and fully accepted as valid by the principals in the movement and by almost all influential Salvationists, officers and lay members alike. There was less agreement as to the courses of action suggested by the proponents of church growth, but enthusiasm for this innovative approach remained widespread. First, as Henry Gariepy wrote in 1984, the corps was "the core of The Salvation Army." The Army's "spiritual life and vitality" depended "in large measure" on the "spiritual health and growth of the corps." Second, Army corps did not have to be small and struggling. As national commander Osborne put it in an official statement at the end of the decade, nothing in the Army's "literature and experience" suggested such a thing. Like many leaders and writers, Osborne rejected the notion that the Army's historic mission was only to win converts and return them to the churches from which they had originally fallen away. It was easy to prove that even if that had been William Booth's original plan, he abandoned it quickly enough — certainly it was no part of official Army policy by the time the work began in the United States in 1880. On the contrary, one of the Army's goals from the start had been to turn as many converts as possible into soldiers. The third premise was that the experience of other small congregations that had enjoyed growth could be adapted to The Salvation Army, and the fourth premise was that this should be done without further delay. Osborne instructed Salvationists to get "in tune with our present emphasis on Corps/Church growth."[60]

Among territorial commanders, the Western leader, Comm. — later, General — Paul A. Rader, himself a graduate of Fuller Seminary, and Comm. Kenneth Hodder in the South, later National Commander, entertained the most dramatic expectations for the new church growth techniques. Both regions were enjoying what Rader called "burgeoning" population growth rates, much of it ethnically diverse and transient and lacking any formal church affiliation. According to the advocates of corps-growth thinking, these elements of the population were ideally suited to the special appeal of the popular and respected Salvation Army. (Parts of the Western and Southern territories also proved attractive to migratory

Salvationists, although the Army's official corps growth manual warned leaders not to count these additions as "real growth." Larsson warned against the "false complacency" into which officers might be lulled by a mere "migration of sheep.") The leaders of the Eastern and Central territories were no less committed to the principles of the new program, and territorial and divisional leaders were hopeful of success, despite the fact that the economic and demographic decline in many parts of these territories made the work of corps growth more difficult. Comm. Harold Shoults of the Central territory announced that corps growth was no mere slogan or fad but a "long haul philosophy of ministry."[61]

The literature laid down four types of growth or, more properly, stages of growth, because in theory the types succeeded each other: internal (or "Christian nurture," in which Christians became more aware of and committed to the teachings of Christ; also called "discipling"); expansion (adding persons to the congregation through a combination of old and new techniques); extension (new churches are started, either from existing ones or from nothing — the "church planting" stage); and "bridging" (carrying the message of one's congregation to another culture — "cross-cultural church planting").[62]

Unfortunately, there were several points at which characteristics of The Salvation Army worked against this cheerful plan. For one thing, many experts believed that a church had to have a certain minimum number of active members to sustain the recruitment aspect of the plan. Opinions differed as to how small this number might be, but there was no disagreement that almost all Salvation Army corps fell below the smallest allowable minimum. For another thing, proper "discipleship" was based on a healthy sense of financial stewardship, which most Salvationists still refused to take seriously. A third major difficulty was that the experts agreed on the necessity of long pastoral appointments — much longer than The Salvation Army had so far been willing or able to achieve. Lyle F. Schaller, for instance, noted that congregations that had experienced a "long series of two or three-year pastorates" tended to be "either numerically declining churches or on a plateau in size. That is a statement of fact," he added, "that can be documented in nearly every denominational family in the second half of the Twentieth Century." Among other problems was the general public's continuing perception of the Army as a charity; among the more knowledgeable minority that recognized the Army as a Christian denomination, there was a perception that its particular appeal was to the poor.[63]

There was nevertheless broad ground upon which the hopeful could graze. As small as they were, the Army's little corps were not much smaller than most Protestant churches in America: Schaller pointed out that over half of all Protestant churches averaged fewer than seventy-five members, and fully one-fourth had fewer than thirty-five on average in worship weekly. The Army's difficulty was that it had almost no large congregations, whereas a majority of American Protestants worshiped in large churches. Still, there was a wave of new interest in the small pastorate among American church leaders in the 1970s and 1980s, and many insights were generated in which Salvationists could find encouragement. Three elements in the literature were especially stimulating to Salvationist optimism: the importance of small groups within the larger congregation, the possibility of stimulating church growth by opening new branches, and the appeal of cross-cultural recruitment. The Salvation Army had considerable experience in all three areas.[64]

Small groups had always functioned effectively within the Salvation Army corps; indeed, most small corps were made up almost entirely of small groups, often with overlapping membership. A given adult might well be a member of the Songster Brigade (choir), the Home League, and the League of Mercy and be serving as a Sunday school teacher, for instance. This was now seen as a great advantage in overcoming the liability of the small size of the general congregation in the average corps. The Army's few large corps still had an advantage in church growth programming, as Camsey pointed out in an important article in June 1990, but effective use of small groups opened a path to success that many smaller corps could travel. Larsson called these small groups "entry" and "holding points" and stated that any "comprehensive evangelistic strategy" must include as many of these points as possible. The presence of the small body of committed Salvationists, the local officers who were the mainstay of every corps, was "essential to this process," according to Rader.[65]

Some groups, like the Home League and the League of Mercy, which were built on contacts with the larger community, were especially well suited to promoting corps growth. Corps were urged to supplement these traditional activities with new programs of visitation, neighborhood outreach, and invitations targeted at special groups. The Delaneys, excited by their triumphs in Norfolk, quickly built up Sunday school attendance in Orlando through systematic visitation. The target group could be even more general. Lt. Jeffery Smith, for instance, adopted "Friend Day," a Church Growth Institute program, for use in Sheboygan, Wisconsin, on

Palm Sunday 1989, and attendance doubled in what Smith described as a "joyous celebration of friendship." One of the most effective and energetic of small groups in many corps was the brass band. William Himes, director of the Central territorial music department, was quick to point out how well this darling of traditional Salvation Army warfare could be adapted to the latest crusade. The little corps band, far from being outdated, was in fact the very model of "small group ministry," providing old member and newcomer alike a "sense of belonging, concern and purpose."[66]

The second arrow in the Army's corps-growth quiver was its century-old experience in the opening of new corps. Although the process had become more complicated and expensive since pioneer days, when eager zealots were sent to open new stations armed only with courage and a few dollars, the Army had embraced the challenge of "opening fire" on new places since 1879. Despite the enormous cost in resources and personnel now required, this policy was widely adopted at the end of the 1980s. *The War Cry* reported early in 1990 that a "new wave of corps openings" was "spreading across the country." The Salvation Army enjoyed a net increase of seventy-seven corps during the 1980s, forty-one of them in the last three years of the decade. Some of the new openings were aimed at the Army's traditional working-class constituency; all five new corps in the Kentucky-Tennessee Division, for instance, were in this category. The Army continued to enjoy success nationwide with the evangelistic, community, and family welfare programs in this type of corps. Many new openings were aimed at attracting new portions of the population, however: "extension" and "bridging" were frequently joined, drawing together the Army's resources for church-planting with its third strength, its equally historic commitment to cross-cultural ministry. This became an integral part of the Army's corps-growth strategy from the outset, and in some regions it was the dominant growth strategy.[67]

The Army's commitment to a broadened ethnic ministry antedated its official embrace of church growth; indeed, The Salvation Army had been throwing out the lifeline to immigrant, minority, and mixed populations since Railton's confident letter to the Army Founder in the summer of 1880 in which he stated that he was about to get the "Americans, Africans and Germans all fairly started." A broadened ethnic ministry was a major theme for the 1980s. In May 1982 Commissioner Needham, the national commander, issued an official statement that "the creation of cross-cultural models and the identification of existing programs must have priority, as should the development of the Corps Community Center, to reflect an indigenous profile in terms of ethnicity, need and language." A special Minority Ministries Committee reported to the NPDC for two years; it was dissolved in 1983 when the commissioners reaffirmed that the special minority emphasis should be conducted on the territorial rather than the national level. In 1985 the Army started sending official delegates to the National Convocation on Evangelizing Ethnic America and to the National Black Evangelical Association Convention.[68]

The Army's top leadership was prepared by 1986 not only to increase the Army's "commitment to the people of the new ethnic America" but to announce an official new "strategy": to make this the "number one priority, without diminishing the traditionally established corps." An annual Salvation Army cross-cultural ministries conference began in 1987. All four territorial headquarters established new cross-cultural ministries bureaus in the years 1987 to 1990. The Eastern territorial office, established in June 1988, sponsored the innovative "City Lights" program, conceived and directed during the next year by Robert Watson, a lay employee of the Army and son of the territorial chief secretary. "City Lights" was intended to introduce teams of young Salvationists to the challenge of cross-cultural ministry in an urban setting. Watson pointed out that the United States had become vastly urbanized and was home to more than two hundred ethnic groups. It was time for the Army to recapture its downtown heritage by "developing new kinds of expertise in studying the unreached" and "effective mission strategies for evangelizing them." A basic strategy of church growth involved identifying special groups among whom the Army's particular type of religious activity might have special appeal. Salvationists had believed since Victorian times that the fact that other churches had not done enough to reach a particular group was sufficient proof that the Army would have a special appeal to it. The Army's success among Scandinavians was an inspiring precedent; an official report in 1983 stated that the Army had excellent "models" for successful work among ethnic minorities in both the Scandinavian and Japanese departments, both gone but clearly not forgotten. There were long-established ministries among African Americans in three territories as well. Fortified by a revived sense of its historic mission, the Army opened important new stations among urban ethnic target groups.[69]

The Army had established successful corps among Hispanics before the new emphasis on corps growth prompted leaders to increase their efforts in these fields. Many new Spanish-speaking corps were opened. Several

Auxiliary Capt. Reginaldo Tippol shares the Gospel with children
at the Los Angeles Central Corps Community Center, 1987.
Source: The Salvation Army National Archives

Hispanic programs replaced their old English-speaking counterparts in once-famous citadels. A notable example was a flourishing Hispanic program that moved into the former Hollywood Tabernacle Corps. Spanish work was advanced in the rest of the country as well. Sometimes the Army's old-time militant flavor was still evident: in March 1989 a "Latino Council of War" was called in Chicago to coordinate the activities of the six Hispanic corps in the area. Miami Citadel Corps, in the heart of the city's "Little Havana" section, became a full-fledged Spanish corps in February 1987, when the English congregation transplanted itself first to Hialeah and then to an entirely new facility when Hialeah became a Spanish-speaking corps. The Army conducted a corps program for Haitians in the Miami area as well, at the Edison corps. An important new Spanish corps was opened in Newark, New Jersey, in July 1990.[70]

The spread of Salvation Army programs among Hispanics necessitated the publication of basic Army materials in Spanish. The work of translation was carried by the Western and Eastern territories, which also added Spanish-language courses at their officer training schools in 1987 and 1988. In 1989 these territories were in a "constant process of translation." The resulting materials were made available to Salvationists nationwide. In 1989 Spanish editions of the Articles of War were distributed in all four territories. By the next year Corps Cadet, Home League, and Bible study materials were available in Spanish; and the West prepared a Spanish-language version of the official *Handbook of Doctrine.* In March 1992 the Army started regular broadcasts of *Maravillosas Palabras de Vida,* a Spanish-language version of its national radio program. Because the Spanish language is widely spoken in other countries where the Army was already established, American Salvationists did not have to start all translation from the beginning: some items were available from the Army's South American territories. The diversity of Spanish culture in the world also meant that Hispanic corps often attracted diverse congregations. Hollywood had soldiers from fourteen different Central American countries, while in Newark the officer, Maj. Aida Garcia, was Cuban, the corps sergeant major was from Peru, and most of the soldiers were Puerto Rican.[71]

Salvation Army work among Asian Americans in the United States had a venerable base. The San Francisco Chinatown Corps was not only one of the most famous corps in the country but was the oldest Chinese corps in the world. Work in this segment of the population was expanded during the 1980s as well. New Chinese corps were opened in Oakland and Monterey in 1985. As we have already noted, San Francisco Chinatown's highly respected officer Check Yee was specially honored early in 1992 with a promotion to lieutenant colonel. In the same year a Filipino officer, Lt. Col. Jose Aguirre, was appointed Western territorial cross-cultural ministries director, reflecting in part an official "increased interest in the expansion of Filipino ministry." The Army's venerable Japanese Division was not forgotten either, despite its sad demise during World War II; in January 1991, the Army revived its ministry among Japanese residents in the United States by opening Kauluwela Japanese Corps in Honolulu. The first commanding officer was a Japanese American, Capt. Faye Nishimura.[72]

The Salvation Army, which had been successfully established in Korea since 1908, was able to open a number of corps among Korean Americans as well. The first of these came in 1980 in the facility previously occupied by the Los Angeles Congress Hall Corps. By the end of the decade the Los Angeles Korean Corps, with 240 Korean soldiers and a twenty-five-piece brass band, had surpassed its once-famous predecessor.

The commissioners soon congratulated themselves for having authorized new evangelistic activity in such a promising field: they noted at their February 1989 conference that Korean Salvationists were "an aggressive group of disciplined planners, devoted to the Army and committed to the primary work of evangelism and soul-saving." Four more Korean corps were opened in the latter half of the decade. In 1985 the Alexandria, Virginia, Korean corps opened officially in facilities shared with the English-speaking corps. The pioneer leaders in this case were Korean Salvationist employees of the Army who later returned to Korea for regular officer training. In November 1989 the first commissioned officers, Capt. and Mrs. Hwang, Sun Yap, were installed. New Korean corps were established in Queens and San Francisco as well. The Chicago Korean Corps was opened in December 1988 by Maj. and Mrs. Paul Kim, who had pioneered Korean Salvationism in Los Angeles in 1980. By the end of the decade, the leadership of all five Korean corps in the United States was in the hands of officers sent for this purpose from the Army's Korea Territory. One leading figure in promoting Salvation Army work among the Korean population of the United States, however, although Korean by birth, had spent much of his active and successful career on the American field. Col. Peter Chang was the first Korean officer to receive an appointment outside his homeland (in Singapore in 1967). He held key positions in two American officer training schools before being promoted to assistant chief secretary in the Western Territory in order to promote and oversee the development of a Korean ministry in that territory. In March 1991 Chang became territorial commander in Korea itself, and in 1994 territorial commander in the Western U.S.A.[73]

The success of the new corps-growth emphasis, which drew on the long-established examples of Army work among Scandinavian, Hispanic, and Asian Americans — and, as the West was quick to remind the other territories, among the Tlingit Indians in Alaska, too — had clearly led the movement into an inviting field. Soon the Army opened its first Laotian corps in Seattle, the only such work among Laotians in the Army world. The pioneer was Aux. Capt. Bounmy Luangamath. A Laotian high school teacher, Luangamath was converted by hearing a Salvation Army missionary in a refugee camp in the Philippines. When he moved to the United States, he attended a local corps; later in Seattle, he started the Army's first Laotian Bible class, became a U.S. citizen, and was made an auxiliary captain in the Army. The Laotian comrades translated the Articles of War, Army songs, and the *Handbook of Doctrine* into French for their own use.

In July 1989 The Salvation Army opened the Seattle Central Corps and Southeast Asian Center with the Luangamaths in command. Within one year average Sunday attendance had grown to 100 persons from local Laotian, Cambodian, Vietnamese, and Thai communities.[74]

Salvation Army outreach programs among Asians, Hispanics, Haitians, Native Americans, and a number of other ethnic populations increased at a rapid rate in the early 1990s, accompanied by repeated official commitments to even greater expansion throughout the remainder of the last decade of the century. In 1992 The Salvation Army was preaching the Christian gospel in twenty different languages within the United States: Cantonese, English, French, Gujarati, Haitian-Creole, Hindi, Ilocano, Japanese, Korean, Laotian, Mandarin, Mohegan, Norwegian, Polish, Portuguese, Seneca, Spanish, Swedish, Tagalog, and Tlingit. The Eastern territory employed the largest number of different languages (thirteen), followed by the West with ten, and the Central and South with four each. The use of three of these languages, English, Korean, and Spanish, was common to all four territories.[75]

One difficulty in the path of the expansion of cross-cultural programs on an even bigger scale was the lack of American officers with the ethnic background of the targeted groups. A shortage of black officers had long frustrated the Army's plans to expand inner-city work, for example. Army leaders, hard pressed for adequate personnel, looked with envious eyes on individuals who had been Salvation Army officers in developing countries before immigrating to the United States on their own initiative. But it was official Army policy that officers who emigrated to the United States without permission would not be allowed to apply for reinstatement as officers for at least five years. In 1984 Norman S. Marshall, the national commander, formally proposed to London headquarters that this policy be overturned so that these immigrant officers could be put back into service in the United States as bona-fide officers. Marshall's reason for the appeal was clear: "We desperately need leadership to help with our establishment of beachhead operations in these ethnic groups." The chief of the staff in London was sympathetic, but Marshall's request was rejected: the effect on officer strength in developing countries might be severe if the Army in effect offered an inducement for these officers to transfer to America. If the American branch of the Army needed ethnic officers, it would have to find local Salvationists from the desired background or urge others to volunteer to serve among that particular group.[76]

The 1980s also brought innovations in personnel recruitment, partly in response to the need for ethnic and other kinds of qualified leadership and partly to provide for converts who wanted to join the Salvation Army leadership team but were unable, for one reason or another, to accept all the requirements for full officership. In the first case, the Army broadened the use of a category of employee that was legally empowered to function like an officer. The rank of "auxiliary captain" was first used in 1975 to describe employees recognized as licensed ministers, but several important questions regarding the status of such persons for tax and other legal purposes were not finally resolved until the Army's legal counsel prepared a detailed clarifying document in 1981. It defined an auxiliary captain as "an individual who is unable, for valid and acceptable reasons, to become a candidate for commissioned officership in The Salvation Army and who is otherwise qualified." The most common "valid and acceptable" reason was the age of the candidate. The Army was eager to draw on the abilities, experience, and dedication of a whole new class of potential helpers who were too old to be accepted into regulation officer training. The use of the auxiliary captain increased markedly during the 1980s. At the same time, a larger number of persons were employed by the Army as "envoys," full-time employees in local leadership positions who lack full officer privileges, and who, unlike auxiliary captains, are not eligible for promotion to commissioned officer status after a certain number of years of successful service. In 1980 there were 137 persons in these two categories on the American field, making up 4 percent of total full-time leadership personnel; by 1990 their number had increased 49 percent to 204 persons, 6 percent of the total.[77]

The Army also broadened the category of membership, making generous use of a classification that had been introduced in the 1960s but little used until the decade of the 1970s, when the Western territory began to enroll numbers of ARC converts as "adherents" of The Salvation Army. The Southern territory increased the use of this category of membership after 1978, when Comm. Arthur Pitcher became territorial leader. Pitcher, a gifted poet and writer and a glowing evangelical speaker, was a native Canadian who explained to his fellow commissioners in 1980 that the use of adherents, widely employed in Canada, was not a statistical ploy to increase membership figures but a means by which persons who did not qualify for soldiership could still have their own "church home" in the Army and a "sense of belonging to the corps by being on the Adherents' Roll." The commissioners established a definite policy on adherents, broadening the category to include not only persons who could not fulfill all the requirements of soldiership (the most common use of the category had been to enroll converts of the Men's Social Services who used tobacco, which was officially forbidden to regular Salvation Army soldiers after 1975).[78]

In May 1981, The Salvation Army in the United States adopted new criteria for adherent status: an adherent was defined as a "person who, by attendance and financial support, considers The Salvation Army to be his place of worship" but who could not become a soldier. Among the reasons why soldiership was not possible were disagreement with some point of Army doctrine (such as nonobservance of sacraments), "inactive" status in some other church (common among people in rest homes), circumstances that made it impossible for the individual to understand or fulfill the requirements of soldiership (e.g., mental disability), and the special case of a Junior Soldier who had passed the age of fourteen — the regulation age at which one became a "senior" (adult) soldier — without feeling ready for the responsibilities of the senior classification. The number of adherents in the United States grew from 9,272 in 1980 to 12,021 in 1990, an increase of 30 percent. In addition to broadening various categories of membership, the Army also stretched its officer resources during the 1980s by making increased use of employees in positions formerly occupied by officers, a policy that not all leaders welcomed.[79]

Corps growth statistics may have benefited from the Army's willingness to bring its "internationalism" home. Despite a brief flurry of controversy over the Army's formal withdrawal from the World Council of Churches on July 31, 1981 — a decision that some Third World Salvationists wished to see reversed but that the American branch of The Salvation Army supported — the international flavor of Salvationism was confirmed in many ways throughout the 1980s, albeit on the Army's own pragmatic terms. The first official "mission statement" for the Army in the United States, issued in May 1982, was careful to describe the organization as "an international religious and charitable movement." In 1991, when the commissioners issued a newly revised and shortened official statement, the description of the Army as "international" was retained. In 1988 the Army in the United States played host to the international leaders of the organization, who gathered in Lake Arrowhead, California, to hear the General proclaim a great new crusade, "Toward 2000 — Vision and Task." American participation in worldwide activities assumed more traditional forms as well: in the summer of 1991 the National Capital Band made a side trip while on a tour of Scandinavia to conduct programs in Estonia —

and thus became the first Salvation Army band to march back into the former Soviet Union.[80]

The American branch of The Salvation Army also made a more practical contribution to the worldwide status of the parent organization. Taken together, the annual Self-Denial collections raised in the four American territories were the largest single source of funds available to international headquarters to support Army programs in less developed countries. In addition, the American national headquarters served as a channel through which funds from the U.S. Agency for International Development (USAID) and other government and private sources were directed to specific overseas projects administered by The Salvation Army. The first USAID grant came in 1978. The funds were used to establish training programs for indigenous Salvationist staff in how to administer local development projects. The USAID grant enabled the Army to create the International Department for Planning and Development at international headquarters in June 1978. At the same time, the Army established a new Salvation Army World Service Office (SAWSO) as part of its national headquarters in the United States. The SAWSO offices were located in Washington, D.C., apart from the rest of national headquarters, which at the time were still in New York City. The first director was Lt. Col. Ernest A. Miller, who helped negotiate the original grant. SAWSO became the official channel through which USAID funds, the proceeds from the annual Combined Federal Campaign ("the only organized fund-raising activity permitted among Federal government employees at their place of work"), and the Army's Self-Denial funds were channeled from the United States to a wide variety of Army overseas programs.[81]

The official rules within which Salvationists had to operate were international as well. The regulations that governed their lives, the lifetime covenants they signed with great solemnity, were issued, as they had been since William Booth's day, in the name of the General in London — although the practice had been established for many years that the General would consult with the world commissioners and territorial leaders in matters of such importance. The Soldier's *Orders and Regulations* were substantially revised in 1977 in this way, but the result was no less binding on Salvationists around the world. The revised edition retained the Army's hierarchy and its militant spirituality and added many references to contemporary social and economic issues but dropped the quaint personal advice and rules of etiquette found in the Victorian original (written by William Booth himself). The "Articles of War," the covenant signed by every Salvationist upon enrolling as an adult member, were revised substantially along the same lines in 1989. The new version was officially introduced on a special "Soldier's Covenant Sunday" on September 10 of that year. The Articles, first issued in 1886, had been changed only once before, in 1975, when a proscription against the use of tobacco was added. The 1989 revision was much more thorough. Indeed, although the general spirit of a worldwide evangelical crusade was preserved and a high standard of personal conduct was proclaimed, none of the awesome absolute pledges of sacrifice, obedience, and Salvation warfare unto the death survived in the new version.[82]

Few mourned these changes in details, but a larger number did express alarm, sometimes through official channels, that the Army's militancy was fading in the era of the yuppie and the baby boomer. Several developments fed these fears. A study commissioned by the Western territory in 1991 officially recommended that the Army open a new branch, stripped of its military structure, imagery, uniforms, and ranks, aimed at the affluent, who were described as having a "pronounced distaste" for these things. While the territorial administration was not prepared to go so far, Western leaders did commit themselves to an innovative approach to church growth that in some aspects deemphasized the Army's old-time militancy in favor of a new style of corps that was more "user-friendly" to a new generation of affluent American suburbanites. The territory embraced a twofold approach to growth. On the one hand it sought to revitalize the traditional corps program by involving much more of the present membership in innovative techniques of evangelism, and on the other hand it sought to open a number of new "centers of worship and service" in areas of rapidly growing populations of persons who, for one reason or another, might be likely prospects for The Salvation Army's innovative approach to Christianity, community, and service. Comm. Paul Rader, writing in the Easter 1992 issue of the territorial newsletter, described the process: "It will mean developing innovative approaches to the establishment of new corps, and finding ways to wrap our programs of caring around the felt needs of the people we serve."[83]

A noteworthy example of this "innovative approach" in the Western Territory could be seen in 1991, when The Salvation Army's decision to open a center in California's Amador Valley (the Livermore-Pleasanton area) was based entirely on sophisticated marketing anlysis. The new Amador Valley center was, according to Maj. Earl McInnes, a staff officer with an international reputation in the practical aspects of church-growth theory, the Army's first "telemarketing corps." The potential membership of the new center was selected through sophisticated market analysis, and the congregation of 130 persons who attended the opening meeting was assembled entirely by telephone solicitation.[84]

In the Southern Territory there was talk of allowing — even en-couraging — large and affluent corps to become magnets for middle-class worshipers from large surrounding areas. Other corps in the South were officially allowed to curtail or abandon traditional Army programs if they could substitute other programs that proved more effective in attracting new members. A considerable variety of innovative and experimental programs were thus advanced in an effort to capture for God a rapidly growing population that had historically overlooked the spiritual possibili-ties offered by The Salvation Army. To those who favored them or were at least willing to give them a chance, the new plans were no more than the old Army spirit in a new, friendlier guise.[85]

Some traditionalists, however, maintained that the latest overtures were compromising at least part of the Army's historic commitment to those people whom other, more fashionable churches ignored or disdained. These officers and soldiers still viewed the Army as an army, a redemptive crusade with a special calling from God, the Great Commander, to lead an uncompromising, militant, and aggressive campaign against sin and suffering. These Salvationists contended that the Army could postpone plans to develop new constituencies until it had brought effective spiritual light to the constituency it already had. Other developments as well caused uneasiness among the militant faction. Sometimes officers in local corps, asked as part of the territorial church-growth program to prepare their own "mission statements" describing the goals of their ministries, neglected to point out the Army's distinctive features; some described it as a church much like any other but with special opportunities for outreach and service. Those who advocated the old-time approach to spiritual warfare might have been encouraged to notice that there were no official statements from top territorial or national leadership to support their fears, and in many ways The Salvation Army explicitly confirmed its militant and aggressive image. For example, Maj. Warren Fulton, the divisional com-mander, chose a theme for the Georgia Divisional Centennial in October 1990 that was still refreshingly typical of The Salvation Army: "Come Join Our Army, to Battle We Go!"[86]

The Salvation Army expended large amounts of its available resources in staff and funding to promote those aspects of its traditional crusading

*A performance of the Salvation Army musical "Take Over Bid,"
by Gowans/Larrson, at the 1983 Western Territory Congress*

spirit that its leaders considered still useful in the great work. Nowhere was that more evident than in the Army's commitment to its musical programs. In personnel alone this investment had no contemporary parallel. No other private religious or charitable organization in the country expended an equivalent share of its resources on music. Each territory had a music department with full-time director (secretary) and staff; in addition, in 1992 twenty-seven of the Army's thirty-eight divisional headquarters had full-time music directors. (In 1992 the figures for divisional music directors were these: six divisions out of ten in the Central; eight out of eleven in the East; eight out of nine in the South; and five out of eight in the West.) All four territorial music secretaries were lifetime Salvationists and accomplished musicians who enjoyed long tenure in their positions: William Himes in Chicago was the first, appointed in 1977; Dr. Richard E. Holz in the Southern territory and Ivor Bosanko in the West were both appointed in 1979; and Ronald Waiksnoris was appointed in New York in 1984. The Salvation Army proclaimed in 1982 that henceforth an annual national "Music Sunday" would be celebrated in every corps on the second Sunday in March.[87]

In the Eastern and Central territories, historic Staff Bands were maintained at a high level of proficiency, still the two most eminent

Salvation Army bands in the country. The Eastern unit retained the venerable name "New York Staff Band" even after the territorial headquarters to which it was attached moved to West Nyack; jokes about the "Nyack [N'York] Staff Band" were, of course, inevitable. In 1990 the Southern Territorial Band was revived to represent that territory at an Army congress in London. The South had lost its full-time staff band during the Depression, but a territorial band had been reassembled from time to time through the years for special events. In 1992 Commissioner Hodder created the Southern Territorial Songsters for the same purposes. The Western territorial staff band, which like the Southern band had been dissolved during the 1930s, was never revived, even on a temporary basis, due in part to the convenience with which territorial headquarters could draw on the services of large and proficient bands in nearby corps to provide music for official events. Progress in maintaining adult brass bands was uneven during the 1980s. Although the overall number of adult brass musicians remained almost constant, there were marked territorial differences: the Eastern and Central territories lost band personnel (the East more severely than the Central), while the West and South gained in band personnel (the South most notably of all). Indeed, overall statistics for all forms of musical activity in the South increased dramatically between 1981 and 1991. There were large, stable, and accomplished divisional youth bands and senior corps bands in all parts of the country during these years, and several notable regional ensembles as well. Of the latter, the oldest and most accomplished was the National Capital Band — the Army's only band representing a single city, as opposed to a corps, region, division, or territory — led since 1985 by Stephen Bulla. In 1988 the National Capital Band became the first Army band in the United States to produce a compact disc.[88]

A considerable body of new instrumental and choral music produced by active and talented Salvationist composers was published by the Army in these years. Some of these artists had been producing important pieces since the 1970s; others had emerged more recently. Among this large and diverse group were Ivor Bosanko, William Gordon, Brian Bowen, Thomas Mack, Harold Burgmayer, James Curnow, Stephen Bulla, William Broughton, and William Himes. In addition, the Army undertook major revisions of its official congregational *Song Book* and accompanying band tune books, which appeared in a new American edition in 1987. Although a separate magazine for Army musicians, *The Musician,* was started in October 1978, it proved unable to attract sufficient subscribers and was discontinued as "cost-ineffective" in May 1989. *The War Cry* and the four territorial newsletters more than filled the gap, providing extensive coverage to musical events throughout the eighties and into the nineties.[89]

Nothing important to The Salvation Army had ever been allowed to take place outside the jurisdiction of its official rules and regulations. The Army's century-plus history of warfare in the United States had confirmed in many ways the organization's basic military structure. In 1988 the commissioners were still finding it worthwhile to conduct a study of the U.S. Navy as a model for decision-making strategies. It is scarcely surprising, then, that this penchant for regulations was applied to an activity of such consequence to the movement as its musical warfare. Acknowledging that the rulebook that governed bands and "songster brigades" (choirs) had become sadly outdated by 1980, the commissioners asked Dr. Richard E. Holz to prepare "a much needed revision" of the official *Orders and Regulations for Bands and Songster Brigades in the United States of America.* Holz was assisted by the other three territorial music secretaries. The mass of detail they had to handle and the importance of the project required slow, painstaking work. In addition, as was the case with revisions proposed for any Salvation Army regulation, every word of the new text had to be reviewed by the commissioners at their own crowded meetings, which were held only three times per year, and the text they approved then had to be sent to London for the approval of the General.[90]

The final version of the new *Orders and Regulations* for musical forces was officially promulgated in 1987. The new rulebook took full account of changed conditions. It provided detailed instructions for the functioning of divisional and territorial music departments, the application of current copyright laws, the production and distribution of recordings, and making provisions for the participation of professional musicians, students, and military personnel in Salvation Army musical groups. It also described the conditions under which wearing new, more casual styles in uniforms were permissible. True to honored form, however, the new *Orders and Regulations* contained much that had not changed in a century: in addition to their playing and singing at all regular indoor and outdoor services — the latter duty was specifically reaffirmed — Salvation Army musicians were reminded that "unusual forms of aggressive salvation fighting should, as far as possible, be planned for and carried out by bands and songster brigades," such as visiting nearby hospitals, rest homes, and prisons "in the spiritual interest of the inmates," sending a portion of the band off to "assist some adjacent small corps," and playing a cheerful concert "outside

the homes of the sick, whether Salvationists or others." Nothing was more
true to the spirit of the pioneer Army, whose ragtag singers and players
had led the glorious advances of the past century, than the renewed
manifesto that opened the regulations:[91]

> Supreme Purposes: Salvation Army bands and songster brigades exist to
> proclaim the Army's message — salvation from sin through Jesus Christ;
> and to accomplish the Army's purposes — the glorification of God and
> the salvation of souls.

> Value of Music: All members of the Army's musical forces should be
> sensitive to the value of the judicious use of instrumental and vocal
> music. Music in itself has no moral or religious quality, yet when
> associated with divine words, thoughts and feelings, and when rendered
> in the power of the Holy Spirit, it is an important agent for stirring the
> emotions and moving the soul, thus helping to lead the people to God.

Advocates of the traditional brass band were prepared to concede
nothing to their comrades who had drawn the conclusion from general
church growth literature that the Army should rid itself of everything
unusual, old-fashioned, or military. William Himes declared the opposite
to be true, writing in an article entitled "The Brass Band: Dynamo or
Dinosaur" that was widely circulated in 1990-1991: "Given the fact that
the largest churches in our country" were "developing instrumental programs at an unprecedented rate, it would be an unfortunate irony to lose
one of our greatest assets." The Army band was still ideally suited to its
two traditional official functions, worship and evangelism. Bands were
flexible, acoustical (a "refreshing" alternative in an age of electronic music),
and practical: with a single set of fingerings, the novice could join the fun
in a short period of time. Official Salvationist corps-growth literature
pointed out the great value of the corps band as one of the small groups
upon which much of the growth program rested. Many smaller corps
supported effective instrumental programs during these years, of which
Warsaw, Indiana, and Augusta, Georgia, were but good examples. Although the "last of the officer-musicians," Comm. Stanley Ditmer, retired
in 1990 after a gala farewell concert in which both the Chicago and New
York Staff Bands appeared on the same platform, new programs were
already in place to recruit and train a new generation of Salvation Army
band personnel. In 1986 Lt. Col. Jack Waters started a "divisional con-

servatory" while serving as divisional commander in Georgia. Based on four to five weeks of individual, self-paced instruction by a highly qualified faculty, with an emphasis on musical service in the corps setting, the program spread rapidly through the South. By 1991 there were eight divisional conservatories in that territory. The results of these and similar efforts nationwide were encouraging: although the number of adult musicians remained almost constant between 1980 and 1990 (declining by just 19, to 3,964), the number of "Junior Bandsmembers" increased by almost 30 percent, to 3,814.[92]

The Army's religious programs for young people enjoyed consistent and widespread success in the decade of the 1980s, during which the organization registered increases of 13 percent in Sunday school attendance and 15 percent in Junior Soldiers (lay members between the ages of seven and fourteen). The well-planned and exciting "divisional youth councils" held annually in each division represented Christian youth activities of a high order, upon which the leaders of much larger denominations continued to look with wistful eyes. In July 1985 the American branch of The Salvation Army even hosted an International Youth Congress, which received attention in the national media. The success of the Army's youth programs was one cause for the cheerful outlook that The Salvation Army carried into the 1990s. There were other encouraging statistical developments in the 1980s, but none which brought more honest joy to Salvationists than a 70 percent increase in the number of converts won in its evangelistic services during the decade.[93]

On top of this happy progress, the public continued to favor The Salvation Army's practical and helpful brand of social service above all others. In November 1991, *The Chronicle of Philanthropy* published the results of an extensive survey of the nation's top four hundred charitable organizations: The Salvation Army was the first among them in annual receipt of donations, the most popular of the "Philanthropy 400." The journal's editors noted the obvious fact that the Army's quaint military ways and its evangelical fervor had not dampened the public's confidence: "the Army's idiosyncrasies" had not "kept it from winning the financial support of donors and the respect of other charity leaders." The Salvation Army faced the end of the twentieth century with the same optimism with which it had said farewell to the nineteenth, its first purpose unchanged. In 1989 the commissioners approved a new nationwide evangelistic crusade "to give emphasis to the Army's commitment to evangelism and soul-saving as it commences the last decade of the twentieth century."[94]

An important element in the Army's official optimism was the recognition on the part of its leaders of the importance of broad-based support
for future planning. The dramatic pronouncements of growth goals and
cheery five-year territorial campaigns were not new to the Army in the
1980s. What had changed was the fact that the Army's top leaders were
willing — and some were more than merely willing — to allow lower-
ranking officer personnel and rank-and-file Salvation soldiers to play an
influential role in planning for the Army's future. A survey of territorial
and divisional leaders in 1991-1992 revealed widespread support among
them for an enlarged role for the soldiers in Army leadership, especially
on the corps level. By this means the leaders hoped to make plans that
would succeed because they reflected in important ways not only the
aspirations of its own members but the resources in "time, talent and
treasure" that they were willing to invest in their projections. The decade
began with the "Second Century Advance," a campaign that outlasted by
several years the Centennial Congress that gave it birth. The Advance,
with its new emphasis on grass-roots participation, had many enduring
effects on The Salvation Army in the United States and proved to have
been a turning point of historic significance. By mid-decade the Army's
leaders recognized that the next logical step was another national forum,
this one devoted as completely to planning as possible. Officers understood
that, whatever the official purpose might be, large numbers of Salvationists
could not have large public meetings without at least some nostalgia and
brassy celebration, but the new forum was designed from the start to be
a serious affair with important results.[95]

The Salvation Army National Forum was held on May 3-7, 1989,
in Atlanta. The 1,400 delegates, divided evenly between officers and soldiers, met in plenary sessions beneath a huge banner inscribed, appropriately enough, "Toward the 21st Century." The Forum had two functions. The first was the discussion, in small groups led by experts, of
institutional, religious, and social issues of importance to the present
ministry and future success of the Army (e.g., its status as a "church," its
official position on AIDS, its doctrinal stand on the use of sacraments,
and the status and tenure of corps officer as factors in church growth).
The second function was the formulation of recommendations on these
topics. Fifty-nine proposals were generated in these sessions, all of which
were then voted on by the entire body of delegates in two plenary sessions.
Each proposal was then solemnly referred to the commissioners' conference
for action — the first time in Salvation Army history that field-level of-

ficers and lay members were given such access to the agenda of the Army's governing board. Furthermore, the commissioners pledged themselves not only to consider all fifty-nine proposals but to take definite action on all of them and to publish the results of these actions in *The War Cry* and the territorial newsletters for all to see.[96]

The commissioners' response to Forum proposals was determined by at least four factors. The first was the merit of the proposal itself. The second factor was the extent to which each proposal was endorsed by the Forum delegates themselves. The results of the voting in the plenary sessions were known in detail to the various commissions to which proposals were initially referred by the commissioners' conference, although these results were not widely circulated otherwise. Strong delegate support for a proposal did not guarantee that it would be enacted into policy, but the opposite was invariably true: any proposal that was voted down by the delegates had thereby received the kiss of death. The results might have surprised some delegates: despite widespread discussion among Salvationists of the desirability of using the word "church" in official descriptions of The Salvation Army, for instance, nearly two-thirds of the delegates at the National Forum rejected this proposal, which received no further attention from the commissioners. The third factor was The Salvation Army's fixed doctrinal, ecclesiastical, and institutional principles. Proposals that violated these parameters were rejected regardless of how popular they had been on the floor of the Forum. One example was a proposal to reintroduce for official discussion the question of the use of sacraments in The Salvation Army. Another was a request that national headquarters provide Salvationists with "non-partisan election promotional materials" so its members could know the Army's official position on political issues — information which, it was hoped, would stimulate Salvationists to "get involved with their government." The fourth factor that guided the commissioners' response to Forum proposals was the leaders' knowledge of the resources actually at the Army's disposal for implementation. Several recommendations about the recruitment, training, and disposition of officer and lay personnel fell into this category.[97]

The Army's leaders took the Forum seriously; the minutes of the commissioners' conference and correspondence of high-ranking officers after 1989 confirmed the public pronouncements of these officials. Their handling of a Forum proposal about field officer tenure could be taken as typical. The fact that many Salvationists disliked the frequent rotation of their pastors had been well known to Army leaders for years — for decades, in fact. The issue was revived with new force in the 1980s. In 1981 the Second Century Advance called for a "five year minimum appointment for officers." The 1989 Forum delegates went farther, voting overwhelmingly in favor of a recommendation to leave corps officers for a "minimum of six years, or longer if possible." The Army's official endorsement of church-growth axioms had been advertised for several years to the entire movement; one of those axioms was that long pastoral appointments were crucial to the success of the whole scheme.[98]

In the end, the commissioners felt compelled to reject the Forum tenure recommendation, but only after lengthy, detailed, and candid discussions that extended over several years. The leaders sympathized with the need for longer appointments, the value of which no one could deny. At their January 1991 meeting the commissioners accepted the recommendation of the Personnel Commission that "everything possible should be done to lengthen the appointment of Salvation Army officers, and that no transfer should be effected without reasonable justification." However, there could be no commitment to any "arbitrary determination of tenure": the Army's system of military-style appointments determined by high-ranking officers had served the Army well for its entire history; the Army's continued success required that leaders be left free to act on their knowledge of the overall needs of the officers, the Army, and its diverse programs. The leaders knew, and reminded the soldiers, that staff officers took the appointment "part of their responsibility very seriously" and that the entire process of making appointments and transfers was "saturated with prayer by the decision-makers." A survey of all territorial and divisional commanders in the United States made in 1992 in connection with the preparation of this volume revealed that almost all of these officers viewed making appointments as their most serious and troubling responsibility. The commissioners and divisional commanders also knew, but did not broadcast, that the single most common reason for the transfer of corps officers was the request of the officers themselves.[99]

The Salvation Army did not pass lightly through an event as important as the National Forum. Despite the ambiguous fate of several popular proposals, the National Forum was a watershed in the history of The Salvation Army in the United States, more important than the Second Century Advance that opened the decade. Comm. Andrew S. Miller (national commander, 1986-1989) predicted soon after the Forum that the Army would "never again be the same." The Forum was widely praised by Salvationists. The commissioners had not yet completed their work on the 1989 proposals when they officially announced that another National Forum would be held five years later, on May 5-8, 1994.[100]

The Army was committed to change nationwide — the official announcement of the "National Growth Goals" came in February 1992 — but there were several interesting regional variations. The Western Territory launched its "VISION 2000" campaign, which embraced as an official goal the doubling of territorial statistics by the turn of the new century. One of the campaign's goals was the development of the "new model Worship and Service Center," designed to reach the rapidly swelling population of baby boomers (persons between the ages of twenty-seven and forty-five). The territory commissioned a religious market research firm in 1991 to conduct a "Target Area Identification and Analysis," which revealed mixed news: The Salvation Army would be able to appeal to this "most spiritually and inwardly reflective" of all generational types, but it would have to make some changes to do so. The baby boomers respected the Army (it had "credibility" with them), but they did not recognize it was a kind of church — or if they knew that it was a church, they looked on it as appealing only to people below them on the social scale. The fact that the target group was indifferent to the religious overtures of The Salvation Army as it was and always had been was not, the research firm assured the Army, the drawback it might seem. In fact, the Army would not even have to drop any of its current programs in order to attract these people: it need only open a new branch, made up of "new model centers," without "military metaphors," designed around the way the baby boomers "live, work, and play." Without its military and downtrodden image, the "new model Salvation Army church" would have no problem succeeding in its fashionable new mission field.[101]

The territorial leaders did not accept all the conclusions of the report — they had never seriously entertained abandoning the Army's traditional style and mission — but they did make use of its demographic research with respect to recommendations for new sites for new Army centers. Although the "new model center" concept continued to receive serious attention early in the nineties, the heart of the territory's "Mission 2000" campaign was its "strong cross-cultural emphasis." Demographic studies showed that by the year 2000, the goal date of the new campaign, 25 percent of all Americans would be nonwhite. The territory proclaimed at Easter 1992 that "the mission call of the world is at our doorsteps!"[102]

The Southern Territory, for its part in promoting change, started "Operation New Treasure" in 1991. The "New Treasure" concept — the name was taken from Matthew 13:52 — was based on streamlining rather than replacing or supplanting the traditional Salvation Army corps. Eleven corps were selected, at least one from each division in the territory, and their officers were sent to the "First Ever Territorial 'Battle School'" in Atlanta in February 1992. The corps were encouraged by the territorial commander, Kenneth Hodder, to introduce innovative new programs at the expense of existing traditional activities so long as the former contributed more to the Army mission of "spiritual redemption and social reformation." The corps would not be the losers for their courage: financial support was guaranteed from territorial "incentive funds," and officers could continue to report the statistics from discontinued programs (on the basis of the monthly returns for 1991) until the "New Treasure" activity began to generate statistics of its own.[103]

The Sherman Avenue Corps in Washington, D.C., was one of the eleven "New Treasure" corps. By extending its daily lunch program to Sunday and inviting the needy to attend morning service, the corps increased average morning attendance from 40 to 225, and attendance at the evening Home League meetings quadrupled. The divisional commander praised the corps officer, Capt. Morgan Lyster, for this "strategic adaptability." Buoyed by this rush of neighborhood interest in The Salvation Army's religious program, Lyster promised thirty new soldiers, twenty-five more recruits, twenty-five more adherents, and six new future officer candidates by the end of 1992! The South also created a promising "Stewardship Campaign" for 1992, in which soldiers were invited to invest their "time, talent, and treasure" in corps programs that advanced the Army's evangelistic crusade. Corps growth strategy and the Army's official designation of 1992 as "Discipleship Year" were combined with the other territorial initiatives to move the territory forward "from Strength to Strength, 1992 to 2000." Helpful overlap among these programs was practically ensured in June 1991, when one headquarters officer, Maj. Jorge Booth, was given responsibility for coordinating all of them.[104]

In the midst of these numerous changes and announcements that it was keeping up with the times — and in the midst, too, of the dazzling marketing campaigns and sophisticated media imaging as one of the nation's largest and most popular institutions — The Salvation Army remained remarkably, touchingly true to its origins and to its historic mission. Armed with computer printouts and video monitors, fax machines and modular phones, its officers were still the spiritual heirs of all the staff captains and senior majors who spent ten times ten thousand Saturday nights singing and praying on downtown street corners, nameless servants lifting the nameless and miserable castoffs of the world into the presence of Christ. The Army's history cast a long shadow: Brig. Stella Young, the doughnut girl whose cheerful smile outlasted the First World War by seventy years, died in March 1989, after a brief moment of glory on ABC's "Good Morning America" program. The Army failed to send a brigade of doughnut makers to comfort the troops in Operation Desert Storm only because the Defense Department felt it was more important that the Army remain home to minister to the families of service personnel overseas. Salvation Army officers and soldiers offered the same practical and imme-diate little acts of mercy in the great earthquakes, fires, and hurricanes at the end of the twentieth century as their predecessors had offered in similar catastrophes throughout its long course, and the leaders of the republic were equally grateful. Traditions that had become dormant were revived as well: in 1991 the Southern territory organized "Fortress," a group of full-time young musicians to carry salvation musical warfare throughout the South. The group's militant spirit, its lifestyle on the road, and its reliance on local funding made it different in no important way from the gallant "Charioteers" of the previous century.[105]

The great names of the Army's past were revived as well and given new relevance: Army authors and leaders stated on numerous occasions that the Army's latest campaigns were based on the teachings of the pioneers who had initiated the movement more than a hundred years before. The important themes in corps growth were discovered to have been invented by William Booth, and Samuel Brengle's resurrection the-ology was revived and admired at Eastertide. The Army even produced and sold its own trivia board game, appropriately called "Beat the Drum!" It was advertised as the "ideal way to develop an appreciation for our Army heritage." It was unlikely, however, that the attention of Salvationists would drift for long from their heritage during the last years of the century. Reminders of the Army's proud traditions were everywhere. The Army's longtime commitment to an equal role for women was officially reaffirmed many times, most notably in 1990, when a new form of address for female officers was introduced: married women officers were allowed to use their own first names, a privilege that had previously been accorded only to male and single female officers. In *Christianity in Action,* published under the auspices of the Army in 1990 and widely praised by its leaders, Col. Henry Gariepy, one of the Army's most prolific writers in this period and one whose work was respected in the broader evangelical community, wrote at length about the "incomputable" contribution made by women "in corps, institutions, and administrative positions." It was, he declared, "a major reason for the vitality and dedicated ministry of the Army."[106]

The organization's continued advocacy of the military approach not only to its operations but to its purpose remained one of its most visible aspects. A "Master List of All Orders and Regulations and Manuals" in use for the Army in the United States was submitted to the commissioners' conference in early 1989 for review. The list contained seventy-eight separate items; twenty-four of these were being revised or updated at the time. The commissioners recommended dropping only six of the total: three because their content was included in other manuals, and three because they were outdated or irrelevant. The complexity of the Army's territorial and national administration had become enormous. To cite a random example, the official minutes of one meeting of the commissioners' conference, during February 9-12, 1987, required 918 pages of single-spaced typed text. The Army's military structure was not only large and intricate but expanding: in 1992 a new position, "Corps Community Service Secretary," was added to the twenty-nine other ranks and positions available to the ordinary soldier in a large American corps. Official statements even affirmed that the old-style uniform and bonnet were still "always appropriate" (1989) and embraced the open-air meeting as "an Army tradition, to bring the gospel to those who need it where they are" (1992).[107]

This militancy was more than a matter of ranks, flags, and the style of uniforms. It was designed to serve the Army's purpose: salvation warfare, against the double curse of humankind, sin and misery. Maj. Philip Needham, in an important series of articles on training school curricula published in the spring of 1990 in a private magazine for Army officers, argued that the Army's military structure had no other justification than militant spiritual warfare; as mere form, the Army's autocratic system was oppressive. In an article in *The War Cry*, Needham reminded Salvationists that the Army's role in the future could be discerned from the "astounding missional effectiveness of our forbearers," based on Christian warfare, "compassionate adaption," and courage. The Army's territorial and divisional officers would have agreed. Surveyed in 1991 and 1992, almost all of these figures expressed wholehearted commitment to a fierce evangelistic crusade. This spirit was embodied in the Army's official worldwide theme for evangelistic campaigns in the year 1990: "With Christ into the Future!" Writing in the Easter *War Cry* in 1990, James Osborne (national commander, 1989-1993) confirmed the timeless theme: Christ "is always the contemporary One. He is always relevant. No generation, however smart or clever, leaves Him behind."[108]

These themes — the Army's mission "to advance the cause of Christ on two levels: spiritual and social" and its unflagging optimism — were brought together in a particularly effective and influential way in 1992, when The Salvation Army announced official new "National Growth Goals." The original concept and much of the groundwork for the formulation of national goals, which drew on territorial projections to inform a truly nationwide campaign, came in 1991 from a special Long Range Planning Committee of the Army's National Advisory Board chaired by Mr. B. Franklin Skinner, president of Southern Bell, who also served as chair of the planning committee. The work was coordinated, in a very detailed way, by the commissioners' conference and the Army's national headquarters. The results were first published in the February 1, 1992, issue of *The War Cry*. The National Growth Goals represented a combination of spiritual integrity, enormous experience, hard work, and optimism restrained (as much as possible) by more sobering analyses of real and projected resources. The results were arguably the most significant development in the history of The Salvation Army in the early 1990s. There was plenty of room for cheering, too. Salvationists would greet the coming turn into the twenty-first century as they had greeted the turn into the twentieth — "rejoicing, bringing their sheaves with them."

Official goals were named in five categories, along with the percentage of each total goal that each territory was expected to contribute. In every case the goals required substantial increases; these expectations were tempered, however, by a thorough knowledge of regional demographics: to achieve their goals in new corps openings, for instance, the Central and Eastern territories were assigned increases of 5 and 11 percent, respectively, while the South and West were expected to grow by 23 and 25 percent, respectively. The expectations for these two territories were in large part based on the assumption that corps growth in these geographic regions would continue mainly among ethnic minorities; a "major emphasis on ministry to ethnic groups" was listed as a particular priority in the corps growth goal. The other four categories to which growth goals were applied were soldiers and adherents, officers and auxiliary captains, attendance at religious meetings, and social services.

The basis for the growth goals was a nine-part "Vision Statement," which, like the goals, was crafted with great care by Skinner's committee

and the commissioners (the actual text was written by Lt. Col. Philip
Needham) — a collaboration *The War Cry* referred to as "an impressive
network of Salvation Army leaders in the U.S." The Vision Statement was
a minor masterpiece of integration of all the elements of the modern
Salvation Army. It would have pleased alike the most single-minded zealot
of the nineteenth century and the young professional advocate of "assistance, rehabilitation, and sensitization" who would grow old in the
twenty-first. The "basis" of the Army was described as "the compelling
message and power of the Christian gospel"; its "focus" was "the world
for whom Christ died," which the Army intended to uplift by its "primary
activity," which was "outreach," defined as "evangelism and social ministry." The Army's "motivation" was the love of God; its "purpose" was to
"advance the cause of Christ in the world on two levels: spiritual and
social." The fact that The Salvation Army continued to have an enormous
capacity to bridge every social, economic, and political barrier, drawing
persons together in love and service, was demonstrated in many ways in
the early nineties. The spiritual part of the Army's ministry consisted of
"evangelism and discipling," in which the corps was reaffirmed as "the
basic, foundational unit." (Institutions were described as "specialized
units," and headquarters, more modestly still, were classified as "resourcing
units.")

The "Social Ministry" had "four significant activities": emergency
assistance, rehabilitation, "sensitization" (which involved awakening "the
social and moral conscience of the general public by taking and furthering
Biblically based positions" on issues that "affect the quality of human life"),
and "character formation" (a term the Army had used for over half a
century to describe its numerous programs that combined religion, fellowship, and useful social activities, such as the Home League, League of
Mercy, indoor youth programs, musical instruction classes, camping, etc.).
The Statement affirmed without qualification that the Army's authority
for all it did was the Bible and its own theological doctrines. Its administration was based on leadership as well as management and had therefore
committed itself to training leaders at every level. ("Soldiers" were placed
at the top of the list, above "officers.") The Army held itself accountable
to its own members for "Christian integrity," to the general public for the
efficient use of funds, and to various government bodies for authority to
operate in various special contexts.[109]

The Army's official commitment to use the funds entrusted to it in the
most efficient way was largely responsible for the decision in September 1992

to sell Booth Memorial Medical Center to New York Hospital. Opened in 1957, Booth Memorial was the largest voluntary hospital in Queens. For thirty-five years the hospital offered the Army a broad field in which to operate its Christian and social-welfare ministries, but it also drew heavily on financial, administrative, and personnel resources. With each passing year the demands on these resources became greater. After lengthy discussions, Army leaders announced that the "Medical Center's future will be enhanced by an organization whose primary expertise and record of achievement is in health care." Maj. Dr. Herbert Rader, medical director at Booth Memorial, called this a "difficult but responsible decision."[110]

A decade earlier a writer for *The Saturday Evening Post* had predicted that, no matter what, The Salvation Army would "certainly be there to mop up the tail end of the 20th Century." Salvationists for their part had no such rearguard action in mind: every divisional and territorial staff officer who responded to a national survey conducted in 1991 and 1992 stated that if the Army's young people would only commit themselves to the cause of Christ, the Army would have a glorious future. Lt. Col. Robert Tobin, personnel secretary for the Western territory, declared in the Easter 1992 issue of the territorial newsletter that those who responded to God's calling to service in The Salvation Army were setting out on "the most exciting adventure of their lives."[111]

The steady growth of the Army's ministry in a region of traditional strength led to an adventure of a different sort as well: on December 21, 1993, the Army's Western territorial headquarters announced the formation of a new administrative division, the first such innovation in seventy-three years. The new Sierra Del Mar Division, with headquarters in San Diego, was formed out of the large Southern California Division. The first divisional commander was Lt. Col. David Riley, a veteran staff officer and former divisional leader for Southern California. The Sierra Del Mar Division was officially scheduled to begin operations on February 1, 1994, with twelve corps. Growth of Salvation Army social and religious activities among the enormous ethnically mixed population of the new division was expected to be rapid.[112]

The Army's leaders were filled with innovative ideas to make the Army's Christian ministry more appealing and effective in all the existing divisions as well. The official recognition that its own social welfare clientele was a mission field of enormous potential was a major theme in The Salvation Army in the 1980s. The creation of the new Corps Community Service Secretary reflected this recognition. So did a proposal made in

1992 by Col. M. Lee Hickam, in charge of personnel in the Central territory, that Salvationist families should "'adopt' an unchurched client-family, using whatever means necessary" — a phrase that would have brought joy to the hearts of the Army's zealous pioneers — "to eventually bring them into the fellowship of the corps." The Army built bridges on the other end of the social scale as well, drawing with equal confidence on its long-standing support among fortune's favorites — and among many "Christian friends" as well — in inviting Mr. Arthur J. Decio, owner of Skyline Corporation and a devout Roman Catholic, to chair its National Advisory Board in 1993. Salvationists' latest "vision statement" and their oldest battle song confirmed their cheerful kingdom-building theme: "So we'll make a thoroughfare for Jesus and his train . . . As we go marching to Glory."[113]

Appendix 1

The Doctrines of The Salvation Army
(as set forth in the Deed Poll of 1878)

1. We believe that the Scriptures of the Old and New Testaments were given by inspiration of God; and that they only constitute the divine rule of Christian faith and practice.
2. We believe there is only one God, who is infinitely perfect — the Creator, Preserver, and Governor of all things — and who is the only proper object of religious worship.
3. We believe that there are three persons in the Godhead — the Father, the Son, and the Holy Ghost — undivided in essence and co-equal in power and glory.
4. We believe that in the person of Jesus Christ the divine and human natures are united; so that He is truly and properly God, and truly and properly man.
5. We believe that our first parents were created in a state of innocency but, by their disobedience, they lost their purity and happiness; and that in consequence of their fall all men have become sinners, totally depraved, and as such are justly exposed to the wrath of God.
6. We believe that the Lord Jesus Christ has, by His suffering and death, made an atonement for the whole world, so that whosoever will may be saved.
7. We believe that repentance toward God, faith in our Lord Jesus Christ, and regeneration by the Holy Spirit are necessary to salvation.

8. We believe that we are justified by grace, through faith in our Lord Jesus Christ; and that he that believeth hath the witness in himself.
9. We believe that continuance in a state of salvation depends upon continued obedient faith in Christ.
10. We believe that it is the privilege of all believers to be "wholly sanctified," and that their "whole spirit and soul and body" may "be preserved blameless unto the coming of our Lord Jesus Christ" (I Thessalonians 5:23).
11. We believe in the immortality of the soul; in the resurrection of the body; in the general judgment at the end of the world; in the eternal happiness of the righteous; and in the endless punishment of the wicked.

Religious Doctrines of The Salvation Army (as set forth in the Salvation Army Act of 1980)

1. We believe that the Scriptures of the Old and New Testaments were given by inspiration of God, and that they only constitute the Divine rule of Christian faith and practice.
2. We believe that there is only one God, who is infinitely perfect, the Creator, Preserver, and Governor of all things, and who is the only proper object of religious worship.
3. We believe that there are three persons in the Godhead — the Father, the Son and the Holy Ghost, undivided in essence and co-equal in power and glory.
4. We believe that in the person of Jesus Christ the Divine and human natures are united, so that He is truly and properly God and truly and properly man.
5. We believe that our first parents were created in a state of innocency, but by their disobedience they lost their purity and happiness, and that in consequence of their fall all men have become sinners, totally depraved, and as such are justly exposed to the wrath of God.
6. We believe that the Lord Jesus Christ has by His suffering and death made an atonement for the whole world so that whosoever will may be saved.
7. We believe that repentance towards God, faith in our Lord Jesus Christ, and regeneration by the Holy Spirit, are necessary to salvation.

8. We believe that we are justified by grace through faith in our Lord Jesus Christ and that he that believeth hath the witness in himself.

9. We believe that continuance in a state of salvation depends upon continued obedient faith in Christ.

10. We believe that it is the privilege of all believers to be wholly sanctified, and that their whole spirit and soul and body may be preserved blameless unto the coming of our Lord Jesus Christ.

11. We believe in the immortality of the soul; in the resurrection of the body; in the general judgment at the end of the world; in the eternal happiness of the righteous; and in the endless punishment of the wicked.

Appendix 2

The Ranks of The Salvation Army,
in Use in the United States of America, 1878-1992

Rank	Adopted	Current/Discontinued
General	gradually assumed from 1878	Current
Chief of the Staff*	1880	Current
Commander**	1896	1948
Commissioner	1880	Current
Lieutenant Commissioner	1920	1973
Colonel	1880	Current
Lieutenant Colonel	1896	Current
Brigadier	1889	1973
Senior Major	1948	1959
Major	1879	Current
Staff Captain	1881	1931
Field Major	1923	1931
Commandant	1916	1931
Adjutant	1888	1948
Ensign	1888	1931

*Not formally a rank but a position held by a Commissioner.

**Not a rank but a title, used for the national commanders of The Salvation Army in the United States from 1896 until 1934. Its official use was revived in 1943 but gradually discontinued during the years 1946-1948. This title was never officially revoked, and has never been declared inappropriate when addressing the national commander.

Senior Captain	1948		1959
Captain	gradually assumed from 1877		Current
(Auxiliary Captain)*	1975		Current
Lieutenant	1879		Current
Second Lieutenant	1948		1959
Probationary Lieutenant	as early as 1917		1973
Cadet	1880		Current

These ranks were never all in use at the same time. During the years 1923-1931 the Army employed the largest number of different ranks (not counting general, chief of the staff, and cadet) in the history of the movement — thirteen, as compared to six in use today. For many years some ranks were reserved only for staff officers. Staff captain, in use from 1881 to 1931, is an example. A more recent example is lieutenant colonel, introduced to the Army in 1896 and regarded as appropriate only for staff officers until 1991.

1890	1930	1950	1990
General	General	General	General
Chief of the Staff	Chief of the Staff	Chief of the Staff	Chief of the Staff
Commissioner	Commander**	Commissioner	Commissioner
Colonel	Commissioner	Lt. Commissioner	Colonel
Brigadier	Lt. Commissioner	Colonel	Lt. Colonel
Major	Colonel	Lt. Colonel	Major
Staff Captain	Lt. Colonel	Brigadier	Captain
Adjutant	Brigadier	Senior Major	Lieutenant
Ensign	Major	Major	Cadet
Captain	Staff Captain	Senior Captain	
Lieutenant	Field Major	Captain	
Cadet	Commandant	Lieutenant	
	Adjutant	Second Lieutenant	
	Ensign	Cadet	
	Captain		
	Lieutenant		
	Cadet		

*An auxiliary captain is not a commissioned officer but an employee discharging the duties of an officer. After a certain number of years of successful service in this rank, the officer may apply to be commissioned in the regulation way as a captain. The form of address for an auxiliary captain is the same as for a regulation captain.

**See note concerning the rank of commander on p. 354.

Appendix 3

National Commanders of The Salvation Army in the United States, 1880-1993

Commander	Years in Command	Disposition
George Scott Railton	1880-1881	Transferred
Thomas E. Moore	1881-1884	Resigned
Frank Smith	1884-1887	Transferred
Ballington Booth, the Marshal, and	1887-1896	Resigned
Maud Ballington Booth	1887-1896	Resigned
Frederick St. George de Lautour Booth-Tucker and	1896-1904	Transferred
Emma Moss Booth-Tucker, the Consul	1896-1903	Died in office
Evangeline Cory Booth, the Commander	1904-1934	Elected General
Edward Justus Parker*	1934-1943	Retired
Ernest I. Pugmire	1943-1953	Died in Office
Donald S. McMillan	1953-1957	Retired
Norman S. Marshall	1957-1963	Retired
Holland French	1963-1966	Retired
Samuel Hepburn	1966-1971	Retired
Edward Carey	1971-1972	Retired
Paul J. Carlson	1972-1974	Retired
William E. Chamberlain	1974-1977	Retired
Paul S. Kaiser	1977-1979	Retired

*National Secretary, 1934-1943; appointed National Commander 1943.

356

Ernest W. Holz	1979-1982	Retired
John D. Needham	1982-1983	Died in Office
Norman S. Marshall	1983-1986	Retired
Andrew S. Miller	1986-1989	Retired
James Osborne	1989-1993	Retired
Kenneth L. Hodder	1993-	Serving

National Commanders of
The Salvation Army in the United States
1880-1993

George Scott Railton
1880-1881

Thomas E. Moore
1881-1884

Frank Smith
1884-1887

Ballington Booth
1887-1896

Frederick Booth-Tucker
1896-1904

Evangeline C. Booth
1904-1934

Edward J. Parker
1934-1943

Ernest I. Pugmire
1944-1953

Donald S. McMillan
1953-1957

Norman S. Marshall
1957-1963

Holland French
1963-1966

Samuel Hepburn
1966-1971

Edward Carey
1971-1972

Paul J. Carlson
1972-1974

William E. Chamberlain
1974-1977

Paul S. Kaiser
1977-1979

Ernest W. Holz
1979-1982

John D. Needham
1982-1983

Norman S. Marshall
1983-1986

Andrew S. Miller
1986-1989

James Osborne
1989-1993

Abbreviations Used in Notes

AWC	The (American) *War Cry,* published by National Headquarters 1881-1921; it covered all SA activities in the United States except those in the Far West; after January 1921 it became *The War Cry* Eastern edition (WCE)
B/F	Biographical file
Busby Coll.	A collection of papers and documents relating to Salvation Army history owned by Col. John Busby, Toronto, Canada
CCM	Commissioners' conference, Minutes of
CN	*Central News* (Central territorial newsletter)
Conq	*The Conqueror,* SA publication, 1892-1896
CTM	Central Territorial Museum, housed at SFOT/C
Damon Diaries	Diaries of Commissioner Alexander Damon, kept throughout his active career as an officer; available for use in SAARC, with advance permission of the officer sons of Lt. Col. Lyell Rader (R), Damon's son-in-law.
Francis Matl.	Items in the personal collection of Lt. Col. William Francis
G/F	General file
Gifford Coll.	A collection of documents preserved by Comm. Adam Gifford, now in the possession of Mr. Harry Sparks; photocopies in SAARC. The collection remained closed, at Mr. Sparks's continuing request, at the time of this writing.
GN	*Good News* (Eastern territorial newsletter)
Holz Coll.	A collection of historical items belonging to the family of Comm. Richard E. Holz. At the time of writing, this large collection was in the hands of Comm. Richard E. Holz (II) and Comm. Earnest W. Holz, grandsons of the first Commissioner Holz.
LD	*The Literary Digest*
Milsaps Coll.	The Milsaps Collection, Circle "M" Collection, housed in Houston Metropolitan Research Center, Houston Public Library. Houston RC: Houston Research Center

Milsaps WCC	Milsaps *War Cry* clipping scrapbooks, five volumes, numbered by volume and page.
Milsaps SB	Milsaps scrapbooks (the numbers following indicate volume and page)
Milsaps Diary	The four Old Series (O.S.) volumes cover the years 1880 to 1883; the sixty-nine New Series volumes cover the years 1896 to 1930.
NF	*New Frontier* (Western territorial newsletter)
SA	The Salvation Army
SAARC	The Salvation Army Archives and Research Center, 615 Slaters Lane, Alexandria, Virginia 22313
SANHQ	The Salvation Army National Headquarters;
	1896-1982: 120 West 14th Street, New York, New York 10011
	1982-1991: 799 Bloomfield Avenue, Verona, New Jersey 07044
	1991-current: 615 Slaters Lane, Alexandria, Virginia 22313
SATHQ/C	Salvation Army Central Territorial Headquarters
	10 W. Algonquin Road, Des Plaines, Illinois 60016
SATHQ/E	Salvation Army Eastern Territorial Headquarters
	40 West Nyack Road, Box C-635, West Nyack, New York 10994
SATHQ/S	Salvation Army Southern Territorial Headquarters
	1424 NE Expressway, Atlanta, Georgia 30329
SATHQ/W	Salvation Army Western Territorial Headquarters
	30840 Hawthorne Blvd., Rancho Palos Verdes, California 90274
Seiler Coll.	Seiler Collection; the largest and most complete collection of SA documents and memorabilia in private hands in the USA; owned by Col. Paul D. Seiler of Ocean Grove, New Jersey; currently administered by his son, Col. Paul D. Seiler II of Brick, New Jersey.
SFOT/C	Salvation Army School for Officers' Training
	700 W. Brompton Ave., Chicago, Illinois 60057
SFOT/E	Salvation Army School for Officers' Training
	201 Lafayette Avenue, Suffern, New York 10901
SFOT/S	Salvation Army School for Officers' Training
	1032 Stewart Ave. SW, Atlanta, Georgia 30310
SFOT/W	Salvation Army School for Officers' Training
	same address as SATHQ/W
SS	*Southern Spirit* (Southern territorial newsletter)
STHC	Southern Territorial Historical Center housed at SFOT/S
WC	*The War Cry*, national edition, 1970-present
WCC	*The War Cry*, Central territorial edition, 1921-1970
WCE	*The War Cry*, Eastern territorial edition, 1921-1970
WCS	*The War Cry*, Southern territorial edition, 1927-1970
WCW	*The War Cry*, Pacific Coast edition, 1883-1921; from 1921-1970 called Western territorial edition

NOTES TO CHAPTER 1

1. Bernard Watson, *Soldier Saint: George Scott Railton, William Booth's First Lieutenant* (London, 1970), p. 59; the quotation is from a private letter shown to Watson by a member of the Railton family.

2. Comm. Frederick de L. Booth-Tucker, *The Life of Catherine Booth: The Mother of The Salvation Army,* 2 vols. (London, 1892), 2:81, 85-86, 88-89; William Booth, "To the Officers and Soldiers of the Salvation Army," *The Salvationist,* 1 October 1879, p. 254, in Seiler Coll.; [George Scott Railton], *Twenty-One Years Salvation Army* (London, [1888]), pp. 7-23, 44; St. John Ervine, *God's Soldier: General William Booth,* 2 vols. (New York, 1935), 1:64, 93, 194, 213, 233-54, 292-94.

3. Watson, *Soldier Saint,* p. 43; Ervine, *God's Soldier,* 1:480-81; Herbert A. Wisbey, Jr., "Religion in Action: A History of The Salvation Army in the United States" (Ph.D. diss., Columbia University, 1951), pp. 22-26; Herbert A. Wisbey, *Soldiers without Swords: A History of The Salvation Army in the United States* (New York, 1955), p. 21; Railton, *Twenty-One Years Salvation Army,* p. 133; Comm. Edward Carey, *It Began in Cleveland, Ohio! The Story of The Salvation Army's First Pioneering Venture outside the British Isles,* SAARC; Dorothy Hitzka, *The James Jermy Story; or, The Earliest Inception of The Salvation Army in America* (Cleveland, n.d.), SAARC; *The Christian Mission Magazine,* August 1870, p. 112; January 1873, p. 15; April 1873, p. 63; September 1873, p. 144; November 1873, p. 164; August 1874, p. 204, in SAARC "James Jermy" file.

4. AWC, 25 August 1888, pp. 6-7, 9.

5. AWC, 4 August 1888, pp. 1-2; AWC, 28 November 1908, p. 11; 5 December 1908, pp. 1, 16; 16 October 1909, pp. 1, 9; "How The Salvation Army Came to America," WCC, 12 September 1925, p. 12; 19 September 1925, p. 14; 26 September 1925, pp. 14-15; interview with Mrs. Russell Crowell (née Everald Eliza Knudsen, granddaughter of Eliza Shirley), Garden Grove, Calif., 8 December 1978; photocopy of AWC, 9 July 1881 [Philadelphia], p. 1, SAARC "Shirley family" file; Wisbey, "Religion in Action," pp. 36, 42, 72, 119; Wisbey, *Soldiers without Swords,* pp. 11-16; Booth-Tucker, *The Life of Catherine Booth,* 2:162-63.

6. George S. Railton, "Salvation Beginnings in America," WCC, 14 March 1925, pp. 4, 15 [written in 1892]; AWC, 24 December 1892, p. 2; Norman H. Murdoch, "Wesleyan Influences on William and Catherine Booth," *Wesleyan Theological Journal* 20 (Fall 1985): 97; Norman H. Murdoch, "Evangelical Sources of Salvation Army Doctrine," *Evangelical Quarterly* 59 (July 1987): 242-43; "The 'Four Books,'" *The Officer* 1 (October 1893): 306-8. This last article presented the results of a survey by the editor of the four books that were the greatest help to the respondents (there were 109 responses); see also "Our Library: Finney's Works," *The Officer* 3 (January 1895): 12.

7. Watson, *Soldier Saint,* pp. 43-45; Ervine, *God's Soldier,* 1:481-85; Eileen Douglas and Mildred Duff, *Commissioner Railton* (London, [1920]), p. 68; Railton, *Twenty-One Years Salvation Army,* pp. 36, 73.

8. Ensign William G. Harris, "Looking Back," WCE, 7 July 1928, p. 11; Hugh Leamy, "Tambourine," *Colliers,* 8 September 1928, p. 12.

9. Holograph note in Railton's hand, in SFOT/E Museum G/F, "Railton"; Douglas and Duff, *Commissioner Railton,* p. 70; Booth-Tucker, *The Life of Catherine Booth,* 2:164.

10. [George S. Railton], "Our American Landing," AWC, 11 April 1896, p. 12; WCC, 10 January 1925, p. 11, quoting from first AWC [St. Louis], 15 January 1881; Harris, "Looking Back," 14 July 1928, p. 11.

11. *New York World,* 11 March 1880, p. 5; Railton, *Twenty-One Years Salvation Army,* p. 135; Harris, "Looking Back," 21 July 1928, p. 11; Wisbey, "Religion in Action," pp. 26-27, 42. The song "With Repentance for Sin" appeared in editions of *The Song Book of The Salvation Army,* published in 1899, 1930, and 1953; the latest edition, published in 1987, does not contain the song.

12. *New York World,* 11 March 1880, p. 5; Railton, *Twenty-One Years Salvation Army,* p. 135; Railton, "Our American Landing," p. 12; AWC, 19 March 1887, p. 1; "The Army of Salvation," *Harper's Weekly,* 3 April 1880, p. 214; *New York Times,* 15 March 1880, p. 8; 16 March 1880, p. 8; 19 March 1880, p. 8; (clippings SFOT/E Museum G/F Railton); AWC, 26 November 1892, p. 12; AWC, 3 March 1900, p. 12.

13. [George Scott Railton], *Heathen England* (London, 1879), pp. 61-79; Railton, "The Army's Advent in the States," AWC, 24 December 1892, p. 2; Leamy, "Tambourine," p. 12. For an account of Harry Hill's concert saloon, see Thomas N. Doutney, *His Life Struggle, Fall and Reformation; also a Vivid Pen-Picture of New York; together with a History of the Work He Has Accomplished as a Temperance Worker; Written by Himself* (Battle Creek, 1891), pp. 358-60, and Luc Sante, *Low Life: Lures and Snares of Old New York* (New York, 1991), pp. 109-11.

14. *New York World,* 15 March 1880, p. 5; "The Army of Salvation," p. 214.

15. Harris, "Looking Back," 21 July 1928, p. 11; WCW, 1 July 1933, p. 12; Col. Wm. H. Cox, "The Salvation Army around the World," *Missionary Review of the World,* August 1919, pp. 586-87. Sgt. B. A. Richardson states that Railton opened New York No. 1 only after he returned from Philadelphia and that only then was Ash-Barrel saved ("Victorious Veterans: The Pioneer Corps of the Central Division," AWC, 29 January 1898, p. 2). Railton, *Twenty-One Years Salvation Army,* pp. 135-37; AWC, 27 March 1886, p. 1; "The First of a Mighty Multitude; or, The Capture of Ash Barrel Jemmy, the First Convert in the U.S.," AWC, 22 April 1893, p. 4. Kemp was made a lieutenant after one year and seven months as a faithful soldier. He was sent to Jersey City No. 1, then promoted to captain and sent to Boston, where he served until he died 11 March 1895 (AWC, 6 April 1895, p. 10; 21 December 1895, p. 11).

16. "A Glimpse at Some of Our Charities," *Harper's Magazine,* February 1878, pp. 441-50, and March 1878, pp. 596-608; "The Gospel and the Poor in Our Cities," *The Homiletic Monthly* 8 (December 1883): 167; J. M. Sherwood, "The Prayer Meeting Service: Oct. 6 — The Conversion of Cities — Luke XXIV:47," *Homiletic Review* 12 (October 1886): 338-39 ("neglect of our cities"); J. M. Sherwood, "Applied Christianity, No. 1: The Relationship of the Church to the Enormous Growth of Our Cities," *Homiletic Review* 13 (January 1887): 25-36; William O. McDowell, "Working-Men and the Church," *Homiletic Review* 13 (February 1887): 779-80; Samuel Lane Loomis, *Modern Cities and Their Religious Problems* (New York, 1887), p. 82 ("everybody knows it"); George F. Pentecost, "Evangelization of Our Cities: A Survey of the Field," *Homiletic Review* 10 (October 1885): 291-92; George F. Pentecost, "Applied Christianity II — How Shall Our Cities Be Evangelized?" *Homiletic Review* 13 (April 1887): 287 ("much discussed"), 288-89, 291-96; Charles A. Dickinson, "The Problem of the Modern City Church," *Andover Review* 12 (October 1887): 362-69, 371 ("to an unusual degree"); "Social Christianity —

The Andover House Association," *Andover Review* 17 (January 1892): 8; "Why the Workingman Does Not Attend the City Churches," *Homiletic Review* 30 (October 1895): 377-78; "Workingmen and the Church," *Homiletic Review* 30 (November 1895): 454-57; Daniel Dorchester, *The Problem of Religious Progress,* rev. ed. (New York, 1895), pp. 418-19; J. H. W. Stuckenberg, "Is the Church an Enemy of Labor?" *Homiletic Review* 31 (May 1896): 457-58; "The Church: The Laborer's Point of View," *Homiletic Review* 32 (October 1896): 362-63. On Roman Catholic success among the working classes, see Rev. Washington Gladden, "The Social and Industrial Situation," *Bibliotheca Sacra* 49 (July 1892): 409, and "Catholicism and the Social Problem," *Homiletic Review* 30 (September 1895): 270-72. James Cardinal Gibbons, the most influential Catholic leader in the United States, wrote to the Holy See in 1887, begging the Pope to refrain from an official condemnation of the Knights of Labor, saying that the Church in America was mostly made up of working-class families and that "the rights of the working classes . . . ought to be especially dear to the Church which our Lord sent to preach His Gospel to the poor" ("The Knights of Labor," in *A Retrospect of Fifty Years,* vol. 1 [Baltimore, 1916], p. 200).

17. One account, for instance, suggests that Atlantic City was not opened until May. See "Forty-Five Years in America: A Brief Historical Sketch," WCC, 12 September 1925, p. 16; "Found — A Member of Railton's Pioneer Party!" WCE, 7 October 1939, pp. 5, 14; Richardson, "Victorious Veterans," p. 2; Wisbey, "Religion in Action," pp. 53-54; *The Salvation News,* Philadelphia, 10 July 1880, p. 2 (SAARC).

18. *New York World,* 17 March 1880, p. 8; Railton, *Twenty-One Years Salvation Army,* 135; Robert Sandall, *The History of The Salvation Army,* 6 vols. (London, 1950), 2:317-18 (Appendix E contains entire ultimatum); *New York Daily Graphic,* 25 March 1880, quoted by Wisbey in "Religion in Action," pp. 51, 59; Crowell interview; "The Army of Salvation," p. 214; AWC, 9 December 1893, p. 10; SFOT/E Museum G/F "Brooklyn," has typed manuscript material on Lewis Pertain, who died 23 March 1922.

19. Railton, "The Army's Advent in the States," p. 2; AWC, 27 February 1892, p. 3; AWC, 2 March 1895, p. 12; Douglas and Duff, *Commissioner Railton,* pp. 75-77; "October 5, 1879," WCE, 7 October 1933, p. 3; *The Salvation War, 1884, under the Generalship of William Booth* (London, [1884]), p. 61; Crowell interview; "Found — A Member of Railton's Pioneer Party!" pp. 5, 14.

20. Railton, in a letter to William Booth, quoted by Douglas and Duff in *Commissioner Railton,* p. 74.

21. *The Salvation News,* 10 July 1880, pp. 1-2; WCW, 21 January 1933, pp. 2, 5.

22. J. Evan Smith, *Booth the Beloved: Personal Recollections of William Booth, Founder of The Salvation Army* (London, 1949), pp. 18-19; Railton, *Twenty-One Years Salvation Army,* p. 138; Douglas and Duff, *Commissioner Railton,* pp. 67-86; *The Baltimore Sun,* 18, 19, and 29 October 1880 and 14 January 1881 (copies sent to author by Brig. Evelyn Allison). The original "Hallelujah Seven" were Capt. Emma Westbrook, Rachel Evans, Clara Price, Mary Alice Coleman, Elizabeth Pearson, Annie Shaw, and Emma Eliza Florence Morris. When Prof. Wisbey interviewed Emma Morris Lambert in February 1949, she could trace only four of the pioneer women; three of these had lived and died in the United States (Wisbey, "Religion in Action," pp. 41, 60). In 1890 only two of the pioneers — Capts. Price and Westbrook — were still serving as officers (AWC, 14 June 1890, p. 2). Eliza Shirley recalled later in life that four of the women had returned to England and resigned as officers, and two remained in the United States, but not as officers (Crowell

interview). The only pioneer who remained an officer throughout the rest of her life was Capt. Emma Westbrook, who retired as a commandant (after 1931, field major) and died in 1933.

23. WCE, 12 September 1925 (orig. AWC, 15 January 1881), p. 12; WCC, 10 January 1925, p. 11.

24. Railton, "The Army's Advent in the States," p. 2; WCC, 10 January 1925, p. 10; George S. Railton to Mrs. Albright, St. Louis, 22 February 1881 (SAARC RG 20.55, 53/3).

25. WCE, 12 September 1925, p. 12.

26. Douglas and Duff, *Commissioner Railton,* pp. 82-86; Watson, *Soldier Saint,* pp. 66-68.

27. The information on Capt. Nancie Weaver was supplied in a letter from Comm. John D. Waldron to Lt. Col. Dennis Philips, Unadilla, New York, 11 July 1990, a copy of which was kindly supplied to the author under cover of a letter from Maj. Marlene J. Chase dated 6 May 1992; Waldron's information came from an article in the English *War Cry* dated 2 June 1881; Wisbey, "Religion in Action," pp. 67-70; Wisbey, *Soldiers without Swords,* pp. 30-31; Ervine, *God's Soldier,* 1:519-20; AWC, 5 March 1887, p. 5; Aaron Ignatius Abell, *The Urban Impact on American Protestantism, 1865-1900* (1943; reprint, Hamden, 1962), p. 120.

28. Booth-Tucker, *The Life of Catherine Booth,* 2:165; Wisbey, "Religion in Action," pp. 74-75; AWC, 14 September 1884, p. 1; Crowell interview; WCE, 8 October 1932, p. 12. Commandant Eliza Shirley Symmonds died 18 September 1932 in Racine, Wisc.

29. "The Army of Salvation," p. 214; C. A. Stork, "The Salvation Army: Its Methods and Lessons," *Lutheran Quarterly* 12 (October 1882): 556; AWC, 6 December 1884, p. 3; *Daily [Columbus] Ohio State Journal,* 12 January 1885 (photocopy sent to author by Brig. Lawrence Castagna).

30. AWC, 4 July 1885, pp. 2-3; 11 July 1885, p. 3; Comm. William Peart, "How We Started in Chicago," WCC, 16 February 1924, p. 8; Comm. Edward Justus Parker, *My Fifty-Eight Years: An Autobiography* (New York, 1943), 9, 39, 54-55, 87-88. An SA document entitled *Disposition of Forces, February 1, 1890,* lists corps by the order of their opening in the United States; Chicago III, opened April 1886, is listed as Corps No. 100 on p. 14.

31. Minute no. 12, 2 August 1890, in Busby Coll.; copies SAARC.

32. WCW, 18 July 1891, in Milsaps WCC, 2:105-6; WCW, 1 July 1887; WCC, 2:271; Milsaps Diary, 4 (O.S.), pp. 243-54; AWC, 2 May 1891, pp. 1-2; Capt. Day, "San Francisco," *Conq.,* September 1893, p. 335; Milsaps Diary, 15 January 1897, p. 14. There were five issues of the Newton *War Cry* (WCW, 22 May 1897, states that there were but four; see WCC, 2:223); they are preserved in the Milsaps material at Houston: WCC, 2:105 (November 1882), 145 (December 1882), 165 (February 1883), and 185 (March 1883) and Milsaps SB, 2, 39 (May 1883).

33. On Milsaps's commission as a "sergeant" in Newton's Army, see Milsaps SB, 2:1, and Milsaps Diary (O.S.), pp. 255, 257-65, 268-69.

34. Day, "San Francisco," pp. 335-36.

35. WCW, March 1884, p. 1; October 1884, p. 2; December 1885, p. 2; February 1886, p. 2; March 1886, p. 2.

36. WCW, November 1886, p. 1; 15 January 1887, p. 1; March 1884; Maj. Alfred

Wells, "An Account of the Opening and Early Days of The Salvation Army on the Pacific Coast," holograph 35 pages, 21 pages typed, in Milsaps unprocessed manuscripts, "California" file; AWC, 2 May 1891, Milsaps WCC, 2:319.

37. Comm. Frank Smith, *The Salvation War in America for 1885* (London, 1886), pp. 149-50; [Maj.] Alfred Wells, "Review of the California Forces," AWC, 10 January 1885, p. 1; WCW, July 1884, p. 1.

38. WCW, 1 July 1887, p. 1; AWC, 10 November 1888, p. 1; WCW, November 1886, p. 2; AWC, 18 December 1886, p. 3; WCW, 1 January 1887, p. 3; 1 June 1887, p. 1; AWC, 19 November 1887, p. 13; WCW, 2 November 1895, p. 2.

39. WCW, July 1884, p. 1; May 1884 [p. 3]; Railton, *Twenty-One Years Salvation Army,* p. 138.

40. Wisbey, "Religion in Action," 97-98; Crowell interview; Ensign Clifford Brindley, "Commissioner Richard E. Holz," WCE, 13 April 1929, p. 11.

41. Entire statement from AWC, 24 July 1884, cited by Wisbey in "Religion in Action," pp. 103-4.

42. Brindley, "Commissioner Richard E. Holz," 13 April 1929, p. 11, and WCE, 20 April 1929, p. 12; SA, *History of Injunction Legislation: The Salvation Army vs. The American Salvation Army* (New York, 1910), pp. 24-33, 37.

43. Brindley, "Commissioner Richard E. Holz," 20 April 1929, p. 12; AWC, 19 March 1887, p. 4; AWC, 22 November 1884, pp. 3-4 (front page missing in SAA copy); Smith, *The Salvation War in America for 1885,* pp. 15-16.

44. [William Booth], *The General's Letters, 1885* (London, [1886]), pp. 51-67, or AWC, 24 and 31 January and 7 February 1885; *The Salvation War, 1884,* pp. 62-64; Norman Murdoch, *Salvationist-Socialist Frank Smith, M.P.: Father of Salvation Army Social Work* (New York, 1978); Kenneth G. Hodder, *Report and Catalogue for Materials Obtained during Research on Frank Smith, M.P. and of the B.B.C. Recording Archives* (New York, 1978), SAARC.

45. WC [Moore edition], 21 May 1881, p. 1; 7 May 1885, p. 1 (SAARC); Staff Capt. Richard E. Holz's diary entries for 5 January and 11-13 March 1887 (SAARC); application form and instructions to candidates (Moore's Army), 21 November 1888 (Holz Coll.).

46. "Personal Reminiscences of Commissioner Gifford," address to Cadets (1927; updated to 1930), unpublished typescript, Gifford Coll.; WCW, October 1886, p. 1; Brindley, "Commissioner Richard E. Holz," 20 April 1929, p. 15; Allan Whitworth Bosch, "The Salvation Army in Chicago: 1885-1914" (Ph.D diss., University of Chicago, 1965), pp. 13, 26.

47. AWC, 13 November 1886, p. 1; 20 November 1886, pp. 1-2; 27 November 1886, pp. 1-2; 4 December 1886, pp. 1-2; 11 December 1886, pp. 1-2; 18 December 1886, pp. 1-2; 15 January 1887, p. 5; Bosch, "The Salvation Army in Chicago," pp. 33-35.

48. AWC, 26 October 1889, p. 8; 2 November 1889, pp. 5, 9; *New York World,* 20 January 1889, p. 2; Brindley, "Commissioner Richard E. Holz," WCE, 4 May 1929, p. 12; SA *Disposition of Forces, November 1, 1889* (New York, 1889), p. 7. *The American War Cry,* official gazette of the American Salvation Army, 9 February 1889, pp. 1-3, contains an explanation for the deposition of Moore (in Seiler Coll.). Twenty-five posts of Moore's Army refused to acknowledge the "Booth yoke" and follow Holz back into the worldwide ranks; these organized under Maj. William Grattan and then under Maj. James William

Duffin as the American Salvation Army, which was incorporated 4 April 1900. Milton K. Light, who had been offered the generalship when Moore was deposed and before Holz accepted, continued to lead a branch of the American Salvation Army in the South. There were eight outposts of this organization in Georgia when the Booth Salvation Army began official operations there in October 1890; these soon folded, and none survived the departure of Light in 1891. See Edward H. McKinley, "Brass Bands and God's Work: One Hundred Years of the Salvation Army in Georgia and Atlanta," *Atlanta History* 34 (Winter 1990-1991): 5-6, 9, 26. By means of lengthy litigation, The Salvation Army forced the American Salvation Army to change its name. It incorporated as the American Rescue Workers, 12 April 1913, and still survives today. On 10 March 1908, William V. Grattan, the last remaining director of the American Salvation Army, surrendered the original and only legal charter of that organization to Commander Evangeline Booth. See the U.S. Department of Commerce, Bureau of the Census, *Census of Religious Bodies, 1936: American Rescue Workers* (Washington, 1940), pp. 1-3, and *The American Rescue Workers Constitution, Orders, Regulations and Book of Rules* (N.p., n.d.), pp. 3-6 (both in SFOT/E Museum, G/F "Moore"); Appellate Division of the Supreme Court, First Division, *The Salvation Army in the United States, Appellant, against The American Salvation Army, Respondent* (New York, [1908]), pp. 454-55, 470-71, kindly loaned by Comm. Richard E. Holz, grandson of the Maj. Holz in the text; "American Rescue Workers" correspondence (Broadway files nos. 1 and 4, SAARC). The best history of the "Moore split" is a recent monograph by Lisa Brennan Kisser and John D. Waldron entitled *Healing Waters: The Story of the Reconciliation of The Salvation Army at Saratoga Springs, New York* (Syracuse, N.Y., 1989); see especially pp. 27-57. The 5 October 1889 letter quoted in text is cited on pp. 39-40. A list of the names of the twenty-nine officers who rejoined with Holz is found on p. 57, which cites AWC, 2 November 1889. Waldron, a retired commissioner, is the Army's most accomplished and respected volunteer historian.

NOTES TO CHAPTER 2

1. Allan Whitworth Bosch, "The Salvation Army in Chicago: 1885-1914" (Ph.D. diss., University of Chicago, 1965), p. 26. The SA *Disposition of Forces* document for February 1890 lists Chicago No. III Corps (West Lake) as Corps No. 100 in the United States, with April 1886 as the date of opening (p. 14).

2. Agnes Maule Machar, "Theological and Religious Intelligence: Red Cross Knights — A Nineteenth Century Crusade," *Andover Review* 2 (August 1884): 205; *Combat Songs of The Salvation Army* [comp. Col. & Mrs. Howard Chesham] (New York, 1976), pp. 4, 10, 12, 20; *The Song Book of The Salvation Army* (New York, 1955), songs 671, 798.

3. Roger Green, "The Theology of William Booth" (Ph.D. diss., Boston College, 1985); Leicester R. Longden, "The Church Militant and the Salvation Army: A Theological Appraisal of William Booth and His Movement" (B.Div. thesis, Union Theological Seminary, n.d.); Philip D. Needham, "Redemption and Social Reformation: A Theological Study of William Booth and His Movement" (M.Th. thesis, Princeton Theological Seminary, 1967); Philip D. Needham, "Mission in Community: A Salvationist Perspective" (D.Min. diss., Candler School of Theology, Emory University, 1981).

4. Comm. Ballington Booth, *From Ocean to Ocean; or, The Salvation Army's March*

from the Atlantic to the Pacific (New York, 1891), p. 102; Maud B[allington] Booth, *Beneath Two Flags: A Study in Mercy and Help Methods,* 4th ed. (Cincinnati, 1894), p. 17; Col. William Evans, "Sanctified Go," *Conq* 1 (February 1892): 9 ("never-ending hell"); Lt. Col. Wesley Bouterse, "Our Holiness Foundations," paper read at Brengle Institute, June 1978, p. 2.

5. [William Booth] in *The Salvationist,* January 1879, reprinted in *The Founder Speaks Again: A Selection of the Writings of William Booth,* ed. Cyril J. Barnes (London, 1960), p. 45; [Ballington Booth], *The Salvation Fight under the Stars and Stripes* (New York, 1888), p. 9; interview with Prof. Roger Green, Wilmore, Ky., 22 March 1979; Green, "The Theology of William Booth," pp. 97-120, especially pp. 108-9. See also Roger Joseph Green, "Theological Roots of *In Darkest England and the Way Out,*" *Wesleyan Theological Journal* 25 (January 1990): 7-14; William Booth, "The Millennium; or, The Ultimate Triumph of Salvation Army Principles," *All the World* 7 (August 1890): 337-43.

6. *All about the Salvation Army by Those Who Know* (New York, 1890), p. 16; Needham, "Mission in Community," pp. 121-24; Bouterse, "Our Holiness Foundations"; E. Schuyler English, *H. A. Ironside: Ordained of the Lord* (Grand Rapids, 1946), pp. 56-58, 68-71 (Ironside was one early officer who resigned over the issue of sinless perfection); Charles Edward Russell, "A Rescuer of Ruined Lives: General William Booth and The Salvation Army," *Missionary Review of the World* 32 (June 1909): 451; Charles A. Briggs, "The Salvation Army," *North American Review* 159 (December 1894): 704.

7. Clarence W. Hall, *Samuel Logan Brengle: Portrait of a Prophet* (Chicago, 1933), pp. 88-89; Comm. S. L. Brengle, *Helps to Holiness* (London, [1896]), pp. 24-25; interview with Lt. Col. Lyell Rader, Ocean Grove, New Jersey, 23 June 1978.

8. A. F. Marshall, "The Salvation Army," *Catholic World* 51 (September 1890): 739, 742-43; Catherine Booth, "Hot Saints," in *Papers on Practical Religion* (London, 1901), p. 174; WCC, 10 January 1925, p. 10 (reprint of AWC, 15 January 1881).

9. Booth, *The Salvation Fight under the Stars and Stripes,* p. 9 ("No! No!" quotation); Philip D. Needham, "Redemption and Social Reformation" and "Mission in Community"; Robert D[avid] Rightmire, "Pneumatological Foundations for Salvation Army Non-Sacramental Theology" (Ph.D diss., Marquette University, 1987), p. 61. See also David Rightmire, *Sacraments and The Salvation Army: Pneumatological Foundations* (Metuchen, N.J., 1991); AWC, 1 December 1888, p. 8; 26 April 1890, cover; Booth, *From Ocean to Ocean,* pp. 103-10; *Salvation Army Song Book* (1953-1986 ed.), 682 (1879) and 479 (1899). "Rescue the Perishing" remained in the 1986 revision of the Army's *Song Book,* but "Throw Out the Lifeline," a favorite of the Army's men's social services program, did not.

10. Booth, *Beneath Two Flags,* p. 130; *All about the Salvation Army by Those Who Know,* pp. 12 ("deficient" quotation), 14-15; Donald Fraser, "The Salvation Army," *Presbyterian Review* 7 (April 1886): 261.

11. "Salvation in London," *The Living Age,* 1 August 1914, p. 313 (quoting *The Nation*); AWC, 19 January 1889, p. 8 ("glad, jolly" quotation); *Salvation Army Song Book,* 798 (1882); WCW, February 1886, p. 1.

12. Capt. Vincent Cunningham, "Railton," WCC, 8 March 1924, p. 7; *Louisville Courier Journal,* 18 May 1883 (copy sent to author by Maj. James Pappas); WCW, October 1884, p. 1; Thomas Easton, *Blood and Fire: The Salvation Army — Its Rise, Progress and Present Standing, and Work of the Fifth N.J. Corps* (New Brunswick, N.J., 1884), p. 17;

Brig. Leland Waldron, "Another Bethlehem Story: The Story of Brigadier and Mrs. John N. Waldron," unpublished typescript (courtesy the author), p. 18; [William Booth], *The General's Letters* (London, 1886), p. 36; English, *H. A. Ironside,* p. 67; "Minutes: The Salvation Army," 3 July 1895, 17 March 1898, and 23 November 1899 Busby Coll.).

13. AWC, 24 September 1892, p. 9; WCW, 1 November 1890 and 15 November 1890 (Milsaps SB, 2:19-22); AWC, 11 July 1891, pp. 1-2; Minutes for 18 June 1891 (Busby Coll.); WCW, January 1886, p. 2. For a new scholarly account of "neurasthenia," see Tom Lutz, *American Nervousness, 1903: An Anecdotal History* (Ithaca, 1991), pp. 1-30 (especially pp. 3-7), 34-35.

14. AWC, 2 August 1890, pp. 1-2; Booth, *From Ocean to Ocean,* p. 175. Norman Murdoch was one of those who suggested that the Army's move away from the urban slums was a betrayal of its mission and a confession of failure. See Murdoch, "The Salvation Army: An Anglo-American Revivalist Social Mission" (Ph.D diss., University of Cincinnati, 1985), p. 309; Minutes for 24 October 1896, ("perfectly at liberty" quotation; (Busby Coll.).

15. *Adrian (Michigan) Daily Times,* 22 March 1883, cited by in a history of the Adrian Michigan Corps compiled by Corps Sgt. Maj. Berten Warren (CTM); Waldron, "Another Bethlehem Story," pp. 30-31; AWC, December 1884, p. 4; Machar, "Red Cross Knights," p. 203; interview with Sr. Maj. Charles A. Schuerholz, Asbury Park, N.J., 30 June 1978.

16. William Booth, *Orders and Regulations for Staff Officers of The Salvation Army* (London, 1904), pp. 252, 277-79; AWC, 29 November 1884, p. 3; 6 December 1884, p. 2; 11 June 189, p. 10; WCW, 15 May 1887, p. 1; 1 June 1887, p. 2; Nora Marks, *Facts about The Salvation Army: Aims and Methods of the Hallelujah Band* (Chicago, 1889), pp. 78-79; Lt. Waggoner, "The Women's Garrison, San Francisco," *Conq* 1 (April 1892): 76 ("skirmishers" quotation); Herbert A. Wisbey, Jr., "Religion in Action: A History of The Salvation Army in the United States" (Ph.D. diss., Columbia University, 1951), p. 78.

17. Needham, "Redemption and Social Reformation," pp. 108-9, 157, 164-65; Longdon, "The Church Militant and the Salvation Army," pp. 49-51; Needham, "Mission in Community," pp. 134-44; Booth, *From Ocean to Ocean,* p. 11 ("phoenix-like"); C. A. Stork, "The Salvation Army: Its Methods and Lessons," *Lutheran Quarterly* 12 (October 1882): 555-60; W. T. Stead, *General Booth: A Biographical Sketch* (London, 1891), p. 68.

18. Booth, *Beneath Two Flags,* pp. 128-29.

19. Minutes for 13 July 1889 and 16 June 1891 (Busby Coll.); AWC, 29 June 1889, p. 5; 10 July 1889, p. 8; "Personal Reminiscences of Commissioner Gifford," 1927, updated to 1930, Gifford Coll.; Comm. Edward Justus Parker, *My Fifty-Eight Years: An Autobiography* (New York, 1943), pp. 50-52; WCW, November 1884, p. 2. See Appendix 2, pp. 354-55 herein, for a list of Salvation Army ranks used during the history of the movement; the author is indebted to Lt. Col. Cyril Barnes of International Headquarters, Mrs. Col. Paul D. Seiler, and Lt. Col. David Moulton for help in compiling this list.

20. [Ballington and Maud B. Booth], *The Soldier's Manual; or, Piety and Practice* (New York, 1889), 33-37. For comments on soldiers who viewed uniform wearing as a "real cross," see *Conq* 2 (September 1893): 369 ("obedience" quote), and Maj. T. C. Marshall, "What Is a Salvationist?" *Conq* 4 (September 1895): 102-3; AWC, 25 July 1885, p. 1; 5 August 1893, pp. 1-10 (especially p. 7). Maj. Milsaps noted in his diary entry for 25 January 1901 that he paid $26 for his new uniform, at the rate of five dollars per week; a major's salary was $10 weekly.

21. Booth, *The Salvation Fight under the Stars and Stripes,* p. 9 ("real battles" quotation); Booth and Booth, *The Soldier's Manual,* p. 23; William Booth, *Orders and Regulations for Field Officers of The Salvation Army* (London, 1901), p. 525 (on "Grading of Field Officers"); WCW, March 1884, p. 1; 1 January 1888, p. 2 ("the great Salvation War").

22. *The Officer* 1 (January 1893): 13.

23. *New York World,* 13 March 1883, p. 1; AWC, 3 January 1885, p. 3; Brindley Boon, *Play the Music, Play! The Story of Salvation Army Bands* (London, 1966), p. 49; photograph and materials on Grand Rapids No. 1 Corps Band in CTM, horizontal files, and in "Grand Rapids Corps History" file; see also Brig. Ronald Rowland, "One Hundred Years of Banding," *The Musician* 1 (October 1978): 6.

24. Ronald W. Holz, *Heralds of Victory: A History Celebrating the Hundredth Anniversary of the New York Staff Band and Male Chorus, 1887-1987* (New York, 1986), pp. 4-5; AWC, 17 January 1885, p. 1; 20 November 1886, p. 2; 16 June 1888, p. 12; 25 January 1891, p. 1; WCW, July 1886, p. 2; June 1889, Milsaps WCC, 1:5; WCW, 7 September 1895, p. 9; Milsaps SB, 2, pocket in back of book, identified photograph, Oakland Citadel corps in 1885; *Danbury Sun Times,* 23 August 1886 (copies sent to author by Lt. William Francis); on East Liverpool, see also WCE, 20 October 1934, p. 15; Sgt. B. A. Richardson, "Victorious Veterans: The Pioneer Corps of the Central Division," AWC, 29 January 1898, p. 2; Booth, *The Salvation Fight under the Stars and Stripes,* p. 20; *The Salvation Army Price List of Publications Outfit Goods and Musical Instruments, October, 1893* (London, 1893), pp. 98, 102-6 (Seiler Coll.). String bands formed a great part of the musical ministry of the Scandinavian corps; see William Booth, *The Salvation Army Orders and Regulations for Bands* (London, 1891), p. 9 (Seiler Coll.).

25. Booth, *The Salvation Army Orders and Regulations for Bands,* pp. 6, 8, 10; Parker, *My Fifty-Eight Years,* pp. 80, 187, 190; Bosch, "The Salvation Army in Chicago," pp. 62-64; AWC, 28 March 1891, p. 7; Ensign Rowland Hughes, "Our Heritage, The Army," WCE, 21 May 1932, p. 3; Lt. Phil Gerringer, diary entries for 25 July and 31 July 1910 (CTM); George Ethelbert Walsh, "The Salvation Army as a Social Reformer," *The Chautauquan* 17 (June 1893): 333 ("amusing" quotation); "About the World: The Salvation Army Crisis," *Scribner's* 19 (May 1896): 657. On Trumble, see Staff Capt. Ed. Trumble [as told to Esther H. Elias], "A Panorama of the Past," WCE, 29 July 1933, pp. 4, 14; and Holz, *Heralds of Victory,* pp. 9-12, 200, 216-17, and the picture facing p. 172.

26. AWC, 5 July 1890, p. 3; Booth, *Beneath Two Flags,* p. 40; Staff Capt. Slater, "The Music of the Salvation Army," *Conq* 4 (January 1895): 34; AWC, 12 December 1885 (Francis matl.); 7 November 1891, p. 3; Machar, "Red Cross Knights," p. 204. See especially "Contraband of War," *Conq* 2 (May 1893): 194-96; (July 1893): 266-67; (August 1893): 314-15; and (November 1893): 434-35; Lt. Col. Charles Skinner, "Is Any Merry? Let Him Sing!" *The Officer* 17 (July 1966): 450-52; Capt. Ernest A. Miller, "The Beat That Communicates," *The Officer,* 15 (December 1964): 832. The first "secular" tune used by the Army with Booth's permission was "Champagne Charlie."

27. Stork, "The Salvation Army," pp. 557, 562; Staff Capt. Marshall, "The United States Press and The Salvation Army," AWC, 7 February 1891, p. 1; *All about The Salvation Army 1884* (Brooklyn, n.d.), pp. 10-12; "A Salvation Army Miracle Play," *Illustrated American,* 23 January 1897, frontispiece and p. 136 (describes the dissection of the devil and the similarity between the Army and medieval Catholic symbolism); John R. Rhemick, "The Theology of a Movement: The Salvation Army in Its Formative Years," *Wesleyan*

Theological Journal 22 (Spring 1987): 81-86; WCW, 30 July 1889, p. 9; 2 September 1893 ("desperately interested" quotation); Milsaps SB, 2:62-63; Lt. Col. T. W. Scott, "How to Advertise Army Meetings," in *Western Congress Addresses* (Chicago, [1906]), pp. 60-62. For an excellent collection of announcements and small posters, see Milsaps WCC, 3:308-49.

28. [George Scott Railton], *Heathen England* (London, 1879), p. 40; Machar, "Red Cross Knights," p. 204.

29. Comm. Frank Smith, *The Salvation War in America for 1886-1887, under the Generalship of Rev. William Booth* (New York [1887]), pp. 20, 105, 119; AWC, 5 March 1887, pp. 1, 4; WCW, May 1884, p. 1; July 1886, p. 1; September 1886, p. 4; AWC, 25 February 1888, p. 6; 30 May 1885, p. 1; 6 June 1885, p. 2; 24 April 1886, p. 1; 22 May 1886, p. 3.

30. AWC, 3 March 1894, p. 5; 28 March 1885, pp. 1-2; WCW, 18 April 1896, p. 8; Bosch, "The Salvation Army in Chicago," pp. 208-9; Parker, *My Fifty-Eight Years,* pp. 107-9, 126-27, 134-42, 144-52, 168-70; Commander [Frederick] Booth-Tucker, *The Consul* (London, 1903), pp. 107-8; Milsaps Diary, 12 February 1897; and AWC, 18 July 1908, p. 16.

31. Catherine Booth, *Aggressive Christianity* (Boston, 1889), p. 59; S. L. Brengle mentions weapons at the altar in an undated letter to his daughter Mrs. H. Chester Reed, SFOT/E Museum G/F, "Brengle."

32. Oscar Handlin, *The Uprooted* (New York, 1951), pp. 117-43; Oscar Handlin, *Immigration as a Factor in American History* (Englewood Cliffs, N.J., 1959), pp. 76-77, 79-84; H. Richard Niebuhr, *The Social Sources of Denominationalism* (1929; reprint, Cleveland, 1962), pp. 200-235; George F. Pentecost, "Evangelisation of Our Cities: A Survey of the Field," *Homiletic Review* 10 (October 1885): 295; Timothy L. Smith, "Religion and Ethnicity in America," *American Historical Review* 83 (December 1978): 1174-77, especially pp. 1176-77. Smith's assertion that many immigrants were drawn to "messianic" and millennial doctrines supports Green's contention that part of the Army's appeal lay in Booth's post-millennialism.

33. AWC, 21 January 1888, p. 4; 25 February 1888, p. 10; 10 March 1888, p. 1; 14 April 1888, p. 15; 16 June 1888, p. 9; 2 July 1888, p. 4; Maj. K. A. Walden, "Through Forty-Five Years: A Review of The Salvation Army's Scandinavian Work in the United States of America, 1887-1933," trans. Lt. Col. T. Gabrielsen (SAARC "Scandinavian" files); AWC, 16 June 1894, p. 13.

34. AWC, 21 July 1889, p. 4; 2 February 1889, pp. 4-5; 9 February 1889, pp. 4-5; 31 January 1891, p. 8; 25 June 1891, pp. 1, 4; 29 October 1892, p. 7; 5 January 1895, p. 12; WCW, 1 April 1944, p. 11; Capt. Percy Soule, "Our Home Mission Work: A Talk with Lt.-Col. Holz," *Conq* 4 (July 1897): 153; "A Short Review of the Scandinavian Work in the United States," *Harbor Lights* 1 (June 1898): 178-79; Leo Alf, "Strang-Orkestern vid Chicago 13," *Conq* II (April 1893), 178-79; Bosch, "The Salvation Army in Chicago," pp. 47, 53, 63; Adjutant Winchell, "Chicago," *Conq* 2 (February 1893), p. 61; WCW, 9 January 1937, pp. 3, 14.

35. "Pushing forward the Swedish War," AWC, 25 August 1894, p. 4; interview with Mrs. Lt. Col. F. William Carlson, Ocean Grove, N.J., 7 August 1978; interview with Col. C. Stanley Staiger, Ocean Grove, N.J., 28 July 1978; interview with Col. William Maltby, Asbury Park, N.J., 30 June 1978. See the novel by Astrid Valley, *Marching Bonnet* (New York, 1948).

36. Railton, quoted by Thomas F. G. Coates in *The Prophet of the Poor: The Life-Story of General Booth* (New York, 1906), p. 130; letter quoted by Eileen Douglas and Mildred Duff in *Commissioner Railton* (London, [1920]), p. 74; *The Salvation News,* 16 October 1880, pp. 1-2; *The War Cry* (Moore edition), 7 May 1885, p. 1; 29 July 1886, p. 1, in SAARC; AWC, 29 October 1887, p. 9; 19 November 1887, p. 11; 7 July 1889, p. 9; 22 October 1892, p. 8; 2 December 1893, p. 5; Ensign Jaeger, "The German-American War," *Conq* 5 (August 1896), p. 357; Mary A. Scherer, "The German Work: Its Rapid Growth and Development in the United Sates," *Harbor Lights* 1 (March 1898): 91; AWC, 16 June 1894, p. 11; 8 June 1895, p. 9; 22 September 1894, p. 2.

37. "The Stranger within Our Gates: A Work among Germans and Italians in the United States," *Harbor Lights* 2 (September 1899): 334-35; AWC, 19 May 1894, p. 1; 16 June 1894, p. 5; Brig. Richard E. Holz, "Scandinavian, German and Italian Department, Notes," AWC, 12 December 1896, p. 3. For a detailed account of the rise and decline of the Army's Scandinavian work from the viewpoint of a dedicated insider, see Edward O. Nelson, *Hallelujah: Recollections of Salvation Army Scandinavian Work in the USA* (Chicago, 1987). For information on the Italian Corps, see Ensign Kupfer, "A Visit to the Italian Corps," *Conq* 5 (September 1896): 420-22; AWC, 17 March 1906, p. 6. For a brief time there was a Russian corps in New York, founded by Envoy John Reut, a Russian Jew converted to Christianity in his homeland in 1892, who moved to New York in 1907 and attended the Bowery corps. He borrowed a drum and a flag, hired a hall with own wages, and opened a corps in a Russian-Jewish neighborhood in New York. The work was heavily opposed: every street meeting required two police officers for protection, and every indoor meeting required three. Reut even produced a crude version of the *War Cry* in Russian, German, and Yiddish. The corps opened formally in March 1909 but soon sank without a trace. See AWC, 13 November 1909, pp. 1, 12; and U.S. Department of Commerce and Labor, Bureau of the Census, *Special Reports: Religion Bodies, 1906,* vol. 1 (Washington, 1910), p. 119.

38. WCW, October 1884, p. 2; March 1885, p. 2; April 1885, p. 2; February 1886, p. 1; 15 December 1887, p. 5; 18 January 1896, pp. 6, 9; 21 March 1896, p. 6; 11 April 1896, pp. 3-4, 6; 11 July 1896, p. 6; 25 July 1896, p. 9; 15 August 1896, p. 4; 26 September 1896, p. 8; 3 October 1896, p. 8; 28 November 1896, p. 6; 18 October 1924, pp. 8-9; *Conq* 5 (August 1896): 385. For an account of the early days of the Army in San Francisco's Chinatown, see Check-Hung Yee, *For My Kinsmen's Sake: A Salvation Army Officer's Quarter Century of Service in San Francisco Chinatown* (Rancho Palos Verdes, Calif., [1986]). On the Pacific Grove mission, see Milsaps Diary, 26 February 1900, 28 February 1900, and 1 March 1900. Milsaps made a special effort to maintain contacts with Fong Foo Sec after he left the Army; see his diary entry for 24 March 1900.

39. St. John Ervine, *God's Soldier: General William Booth,* 2 vols. (New York, 1935), 1:480-81; Douglas and Duff, *Commissioner Railton,* p. 74; AWC, 18 July 1885, p. 1.

40. WCW, November 1884, p. 4; AWC, 11 July 1885, p. 1; 18 July 1885, p. 1; 22 August 1885, p. 1; 29 August 1885, p. 4; 19 September 1885, p. 1; 26 September 1885, p. 2; 3 October 1885, p. 1; 5 September 1885, p. 1; 31 October 1885, p. 3; 21 November 1885, p. 3; 28 November 1885, p. 1 (dismissal of Braithwaite); 5 December 1885, p. 1; 12 December 1885, p. 1; 26 December 1885, p. 7; 23 January 1886, p. 1; 6 February 1886, p. 1; 3 April 1886, p. 1; Comm. Frank Smith, *The Salvation War in America, 1885* (New York, 1886), pp. 135-37, 11; George Scott Railton, *Twenty-One Years*

Salvation Army (London, 1888), p. 140; AWC, 8 January 1887, p. 9; 14 May 1887, p. 1; SA *Disposition of Forces: March 1888,* p. 3; *April 1888,* pp. 4, 18.

41. AWC, 3 October 1891, p. 11; 14 May 1892, p. 13; 7 September 1889; WCW, 18 April 1896, p. 8; AWC, 25 August 1888, p. 4; 31 January 1891, p. 4; William J. Brewer, *Lifting the Veil; or, Acts of the Salvationists* (Boston, 1895), n.p.; AWC, 25 August 1900, p. 7; 20 August 1887; letter from S. L. Brengle to Adjutant David Farrar, St. Petersburg, Fla., dated 12 February 1936 (Francis matl.); Hall, *Samuel Logan Brengle,* p. 84; Milsaps Diary, 5 March 1898 and 9 March 1898. On Capt. Beck, see SA *Disposition of Forces: June 1896,* p. 13; and *Disposition of Forces: February 1897,* p. 29; the *Disposition of Forces* volumes for January through December 1898 list Beck as "on furlough," after which his name disappears from the record. The author is indebted to Prof. Ronald Holz for the following information: the song "My Lord, What a Mourning, When the Stars Begin to Fall," which was widely used by the pioneer Salvationists in the United States, was probably introduced into The Salvation Army by those who first heard the song, and other black choral music, during the days of the Christian Mission, when such groups as the Hampton Student Choir and the Fisk Jubilee Singers toured Britain. See *Jubilee and Plantation Songs, Characteristic Favorites as Sung by the Hampton Students, Jubilee Singers, Fisk University Students, and Other Concert Companies* (Boston, 1887), p. 72; and *The Salvation Army Band Music* (London, 1891), no. 56. As noted in Chap. 1, Eliza Shirley sang this song to great effect in the early days in Philadelphia.

42. AWC, 14 July 1894, p. 8; 21 July 1894, p. 8; 28 December 1895, cover and p. 2; 20 May 1899, p. 8.

43. AWC, 28 July 1894, cover; 23 June 1894, p. 9; 7 July 1894, p. 12; WCW, 30 June 1894, p. 7; "Our Apostle to the Colored People," *Conq* 5 (October 1896), p. 474; "Colonel Holland, Our New Apostle to the Colored Race," AWC, 22 August 1896, pp. 1-2; "Colonel Holland: An Interview," *Conq* 6 (January 1897): 13; Booker T. Washington in a letter to Maj. T. C. Marshall, Tuskegee, Alabama, dated 28 July 1896 and printed in *Conq* 1 (October 1896): 475. See also Norris Alden Magnuson, "Salvation in the Slums: Evangelical Social Welfare Work, 1865-1920" (Ph.D. diss., University of Minnesota, 1968), pp. 324-44, 459-60; and Needham, "Redemption and Social Reformation," p. 73.

44. Matt. 25:31-46; Maud Ballington Booth, "Salvation Army Work in the Slums," *Scribner's Magazine* 17 (January 1895): 103.

45. *Mended Links: The Annual Report of The Salvation Army's Rescue Work in the United States 1903* (New York, n.d.), n.p. (SAARC); Comm. Frank Smith, *The Salvation War in America, 1885* (New York, [1886]), pp. 126-27; *Danbury News-Times,* 21 April 1887 (Francis matl.); WCW, August 1886, p. 3; 1 March 1887, p. 1.

46. AWC, 9 October 1886, p. 1; 5 February 1887, p. 8; 19 March 1887, p. 5 (at that time, the rescue home was the only Army institution beyond the corps); 2 July 1887, p. 8; 30 July 1887, p. 9; 28 April 1888, p. 12; 27 October 1888, p. 4; 16 April 1892, p. 2 and illustration; 25 June 1892; 15 July 1893, p. 2; WCW, 1 February 1887, pp. 1-2; 1 April 1887, p. 1; 1 August 1887, p. 1. Finding qualified officers for these homes was a constant problem. See William Evans to Maj. [R. E.] Holz, New York City, 7 October 1890 (Holz Coll.).

47. Daniel Dorchester, *Christianity in the United States from the First Settlement down to the Present Time* (New York, 1888), pp. 710-17 (quotation p. 711); AWC, 5 July 1890, p. 8.

48. AWC, 10 August 1889, p. 14; 31 August 1889, p. 8; 12 October 1889, p. 9; 19 October 1889, p. 13; 30 November 1889, p. 5; 1 March 1890, pp. 2-3 (reprinted from the *New York World*); AWC, 30 August 1890 (reprinted from *Illustrated American*); Harry B. Wilson, "Contrasting Methods of Salvation Army Warfare," *Harper's Weekly,* 22 December 1894, p. 1219; Maj. Bown, "Glimpses of Slum Operations," *Conq* 4 (January 1895), p. 19; Maud Ballington Booth, "The Church of the Black Sheep: An Article on The Salvation Army," *Harper's Weekly,* 15 March 1896, p. 250; Ballington Booth, "Salvation Army Work in the Slums," p. 107 ("no food" quotation), 109-11; Edwin Gifford Lamb, *The Social Work of The Salvation Army* (New York, 1909), pp. 117-18, 120, 132; Lyman Abbot held the slum sisters up as an example of the way in which Christ shared the poverty of His followers (*Christianity and Social Problems* [Boston, 1896], pp. 20-21).

49. William Booth, *In Darkest England and the Way Out* (London, 1890), pp. 26-27, 278; AWC, 22 November 1890, pp. 2-3, 8; 6 December 1890, p. 2; Albert Shaw, "A Year of General Booth's Work," *The Forum,* February 1892, pp. 766-67; Commander Ballington Booth, "The Salvation Army: Its Work among the Poor and Lowly — The Work of the Shelter Brigade," *Harper's Weekly,* 30 December 1890, p. 1257.

50. *The Congregationalist,* 1 January 1891, p. 4; *Homiletic Review* 21 (January 1891): 93; W. J. Ashley, "General Booth's Panacea," *Political Science Quarterly* 6 (September 1891): 537 (quotation); see also pp. 541-42, 547-48. Army leaders in the United States looked on the publication of Booth's book as one of the major events of the year 1890. See, e.g., Booth, *From Ocean to Ocean,* pp. 138-74.

51. K. S. Inglis, *Churches and the Working Class in Victorian England* (London, 1963), pp. 194-204, 212-14, 259-60. "It was Booth's anxiety about the Army's lack of penetrating power among slum dwellers that turned him towards social reform," wrote Inglis (p. 197). A "letter from London" informed the readers of *The Nation* in 1883 that the Army "appealed with great success to the ordinary beliefs of orthodox English Protestants" (A. V. Dicey, "The 'Salvation Army' as an Index of English Opinion," *The Nation,* 25 January 1883, pp. 77-78). Inglis also cites contemporary statements. [George Scott Railton], *Heathen England* (London, 1879), p. 11 ("Labouring classes"); "What Is a Salvationist?" *Conq* 4 (March 1895): 101-4 ("all kinds"); Booth, *Beneath Two Flags,* pp. 17, 28, 152 (quotation), 268; Ballington Booth, "Out of the Depths; or, Reaching the Submerged," AWC, 6 February 1892, p. 9 (quotation); Victor Bailey, "'In Darkest England and the Way Out': The Salvation Army, Social Reform and the Labour Movement, 1885-1910," *International Journal of Social History* 29 (1984): 135-36, 141; Norman H. Murdoch, "William Booth's *In Darkest England and the Way Out:* A Reappraisal," *Wesleyan Theological Journal* 25 (Spring 1990): 106-16; Murdoch, "The Salvation Army," pp. 249-57, 282, 286, 309, 323-24, 378-79, 384, 398-99, 406-8, 435-514. See also Norman H. Murdoch, "The Salvation Army and the Church of England, 1882-1883," *Historical Magazine* 55 (March 1986): 32.

52. Roger J. Green, *War on Two Fronts: The Redemptive Theology of William Booth* (Atlanta, 1989), pp. 100-102; Roger J. Green, "Theological Roots of *In Darkest England and the Way Out,*" pp. 83-105; Roger J. Green, "The Theology of William Booth," pp. 13-15, 19, 25, 30-31, 96-99, 126-49. Even Inglis offers evidence to support Green's thesis, with a catalogue of all the Army's social-relief activities in the decade before the "Darkest England" scheme was announced (see *Churches and the Working Class in Victorian England,* pp. 197-99); Needham, "Mission in Community," pp. 112-73.

53. Amos G. Warner, *American Charities* (New York, 1894), pp. 244-62; Wilbur F. Crafts, "The Age of Reforms," *Homiletic Review* 19 (May 1890): 480 ("promiscuous alms-giving" quotation); Capt. McFee, "The San Francisco Lifeboat," *Conq* 4 (January 1895): 29; AWC, 6 February 1892, pp. 1, 4-5; 18 March 1893, p. 11; "Our New York Lighthouse," *Conq* 1 (February 1892): 11; Lt. Col. Norman J. Winterbottom states that the use of kettles began in San Francisco in 1893 ("The Salvation Army Western Territory . . . Chronology," manuscript in SATHQ/W, Personnel Dept.).

54. Parker, *My Fifty-Eight Years,* pp. 154-55; Lyman Abbott, "The Personal Problem of Charity," *The Forum,* February 1894, pp. 667-68; "Social Progress in the United States," *Harbor Lights,* May 1898, p. 142; Bosch, "The Salvation Army in Chicago," pp. 277-85; Comm. Frederick Booth-Tucker, *The Salvation Army in the United States* (New York, 1899), n.p. (contains a complete survey of SA social activities in 1899); "Odds-and-Ends Charity," *Harper's Weekly,* 2 December 1899, p. 1220 plus illustration; Order No. 20, "The Salvation Army Special Orders to Social Officers," gold-stamped binder, signed by Edward J. Parker and dated 1 December 1910, SAARC; interview with Sr/Maj. Railton F. Spake, Los Angeles, 11 December 1978.

55. AWC, 16 June 1894, p. 11; 28 July 1900, p. 5; Minutes for 1 March 1897 (Busby Coll.).

56. Jacob A. Riis, *The Making of an American* (New York, 1902), pp. 387-88; William T. Stead, *If Christ Came to Chicago* (Chicago, 1894), p. 269; William Hayes Ward, "The Salvation Army," *Harper's Weekly,* 2 December 1893, p. 1147; Walter Besant, "The Farm and the City," *Living Age,* 29 January 1898, pp. 306, 314; Walter Rauschenbusch, *The Social Principles of Jesus* (New York, 1916), p. 5; Richard T. Ely, "The Simple Gospel of Christ," in *Social Aspects of Christianity and Other Essays* (New York, 1889), pp. 27-29; Washington Gladden, "Religion and Wealth," *Bibliotheca Sacra* 52 (January 1895): 160; Henry F. May, *Protestant Churches and Industrial America* (1949; reprint, New York, 1963), pp. 91-111, 121-22.

57. Rev. Newell Woolsey Wells, "The Lawful Limitations of Charity," *Homiletic Review* 18 (August 1889): 123-26; Warner, *American Charities,* pp. 437-56; "Organized Help," *Charities* 1 (December 1897): 4; John R. Commons, *Social Reform and the Church* (New York, 1894), pp. 13-14, 17, 20-21, 24-26, 46-47, 58-63; Edward T. Devine, "Co-operation among Societies," *Charities* 1 (October 1898): 8. For the assertion that the COS had become alms-givers, see Alexander Johnson, "Concerning Certain Wise Limits to Charity Organization Society Work," *American Journal of Sociology* 5 (November 1899): 322-28 (quotation); and Charles Meredith Hubbard, "Relations of Charity-Organization Societies to Relief Societies and Relief-Giving," *American Journal of Sociology* 6 (May 1901): 783-84, 786; Lamb, *The Social Work of The Salvation Army* (New York, 1909), pp. 133-34. See also Inglis, *Churches and the Working Class,* pp. 200-201.

58. Winchell, "Chicago," p. 58; AWC, 16 September 1893; 15 September 1894, p. 8; 20 October 1894, p. 2; Bosch, "The Salvation Army in Chicago," pp. 115-16, 121-23; James E. Beane: *'That Terrible Summer': The Salvation Army and the Great Pullman Strike of 1894* (New York, 1977), SAARC.

59. Victor Bailey speaks of the "profoundly ambiguous" relationship between the Army and London radicalism in the 1880s ("The Salvation Army, Social Reform and the Labour Movement, 1885-1910," pp. 133-35, 137-38). See also Gertrude Himmelfarb, *Poverty and Compassion: The Moral Imagination of the Late Victorians* (New York, 1991),

pp. 226-27; Booth, *The Salvation Fight under the Stars and Stripes,* p. 45; WCW, 20 July 1895 (Milsaps WCC, 1); 14 September 1897, pp. 6, 14 (labor quotes); AWC, 27 June 1891, p. 6; Josiah Strong, *Religious Movements for Social Betterment* (New York, 1900), p. 33 ("Now it is very significant that the working multitudes who shun the churches flock to the meetings of the Salvation Army"); AWC, 28 April 1888, p. 8 (labor made tractable). The Army was remarkably frank about its value to captains of industry in this regard; see "The Capitalist's Debt to the Salvation Army," LD, 3 January 1914, p. 24 (quoting Evangeline Booth, "Why the Capitalist Should Help the Salvation Army," AWC, 27 December 1913). A contemporary history text made special note of the fact that The Salvation Army avoided "any programme of social or political reform," and did not announce "any manifesto of human rights," yet "uplifted hordes of the fallen, while drawing to the lowliest the notice, sympathy, and help of the middle classes and the rich" (E. Benjamin Andrews, *History of The United States from the Earliest Discovery of America to the End of 1902,* vol. 5 [New York, 1903], p. 120). For developments out West, see the issue of the *Pacific Union Printer,* San Francisco, for February 1895 (Milsaps SB 2:71) and Milsaps Diary, 4 November 1897.

60. AWC, 25 December 1886, p. 1; Milsaps WCC, 2:303, 353, and *passim;* Magnuson, "Salvation in the Slums," pp. 124-25, 129.

61. Staff Capt. Crafts, "Dollars and Cents," *Conq* 3 (July 1895): 309 ("self-support" quotation); "Are Our People Generous?" *The Officer* 3 (April 1895): 115 ("remarkably low" quotation); Booth, *Order and Regulations for Staff Officers, 1904,* p. 81; notarized financial statement issued by Frank Smith, 1 December 1884–31 July 1885, showing that WC sales amounted to 52 percent of all Army income (item in SFOT/E Museum, G/F "Moore"). For this reason it was practically impossible for an officer to reduce his weekly order for *War Crys:* see AWC, 4 February 1888, p. 5; Milsaps Diary, 20 July 1901; "Old Facts for New Friends," *Conq* 2 (May 1893): 182 (last quotation).

62. On Auxiliaries, see AWC, 20 August 1887, p. 9; WCW, 15 November 1887; 15 December 1887, p. 7; 9 March 1889, pp. 8-9; 18 January 1890, p. 13; 15 October 1892; Dr. Lyman Abbott, "Why I Am an Auxiliary," *Conq* 4 (January 1895): 41; Maj. T. C. Marshall, "The Auxiliary League," *Conq* 6 (May 1897): 109; *Harper's Weekly,* 22 December 1894, p. 1216; Wisbey, "Religion in Action," pp. 94, 197-98.

63. *The Conqueror* 1 (February 1892), frontispiece, pp. 1-3; Walsh, "The Salvation Army as a Social Reformer," p. 329 (Chautauqua quotation); AWC, 3 April 1886, pp. 1, 4 (Cleveland), also in Railton, *Twenty-One Years Salvation Army,* p. 142; AWC, 10 December 1892, p. 3 (Harrison); also WCW, 9 May 1892 in Milsaps SB 2:28-29; WCW, 18 January 1896, p. 4 (McKinley); and AWC, 14 August 1897, pp. 8, 13.

64. Robert Sandall, *The History of The Salvation Army,* 6 vols (London, 1950), 2:241; AWC, 7 April 1894, p. 13; 25 November 1893, pp. 8, 12; "Personal Reminiscences of Commissioner Gifford," pp. 35-36; Booth, *Beneath Two Flags,* p. 63; "The Major of the Empire State," *Conq* 2 (January 1893), p. 29; Hughes, "Our Heritage, The Army," pp. 3, 15; Booth, *The Salvation Fight under the Stars and Stripes,* pp. 37-38; AWC, 31 October 1903; 2 May 1891, in Milsaps WCC, 3:163, 320; Milsaps Diary, 14 May 1898; AWC, 31 July 1886, p. 1; 22 March 1890, pp. 1-2; "A Maid of Connecticut," *Conq* 4 (February 1895): pp. 62-63; Milsaps SB, 2:25 ("dina might" letter).

65. WCW, 15 February 1887, p. 1; Brewer, *Lifting the Veil,* p. 11; WCW, 1 February 1887; Milsaps WCC, 1:1-2; interview with James T. Stillwell, Suffern, N.Y., 12 July 1978;

"Maid of Connecticut," pp. 63-65; AWC, 30 May 1885, p. 3; 1 August 1885, p. 1; 24 July 1886, p. 1; 28 July 1888, p. 9; 18 August 1888, p. 12; 11 January 1890, pp. 1-2; Marks, *Facts about the Salvation Army,* pp. 202-9; Railton, *Twenty-One Years Salvation Army,* p. 141 (quote).

66. "The Gospel and the Poor in Our Cities," *Homiletic Monthly* 8 (December 1883): 168-70 (quotation); Samuel Lane Loomis, "Christian Work in London, II — Dissenting Churches — Other Movements," *Andover Review* 8 (July 1887): 31. For examples of advocacy of at least some of the methods adopted by the Army, see George F. Pentecost, "Evangelization of Our Cities: Obstacles on the Way," *Homiletic Review* 10 (November 1885): 401-3; George F. Pentecost, "Evangelization of Our Cities: How Shall We Evangelize Them?" *Homiletic Review* 10 (December 1885): 476-81; George F. Pentecost, "Applied Christianity II — How Shall Our Cities Be Evangelized?" *Homiletic Review* 13 (April 1887): 287-96; Loomis, *Modern Cities and Their Religious Problems,* pp. 182-211; and Charles A. Dickinson, "The Problem of the Modern City Churches," *Andover Review* 12 (October 1889): 366-67. On Catholic opinion, see "The 'Salvation Army' in Great Britain," *Catholic World* 36 (October 1882): 178 (quotation), 181-85. For other examples of Catholic opinion, see Gilbert Simmons, "The Salvation Army and Its Latest Project," *Catholic World* 52 (February 1891): 633, 642-43. See also Bosch, "The Salvation Army in Chicago," pp. 83-85.

67. Royal L. Melendy, "The Saloon in Chicago," *American Journal of Sociology* 6 (November 1900): 292-93.

68. Three saloons folded in Danbury during the Army's first two years there. See *Danbury News Times,* 12 November 1887 (Francis matl.); Booth, *The Salvation Fight under the Stars and Stripes,* p. 7 (quotation); Ernest H. Crosby, "The Saloon as a Political Power," *Forum,* May 1889, p. 325. See also Charles F. Deems, "The First National Temperance Congress," *Homiletic Review* 21 (January 1891): 30-31; H. L. Wayland, "The Privileged Law-Breaker, the American Saloon," *Homiletic Review* 22 (October 1891): 382-83; and "Law: Case of Interest," *Christian Advocate,* 24 March 1898, p. 501. The figures on political meetings in saloons are from "Liquor Traffic," in *The Encyclopedia of Social Reforms,* 2d ed., ed. William D. P. Bliss (New York, 1899), p. 821; Charles H. Sheldon, *In His Steps* (1896; reprint, Grand Rapids, 1967), pp. 88-96, 110, 113-15; James F. Richardson, *The New York Police: Colonial Times to 1901* (New York, 1970), pp. 182-85, 280-84; Sandall, *The History of The Salvation Army,* 2:239-40; Stead, *If Christ Came to Chicago* pp. 49-68, 303-7, 379; Herbert Asbury, *The Barbary Coast* (New York, 1933), p. 245; Bosch, "The Salvation Army in Chicago," pp. 22-23; Booth, *From Ocean to Ocean,* pp. 91-92; Smith, *Salvation War in America, 1885,* pp. 17-50; *Facts Concerning the Recent Outrage upon Religious Liberty at Galion, O* (Cleveland, 1893), Seiler Coll.; WCW, 18 July 1891 (Milsaps WCC, 2:106), states that it was "simply impossible" to list all of those who were arrested "because so many have suffered that way for Christ." The Army was not the only victim of police persecution; any group of street evangelists whose message of temperance and moral reform was likely to penetrate saloons and "infamous houses" was liable to be arrested. In 1904 and 1905 a group of evangelists, pastors, and reformers who staged midnight gospel meetings in Chicago's Custom House Place were arrested by police whom the evangelists believed had been brought on the scene by the saloon keepers and procurers whose trades were threatened (see Ernest A. Bell, "Slum Missions — Street Evangelism — Mid-Night Meetings," in *Catching Men: Studies in Vital Evangelism,* ed. J. P. Brushingham [Cincinnati, 1906], pp. 115-16).

69. The references to Joe the Turk in Army literature and reminiscences are voluminous. See, e.g., Capt. Joseph Garabed, "Joe the Turk," AWC, 26 March 1892, p. 4; Capt. Joseph Garabed, "In Prison Oft: Joe the Turk Still 'Moves Around,'" *The Officer,* October 1895; Adj. William Harris, "Joe the Turk," WCE, 6 January 1934, p. 4; WCW, 30 October 1937. Joe's entire Army career was spent as a "spiritual special," although he was given an official appointment as a traveling salesman for the Trade Department. He retired in 1925 as a staff captain and died in 1937.

70. WCW, 31 December 1892, p. 1 ("dangers" quotation); *Harbor Lights* (January 1898), p. 27 ("felicitous feature" quotation); AWC, 10 December 1892, p. 4; letter from Ballington to all divisional officers, New York City, 22 November 1889 (Holz Coll.); *The Salvation Army and Its Lessons* (New York, [1892]), p. 3. On the fact that Army leaders welcomed persecution, see Railton, *Heathen England,* p. 38; and Booth, *Orders and Regulations for Field Officers, 1901,* pp. 245-70: "In any real work for God the F.O. must expect opposition. War supposes this." AWC, 30 May 1885, p. 1 (Smith at Newark).

71. WCW, 11 June 1892, pp. 1-3, 6-7, 8-9; 18 June 1892, pp. 3-5, 9; 25 June 1892, pp. 1-7; 2 July 1892, pp. 3-5; Cadet M. W. Flaherty, "Behind Steeds of Salvation," *Conq* 3 (August 1894): 315; letter from T. E. Wood to the author, Ocean Grove, N.J., dated 15 September 1978; Commandant Julius H. Abrams, *Out of the House of Judah* (New York, 1923), pp. 84-85, 119-29, 145-47. For a photograph of the eleven-piece Charioteers' Band taken during the summer of 1893, see Milsaps WCC, 3:181. On disbanding the Charioteers, see WCW, 29 February 1896 and 7 March 1896, p. 7,

72. Brian W. Dippie, "Charlie Russell's Lost West," *American Heritage* 24 (April 1973): 7-9, 12.

73. AWC, 23 June 1894, pp. 1, 13; 8 September 1894, p. 5; 15 September 1894, p. 8; 3 November 1894, p. 13; WCW, 7 July 1894, pp. 1-2; 8 September 1894, cover (shows the "Advance on Hawaii"; Milsaps WCC, 1:51); 15 September 1894, pp. 1-3; 13 October 1894, pp. 1-3; "The Salvation Army in Hawaii" (material collected from state archives by Lt. Col. N. J. Winterbottom, 1963, and held in a brown binder, SATHQ/W Personnel Department. As early as 1887 a Sgt. Rutherford of Sausalito corps went off to evangelize Hawaii, but he seems to have disappeared in the process. WCW, 15 February 1887, p. 3.

74. WCW, 13 October 1894, p. 2; AWC, 22 September 1888, p. 7; Brig. Alice Lewis, "The Naval and Military League," *Conq* 5 (October 1896): 476; Booth, *Orders and Regulations for Staff Officers, 1904,* pp. 181-82 ("The Naval and Military Secretary"); WCW, 10 October 1896, p. 2.

75. AWC, 21 May 1898, cover; 14 May 1898, pp. 4, 9; 21 May 1898, pp. 4, 16; 28 May 1898, pp. 4-5; 4 June 1898, pp. 4-5; 25 June 1898, pp. 4-5; 2 July 1898, p. 5; 9 July 1898, p. 4; *Harbor Lights,* June 1898, p. 183; July 1898, p. 213; WCW, 11 June 1898, pp. 1-2.

76. AWC, 21 May 1898, p. 5 (Olympia); Milsaps Diary, 19 May–25 June 1898; for orders and preparations for sailing, see vol. 4, pp. 1-5.

77. Milsaps SB, vol. 3 contains letter from Col. W. Evans for Milsaps to use as an authorization ("attend" quotation); Milsaps Diary entry for 29 June 1898 describes his twenty months of work in the Philippines; Maj. John Milsaps, "Reminiscences," WCC, 23 April 1921 through 22 January 1922 (19 articles); Maj. John Milsaps, "The Salvation Army Sails with General Merritt's Expedition for the Philippines," *Harbor Lights* 1 (August 1898): 231-34; "In the Philippines," *Harbor Lights,* November 1898, pp. 337-41; Decem-

ber 1898, pp. 375-77; and "Five Memorable Nights in the Philippines," July 1899, pp. 219-22; August 1899, pp. 255-59.

NOTES TO CHAPTER 3

1. Ensign [J. C.] Ludgate, "A Typical Open-Air Meeting," AWC, 14 March 1898, p. 13; *All about The Salvation Army, by Those Who Know* (New York, 1890), p. 5 (quotation); AWC, 22 August 1896, entire issue; on Price oration at Baker, see AWC, 9 July 1892, p. 15; "Thirty-Fourth Annual Commencement of Baker University, 1892" [program], kindly provided by Maxine Kreutziger, Kansas East Commission on Archives and History, Baker University, Baldwin City, Kans., under cover of letter to author, Baldwin City, 11 February 1992; Prof. Charles A. Briggs, "The Salvation Army," *North American Review* 159 (December 1894): 710 (quotation).

2. AWC, 10 December 1892, pp. 4, 9; WCW, 22 February 1897; Cmdr. Ballington Booth, *A Manifesto for 1895 to the Staff and Field Officers of The Salvation Army in the United States* (New York, 1895), n.p. (Seiler Coll.). Contemporary writers often criticized the Army's statistical methods. See Rev. Donald Fraser, "The Salvation Army," *Presbyterian Review* 7 (April 1886): 262; and "The Churches Are Described by Themselves," *Christian Advocate,* 20 January 1898, p. 92.

3. "The Headquarters of The Salvation Army," *Harper's Weekly,* 30 March 1895, p. 293; WCW, 3 August 1895, p. 7; AWC, 17 June 1893, p. 9; 1 September 1894, pp. 1, 4-5; Herbert A. Wisbey, Jr., "Religion in Action: A History of The Salvation Army in the United States" (Ph.D. diss., Columbia University, 1951), pp. 194-95. William Booth started the Self-Denial Fund in 1886; see WCE, 19 March 1932, p. 2.

4. J. J. Keppel to Booth-Tucker, Chicago, 18 September 1898, Wood Coll., SAARC ("everlasting beg"); Ensign William Harris, "Looking Back Long Liberty Trail," WCE, 11 August 1928, p. 11; "The Reminiscences of Commissioner Gifford," [1930], private collection, pp. 39-43. On the training process, see *All about The Salvation Army* (Brooklyn, 1884), p. 14; George Ethelbert Walsh, "The Salvation Army as a Social Reformer," *The Chautauquan* 17 (June 1893): 330; menu at Jersey City in 1894 found in "Another Bethlehem Story: The Story of Brigadier and Mrs. John Waldron," ed. Brig. Leland Waldron, undated 96-page photocopy, p. 20, courtesy Brig. Leland Waldron.

5. AWC, 27 August 1887, p. 5; William Hayes Ward, "The Salvation Army," *Harper's Weekly,* 2 December 1897, p. 1147. On the Montgomeries, see "Mr. & Mrs. Montgomery," AWC, 11 June 1892, pp. 1, 4; and Carrie Judd Montgomery, "The Wing Life," *Conq* 3 (March 1894): 85-87. On the Vapo-Cresolene endorsement, see *Munsey's Magazine,* June 1896, p. 57. The product was also advertised in the SA's own catalogue of trade goods; see *The Salvation Army Price List of Publications, Outfit Goods, Musical Instruments, Etc.* (New York, n.d. [pre-1896]), p. 42.

6. *The Musical Pioneer* (New York, 1890), pp. 1-2, in SATHQ/E, Music Dept; SA *Songbook,* 1987 Edition, no. 758 ("Cross Is Not Greater"); AWC, 3 September 1887, p. 8; Maud Ballington Booth to "My dear and prayed for Girl," New York City, 31 May 1888 (SAARC RG 20.47, 47/1); Maud B. Booth to Mrs. R. E. Holz, New York, 23 January 1890 (a note of concern about sick children, signed "Your sister in sympathy and in love of the War, which Christ is helping us to wage"), Holz Coll.

7. Comm. Ballington Booth, *From Ocean to Ocean; or, The Salvation Army's March from the Atlantic to the Pacific* (New York, 1891), autograph inscription in flyleaf, copy in Circle "M" Collection, Houston RCC, M267.15B ("who daily yearns"); Lt. Col. Wallace Winchell, "Shall the Saloon Come Back?" WCE, 9 July 1932, p. 3; Ballington's *Herald* articles were later reprinted as *New York's Inferno Explored* (New York, 1891), SFOT/E library; Jno. Gilmer Speed, "The Salvation Army Congress," *Harper's Weekly*, 3 December 1892, p. 1166.

8. J. J. Keppel to Booth-Tucker, Chicago, 16 September 1898, Wood Collection, SAARC: "The Ordination of Ballington Booth," *The Outlook*, 3 October 1896, pp. 618-19.

9. The diary of Maj. John Milsaps is filled with references to what he and others derided as "Boothism," a charge he leveled not only at Ballington but at his successors the Booth-Tuckers and Evangeline Booth as well. See diary entries for 25 April 1900, 5 June 1900, 11 October 1900, and 18 May 1901 for samples; the diaries are filled with similar sentiments, which Milsaps claimed were widespread among American officers.

10. SFOT/E Museum, B/F, "Split--Ballington," statement regarding resignation.

11. AWC, 14 April 1894, p. 5; 22 September 1894, p. 16; 29 September 1894, pp. 1, 4; 27 October 1894, *passim;* original poster and Booth's handwritten instruction to printer in Seiler Coll.; "The General's Journeys in North America," *Conq* 4 (April 1895): 153-65; "The Salvation Army Jubilee," *Harper's Weekly*, 3 November 1894, p. 1048; William Booth to Emma Booth-Tucker, London, 22 April 1896 ("Yankee Doodleism"), in SFOT/E Museum B/F, "Split — Ballington." On the pulpit warning, see AWC, 17 November 1894, p. 9.

12. Maud B. Booth, *Beneath Two Flags* (New York, 1890), pp. 130, 215; Col. [William] Evans, "At '111,' " AWC, 22 October 1892, p. 9. For a list of all divisional staff leaders at this time, see AWC, 9 January 1892, p. 13; 19 March 1892, p. 13. Only three of the eighteen divisional leaders appeared on Evans's list in the October 22 article; "Old Facts for New Friends," *Conq* 2 (May 1893): 182; see also Milsaps Diary references in note 21 below. On English officers and native converts, see, e.g., the account in Edmund M. Gagey, "General Booth with His Big Bass Drum Enters into Haverhill, Massachusetts," *New England Quarterly* 45 (December 1972): 510. For the "English, You Know" song, see George Ethelbert Walsh, "The Salvation Army as a Social Reformer," *The Chautauquan* 17 (June 1893): 333. For samples of public comment on foreign control or influence over the Army, see Rev. Donald Fraser, "The Salvation Army," *Presbyterian Review* 7 (April 1886): 263; and "Salvation by Noise," *The Nation*, 3 June 1897, p. 411.

13. Susan Fulton Welty, *Look Up and Hope! The Life of Maud Ballington Booth* (New York, 1961), pp. 90-95, 100-105; R. V. Trevel, "Maud Ballington Booth," in *Heroines of Modern Religion,* ed. Warren Dunham Foster (New York, 1913), pp. 242-44; printed letters from Ballington Booth, dated 29 February 1896 and 4 March 1896, Seiler Coll., binders; "Good American Salvation," *The Nation*, 5 March 1896, p. 191.

14. AWC, 8 February 1896, p. 9; WCW, 15 February 1896, p. 7. The last word from the Booths in the WC was a letter to the American troops announcing their farewell; there was no hint of resignation.

15. *New York Herald*, 2 March 1896, p. 6; "The Salvation Army Troubles," *The Outlook,* 7 March 1896, p. 426; "Good American Salvation," p. 190; WCW, 21 March 1896, p. 8; Brig. E. Fielding to Gen. William Booth, Chicago, 23 February 1896, Busby

Coll. and SAARC; "Salvation by Noise," p. 411 ("element of nationality"); "The Salvation Army," *Homiletic Review* 31 (April 1896): 385 ("despotism"); "About the World: The Salvation Army Crisis," *Scribner's Magazine,* May 1896, p. 658.

16. WCW, 11 April 1896, p. 6; AWC, 4 April 1896, p. 9; supplement to AWC, 2 May 1896, following p. 8; Adam Gifford to Ballington and Maud Booth, 10 January 1896, Gifford Coll.; J. Garabed to Mrs. Ballington Booth, Boston, 5 May 1896 (SFOT/E Museum, G/F, "Joe the Turk, Correspondence").

17. Maud B. Booth, *Beneath Two Flags: A Study in Mercy and Help Methods* (1889; reprint, Cincinnati, 1894), p. 215; *New York Herald,* 2 March 1896, p. 6. Maj. Milsaps, the California pioneer, was a mainstay of loyalty; see Milsaps Diary entries for 15 January 1917, 2 April 1897, 11 April 1897, 25 May 1897, 1 March 1898, 1 April 1898, 12 June 1898, and 5 October 1898; A. M. Nicol, *General Booth and The Salvation Army* (London, n.d.), pp. 233-49; [Maj. T. C. Marshall], "The Editor's Pen," *Conq* 4 (April 1896): 172 ("grandest examples"); Sallie Chesham, *Born to Battle: The Salvation Army in America* (New York, 1965), p. 98; Ronald W. Holz, *Heralds of Victory: A History Celebrating the 100th Anniversary of the New York Staff Band and Male Chorus, 1887-1987* (New York, 1986), p. 12; interview with Lt. Col. Edward Laity, Atlanta, 24 November 1978; Brig. Richard Holz to Ballington Booth, Binghamton, N.Y., 24 July 1896, and Ballington Booth to Holz, New York City, 22 June 1896, both in Seiler Coll., binders.

18. AWC, 11 June 1887, p. 8; WCW, 21 March 1896, p. 8; interview with Col. Bertram Rodda, Oakland, 12 December 1978; material on Capt. William Brewer in SA Editorial Department, *Odds against Him: A Brief Sketch of the Career of Colonel Arthur T. Brewer Prepared for the Occasion of His Honorable Retirement on April 24, 1933* (1933; reprint, Chicago, 1989), pp. 33-34; letter to author from Mrs. Comm. Robert Rightmire, Whiting, New Jersey, 5 February 1992; Allan Whitworth Bosch, "The Salvation Army in Chicago: 1885-1914" (Ph.D. diss., University of Chicago, 1965), p. 135; Clarence W. Hall, *Samuel Logan Brengle: Portrait of a Prophet* (Chicago, 1933), pp. 96-99; Chesham, *Born to Battle,* pp. 98-99; Comm. Samuel Logan Brengle, *The Soul-Winner's Secret* (London, n.d.), p. 55 (last quotation).

19. AWC, 28 March 1896, pp. 8-9; "Consul and Commander Booth-Tucker," *Conq* 5 (May 1896): 203-4; preface by Booth-Tucker in *The Officer* 1 (January 1893); Commander [Frederick] Booth-Tucker, *The Consul* (London, 1903), pp. 106-7; interview with Mrs. Edmund C. Hoffman, Asbury Park, N.J., 23 June 1978; WCE, 3 January 1948, pp. 1, 3, (on the death of Gen. Higgins, who served as a staff officer on the American field 1896-1905). Gertrude Himmelfarb refers to Booth-Tucker as the first "gentleman" to join Booth's Army in London in a note on p. 223 of *Poverty and Compassion: The Moral Imagination of the Late Victorians* (New York, 1991).

20. *New York Herald,* 2 April 1896, p. 5; AWC, 4 April 1896, p. 9; SFOT/E Museum, B/F, "Split — Ballington," has several pieces of important correspondence on the crisis; Mrs. Col. Carpenter, "Consul Emma Booth-Tucker," in *Some Notable Officers of The Salvation Army* (London, 1926), p. 26; AWC, 5 March 1904, pp. 1, 8, on the death of Sen. Mark Hanna.

21. "Salvation by Noise," p. 411; Milsaps Diary, 8 March 1897, 10 March 1897, 21 February 1899, 11 April 1899, 22 June 1899, 13 July 1899, 2 June 1902; Booth-Tucker, *The Consul,* p. 116; WCW, 11 April 1896, pp. 1, 6-7; 2 May 1896; 9 May 1896, *passim;* 23 May 1896, pp. 1, 2, 6-7; Bosch, "The Salvation Army in Chicago," pp. 133-38.

22. James E. Beane, *The Incorporation of The Salvation Army in the United States, 1882-1899* (New York, 1975), pp. 10-11 (SAARC); Frederick Booth-Tucker to the Chief of the Staff, New York, 22 December 1898 ("boodlers"), in SFOT/E Museum, G/F, "Moore"; AWC, 13 May 1899, p. 8; *The Salvation Army Incorporated in the State of New York, Certificate of Incorporation and By-laws* (New York, n.d.), courtesy Col. William Bearchell.

23. Rev. Josiah Strong, "The Salvation Army in the United States," AWC, 22 December 1900, p. 3; Maj. J. C. Ludgate, "Conducting Open-Airs Singlehanded," AWC, 23 August 1902, p. 5; WCW, 7 April 1900, p. 3; 15 June 1897 in Milsaps WCC, 1:81; Minute no. 61, 25 March 1898, on uniform, in Busby Coll. and SAARC; see also no. 77, 10 October 1901. For a sample of references to the Army in professional reform literature, see C. R. Henderson, *The Social Spirit in America* (Meadville, Pa., 1897), pp. 317-19; William D. P. Bliss, *The Encyclopedia of Social Reforms,* 2d ed. (New York, 1898), pp. vi, 1212-13; Edward Allsworth Ross, "Social Control, VI," *American Journal of Sociology* 2 (January 1897): 559-60; "Century Advance, July 1, 1899–December 31, 1900, Plan of Campaign, by Commander Booth-Tucker" (brochure in Holz. Coll.; photocopy SAARC); *Guide to the Fall and Winter Red Crusade of 1903-1904 by the Commander,* Seiler Coll. binders; Booth-Tucker, *The Consul,* 139; AWC, 29 January 1898, p. 8 ("we met").

24. Booth-Tucker lists many of the powerful friends of the Army who paid tribute to the Consul at her funeral in *The Consul,* pp. 107-8, 125, 130-31, 164-66, 177, 178-79. On the flow of directives, see Minutes, no. 45, 3 December 1895; no. 46, 11 August 1896, Busby Coll. and SAARC.

25. "The Great Inauguration Council," *Conq* 5 (August 1896): 350-52; "The Training of Officers," *Harbor Lights,* October 1899, pp. 302-6.

26. "The Social Reform Work of The Salvation Army," in *The Encyclopedia of Social Reforms,* 2d ed., ed. William D. P. Bliss (New York, 1898), pp. 1212-15; Commander [Frederick] Booth-Tucker, *The Salvation Army in the United States* (New York, 1899), n.p.; Bosch, "The Salvation Army in Chicago," pp. 251-55, 302-5; *Mended Links: The Annual Report of The Salvation Army's Rescue Work in the United States, 1903* (New York, [1903]), p. 17 (SAARC); AWC, 23 August 1902, pp. 1, 9; 31 August 1901, pp. 9, 12; 5 September 1908, cover; 15 November 1902, p. 4; 13 December 1902, p. 14; 31 January 1903, p. 5; 14 February 1903, p. 5; 21 February 1903, p. 4; WCW, 28 November 1896, pp. 1-3; Maj. [Samuel L.] Brengle, "A Few Notes on My Western Trip," *Conq* 6 (November 1897): 259; Staff Capt. Merriweather, "A Jail Conversion," *Harbor Lights* 1 (April 1898): 128; WCW, 18 August 1900, p. 3; Booth-Tucker, *The Consul,* p. 118.

27. Minutes, no. 84, 20 June 1902 (Busby Coll. and SAARC); *The Little Soldier,* 26 November 1885, pp. 2, 4 (Seiler Coll., binders); AWC, 22 January 1887, p. 8; interview with Mrs. Edmund C. Hoffman, and see her testimony in WCE, 1 June 1929, pp. 4, 11.

28. Minutes, no. 28, 6 October 1891 (Busby Coll.); AWC, 16 June 1894, p. 13; *The Salvation Army Band of Love International Music Drills* (London, 1899), SFOT/E Museum, G/F, "Band of Love"; Staff Capt. Winant, "The American Junior Soldier War," *Conq* 5 (January 1896): 10-11; Minutes, no. 64, 13 May 1898 (Busby Coll.); Brig. William Halpin, "The Children for Jesus," *Harbor Lights* 1 (April 1898): 124-25; AWC, 3 June 1899, pp. 2-3.

29. "East Side Babies of New York," *Harbor Lights* 3 (August 1900): 235-37 ("portal" quotation); Maud Ballington Booth, "Salvation Army Work in the Slums,"

Scribner's Magazine 17 (January 1895): 112-13 ("first day nursery"); AWC, 12 November 1904, p. 10; G. D. Whelpley, "Salvation Army Colonies," *Harper's Weekly*, 7 September 1901, p. 902; AWC, 27 August 1898, p. 11; photographic album of Lytton Boys and Girls Home, SATHQ/W Property Dept., SAARC; AWC, 6 October 1900, pp. 4, 8; 13 October 1900, p. 4; 20 October 1900, p. 7 (on Cincinnati fire).

30. On the common practice of visiting New York slums in disguise, see Luc Sante, *Low Life: Lures and Snares of Old New York* (New York, 1991), pp. 128-29, 283-86, 295-96; Sante states that by the late 1890s, tours of slums, dives, and Chinatown had become a cottage industry: New York was a kind of "theme park of squalor." A notorious local character, Steve Brodie, even took William Booth on a tour of Chinatown on one of his American tours! AWC, 23 May 1896, pp. 1-2; *New York Herald*, 24 April 1896, p. 12; 29 April 1896, p. 5; "Salvation by Noise," p. 411; WCW, 15 August 1896, p. 4; Aaron Ignatius Abell, *The Urban Impact on American Protestantism, 1865-1900* (1943; reprint, Hamden, Conn., 1962), p. 135; WCW, 18 July 1896, p. 8; Minutes, no. 47, 21 October 1896, allowing divisional officers to staff corps with persons who had not completed the "usual six months' training" (Busby Coll. and SAARC). See also Milsaps Diary, 31 May 1898.

31. Booth-Tucker, *The Salvation Army in the United States;* Milsaps Diary, 4 November 1897; Minutes, no. 52, 30 November 1896; no. 54, 7 June 1897; no. 70, 10 October 1898; no. 74, 20 October 1900; no. 81, 20 June 1902 (all on Mercy Box league); for attitude on appeals, see Minutes, no. 80, 20 February 1902 (Busby Coll.); Adjutant Maltby, *The Poor Man's Church: Report of The Salvation Army (Incorporated) in Meadville, for the Year Ending March 25, 1900* (Meadville, Pa., 1900), courtesy Col. Maltby.

32. William Booth, *In Darkest England and the Way Out* (London, 1890), pp. 100-159.

33. Lyman Abbott, "The Personal Problem of Charity," *The Forum*, February 1894, pp. 663-65; Josephine Shaw Lowell, "The True Aim of Charity Organization Societies," *The Forum*, June 1896, p. 495; Norris Alden Magnuson, "Salvation in the Slums: Evangelical Social Welfare Work, 1865-1920" (Ph.D. diss., University of Minnesota, 1968), p. 283; Marvin E. Gettleman, "Charity and Social Classes in the United States, 1874-1900," *American Journal of Economics and Sociology* 22 (April 1963): 327-29 and (July 1963): 417-18; "How to Help the Colony Funds," *Harbor Lights* 3 (October 1900): 308-9; Cmdr. [Frederick] Booth-Tucker, *The Social Relief Work of the Salvation Army in the United States* (Washington, 1900), p. 28; Staff Capt. Wm. H. Cox, "At the Lighthouse," AWC, 6 February 1892, p. 4.

34. "The Little Laborers of New York City," *Harper's Magazine* 47 (August 1873): 330 (quotation); "A Glimpse of Some of Our Charities," *Harper's Magazine* 56 (February 1878): 448 and (March 1878): 606; Henry George, *Progress and Poverty: An Inquiry into the Cause of Industrial Depressions, and of Increase of Want with Increase of Wealth; The Remedy* (New York, 1882), *passim;* Booth, *In Darkest England and the Way Out*, pp. 70, 83, 136; AWC, 10 October 1896, p. 8; 20 February 1897, p. 8; Frederick de Lautour Booth-Tucker, "The Farm Colonies of the Salvation Army," *The Forum*, August 1897, p. 752; [William H. Cox], "The Proposed Colonization Scheme: The Substance of an Interview with Commander Booth-Tucker," *Conq* 6 (September 1897): 201-2.

35. Booth-Tucker, *The Social Relief Work of the Salvation Army in the United States*, pp. 29-37; WCW, 25 August 1900, cover; "Draft Outline for Regulations for Vacant Lot

Farms," Holz Coll.; AWC, 27 March 1897, p. 14; 8 May 1897, pp. 10-11; 18 December 1897, pp. 2-3.

36. AWC, 21 January 1899, p. 5; Whelpley, "Salvation Army Colonies," p. 902; Booth-Tucker, *The Social Relief Work of the Salvation Army in the United States,* pp. 35-36; Milsaps Diary, 1 January 1898; Frederick Booth-Tucker, *Farm Colonies of The Salvation Army* (Washington, 1903), pp. 983-84; Dorothy Hitzka, *Farm Colonies of the Salvation Army and in Particular the Ft. Herrick Colony, Mentor, Ohio* (Cleveland, 1976), p. 6; SFOT/E Museum, G/F, "Farm Colonies (General)"; on the bill, see AWC, 9 April 1904, p. 8; 14 May 1904, p. 5; *The Congressional Record,* 3454-55 (1904), information courtesy Lt. Col. Ernest Miller; Clark C. Spence, "The Landless Man and the Manless Land," *Western Historical Quarterly* 16 (October 1985): 397-412; Clark C. Spence, *The Salvation Army Farm Colonies* (Tucson, 1985).

37. Staff Capt. (Jay Bee) Burrows, "Fort Amity, Col.," *Harbor Lights* 1 (June 1898): 172-73; AWC, 9 July 1898, p. 5; 29 March 1902, p. 4; 12 August 1905, p. 13; "Successful Farm Colonies," *The Outlook,* 11 July 1903, pp. 640-41; Whelpley, "Salvation Army Colonies," p. 902; interview with Mr. James T. Stillwell, Suffern, N.Y., 12 July 1978; SFOT/E Museum, G/F, "Farm Colony-Amity"; H. Rider Haggard, *The Poor and the Land: Being a Report on the Salvation Army Colonies in the United States and at Hadleigh England with Scheme for National Land Settlement* (London, 1905), pp. 67-72; Edwin Gifford Lamb, "The Social Work of The Salvation Army" (Ph.D. diss., Columbia University, 1909; privately printed), pp. 99-116; Marie Antalek, "The Amity Colony" (M.A. thesis, Kansas State Teachers' College, Emporia, 1968), pp. 37-76.

38. AWC, 17 September 1898, p. 9; Hitzka, *Farm Colonies of the Salvation Army,* pp. 10, 12-13, 30; *Church of the Black Sheep: Annual Report of The Salvation Army in Cleveland, 1898-1899,* n.p.; Haggard, *The Poor and the Land,* pp. 115-16, 119; Antalek, "The Amity Colony," pp. 34-36; R. E. Holz, national social secretary, to Cmdr. Booth-Tucker, New York, 8 March 1899 ("grumbling"), in Holz Coll.; AWC, 27 September 1913, pp. 1, 9.

39. AWC, 16 October 1897, p. 4; WCW, 23 October 1897 (in Milsaps WCC, 1:297); WCW, 9 October 1897, pp. 101-2; Haggard, *The Poor and the Land,* pp. 38-66; WCW, 11 August 1900, p. 7; 18 August 1900, p. 3; 28 July 1900 (in Milsaps WCC, 1:3); Milsaps Diary, 22 March 1897, 16 May 1897, 20 October 1897, 10 February 1898; Antalek, "The Amity Colony," pp. 30-34.

40. C. C. Carstens, "Shall Salvation Army Take the Public into Its Confidence?" *Charities,* 27 April 1907, p. 118; C. C. Carstens, "The Salvation Army — A Criticism," *Annals of the American Academy of Political and Social Science* 30 (November 1907): 126-27; Milsaps Diary, 2 June 1900, 28 August 1900, 31 January 1901 (quotation); Spence, "The Landless Man and the Manless Land," pp. 402-3; Spence, *The Salvation Army Farm Colonies,* pp. 59, 63, 74.

41. Booth-Tucker, *The Consul,* pp. 9, 155-57, 176; AWC, 14 November 1903 and 21 November 1903, *passim;* 20 February 1904, pp. 1, 9; details about the two funerals of Emma Booth-Tucker were found in the diary of Brig. Alexander Damon (entries for 29-30 October and 1 and 3 November 1903), held in SAARC (RG 20.38, 229/5, Damon Diary 1903) and used with the kind permission of the Rader family; interview with Mrs. Edmund C. Hoffman, who attended the funeral; SA *Songbook,* 1953 ed., no. 457, and 1987 ed., no. 507; Seiler Coll. binders contain one of the purple-trimmed funeral programs.

42. "The Power of Organization," *Christian Advocate,* 5 March 1904, p. 325 (statistics); "Work in Other Churches: The Salvation Army in the United States," *Christian Advocate,* 22 December 1904, p. 2090; "Personal" column, *Christian Advocate,* 10 November 1904, p. 1832, and 24 November 1904, p. 1911 (statistics — which were almost certainly supplied by the Army); AWC, 27 August 1904, p. 8; Harry Edward Neal, *The Hallelujah Army* (Philadelphia, 1961), pp. 12-13.

43. The account of Eva's boarding the train in Buffalo came from the Damon Diary entry for 31 October 1903 (SAARC RG 20.38).

44. Commission issued to Evaline Cory Booth by Gen. William Booth, 9 November 1904 (Busby Coll.); Milsaps Diary, 6 January 1905; AWC, 26 November 1904, p. 9; 3 December 1904, p. 16; Damon Diary, entries for 19 January 1904 and 4 November 1904 (SAARC RG 20.39 229/G, Damon Diaries 1904).

45. Letter from William Booth to William McKinley, New York City, 4 April 1898 (SAARC RG 20.34, ARC 427, folder 15); AWC, 7 March 1903, pp. 6, 8; 23 April 1904, p. 7; William Hamilton Nelson, *Blood and Fire: General William Booth* (New York, 1929), pp. 228-30; Brig. Ashley Pebbles, "Our Responsibility for Those Who Have Failed Socially," *[SA] Western Congress Addresses* (Chicago, [1906]), p. 105; Charles Michael Williams, "The Drum: The Story of the Reclamation of a Young American Heathen," *Munsey's Magazine,* March 1903, pp. 895-98; Rick Mitchell, "The Salvation Army and Motion Pictures Project: First Draft Script by Rick Mitchell," unpublished typescript, 18 April 1988, p. 5, and letter from Rick Mitchell to Capt. Robert R. Hostetler, Los Angeles, 23 August 1991, both sent to the author under cover of a letter from Capt. Robert R. Hostetler, Youngstown, Ohio, 4 November 1991; Ronald W. Holz, "A History of the Hymn Tune Meditation and Related Forms in Salvation Army Instrumental Music in Great Britain and North America, 1880-1980" (Ph.D. diss., University of Connecticut, 1981), p. 274; Bosch, "The Salvation Army in Chicago," pp. 232-33.

46. Royal L. Melendy, "The Saloon in Chicago, II," *American Journal of Sociology* 6 (January 1901): 453-54; Lamb, "The Social Work of The Salvation Army," 69-70; Comm. Edward Justus Parker, *My Fifty-Eight Years: An Autobiography* (New York, 1943), pp. 152-53; Henry Jarvis, "A People's Palace," *The Outlook,* 2 June 1906; AWC, 4 February 1905, p. 7; 1 May 1915, p. 11; Bosch, "The Salvation Army in Chicago," p. 255; Ernest A. Bell, *Fighting the Traffic in Young Girls; or, War on the White Slave Trade* (Chicago, 1910), pp. 442-45, 475.

47. AWC, 23 August 1902, p. 2; 20 October 1906, p. 5; 27 October 1906, pp. 6-7; 31 July 1909, pp. 1-8; 26 August 1911, pp. 1, 8-9; Bosch, "The Salvation Army in Chicago," pp. 242-48; Col. R. E. Holz, "Brief on Ohio, Pittsburgh & Southern Providence, 1908," large brown binder, n.p., SAARC (account of Euclid Park trip, 9 July 1908); AWC, 25 July 1908, p. 3.

48. AWC, 14 August 1897, p. 7; 8 November 1913, p. 8.

49. Edwin L. Earp, *Social Aspects of Religious Institutions* (New York, 1908), pp. 54-67 (quotation pp. 54-55). For additional praise of the Army, see "Worthy of Honorable Mention," *Christian Advocate,* 23 October 1902, p. 1686; Frederick W. Farrar, "The Promise of Present Efforts to Reach the Submerged Masses," *Homiletic Review* 45 (January 1903): 8; "What the Salvation Army Is Doing," *Missionary Review of the World* 26 (February 1903): 149; "Starving in the Heart of Great Cities," *Christian Advocate,* 14 January 1904, pp. 44-45; Rev. Edward Judson, "The Church in Its Social Aspect," *Annals of the American*

Academy of Political and Social Science 30 (November 1907): 435. For an account of the Army's efforts during the Christmas season of 1899 (the Army claimed to have fed 130,000 at that time), see "How the Army Fed the Multitudes at Christmas," *Harbor Lights* 3 (February 1900): 40-42. The critical materials include "New York Letter," by "Stylus," in *Christian Advocate,* 2 January 1902, p. 18 ("shivering bell ringer" and "honestly worthy"); C. C. Carstens, "The Salvation Army — A Criticism," *Annals of the American Academy of Political and Social Science* 30 (November 1907): 545-56; and John Manson, *The Salvation Army and the Public* (New York, 1906), pp. 3-4, 17-37, 176-98. Edwin Gifford Lamb, *The Social Work of the Salvation Army* (New York, 1909), pp. 26, 133-38. On the Boston dispute, see AWC, 27 November 1909, pp. 8, 13; and 11 December 1909, pp. 1, 8-9, 12. See also Peter W. Stine, "Loaves and Fishes in Boston: A Modern Miracle" (New York, 1978), SAARC. On SA funding procedures, see Rev. S[tephen] B. Williams, *The Salvation Army Today* (Lincoln, Nebraska, 1914), pp. 19-20. For a favorable assessment of Army accounting procedures, see "The Business Methods of the Salvation Army," *Homiletic Review* 54 (December 1907): 426-28. Maj. John Milsaps disliked the Army's fund-raising policies and apparently knew of others who felt the same way; see Milsaps Diary, 21 August 1901 and 28 November 1902.

50. W. J. Ashley, "General Booth's Panacea," *Political Science Quarterly* 6 (September 1891): 459-550; WCC, 5 November 1927, p. 13; Bosch, "The Salvation Army in Chicago," pp. 192-96; SA cash account book, Princeton, Indiana, 1912-1916, in CTM; William Booth, *Orders and Regulations for Field Officers, 1901* (London, 1901), pp. 401, 525.

51. U.S. Department of Commerce, Bureau of the Census, *Special Reports: Religious Bodies: 1906,* 2 vols. (Washington, 1910), 2:613-20; George A. Coe, "Notes on the Recent Census of Religious Bodies," *American Journal of Sociology* 15 (May 1910): 806-9; Brig. W. F. Jenkins, "The Making of Soldiers," *Western Congress Addresses,* pp. 36-37; Holz, "Brief on Ohio, Pittsburgh and Southern Providence, 1908"; WCW, October 1884, pp. 1-2.

52. "A North-American 'Hard Nut': How Shall It Be Cracked?" *The Field Officer,* November 1902, p. 487; Jenkins, "The Making of Soldiers," pp. 38, 41-42.

53. Harold Begbie, *Life of William Booth: The Founder of The Salvation Army,* 2 vols. (London, 1925), 2:163 ("better sort"); interview with Lt. Col. William Bearchell, Asbury Park, N.J., 30 June 1978; interview with Lt. Col. Wesley Bouterse, Atlanta, 28 November 1978; Mrs. Col. Norman S. Marshall, *History of the Home League in the Eastern Territory* (New York, 1976), SAARC; AWC, 20 February 1915, p. 9. Norman Murdoch points out that in the 1880s, Army leaders in Britain lamented the fact that the Army lacked the capacity to nurture its own members in the faith, with the result that few converts became members ("The Salvation Army: An Anglo-American Revivalist Social Mission" [Ph.D. diss., University of Cincinnati, 1985], p. 382).

54. "An Open Letter to a Troubled Young Officer," carbon copy, SFOT/S Museum, book of papers relating to Brengle; AWC, 21 February 1903, p. 8; 28 February 1903, p. 4; 31 October 1903, p. 2; 19 April 1913, p. 12; Holz, "Brief on Ohio, Pittsburgh and Southern Providence, 1908."

55. AWC, 23 April 1887, p. 6; Mrs. Brig. Cozens, "Our Invasion of Kentucky," *Conq* 4 (June 1895): 259; AWC, 22 August 1896; *Philadelphia Sunday Press,* 3 November 1903, p. 6 (clipping in SFOT/E Museum, G/F, "USA History"); AWC, 5 March 1904,

p. 7; William E. Barton, "The Church Militant in the Feud Belt," *The Outlook,* 10 October 1903, pp. 351-52. See also Ensign Clifford Brindley's extensive biography of Richard Holz, "Commissioner Richard E. Holz," WCE, 13 April–31 August 1929.

56. U.S. Department of Commerce, Bureau of the Census, *Religious Bodies: 1916,* 2 vols. (Washington, 1919), 1:76, 2:662; U.S. Department of Commerce, Bureau of the Census, *Religious Bodies: 1936,* 2 vols. (Washington, 1941), 1:334-35 (interesting summary figures); AWC, 30 January 1904, p. 5; 2 March 1907, pp. 1, *passim;* WCW, 8 November 1941, p. 13.

57. AWC, 25 May 1889, p. 8 (cited by Bosch in "The Salvation Army in Chicago," pp. 72-73); AWC, 29 June 1889, p. 1; 10 March 1900, p. 16; WCW, 13 October 1900 (Milsaps WCC, 1:6); AWC, 22 September 1900, pp. 9, 8; 29 September 1900, p. 9; 6 October 1900, pp. 1, 8-9; 13 October 1900, pp. 9, 12; 20 October 1900, p. 5.

58. AWC, 19 May 1906, pp. 1, *passim;* 2 June 1906, pp. 3-4, 6-7.

59. AWC, 5 May 1906, pp. 1, 9, 12; 26 May 1906, pp. 4-5, 13; 16 June 1906, p. 4; 30 June 1906, pp. 4-5, 8-9; 14 July 1906, p. 8; 13 April 1907, p. 5; 20 April 1907, p. 2.

60. AWC, 16 June 1906, p. 8; 23 June 1906, pp. 2, 8, 12; 11 May 1907, pp. 9, 13.

61. AWC, 16 March 1907, p. 6; 31 August 1907, p. 12; 28 September 1907, pp. 1, *passim;* 16 November 1907, p. 13; 23 November 1907, p. 9; 12 October 1908, pp. 8-9, 12. For details on the relationship between McKinley and The Salvation Army in Canton, Ohio, and on the remarkable portrait window, which is on display in the present Army corps building at 420 S. Market Ave, see Dorothy Hitzka, "Great Is Our God: The Canton, Ohio, Story," unpublished, undated manuscript, especially pp. 20-21 (SAARC RG 20.7 208/16).

62. *All about The Salavation Army* (1884), p. 22; AWC, 20 August 1892, p. 5; 3 September 1892, p. 8; *Orders and Regulations for Field Officers, 1901,* pp. 242-44.

63. AWC, 11 December 1909, p. 12; "Boozers' Convention," SFOT/E Museum, G/F; Clarence W. Hall, *Out of the Depths: The Life-Story of Henry F. Milans* (Westwood, N.J., 1930), pp. 126-38, 139-48, illustration facing p. 132; broadside song sheet, "Jim and Me," undated, Holz Collection.

64. AWC, 26 December 1908; WCS, 23 April 1927, cover. Fine examples of the Falk Studio portrait were loaned to author by Mr. Tom McMahon of Ocean Grove, N.J.; see the photograph on p. 136 herein.

65. Comm. Frank Smith, *The Salvation War in America for 1885* (New York, [1886]), p. 74 (quotation); for sources of figures of SA real-estate holdings, see note 66; Minutes, no. 32, 8 March 1892 and no. 39, 6 August 1894 (Busby Coll. and SAARC). The Salvation Army Certificate of Incorporation lists the value of all Army property in 1899. The only sizable piece of property was the national headquarters building; the farm colonies were owned by the colonists, on Army-held leases and mortgages.

66. For statistics on Army ownership of properties, see U.S. Bureau of the Census, *Religious Bodies: 1906,* 1:617; *Religious Bodies: 1916,* 1:43, 46, 2:661-62; Minutes, no. 77, 10 October 1901 (Busby Coll.); Field Minutes, no. 3, 1 January 1911 (SAARC); Catherine Baird, *William McIntyre: God's Harvester* (London, 1948), pp. 30-32; AWC, 25 May 1907, p. 8 ("lofty pedestal"); Holz, "Brief on Ohio, Pittsburgh and Southern Providence, 1908"; Col. W. A. McIntyre, *Twenty Years Housing The Salvation Army* (New York, 1920), p. 9;

Agnes L. Palmer, *The Time Between: 1904-1926* (New York, 1926), pp. 19-28, 10; AWC, 25 February 1911, pp. 1, 6-7 (Flint); SATHQ/W, Property Dept. files (Oakland). On Army property holdings in 1917, see WCE, 2 June 1917, p. 13.

67. "William Booth — Soldier of the Cross," *Christian Advocate,* 29 August 1912, p. 1242; diary of Lt. Phil Gerringer, CTM; Ensign Cornelia A. Goss, *'Neath the Waters: From Modiste to Salvation Army Officer* (Cincinnati, 1923), pp. 38-42 (refers to the years 1902-1903). See also Milsaps Diary entries for 6 April 1900, 8 June 1900, 10 August 1900, 2 February 1901, and 20 August 1902; and Holz, "Brief on Ohio, Pittsburgh and Southern Providence, 1908."

68. E. H. McKinley, *Somebody's Brother: A History of The Salvation Army Men's Social Service Department, 1891-1985* (Lewiston, Me., 1986), pp. 66-72. On *Titanic* activities, see Robert M. DiSogra, "They Were There: Salvation Army Answered Survivors' Call at Pier 54," *Voyage* 7 (February 1991): 162-64; and Robert M. DiSogra, "They Were There: Britain's Salvation Army Leads *Titanic* Relief Efforts," *Voyage* 8 (June 1991): 109.

69. Edward Allsworth Ross, "Social Control, VI," *American Journal of Sociology* 2 (January 1897): 559-60; "William Booth — Soldier of the Cross," *Christian Advocate,* 29 August 1912, cover and pp. 1242-43 (representative of tributes in the religious press); Booth cited by Chesham in *Born to Battle,* p. 133; WC (London), 31 August 1912, p. 5 ("kiss him for me"); Nicholas Vachel Lindsay, "General William Booth Enters into Heaven," *Poetry* 1 (January 1913): 101-3. See also LD, 8 March 1913, pp. 541-42.

70. SA, *The Why and Wherefore of The Salvation Army Orders and Regulations, Intended Especially for the Use of Candidates for Officership and Cadets in the Training Colleges* (London, 1914), p. 7.

71. AWC, 6 June 1914, p. 10; 13 June 1914, pp. 11, 13; 27 June 1914, pp. 8-9, 12; "The Salvation Army Congress of the Nations 1914: Celebration at the Crystal Palace, Tuesday, June 23rd: Official Programme," Seiler Coll., binders.

NOTES TO CHAPTER 4

1. When Evangeline Booth was interviewed in 1935 for a biography, she was questioned about the fact that the American *War Cry* carried no news about the coming war. Her reply was that the Army had its *own* news in 1914: the approaching Congress in London! P. Whitwell Wilson, *General Evangeline Booth* (New York, 1935), pp. 65-66; *You Should Know These Things* (New York, 1915), p. 6; Frances Ross-Shannon, "Music and Memories," *Christian Advocate,* 14 June 1945, pp. 15-16 (San Bernadino); Ronald W. Holz, *Erik Leidzen: Band Arranger and Composer* (Lewiston, 1990), p. 17.

2. *Where Shadows Lengthen: A Sketch of The Salvation Army's Work in the United States of America* (New York, 1907), pp. 52-53; Edward H. McKinley, *Somebody's Brother: A History of The Salvation Army Men's Social Services Department, 1891-1985* (Lewiston, Me., 1986), pp. 70-78; J. Stanley Sheppard, *The Prison Work of The Salvation Army* (New York, 1948), pp. 29-30, 77-80; *Close-Ups from Humanity's Scrapheap: Being the Annual Prison Report of The Salvation Army, 1921-1922* (New York, 1922), p. 87; AWC, 3 February 1917, pp. 8-9.

3. *Service: An Exposition of The Salvation Army in the United States* (New York, 1941), pp. 12-13; Charles Edward Russell, "A Rescuer of Ruined Lives: General William

Booth and The Salvation Army," *Missionary Review of the World* 32 (June 1909): 456; Raymond Arthur Dexter, "Officer Training in the Salvation Army: An Institutional Analysis" (Ed.D. diss., Stanford University, 1962), pp. 16-17; "The Salvation Army's Campaign," *The Outlook,* 26 April 1916, p. 943; Theodore Roosevelt, "The Salvation Army," *The Outlook,* 23 August 1913, pp. 892-93. The use of the beguiling term "University of Humanity" continued to appeal to Army leaders: in 1931 it was used in a major campaign to raise $500,000 for a new territorial training college in Chicago; see the brochure "University of Humanity: 1931," in CTM horizontal files, "Training College Manuals and Documents."

4. Milsaps Diary, 5 March 1898; Holz Diary, 15 August 1892 (SAARC); Findings of the Commissioners' Conference Presided over by Commander Evangeline Booth, New York, September 14th, 15th, 16th, 1922, "Fake Armies" on p. 12; Commissioners' Conference Minutes (CCM) for the years 1921 to 1940 in SAARC on microfilm ARC 191; for years to 1978 also on microfilm; Minutes for years 1978 to the present in Records Bureau, Salvation Army National Headquarters; both agencies in Alexandria, Va. References to the Commissioners' Conference Minutes hereinafter cited as CCM; correspondence on these "spurious concerns" in two Broadway files boxes, "No. 4," and "G," in SAARC, which also has catalogued the complete correspondence of Brig. Madison J. H. Ferris; Nels Anderson, *The Hobo: The Sociology of the Homeless Man* (1923; reprint, Chicago, 1961), p. 250.

5. AWC, 29 August 1914, p. 8; 12 September 1914, pp. 8, 12.

6. AWC, 14 November 1914, pp. 8-9, 12; 2 January 1915, p. 9; George Taggart and Wallace Winchell, *A Yankee Major Invades Belgium* (New York, 1916), pp. 7-12.

7. Taggart and Winchell, *A Yankee Major Invades Belgium,* pp. 25-27, 43-44, 49, 71, 134-35, 144-46, 172-73, 194, 108-9.

8. Editorial, AWC, 24 March 1917, p. 8 ("contending camps"); Evangeline Booth, "The Salvation Army and the War," AWC, 21 April 1917, p. 9; the cartoon appears in AWC, 5 May 1917, p. 10; Col. [Samuel L.] Brengle, "Hold Fast," AWC, 26 May 1917, p. 7.

9. AWC, 21 April 1917, p. 8 ("steps"); 28 April 1917, p. 9 ("huts or rest-rooms"); 5 May 1917, p. 9; 12 May 1917, pp. 8-9; 2 June 1917, p. 8 ("cheering, blessing"); on the vacant lot farms, see AWC, 5 May 1917, p. 8; 12 May 1917, p. 9; and 9 June 1917, p. 13; "Salvationist 'Soldiers of the Soil,'" LD, 6 June 1917, p. 1748; SA, "Soldiers of the Soil," pamphlet dated 1919; SFOT/E Museum, G/F, "Farm Colonies/General."

10. William Howard Taft, *Service with Fighting Men: An Account of the Work of the American Young Men's Christian Associations in the World War,* 2 vols. (New York, 1922), 1:viii, 26, 38, 48-50, 130; 2:499, 627-29; Herbert A. Wisbey, Jr. "Religion in Action: A History of The Salvation Army in the United States" (Ph.D. diss., Columbia University, 1951), p. 326.

11. Taft, *Service with Fighting Men,* 1:387; 2:44; 1:96n.1; 2:409, 504, 511-19; *War Service Herald,* 11 November 1917, p. 7; 4 April 1919, pp. 8-9 (SAARC); AWC, 4 August 1917, p. 16; Weldon B. Durham, "'Big Brother' and the 'Seven Sisters': Camp Life Reforms in World War I," *Military Affairs* 42 (April 1978): 58-60; Evangeline Booth, "Mothering the Boys at the Front," *The Forum,* September 1918, p. 305.

12. Evangeline Booth and Grace Livingston Hill, *The War Romance of The Salvation Army* (Philadelphia, 1919), p. 44, illustration facing p. 48; AWC, 26 July 1917, p. 6.

13. Booth and Hill, *The War Romance of The Salvation Army*, pp. 45-47; on the Lee-Pershing incident, see a letter from Maude D. Dart to Comm. Holland French, Los Angeles, dated 19 October 1964 (SANHQ/chief secretary's office).

14. Booth and Hill, *The War Romance of The Salvation Army*, pp. 55-56, 82; AWC, 30 June 1917, pp. 9, 11; 11 August 1917, cover, p. 11; 25 August 1917, pp. 1, 2, 9; on special war commissions, see SFOT/E Museum, G/F; Wisbey, "Religion in Action," p. 330.

15. Col. William McIntyre to Ensign Helen Purviance, New York City, 2 August 1917 (SAARC, RG 20.68 68/1); *Akron Beacon Journal*, 11 November 1976, p. B-10; Sr. Maj. Helga Ramsay, "War Service in France and Army Occupation in Germany," typescript from dictation (SFOT/E Museum, G/F, "World War I"); Taft, *Service with Fighting Men*, 1:147-48; 2:505; Wisbey, "Religion in Action," pp. 336-37; Dorothy Hughes Post, "The Legacy of the Doughnut Girls," WC, 11 November 1989, pp. 16-21. For information on officer and non-officer SA personnel in World War I, see *War Service Herald*, 6 July 1919, pp. 8-9 and 7 August 1919, pp. 8-9.

16. Booth and Hill, *The War Romance of The Salvation Army*, pp. 59-61, 91, 97; diary entry of Ensign Lydia Margaret Sheldon for 1 October 1917 (in SFOT/E Museum horizontal drawer case "World War I"); Taft, *Service with Fighting Men*, 1:127, 560-61, 571; "Salvation Army Pie and Prayers at the Front," LD, 19 October 1918, p. 67; Booth, "Mothering the Boys at the Front," p. 305; Commandant Joseph Hughes, "A Salvationist in the War," WCC, 4 August 1923, p. 13.

17. AWC, 6 July 1918, p. 4; 23 February 1918, p. 16; Booth and Hill, *The War Romance of The Salvation Army*, pp. 109, page facing 228, 259; Frank Freidel, *Over There: The Story of America's First Great Overseas Crusade* (New York, 1963), pp. 293-97, 300-302; "Imperfect Religion in the YMCA," LD, 16 November 1918, pp. 32-33; Taft, *Service with Fighting Men*, 1:249-50; interview with Mr. James Stillwell, Suffern, N.Y., 12 July 1978; [Federal Council of Churches] Committee on the War and the Religious Outlook, *Religion among American Men, as Revealed by a Study of Conditions in the Army* (New York, 1920), pp. v-x, 25-32. This report was based on extensive surveys and interviews during the war and includes special praise for The Salvation Army. See also Ray H. Abrams, *Preachers Present Arms* (1933; reprint, Scottdale, Pa., 1969), p. 176; John F. Piper Jr., *The American Churches in World War I* (Athens, Ohio, 1985), pp. 10, 12-12, 51-75.

18. Booth, "Mothering the Boys at the Front," p. 309; undated clipping from the *Omaha Daily News* magazine and letter from Comm. Thomas Estill to Martha Porter, Chicago, 16 June 1919, on grave decoration, both in SFOT/E Museum, G/F, "WWI"; Adjutant Helen Purviance, "A Doughgirl on the Firing Line," *The Forum*, December 1918, p. 654; Booth and Hill, *The War Romance of The Salvation Army*, pp. 51-52; Taft, *Service with Fighting Men*, 1:100-101; Staff Capt. L. Allison Coe, "With the American Expeditionary Forces in France," AWC, 23 February 1918, p. 16.

19. Booth and Hill, *The War Romance of The Salvation Army*, p. 13; Evangeline Booth, "Around the World with The Salvation Army," *National Geographic Magazine*, April 1920, p. 347; Purviance, "A Doughgirl on the Firing Line," p. 649; for detailed information on Purviance's important role in the development of the famous doughnut, see her correspondence (in SAARC, RG 20.68), her typed notes for "War Talk" (1930), and a letter from Sudiem M. Zuber to Purviance, Auburn, Ala., 24 September 1939; Braxton Zuber to Bert Nevins Association, n.p., n.d.; interview with Margaret Sheldon, St. Petersburg, Fla., 10 May 1976; letter from Stella Young to Col. Purviance, Old Orchard Beach, Me.,

27 November 1979; Wisbey, "Religion in Action," p. 332; Booth and Hill, *The War Romance of The Salvation Army,* pp. 76-78; "Salvation Army Pie and Prayers at the Front," pp. 63-64; interview with Col. Florence Turkington, Asbury Park, N.J., 9 August 1978 (Turkington also provided the author with the list of World War I personnel); [Adjutant Raymond C. Starbard], "Pies and Doughnuts: A New Kind of War Munitions Furnished by the Salvation Army — Special Correspondent of the Outlook," *The Outlook,* 5 June 1918, p. 220; Freidel, *Over There,* p. 295; Ramsay, "War Service in France and Army Occupation in Germany," p. 2.

20. Starbard, "Pies and Doughnuts," pp. 220-21; "Salvation Army Pie and Prayers at the Front," p. 64; Purviance, "A Doughgirl on the Firing Line," p. 650; Ramsay, "War Service in France and Army Occupation in Germany," pp. 3, 6; AWC, May 4, 1918, 4; Hughes, "Salvationist in the War," WCC, 30 June 1923, p. 16; interviews with Stillwell, Col. Turkington.

21. Starbard, "Pies and Doughnuts," p. 220; Booth and Hill, *The War Romance of The Salvation Army,* pp. 258-59, 66-67, 75.

22. AWC, 4 August 1917, p. 9; 16 February 1918, pp. 12-13; 22 March 1919, p. 2; "Salvation Army Pie and Prayers at the Front," p. 64; Booth and Hill, *The War Romance of The Salvation Army,* pp. 100-106; Wisbey, "Religion in Action," pp. 339-40.

23. Freidel, *Over There,* p. 293; "Salvation Army Pie and Prayers at the Front," p. 63; *Echoes from Over There,* ed. Craig Hamilton and Louise Corbin (New York, 1919), pp. 31-32, 176; AWC, 26 January 1918, p. 8; 2 February 1918, p. 2; 9 February 1918, p. 16; Commander Evangeline Booth, "That Million Dollars," AWC, 16 February 1918, p. 8 (see also p. 16); 23 March 1918, p. 9; 8 June 1918, p. 9; 17 August 1918, p. 2; Booth, "Mothering the Boys at the Front," p. 307; "What the Salvation Army Has Done," LD, 16 March 1918, pp. 38-39.

24. Booth and Hill, *The War Romance of The Salvation Army,* pp. 35-40; Herbert Adams Gibbons, *John Wanamaker,* 2 vols. (1926; reprint, Port Washington, N.Y., 1971), 2:420-21.

25. AWC, 30 June 1917, p. 9; 16 February 1918, pp. 8-9, 12-13; 2 June 1917, p. 9; 4 August 1917, p. 16; 6 July 1918, p. 5; Durham, "'Big Brother' and the 'Seven Sisters,'" p. 59.

26. AWC, 17 May 1917, pp. 3-5; 26 May 1917, pp. 9, 12-13, 16; 2 June 1917, pp. 9, 12, 16; 19 January 1918, cover, p. 2; Col. S. L. Brengle, "Can We Have Revivals in War Time?" AWC, 2 March 1918, pp. 9, 12; McKinley, *Somebody's Brother,* pp. 78-80.

27. AWC, 22 December 1917, p. 21; 18 May 1918, pp. 8, 9, 16; 25 May 1918, p. 4; autograph album of Ensign Lydia Margaret Sheldon (in SFOT/E Museum horizontal drawer case "World War I"); AWC, 19 April 1919, pp. 2, 12; 3 May 1919, pp. 4, 16; 17 May 1919 (entire "Home Service Campaign" issue); *War Service Herald,* 1 August 1917, p. 15; 5 May 1919, pp. 1-2, 4-5, 10; *Stars and Stripes,* 2 May 1919, (clipping in SFOT/E Museum G/F, "WWI"; "The Motherly Salvationists," LD, 11 May 1918, p. 32; "Salvation Army Drive for a 'Home-Service Fund,'" LD, 26 April 1919, p. 30; "The Salvation Army Drive," *The Outlook,* 28 May 1919, p. 140; "Salvation Army Home Service Meeting, Madison Square Garden, May 18, 1919" (program, SFOT/E Museum, B/F, Evangeline Booth).

28. AWC, 30 November 1918, p. 8; 15 January 1919, p. 9; 22 March 1919, p. 16; 14 August 1920, pp. 12, 14.

29. "Salvation Army Has Fought Satan Fifty-Four Years," LD, 19 July 1919, p. 34; WCS, 27 October 1928, cover; AWC, 14 August 1920, p. 12; "Millions for the Salvation Army," LD, 7 June 1919, p. 39; J. Ray Johnson, "Campaigning with The Salvation Army," AWC, 5 July 1919, pp. 10-11; collection of sheet music and song posters belonging to Lt. Col. Richard Norris, Adult Rehabilitation Center Commander, Atlanta (STHC); letter on Armistice Day celebration from Comm. R. E. Holz to Adjutant Helen Purviance, New York City, 26 October 1921 (SAARC, RG 20.68, 68/1); letter from Bruce Barton in *Now We Are Sixty: Anniversary Greetings to The Salvation Army* (New York, 1940), n.p.

30. AWC, 22 August 1896, p. 6; WCW, 16 July 1898, pp. 1-3, 4-5; Capt. Masasuke Kobayashi, "The Salvation Army among the Japanese of the Pacific Coast," AWC, 25 September 1920, p. 4.

31. AWC, 25 September 1920, pp. 8-9; WCW, 9 April 1921, pp. 12-13; 12 May 1923, p. 11; 16 June 1923, pp. 8-9, 13; 1 September 1923, p. 3; 5 April 1924, p. 5; 13 September 1924, p. 10; 27 September 1924, pp. 8-9; "The Romance of the Japanese Work in America: An Interview with Staff-Captain M. Kobayashi," WCE, 7 April 1928, pp. 11-13; Gen. Bramwell Booth to Comm. Adam Gifford, London, 28 April 1921 (Gifford Coll., SAARC); interview with Brig. Masahide Imai, Santa Clara, Calif., 12 December 1978; Brig. Masahide Imai, "The Salvation Army," in *A Centennial Legacy: History of Japanese Christian Missions in North America, 1877-1977,* vol. 1, ed. Sumio Koga (Chicago, 1977), pp. 62-65.

32. Brian Masaru Hayashi, "The Japanese 'Invasion' of California: Major Kobayashi and The Japanese Salvation Army, 1919-1926," *Journal of the West* 23 (January 1984): 79-82.

33. WCW, 19 November 1921, pp. 2, 5, 8-9, 10-11; 26 November 1921, p. 5; 12 May 1923, p. 11; 16 June 1923, pp. 8-9, 13; 1 September 1923, p. 3; 5 April 1924, p. 5; 13 September 1924, p. 10; 27 September 1924, pp. 8-9; Imai interview; Imai, "The Salvation Army," pp. 62-65.

34. Col. William H. Cox, "The Salvation Army around the World," *Missionary Review of the World* 42 (August 1919): 585; and the following items from the Fritz Nelson Materials, CTM, Drawer 14: undated clippings; "Mariners' League: Regular Membership" (certificate), item 88.67; "The Mariners' League of The Salvation Army" (brochure), item 87.39; "The International Fraternity of Christian Mariners" (brochure), item 87.43.

35. SA, *Orders and Regulations Governing the Retirement of Officers* (London, 1945), pp. 3, 7; "The Salvation Army West Point," LD, 4 August 1923, p. 40; Col. Richard E. Holz, "Historical Sketch of The Army in America," WCE, 12 September 1925, p. 14; "Salvation Army Training," *Missionary Review of the World* 48 (November 1925): 893; U.S. Department of Commerce, Bureau of the Census, *Religious Bodies: 1916,* 2 vols. (Washington, 1919), 2:334-35; Bureau of the Census, *Religious Bodies: 1926,* 2 vols. (Washington, 1929), 2:1279, 1283; Bureau of the Census, *Religious Bodies: 1936,* 2 vols. (Washington, 1941), 1:334-35.

36. AWC, 7 August 1920, pp. 8-9; 14 August 1920, p. 1; 2 October 1920, pp. 1, 8; information on change in titles based on research in SA *Disposition of Forces* volumes for 1920-1929, from Susan Mitchem, SAARC, by telephone to the author, 8 May 1992; see also discussion of the "Commandership" in Chap. 5 below; Memorandum of Appointment, Lt. Comm. Adam Gifford, Territorial Commander of the West, 3 February 1921 (Gifford Coll., SAARC); Porter R. Lee and Walter W. Pettit, *Social Salvage: A Study of the*

Central Organization and Administration of The Salvation Army (New York, 1924), pp. 11, 33-34.

37. Norris Alden Magnuson, "Salvation in the Slums: Evangelical Social Welfare Work, 1865-1920" (Ph.D. diss., University of Minnesota, 1968), pp. 429-31, 434; Phil Collier, WC assistant editor, kindly provided information on the publication, 2 April 1979.

38. WCC, 16 April 1923, p. 4; Sigmund A. Lavine, *Daughter of Salvation* (New York, 1970), p. 93 (BPOE cable); *New York World*, 9 September 1922, pp. 1, 6; 12 September 1922, p. 8; "The Recall of Evangeline Booth," LD, 7 October 1922, p. 34; "An Army, Not an Association," *The Outlook*, 27 September 1922, pp. 134-36; *New York World*, 14 September 1922, p. 5.

39. Evangeline C. Booth (ECB) to Adam Gifford, New York, 28 September 1922; Gifford to E. Higgins, San Francisco, 14 October 1922; ECB to Gifford, White Plains, telegram, 4 November 1922 (in which she describes herself as "nearly distracted" and the situation with Bramwell as "intolerable"); Col. Walter Jenkins to Gifford, New York, 14 November 1922 (in which he mentions the danger of "brain fever" in ECB, says that she has been "broken down" by ordeal, and suggests that Gifford send a "heartening wire" — Gifford Coll., SAARC, closed); table of ranks of The Salvation Army in Appendix 2, pp. 354-55 herein.

40. Brig. Richard Griffith to Gifford, White Plains, N.Y., 14 November [1922], with "Brown-Cory" code (Gifford Coll., SAARC, closed).

41. There is an interesting exchange of letters on Manifesto no. 1 in Gifford Coll., SAARC. Comm. Edward Higgins, the chief of the staff, wrote to the territorial commanders stating that these manifestos had been received all over the Army in America and Britain, that the General had decided not to make any public comment, and that he, the chief, would be glad to know what "effect," if any, the manifestos were having on American officers. On 6 April 1925, ECB telegraphed the American commissioners and instructed them on how they should respond to inquiries from London: they were to equivocate, to avoid saying that the manifestos were simply being ignored or that nobody was taking them seriously, and to say rather that they were being "fully discussed" by officers, that it was too early to know what their reaction would be. They were to use their "own language" in these responses. As a result, Adam Gifford wrote to Higgins that there was "no question" in his mind that the manifesto was "being fully discussed," but a "large majority" of the officers remained "dead silent." To date, he offered, there had been no statements of "disloyalty," but in his judgment "many minds" were "somewhat disturbed." Higgins to Gifford, London, 24 March 1925; ECB to Gifford, New York, 6 April 1925; Adam Gifford to ECB, San Francisco, 8 March 1925; Gifford to Edward Higgins, San Francisco, 9 April 1925 (all in Gifford Coll., SAARC, closed). On "Atwood" writings, see F. A. MacKenzie, *The Clash of the Cymbals: The Secret History of the Revolt in the Salvation Army* (New York, 1929), pp. 72-73; Lee and Pettit, *Social Salvage*, p. 71; " 'Wilful Will' Booth and His Salvation Army," LD, 9 February 1929, pp. 38-50; "An American Salvation Army," *The Outlook*, 24 November 1926, pp. 392-93; interview with Col. William Maltby, Asbury Park, N.J., 30 June 1978. Before Col. Maltby went to London in 1925 on business, the Commander instructed him to answer any question there about ECB's status in the United States by saying that the American people loved her. For praise of Gen. Booth from the unsuspecting rank and file, see WCC, 27 March 1926, pp. 7, 10-11; 1 May 1926, pp. 8-9; and E. Irena Arnold, *Poems of a Salvationist* (New York, 1923), p. 19.

42. WCS, 5 February 1938, p. 13; WC, 30 December 1978, pp. 12-13; WCE, 3 February 1923, pictorial section; WCS, 17 December 1927, p. 15; WCC, 12 December 1925, p. 3; Dr. Charles Wheeler, "Through the Hole in the Doughnut," WCC, 29 January 1921, p. 7; Edward Justus Parker, *My Fifty-Eight Years: An Autobiography* (New York, 1943), pp. 176-77; Agnes L. Palmer, *The Time Between: 1904-1926* (New York, 1926), pp. 50-51.

43. AWC, 19 April 1919, p. 3; the inscription was found on the framed photograph (STHC, item 91.42.02); see "Shall We Forget the War?" WCC, 10 November 1923, p. 6; Virginia Mack, "Redeemed," WCC, 30 June 1924, p. 13; "Forty-Five Years in America: A Brief Historical Sketch," WCC, 12 September 1925, p. 12; *Ten Talks on The Salvation Army: The Sesqui-Centennial International Exposition, Philadelphia, June 1–December 1, 1926* (New York, 1926), pp. 74-75; WCS, 26 March 1927, p. 3; WCS, 23 April 1927, p. 5; WCS, 30 July 1927, p. 2; Evangeline Booth, *Let Us Live: An Address Delivered to the American Legion Convention, Trocadero Palace, Paris, September 21, 1927* (New York, 1928), pp. 5-7; on clubs, see WCC, 30 July 1921, p. 13; WCW, 10 September 1921, p. 11; WCC, 23 January 1926, p. 5; WCC, 23 February 1929, p. 10; WCW, 14 July 1923; Lt. Col. C. W. Bourne, "Thirty-Three Years in Uniform," WCC, 13 September 1924, p. 11; minutes of the Territorial Trade Board for 9 February 1927 (officer's dues), Transfer Trade Finance Board Minutes, SATHQ/S, office files of trade secretary.

44. CCM, 3-4 January 1921, pp. 1-3 (SAARC, ARC 191); two clippings from the *Adrian [Michigan] Daily Telegram* dated 18 February 1921 and 25 February 1921 contain detailed accounts of the start of the advisory boards (Adrian, Mich., Corps History file, CTM); Col. Richard E. Holz, "Historical Sketch of The Army in America," WCE, 12 September 1925, p. 14.

45. [Mary Ross], "Social Practice: Salvation First," *The Survey,* 15 November 1924, 195; SA, *Orders and Regulations for Officers* (London: International SA Headquarters, 1925), p. 149; WCE, 17 January 1925, p. 3 ("Storm the Forts"); Sallie Chesham, *Born to Battle: The Salvation Army in America* (Chicago, 1965), pp. 179-81; Damon Runyon, "The Idyll of Miss Sarah Brown," in *Runyon à la Carte* (Garden City, N.Y., 1945), pp. 94-96; Damon Runyon, *Guys and Dolls* (New York, 1931); ECB to Gifford, New York City, 30 October 1922 (Gifford Coll., SAARC); interview with Brig. Christine McMillan, 26 June 1978.

46. WCW, 3 February 1923, p. 5; WCC, 29 October 1922, p. 9.

47. WCC, 18 November 1922, p. 2; ECB to Adam Gifford, telegram, New York, 4 November 1922; Gifford to ECB, San Francisco, 6 November 1922 (Gifford Coll., SAARC); WCC, 26 July 1924, p. 8.

48. Ensign W. W. Bouterse, "The Salvationist in High School," *The Young Soldier,* 11 February 1928, p. 2; "Southern Territorial Staff Council, Memoranda of Decisions and Suggestions, Bryson City, North Carolina, June 22, 27, 1927," transcript copy, p. 9 (Holz Coll.).

49. Information on conditions in corps during the 1920s was derived from interviews by the author with the following: Col. Frank Guldenschuh, Asbury Park, N.J., 16 June 1978; Brig. Fred Crossley, Asbury Park, 30 June 1978; Sr. Maj. Charles A. Schuerholz, Asbury Park, 30 June 1978; Sr. Maj. and Mrs. Carl Blied, Asbury Park, 14 July 1978; Mrs. Annie Breen, Asbury Park, 14 July 1978; Brig. and Mrs. Ernest Baxendale, Asbury Park, 7 August 1978; Lt. Col. Edward Laity, Atlanta, 24 November 1978; Sr. Maj. Bertha Shadick, Los Angeles, 15 December 1978; Mrs. Sr. Maj. George Watt, Los Angeles, 15 December 1978; Allan Whitworth Bosch, "The Salvation Army in Chicago: 1885-1914"

(Ph.D. diss., University of Chicago, 1965), p. 258; Pamela Search, *Happy Warriors: The Story of the Social Work of The Salvation Army* (London, 1956), p. 162.

50. WCW, 22 October 1921, pp. 5-9, 10, 11-12; 29 October 1921, p. 10; WCC, 12 August 1922, pp. 1, 11; Bureau of the Census, *Religious Bodies: 1926,* 2:1287 (statistics); Ross, "Social Practice: Salvation First," pp. 195-98; Lee and Pettit, *Social Salvage,* p. 94 ("have little significance"); [Brig.] Ferdinand Braun, "We Still Save Men," *North American Review* 227 (March 1929): 316-17. For an account of the men's social services during the 1920s, see McKinley, *Somebody's Brother,* pp. 81-89.

51. Capt. Karl E. Nelson, "The Organization and Development of the Health Care System of The Salvation Army in the United States of America" (thesis prepared for the Committee on Credentials in partial fulfillment of the requirements for Fellowship, American College of Hospital Administration, 1973), p. 24 (SAARC); *Ten Talks on The Salvation Army,* pp. 52, 54-56; Lee and Pettit, *Social Salvage,* pp. 25-26, 80; interview with Sr. Maj. Magna Sorenson, Los Angeles, 15 December 1978; interview with Brig. Emma Ellegard, Asbury Park, N.J., 16 June 1978.

52. Parker, *My Fifty-Eight Years,* pp. 160-62; "The Salvation Army's 'Lost Drunks'," LD, 18 September 1920, p. 38; "A Salvation Army Report on Prohibition," LD, 8 October 1921, p. 32; Anderson, *The Hobo,* pp. 27-28, 261-62; Evangeline Booth, "Results of Prohibition in the United States," WCC, 3 September 1921, p. 11; Evangeline Booth, *The Salvation Army Appraises Prohibition* (New York, 1929).

53. AWC, 26 June 1920, p. 3; WCW, 30 July 1921, p. 16; articles by Evangeline Booth on prohibition in WCC, 27 August 1921, p. 4; 3 September 1921, p. 11; 10 September 1921, p. 13; WCE, 20 January 1923, p. 16; WCC, 20 January–10 March 1923, later printed as a 30-page booklet; appeared also in WCC, 1 November–20 December 1924; WCW, 1 August 1925, p. 9; WCE, 7 July 1928, p. 3; 14 July 1928, p. 3; "Salvation Army Report on Prohibition," p. 32; *The Salvation Army Yearbook, 1922,* p. 71; *1924,* p. 80; *1926,* p. 108; WCS, 16 July 1927, pp. 8, 10; 23 July 1927, p. 5; *Bridging the Gulf: Being a Description of the Prison Work of The Salvation Army, Coupled with the Annual Report for 1924-1925* (New York, 1925), pp. 12-13, 24, 46; WCC, 14 July 1923, p. 8; WCC, 7 July 1928, p. 3 (Republicans); WCC, 14 February 1931, p. 10 (Hoover); Evangeline Booth, "The Army's Jubilee in the United States: Address to Staff Officers," *The Staff Review* 11 (January 1931): 5-7; Arnold, *Poems of a Salvationist,* p. 22; WCW, 18 August 1923, p. 10; WCC, 28 November 1925, p. 8; 25 October 1930, pp. 7, 15.

54. WCC, 27 August 1921, p. 2; *Close-Ups from Humanity's Scrapheap,* p. 26.

55. AWC, 30 October 1920, p. 3; WCC, 26 March 1921, p. 5; 3 December 1921, p. 8; 10 July 1924, p. 11; 17 May 1924, p. 5; *What Is The Salvation Army?* (New York, 1924), pp. 66-67; *Bridging the Gulf,* pp. 56-58; *Broken Souls: Being the Report of Prison Welfare Work during the William Booth Centenary Year* (New York, 1929), p. 32; *Close-Ups from Humanity's Scrapheap,* p. 27.

56. *Broken Souls,* pp. 3-5 (prelude by Commander Booth).

57. *Broken Souls,* pp. 23, 16-18, 26-27; *Bridging the Gulf,* pp. 26-27, 33, 73-80, 104; "Our Prison Work," WCC, 2 February 1924, pp. 5, 15; Palmer, *The Time Between,* pp. 96-102.

58. WCC, 15 December 1923, p. 11; WCW, 20 September 1924, pp. 8-9, 10; Ronald W. Holz, *Heralds of Victory: A History Celebrating the 100th Anniversary of The New York Staff Band and Male Chorus, 1887-1897* (New York, 1986), pp. 35, 257; Capt. Ray

Steadman-Allen, "The Evolution of Salvation Army Music," *The Musician* (London), 24 July 1965, p. 471.

59. WCC, 5 May 1928, p. 13; letter to author from Lt. Col. Ray Steadman-Allen, London, 2 February 1978; interview with Comm. Richard Holz, Rancho Palos Verdes, Calif., 13 December 1978; interview with Lt. Col. Wm. Bearchell, Asbury Park, N.J., 30 June 1978; James Neilson, "The Salvation Army Band," *The Etude* 67 (February 1949): 122-23; Ronald W. Holz, "A History of the Hymn Tune Meditation and Related Items in Salvation Army Instrumental Music in Great Britain and North America, 1880-1980" (Ph.D. diss., University of Connecticut, 1981), pp. 153-54, 181-82. For a description of the congregational songbooks that accompanied Salvation Army band tune books through the years, see Gordon Taylor, *Companion to the Song Book of The Salvation Army* (London, 1989), pp. xiii-xviii.

60. "Salvation Limited," *The Nation,* 30 January 1929, p. 124; Lt. Cmdr. John Philip Sousa, USNRF, "Why the World Needs Bands," *The Etude* 48 (September 1930): 657; WCC, 1 September 1928, p. 9.

61. Lee and Pettit, *Social Salvage,* pp. 95-97; Comm. W. A. McIntyre, "Story of the Southern Territory, USA," unpublished typescript (1930), kindly lent to the author by Mrs. Col. William Noble (the community chest reference appears on p. 8); for commissioners' conference quotation, see CCM, 14-16 September 1922 (SAARC, ARC 191).

62. Interviews with Sr. Maj. Charles Schuerholz and Sr. Maj. Bertha Shadick; letter to the author from M. C. Tunison, Saratoga Springs, N.Y., 16 April 1979.

63. WCW, 20 January 1923, p. 5; *What Is The Salvation Army?* pp. 71-74; Lee and Pettit, *Social Salvage,* pp. 91-97, 72-73; *Ten Talks on The Salvation Army,* 90; Southern staff council memorandum, June 1927, pp. 13-17 (Holz Coll.).

64. William E. Kerrish, "Catholic Action on the Street Corner," *America,* 16 March 1929, p. 545; see also Rev. Worth M. Tippy, "The Field of the Church in Social Work and Public Welfare," *Annals of the American Academy of Political and Social Science* 105 (January 1923): 68; *The Life-Saving Guards' Notebook and Diary for 1928,* pp. 5-6, 8-14, 57 (SAARC, RG 20.18, 211/8); for official statements about building membership, see "Notebook Compiled Especially for the Use of the Individual Cadet," ed. Thomas Stanyon [1925], n.p. (CTM, Horizontal file "Training College Manuals and Documents"); for lectures that include such references, see Col. Stanyon, "Object of Training"; "The Salvation Army: Its Purpose"; "An Ideal Corps"; "A Useful Officer and Requirements"; Col. Holz, "Army Making #5"; Mrs. Col. Stanyon, "Visitation"; and Col. Brewer, "Your Vows"; Palmer, *The Times Between,* p. 6; WCC, 10 July 1926, pp. 3-5; Bureau of the Census, *Religious Bodies: 1936,* 1:334-35; "Samptown, a 100 Per Cent Army Village," WCC, 22 November 1924, p. 5; "A Whole Community at the Drumhead," LD, 25 October 1924, pp. 33-34; WCE, 5 September 1925, p. 13 ("still the style").

65. WCC, 23 October 1926, pp. 5, 8, 13 (map, announcement); WCE, 23 October 1926, pp. 4, 6, 9, 13; Col. Bertram Rodda, "Draft of Material in re: Birth and Re-Birth of Southern Territory," unpublished typescript, n.d. (SATHQ/S, Publications Dept.); for the breakdown of the new divisions, see the SA *Disposition of Forces, Southern Territory, Feb. 1927,* pp. 10-20; interview with Col. Bertram Rodda, Oakland, Calif., 12 December 1978; Edward H. McKinley, "Brass Bands and God's Work: One Hundred Years of the Salvation Army in Georgia and Atlanta," *Atlanta History: A Journal of Georgia and the South* 34 (Winter 1990-1991): 11-13.

66. Interview with Mrs. Col. Lillian Hansen Noble, Atlanta; see also McIntyre, "Story of the Southern Territory, USA," and Comm. William A. McIntyre, *Christ's Cabinet: Character Stories of the Twelve Apostles* (Chicago, 1937), an engaging little book that tells one as much about McIntyre as it does about the apostles.

67. Interviews with Col. Rodda and Lt. Col. Laity; McIntyre, "Story of the Southern Territory, USA," pp. 12-13.

68. WCS, 26 March 1927, p. 3 (inaugural issue); WCS, 1 October 1927, pp. 8-9; Catherine Baird, *William McIntyre, God's Harvester* (London, 1948), pp. 38-39.

69. WCS, 9 July 1927, p. 7; "Inaugural Program, Southern Territorial Staff Band, Thanksgiving Day, November 24, 1927" (SATHQ/S, publications dept.); McIntyre, "Story of the Southern Territory, USA," p. 7; and WCS, 9 April 1927, p. 10 (weak corps). In 1925 the top thirty-four corps in the Self-Denial fund collection were listed in *The War Cry,* and five of them were in the South (the five listed in the text, except for Atlanta) — see WCE, 18 July 1925, pp. 13, 16; see also McKinley, "Brass Bands and God's Work," pp. 11-13; Southern Trade minutes, 28 November 1928, p. 2; WCC, 26 May 1928, p. 10.

70. Col. Richard E. Holz, "The Salvation Army and the Negroes of the Southern States of North America," *The Officer* 22 (July 1914): 479 (quotation); AWC, 14 August 1920, pp. 12, 14; material on integration of large meetings in South in 1920s was drawn from interviews with Comm. Ernest W. Holz, Atlanta, 23 November 1978; with Col. Bertram Rodda; and with Lt. Col. Laity. The Southern *Disposition of Forces,* February 1927, listed as "colored" the Washington No. 2 Corps in the Potomac Division and the Service-man's Hotel at Seventh and P Streets (p. 18). For figures on black corps, see Bureau of the Census, *Religious Bodies: 1926,* 1:708-9, 720-21, and *Religious Bodies: 1936,* 1:902-3. The Army listed five "negro churches" in 1926 with 495 members and three churches in 1936 with 436 members.

71. Col. W. A. McIntyre, *Twenty Years Housing The Salvation Army* (New York, 1920), p. 13 (SAARC); WCC, 11 June 1921, p. 2; WCE, 25 November 1922, pictorial section; WCE, 17 November 1923 (pictorial section); "The Salvation Army Eastern Territory, Opening Dates of Women's Social Institutions," comp. Brig. Hester Dammes (SAARC); interview with Brig. Emma Ellegard.

72. For interesting correspondence regarding advisory board protests over the transfer of the corps officer in New Kensington, Pa., in June 1927, see SAARC, New Kensington Correspondence, RG 4.3, 206/15; "The Salvation Army Soars," *The Survey,* 15 June 1930, p. 259; WCC, 12 July 1930, p. 6. SANHQ was housed in this building until 1982, when the National Headquarters moved to Verona, N.J. In 1991 the National Headquarters moved to Alexandria, Va. The former headquarters building on West Fourteenth Street was occupied by Eastern Territorial Headquarters until 1991, when it moved to West Nyack, N.Y. The same building, which stands unaltered at 120 West Fourteenth St., is now occupied by the Army's Greater New York Metropolitan Command.

NOTES TO CHAPTER 5

1. St. John Ervine, *God's Soldier: General William Booth,* 2 vols. (New York, 1935), 2:1046-49 (Appendix 1, pp. 351-53 herein = Deed Poll of 1878).

2. Ervine, *God's Soldier,* 1:1078-90 (Appendix 6 = Supplementary Deed Poll of 1904); SA *Orders and Regulations for Officers,* 1925, pp. 11-12.

3. Lt. Col. J. Morgan, "General Bramwell Booth 'Behind the Scenes,'" *The Officer* 7 (March/April 1956): 83; *The Salvation Army Telegraph Code No. 2* (London, 1925), pp. 461-63, 610-13. The code books were designed to provide a vast catalogue of standard phrases that could be transmitted by telegraph using five-letter code words, a procedure that realized great savings in telegraph rates. The list of expected compliments appeared in the 1930 edition of the code book as well, but the more fulsome and personal were omitted in the later edition, issued after Bramwell had been removed from office. *The Salvation Army Telegraph No. 3* (London, 1930), pp. 435-36. These code books were kindly provided to the author by Comm. Robert E. Thomson in April 1992. The Commissioner discovered the books when supervising the transfer of headquarters records from 120 West 14th St. to the new facilities in West Nyack, N.Y.

4. Frederick Booth-Tucker to Samuel L. Brengle, London, 21 June 1927 (Gifford Coll., SAARC, closed); F. A. MacKenzie, *Booth-Tucker: Sadhu and Saint* (London, 1930), pp. 233-35, 238, 249; F. A. MacKenzie, *The Clash of the Cymbals: The Secret History of the Revolt in the Salvation Army* (New York, 1929), pp. 90-91, 122; interview with Comm. Richard E. Holz, Los Angeles, 13 December 1978.

5. "An American Salvation Army," *The Outlook,* 24 November 1926, p. 392; "The Salvation Army Revolution," LD, 4 December 1926, pp. 21-32; "Why the Salvation Army Revolted," LD, 9 February 1929, p. 25; "Colony or Dominion?" *The Outlook,* 13 March 1929, p. 421; MacKenzie, *The Clash of the Cymbals,* pp. 64, 115-17, 164-68. For correspondence containing specific statements about the feelings of Evangeline and her circle against Bramwell and their plans to alter the Army structure, see R. Griffith to Comm. Henry Mapp, New York, 22 November 1927; Lt. Col. [Richard Griffith] to [Comm. Adam] Gifford, New York, 5 December 1927; Evangeline Cory Booth (ECB) to Gifford, New York, 17 February 1928, conveying Exhibits "A," "B," and "C," her "Notes for an Interview with the General," his response to her dated 24 November 1927, and her twenty-one-page response to him dated 9 February 1928; William Peart to Gifford, New York, 14 May 1928 and 28 May 1928; Peart to Gifford, New York, 13 June 1928 and 19 September 1928 (if the Army's second-in-command refused to call the Council, Evangeline wished to know what the reaction would be of the American commissioners if she organized a meeting between all of them and the General to "consider the whole situation"; if he refused, and if the chief of the staff were still "unfavorable" to calling the Council, "there is still the possibility of the Commander calling together the High Council"); telegram [undated] from Gifford to all Western divisional commanders urging them to wire the Commander with their honest personal views concerning "change of method of successorship." All this correspondence in Gifford Coll., SAARC, closed. Comm. William McIntyre to all officers in the South, Atlanta, 12 December and 14 December 1928, urging them not to make comments to the press and to support "our beloved Commander, Evangeline Booth," who was "fully capable" of leading the U.S. branch of the Army "in the right direction in this important matter," owned by Lt. Col. Edward Laity, Atlanta.

6. Frank Smith, *The Betrayal of Bramwell Booth: The Truth about the Salvation Army Revolt* (London, 1929), pp. 51-65, 89, 92-93; Comm. Catherine Bramwell-Booth, *Bramwell Booth* (New York, 1932), pp. 474-76, 484-99, 500-503, 509, 517; MacKenzie, *The Clash of the Cymbals,* p. 64.

7. Ervine, *God's Soldier,* 2:1100-1120 (Appendices 8-11 = Atwood bulletins); W. L. Atwood to Adam Gifford, Wichita Falls, Tex., 1 December 1927, and a form soliciting articles for a new magazine, the "International Salvationist," to be published by Atwood, in Gifford Coll. There is no record of Atwood in the corps records of the Wichita Falls corps, which are "reasonably complete" back to 1928. When asked by the corps officer in 1979, two elderly soldiers remembered that Atwood attended services at the corps occasionally in the 1920s but was never a soldier. Lt. Marshall Gesner to the author, Wichita Falls, 22 June 1979.

8. MacKenzie, *The Clash of the Cymbals,* pp. 181-84; Ervine, *God's Soldier,* 2:905-6; Bramwell-Booth, *Bramwell Booth,* 485-86.

9. Bramwell Booth to ECB, London, 24 November 1927, Gifford Coll.

10. ECB to Bramwell-Booth, New York, 9 February 1928, pp. 12, 15 (quotations), in Gifford Coll.; Bramwell-Booth, *Bramwell Booth,* 489, 521.

11. Telegram, Comm. W. A. McIntyre to Col. A. Kimball, Atlanta, 14 November 1928, announcing that the General is "dying" and that the Commander, inviting all American commissioners to accompany her to London, and inviting the divisional commanders to express their views on successorship to her directly by wire — just as Gifford asked his officers to do (see n. 5 above), in Seiler Coll., binders; WCS, 1 December 1928, p. 8.

12. WCC, 23 February 1929, p. 8; MacKenzie, *The Clash of the Cymbals,* p. 137.

13. WCC, 19 January 1929, p. 8; 26 January 1929, pp. 8-11; 2 February 1929, pp. 9-10; 9 February 1929, p. 9; 16 February 1929, p. 9; WCS, 26 January 1929, pp. 6, 8-9; 2 February 1929, p. 4; 9 February 1929, p. 4; "Religious Dynasty," *The Outlook,* 9 January 1929, p. 60; Bramwell-Booth, *Bramwell Booth,* pp. 489, 521; Col. W. S. Barker (chief secretary for the Western Division, 1926-1930] to ECB, San Francisco, 17 December 1928 (urging her not to run for the office), Gifford Coll.; interview with Mrs. Col. William Noble, Atlanta, 27 November 1978, included the recollection that the Bramwell crisis broke McIntyre's heart; interview with Col. Bertram Rodda (daughter-in-law of Col. Jenkins, the national secretary during the crisis), Oakland, 12 December 1978, included the assertion that ECB allowed herself to be deceived into counting on her own election as Bramwell's successor; Ervine, *God's Soldier,* 2:1000-1001 (conveys the same version); Col. John Waldron, "Brengle and the Future of the Army," *The Officer* 27 (July 1976): 302-3 (on Brengle's role in the crisis of 1929). For Brengle's statements and observations as to why the other commissioners did not want to elect Booth, see his letter to Col. Jenkins, London, 15 January 1929 (SAARC, RG 20.5 206/12); quotation in cable to Damon in Damon Diaries, entry for 14 February 1929 (SAARC, RG 20.38, Damon 1929).

14. For the details of Brengle's visit to Gen. Bramwell Booth, see his thirty-page handwritten letter to Col. Jenkins, Sunbury Court, England, 14-21 January 1929 (SAARC, RG 20.5, 206/12).

15. WCE, 1 March 1929, p. 4; 23 March 1929, p. 9; "Why the Salvation Army Revolted," p. 25; Charles T. Hallinan, "The Overthrow of General Booth," *The Survey,* 1 March 1929, p. 712; "General Booth Goes to Court," *Commonweal,* 13 February 1929, pp. 413-14. An adequate, unbiased, and complete account of the overthrow of Gen. Bramwell Booth has not yet appeared in print. It is interesting to note that there were predictions of serious trouble about who would succeed Bramwell even before Gen. William

Booth died. See Agnes Maule Machar, "Red Cross Knights — A Nineteenth Century Crusade," *Andover Review* 2 (August 1884): 208; see also "General William Bramwell Booth and the Salvation Army," *The Outlook,* 15 November 1913, p. 562. Some American staff officers were privately relieved that Evangeline was not elected General.

16. WCC, 5 January 1929, pp. 8-9; 28 December 1929, p. 9; 22 February 1930, p. 6; 5 April 1930, p. 9; 10 May 1930, p. 3; WCC, 7 June 1930 ("Jubilee Number"); WCW, 21 January 1933, p. 5; interview with Lt. Col. Wm. Bearchell, Asbury Park, N.J., 30 June 1978; *Musical Salvationist,* July 1938, pp. 74-75.

17. U.S. Department of Commerce, Bureau of the Census, *Religious Bodies: 1906* (Washington, 1910), 2:613-20; Bureau of the Census, *Religious Bodies: 1926* (Washington, 1929), 2:1279; Bureau of the Census, *Religious Bodies: 1936* (Washington, 1941), 1:334-35; 2/2:1555.

18. Herbert A. Wisbey, Jr., "Religion in Action: A History of the Salvation Army in the United States" (Ph.D. diss., Columbia University, 1951), p. 378 (700 percent); WCE, 17 November 1934, pp. 8-9; WCS, 25 December 1936, pp. 21, 25; interview with Col. Frank Guldenschuh, Asbury Park, 28 June 1978; interview with Lt. Col. Charles Southwood, New York City, 3 August 1978; interview with Lt. Col. Wesley Bouterse, Atlanta, 28 November 1978. For an extended treatment of this period, see E. H. McKinley, *Somebody's Brother: A History of The Salvation Army Men's Social Service Department, 1891-1985* (Lewiston, Me., 1986), pp. 93-102.

19. Interview with Brig. Emma Ellegard, Asbury Park, N.J., 16 June 1978; interview with Sr. Maj. Magna Sorenson, Los Angeles, 15 December 1978; Brig. Hester Dames, "The Salvation Army, Eastern Territory, Opening Dates of Women's Social Institutions," SAARC, n.p.

20. Edward Higgins to Adam Gifford, London, 15 June 1931 (Gifford Coll.); interviews with Lt. Col. Bearchell and Col. C. Stanley Staiger, Ocean Grove, Calif., 28 July 1978; interview with Mrs. Col. William Noble, Atlanta, 27 November 1978; interviews with Lt. Col. Bouterse and Lt. Col. Norman Winterbottom, Santa Rosa, Calif., 13 December 1978; on the decision to close the training colleges, see the article by Comm. William Peart in WCE, 18 June 1932, p. 9; see also Lt. Col. William H. Barrett, "Anxious Candidates," WCE, 23 July 1932, p. 9; "Southern Trade Minutes," transfer file, SATHQ/S, trade dept., for 14 May 1931, p. 1. For data from commissioners' conference meetings, see CCM, 24-26 May 1932; 28 April 1933; and 13 November 1937 (SAARC, ARC 191).

21. Cyril W. Grace and Mrs. Cyril W. Grace, "A Survey of The Salvation Army of Minneapolis, Minnesota; September 4, 1937: A Summary" (Minneapolis, 1937), pp. 39, 52, (CTM, file drawer 11). The cited figures are for 1936. Capt. A. Kenneth Wilson, in his excellent corps history of Pottsville, Pa., states that the corps faced the end of the 1930s in debt to every merchant in town and in danger of losing the corps building, which was heavily mortgaged ("The Salvation Army in Pottsville, Pa.: A Centennial History — 1886-1986," unpublished typescript, p. 111).

22. Interview with Col. C. Emil Nelson, New York City, 24 October 1977; interview with Brig. Fred Crossley, Asbury Park, N.J., 30 June 1978; interview with Sr. Maj. Charles Schuerholz, Asbury Park, N.J., 30 June 1978; with Lt. Col. Laity; interview with Mrs. Col. Noble; interview with Sr. Maj. Railton Spake, Los Angeles, 15 December 1978; WCC, 9 May 1931, p. 13; WCS, 11 December 1937, p. 5; WCW, 28 January 1933, pp. 5, 14, 16; Bureau of the Census, *Religious Bodies: 1926,* 2:1279; Bureau of the Census,

Religious Bodies: 1936, 2/2:1555; Damon Diary, entries for 2 January 1933 (Waycross), 6 March 1933, and 11 May 1933 (cars) in SAARC, RG 20.38, 233/4, Damon 1933.

23. *The Young Soldier* (Central), 11 January 1930, p. 5 ("Golden Jubilee Crusade"); WCE, 9 January 1932, cover; WCE, 27 February 1932, p. 8 ("Fight It Through"); WCE, 18 February 1933, p. 16; Col. Fletcher Agnew, "Try Religion: A Special Campaign Article," WCE, 1 October 1932, p. 13; 25 February 1933, cover ("Try Religion"); WCE, 16 February 1935, p. 6 ("The World for God"); WCC, 27 January 1934, cover, p. 2 (build a wall); WCE, 5 February 1938, pp. 5, 14 (open-air figures and quotation); "The Man in the Street: Does He Still Get Converted at the Army Drumhead?" WCE, 26 February 1938, p. 4 (Dimond); *The Salvation Army's Contribution to a Century of Progress* (Chicago, [1933]), brochure, n.p. (CTM, Director's office files); WCC, 29 June 1968, p. 15 (information on Warner Sallman).

24. John Steinbeck, *The Grapes of Wrath* (1939; reprint, New York, 1972), pp. 349-50; Rick Mitchell, "The Salvation Army and Motion Pictures Project: First Draft Script," unpublished typescript, pp. 5-6, sent to the author by Capt. Robert R. Hostetler, Youngstown, Ohio, 4 November 1991.

25. Comm. William A. McIntyre, "The Homeless and Transient Problem in the United States," WCE, 15 July 1933, pp. 8, 12 (copy of an address to NCSW). For representative news items on depression relief, see WCE, 22 November 1930, p. 9; WCC, 10 January 1931, p. 13; 17 January 1931, pp. 4, 13; 29 November 1930, p. 8; WCE, 14 November 1931, pp. 8-9; WCS, volume for 1933 *passim;* WCE, 17 June 1933, p. 8; interview with Col. William Maltby, Asbury Park, N.J., 30 June 1978; interview with Mrs. Col. Noble; interview with Sr. Maj. Bertha Shadick, Los Angeles, 15 December 1978; "Nostalgem" WC, 19 May 1979, p. 6. For items about the *SS Broadway,* see Col. Fritz Nelson material, CTM, horizontal files.

26. WCE, 24 October 1931, cover, pp. 7, 14; WCC, 29 November 1930, p. 4.

27. WCE, 13 August 1932, p. 7 (Massilon); Col. Davis quoted in "The Drunkard Disappearing," LD, 2 April 1932, p. 21; "How Prohibition Saved the Bowery," LD, 17 May 1930, pp. 25-26 (quoting Evangeline Booth); WCE, 24 October 1931, p. 3; WCE, 13 May 1933, p. 11 (Winchell); "The Commander's Prohibition Address," WCE, 23 July 1932, p. 6 ("party").

28. WCC, 29 November 1930, p. 1; 10 December 1932, pp. 12-13; Maltby and Bearchell interviews; Brig. Edwin Clayton, "The Glory of Hard Times," WCC, 13 August 1932, p. 8; "Is God Speaking through the Depression?" WCE, 6 February 1932, pp. 2, 14; Adjutant Vincent Cunningham, "Stop Talking Depression," WCC, 21 May 1932, p. 5; Comm. S. L. Brengle, "What This Country Needs Is a Revival," WCC, 3 December 1932, pp. 8, 12.

29. Interviews with Brig. Crossley, Sr. Major Spake, Comm. Richard E. Holz; Ronald W. Holz, *Heralds of Victory: A History Celebrating the 100th Anniversary of The New York Staff Band and Male Chorus, 1887-1987* (New York, 1986), p. 54; "Salvation Plus Music," *Newsweek,* 15 December 1941, p. 69; interview with Sr. Maj. Carl Blied, Asbury Park, N.J., 14 July 1978; WCW, 9 January 1937, pp. 3, 14.

30. WCC, 17 February 1934; WC International, 18 January 1936; WCE, 2 January 1954, pp. 9, 14.

31. WCC, 17 February 1934, p. 12; CTM — Corps Histories — Norridge Citadel; WCS, 26 December 1936, p. 4, picture no. 2; interview with Col. Giles Barrett, Asbury

Park, N.J., 10 August 1978; Lt. Col. Charles Southwood, "Deployment of Officer Personnel in the Eastern Territory, December 2, 1976," Chart "G" (SATHQ/E, officer of Field Secretary for Personnel). On the Madsen recommendation, see "Facts and Reasons for a United Scandinavian-American Command," unpublished typescript, n.d. (RG 20.28, 218/9 Madsen Correspondence, SAARC).

32. Brief, "The Salvation Army Motorcade, Adjutant William Harris," [2-7 July 1931] (SFOT/E Museum, B/F, Evangeline Booth); WCE, 18 July 1931, p. 13; Bearchell interview; Laity interview (nose story).

33. "Presenting Leidzen and the Metropolitan Ensemble," WCE, 22 November 1930, p. 7.

34. Bandmaster Erik Leidzen, "'Songs of the Evangel': A Review," WCS, 30 April 1927, p. 5 ("handmaiden"); account of Leidzen vs. Eva episode from the private diary of Lt. Col. William Bearchell, interview with Comm. Richard Holz, and interview with Lt. Col. David W. Moulton, Wilmore, Ky., 15 May 1978; program, "Friday Evenings at the Temple, October to May, 1932-1933," and separate program for 26 May 1933 (Busby Coll.); Leslie Fossey, *This Man Leidzen* (London, 1966), pp. 24-26. The best biography of Leidzen is Ronald W. Holz's *Erik Leidzen: Band Arranger and Composer* (Lewiston, Me., 1990); the 1933 incident is described on pp. 26-32.

35. "Briefs, Star Lake Music Camp, 1935-1977," SATHQ/E, Music dept.; WCW, 14 December 1940, p. 13.

36. On Brown, see WCS, 18 December 1937, p. 5; 3 July 1948, pp. 8, 15; 3 January 1948, p. 8 (Order of Founder); 3 January 1959, p. 6 (obituary). The SATHQ/S publications bureau has a file labeled "Mountain Mission" that contains a retirement program and a pamphlet entitled "Maid of the Mountains" (Atlanta, 1947). On Mexico, see WCS, 2 October 1937, p. 16; 16 October 1937, p. 6; 23 October 1937, p. 8; 5 March 1938, p. 3; 3 December 1938, p. 8; 10 December 1938, pp. 8, 11, 13, 15; 8 May 1948, p. 13; interview with Comm. Ernest W. Holz, Atlanta, 23 November 1978; Brief, "Inauguration of Mexico and Central America Territory, Commissioner Ernest W. Holz," n.d. (Holz Coll.).

37. WCE, 8 October 1932, p. 12 (Symmonds); WCE, 31 December 1932, p. 10 (Milsaps); WCE, 21 January 1933, pp. 8-9 (Westbrook); WCE, 20 October 1934, pp. 8, 15 (Winchell); WCE, 16 March 1935, p. 12 (quotation on Parker); WCW, 30 October 1937, pp. 3, 14 (Joe the Turk); "Found — A Member of Railton's Pioneer Party!" WCE, 7 October 1939, pp. 5, 14. On Army ranks, see Appendix 2, pp. 354-55 herein, and WCC, 10 January 1931, p. 9.

38. WCE, 22 September 1934, cover, pp. 8-9; Ervine, *God's Soldier*, 2:1017-18. On the Higgins-ECB quarrel, see exchanges between Higgins and ECB and both with Gifford, 12 June 1930 and January-April 1931. A cable dated 20 April 1931 from ECB to seven international commissioners who had cabled her read, "My concern is that my dependence upon International respecting myself and America is worn threadbare. Records hold proof of repeated slights. Think possibly my ideas of loyalty have reached exaggerated degree." On the Bill itself, see WCC, 10 January 1931, p. 9. Gifford sought to calm the fears of divisional officers with a telegram he sent 5 March 1929 in which he indicated that she supported Higgins. "Not an atom of truth in published reports that Commander intends seceding and establishing independent organization. . . . Perfect harmony and unanimity exists" (Gifford Coll., SAARC).

39. Wisbey, "Religion in Action," p. 385; "National Tribute of Farewell to Evangeline Booth, General-Elect of The Salvation Army, New York City, October 31–November 2, 1934," program (Seiler Coll., binders); WCE, 22 September 1934, cover, pp. 8-9, 10; 29 September 1934, pp. 9, 13, 15; brief of appointment as territorial commander of the South, Comm. William Arnold, 27 March 1939, p. 3 (Busby Coll.); "Evangeline Booth Commands The Salvation Army," *Christian Century,* 12 September 1934, p. 1132; "Greatest Army: Evangeline Booth Inspecting Outposts of 3,000,000 Salvationists," LD, 21 November 1936, p. 20. On the lack of reform, see "Army Now Obeys 'General Eva,'" *Christian Century,* 26 September 1934, p. 1221; and "Electing a Successor to Evangeline Booth," *Current History,* June 1939, p. 49.

40. "Scrap Book, 1937 American Tour of General Evangeline Booth: The Voice of the South," compiled by Russell R. Whitman, public relations counsel for Southern tour, 1 October 1937 (SFOT/E Museum); WCS, 29 October 1938, p. 9.

41. WCS, 4 June 1938, pp. 8-9, 13; 18 June 1938, p. 15 (quotation), 14.

42. WCW, 22 March 1937, pp. 9, 14; 2 November 1940, p. 13.

43. WCE, 22 July 1939, p. 9; WCE, 9 September 1939, pp. 9, 14; WCE, 23 September 1939, pp. 8-9, 14; Evelyn Roe, "She 'Caught the Flame': General Evangeline Booth Soon to Retire from Many Years of Salvation Army Service," *Christian Science Monitor Magazine,* 19 August 1939, p. 7 ("slows down"); "Salvationists Curb Autocracy with Election of New Leader," *Newsweek,* 4 September 1939, p. 37; "Salvationist Problem: Autocracy-Democracy Issue Again Raised in Election," *Newsweek,* 28 August 1939, pp. 26-27; "The Salvation Army Has a New General," *Christian Century,* 6 September 1939, pp. 1059-60.

44. "The Salvation Army Carries On," *Newsweek,* 25 September 1939, p. 32; WCE, 30 July 1938, p. 7; WCE, 15 April 1939, cover ("spirit of love"); WCE, 14 October 1939, p. 8, and 20 May 1939, p. 15 (SA day at Fair); WCE, 25 November 1939, p. 8 (Armistice Day).

45. "School for Salvage," LD, 11 September 1937, pp. 16-17; Brig. Norman S. Marshall, "The Enthusiasts' Session of Cadets: A Saga of Accomplishment," WCE, 18 June 1938, pp. 8-9; WCE, 10 June 1939, p. 8; Richard O. Boyer, "A Reporter at Large: Hold Fast! Hold Fast!" *The New Yorker,* 13 April 1940, p. 65. For figures for the denomination as a whole, see Bureau of Census, *Religious Bodies: 1936,* 1:96.

46. SA, *The 1944 Institutes of the Men's Social Service Department* (New York, 1944), p. 137; interview with Lt. Col. Peter J. Hofman, Asbury Park, N.J., 1 August 1978; McKinley, *Somebody's Brother,* pp. 112-15.

47. "The Salvation Army Carries On," *Newsweek,* 25 September 1939, p. 32 (quotation); *What Is The Salvation Army?* (New York, 1945), pp. 13-15; interview with Col. Giles Barrett; details of the commissioners' conference meeting of 18-19 March 1941 in CCM, SAARC ARC 191, p. 3; see also CCM, 13-14 April 1942, SAARC ARC 191 (dancing quotation); "Militant Christians," *Time,* 9 November 1942, p. 64; Comm. Edward Justus Parker, *My Fifty-Eight Years: An Autobiography* (New York, 1943), pp. 283-98, 300-305; Sallie Chesham, *Born to Battle: The Salvation Army in America* (Chicago, 1965), pp. 221-22, 227.

48. Interview with Comm. R. E. Holz; Wisbey, "Religion in Action," pp. 406-7; WCW, 9 November 1940, p. 9.

49. WCW, 6 December 1941, p. 9; *The Red Shield,* February 1943, p. 1 (SAARC).

50. WCW, 9 November 1940, p. 8; Lt. Col. Norman J. Winterbottom, "Territorial Chronology, Western Territory, USA," n.p. (SATHQ/W, personnel dept.); CCM, 13-14 April 1942, p. 13 (suggestion that the Western territorial Scandinavian work should be amalgamated); SA, *Disposition of Forces, Western Territory, October 1940*, p. 36; *Disposition of Forces, Western Territory, April 1941*, pp. 11-13; *Disposition of Forces, Western Territory, October 1941*, pp. 11-13, 22-24; interview with Brig. Masahide Imai, Santa Clara, Calif., 12 December 1978; interview with Lt. Col. R. Eugene Rice, Los Angeles, 7 December 1978.

51. Interview with Col. Orval Taylor, New York City, 4 August 1978; interviews with Lt. Col. Rice and Lt. Col. Winterbottom.

52. Interview with Brig. Imai; Capt. Lawrence Shiroma, "The Story of the Japanese Division," NF, 24 August 1991, pp. 1, 4-5. Additional material was kindly supplied by Capt. Shiroma under cover of his letter to the author, San Francisco, 16 September 1991. Included in this material was a copy of an oral interview conducted by Yoshino Tajiri Hasegawa for the Fresno County Free Library 14 July 1983 ("Brigadier Masahide Imai: An Oral Interview," Fresno County Public Library, Samuel Suhler Memorial Oral History Collection, 1984).

53. Shiroma, "The Story of the Japanese Division," p. 4.

54. *What Is The Salvation Army?* pp. 13-15; SA, *Disposition of Forces, Southern Territory, December 1942*, p. 14, *Disposition of Forces, Southern Territory, September 1943*, p. 16, *Disposition of Forces, Southern Territory, November 1944*, p. 16, *Disposition of Forces, Southern Territory, November 1945*, p. 16, *Disposition of Forces, Southern Territory, October 1946*, p. 14, interviews with Col. Maltby, Lt. Col. Winterbottom, Comm. R. E. Holz; "Militant Christians," *Time*, 9 November 1942, p. 64; Brig. William J. Parkins, "The USO Work of The Salvation Army," *Journal of Social Hygiene* 29 (January 1943): 11-13; WC, 10 November 1990, p. 2.

55. *1944 Institutes, Men's Social*, pp. 3, 61, 115, *passim;* interviews with Col. Frank Guldenschuh and Lt. Col. Hofman; for a detailed treatment of the development of the "Service to Man" program, see McKinley, *Somebody's Brother*, pp. 119-34; see also "Activities of the Research Council on Problems of Alcohol," *Quarterly Journal of Studies on Alcohol* 1 (June 1940): 104-5 (journal hereinafter cited as *QJSA*); Walter L. Voegtlin and Frederick Lemere, "The Treatment of Alcohol Addiction: A Review of the Literature," *QJSA* 2 (March 1942): 724-28; E. H. L. Corwin and Elizabeth V. Cunningham, "Institutional Facilities for the Treatment of Alcoholism: Report of a Study by the 'Committee on Hospital Treatment of Alcoholism' of the American Hospital Association," *QJSA* 5 (June 1944): 57-59 (quotation on p. 59); Rev. Francis McPeek, "The Role of Religious Bodies in the Treatment of Inebriety in the United States," *QJSA* (1945): 414-15 (sympathetic account of the traditional Salvation Army program for alcoholics); Rev. Roland H. Bainton, "The Churches and Alcohol," *QJSA* 6 (June 1945): 57-58 (makes no mention of the Army).

56. Interview with Brig. Ruth E. Cox, RN, Los Angeles, 11 December 1978; interview with Sr. Major Sorenson; letter from Dr. Alvin H. Darden to Gerald White, Cincinnati, Ohio, 30 September 1968, covered by Capt. Israel Gaither to Maj. Dorothy Breen, New York City, 25 May 1979 ("Black Salvationist" research, SAARC); letter from Matthew S. Borman (asst. archivist, SAARC) to the author, New York, 27 May 1983. The complete records for the Evangeline and Catherine Booth hospitals for these years are housed in the SAARC.

57. WCW, 31 January 1942, p. 3; WCE, 27 December 1941, pp. 10, 15; *Red Shield,* January 1942, p. 1; interview with Brig. Henry Dries, Asbury Park, N.J., 3 July 1978.

58. WCW, 27 December 1941, p. 10; 14 February 1942, p. 9; Comm. Samuel L. Brengle, "Killing in Battle: Is It Murder?" WCW, 31 January 1942, p. 5; on Hester Pottinger, consult CTM Oral History collection, Hester Pottinger (September 1982); on Goodier, see Edward H. McKinley, "Brass Bands and God's Work: One Hundred Years of the Salvation Army in Georgia and Atlanta," *Atlanta History: A Journal of Georgia and the South* 34 (Winter 1990-1991): p. 19; "Report to the Advisory Board of The Salvation Army of Augusta, Ga., January 3 to December 26, 1943," in Divisional File, Augusta, in Salvation Army Georgia Divisional Headquarters, Atlanta.

59. WCW, 9 January 1943, p. 10; interview with Brig. Dries; interview with Bandmaster Alfred V. Swenarton, Asbury Park, N.J., 10 July 1978; interview with Brig. Crossley; McKinley, "Brass Bands and God's Work," p. 18; *Red Shield,* February 1942, pp. 1-2; March 1942, p. 1; *What Is The Salvation Army?* pp. 35-36; Chesham, *Born to Battle,* p. 226; *Red Shield,* October 1942, pp. 2-3; *Worker's Index for the 1943 Salvation Army Campaign for Wartime Activities and Welfare Needs* (New York, 1943), SFOT/E Museum, G/F, "WW II."

60. WCW, 3 January 1942; 17 April 1943, pp. 9, 12; 18 March 1944, p. 10; *Red Shield,* January 1942, p. 1; WCW, 20 February 1943, p. 12; interview with Lt.-Col. Eric Newbould, Los Angeles, 6 December 1978; Winterbottom, "Territorial Chronology, Western Territory, USA," n.p., "Hawaii Division"; interview with Brig. Olive McKeown, Asbury Park, N.J., 2 August 1978.

61. WCW, 15 April 1944, p. 3; 27 May 1944, p. 11; 28 April 1945, p. 13; [Lt. Col.] Chester O. Taylor, "Nah-Kee-Ahn-Sa-Kol-Neek: A Northland Story," unpublished typescript, SFOT/W Library, pp. 10-30, 34-40; interview with Lt.-Col. Chester O. Taylor, Hayward, Calif., 12 December 1978; O. M. Salisbury, *The Customs and Legends of the Tlinget Indians of Alaska* (reprint, New York, 1962), pp. 99-106, photos facing p. 20; WC, 5 August 1978, pp. 13-14; "Beginnings of The Salvation Army in Alaska," cassette recording, Lt. Col. Walter Carruthers, SATHQ/W, chief secretary's office.

62. In a letter to Prof. Wisbey dated 27 September 1948, the Chief of Chaplains, U.S.A., indicates that there was a total of thirty SA chaplains in World War II ("Religion in Action," p. 406, n. 2); Comm. R. E. Holz states that it was thirty-two (interview).

63. Interviews with Comm. R. E. Holz, Col. Giles Barrett; Comm. Richard E. Holz, "Bombed Out on Christmas Eve: An Actual World War 2 Adventure," WC, Christmas, 1978, pp. 8-9.

64. All correspondence cited in the treatment of the matter of the national commandership found in SANHQ File Box 11, Acc. 89-56, "Correspondence, 1943-1946" (national chief secretary), unprocessed, file "Commandership," viewed by permission of Comm. Kenneth Hood, National Chief Secretary, March 1992. The author is grateful to Maj. Judith B. Small for bringing this important correspondence to his attention during his research trip to National Headquarters in March 1992. Charles Baugh, Chief Secretary, to E. I. Pugmire, London, 8 December 1943 and 13 December 1943 (quotations).

65. Lt. Comm. Donald McMillan to John L. McNab, San Francisco, 17 November 1943 (telegram); Ernest I. Pugmire to Charles Baugh, New York City, 19 November 1943; Baugh to Pugmire, London, 8 December 1943 and 13 December 1943; "Bulletin, Terri-

torial Headquarters" (New York City), 14 December 1943; Edward J. Parker to Gen. George Carpenter, New York City, 15 December 1943 (cable); [E. I. Pugmire] to Charles Baugh, New York City, 3 January 1944; George Carpenter to Pugmire, London, 21 February 1944; [Carpenter] to E. I. Pugmire, London, 13 December 1944, conveying Memorandum of Appointment (M.O.A.) as Commander; "Memorandum from Commissioner Donald McMillan Re: Corporations of The Salvation Army in the United States" [28 September 1945], unpublished typescript; Baugh to Pugmire, London, 19 October 1945; Pugmire to Baugh, New York City, 27 November 1945. All mmaterials described here were found in the SANHQ files cited in note 64.

66. Baugh to E. I. Pugmire, London, 4 March 1946 ("a little natural reluctance"); on Pugmire's preference for the title "national commander," see Pugmire to Baugh, New York City, 27 November 1945; for the official (negative) response, see Baugh to Pugmire, London, 11 December 1945, insisting on the "Commander" title that was required by the Army's acts of incorporation and "that Commander Evangeline used for so long"; SA, *Disposition of Forces, Eastern, April 1943,* p. 1 (first use of "National Commander" for Comm. Edward J. Parker); *Disposition of Forces, Eastern, August 1947,* p. 1; *Disposition of Forces, Western, July 1947,* p. 1; *Disposition of Forces, Central, October 1948,* p. 1; *Disposition of Forces, Southern, November 1949,* p. 1. See also many of the items cited in note 65 above.

67. WCE, 22 December 1945, cover; "New General: Salvation Army's World Leader Is a Straight-Talking Preacher from Street Corners of London," *Life,* 4 November 1946, pp. 85-88; [Gen.] Albert Orsborn, *The House of My Pilgrimage* (London, 1958), pp. 146-48, 185-86.

68. *The Salvation Army Social Service for Men: Standards and Practices* (New York, 1948), p. 5; SA, *Orders and Regulations for Local Officers* (London, 1946), pp. 1-3; for officer ranks, see Appendix 2, pp. 354-55 herein.

69. Beulah Amidon, "Front Line Officer," *Survey Graphic* 37 (October 1948): 430-32, 439-40.

70. James Neilson, "The Salvation Army Band, Part One," *The Etude* 67 (January 1949): 20 (quotations); "The Salvation Army Band, Part Two," *The Etude* 67 (February 1949): 123; WCW, 29 June 1946, pp. 9, 15 (first in the air). The Flint Citadel Band mistakenly made a claim to be the first band to fly to an engagement, based on a 1950 trip; see WC, 22 April 1978, p. 6.

71. Neilson, "Salvation Army Band, Part Two," pp. 81, 123; interviews with Comm. R. E. Holz and Bandmaster Alfred Swenarton; "Brief, Star Lake Camp, 1949," SATHQ/E Music Dept.; Vernon Post, comp., *An Index to the Compositions of Erik Leidzen by Title* (New York, n.d.); Holz, *Erik Leidzen,* pp. 52-78, 89-90, 111-19; Ronald W. Holz, "A History of the Hymn Tune Meditation and Related Forms in Salvation Army Instrumental Music in Great Britain and North America, 1880-1980" (Ph.D. diss., University of Connecticut, 1981), pp. 79-83; "The Talk of the Town: To Ennoble the Soul," *The New Yorker,* 23 April 1949, pp. 13-14.

72. Interview with Lt. Col. Laity, in which the author was shown the program for the first Brengle Institute; WC, 8 April 1978, p. 8 (obituary for Col. Albert Pepper); CTM, Drawer 13, "Brengle and Sessions," contains lists of all delegates to all sessions of the Brengle Institute starting in 1947.

73. *Red Shield,* July 1943, p. 1; *War Service Bulletin,* March 1945, p. 2; July 1945, p. 4; WCS, 10 January 1948, p. 15; 31 January 1948, p. 4; 29 May 1948, p. 11; interviews

with Comm. Ernest W. Holz and Lt. Col. Laity; "The History of Sherman Avenue Corps (Including No. 2 and Central Corps) Washington, D.C.," comp. Linda B. Murray for Capt. Allan Wiltshire, Sherman Ave. Corps, 4 December 1978, pp. 2-3, 4 (SAARC); McKinley, *Somebody's Brother,* pp. 184-85; Amidon, "Front Line Officer," p. 432.

74. WCS, 24 April 1948, pp. 8-9, 13; 15 May 1948, p. 7; 12 June 1948, p. 5; 19 June 1948, p. 5; 3 July 1948, p. 11; 24 July 1948, p. 6; 14 August 1948, p. 13; 25 September 1948, p. 15; interview with Lt. Col. Laity; Arnold's appointment memorandum as territorial commander of the South included these instructions: "The needs also of the large population of coloured people must not be overlooked" (27 March 1939, p. 4 — Busby Coll.).

75. "Shock Troops," *Time,* 26 January 1948, p. 71; "I Was a Stranger," *Time,* 26 December 1949, pp. 39, 41 (clipping courtesy Col. C. S. Staiger); "How to Meet Better People," *Time,* 7 February 1949, p. 16; "Frank and the Nice People," *Newsweek,* 7 February 1949, pp. 22-23.

76. Interviews with Col. Nelson and Col. Guldenschuh; interview with Lt. Col. Lyell Rader, Ocean Grove, N.J., 23 June 1978.

77. Evangeline C. Booth to Ensign Wm. Maltby, New York City, 16 January 1928; ECB to Brig. Wm. Maltby, Hartsdale, 29 November 1948 (both in the possession of Col. Maltby, who kindly provided much of the information for this episode). "Program, Musical Festival Featuring the Compositions of Evangeline Booth, Friday Evening at the Temple, November 19, 1948," in SFOT/E Museum, B/F, Evangeline Booth.

78. "Evangeline Booth Is Promoted to Glory," *Life,* 31 July 1950, pp. 72-73; Maj. Christine E. McMillan, "The Founder's Daughter," WCE, 12 August 1950, p. 7 (and see the rest of the issue as well).

NOTES TO CHAPTER 6

1. *Time,* 26 December 1949, cover and pp. 38-41; see Lt. Col. Rowland D. Hughes, "Behind the Banners and Bonnets," WCE, 27 November 1954, pp. 5, 14.

2. *Guys and Dolls,* story by Damon Runyon, music and lyrics by Frank Loesser, book by Jo Swerling and Abe Burrows; Charlotte and Denis Plimmer, "Marching as to War," *Reader's Digest,* November 1961, p. 186 (quotation); Kurt Tetzeli v. Rosador, "The Natural History of *Major Barbara,*" *Modern Drama* 17 (June 1974): 153, nn. 32-39; "Mercenaries for Christ," *Newsweek,* 27 December 1971, p. 50.

3. Sr. Capt. Don Pitt, *Pilgrim's Progress — Twentieth Century: The Story of Salvation Army Officership* (New York, 1950), p. 19; WCE, 9 January 1954, p. 12 (Frankfort); WCE, 18 September 1954, p. 11 (Niagara Falls funeral; the sergeant major was Edward V. Mateer). See also "Salvation Army Street Fighters," WCE, 20 March 1954, p. 3.

4. There was one exception to the general renaming: the New York Bowery Corps retained its original name, since the Army decided the name was "distinctly linked with a street of the city." See *The Salvation Army Yearbook for 1950* (London, 1951), p. 90; Paul Robb, "Cap'n Tom — The Other Side of Skid Row," *Reader's Digest,* April 1952, pp. 95-96; "Shock Troops," *Time,* 26 January 1948, p. 71; Albert Orsborn, *The House of My Pilgrimage* (London, 1958), pp. 188-90; *Time,* 26 December 1949, p. 39; interview with Brig. Olive McKeown, Asbury Park, N.J., 2 August 1978.

5. Interview with Col. Frank Guldenschuh, Asbury Park, N.J., 16 June 1978; interview with Col. Giles Barrett, Asbury Park, N.J., 10 July 1978; interview with Lt. Col. Peter J. Hofman, Asbury Park, N.J., 1 August 1978; Howard J. Clinebell, Jr., *Understanding and Counseling the Alcoholic through Religion and Psychology* (New York, 1956), pp. 83-93.

6. Leonard Blumberg, Thomas E. Shipley Jr., and Irving W. Shandler, *Skid Row and Its Alternatives: Research and Recommendations from Philadelphia* (Philadelphia, 1973), pp. 148-49; *The Salvation Army Yearbook, 1956* (London, 1956), p. 135 ("trophy"); on Cleveland, see WCE, 19 June 1954, p. 16, and 17 July 1954, p. 16.

7. Interview with Lt. Col. Hofman; "Bargain Buys from the Salvation Army," *Good Housekeeping,* January 1959, p. 95.

8. Interview with Lt. Col. Hofman; *Minutes of the Men's Social Service Secretaries' Conference, October 3, 4, 5, 1956* (New York, 1956), pp. 6, 9-11, 34, 39-45, 58-59, 69, 73, *passim;* The Salvation Army Men's Social Service, *Handbook of Standards, Principles and Policies* (New York, 1960), pp. 7-14, 61-62, 249-54, *passim;* Blumberg et al., *Skid Row and Its Alternatives,* pp. 19-20; the current edition is *The Salvation Army Men's Social Service Handbook of Standards, Principles and Policies,* approved by the Commissioners' Conference, October 1987 (New York, 1987). For an extensive treatment of the relationship between the Fair Labor Standards Act and The Salvation Army Men's Social Services in these years, see E. H. McKinley, *Somebody's Brother: A History of The Salvation Army Men's Social Services Department, 1891-1985* (Lewiston, Me., 1986), pp. 112-14, 126, 129, 140-52, 161-69.

9. Herbert W. Wisbey, *Soldiers without Swords: A History of The Salvation Army in the United States* (New York, 1955), p. 209; Herbert W. Wisbey, "Religion in Action: A History of The Salvation Army in the United States" (Ph.D. diss., Columbia University, 1951), p. 412; Sr. Maj. Jane E. Wrieden, "To Strengthen Maternity-Home Service for Unmarried Mothers, II," *The Officer* 5 (March-April 1954): 86-87; *The Salvation Army Services to Unmarried Parents and Their Children — Maternity Homes and Hospitals: Handbook of Information* (New York, 1962), pp. 56-57, 18-21, 23-29 (quotations pp. 19 and 24), hereinafter cited as *Homes and Hospitals Handbook;* interview with Brig. Ruth E. Cox, R.N., Los Angeles, 11 December 1978; Richard Armstrong, "An Army of Gentle Warriors," *Saturday Evening Post,* 15 December 1962, p. 17.

10. WCE, 27 November 1954, cover, pp. 2-3 (seventy-fifth anniversary); Maj. Christine E. McMillan, "Those Were the Pioneers," WCE, 27 November 1954, p. 2 (quotation); WCE, 27 November 1954, p. 15 (radio program and recordings); Comm. Norman S. Marshall, "The Army Is Still 'On The March,'" WCE, 10 July 1954, p. 3; Comm. Richard E. Holz (R), "My Favorite Bandsman," WC, 12 March 1983, pp. 12-13 (Frank Fowler); "To Spread Gospel via Radio," WCE, 1 January 1955, p. 6 (Rader); WCE, 9 April 1960, p. 7 ("Today"). For use of the corps numbering system, see *Young Salvationist* (Central edition) 9 January 1954; WCE, 4 December 1954, p. 9 ("Army of Stars"); WCE, 26 March 1960, p. 15 (33 rpm).

11. J. Stanley Sheppard, *The Prison Work of The Salvation Army* (New York, 1948), p. 23; SFOT/E Library, pamphlet files, "Penology," for reports of Salvation Army Congress of Corrections, 1959-1967; WC, 4 March 1978, p. 15; interview with Lt. Col. Chester Taylor, Hayward, Calif., 12 December 1978; on Nightingale, see "Twenty Years in San Francisco's Shadows," WC, 3 January 1970, pp. 12-13; on Alpha, see Anthony W. Zum-

petta, "ALPHA Doesn't Sell Paroles — It Builds Self-Confidence and Respect," *American Journal of Correction* 37 (March-April 1975): 34, 40.

12. *Testament to Youth: The Salvation Army's Report to the Mid-Century White House Conference on Children and Youth* (New York, 1950), pp. 9-16, 36, 37-39; all four WC editions for 28 October 1950; Lt. Col. Charles Southwood, "Deployment of Officer Personnel in Eastern Territory, December 2, 1976," charts F and G; for the figures of the decline, see *The Salvation Army Yearbook, 1955* (London, 1956), p. 121, and sources for national statistics cited in the bibliographical essay; Armstrong, "An Army of Gentle Warriors," p. 22.

13. "Brief: Eastern Territory Public Relations Department," compiled by Lt. Col. H. E. Weatherly, 28 March 1963, pp. 2-3 (SAARC); *Action! The Salvation Army Manual for Emergency Disaster Service* (New York, 1972), p. 7 (quotation); Wisbey, "Religion in Action," p. 315; *The Salvation Army Definitive Statement of Service and Activities* (New York, 1960), p. 19.

14. Orsborn, *House of My Pilgrimage,* p. 191; Pitt, *Pilgrim's Progress,* p. 15; *Salvation Army Yearbook 1955,* p. 122; WCE, 2 January 1954, pp. 9, 14 (SAROL); Maj. David Baxendale, "These Are My People!" *The Officer* 24 (December 1973): 542.

15. Herbert Newton, "Is the Army Policy Scriptural?" *Conq* 2 (February 1893): 55 ("pigeon-holed"); Capt. John Waldron, "Statistics Tell a Story," *The Officer* 4 (September-October 1953): 294; Wisbey, "Religion in Action," pp. 410-11; Wisbey, *Soldiers without Swords,* p. 208; "Management: Salvation Army Beats a Bigger, Better Drum," *Business Week,* 19 June 1965, pp. 116, 123 (quotation).

16. Wisbey, "Religion in Action," pp. 385-88; Wisbey, *Soldiers without Swords,* pp. 194-96; "The New Army," *Time,* 30 June 1958, p. 68.

17. Wisbey, "Religion in Action," p. 172; Wisbey, *Soldiers without Swords,* p. 82; Lt. Col. Norman J. Winterbottom, "Territorial Chronology: The Salvation Army Western Territory, USA," 1963-1967, "Divisions Discontinued, No. 5: Scandinavian Division" (SAARC, "Eastern Scandinavian" file); SA, *Disposition of Forces, Eastern Territory, November 1960,* pp. 64-66; *Disposition of Forces, Eastern Territory, October 1961,* p. 6; *Disposition of Forces, Central Territory, November 1963,* pp. 50-52; *Disposition of Forces, Central Territory, November 1964,* pp. 42-45; *Disposition of Forces, Central Territory, October 1965,* pp. 48-52; WCE, 18 February 1961, p. 10; WCE, 21 January 1961, p. 15; Edward O. Nelson, *Hallelujah: Recollections of Salvation Army Scandinavian Work in the USA* (Chicago, 1987), pp. 131-35; Lt. Col. Olof Lundgren to author, New York City, 19 June 1978; Comm. Robert Rightmire to author, Whiting, N.J., 5 February 1992.

18. The quoted survey is cited in Vincent W. Erickson, "Doers of the Word in Today's Congregations," *Lutheran Quarterly* 17 (August 1965): 260; "Booth Led Boldly with His Big Bass Drum," *Christian Century,* 14 July 1965, p. 886; Pitt, *Pilgrim's Progress,* p. 50; Armstrong, "Army of Gentle Warriors," p. 22.

19. On affiliation with the NHA, see *The Salvation Army Yearbook 1960* (London, 1961), p. 129, and WCE, 4 June 1960, pp. 2-8; WCE, 2 July 1960, pp. 7, 14. On the resurrection of messages by pioneer Army leaders, see the late Comm. Samuel L. Brengle, "We Need a Revival," WCE, 16 January 1960, pp. 5, 14; George Scott Railton, "More Conquests! A Message for Today Written in 1894," WCE, 2 January 1960, p. 2; "Go — by the Founder," WCE, 2 January 1960, p. 4. On the Army's traditional programs, see Comm. Edward Carey, "'Is the Army in America . . . ?'" *The Officer* 19 (March-April

1968), p. 83; Capt. Frances Anderson, "A Bonnet for All Seasons," WCE, Easter 1967, pp. 12-13 (quotation). On lay commissions and Glen Eyrie, see WCE, 6 May 1967, p. 15; WCE, 13 May 1967, pp. 2-3; WCE, 27 May 1967, p. 16. On Army programs to hippies and street people, see Mrs. Brig. Howard F. Chesham, "The Old Hat," WCC, 4 November 1967, pp. 12-15; Sgt. Maj. Thomas C. Maier, "Boardwalk Evangelists," WCE, 8 July 1967, pp. 7, 10; Lt. Col. Kay McClelland, "New Sight in San Francisco," WCE, 17 June 1967, pp. 12-13; McCandlish Phillips, "Salvation Army Has 'Answer' for Hippies," WCE, 30 September 1967, pp. 20-21 (reprint of article in *The New York Times*); Allen Satterlee, *Sweeping through the Land: A History of The Salvation Army in the Southern United States* (Atlanta, 1989), pp. 215-16; also WCE, 18 February 1967, p. 8; WCE, 15 July 1967, p. 14; WCE, 7 January 1970; WCE, 12 September 1970, p. 19.

20. "Evangelism: Steady as Before," *Time*, 11 October 1963, pp. 86-88; Lt. Kenneth L. Hodder, "How Much Can a Vietnam Day Hold?" WCE, 17 May 1967, pp. 4-5; 8 April 1967, p. 17; Capt. Paul Kelly, "They Wear Another Uniform," WCE, 4 February 1967, p. 11; Lawrence P. Fitzgerald, "Viet-Nam: What More Can the Churches Do?" WCE, 11 February 1967, pp. 7-8, 15; "Religion in the News: Clergymen Can't Agree on Vietnam," WCE, 11 March 1967, p. 17; research material files, "Viet-Nam," unprocessed, in SAARC, under cover of letter Col. Norman S. Marshall to Maj. Dorothy Breen, New York City, 6 September 1977. For a reflection of the effect of the Army's military image in the 1960s, see Verne Becker, "Saved by the Bell," *Christianity Today*, 17 December 1990, p. 18. On the dismissal and lawsuit issues, see Trevor Beeson, "Salvation by Censorship," *Christian Century*, 1 July 1970, p. 812; "Crisis for Salvationists," *Christian Century*, 23 September 1970, p. 114; "Salvation Army Officer Ousted in Dispute over Book," *Christian Century*, 4 November 1970, p. 1312; J. D. Douglas, "Breaking Ranks," *Christianity Today*, 6 November 1970, p. 58; "S*E*X in the Army," *Christianity Today*, 9 October 1970, pp. 40-41; "High Court Refuses to Act on Women's Rights Issue," *Christian Century*, 1 November 1972, p. 1091; Comm. William E. Chamberlain, "Memorandum: Mrs. Billie B. McClure vs The Salvation Army," Atlanta, 5 January 1973 (SAA); Satterlee, *Sweeping through the Land*, pp. 213-14; "Concerned Officers' Fellowship" file, National Headquarters Correspondence (national chief secretary), unprocessed, SAARC, Acc. 89-56, Box 11, reviewed by permission of the national chief secretary; this file also contains references to several "bulletins," and numerous important letters: Lt. Comm. William J. Parkins to Comm. Samuel Hepburn, San Francisco, 16 March 1967; Comm. William Davidson to Comm. Samuel Hepburn, New York City, 17 March 1967; and William J. Moss to Lt. Comm. John Grace, New York City, 6 February 1968 (urging that the Army take no official action regarding the "COF"); see also CCM, 8 November 1967, cited in Moss's letter to show that the commissioners' decided to take no action.

21. Capt. Philip Collier, "Someone Saw the Need," WCE, 28 May 1960, pp. 3, 14; Brig. Paul S. Kaiser, "Candidates' Corner: Service in the Sixties," WCE, 11 June 1960, p. 3. On the establishment of the two-year program, see "The New Army," *Time*, 30 June 1958, pp. 67-68; Sr. Maj. Henry Koerner, "Candidates: An American Contribution to an Ever-Relevant Discussion," *The Officer* 7 (March-April 1956): 116-17; Raymond Arthur Dexter, "Officer Training in The Salvation Army: An Institutional Analysis" (Ed.D. diss., Stanford University, 1962), pp. 139-40; "The Salvation Soldiers," *Newsweek*, 6 June 1960, p. 85; *The Salvation Army Definitive Statement of Service and Activities*, p. 11.

22. Dexter, "Officer Training in The Salvation Army," note on p. 150; Morton

Yarmon, "About The Salvation Army," *New York Times Magazine,* 28 November 1954, p. 20; "The Hallelujah Army Observes Its 75th Christmas," *Life,* 27 December 1954, p. 10; Gilbert Millstein, " 'Sinner, Will You Let Him In?' " *New York Times Magazine,* 21 May 1961, p. 30; Richard Armstrong, "An Army of Gentle Warriors," *Saturday Evening Post,* 15 December 1962, p. 20; Southwood, "Deployment of Officer Personnel in Eastern Territory, December 2, 1976"; interview with Comm. Ernest W. Holz and Col. John Paton, Atlanta, 23 November 1978; statistics from annual editions of the SA *Yearbook.*

23. James Francis Cooke, "Pennies in the Tambourine: An Editorial," *Etude,* July 1953, p. 59; *An Index of the Compositions of Erik Leidzen by Title,* comp. Vernon Post (New York, n.d.); SA Eastern Territorial Music Bureau, *Catalog and Price List for Instrumental Music and Vocal Music* (New York, 1977); Ronald W. Holz, "A History of the Hymn Tune Meditation and Related Forms in Salvation Army Instrumental Music in Great Britain and North America, 1880-1980" (Ph.D. diss., University of Connecticut, 1981), pp. 87-109 (quotation, p. 97).

24. Sallie Chesham, *Born to Battle: The Salvation Army in America* (Chicago, 1965), p. 254; Wisbey, "Religion in Action," p. 129; Wisbey, *Soldiers without Swords,* p. 62; *Testament to Youth,* pp. 37-38.

25. Interview with Comm. Ernest W. Holz; SA, *Disposition of Forces, Southern Territory, June 1952,* p. 26; *Disposition of Forces, Southern Territory, November 1952,* p. 26; *Disposition of Forces, Southern Territory, April 1951,* p. 23; *Disposition of Forces, Southern Territory, November 1951,* p. 24; Helen G. Purviance to Brig. Edward Carey, New York City, 24 March 1949, filed with Capt. George H. Evans, " 'The Black Salvationists' (Work in Progress) Regarding the Cleveland (Central Area Corps), Ohio," part of material on African American Salvationists presented by Capt. Israel Gaither to the SAARC; information on Victor Wilson based on private interview with the author, Sherman Avenue Corps, Washington, 8 March 1992.

26. WCS, 8 January 1955, p. 4; WCS, 15 January 1955, p. 10; WCS, 5 February 1955, p. 9; WCE, 21 January 1961, p. 8; interview with Brig. Emma Ellegard, Asbury Park, N.J., 16 June 1978; interview with Sr. Maj. Railton Spake, Los Angeles, 11 December 1978.

27. "A Position Statement: The Salvation Army and Inter-Group Relations," approved by the commissioners' conference, May 1964; Chesham, *Born to Battle,* pp. 253-54.

28. WCE, 18 May 1963, pp. 20-21; WCE, 10 September 1966, p. 20; Baxendale, "These Are My People!" p. 359.

29. Lt. John Merritt, "The Salvation Army in the Inner City," *The Officer* 20 (August 1969): 565; Brig. Christine McMillan, "Opportunity Unlimited at the Harlem Temple Corps," WCE, 11 March 1967, and "The Harlem That Doesn't Make the Headlines," WCE, 11 February 1967; Capt. David Holz to Maj. Carl Hansen, Richmond, Va., 31 May 1968, in SATHQ/S Publications Bureau files, "SA and Blacks"; WC, 10 March 1979, pp. 12-13; *The Musician* (New York), May 1979, p. 11.

30. Maj. Dorothy E. Breen, "The Army and Deprived Children," *The Officer* 22 (June 1971): 367; Maj. Henry Gariepy, *Urban Challenge and Response* (New York, 1973), pp. 9-13; WCE, 22 November 1969, p. 19; 6 December 1969, pp. 14-18; 5 September 1970, pp. 12-13; interview with Col. Giles Barrett. For a complete account of the Hough project, see Henry Gariepy, "Challenge and Response: A Dramatic Docmentary on Christianity in Action in the Inner City," unpublished typescript (copy dated March 27, 1992, kindly provided to author by Col. Gariepy).

31. Interview with Mrs. Col. William Noble, Atlanta, 27 November 1978; Breen, "The Army and Deprived Children," pp. 367-68; WCE, 9 March 1968, pp. 16-17; SA, *Disposition of Forces, Central Territory, November 1976,* pp. 29-30.

32. Maj. Robert A. Watson, *Report: Services to Minorities and the Inner City — The Salvation Army Eastern Territory, July, 1973* (New York, 1973), *passim* (quotations on pp. 6, 8, 10); Maj. Robert A. Watson, *Urban Conditions and the Leadership Challenge* (New York, 1973), pp. 3, 8-9, *passim* (SAARC).

33. Maj. Dorothy A. Purser, *Report on the Meeting of Active Black Officers Serving in the Eastern Territory: The Salvation Army Territorial Congress, June, 1969* (New York, 1969), pp. 3-4; Brig. B. Barton McIntyre to Col. J. Clyde Cox, New York City, 26 May 1969 (SAARC "Black Salvationists" file).

34. WC, 10 March 1979, pp. 12-13; 31 March 1979, pp. 12-13; 16 June 1979, pp. 12-13; WCS, 1 June 1968, p. 2; "Black Salvationist" files, SAARC, SFOT/E Library; interviews with Brig. Emma Ellegard, Col. Frank Guldenschuh, Brig. Fred Crossley, Col. William Maltby, Brig. Henry Dries (Asbury Park), Comm. William E. Chamberlain, Comm. Paul J. Kaiser (New York), Comm. Ernest Holz, Lt. Col. Edward Laity, Mrs. Col. William Noble, Lt. Col. Wesley Bouterse (Atlanta), and Col. Bertram Rodda (Oakland); SA, *Disposition of Forces, November 1991* (West Nyack, N.Y., 1991), p. 109.

35. WCW, 17 August 1940, p. 8; interview with Maj. Leroy Pederson, Los Angeles, 15 December 1978.

36. WCE, 21 January 1961, p. 13; 25 March 1961, p. 10; Gariepy, *Urban Challenge and Response,* pp. 8-9; Watson, *Report: Services to Minorities and the Inner City,* pp. 2, 4, 6, 8, 9-10.

37. WCW, 21 March 1896, p. 6; 5 May 1923, pp. 1, 8, 13; 23 August 1924, pp. 10, 13; 20 April 1940, p. 8; Capt. Check Hung Yee, "Songs under the Lanterns," *The Officer* 17 (November 1966): 744-45; Capt. Check Hung Yee, "Preaching Christ in the Chinese Way," *The Officer* 19 (January-February 1968): 11; WC, 4 March 1978, pp. 12-13.

38. Porter R. Lee and Walter W. Pettit, *Social Salvage: A Study of the Central Organization and Administration of The Salvation Army* (New York, 1924), pp. 85-86 (quotation); Pitt, *Pilgrim's Progress,* pp. 22-24; "The New Army," *Time,* 30 June 1958, pp. 67-68; Dexter, "Officer Training in The Salvation Army," pp. 13, 25-27, 83, 196-205; interview with Mrs. Lt. Col. F. William Carlson, Ocean Grove, N.J., 7 August 1978.

39. E. H. McKinley, "A Preliminary Report, on the Relationship between Asbury College and The Salvation Army, 1924-1973," 11 May 1973 (SAARC); Comm. William E. Chamberlain, *Relationships between Asbury College and The Salvation Army, Southern Territory* (Atlanta, 1973), SAARC; Kenneth Baillie and Lyell Rader, *Statistical Study to Determine the Effect of Attendance at Asbury College on Commitment to Officership in The Salvation Army, 1957-1965* (New York, 1965), SAARC; interview with Comm. William Chamberlain; *Education into the Second Century: The Salvation Army School for Officers' Training, Chicago, Illinois — Asbury College, May 23, 1979* (Chicago, 1979); WC, 17 June 1978, p. 6; *The Salvation Army Yearbook, 1978* (London, 1978), p. 173; "Student Witness," *The Officer* 15 (August 1964): 574-76; Col. Dorothy Phillips, "Education in the United States (2)," *The Officer* 22 (April 1971): 248-49.

40. WC, 15 October 1977, pp. 12-13; WC, 25 February 1978, pp. 12-13; *The Musician* (New York), November 1978, pp. 5, 6, 11; December 1978, pp. 3, 6-7; January

1979, p. 6; February 1979, p. 7; March 1979, p. 12; April 1979, p. 8; *The Musician* (London), 4 February 1978, p. 73; Ronald W. Holz, "A History of the Hymn Tune Meditation," p. 18 (contains list of noted and active American Salvationist composers); "Under Two Flags," WC, 12 September 1992, pp. 16-17.

41. Bandmaster Charles Hansen, "Are SA Bands Fading Out? Definitely Not!" WCE, 15 February 1967, p. 11; WCS, 33 February 1968, pp. 12-13; Capt. Ernest A. Miller, "The Beat That Communicates," *The Officer* 15 (December 1964): 833; Maj. David A. Baxendale, "Blueprint for Teenage Evangelism," *The Officer* 22 (November 1971): 602-3. For statistics, see "The Salvation Army in the USA," WCE, 28 May 1960, pp. 6, 14, and the statistical reports cited in the bibliographical essay (pp. 431-34 herein).

42. Statistics from national composites; SA, *Disposition of Forces, Southern Territory, October 1978,* p. 133; *The Salvation Army Band Tune Book Supplement* (London, 1954), p. [iv] (quotation). And see the complete run of *The Musician* (New York), October 1978–May 1989.

43. Frederick Coutts, "The Army Marches On," *Christianity Today,* 1 January 1965, p. 7; WCS, 3 February 1968, pp. 12-13; Capt. Ernest A. Miller, "The Beat That Communicates," *The Officer* 15 (December 1964): 833; Maj. David A. Baxendale, "Blueprint for Teenage Evangelism," *The Officer* 22 (November 1971): 602-3; Mrs. Captain Howard Chase, "The Sound of Music . . . NOW," *SAY* 1 (July 1975): 14-19.

44. *Homes and Hospitals Handbook,* foreword (quotation); Capt. Karl E. Nelson, "The Organization and Development of the Health Care System of The Salvation Army in the United States of America" (fellowship thesis, American College of Hospital Administrators, New York, 1973), p. 57; interview with Comm. W. R. H. Goodier, New York, 3 August 1978; interview with Comm. Ernest W. Holz and Col. John Paton, Atlanta, 23 November 1978; interview with Brig. Ruth E. Cox, R.N.; interview with Col. Florence Turkington, Asbury Park, N.J., 9 August 1978; telephone interview with Lt. Col. Mary Verner, 10 July 1979; Lt. Col. Mary E. Verner, "Analysis of Decreased Utilization of Salvation Army Maternity Homes and Hospitals 1967-1975 and Contributing Factors" (fellowship thesis, American College of Hospital Administrators, 1976), pp. 11-18, 32-34, 42-45, 99-100.

45. "Misdemeanant Probation Program: Historical Perspective," in *The Salvation Army Correctional Services in Florida, 1988-1989* (Tampa, 1989), n.p. (this volume also contains sections entitled "Federal and State Pre-Release Program Summary" and "Misdemeanant Probation Program Description"); see also "The Salvation Army Act," Florida SB925 (amending §945.30 of the Florida Statutes), passed 2-3 June 1976 and signed into law 23 June 1976 to take effect 1 October 1976 (these materials supplied to author by Lt. Col. John Busby, Florida divisional commander, Tampa; [Philip B. Taft], "The Salvation Army Conquers Florida," *Corrections Magazine* 9 (February 1981): 40-41 (quotation); Steve Hicks, "A Comprehensive Correctional Program," WC, 7 July 1990, pp. 6-8.

46. Author visits to the Chicago Freedom Center in May 1976 and to the St. Louis Harbor Light Center 19 May 1979; Maj. Edward V. Dimond, "Syncopated Salvation," WCC, 18 January 1969, pp. 12-13; Maj. Edward V. Dimond, "Full Throttle Heavenward," WC, 18 April 1970, pp. 12-13; Maj. Edward V. Dimond, "Darkest England Revisited," *The Officer* 41 (August 1990): 344-48 and (September 1990): 395-401.

47. *Salvation Army Men's Social Service Handbook,* pp. 65-68.

48. Commissioners' Conference Minutes, 25-27 May 1977, p. 201 (SATHQ/E);

interview with Comm. W. R. H. Goodier; interview with Comm. Richard E. Holz, Los Angeles, 13 December 1978; interview with Lt. Col. Hofman; Blumberg et al., *Skid Row and Its Alternatives,* p. 12.

49. On the creation of the Salvation Army Archives and Research Center, see the issues for October 1987 and April 1990 of the Center's journal *Historical News-View.* The concept of a national repository of Salvation Army historical materials was cherished and advocated for many years by Brig. Christine McMillan, who served many years at the Center as an unofficial Army historian. McMillan died 15 September 1987. On the stained glass windows, see "Salvation Army Stained Glass," WC, 3 February 1990, pp. 10-16.

50. Booz, Allen, and Hamilton, *General Survey of Administration and Operations: The Salvation Army in the United States,* report dated 19 April 1968 (SAARC), pp. 5-14, 19-21 (chart), 38-39, 42; interview with Commander James Osborne, Alexandria, Va., 10 March 1992; "National Commissions, Committees and Planning Committees, Membership" (document provided by Lt. Col. Myrtle Ryder, Assistant National Chief Secretary); on officer training, see Dexter, "Officer Training in The Salvation Army," p. 188; interview with Col. Orval Taylor, New York City, 4 August 1978; "A Feasibility Study . . . National SFOT, November 1970" (STHC, item 86.07.19, box 5, folder 5); *Progress Report Territorial Headquarters Reorganization: The Salvation Army Eastern Territory, August 29, 1973* (New York, 1973), SAARC.

51. For data on the new training program, see CCM, 9-11 October 1974, p. 141; 25-27 May 1977, p. 18; 24-25 May 1978, pp. 26-34; 18-20 October 1978, p. 6; 23-25 May 1979, p. 32; 28-29 February 1980, p. 25; 27-31 October 1980, pp. 4-6, 8-9; and 23-26 October 1989, pp. 100-103.

52. [Maj. Robert E. Thomson], "A New Look but the Same Message," WC, 3 October 1970 (the inaugural issue), p. 2; *SAY* 1 (January 1975); *The Musician* 1 (October 1978); WC, 12 March 1983, p. 4.

53. Since 1973 The Salvation Army chain of command has been equivalent to that of the U.S. military for the first five rank-levels: lieutenant, captain, major, lieutenant colonel, and colonel, which are the only ranks with which the public has much contact. The two remaining ranks are commissioner (only one per territory, and one or two at the national headquarters level) and general (only one Salvation Army officer holds this active rank at a time). Along with the rank changes of 1973, quotas for command ranks were fixed for each territory at, say, one commissioner, one colonel, and eight lieutenant colonels, so that most officers would expect to rise no higher than major before retirement. In 1991 this policy was liberalized, and a larger number of promotions to the rank of lieutenant colonel and colonel were allowed in each territory (on which, see Chap. 7). For a brief history of the fate of the Young People's Legion, see CCM, 18-22 October 1982, pp. 286-89, and 7-10 February 1983, pp. 322-23. On the new National Statistical System, see CCM, 18-22 October 1982, p. 286; and *The Salvation Army National Statistical System,* issued by authority of Commissioners' Conference, February 1988 (Verona, N.J., 1988), pp. 1-2, 9-42.

54. Col. John D. Waldron, Chief Secretary, New York City, to divisional commanders and department heads, 20 June 1975 (SFOT/E Museum, general files, "SA Symbols"); interview with Comm. Goodier; "Salvation Army Stained Glass," pp. 10-16.

55. Mrs. Lt. Comm. Winifred Gearing, "Though Mountains Shake . . . ," *The Officer* 21 (November 1970): 730-42; *Action! The Salvation Army Manual for Emergency*

Disaster Service, pp. 13, 53, 55-61; Vincent W. Erickson, "Doers of the Word in Today's Congregations," *Lutheran Quarterly* 17 (August 1965): 261; interview with Maj. Don Pack, Los Angeles, 13 December 1978; interview with Comm. Holz, Atlanta; interview with Lt. Col. Hofman; interview with Brig. Henry Dries, Asbury Park, N.J., 3 July 1978; interview with Maj. Harold Hinson, Atlanta, 29 November 1978; Ellwyn R. Stoddard, "Some Latent Consequences of Bureaucratic Efficiency in Disaster Relief," *Human Organization* 28 (Fall 1969): 180-88; "Biting the Hand That Feeds You," *Trans-Action,* April 1970, p. 4; and, in reply, [Maj. Edward Fritz], "More Than Coffee and Doughnuts," *Trans-Action,* October 1970, pp. 60-63; James L. Ross, "The Salvation Army: Emergency Operations," *American Behavioral Scientist* 13 (January/February 1970): 407-13.

56. "Brief of Appointment, 1973," SA National Public Affairs Office, Washington, D.C., covered, and other information supplied, by letters to author from Mrs. Brig. W. Kenneth Wheatley, Clearwater, Fla., 25 April 1991 and 10 May 1991.

57. H. Rider Haggard, *Regeneration: Being an Account of the Social Work of The Salvation Army in Great Britain* (London, 1910), p. 13; for an account of Booth-Tucker and farm colonies, see Chap. 3 herein; Chesham, *Born to Battle,* p. 264; *Chicago Tribune,* 5 July 1979, sect. 6, pp. 1-2.

58. Interviews with Comm. Ernest Holz, Comm. W. R. H. Goodier, Comm. William Chamberlain, Comm. Paul Kaiser, Col. Orval Taylor, Col. John Paton, Maj. Leroy Pederson; letter from Capt. Stanley Jaynes to the author, Jackson, Miss., 28 March 1978; Sheila B. Kamerman and Alfred J. Kahn, *Social Service in the United States: Policies and Programs* (Philadelphia, 1976), pp. 18-19, 532; letter from Lt. Col. Ernest A. Miller to the author, Washington, D.C., 20 July 1978; WC, 29 July 1978, pp. 6-7; *The Role of the Corps Officer in the United States of America: Guidelines for Corps Officers of The Salvation Army in the United States of America,* approved by the Commissioners' Conference, U.S.A., October 1972 (New York, 1972), pp. 8, 11, 12, 19, 41.

59. Jaynes letter, 28 March 1978; "Report on Realignment of Divisional Boundaries" (Eastern territory, November 1971), schedules 1-13 (SAARC); American Association of Fund-Raising Counsel, Inc., *Giving USA: 1977 Annual Report,* p. 39.

60. *Working Together: Principles of Cooperation for Salvation Army Participation in United Appeals,* adopted by Commissioners' Conference, October 1975 (New York, 1975); "Street Corner Carolers," WCE, 3 December 1960, pp. 7, 14; WC, 31 December 1977, pp. 12-13; "United Way: Are the Criticisms Fair?" *Changing Times,* October 1977, p. 31; SA National Soldiers' Commission, U.S.A., *Report and Recommendation to the Commissioners' Conference, May 22-25, 1967* (Chicago, 1967), pp. 15-19.

61. WC, 19 November 1977, pp. 12-13, 18-19; 21 April 1979, p. 19; 12 May 1979, pp. 12-13; *The Role of the Corps Officer in the United States of America,* p. 11.

62. *United Methodist Reporter,* 17 June 1977, p. 5; U.S. Department of Commerce, Bureau of the Census, *Census of Religious Bodies, 1936: The Salvation Army* (Washington, 1940), pp. 1-2. An important series of figures appears in the annual *Yearbook of American and Canadian Churches* under the heading of "enrollment," which refers to the number of regularly enrolled members. The figures for The Salvation Army fluctuate from year to year but show a slow but steady increase over the years through 1967: the figure for 1965 was 164,384 and for 1966 was 167,725; in 1967 the figure dropped to 133,980. In 1970 the figure was 119,363; in 1982, 103,258; in 1989, 110,584. See *Yearbook of American and Canadian Churches, 1965,* ed. Benson Y. Landis (New York, 1965), p. 95; *Yearbook*

of American and Canadian Churches, 1966 (New York, 1966), p. 92; *Yearbook of American and Canadian Churches, 1970* (New York, 1970), p. 72; *Yearbook of American and Canadian Churches, 1982,* ed. Constant H. Jacquet Jr. (New York, 1982), p. 88; *Yearbook of American and Canadian Churches, 1989* (New York, 1989), p. 103; Douglas W. Johnson, Paul R. Picard, and Bernard Quinn, *Churches and Church Membership in the United States: An Enumeration by Region, State and County* (Washington, 1974), pp. ix-xi, 1-2; SA *Yearbook, 1951,* p. 90; SA *Yearbook, 1961,* p. 128; SA *Yearbook, 1971,* p. 191; WCE, 17 November 1934, p. 9; Southwood, "Deployment of Officer Personnel"; *Religions in America: Ferment and Faith in an Age of Crisis — A New Guide and Almanac,* ed. Leo Rosten (New York, 1975), pp. 437, 441, 458-60; Baxendale, "Blueprint for Teenage Evangelism," p. 601; Maj. Herbert Luhn, "Diminishing Corps and the Way Out," paper delivered to The Salvation Army National Social Services Conference in Dallas, 1978, p. 2. Current statistics were supplied by SANHQ 19 July 1979 and in a composite report, "National Composite Territory, Statistical Report to USA National Headquarters for Year Ending Dec. 30, 1980." This and all current statistical data were kindly supplied to the author by Comm. Kenneth E. Hood, national chief secretary at the time of revision of the text. For a description of the sources for statistical material, see also the bibliographical essay herein.

63. *Report and Recommendation to the Commissioners' Conference, May 22-25, 1967,* p. 23 (quotation); Booz, Allen, and Hamilton, *General Survey,* p. 16; Col. Paul S. Kaiser, "Our Evangelistic Outreach," *The Officer* 17 (November 1966): 731; interview with Brig. Ellegard; interview with Lt. Col. William Bearchell, Asbury Park, N.J., 20 June 1978; interviews with Col. William Maltby, Comm. Goodier, Comm. Chamberlain, Comm. Kaiser, Col. John Paton, Comm. Richard Holz.

64. Luhn, "Diminishing Corps and the Way Out," pp. 2, 4; Capt. Philip D. Needham, "Preach or Perish," *The Officer* 23 (July 1972): 314-15, 319; T. J. Carlson, *A Viewpoint concerning Goals and Objectives of The Salvation Army as It Enters Its Second Century* (New York, 1966), p. 11.

65. Johnson, Picard, and Quinn, *Churches and Church Membership in the United States,* pp. xi, 1-2, 229-33; Baxendale, "Blueprint for Teenage Evangelism," p. 601 (quotation).

66. Memorandum for the Ruling Division, IRS, submitted in behalf of the Salvation Army by Cadwalader, Wickersham, and Taft, 1 August 1955, p. 9 (Holz Coll.); "The Salvation Army as a Religious Organization," memorandum by William J. Moss of Cadwalader, Wickersham, and Taft for the commissioner's conference, 19 October 1978 (Holz Coll.); Lloyd Billingsley, "The Salvation Army: Still Marching to God's Beat after 118 Years," *Christianity Today,* 16 December 1983, p. 21.

67. CCM, May 1977, pp. 368-73; memorandum of appointment of Comm. William E. Chamberlain as national commander of The Salvation Army in the United States, 20 November 1974, (*National Headquarters Manual,* SATHQ/W, Personnel Dept.), p. 3 (lists the forty-one organizations); Comm. William E. Chamberlain to Gen. Michael S. Davidson, New York City, 8 December 1976, in chief secretary's office, SANHQ (resigning from USO). The Army had serious concerns about its membership in the World Council of Churches even before the 1978 decision to withdraw; in 1975, for instance, the Army protested a clause in the proposed revision of the WCC Constitution that called for "visible unity in one faith and in one eucharistic fellowship." See "Search for Meaning," *Christianity Today,* 9 April 1976, pp. 44-45.

68. Articles of Organization and By-Laws, Laymen's and Officers' Councils, SATHQ/W; interview, Col. Orval Taylor, New York City; *Chosen to Be a Soldier: Orders and Regulations for Soldiers of The Salvation Army* (London, 1977), pp. 3, 32-38; Col. W. R. H. Goodier to territorial chief secretaries, New York City, 30 January 1975, filed with *National Headquarters Manual.*

69. Brig. Maro Smith, "The D.C. as Pastor (2)," *The Officer* 24 (November 1973): 495.

70. These officers were Comms. Goodier, E. Holz, R. Holz, Needham, Chamberlain, and Kaiser, and Cols. Albert Scott, John Paton, Will Pratt, Andrew Miller, Emil Nelson, and Orval Taylor.

71. The officers named in the text have all provided the author with invaluable assistance in the preparation both of the original edition and the revised edition of this volume.

NOTES TO CHAPTER 7

1. SA, "National Centennial Congress, 1880-1980" (program), pp. 12-40 ("Service of Praise" on pp. 18-19); Lt. Col. Robert Thomson, "Confessions of a Reluctant Flag Waver," *The Officer* 31 (October 1980): 471-72.

2. "National Centennial Congress" program, pp. 18-19, 26, 38-39, 40; Maj. William MacLean, "Neshan Garadean Was Perhaps the Army's 'Most Unforgettable Character,'" WC Centennial Edition, 10 May 1980, pp. 10-11; Maj. Henry Gariepy, "Will the Real Salvation Army Please Stand Up?" *The Officer* 31 (March 1980): 118-19; *The Salvation Army in America . . . The Second Hundred Years* (n.p., n.d.), pp. 10-11.

3. SA, *Second Century Advance: Recommended Action Plans for The Salvation Army as Prepared by the National Committee of Task Force Chairmen, October 26, 1981* (New York, 1981), pp. i (Fleming quotation), iii (list of personnel); International Marketing Group, Inc., *The Second Hundred Years: A Strategy Plan for The Salvation Army, U.S.A.* (McLean, Va., 1980), and *Appendix: Summary of Research Findings and Conclusions* (McLean, Va., 1980), 46 (on lack of religious motivation among advisory board members).

4. SA, *Second Century Advance,* pp. 1-2, 3-4 ("Bible-based growth program"), 21-22 ("purpose of all Salvation Army social services"); see also pp. 26-27, 37 ("broad spiritual foundation"), 40 (minorities), and *passim;* Jean Caffey Lyles, "New Battle Plan for Booth's Army," *Christian Century,* 27 August–3 September 1980, p. 811.

5. Dale Hanson Bourke, "The Salvation Army Seeks a New Image," *Christianity Today,* 11 December 1981, pp. 40-41; "The Salvation Army Mission Statement; Approved by the Commissioners' Conference, USA, May 1982"; CCM, 8-12 February 1982, pp. 598-603 (quotation on p. 598); CCM, 16-19 May 1983, p. 612.

6. On "Americanizing" the language of position statements, see CCM, 21-25 September 1981, pp. 589-90, and 24-28 May 1982, pp. 545-57, which contain the texts and revisions of the five statements revised and sent to London for approval; for the final text, see SA, *Positional Statements* (London, [1987]); Ian Adnams, "Into Year Ten for OMM," *Video Capsule* newsletter, 9/1 [1990]: n.p.; *Wonderful Words of Life: A Worldwide Radio Ministry of The Salvation Army* (series 76 newsletter), Winter 1992, n.p. (states that by 1992 the program was heard on 204 different radio stations in 46 states and 14

foreign countries); "Wonderful Words of Life Growth Surge," WC, 9 June 1990, pp. 11-14; WC, 9 June 1990, p. 16; SS, 12 February 1990, p. 1; WC, 3 March 1984, p. 7; letter to the author from Maj. James Hylton, Atlanta, 4 May 1992. On the National Communications Department, see also CCM, 13-17 February 1984, p. 449; CCM, 3-8 March 1986, pp. 259-71 (for "National Communications Guidelines"), 263, 266 (for quotation and goals).

7. CCM, 27-31 October 1980, pp. 376-81; 13-17 February 1984, p. 451 (quotations). In an interview with the author, Comm. James Osborne, national commander, stated that he regarded the Second Century Advance as a major success for the reasons cited in the text. On the changes to NPDC cited, see CCM, 13-17 February 1984, p. 451; CCM, 9-12 February 1987, pp. 714-15; and CCM, 18-21 May 1987, p. 280.

8. CCM, 27-31 October 1980, pp. 373-74; CCM, 2-6 February 1981, pp. 490-92; letter to the author from Col. Leon Ferraez, Alexandria, Va., 16 April 1992; letters to the author from Col. Leon Ferraez, Alexandria, Va., 1 and 2 June 1992. The June 1 letter included a 16-page typescript entitled "'White Paper' on NAC/NAB for Commissioner Needham" written in 1983, which contains information on the NAC during the formative years 1976-1982.

9. CCM, 18-22 October 1982, pp. 429, 448-50 (the text of the "Manual of Advisory Organizations, National Advisory Board" appears on pp. 452-85); CCM, 3-6 November 1986, p. 339; "'White Paper' on NAC/NAB," pp. 11-12, 1A-4A.

10. CCM, 17-21 October 1983, p. 490; 13-17 February 1984, pp. 462-75; 12-16 October 1987, p. 427; WC, 10 March 1984, p. 3 ("year of destiny"); The Young Salvationist 90 (January 1984): 2 ("all new"); The Young Salvationist was regarded as a continuation of The Young Soldier, which ceased separate publication with no. 4289 [December 1982]); SAY 9 (December 1983): 26-27; WC, 27 October 1990, p. 14 ("programaids").

11. CCM, 13-17 February 1984, pp. 376-82 (includes a letter from J. L. Tarr, chief scout executive, to Comm. Norman S. Marshall, national commander, Irving, Tex., dated 20 September 1983); WC, 4 February 1984, pp. 3, 5; 21 December 1989, p. 9; statistics from "Statistical Report to USA National Headquarters for the Year ending December 31, 1990."

12. Quotation by Comm. Robert E. Thomson from notes he prepared for the dedication ceremony of the Eastern territorial headquarters, kindly supplied to author by the commissioner under cover of letter to author dated 31 December 1991.

13. For details on changes in locations of Army headquarters, see WC, 7 July 1990, p. 2; 13 October 1990, pp. 12-13; GN, October 1990, pp. 1-2; interview with Comm. James Osborne, Wilmore, Ky., 4 October 1990. CCM, 27-31 October 1980, pp. 481-82; CCM, 21-25 September 1981, p. 585; CCM, 28 January–1 February 1991, pp. 580-81, 622-25; interview with Comm. Kenneth Hood, Alexandria, Va., 10 March 1992.

14. CCM, 27-31 October 1980, pp. 462-70 (quotation on p. 467); CCM, 18-22 October 1982, p. 319; CCM, 17-21 October 1983, pp. 245, 620-22; CCM, 21-25 October 1985, pp. 352-64 (revision of "The Uniform . . . Wear It Proudly" brochure); CCM, 13-16 February 1989, pp. 20, 168-69; WC, 17 September 1983, cover, pp. 12-15; Maj. Paul Marshall to Col. Edward J. Johnson, Chicago, 11 January 1989 (in box file labeled "Conservation of Uniforms Policy," CTM office files). When Gen. Eva Burrows visited the White House in November 1990, First Lady Barbara Bush complemented her on her bonnet; see WC, 24 November 1990, pp. 3, 6.

15. CCM, 8-12 February 1982, p. 561 (quotation on Glen Eyrie); statistics from National Composite for years ending 31 December 1970, 1980, and 1990 supplied by SANHQ.

16. On Purdell, see WC, 10 September 1988, back cover; Capt. John R. W. Purdell to the author, Van Nuys, Calif., 22 October 1988. For three years Purdell conducted a course called "Outdoor Evangelism" at the Army's annual National Seminar on Evangelism in Glen Eyrie, Col.; letter to the author from Cadet Tom Bailey, Atlanta, 18 September 1991 (the three cadets in Joyful Noise were Mike Anderson, Tom Bailey, and George Hackbarth); Cadet Grant Overstake, "Salvation War Correspondent," unpublished type-script [3 November 1990].

17. On American Rescue Workers, see CCM, 7-10 February 1983, pp. 443-48 (includes a letter from William J. Moss to Paul E. Martin, New York City, 5 November 1982); "Report of the Archives Advisory Committee, January 1–August 31, 1983," in National Archives Advisory Committee files, CTM; WC, 29 May 1983, pp. 3-8 (Western centenary); *Historical News-Views,* January 1989, n.p.

18. Lt. Col. Robert E. Thomson, "The Semantics of Salvationism," *The Officer* 34 (June 1983): 282 (quotation).

19. Comm. Edward Carey, " 'Is the Army in America . . . ?' " *The Officer* 19 (March-April 1968): 78-83; letter to the author from Comm. Edward Carey, Clearwater, Fla., 4 March 1992.

20. SA, *Second Century Advance,* p. 21; CN, April 1990, n.p.; [Gordon Bingham], *Structuring Community Service Ministries So That Participants Have an Opportunity to Receive Spiritual Guidance* (Verona, N.J., 1988), p. 1; on this document and others, see also CCM, 8-11 February 1988, pp. 504-12.

21. Roger J. Green, *War on Two Fronts: The Redemptive Theology of William Booth* (Atlanta, 1989), p. 68 (quotations), pp. 58-75; Philip D. Needham, "Mission in Commu-nity: A Salvationist Perspective" (D.Min. diss., Emory University, 1981), pp. 120, 124-25, 147, 167, 176-82, 203-4; Maj. Philip Needham, "Toward a Re-Integration of the Sal-vationist Mission," in *Creed and Deed: Toward a Christian Theology of Social Services in The Salvation Army,* ed. John D. Waldron (Oakville, Ont., 1986), pp. 121-58.

22. Roger J. Green, *War on Two Fronts;* Philip Needham, *Community in Mission: A Salvationist Ecclesiology* (Atlanta, 1987).

23. Judith Brigham, "The Salvation Army: Santa All Year Long," *Saturday Evening Post* 253 (December 1981): 61 (quotation); Jack Fincher, "An Army Salutes Its Hundred Years' War with Satan," *Smithsonian* 11 (December 1980): 79; [Maj.] Peter J. Hofman and Elma Phillipson Cole, "Bridging the Gap between Youth and Community Services: A Life Skills Education Program," *Education Today* 12 (May/June 1983): 17-21; F. Ellen Nelting, "Church-Related Agencies and Social Welfare," *Social Service Review,* September 1984, pp. 410-14; statistics from "Statistical Report to USA National Headquarters" (national com-posites for years ending 31 December 1980 and 31 December 1990 in total case loads, holiday meals, and community center participation); letter to the author from Lt. Col. Beatrice Combs, Verona, N.J., 28 November 1990, including a three-page typescript entitled "The Salvation Army National Social Services Award" and scripts for awards for 1988, 1989, and 1990. On SHARE, see Edward H. McKinley, "Brass Bands and God's Work: One Hundred Years of the Salvation Army in Georgia and Atlanta," *Atlanta History: A Journal of Georgia and the South* 34 (Winter 1990-1991): 29.

24. Lt. Col. Ernest A. Miller, "The Homeless in America," WC, 28 February 1987, p. 4 (this entire issue of the WC was dedicated to the SA's ministry to the homeless); Comm. Norman S. Marshall, "Historical Perspective of Homelessness," paper read at The Salvation Army National Social Services Conference/PHWA in New Orleans, 14 March 1987; NF, 31 December 1989, pp. 4-5; William Booth, *In Darkest England and the Way Out* (London, 1890), pp. 129-31 (on Booth's plans for special provision for military veterans in SA shelters and programs); "Emergency Shelter," *Christian Century,* 16 December 1987, p. 1137.

25. Patty Tara, "Street Kids to Have 'Family' Thanksgiving," NF, 18 November 1989, pp. 1, 6; NF, 31 December 1989, p. 5; SS, 10 September 1990, p. 2; [James C. Kisser], "A Slum Sister's Story," GN, January 1991, p. 3.

26. SA, *The Salvation Army and AIDS: Guidelines, Programs, Services* (New York, 1988), pp. 1, 5, 6 (quotations), 8 (task force personnel).

27. CN, January 1990, n.p.; NF, 31 May 1990, pp. 1, 11; NF, 28 July 1990, pp. 1, 7; NF, 8/12 [1990]: 7; Beverly Cubbage, "Army AIDS Consultation Plans New International Intervention Strategy," WC, 28 July 1990, pp. 1, 7; Aux. Capt. Michael Olsen, "A Salvationist Response to AIDS," WC, 28 July 1990, p. 7. See also "Army Ministers to AIDS Patients," WC, 10 November 1990, p. 11 (reprinted from British WC); CCM, 12-16 October 1987, pp. 348-50; CCM, 28 January–1 February 1991, pp. 487-89.

28. Mark Olsen, "A Giver's Guide," *The Other Side,* March 1983, pp. 8-9 (quotation); on the Olsen article, see also Lloyd Billingsley, "The Salvation Army: Still Marching to God's Beat after 118 Years," *Christianity Today,* 16 December 1983, pp. 21-22); Booth, *In Darkest England and the Way Out,* pp. 17-18 (quotation).

29. CCM, 13-17 February 1984, pp. 612-41, contain the following items: clippings from the *New York Times* of 22 and 23 December 1983 (pp. 628-29); a letter from Merrick T. Rossein (assistant director of New York City's Bureau of Labor Services) to Robert M. Gutheil, New York City, 23 December 1983 (pp. 625-27); and a letter from William J. Moss to Lt. Col. Roland G. Schramm, New York City, 29 December 1983 (pp. 617-24).

30. CCM, 13-17 February 1984, p. 613 (quotations from "A National Statement by The Salvation Army regarding Employment"); CCM, 21-25 May 1984, p. 590; CCM, 22-26 October 1984, p. 494; CCM, 20-23 May 1985, pp. 398-420 (contains a letter from Lt. Col. Wallace Conrath to the Most Rev. John J. O'Connor, New York City, 4 April 1985 [pp. 400-402]); "Salvation Army Loses City Funds over a Gay Rights Disagreement," *Christianity Today,* 18 May 1984, p. 79.

31. For items relating to San Francisco cases, see CCM, 20-23 May 1985, p. 416; CCM, 3-6 March 1986, pp. 452-54 (quotation on "untraditional moral values"), 508, 514; CCM, 19-22 May 1986, pp. 424-31; CCM, 3-6 November 1986, pp. 417-18. On the Moss award, see CCM, 20-23 May 1985, p. 440; information on his career was kindly supplied by Mr. Moss in a letter to the author dated 1 April 1992.

32. WC, 7 July 1990, pp. 2, 6-8, 17; 3 November 1990, p. 3; NF, 31 December 1989, p. 3; "Tremont Older Persons Program," WC, 24 November 1990, pp. 11-13, 15-17.

33. Letters to the author from Lt. Col. Harold Anderson, Oklahoma City, dated 13 and 24 February and 9 March 1992; the latter covered several items: a six-page typescript entitled "Kindred Session: 'In Praise of Age' 'From One to Nineteen-Twenty' Washington,

D.C. April 12, 1988," an undated document entitled *The Salvation Army Senior Centers of Greater Oklahoma City,* and a four-page typescript by Kendra Sebo entitled "The Wind Beneath Our Wings: A Memorial to Nina Willingham, *The War Cry* August 30, 1991"; letter to the author from Linda Soos (executive director of SA Senior Centers), Oklahoma City, 26 March 1992, which covered a seven-page typescript entitled "The Salvation Army Senior Centers Program Prospectus" [1988]; "General visits Oklahoma City," SS, 31 December 1990, pp. 1, 4-5.

34. Eve P. Smith and Robert H. Gutheil, "Successful Foster Parent Recruiting: A Voluntary Agency Effort," *Child Welfare* 67 (March/April 1988): 137-43. On Maj. Hickam's report, see Maj. M. Lee Hickam, "Report on Conference on Pornography & Obscenity, November 17, 1983, Cincinnati, Ohio, compiled by Major M. Lee Hickam, Divisional Commander, Indiana Division," in CCM, 21-25 May 1984, pp. 600-607. See also CCM, 21-25 October 1985, pp. 509-11; CCM, 3-6 March 1986, p. 651. On the Call to Action by the Religious Alliance Against Pornography, see WC, 3 February 1990, p. 2, and C. Everett Koop, "Pornography and Public Health," WC, 3 March 1990, p. 21; "A Position Statement: The Salvation Army's Position on Abortion, Approved by the Commissioners, March 1986."

35. See chap. 6 of E. H. McKinley's *Somebody's Brother: A History of The Salvation Army Men's Social Services Department, 1891-1985* (Lewiston, Me., 1986); statistics from "Statistical Report to USA National Headquarters for year ending December 31, 1990."

36. Letters to the author from Maj. Travis Israel, Atlanta, 2 March 1989 and 8 March 1989; letter to the author from Lt. Col. Raymond E. Howell, New York City, 27 February 1989; letter to the author from Lt. Col. Marcus Stillwell, Chicago, 10 March 1989. It is interesting to note that one of the largest private salvage businesses in the country was operated in the 1980s by a family named Ellison, the founders of which were trained in The Salvation Army; see David Johnson, "Charity Thrifts: Donated Goods Form Heart of Billion-Dollar Family Empire," *Los Angeles Times,* 27 September 1987, VI:1, 11.

37. Comment on the FLSA crisis from author's interview with James Osborne, national commander, Alexandria, Va., 10 March 1992, and Robert Docter, "U.S. Labor Department Misinterprets ARC Program," NF, 28 September 1990, pp. 2, 10 (see also p. 1); NF, 22 October 1990, p. 2; WC, 27 October 1990, p. 7; *Lexington (Ky.) Herald Leader,* 18 September 1990, p. A5.

38. Maj. and Mrs. Robert H. Johnson, "Serving the Total Man at Minneapolis," WC, 21 June 1986, pp. 4-5 (this entire issue was dedicated to ARC programs nationwide); Lt. Col. Raymond Howell, "Spiritual Emphasis Still Focus of Adult Rehabilitation Center Program," GN, November 1990, p. 1; SS, 26 February 1990, n.p.; SS, 18 June 1990, n.p.; NF, 14 March 1990, p. 5; NF, 3 November 1990, p. 7; GN, November 1990 (entire issue dedicated to ARC program); *Recycling and Rehabilitation* (Southern territorial newsletter), 19 November 1990, n.p.; CN, September 1990, p. 7; WC, 26 May 1990, p. 12 (Pittsburgh clowns); *The Salvation Army Harbor Light Drum Beat* (Cleveland Harbor Light Corps newsletter), September/December 1989; January/March 1990; Capt. Jack Bennett, "Road to Recovery at Harbor Light Complex," WC, 28 February 1987, pp. 7-8; "God's Grace on the Bowery," WC, 23 June 1990, pp. 12-15.

39. Bill Carlton, "The 'A' Captain," WC, 10 November 1990, pp. 16-17; SS, 30 December 1991, p. 6 (name change); see also "Southern Territory Official Gazette," 30 December 1991, p. 1; "Western Territory USA Official Gazette," 30 January 1992, p. 2.

40. CCM, 16-19 May 1983, p. 413 (on kettles); CCM, 22-26 October 1984, p. 167 (DeBartolo); CCM, 23-26 October 1989, p. 435; CCM, 28 January–1 February 1991, p. 357.

41. CCM, 27-31 October 1980, pp. 438-40; CCM, 18-22 May 1981, pp. 486-92; CCM, 12-16 October 1987, pp. 390-91; *Working Together* (Verona, N.J., 1983); "Guidelines for Relationships between The Salvation Army and Other Groups and Organizations," kindly provided by Col. Leon Ferraez, SA National Communications Department; *Corps Community Center Profile* (Verona, N.J., 1983), p. 19 (quotation). On the Corps Stewardship Secretary, see CCM, 7-10 February 1983, p. 259.

42. Although reports to the commissioners conference throughout the decade indicated that the Army's relationship with the United Way was generally good nationwide, the percentage of the Army's annual income nationwide that came from the United Way declined through the decade to 8.4% by 1990 (CCM, 22-25 May 1989, pp. 793-94). "The Salvation Army Combined National Operating Statement, Year Ended December 31, 1990," courtesy of national chief secretary, 10 March 1992; interview with Comm. Osborne, 10 March 1992; letter to the author from Col. G. Ernest Murray, Belfair, Washington, 20 February 1992; SS, 27 August 1990, pp. 1, 6; Gwen Kinkead, *America's Best-Run Charities* (New York, 1987), n.p. (reprint of *Fortune* magazine, 9 November 1987).

43. "The Salvation Army," in *The Encyclopedia of American Religions,* 3d ed., ed. J. Gordon Melton (Detroit, 1989), p. 334 (quotation); SA, *Second Century Advance,* pp. 1-29.

44. SA, *Second Century Advance,* pp. 12-16 (Rader quotations); see also Paul Alexander Rader, "The Salvation Army in Korea after 1945: A Study in Growth and Self-Understanding" (D.Miss. diss., School of World Mission and Institute of Church Growth, Fuller Theological Seminary, 1973).

45. SA, *Second Century Advance,* pp. 1-63; Col. Rowland D. Hughes (R), "Let's Kick the Habit," *The Officer* 33 (December 1982): 538-40; Maj. Lloyd F. Stoops, "Are the Preliminaries Too Long?" *The Officer* 40 (January 1989): 37-38.

46. Lt. Col. Charles Southwood, "The Care and Shepherding of Officers," *The Officer* 32 (July 1981): 307 (quotation); SA, *Second Century Advance,* pp. 24-25; Eastern Territorial Headquarters "Bulletin," dated 18 October 1991, on Pastoral Care Department (Damon Rader); interview with Lt. Col. Warren H. Fulton, Washington, D.C., 11 March 1992. On area coordinators, see CCM, 7-10 February 1983, pp. 28-29.

47. SA, *Second Century Advance,* p. 3; CCM, 7-10 February 1983, pp. 24-25 (quotation), 30-31 (five-year appointments). In an interview with the author on 12 March 1992, Lt. Col. Fulton explained the many difficulties that made it impossible for SA leaders to commit themselves to a fixed tenure in officers' appointments. For one thing, experienced officers sometimes had to be reassigned to fill gaps. Some officers requested transfers without informing the soldiers under their command, and some who were unable to get requested transfers elected to resign; in the natural course of things, officers retired, fell ill, and died before retirement; and in some cases, promising officers might better serve the cause by using their talents in staff positions. Positions vacated in these ways had to be refilled, and since no divisional or territorial leader had any "spare" officers on hand, filling one position entailed emptying another or several others, setting in train a number of transfers. These "changes in appointment" often came as a surprise to all concerned.

48. "Major Check Yee Promoted to Lt. Colonel," NF, 15 January 1992, pp. 2, 10.

On quotas for high rank, see CCM, 8-12 February 1982, p. 741; CCM, 16-19 May 1983, pp. 710-11; and CCM, 28 January–1 February 1991, pp. 643-44. The system was described by Comm. James Osborne (national commander) and Comm. Kenneth Hood (national chief secretary) in interviews with the author on 10 and 13 March 1992.

49. CCM, 27-31 October 1980, p. 263; CCM, 17-21 October 1983, pp. 165, 424-27 (pp. 166-93 for approved text); SA, *Corps Community Center Profile* (Verona, N.J., 1983), foreword, p. 1 (quotation).

50. SA, *Corps Community Center Profile,* pp. 2, 10-11, *passim.*

51. On the Needham volume, see CCM, 13, 15-17 October 1990, pp. 6-10; CCM, 28 January–1 February 1991, p. 43; Comm. Kenneth Hood kindly provided the author with a copy of the preliminary text of *Mission and Method* under cover of a letter dated 7 May 1992, noting that the text was not yet in final form; the review of this material by the commissioners' conference was scheduled for August 1992. Pagination in the proposed manuscript will not conform to that in the printed volume, and is therefore not cited. Lt. Col. Needham also provided helpful information.

52. SA, *Second Century Advance,* pp. 51-52; CCM, 23-25 May 1979, p. 32; CCM, 18-22 May 1981, pp. 6-7; NF, 18 February 1984, p. 1 (Pratt quotation); GN, October 1990, p. 9; WC, 13 October 1990, p. 11; CTM, horizontal files, "Training College Manuals and Documents" (contains selection of "Training Manuals" for 1981-1986); letters to the author from Lt. Col. Howard R. Evans, Suffern, N.Y., 8 January 1992; and Maj. Richard T. Ulyat, Atlanta, 11 February 1992.

53. Letter to the author from Maj. John R. Rhemick, Des Plaines, Ill., 20 February 1992 (Maj. Rhemick's letter covered a number of helpful documents concerning the development of the continuing education program, including the *Olivet Nazarene University 1990-1991 Bulletin: School of Graduate and Adult Studies* [Kankakee, Ill., 1990], pp. 46-51, 99-108; there is also a provision for an officer to earn a master's degree from Olivet); letter to the author from Maj. Edward Russell, West Nyack, N.Y., 21 February 1992.

54. Letter to the author from Maj. Richard T. Ulyat, Atlanta, 11 February 1992, covered a brochure entitled "CAMS: Certification of Advanced Ministry Skills — A Joint Program of The Salvation Army, Southern Territory, and Asbury Theological Seminary"; letter to the author from Maj. Wesley Sundin, Rancho Palos Verdes, Calif., 17 February 1992; NF, 31 January 1990, p. 1.

55. The calculation of the percentage of officers with college experience is based on information from the 1979 survey of 2,720 officers conducted by the International Marketing Group, Inc., which revealed that 31.4% had "attended some college" (*Appendix: Summary of Research Findings and Conclusions* [McLean, Va., 1980], p. 6) and letters to author from the field secretaries for personnel of three territories, which revealed that for those territories an overall average of 56.7% officers had some college experience (letters to the author from Lt. Col. Robert Tobin, Rancho Palos Verdes, 24 January 1992; Col. Paul M. Kelly, West Nyack, N.Y., 6 February 1992; and Col. M. Lee Hickam, Des Plaines, Ill., 10 February 1992). On Asbury, see WC, 23 April 1983, cover, pp. 6, 8, 12-13; 19 November 1983, pp. 3-7. On Houghton, see WC, 10 November 1990; letter to author from Maj. Edward C. Russell, West Nyack, N.Y., 21 February 1992. The list of SASF chapters and Salvationist enrollment at various institutions was assembled from information gathered in the author's telephone conversations on 6 May 1992 with Maj. R. William Hunter, Maj. Dale Hill, Capt. Mrs. Jacalyn Bowers, and Ms. Pat Germany.

56. "The Salvation Army Fighting and Loving to Reach Humanity," *Fundamentalist Journal* 5 (July/August 1986): 62.

57. WC, 4 June 1983, pp. 12-21 (League of Mercy); WC, 23 October 1982, pp. 12-20 (Men's Fellowship Clubs); WC, 20 October 1982, pp. 14-23 (Home League); Carol R. Thiessen, "Refiner's Fire: On the Street Corner or in the Concert Hall, Philip Smith Plays to the Glory of God," *Christianity Today*, 16 December 1983, p. 49 (for more on Philip Smith, see WC, 12 March 1983, pp. 3, 7); Michael Haggerty, "Marching as to War," *Atlanta Weekly*, 25 January 1981, pp. 8-10, 18-19, 22 (Atlanta Temple); WC, 3 March 1984, pp. 12-13 (Ft. Lauderdale); "The Great Awakening," WC, 3 December 1988, pp. 10-16 (Royal Oak); "Night and Day in Lexington, Ky," WC, 28 October 1989, pp. 12-19; Lt. Col. Donald A. Rose, "A Place Where 'Jesus Shall Reign,'" WC, 28 April 1990, pp. 12-15 (Clearwater); "A Place of Service, Place of Prayer," WC, 21 July 1990, pp. 11-15 (Rockford Temple); see also "Whitened Fields," WC, 20 January 1990, pp. 12-18; WC, 26 May 1990, p. 13.

58. Jack Fincher, "An Army Salutes Its Hundred Years' War with Satan," *Smithsonian* 11 (December 1980): 86. The Army gained a net of 8,501 senior and junior soldiers in the ten years between 1980 and 1990, an increase of about 8 percent; the overall national population increased by 24 million, or 11 percent.

59. Fincher, "An Army Salutes Its Hundred Years' War with Satan," pp. 86, 88; CCM, 7-10 February 1983, p. 28; CCM, 3-6 March 1986, p. 448; CCM, 17-20 October 1988, pp. 163-67; GN, May 1989, p. 9; CN, January 1989, n.p.; CN, March 1989, n.p.; Robert Docter, "West Goes for Growth," NF, 14 November 1987, p. 1; Aux. Capt. Terry Camsey, "Strategy Guide: Corps May Design Own Unique Plans," NF, 14 November 1987, pp. 3-6; "Growth: The Western Story of the Eighties," NF, 31 December 1989, p. 1; NF, 30 June 1990, pp. 4-5, 9; "Whitened Fields," pp. 12-13; Maj. Herbert Luhn, "International Growth Conference," WC, 20 January 1990, p. 20; WC, 20 January 1990 (entire issue devoted to corps growth); WC, 13 October 1990, p. 14; John Larsson, *How Your Corps Can Grow: The Salvation Army and Church Growth* (London, 1988).

60. [Henry Gariepy], "Hallmarks of a Great Corps," WC, 3 March 1984, p. 3 (quotation); James Osborne quoted in WC, 20 January 1990, p. 2.

61. Comm. Paul A. Rader, "We Are Committed to Growth," NF, 30 June 1990, pp. 1-2 (see also material on the "Mission 2000" campaign later in the text); SS, 29 January 1990, pp. 1, 4-5; Larsson, *How Your Corps Can Grow*, p. 32 (quotations); Comm. Harold Shoults, "Official Greetings," *Beanstalk* 1 (January 1990): n.p.

62. Larsson, *How Your Corps Can Grow*, pp. 8-9, 23-24; "The Salvation Army Corps Growth Seminar, Atlanta, Georgia, June 3-4, 1988, Dr. Carl F. George," a series of ten tape recordings kindly provided to author by Maj. Paul Kellner of Atlanta. Citations are from tapes 2 and 3.

63. For opinions about the minimum size of a viable congregation, see Larsson, *How Your Corps Can Grow*, p. 23; Paul O. Madsen, *The Small Church: Valid, Vital, Victorious* (Valley Forge, Pa., 1975), pp. 10, 16-17; Carl S. Dudley, *Making the Small Church Effective* (Nashville, 1978), pp. 19-21. Many experts settled on two hundred people as the minimum; in 1990, only 7 of the 275 corps in the Central territory had as many as 150 members. See *The Beanstalk* 1 (June 1990): n.p.; Lyle F. Schaller, *The Small Church Is Different!* (Nashville, 1982), p. 71 (quotation).

64. Schaller, *The Small Church Is Different!* p. 58; Madsen, *The Small Church,* p. 19; David R. Ray, *Small Churches Are the Right Size* (New York, 1982), pp. 30-31, 34; *New Possibilities for Small Churches,* ed. Douglas Alan Walrath (New York, 1983), pp. ix-x; George, "The Salvation Army Corps Growth Seminar," tape 2.

65. Capt. Terry Camsey, "Booth's Growth Principles Work Today," NF, 30 June 1990, pp. 5, 9; Rader, "We Are Committed to Growth," p. 2; Rev. Carl E. George, "Salvation Army Urged: Make Growth Top Priority of the 1990's," WC, 20 January 1990, p. 21.

66. WC, 24 November 1990, p. 14 (Orlando "Super Sunday"); Lt. Jeffery Smith, " 'Friend Day' at Sheboygan Corps," *Beanstalk* 1 (June 1990): n.p.; William Himes, "Music and Corps Growth — Partners in Progress," CN, February 1990, n.p.

67. "Whitened Fields," p. 18 (quotation); for statistics, see sources listed in the bibliographical essay; CN, September 1990, n.p.

68. Railton, quoted by Eileen Douglas and Mildred Duff in *Commissioner Railton* (London, [1920]), p. 74; CCM, 18-22 October 1982, pp. 426-27 (Needham statement; see also p. 580); CCM, 16-19 May 1983, pp. 593-95, 606-8 (Minority Ministries Committee); CCM, 17-21 October 1983, pp. 416-20; CCM, 21-25 May 1984, p. 652 (official delegates); CCM, 21-25 October 1985, p. 508.

69. CCM, 3-6 March 1986, pp. 454-56 ("Commitment" quotation; see also CCM, 17-20 October 1988, pp. 168-70); Larsson, *How Your Corps Can Grow,* pp. 69-77; *America the Beautiful: The 1991 City Lights Program* (West Nyack, N.Y., 1990); Robert Watson, "City Lights Cherishes Army Heritage," transcript of article for WC, December 1990; Robert Watson, "Cross-Cultural Ministries: This Is My Father's World," GN, May 1990, p. 6; Robert Watson, "City Lights and the Neighborhood of God," GN, June 1990, p. 7; "Cross Cultural Ministries Bureau Report, Eastern Territory, USA, April 24, 1990," sent to author under cover of letters from Robert Watson, West Nyack, N.Y., 7 May 1990; 24 September 1990; 15 November 1990.

70. Lloyd Billingsley, "The Salvation Army: Still Marching to God's Beat after 118 Years," *Christianity Today,* 16 December 1983, p. 22; CN, January 1990; CN, September 1990; GN, October 1990, p. 6; NF, 31 December 1989, pp. 4, 7; WC, 10 June 1989, p. 19; WC, 15 September 1990, p. 22; WC, 2 March 1991, p. 21.

71. April Foster, "Keeping Army Curriculum Current," GN, November 1988, p. 3; Maj. Jorge Booth, ". . . Into All the World," in *Wonderful Words of Life* (newsletter), Spring 1992, n.p., sent to author under cover of letter from Maj. James Hylton, Atlanta, 4 May 1992 (Spanish version of "Wonderful Words of Life" radio program); CCM, 18-21 May 1987, p. 273 (commissioners' actions on translations); CCM, 8-11 February 1988, p. 425; CCM, 23-26 October 1989, pp. 207 ("constant process" quotation), 252, 262, 392-93; CCM, 13, 15-17 October 1990, p. 209; CCM, 28 January–1 February 1991, pp. 155, 383; WC, 15 September 1990, p. 22; GN, October 1990, p. 6.

72. "Major Check Yee Promoted to Lt. Colonel," NF, 15 January 1992, pp. 1, 2, 10; "Changing Populations Demand Strong Cross-Cultural Emphasis," NF, Easter 1992, p. 10 (quotation on Aguirre); letter to the author from Capt. Faye Nishimura, Honolulu, 18 March 1992.

73. CCM, 13-16 February 1989, p. 349 (quotation by commissioners on Korean Salvationists); "Koo Sei Kun Comes to Town," WC, 15 September 1990, pp. 8-14, 16-17; WC, 15 September 1990, pp. 2-3; CN, February 1990, n.p.; SS, 15 January 1990, p. 1.

74. CCM, 12-16 October 1987, p. 150 (Tlingits); WC, 11 November 1989, p. 15; "Tatto of Death, Mission of Life," WC, 31 March 1990, pp. 12-14; CCM, 13-16 February 1989, p. 349.

75. *The Salvation Army Yearbook* (London, 1991), pp. 200, 205, 213, 218.

76. Letter from Norman S. Marshall to Comm. Albert Scott, Verona, N.J., 11 October 1984 (quotation); letter from Albert Scott (international secretary for the Americas) to Norman S. Marshall, London, 24 September 1984, both in CCM, 22-26 October 1984, pp. 456-58.

77. CCM, 18-22 May 1981, pp. 29-35; CCM, 21-25 September 1981, pp. 18-26 (contains letter from W. J. Moss to G. Ernest Murray, New York City, 29 May 1981, covering "Employment Statement of Auxiliary Captains" [pp. 20-26]); CCM, 8-12 February 1982, pp. 20-42 (quotation with definition, p. 21). Statistics from National Composite, Statistical Report to the National Headquarters for the Year Ending 31 December 1980 and 31 December 1990, courtesy SANHQ.

78. On the enrollment of ARC converts as adherents in the Western territory, see Chap. 6 herein; CCM, 31 October–2 November 1979, p. 566; CCM, 22-23 May 1980, p. 410 (Pitcher quotation); CCM, 27-31 October 1980, pp. 475-76.

79. CCM, 18-22 May 1981, pp. 518-22; *Definitive Statement of The Salvation Army Services and Activities in The United States of America* (Verona, N.J., 1989), p. 20 (definition of adherent); statistics from National Composites for 1980 and 1990, courtesy SANHQ. On the use of employees, see CCM, 7-10 February 1983, p. 33; CCM, 20-23 May 1985, pp. 24-25.

80. On the Army withdrawal from the World Council, see Bruce Best, "Salvation Politics in the Sports Reports," *One World* 70 (October 1981): 11; [Susan Woolfson], "Who Says What Is Political?" *Worldview* 24 (December 1981): 4; see also CCM, 21-25 September 1981, p. 625. For expressions of unease that the Army's international leaders might succumb to pressure to rejoin the World Council, see CCM, 7-10 February 1983, pp. 455-57; on Gen. Wahlstrom's conciliatory response, see the letter from Jarl Wahlstrom to John Needham, London, 25 March 1983, in CCM, 16-19 May 1983, pp. 683-84; "The Salvation Army and the World Council of Churches," *One World* 90 (October/November 1983): 18-20; Billingsley, "The Salvation Army: Still Marching to God's Beat after 118 Years," p. 21; interview with Comm. James Osborne, 4 October 1990. On the Lake Arrowhead conference, see NF, 10 September 1988, pp. 1, 11; GN, November 1988, pp. 1, 6-7. On the National Capital Band, see WC, 17 August 1991, pp. 18-19; letter to the author from Lt. Col. Warren Fulton, Washington, D.C., 29 April 1992.

81. On U.S. role in Self-Denial funding, see WC, 15 September 1990, p. 3; SA, *Yearbook 1992* (London, 1991), p. 44. The *Yearbook* lists forty-eight countries as having made donations to international Self-Denial funds and Special Projects; the funds listed as having come from the four American territories constituted 52 percent of the total amount from all sources. On SAWSO, see the letter to the author from Lt. Col. Ernest A. Miller, Washington, D.C., 20 July 1978; SA, *A New Program for World Service* (New York, 1978); SA World Service Office, "News Bulletin" [1978]; letter from W. S. Cottrill (chief of the staff) [to E. A. Miller], London, 22 March 1978 (copy sent to author). See also CCM, 24-28 May 1982, pp. 473-74; CCM, 16-19 May 1983, pp. 577-79; CCM, 3-6 March 1986, p. 462; CCM, 13, 15-17 October 1990, p. 607; WC, 5 January 1991, pp. 4-6. Col. Walter French replaced Miller in 1990 when the latter retired; the executive

director of SAWSO during these years was Dean Seiler, a Salvationist layperson. Comm. Kenneth Hood (national chief secretary) included an explanation of SAWSO funding in an interview with the author, 10 March 1992; Dean Seiler also explained this to the author in an interview, 12 March 1992, both at SANHQ, Alexandria, Va.; SA World Service Office, *SAWSO Annual Report 1990* (Washington, 1990), pp. 16-17.

82. Maj. Barbara Bolton, "Battle Orders for a New Age," SA, *Yearbook 1991* (London, 1990), p. 20; CN, October 1989, pp. 1-2; SA, *Chosen to Be a Soldier: Orders and Regulations for Soldiers of The Salvation Army,* rev. ed. (London, 1977), *passim* (the traditional Articles of War appear on pp. 4-6); "The Salvation Army, Articles of War, A Soldier's Covenant," current issue, courtesy SATHQ/S; SA, *Salvation Army Ceremonies* (London, 1989), pp. 4-5 (the new enrollment ceremony, using the revised Articles); letter to author from Col. William Rivers, London, 13 June 1989; CN, October 1989, pp. 1-2; CCM, 13-16 February 1989, pp. 429-30; CCM, 23-27 May 1989, pp. 243-46.

83. Church Information and Development Services, *TIER Final Report* (Costa Mesa, Calif., 1991), pp. 2-3, 9-11; there is more on these developments later in the text. Comm. Paul A. Rader, "The Risen Christ Throws Open the Doors to the Challenging World of MISSION 2000," NF, Easter 1992, pp. 1-2 (quotation); "Potential New Sites Revealed," NF, Easter 1992, pp. 1, 4; letter to the author from Comm. Paul A. Rader, Rancho Palos Verdes, Calif., 21 April 1992; letter to author from Capt. Terry Camsey, Rancho Palos Verdes, Calif., 8 April 1992.

84. Information on Amador Valley and a helpful explanation of the practical aspects of corps growth were provided to the author by Maj. Earl McInnes, general secretary for Church Growth and Evangelism, Northern California–Nevada Division, in an interview 9 May 1992.

85. See more below on the South's "New Treasure" corps; the reference to "regional corps" appeared in a survey of divisional commanders conducted by the author in preparing for this volume.

86. Corps mission statements in each issue of *Beanstalk;* WC, 5 January 1991, p. 17 (Fulton quotation); letter to author from Maj. Herbert Luhn, Des Plaines, Ill., 2 April 1992.

87. Data on the divisional music directors in each territory were supplied to author by the four territorial music secretaries in correspondence and telephone conversations, February-May 1992. On the decision to establish national Music Sunday, see CCM, 16-19 May 1983, p. 562; WC, 10 March 1984, pp. 3, 15; 3 March 1990, p. 15; 2 March 1991, pp. 4-5.

88. Statistics on levels of brass band personnel in the four territories were derived from territorial composites sent to the Army's national headquarters and supplied to author for the years since 1960 by Maj. Norman Nonnweiler, SANHQ, 2 March 1992. The developments in the Southern territory were described in a letter to the author from Dr. Richard Holz, Atlanta, 25 February 1992. On National Capital Band, see "National Capital Band History," unpublished typescript provided by National Capital/Virginia Divisional HQ, 12 March 1992.

89. Data on prominent composers in each territory was provided by the territorial music secretaries in correspondence and telephone conversations with the author, February-May 1992; *The Musician* 1/1 (October 1978) to 12/5 (May 1989); (on the decision to cancel *The Musician,* see CCM, 24-28 May 1982, pp. 399-400); CCM, 17-20 October

1988, p. 436; CCM, 13-16 February 1989, pp. 642-45; CCM, 22-25 May 1989, pp. 844-45; Ronald W. Holz, "A History of the Hymn Tune Meditation and Related Forms in Salvation Army Instrumental Music in Great Britain and North America, 1880-1980" (Ph.D. diss., University of Connecticut, 1981), pp. 166, 177; SS, 12 February 1990, pp. 1, 8; letter to the author from Dr. Richard E. Holz, Atlanta, 25 February 1992.

90. CCM, 23-27 May 1988, pp. 303-5 (the Navy model); CCM, 27-31 October 1980, pp. 520-21 (revision of music regulations); CCM, 8-12 February 1982, p. 570; CCM, 16-19 May 1983, pp. 344-561 (revised text).

91. *The Salvation Army Orders and Regulations for Bands and Songster Brigades in the United States of America* (Verona, N.J., 1987), pp. 1 (block quotation), 3 (other quotations), *passim;* letter to the author from Dr. Richard E. Holz, Atlanta, 30 March 1992. The author is especially indebted to Dr. Holz for his prompt and courteous assistance in preparing much of the material in the text relating to recent developments in Army music.

92. William Himes, "The Brass Band: Dynamo or Dinosaur?" CN, April 1990, n.p. (reprinted NF, 11 January 1991, p. 7); Needham, *Community in Mission,* pp. 60-61, 81-83; Larsson, *How Your Corps Can Grow,* pp. 98-99; "Still in God's Hands," WC, 3 March 1990, pp. 14-15 (Ditmer quotation); Dr. Richard E. Holz, "Divisions Promote Musical Excellence with Conservatories," SS, 7 October 1991, p. 8; WC, 10 November 1990, p. 14 (Augusta); "History of Music in the Warsaw Indiana Corps" (1984), in CTM, drawer 11; WC, 3 March 1990, pp. 12-13 (Ditmer retirement); statistics on National Composites were supplied by SANHQ.

93. Statistics from National Composites for years ending 31 December 1980 and 31 December 1990. The number of "converts" referred to in the text was taken from the combined totals for "Number I" and "Number III" seekers. The former is defined by The Salvation Army as a person fourteen years of age or older who has not been a "seeker" within the past year and is "not listed on the Recruits' or Soldiers' Roll of any Salvation Army Corps"; a "Number III" seeker is the same, but younger: under the age of fourteen and not a Junior Soldier (*The Salvation Army National Statistical System,* 1988, line items 1005 and 1015, p. 9).

94. "The Philanthropy 400," *Journal of Philanthropy,* 19 November 1991, pp. 1, 20-26, 30 (quotation on p. 23); CCM, 22-25 May 1989, pp. 247-48 (quotation).

95. Survey conducted by the author of all territorial and divisional leaders in the United States in preparation of this volume, 1991-1992; CCM, 19-22 May 1986, pp. 315-31.

96. "National Forum — A Watershed Event," WC, 10 June 1989, pp. 2-3, 9-14, 15; NF, 19 May 1989, pp. 1, 5, 8; NF, 31 May 1989, pp. 6-8; SS, 19 June 1989, pp. 1, 4-5, 7; "Forum Update," WC, 21 July 1990, pp. 3-6.

97. CCM, 23-27 May 1988, pp. 313-28; CCM, 22-25 May 1989, pp. 787-92; "National Forum Recommendations and Research Committee Responses," in "Revised Minutes: National Planning and Development Commission, Research Committee; June 26-27, 1989," iii-xl; WC, 21 July 1990, pp. 3-6.

98. SA, *Second Century Advance,* pp. 45-47; CCM, 28 January–1 February 1991, pp. 119-22; Larsson, *How Your Corps Can Grow,* pp. 23-24; Maj. Herbert Luhn, "Toward More Selective Moves," *The Officer* 41 (July 1990): 333-34.

99. Interviews by the author with Comm. James Osborne (national commander)

and Lt. Col. Warren H. Fulton (divisional commander in National Capital/Virginia) in March 1992 were particularly helpful in shedding light on the complexity of decisions regarding officer transfers.

100. WC, 10 June 1989, p. 2 (Miller quotation); CCM, 13, 15-17 October 1990, pp. 234-35 (new National Forum).

101. SA Western Territory *TIER Final Report*, pp. 2, 4, 9-12 (quotations), 38-55, *passim.*

102. "Potential New Sites Revealed," NF, Easter 1992, pp. 1, 4; "Changing Populations Demand Strong Cross-Cultural Emphasis," NF, Easter 1992, p. 10 (quotations).

103. "USA Southern Territory 'Battle School' 1992" (brochure); *The Southern Territory Operation New Treasure* (newsletter), January 1992, n.p.; "Guidelines — Territorial Incentive Fund," dated 26 October 1990, in *New Treasure* binder in divisional office, National Capital/Virginia Division, Washington D.C.; this binder also contains a letter from Maj. Paul S. Kellner to Corps Officers, Operation New Treasure, Atlanta, 28 March 1991, containing instructions on statistical procedures.

104. Lt. Col. Warren H. Fulton, "A New Treasure Mandate," unpublished typescript dated 6 November 1991 reporting on the Sherman Avenue Corps (the author visited the Sherman Avenue Corps 8 March 1992); "The Salvation Army Southern Territory, Atlanta, Georgia, Fifth Year Officers Seminar: Church Growth" (syllabus). Maj. Jorge Booth kindly provided materials associated with the Southern Territory's 1992 "Stewardship Campaign" and the 1992 "Discipleship Year."

105. NF, 31 May 1989, p (Stella Young). On the Army's role in Desert Storm, see CCM, 20-24 May 1991, pp. 514-16; NF, 28 December 1990, pp. 1, 4-5; and WC, 5 January 1991, cover, p. 2. On disaster relief and Pres. George Bush's endorsement of the Army's role in it, see NF, 31 December 1989, p. 2; see also SS, 15 January 1990, p. 7. On Fortress, see SS, 3 June 1991, pp. 1, 6.

106. Capt. Terry Camsey, "Booth's Growth Principles Work Today," NF, 30 June 1990, pp. 5, 9; S. L. Brengle, "The Resurrection," GN, April 1990, pp. 1, 8; GN, December 1989, p. 10 ["Beat the Drum"]; "Women at Work," NF, 3 November 1990, p. 1; Mrs. Lt. Col. Fay Howell, "The Changing Role of Women in the ARC," GN, November 1990, pp. 11, 13; Henry Gariepy, *Christianity in Action: The Salvation Army in the USA Today* (Wheaton, Ill., 1990), pp. 24 (quotation), 25, 27, 70; on the book, see WC, 3 February 1990, p. 3; Maj. Della Rees, "Reflections of a Single Woman Officer," *The Officer*, 36 (January 1985): 35-39.

107. "Master List of All Orders and Regulations and Manuals," in CCM, 13-16 February 1989, pp. 344-47; SS, 24 February 1992, pp. 1, 6 (new rank); SA, *Orders and Regulations for Local Officers* (London, 1986), 5-7 (list of current local officer ranks and positions); *Southern Territory Minute Book*, no. 10, rev. 25 July 1989, National Capital/Virginia Division office (uniform); Leon Ferraez, "The Salvation Army," in *An Encyclopedia of Religions in the United States: One Hundred Religious Groups Speak for Themselves*, ed. William B. Williamson (New York, 1992), p. 296 (open-airs).

108. Maj. Phil Needham, "The Training Programme in the 1990's," *The Officer*, March 1990, p. 114 (the entire series appeared in the February, March, and April issues of the magazine); Maj. Phil Needham, "Army Called to Be 'Mobilized for Mission,'" WC, 28 July 1990, p. 5 (quotation); CN, January 1990, p. 2; James Osborne, "The Notable Exception," *War Cry*, Easter 1990 ed., p. 3 (quotation).

109. "Writing the Vision: The Salvation Army in the U.S. Crafts a Vision Statement and National Goal," WC, 1 February 1992, pp. 16-19 (all quotations; charts and graphs on pp. 17-18).

110. SATHQ/E bulletin, dated 30 September 1992 (quotation); Booth Memorial Medical Center, official news release, dated 30 September 1992; these items kindly supplied to the author by Maj. Dr. Herbert Rader by fax, 30 September 1992; the quotation of Maj. Rader is taken from a telephone conversation with the author, 30 September 1992.

111. Judith Brigham, "The Salvation Army: Santa All Year Long," *Saturday Evening Post,* December 1981, p. 118 (quotation); Lt. Col. Robert Tobin, "New Openings Require New Leaders: Staffing Needs Explored," NF, Easter 1992, p. 4 (quotation).

112. "Third California Division Slated," NF, 15 September 1993; telephone interview with Ms. Becky Briggs (secretary to Lt. Col. David Riley), 22 December 1993.

113. Col. M. Lee Hickam, "On Building Bridges," CN, April 1992, n.p. The song "Marching to Glory" was written by George Scott Railton, to be sung to the tune "Marching through Georgia"; it appeared in *The Salvation Army Song Book* in the 1890 edition as number 598 (five verses), in the 1953 edition as number 866 (reduced to three verses), and in the 1987 edition as number 815 (same three verses).

Bibliographical Essay

The following brief remarks are meant to supplement the more complete bibliographical information cited in the notes. The major source of primary materials for research in the history of The Salvation Army in the United States is the Army's official archival collection, housed in The Salvation Army Archives and Research Center (SAARC) at National Headquarters in Alexandria, Virginia. There are extensive collections of documents in each of the four territorial museums as well, although the majority of items in these collections are artifacts and memorabilia. All four territorial museums and historical collections are housed at the territorial School for Officers' Training in Chicago; West Nyack, New York; Atlanta; and Rancho Palos Verdes, California. Maj. John Milsaps assembled a large and valuable collection of Salvation Army historical items throughout his long and active lifetime and donated it to Houston's Public Library, where it is currently housed in the Circle "M" collection of the Houston Metropolitan Research Center. Major Milsaps's personal diary, an invaluable source for Army historians, has been microfilmed and is available at the SAARC. The detailed and extensive personal diary of Comm. Alexander Damon, also housed in the SAARC, is equally valuable, but is available to researchers only with permission of the officer sons of Lt. Col. Lyell Rader (R), Damon's son-in-law. The largest and most valuable private collection of Salvation Army historical documents and memorabilia in the United States belongs to Col. Paul Seiler of Ocean Grove, New Jersey; the Seiler Collection is currently administered by Col. Paul D. Seiler Jr. of Brick, New Jersey. Among other large and valuable collections of original documents (and in some cases of artifacts as well) in private hands are

431

those of Lt. Col. Richard Norris, Adult Rehabilitation Center Commander for the Southern Territory; Lt. Col. John Busby, divisional commander for the Florida Division, Tampa, Florida; Brig. Lawrence Castagna of Columbus, Ohio; and Comm. Ernest W. Holz, Mrs. Comm. Richard E. Holz, and Mr. Harry Sparks of Los Angeles. Several other officers and soldiers have small collections of items of historical interest as well.

The Salvation Army archives contain the most complete set available anywhere of all Salvation Army publications issued in the United States throughout the history of the movement in this country, including sets of territorial publications and a nearly complete set of the Moore edition of *The War Cry.* Almost all of these items, which are cited in detail in the text and endnotes herein, are available on microfilm. The archives also contain sets of *The Conqueror, All the World, Harbor Lights, The Young Salvationist, The Young Soldier, SAY, Social News, The Staff Officer's Review, The Field Officer,* and *The Officer* magazines and the Army's wartime publications, *The War Service Herald* (published from August 1917 to September 1919) and *The Red Shield* (published from January 1942 to December 1943), which became the *War Service Bulletin* (published from January 1944 to December 1945). The national publications office at national headquarters contains complete sets of the four territorial editions of *The War Cry* in addition to a continuing set of the national *War Cry* microfilm. Each of the four territorial Officers' Training schools has a complete set of editions of its territory's *War Cry* and its territory's newsletters (which began publication in all four territories in the mid-1980s), and their libraries also contain collections of old books, pamphlets, and memorabilia. All four Schools have full-scale museum programs as well, with many items available for consultation.

Scholars have produced a number of dissertations and books on The Salvation Army, all but one of them fairly recent (several of the most important having appeared since 1980). Lamb's excellent dissertation of 1909 has been joined by those by Wisbey (1951), Bosch (1965), Magnuson (1968), Holz (1981), Rhemick (1984), and Murdoch (1985), all serving to place the Army in a historical context. Dissertations by Needham (1967 and 1981), Green (1985), and Rightmire (1987) focus on Army theology. The works of Green, Needham, Murdoch, and Rhemick were especially valuable to the author. In addition, Verner and Nelson have produced dissertations on Army hospital work; Mehling, Wrieden, and Thompson on social case work; and Dexter on officer training programs. Hodder has done extensive research on Frank Smith and produced a valuable report on the organizational development of the Army. The work of The Salvation Army in opening opportunities for ministry to women and the relation of the Army in this regard to other contemporary evangelical and charitable organizations with disproportionately large percentages of active female members has been discussed in several articles; it is a subject that will repay expanded study.

The published writing of Salvationists about themselves and their work is vast in quantity and uneven in quality; much of it is cited in the text. Ballington Booth was a fine writer, and many other early officers had great hearts and vivid prose styles. The later work of Watson, Chesham, Sandall, Frederick Coutts, Barnes, Hall, Pitt, and Hughes and the very recent writing of Thomson, Gariepy, Troutt (Evangeline Booth), Carey, Wilson, Waldron, Satterlee (Southern territorial history), Spence (farm colonies), McKinley (men's social services), and the *War Cry* articles of these authors and Brindley, Harris, Hughes, Richard E. Holz (I), Cunningham, and the Booths and Booth-Tuckers are of value. Among corps histories, those of Corps Sgt. Maj. Berton Warren (Adrian, Mich.) and Capt. A. Kenneth Wilson (Pottsville, Pa.) are outstanding. Careful reporting on the Army by those outside its ranks has also found its way into print, and some of this material is of great value as well. The two volumes by Ervine have not yet been surpassed, and the more narrow work of Lamb, Lee, and Pettit and the reports by Booz, Allen, and Hamilton and International Marketing, Inc., were indispensable in preparing this history. The work of Inglis, Bailey, and Himmelfarb, among others, on the Army's British context were very useful. Four early works deserve special notice: Nora Marks's *Facts about The Salvation Army: Aims and Methods of the Hallelujah Band* (Chicago, 1889) is based on Marks's observations of the Army in 1888, which she collected while studying the Army (disguised as an officer) to collect material for articles in the *Chicago Tribune;* it should be required reading for anyone interested in the early Army. The same is true for two perceptive and sympathetic descriptions of the Army in its early years in the United States: Agnes Maule Machar, "Red Cross Knights — A Nineteenth Century Crusade," *Andover Review,* August 1884, pp. 193-210, and Charles Augustus Briggs, "The Salvation Army," *North American Review* 159 (December 1894): 697-710. For a wise and knowledgeable discussion of Salvation Army music at a time when it was attracting widespread criticism for its vulgarity, see Ch(arles) Crozat Converse, "The Salvation Army's Music," *Homiletic Review* 25 (June 1893): 560-62. There is an extensive and growing body of literature on Army programs in specialized journals treating such topics as alcoholic rehabil-itation, corrections, senior citizens activities, and the like, much of it cited in the text. In 1990 an entire issue of *Christian History* (vol. 9, no. 2, issue 26) was devoted to The Salvation Army; it contains nine articles by writers in this field, including several cited in this volume.

In addition to being referred and alluded to in an amazing number of theatrical productions, popular works of fiction, motion pictures, tele-vision programs, and magazine cartoons, The Salvation Army was the featured subject of two modern novels, *Salvation Johnny,* by Natalie Ander-son Scott (Garden City, 1958), and Astrid Valley's *Marching Bonnet* (New York, 1948).

The statistics used in the preparation of this book come from a wide variety of sources. Every effort was made to establish clear, accurate, and consistent statistics, but this was not always possible for data from the Army's early days; where there is uncertainty about figures, it is indicated in the text. The annual *Salvation Army Yearbook* and the numerous editions of *The Salvation Army Disposition of Forces,* which for many years appeared several times per year, were often used as sources for figures. When officers were asked for information by outside inquirers, or when they volunteered information for publicity purposes, it was to these official Army publica-tions that they typically turned for specific figures. There is no other source of reliable statistical information on The Salvation Army during much of its history in the United States. Of great value to historians of American religious life are the five major surveys undertaken by the U.S. Bureau of the Census in the years 1890, 1906, 1916, 1926, and 1936. The figures published in the *Religious Bodies* volumes were based on standard defini-tions and were consistent over time. The annual volumes of the *Yearbook of American and Canadian Churches* offers the same advantage. Detailed and extensive information on Salvation Army statistics since 1960 were very kindly provided the author by Maj. Norman Nonnweiler Jr., the Army's national financial secretary, on March 2, 1992, and by Comm. Kenneth Hood on several occasions during 1991 and 1992. The most useful report, and one that is cited frequently in this volume, is the "National Composite: Statistical Report to USA National Headquarters for the Year Ending December 31," for the years in question. There are annual composites from each of the four territories as well, and these, too, were used extensively. The Salvation Army has used the same consistent standard definitions in its statistical reporting, both internally and to the public, since the adoption of its National Statistical System (NSS) in 1977.

Index

435